FLASH MX

SAVVY™

FLASH™ MX

ETHAN WATRALL | NORBERT HERBER

SAN FRANCISCO | LONDON

SYBEX®

Associate Publisher: DAN BRODNITZ
Acquisitions and Developmental Editor: MARIANN BARSOLO
Editors: JIM GABBERT, KIM WIMPSETT, CAROL HENRY
Production Editor: DENNIS FITZGERALD
Technical Editors: ERIC BELL, DENISE TYLER
Production Manager: AMY CHANGAR
Cover, Interior, and Technical Illustration Designer: CARYL GORSKA
Icon Illustrator: TINA HEALEY ILLUSTRATIONS
Compositor: MAUREEN FORYS, HAPPENSTANCE TYPE-O-RAMA
Proofreaders: AMEY GARBER, DAVE NASH, LAURIE O'CONNELL, NANCY RIDDIOUGH, SUZANNE STEIN
Indexer: TED LAUX
CD Coordinator: DAN MUMMERT
CD Technician: KEVIN LY
Cover Photographer: PETER PURDY, HULTON ARCHIVE

About the Authors

Born in Regina, Saskatchewan, Canada, Ethan Watrall completed his bachelor's degree with distinction at the University of Regina, with a double major in anthropology and history. While an undergraduate, he participated in many archaeological excavations in Saskatchewan, Manitoba, and Indiana.

After graduation, Ethan was accepted into the Ph.D. program in anthropology at Indiana University. There, he has directed his academic energies toward two main subjects. The first, which represents a culmination of years of archaeological experience, is household craft production in Predynastic Egypt. He has worked at both Nabta Playa (an extremely large Neolithic habitation site in the Egyptian Western Desert) and Hierakonpolis (arguably the most important extant Predynastic site in all of Egypt), where he has excavated such cool things as prehistoric wells, clay mines, households, animal enclosures, pottery kilns, and cemeteries. His current research at the HK11 locality, a Late Predynastic village at Hierakonpolis, has consistently yielded information that challenges and greatly expands the current understanding of Predynastic Egyptian households.

The second subject that Ethan has focused on is the place of interactive media in archaeology. Whether from the standpoint of an educational tool, a method for scholarly publication, or simply an issue deserving academic discussion, Ethan has dedicated himself to expanding the dialog surrounding interactive media and archaeology. He is particularly interested in the role that interactive entertainment plays in the public perception of archaeology—a topic on which he has published and delivered papers targeted to both professional archaeologists and professional game designers. Not content to simply comment on the situation, Ethan preaches active involvement on the part of academics in the interactive entertainment industry.

Beyond academia, Ethan is also an active practitioner of interactive media. He is a faculty member at both Ivy Tech State University, Columbus (Indiana), and Ivy Tech State College, Bloomington (Indiana), where he teaches classes in interactive design and multimedia. Ethan's first book, *Dreamweaver 4/Fireworks 4 Visual JumpStart*, was published by Sybex, Inc., in February 2001 and has been translated into Chinese and Greek. He is also writing his third book, *Dreamweaver MX: Design and Technique,* which will be published by Sybex in the summer of 2002.

Ethan's digital alter ego can be found hanging out at www.captainprimate.com.

Norbert Herber grew up in Minneapolis/St. Paul, Minnesota. At 16, he began his musical career as a jazz saxophonist, trading sets with the swing tenor legend Irv Williams. After cutting his teeth in the Twin Cities, he entered the Indiana University School of Music, Bloomington. Here, he continued his studies of jazz with David Baker, pursuing interests in improvisation, arranging, music theory, woodwinds, and composition.

After graduation, Norbert worked as a freelance musician and arranger while founding his own group, the *x-tet*, and writing a score for the short film *Jambalaya*. His musical interests soon merged with digital media. Yearning to explore the relationships between sound, text, imagery, and storytelling, he returned to Indiana University for graduate work in the MIME program in the Department of Telecommunications. Here, he began an intense, concentrated study of electronic music, film scoring, sound design, and interactive musical composition.

Currently, Norbert is pursuing several interactive, digital media projects, including *Word Is Virus*, a sonic exploration of the writings and techniques of William S. Burroughs. His interests are centered around the use of audio in interactive environments, nonlinear music composition, and the effects of the sound–picture relationship in both linear and nonlinear media. Norbert is an instructor at the International Academy of Design and Technology in Chicago, where he teaches classes in multimedia development and scripting, interactive design, and digital audio.

For information on Norbert's current and past projects, visit `www.x-tet.com`.

Dedication

To Taylor, with the hope that someday she'll write books far better than this one.

—ECW

This book goes out to Jenny. Your patience, love, and understanding made this possible.

—NFH

Acknowledgments

As with any book—especially one of this size—there are quite a number of people who deserve thanks for their help in bringing this project to fruition. ■ First and foremost, I must extend my thanks to my friend, coauthor, and partner in many digital shenanigans: Norb Herber. A hefty book (covering an application of Flash MX's complexity) in which two authors share writing duties is an undertaking rife with possibilities for disaster. Instead, we managed to create a book with some serious neckwear punch. Here's to many more fruitful collaborations! ■ To all those who graciously gave permission to use their work as Inspirational Design Models or in the Color section (there are way too many folks to list by name—they know who they are), I offer my profound thanks. I especially want to thank Joost van Schaik and Brian Taylor, whose contributions and help were above and beyond the call of duty. ■ On a more personal level, as always I want to express my profound love and gratitude to Jenn. She graciously put up with my lunacy and long hours on the computer during the year that this book was being written, rewritten, revised, re-revised, and so on, and so on. Thanks also to both Mom and Dad and my good friend Neil Birch for their support during this project. Finally, a special thank-you (and a good tummy rub) to my dog, Oscar; nothing brings you down to earth like a puppy who wants nothing more in life than to play. ■ Lastly, my sincere apologies to anyone whom I managed to forget. Thanks, everybody!

Ethan Watrall

Not only was this book a team effort by two authors, but each of us had our own "support staff" to help us through many late nights with the digital quill and ink. For starters, I extend my thanks to Bill Frisell, Miles Davis, James Brown, and many others for providing the musical catalyst that inspired much of this text. Thanks also to Peet's Coffee and Tea for the fuel behind many long hours of working with ActionScript, and to the Laughing Planet Cafe and Soma (in Bloomington, Ind.) for hosting several long meetings about the book. ■ Cheers to those who shared their work as Inspirational Design Models, especially Nico Stumpo, Jean-luc Lamarque, NPFC, Joe Sparks, and Donna Durant at LEGO Systems, Inc. Also, a round of applause for Shannon Zastrow and Ryan Douglas of DoReMedia for providing the ideas and material that went into the Hands On 6 section. ■ Thanks to my colleagues in Chicago: Tim Arroyo and Bernie Mack at IADT for their contributions to this book, and Brian Hrastar at Opt1mus for video consultations and a sampling of the family footage. ■ A huge thanks to my partner in crime, Ethan Watrall, for convincing me to do this in the first place. I knew it would work, since there were no twin brothers involved! Thanks for your endless diligence and resourcefulness. I must also thank my wonderful, supportive family: Mom and Dad, Genevieve, Lyla, Susan, Hasan, and, most of all, my dearest Jenny. Thanks for listening to story after story about "the book." ■ Finally, thank *you* for reading this!

Norbert Herber

Both of us want to acknowledge lots of other people who helped make this book a reality. ■ Many thanks go to our agent, David Fugate of Waterside Productions, Inc. As always, we are forever in his debt for all the work he put in and for the advice he provided during this project. At Sybex, Dennis Fitzgerald, Jim Gabbert, Carol Henry, Kim Wimpsett, Dan Schiff, Dan Mummert, and Maureen Forys deserve praise for all their help and hard work. Kudos to technical editor Denise Tyler, who was of great help during the writing process, and to Eric Bell for his technical insight. Without the help of Mariann Barsolo, our acquisitions and developmental editor at Sybex, this project might well have exploded very early. She was always there with great advice, tons of help, and an incredibly understanding attitude, especially during the really nutty periods. ■ A resounding thanks to Thom Gillespie for helping with the book's foreword, and to Brian Taylor (Rust Boy & XL5 Design), Virginia Mielke (Nelvana), Derek Mosher (Sony Screenblast), and Joost van Schaik (Djojo Studios) for their kind endorsements. ■ We also want to extend our gratitude to those individuals who helped with the software and hardware that either appears on the CD or was used while we were writing the book: William Reeb (of Wacom), Philip Staiger (Eovia), Paul Babb (Maxon), Karen Carpenter (Curious Labs), Stefan Moss (Ideaworks3D), Ben Yoder (Electric Image), Dave Klein (Electric Rain), Steve Foldvari (Sonic Foundry), Daniel Brown (Adobe Systems Incorporated), and Zac Wheatcroft (BIAS, Inc.).

CONTENTS AT A GLANCE

Contents

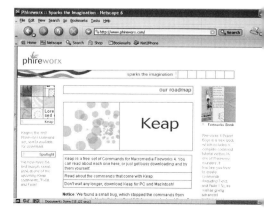

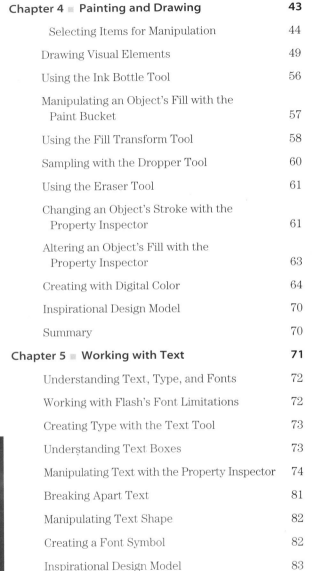

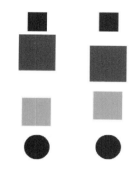

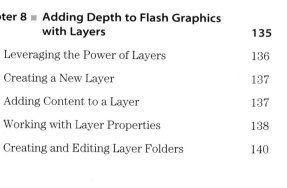

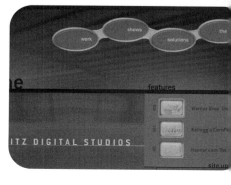

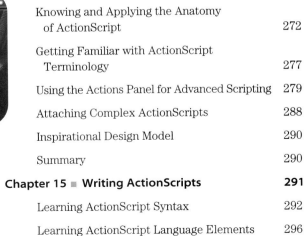

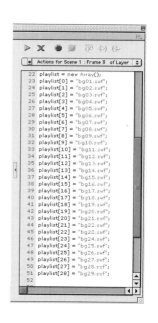

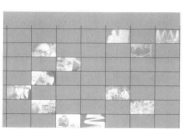

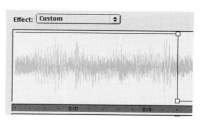

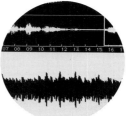

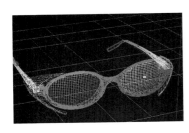

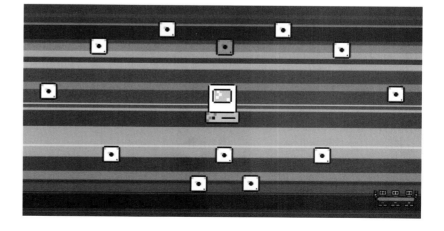

Foreword

When FutureSplash first splashed down, I and most of the known "newMedia" world thought Director was the be-all and end-all of newMedia. Suddenly, there was this wacko animation tool floating around the Net. I downloaded it and played with it. It looked sorta like Director since it had a timeline, but it seemed to work the opposite of Director in every way, which made it difficult to use. I was amused by simple morphing—making eyes blink and balls roll. FutureSplash was fun, but obviously inconsequential. So I went back to struggling with bitmaps, sounds, and Lingo. I knew the future.

A couple of years later, I created the MIME program in interactive media at Indiana University. Two of my first students were Ethan and Norbert. Ethan was doing his Ph.D. in archaeology, and Norbert was a jazz sax player. Ethan alternated between newMedia and digging things up in the Nile Valley. Norbert made funny sounds. They were very nice, creative, and obviously smart guys, but not really technologists. I figured they might be useful folks, but I had to get back to working with the real technologists. I knew the future.

Actually, I didn't have a clue about the future. Flash is much more important than Director ever was, and Ethan and Norb have gone on to do lots of interesting things with all sorts of technology, by virtue of the fact that they're *not* technologists. And now they've written this book for creative, smart folks who aren't interested in technology for technology's sake, but as a tool to get real work done.

This book isn't your traditional loops-and-variables techno book; nor is it a look-what-we-can-do, over-glossed guide to eye candy. An exceptional difference between this book and other Flash books is its substantial amount of sheer information on integrating Flash with audio and sound. Flash MX includes better sound control, and *Flash MX Savvy* explains how to use these new tools to boost the auditory experience.

Ethan understands human culture—how people have lived, worked, and learned. Norb is a musician who has augmented his living as an interactive designer, graphic artist, and educator. When writing about Flash, they bring more to the table than mere technologists would. They've written a very good book about using Flash to get real work done in the real world.

Dr. Thom Gillespie, Director of MIME (www.mime.indiana.edu)

Associate Professor, Telecommunications, Indiana University

Introduction

In the summer of 1996, a little-known company named FutureWave shipped a small program called FutureSplash Animator, a relatively simple application that was designed to create linear, vector-based animations. After its release, the application attracted considerable attention when it was used in the design of both Microsoft's web version of MSN and Disney's subscription-based Disney Daily Blast. In November 1996, Macromedia approached FutureWave about the possibility of working together. For FutureWave, which was still a tiny company of six employees, this was an incredible opportunity. So, in December 1996, FutureWave sold the technology to Macromedia, who released Flash 1 in early 1997. The rest, as they say, is history.

Fast-forward to 2002. Six versions later, Flash (now dubbed Flash MX) is arguably one of the most popular interactive authoring applications. With it, you can create not only unbelievably cool-looking animations but incredibly complex interactive experiences that feature rich media and the integration of dynamic, database-driven applications.

Not only are today's Web-based Flash creations a quantum leap beyond anything that could have been conceived previously for online media, but they are pushing the boundaries of interactive digital media. Although Flash was originally intended for the Web, its sheer popularity (and phenomenal power) has taken it far beyond the online domain. These days, you can see the integration of Flash as an authoring tool in mobile devices, broadcast media, and console games.

To really understand the penetration of Flash into the world of interactive digital media, you only need to look at the number of people who have downloaded the Flash Player over the years: more than 430 million. Yup, that's right—nearly half a billion! Need we say more?

About This Book

This book was written with a lot of love, blood, sweat, and tears...seriously. We don't want to give you the impression that we are "tortured authors," holed up in a dingy loft pouring over manuscripts and surrounded by bottles of wine and take-out containers. However, we did put a lot of thought and planning into the writing process. Our objective was to create the most intuitive, learning-focused Flash reference imaginable.

Unlike many Flash books, this one was written with the intention of not only explaining *how* to work with Flash MX but *why*. Knowing why you do things is a crucial step in the learning process because it gives you the means to creatively apply your newfound skills to original ideas of your own. The techniques outlined in this book will give you the basic concepts to create an enormous variety of things in Flash. Additionally, all techniques are presented with the mind-set that "this is just the beginning." Our hope is that you will use these lessons as a point of departure for your own creative ideas. As educators, we approached this book in much the same way we would approach a class.

This book will be equally effective for Macintosh and Windows users. As a writing team, we are split: Norbert is "the Mac guy," and Ethan "the Windows guy." We tried as much as possible to present a balanced approach so that regardless of your platform, the book will fit your specific needs and illustrate each technique clearly.

Who Needs This Book?

Every man, woman, and child on the planet needs this book!

But seriously, folks, it's impossible to write a book that is all things to all people. That being said, we did our best to write a book that is many things to a lot of different people. We carefully selected the topics discussed, and crafted the way we discussed them so that many different types of people, with varying levels of expertise and different goals, could pick the book up and find it useful. Granted, if worse comes to worse, the book is large enough to prop up the wobbly leg on your bed or serve as a pretty decent doorstop.

If you were to corner us in a dark alley, we would feel comfortable (*relatively* comfortable, that is, since we're not used to being cornered in dark alleys by our readers) in saying that the range of people who will get the most out of this book will vary between the savvy computer user who "gets" Flash but has never actually worked with the program and someone who is experienced in the basics of Flash and wants to obtain intermediate and low-level advanced skills.

We feel strongly that this book isn't really appropriate for people who already have advanced Flash skills. We certainly don't want to discourage any interested individual from using the book—quite the contrary! It covers a lot of stuff that even the most advanced user might not be familiar with. However, we feel that those more-experienced Flash users might not find in this book exactly what they are looking for, and would therefore be disappointed—something we definitely don't want.

Having said that, we think that anyone who is eager to take part in the Flash revolution and become a dyed-in-the-wool "Flasher" should read this book! That includes any student wanting to put their class project on the Web, any animator or artist wanting to go digital with their creations, anyone who is frustrated by the inherent design limitations of HTML, anyone enamored with the "wow" factor of vector animation and interactivity—in short, anyone who is excited about the endless possibilities and phenomenal power of Flash, but who is a little befuddled about where they should start or is a bit unsure about their skills. If you're one of those types, this book is for you!

How This Book Is Organized

There is a natural progression of skills involved in working with Flash MX. The chapter-by-chapter structure of this book is designed to emulate this progression. Although each chapter builds on the previous one to a certain extent, the book can, in fact, be used as a reference for those wishing to tackle specific problems.

 We've been careful to point out which features are new in Flash MX—this will be useful if you've used Flash 5 and are completely new to MX. Be on the lookout for the handy "new to MX" icon.

Here's a quick look at what you can expect to explore in each chapter.

PART I ■ Getting to Know Flash

Part I sets the stage for all your future work in Flash. In **Chapter 1**, you'll start off by getting a nice introduction to the world of Flash. You'll bone up on the venerable history of Flash (including the advances in each version), explore the difference between vectors and bitmaps, and get a snapshot of what kinds of cool stuff are being created with Flash. In **Chapter 2**, you'll explore the great updates that Flash MX features. Finally, in **Chapter 3**, you'll delve deeply into the Flash MX interface and get your hands dirty exploring how you can manipulate your working environment.

PART II ■ Creating and Manipulating Visual Content

Part II is geared toward teaching you the fundamentals of creating and manipulating all things visual in Flash MX. In **Chapter 4**, you'll become intimately familiar with all of Flash

MX's painting and drawing tools. From there, **Chapter 5** covers the process of creating and manipulating text. In **Chapter 6**, you'll learn how to use objects (a blanket term for just about anything graphical in Flash MX) to your advantage. **Chapter 7** features an in-depth discussion about working with reusable content—primarily symbols and the Library. Finally, **Chapter 8** explores how to work with layers—a vital subject if you want to create animations having any degree of complexity.

PART III ▪ Animating with Flash

Part III is designed to teach you just about everything you need to know about creating animation in Flash MX. First, **Chapter 9** thoroughly explores how to use the Timeline to add the dimension of movement to your Flash creation. From there, you'll learn how to work with Movie Clips—arguably one of the most important elements in Flash—in **Chapter 10**. Finally, **Chapter 11** will teach you how to work with scenes, a vital tool for partitioning and organizing animated content.

PART IV ▪ Scripting for Interactivity with ActionScript

This section of the book will introduce you to one of the most compelling and important aspects of Flash development: ActionScript. **Chapter 12** introduces the basic concepts of the ActionScript language and the techniques for adding scripts to control the interactivity of your movies. **Chapter 13** presents a discussion on the creation and design of interactive controls, an essential part of any interactive experience.

PART V ▪ Adding Advanced Interactivity with ActionScript

If you love Flash but have been hesitant to take the plunge into the world of Flash-based scripting, Part V is for you. **Chapter 14** discusses some beginning concepts of programming and explains how ActionScript works inside a Flash movie. **Chapter 15** provides details on the syntax, structure, and elements of ActionScript, while **Chapter 16** presents a variety of inspiring and useful in-context examples that use ActionScript to add all sorts of functionality to your Flash movies. In **Chapter 17**, you'll explore how to make Flash dynamic (either alone or with other database-driven technologies) by sending data out or bringing data in. We feel that it's important to keep this book realistic; as a result, **Chapter 18** discusses the techniques and tools that you can use to troubleshoot ActionScripts that aren't performing as expected.

PART VI ■ Working with Audio

Part VI covers one of the most important (and sadly neglected) aspects of multimedia development: audio. **Chapter 19** provides useful information on the basics of digital audio and serves as a primer for anyone who is new to working with sound and music on their computer. With the essentials of digital audio under your belt, you can read **Chapter 20** to learn how audio works inside Flash and how to publish "sonified" Flash movies. Because getting your audio to synchronize with any variety of events is a crucial part of animation and interactive development, **Chapter 21** discusses the various techniques for audio/visual synchronization. Finally, **Chapter 22** ups the ante, showing you how to control audio elements interactively via ActionScript.

PART VII ■ Integrating Flash with Other Programs

In Part VI, you'll learn how you can integrate Flash with lots of other applications. **Chapter 23** discusses Flash in the context of Macromedia's other multimedia powerhouse: Director. In **Chapter 24**, you'll learn how to integrate Flash MX with Macromedia's popular vector-illustration program, FreeHand. **Chapter 25** discusses different ways that you can use third-party audio applications to edit sounds, compose music, and engineer your digital audio files before integrating them with your Flash masterpiece. Finally, in **Chapter 26**, you'll get a taste of how to integrate 3D with your Flash creation. The chapter covers both third-party 3D software and techniques for simulating 3D with Flash's painting and drawing tools.

    The book's companion CD-ROM contains a full-length chapter (in Adobe Acrobat PDF format) about integrating Flash with Macromedia's Dreamweaver.

PART VIII ■ Publishing and Distributing Flash Movies

Part VIII focuses on how you go about actually getting your beautiful Flash creations to your audience. In **Chapter 27**, you'll learn how to publish your Flash movies to several formats that are suitable for distribution. Flash MX is the first version that has real support for digital video. **Chapter 28** discusses the techniques involved in publishing Flash movies that include video, and publishing Flash movies *as* digital video in either QuickTime or AVI format. You'll also learn how to transfer your Flash movies to VHS tape using Adobe Premiere. And finally, **Chapter 29** discusses the ins and outs of developing Flash movies for delivery on CD-ROM.

Inspirational Design Models

Every creative endeavor—and that includes a Flash MX movie—definitely benefits from a little inspiration now and then. Let's face it, folks, even the most innovative person on the planet sometimes feels a bit "creatively constipated."

To help, we've included an Inspirational Design Model (IDM) at the end of almost every chapter. Each IDM highlights one of the best Flash creations and is loosely tied to the subject of the chapter. For example, in Chapter 5, "Working with Text," the IDM is Jimmy Chen's typographic.com, a beautiful fusion of type and Flash. Ultimately, the IDMs give you not only helpful nudges along the path of creativity but also a good feel for the terribly groovy possibilities of the application.

Hands On Sections

This book offers eight Hands On sections. As the name suggests, these are included to put your skills to work in the context of projects that are larger and more in-depth than those encountered within the chapters. **Hands On 1** shows you how to change keyboard shortcuts in Flash MX with the Keyboard Shortcuts editor. **Hands On 2** features a step-by-step tutorial on using Flash MX's painting and drawing tools to create a static garden scene. **Hands On 3** walks you through the creation of a short science-fiction animation. **Hands On 4** shows you how to create an interactive resume using basic ActionScript techniques. **Hands On 5** delves deeper into ActionScript, showing you how to work with a movie that uses multiple SWF files in a single Flash movie. **Hands On 6**, which focuses on audio, demonstrates how you can use DoReMedia Sound Families to create a dynamic soundtrack for your Flash movies. **Hands On 7** shows you how to create an animated 3D logo and place it in an HTML document using Amorphium Pro and Macromedia Dreamweaver. And to top it all off, **Hands On 8** teaches you how to burn a hybrid (cross-platform) CD-ROM using Toast 5 Titanium.

ActionScript Reference

The ActionScript Reference section of this book provides you with the correct syntax, contextual examples, and tips for working with many ActionScript terms. This isn't a complete reference; rather, it contains what we consider to be *essential* ActionScript elements. It should prove to be very helpful when you're composing scripts from the ground up.

Appendix

Appendix A, "Adding Cool Bells and Whistles," features step-by-step tutorials that didn't quite fit into other parts of the book. These tutorials will show you how to create some of the coolest Flash widgets and doohickeys. Included are navigational widgets, preloaders, and array-based doohickeys.

Color Section

The color section is a gallery containing some of the most innovative, beautiful, and interesting Flash work on the Internet today. Pieces were selected not only because they are visually stunning but because they demonstrate the true potentials of this application, from concept and artistry to interactivity and entertainment.

How to Use This Book

This book can be used in two ways. The first, as mentioned earlier, depends on the fact that the material presented follows a logical learning curve. As a result, someone can easily read the book from cover to cover, confident that when they're finished, they'll have a solid foundation in basic, intermediate, and some advanced Flash MX techniques.

The book can also be used as a reference. If you want to solve certain problems or learn specific skills, you can simply locate the information you desire by using the index or the table of contents.

The bottom line is that whatever way you decide to use this book, you'll learn the skills necessary to continue your journey in the wonderful world of Flash MX.

Fire up your computer and grab hold of something nailed down. It's going to be a wild ride!

About the CD

As with many computer books, *Flash MX Savvy* comes with a handy-dandy companion CD-ROM, which is compatible with both Macintosh and Windows platforms. Although the CD would probably make a pretty decent Frisbee, we've gone to great lengths to include some really useful stuff.

First, you'll find a whole bevy of demo and trial software. Most, if not all, of these applications were chosen because they are discussed in the book; some of them are needed for the successful completion of the Hands On tutorials. Second, the CD contains all the necessary support and example files that are used in the chapters and the Hands On sections. Third, there's an additional chapter, "Working with Flash and Dreamweaver." And finally, you'll find a host of links to extremely useful online Flash resources.

Any time we want to point you toward files on the CD, the text will appear next to a cool little CD icon like this. Feel free to use these files as starter files for your own unique Flash creations. It is recommended that you open all Flash MX documents (FLA files) from within Flash MX. Simply choose File → Open and browse to the file you need.

Getting in Touch and Staying Connected

We have developed a community resource for the readers (and potential readers) of this book. Visit www.vonflashenstein.com to learn about Flash in the laboratory of Dr. Helmut von Flashenstein and his faithful lab assistant, Müvie Klip. In the depths of his lab, Dr. von Flashenstein will introduce you to various Flash oddities, lessons, and other material in support of this book.

The website includes:

- An expanded Inspirational Design Model section
- An ActionScript-of-the-week example and source FLA files
- Opportunities to sign up for receiving news and events via e-mail
- Access to bonus tutorials and articles

We said that this book was constructed like a class. But there's one exception: You can't raise your hand to ask a question or offer feedback. In case you'd like to get in touch with us, here are our addresses:

norbert@vonflashenstein.com

ethan@vonflashenstein.com

PART I

Getting to Know Flash

Flash began its career humbly as a great tool for adding low-bandwidth animations to websites. To say the least, the application has grown by leaps and bounds! Yes, Flash can still animate, but it can also be used to create complex, interactive navigational schemes, dynamic and data-driven websites, cartoon serials, games, music videos, music players…the list goes on and on. Flash has evolved from "simple animator" to "multimedia authoring juggernaut." In fact, it would be hard to imagine the Internet today without Flash and what it offers to contemporary digital media.

Part I of this book will take you on a guided tour of Flash. You'll learn about the history of the software, explore its role in digital media today, and get a glimpse of how the application may evolve in the future. And of course, you'll be introduced to Macromedia's latest addition to the Flash pedigree: Flash MX. This sixth version of the application also has a terrific new interface that makes working with the program more intuitive than ever before. Whether you're a veteran Flash developer or a first-time user, this section of the book will show you the now, then, and possibly tomorrow of Flash.

CHAPTER 1

Introduction to Flash

As one of the most popular and versatile applications for creating digital multimedia, Flash wears (and has worn) many hats. Flash has always been at the cutting edge of technology for the delivery of compelling animated content. And, as a vector-based medium, Flash is able to deliver the goods at a fraction of the bandwidth required by other animated media. What many people don't know is that Flash can do much more that simply create bandwidth-efficient vector animation. As the application continues to evolve, its scope broadens more and more. Flash is now one of the more flexible authoring tools available, offering the capabilities to run not only on the Internet and contemporary desktop computer platforms, but on game consoles and mobile devices as well. It is truly, *multi*media.

To get a sense of what Flash really is, it can be helpful to know its lineage, makeup, and current scope of possibilities. In this chapter, you will learn:

- **The history of Flash**

- **The differences between raster and vector formats**

- **The many faces of Flash**

A History of Flash

Before you dig into today's Flash, it's a good idea to cast your eye back and get an idea of how this virtual revolution in interactive multimedia came about. Besides, it's a cool story.

So, turn the "way back" machine to the late 1980s. The stage for our little story has been set with four companies. The first, Macromind, was a Chicago-based software company whose primary product was an application called VideoWorks. The second, Paracomp in San Francisco, was best known for its Macintosh 3D application, Swivel3D. The third company was Authorware, a Minnesota-based company best known for its CBT/multimedia authoring application, Authorware. In 1991, Macromind, which had moved to San Francisco, merged with Paracomp to form Macromind-Paracomp. Authorware then moved from Minnesota and joined Macromind-Paracomp in Redwood Shores, California, to found the mighty Macromedia—the beginning, so to speak.

As you may have noticed, this accounts for only three of the four players in our story. To learn about the fourth member of the cast, we look back to January 1993. Jonathan Gay, who had put himself through college writing such venerable early Mac games as *Dark Castle* and *Beyond Dark Castle,* convinced his buddy Charlie Jackson (founder of Silicon Beach Software) to invest some money and help form a company called FutureWave. The whole point of the company, whose first product was an application called Go, was to produce software that would dominate the pen computer market. Well, unfortunately, the early pen computers failed to really catch on, and there was some corporate interference by AT&T, so Go became an application without a market.

So FutureWave found itself in serious trouble. It was a small software company with no income and had spent a year developing an application that would never see the light of day. Their salvation came in the form of a small drawing program called SmartSketch that they had developed as a sideline to Go. FutureWave began marketing SmartSketch as a computer-based drawing solution for both Macintosh and Windows platforms. It wasn't long before people were asking why FutureWave didn't turn SmartSketch into a 2D animation program. In perhaps one of the most stunning examples of technological foresight, FutureWave shifted the focus of SmartSketch from a static image–creation program to an animation program. This shift was based solely on the hope that the Internet—something that everyone was beginning to talk about—would be a great medium for delivering 2D animation.

After both Adobe and Fractal Design declined to buy the technology (they must be kicking themselves now!), FutureWave shipped its FutureSplash Animator in the summer of 1996. FutureSplash Animator was a relatively simple application for creating linear vector-based animations. After its release, the application gained some attention when it was used in the design of both Microsoft's web version of MSN, and Disney's subscription-based Disney Daily Blast. In November 1996, Macromedia approached FutureWave about the possibility of the two firms working together. For FutureWave, which was still a tiny company with only six employees, this was an astonishing opportunity. So, in December 1996, FutureWave sold the technology to Macromedia, which released the first Flash in early 1997. The rest, as they say, is history.

Once it was picked up by Macromedia, Flash began to evolve as a software tool. Each new version offered significant advances in the application's capabilities and usability:

Flash 1 Flash 1, which was really just a rebranded version of FutureWave's FutureSplash, featured very basic (by Flash MX's standards) timeline-based vector animation. Its primary strength was that, with the help of either a Netscape plug-in or an Internet Explorer ActiveX control, the user could mount animations on the Web for anyone to view and enjoy.

Flash 2 Flash 2 was a major step for the application. Generally speaking, it began the transformation of Flash from a straight linear-vector animation program to an interactive media-design program. The shift resulted from the integration of such features as reusable button symbols, embedded graphics, vector fonts, very basic actions, and stereo audio. Flash 2 also supported the import of an impressive selection of file formats, including EPS, GIF, JPEG, AutoCAD DXF, BMP, Enhanced Metafile, AIFF, Windows Metafile, and Shockwave.

Flash 3 One of the most significant additions to Flash 3, besides the continual improvement to the user interface, was the increasing importance and integration of actions. Based loosely on JavaScript, actions (which would later evolve into ActionScript) enabled users to add a certain measure of control and interactivity into their movies. In addition, the integration of masks, shape tweening, and transparency allowed users to exert much more control over how their Flash creations actually looked.

Flash 4 One of the most exciting improvements in Flash 4 was the ability to implement compressed MP3 audio files in the context of a Flash movie. Flash 4 also boasted improved ActionScript, which made it easier to create interactive games and interfaces. Other enhancements included editable text fields, an improved user interface, and a simplified publishing process.

Flash 5 The greatest advance in Flash 5 was definitely ActionScript. By aligning itself with the ECMA-262 standard, Macromedia announced to the world that Flash and ActionScript were ready to compete with the "big dogs." Other changes in this version were in the user interface: additional art tools, the introduction of panels, the Movie Explorer, the Macromedia Dashboard (for online help and updates), and user-customizable keystrokes for common tasks and functions.

Flash has clearly come a long way. Features that once seemed amazing and unbelievable in one version pale in comparison to the possibilities offered in subsequent upgrades. As you will soon discover, Flash MX is another significant step forward. Like the upgrades that came before it, Flash MX offers options and features that will continue to keep Flash at the forefront of digital media and Internet development.

FLASH MX: WHAT'S IN A NAME?

One of the most startling changes to this latest version of the Flash software is the departure from its traditional naming scheme. According to Macromedia, they made the switch to *MX* in order to inform developers that the software presents integrated solutions to Internet-based digital media. Because Macromedia's tools (Flash, Dreamweaver, ColdFusion, and so on) can be so tightly integrated, the company felt it was only appropriate that the authoring applications carry the same moniker. *MX* is simply a label used for this family of Macromedia tools. The Flash Player (the application that hosts any Flash movie, either as a plug-in or stand-alone) still carries the current version number in its title (Flash Player 6), but the software does not.

The initials MX don't seem to "stand for" anything in particular, and the Flash community simply has to accept this change at face value. Whether you like the name change or not, it's a moot point at this stage of the game. The good news is, regardless of Macromedia's master plan for marketing, Flash MX is a fine upgrade and will serve you well until the next version comes along. The title of that one is anybody's guess!

Raster vs. Vector Formats

Computers can store and display graphics in two main formats: *vector* and *raster*. To better understand how Flash works and why it presents advantages over other kinds of animation applications, it's helpful to understand the differences between these two graphic formats.

One of the aspects of Flash that makes it unique is its use of *vectors* to display much of its animated content. Vectors are line representations of an image. Like cartoons, they resemble an actual image but don't look completely realistic. The vectors that create an image give it shape and color. The curves of the vectors give an object its shape and contour. Every vector has two color properties: stroke (or outline) and fill; these properties (see Figure 1.1) give a vector image both its outline and overall color.

The kicker about vector images is that stroke and fill are calculated mathematically. This is very important when it comes to animation.

Raster images are very different from vector images. A raster image is created by a collection of pixels. *Pixel*, a hybrid word combining *picture* and *element*, is a colored dot or tile. A raster image, which can contain millions of pixels, works like a mosaic. Each little colored tile, which consumes a fixed amount of memory, plays a role in creating the overall color makeup and detail of the image. For an illustration of raster format, see Figure 1.2.

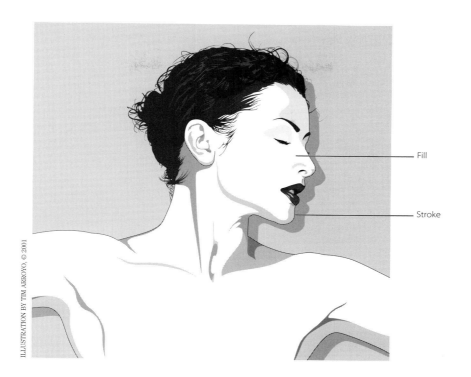

Fill

Stroke

Figure 1.1

The stroke and fill of a vector image give it its overall graphic properties.

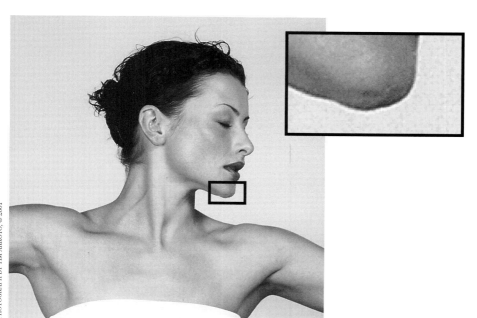

Figure 1.2

A raster image is created using a series of colored tiles, or pixels, arranged in a grid format.

One of the major differences between vector and raster graphics is in their scalability. Because the components of a vector image (stroke, fill, and so on) are calculated mathematically, they can be scaled, stretched, and manipulated by the computer without any loss of the image's clarity or resolution. The same is not true for raster images, however. They have a preset grid configuration, so any change in size alters the grid. When the size of a raster image is increased, the computer must interpolate (make an educated guess for) the additional pixels needed to make a larger grid. This can result in unwanted "chunkiness" or "blockiness" in the enlarged raster graphic.

The Many Faces of Flash

As you probably know by now, Flash isn't just an animation tool. So, what *is* it, then? Rather than try to define Flash, it's better to exemplify what it can do. Its presence and application around the world speak volumes.

Broadcast Media

Even though Flash is probably most "at home" on the Web, it has also made its way to broadcast media in recent years. This transition shouldn't come as a surprise. After all, Flash has proven to be a powerful animation tool and can be exported to a variety of file formats.

Flash has been used for several broadcast applications, both in Europe and the United States. In the U.K., the web design firm Kerb developed one of the first broadcast cartoon series that was created entirely in Flash. You can read more about the series, *Hellz Kitchen*, an irreverent and hilarious look at a group of slightly deranged talking vegetables, in the "Inspirational Design Model" of Chapter 28.

In the United States, Flash can be seen in the intro animation of *The Rosie O'Donnell Show*. For more information on this and other uses of Flash as a "convergent media," see www.macromedia.com/macromedia/proom/pr/2000/converge.html

Mobile Computing/Communications

As computers continue to become both smaller and more communicative, Flash will be part of the revolution. The Flash Player is poised to deliver content to a wide variety of Web-ready gadgets and devices. This includes business applications and commerce, news, entertainment—the works!

One of the first platforms to support Flash was Microsoft's Pocket PC. You can read more about Flash for the Pocket PC platform at www.macromedia.com/software/flashplayer/pocketpc.

The science fiction doesn't stop there. Flash is also being developed for implementation on mobile phones and other handheld or portable computing devices. For more information, see www.macromedia.com/software/flashplayer/resources/devices.

Gaming Consoles

Arguably one of the most unexpected applications of Flash has been in the interactive entertainment industry—console games, to be precise.

The most noteworthy example was the use of Flash to create the user interface for
LucasArts's popular "Star Wars: Starfighter" game for PlayStation 2 and Xbox. Although
LucasArts had designed the in-game interface for "Starfighter," they encountered a serious
problem near the end of their development cycle when they realized that they were lacking a
functional out-of-game user interface. Enter Macromedia Flash. LucasArts partnered with two
companies, Secret Level (`www.secretlevel.com`) and Orange Design (`www.orangedesign.com`), to
design the out-of-game interface using Flash. Released in February of 2001, the game serves as a
milestone in Flash history. Hopefully such future collaborations will open new avenues for Flash
and its development community. For more information on how Flash was used in "Star Wars:
Starfighter," see the Gamasutra article at `www.gamasutra.com/features/20010801/corry_01.htm`.

Interestingly, in May 2001, Macromedia and Sony announced a partnership geared toward
bringing the Flash Player to the Sony PlayStation 2. Facilitating in-game visual design, like
that featured in "Star Wars: Starfighter," was high on the partnership's list of goals. Offering a
complete range of Flash-facilitated connected entertainment experiences in the emerging
broadband era is also an important focus for the new partners.

The Internet

Flash started as a tool for deployment of animated content on the Internet, and, well, some
things will never change. No matter how Flash continues to advance in the areas of connec-
tivity, media authoring, and audience interactivity, it will always be a web development tool
at heart. To get a sense of this tradition, see the Inspirational Design Model sections throughout this book. Most of these projects are web-based and present a very rounded view of the
possibilities that this application presents.

In addition to delivering information and entertainment, Flash is used for advertising. To
read how Flash can track advertisements, see the article at `www.macromedia.com/resources/`
`richmedia/tracking`.

Web Games and Cartoons

Flash is great for creating multimedia and interactive navigation, but it is *superb* for creating
fun stuff! Why do we try to pass Flash off as such a "serious" application, when a large portion of its development community is dedicated to doing work that is meant to be anything
but serious! Games and cartoons are another important part of the Flash oeuvre.

It's fair to say that these kinds of Flash movies provide some of the most stimulating and
memorable Flash work on the Internet today. This book contains several excellent examples
for you to discover, including "Goodnight Mr. Snoozleberg" (Chapter 14), "Radiskull & Devil

Doll" (Chapter 20), the Mondo Media website (Chapter 11), the Atomic Cartoons website (Chapter 7), and the Camp Chaos website (this book's Color section).

Kiosk Development

A *kiosk* is a piece of custom computer hardware that delivers a fixed body of information, usually through a very user friendly interactive interface. Kiosks are most commonly used in situations where an organization wants to let the user control the access to information (usually through a touch screen or a mouse-driven interface) that would traditionally be delivered by a receptionist or another such individual. Because Flash can create powerful interactive experiences that are both complex and beautiful, it naturally lends itself to creating kiosks.

Although it would be difficult to provide a representative list of all the kiosks that have been developed with Flash, there is one very noteworthy example that we absolutely must mention. In late 2000, Moccu (whose corporate website is featured in the Color section of this book) presented the prototype for a touch screen, Flash-based petrol pump at CeBit in Hannover, Germany. Designed to let motorists search for information on travel routes and traffic situations, browse special shop offers, and even send e-mail while they're filling their tank, the CeBit pump prototype has yet to be implemented. It will be an outstanding and exciting example of the possibilities of merging Flash content with nontraditional computing environments such as kiosks (and even Web-enabled appliances).

Digital Art

Some Flash work defies description and needs no explanation. As the audience, you can take away from the experience whatever you like. Works of this nature can only be called one thing: art.

There are many individuals who are pushing the boundaries of Flash in ways that challenge current thinking about interactive, digital media. Two of these individuals are featured in this book: Maruto (Josh Davis), and Yugo Nakamura. See the Color section for a glimpse into their work and for links that will allow you to experience it firsthand at your computer.

Summary

In this chapter, you had a chance to make a closer examination of Flash as an application. This look at the range of its possibilities will be a helpful framework for your learning experience as you work through the lessons of *Flash MX Savvy*. Not only do you get to learn the history and tradition of the software and its community, but you'll be given hands-on experience with the amazing possibilities Flash has to offer. Now that you're prepared, you're ready to dig into the rest of this book and learn how to make the application work for you. Good luck, and have fun!

CHAPTER 2

What's New in Flash MX

Well, it's official: Flash MX has some truly cool features. With its release, Macromedia has upheld its longstanding tradition of meaningful software updates. By introducing a horde of new and exciting features, Macromedia has once again managed to push the boundaries of cutting-edge interactive design tools. This chapter details the latest and greatest additions.

Topics covered include the following:

- **Enhancing workflow and usability**
- **Using new tools for visual creativity**
- **Integrating rich media**
- **Exploring ActionScript advancements**
- **Introducing new publishing and distribution features**

Enhancing Workflow and Usability

Great software is easy to use and easy to customize. As such, Macromedia has included the following additions in Flash MX in order to increase its usability and streamline your workflow:

New user interface Flash MX's new user interface, in which all panels are fully dockable and collapsible/expandable, maximizes workflow so that you can focus on what is most important: creativity. For more information on Flash MX's new interface, see Chapter 3.

Improved Timeline Flash MX's most vital tool for animation, the Timeline, now includes such innovations as layer folders. For more information on the new and improved Timeline, see Chapter 9.

Starter templates Flash MX now lets you create documents from a library of templates, thereby bypassing many of the common tasks required in starting a new movie. You can also save existing movies as templates and distribute them to colleagues.

Property Inspector Replacing many of the panels from Flash 5, the Property Inspector is a dynamic tool that lets you efficiently edit all aspects of your movie from one central location. The Property Inspector is introduced in Chapter 3, but you'll see it used throughout the entire book.

Editing symbols in place Gone are the days when you had to leave the main Timeline to create and manipulate symbols. Now, you can work with your movie's symbols directly from the Stage. To learn more about editing symbols, refer to Chapter 7.

Shared Library enhancements Now you can employ Shared Library assets that are either integrated into your movie at runtime (when they're on a web server) or at author-time (when you're creating them on a local computer). For more information on the new Shared Library enhancements, see Chapter 7.

Components For developers who create highly interactive or content-driven movies, Components are a welcome addition. They enable you to add standard interface controls through a simple drag-and-drop procedure, and they include a check box, a drop-down menu, a scrolling menu, push buttons, radio buttons, a scroll bar, and a scroll pane. Flash MX makes it possible to customize the default Components and to create and distribute original Components that fit your specific needs. To learn more about Components, see Chapter 16.

Lessons and tutorials Macromedia knows that learning Flash MX can be a complicated process. As a result, it has included a series of enhanced and interactive tutorials and lessons geared toward getting developers and designers up to speed as quickly as possible on Flash MX's new features. Select Help → Tutorials to peruse your options.

Using New Tools for Visual Creativity

Flash MX includes many tools and enhancements for the drawing and design process, thereby helping you make the most of your creative skills:

Color Mixer enhancements Recognizing that the efficient use of color is one of the most important aspects of a successful Flash movie, Macromedia has enhanced the Color Mixer so that it's easier to mix, manipulate, and use colors and gradients. If you are interested in learning more about the Color Mixer, see Chapter 4.

Free Transform tool The Free Transform tool is a handy-dandy one-stop tool for all your object transformation and manipulation needs. Rotating, skewing, scaling—the Free Transform tool does it all. Chapter 6 covers the Free Transform tool.

Envelope Modifier tool A subset of the Free Transform tool, the Envelope Modifier tool (also referred to as the *Edit Envelope tool*) is a marvelous little gadget that lets you warp and distort the shape of the bounding box around an object—and therefore the object itself. For more information about the Envelope Modifier tool, see Chapter 6.

Distribute to Layers The Distribute to Layers command lets you take any number of selected objects and quickly distribute them to their own individual automatically generated layers— a definite must for complex animation. To learn more about how to distribute to layers, see Chapter 8.

Enhanced text With Flash MX's Text tool (in conjunction with the Property Inspector), you can exert a great deal more control over the way in which the type in your movie looks. Included are new features such as vertical text (great for creating Asian-language content). For more information about Flash MX's new enhanced text control, see Chapter 5.

Integrating Rich Media

What is Flash without rich media? These improvements and new features help you integrate Flash MX with all sorts of other cool media formats:

Enhanced audio support Flash MX has additional ActionScript elements that will further expand the sound possibilities of your Flash movies. The Sound object has added support that makes it possible to preload individual streaming sound files, monitor a sound's duration and playback position, and manage events when a sound loads or finishes playing. These new sound-related ActionScript terms make it easier than ever to distribute and manage high-quality audio content in a Flash movie. Flash MX's audio tools are covered fully in Part VI.

Support for external images Flash MX now makes it possible for you to load JPEG files from an external source. This feature is a welcome addition for developers who are creating interactive slide shows and other image-intensive movies. To learn about loading external JPEGs, see Chapter 17.

Video support For the first time, Flash MX offers real support for video. Flash has the capability to import many digital video formats and either embed or link them to a Flash movie. Embedded video takes advantage of Sorenson Spark, a video encoder/decoder that allows video to play within your Flash movies. As an element of your movie, video can then be controlled by ActionScript to create interactive movie players and editors. For more information on working with video in Flash, see Chapter 28.

Exploring ActionScript Advancements

Flash MX's scripting language, ActionScript, is probably one of the most powerful tools at your fingertips during the creative process. You'll see incredible enhancements to ActionScript in Flash MX.

Flash MX's new ActionScript enhancements are discussed throughout Part IV and Part V.

Some of the improvements to ActionScript include the following:

Better scripting environment Flash MX boasts a re-designed Actions panel that will make even the most squeamish animator take the plunge into the world of ActionScript. Enhancements include a new ActionScript Toolbox organization, a Jump menu for script navigation, code hint scripting shortcuts, a customizable script display, and an improved Debugger window that allows you to examine scripts in a line-by-line fashion.

Scripting for text and text fields To increase the control over text elements in your movies, Flash MX offers many ActionScript elements for manipulating text fields and text formatting parameters. This enhancement will increase the possibilities for displaying Dynamic Text in a movie.

Drawing with Movie Clips The Movie Clip object now has several new methods that allow you to paint and draw with ActionScript. To read about these new terms, see the ActionScript Reference section.

Expanded button scripting Buttons have always been symbols in Flash; in Flash MX they are also objects. As objects, buttons have been given an entire collection of ActionScript elements that enhance their functionality and interactivity. To learn more about the Button object, see Chapter 16 and the ActionScript Reference section.

Playback support The new Capabilities and Stage objects allow you to monitor the playback conditions of your movie and change its content accordingly to give your audience the best show possible. Read more about the Capabilities object and Stage object in the ActionScript Reference section.

Introducing New Publishing and Distribution Features

Flash MX broadens the possibilities of where and how you publish your creations. The new enhancements include the following:

Creating accessible content Using the new Accessibility panel, you can create and publish movies in Flash MX that are accessible by disabled individuals who use adaptive technology such as screen readers. For more information on creating and publishing accessible content, see Chapter 27.

SWF compression The Z-Lib compression codec greatly improves the download time for SWF files that contain particularly complex content.

Saving as Flash 5 Although Flash MX is a marvelous tool, there are people still working in the Flash 5 authoring environment. With the Save as Flash 5 option, you can upgrade to Flash MX and still collaborate with colleagues and teammates who haven't taken the plunge into the latest version.

Summary

In this chapter you got a brief, whirlwind tour of all the cool new enhancements of Flash MX. These included improvements to workflow and usability, visual creativity tools, rich media integration, ActionScript, and publishing features. You are now set to venture forth into the wonderful world of Flash MX.

CHAPTER 3

A Tour of the Flash Interface

After you've double-clicked the Flash program icon, you'll face a multitude of panels and windows. Have no fear, fellow Flasher, for by the end of this chapter, you'll be well acquainted with the Flash interface and know how to bend it to your will! To accomplish this amazing feat, you'll start by exploring the main program menu, the toolbars, and the Toolbox. From there, you'll look at the areas of the interface where you'll produce the majority of your creative masterpieces: the Stage and the Timeline. Then you'll look at the myriad of panels in Flash that help you streamline your workflow and leverage your creative potential. Finally, you'll delve into customizing Flash and using the Flash help system.

Topics in this chapter include:

- Using the main menu
- Working with the toolbars
- Digging into the Toolbox
- Using the Stage and work area
- Using the Timeline
- Understanding the Property Inspector
- Working with panels and windows
- Getting help

Getting Comfortable with Flash's Working Environment

One of the great joys of Flash is its interface. The program boasts an incredible collection of tools, all of which can be at your fingertips at a moment's notice. The interface, which accommodates a wide range of expertise and working styles, lets you maximize what's really important—creativity. So, let's launch Flash and take a quick tour of the tools you'll be using.

By default, Flash loads with a preset configuration of tools. Don't worry about this for the moment because, by the end of the chapter, you'll have learned how to get the interface looking exactly how you want.

Navigating the Main Menu Bar

Like many other programs, the main program menu bar lets you access many of Flash's functions, tools, and commands. The main program menu bar appears at the top of the program's interface (see Figure 3.1).

Many of the commands in the main program menu bar have hot keys associated with them—all of which are customizable. For more information on customizing keyboard shortcuts, see the "Customizing Shortcuts" section later in this chapter. To get a hands-on, step-by-step approach to customizing your keyboard shortcuts, see Hands On 1, "Customizing Keyboard Shortcuts," which follows this chapter.

File Menu

The File menu contains many of the primary file-related operations. Because most, if not all, of your Flash projects will either start or finish with one of the options in the File menu, it's good to become familiar with it. The File menu contains the following commands (many of which are covered in subsequent chapters): New, New from Template, Open, Open as Library, Close, Save, Save as, Save as Template, Revert, Import, Import to Library, Export Movie, Export Image, Publish Settings, Publish Preview, Publish, Page Setup, Print Preview, Print, Send, Recent File, and Exit.

Edit Menu

The Edit menu contains commands that let you handle data and manipulate the Flash environment to one degree or another. The commands include Undo, Redo, Cut, Copy, Paste, Paste in Place, Paste Special, Clear, Duplicate, Select All, Deselect All, Cut Frames, Copy Frames, Paste Frames, Clear Frames, Select All Frames, Edit Symbols, Edit Selected, Edit in Place, Edit All, Preferences, Keyboard Shortcuts, and Font Mapping.

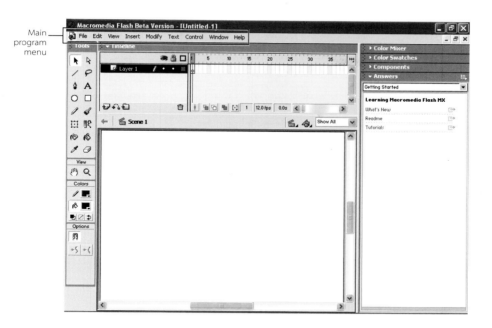

Figure 3.1

The main program menu

View Menu

The View menu gives you access to a number of commands that let you control how movies (as well as some tools) are viewed. These commands include Goto (with submenu commands First, Previous, Next, Last, and Scene), Zoom In, Zoom Out, Magnification (with submenu commands 25%, 50%, 100%, 200%, 400%, 800%, Show Frame, and Show All), Outlines, Fast, Antialias, Antialias Text, Timeline, Work Area, Rulers, Grid (with submenu commands Show Grid, Snap to Grid, and Edit Grid), Guides (with submenu commands Show Guides, Snap to Guides, and Edit Guides), Snap to Pixels, Snap to Objects, Show Shape Hints, Hide Edges, and Hide Panels.

Insert Menu

The Insert menu lets you add the elements that make a Flash animation. The Insert menu includes Convert to Symbol, New Symbol, Layer, Layer Folder, Motion Guide, Frame, Remove Frames, Keyframe, Blank Keyframe, Clear Keyframe, Create Motion Tween, Scene, and Remove Scene.

Modify Menu

While the Insert menu lets you insert various elements of a Flash project, the Modify menu enables you to alter those elements. The Modify menu contains the following commands:

Layer, Scene, Document, Smooth, Straighten, Optimize, Shape (with submenu commands Convert Lines to Fills, Expand Fill, Soften Fill Edges, Add Shape Hints, and Remove Shape Hints), Swap Symbol, Duplicate Symbol, Swap Bitmap, Trace Bitmap, Transform (with submenu commands Free, Distort, Envelope, Scale, Rotate and Skew, Scale and Rotate, Rotate 90° CW, Rotate 90° CCW, Flip Vertical, Flip Horizontal, and Remove Transform), Arrange (with submenu commands Bring to Front, Bring Forward, Send Backward, Send To Back, Lock, and Unlock All), Frames (with submenu commands Reverse, Synchronize Symbols, Convert to Key Frames, and Convert to Blank Key Frames), Group, Ungroup, Break Apart, and Distribute to Layers.

Text Menu

The Text menu contains the commands for manipulating text attributes and alignment. These include the following: Font (with a submenu of all the available fonts on your system), Size (with a submenu of point sizes), Style (with submenu commands Plain, Bold, Italic, Subscript, and Superscript), Align (with submenu commands Align Left, Align Center, Align Right, and Justify), Tracking (with submenu commands Increase, Decrease, and Reset), and Scrollable.

Control Menu

The Control menu contains all the commands you'll need to control the playback of your Flash movie. These include Play, Rewind, Go to End, Step Forward, Step Backward, Test Movie, Debug Movie, Test Scene, Loop Playback, Play All Scenes, Enable Simple Frame Actions, Enable Simple Buttons, Mute Sounds, and Enable Live Preview.

Window Menu

The Window menu gives you access to some of Flash's most important tools—primarily panels and dialog boxes. It includes the following commands: New Window, Toolbars (with submenu commands Main, Status, and Controller), Tools, Timeline, Properties, Answers, Align, Color Mixer, Color Swatches, Info, Scene, Transform, Actions, Debugger, Movie Explorer, Reference, Output, Accessibility, Components, Component Parameters, Library, Common Libraries (with submenu commands Buttons, Learning Interactions, and Sounds), Sitespring, Panel Sets (with submenu commands Default Layout, Designer [1024×768], Designer [1280×1024], Designer [1600×1200], Developer [1024×768], Developer [1280×1024], and Developer [1600×1200]), Save Panel Layout, Close All Panels, Cascade, and Tile. A selection list of currently open windows appears at the bottom.

Help Menu

The Help menu offers you access to a myriad of resources to help you out. These include Welcome, What's New, Lessons, Tutorials, Using Flash, ActionScript Dictionary, Flash Exchange, Manage Extensions, Samples, Flash Support Center, and About Flash.

Accessing the Toolbars in Windows

Flash's toolbars are available only on the Windows operating system (sorry, no toolbars on the Mac). The series of toolbars contain shortcuts for popular menu commands.

> As you can easily access many of the commands in the toolbars through the main program menu, it's best to leave them turned off to conserve precious screen real estate.

Main Toolbar

The Main toolbar, accessible through Window → Toolbars → Main, is similar to the edit/production toolbar of many graphics programs. The default tools (from left to right) include the following: New, Open, Save, Print, Print Preview, Cut, Copy, Paste, Undo, Redo, Snap to Object, Smooth, Straighten, Rotate, Scale, and Align.

> Although the default location of the Main toolbar is just above the Timeline, it can also float free of the interface or be placed along the left or the right side of the interface. To move it from its default location, simply click it (anywhere off its various buttons) and drag it to the desired location.

> Many of the commands in the Main toolbar (Copy, Cut, Paste, Smooth, Straighten, Rotate, and Scale) are only accessible if you have an object selected on the Stage.

Status Toolbar

Unlike the Main toolbar, which can either float or be docked to the top or sides of the Flash interface, the Status toolbar resides at the bottom of the Flash interface (see Figure 3.2). Essentially, the Status toolbar provides tooltips for various Flash interface elements. You can access it by selecting Window → Toolbars → Status.

Controller Toolbar

The Controller toolbar, accessible through Window → Toolbars → Controller, gives you access to a series of VCR-like buttons, which enable you to control and test your animation in the Flash Movie Editor. From left to right, the buttons in the Controller toolbar are Stop, Rewind, Step Back, Play, Step Forward, and Go to End.

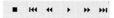

> Like the Main toolbar, the Controller toolbar can also float free of the interface or be placed along the left or the right side of the interface. To move it from its default location, simply click its surface (avoiding its various buttons), and drag it to the desired location).

Figure 3.2

The Status toolbar

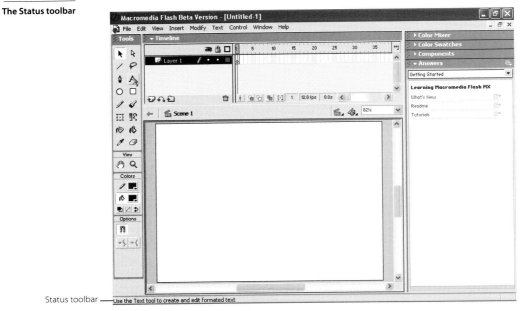

Status toolbar — Use the Text tool to create and edit formated text

If your Flash movie doesn't actually feature any kind of animation, the buttons in the Controller toolbar won't be accessible.

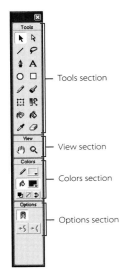

Tools section

View section

Colors section

Options section

Digging into the Toolbox

Imagine you are a cross between an artist and a handyman (or handywoman). I know the idea is a little silly, but for this section, it's apt. Now, to carry out your job, you need all manner of tools designed both to create art as well as to repair and modify your creations. Where would you find such an odd set of tools in one place? Look no further, for the Flash Toolbox is just what you need!

Essentially, the Flash Toolbox (Windows → Tools), which is partitioned into four sections, is a central location for a whole host of drawing, painting, selection, and modification tools. Let's have a look at each of the sections separately.

Tools Section

This section of the Toolbox contains tools for drawing, painting, and selecting. Don't worry about understanding how each of the individual tools work at this point, as they'll all be covered in subsequent chapters.

View Section

The View section of the Toolbox contains the necessary tools for zooming in on and panning your Flash movie.

> The Hand tool is "handy" for panning your movie if you've magnified the Stage to such a degree that all of it isn't visible. A little confused as to what exactly the Stage is? See the "Discovering the Stage and Work Area" section to find out.

To pan your Flash movie, follow these steps:

1. Select the Hand tool from the View section of the Toolbox (or simply hit H).
2. Click anywhere on the Stage, hold down your mouse button, and drag the Stage to the location you want. When you are finished, release your mouse button.

To zoom in on a specific location in your movie, follow these steps:

1. Select the Zoom tool from the View section of the Toolbox (or simply hit either M or Z).
2. Move the Zoom tool over the Stage, click and drag the mouse so that the line encloses the area you want to magnify, and release the mouse button.

To zoom out, simply hold down the Option/Alt key. You'll notice that the magnifying glass icon changes to contain a minus sign instead of a plus sign. From here, click your mouse button until you are zoomed out to where you want.

> Alternatively, instead of using the Option/Alt key to zoom out, you can click the Reduce button (the one with the minus sign), which appears in the Options section of the Toolbox when the Zoom tool is active.

Colors Section

As you would expect, the Colors section of the Toolbox deals exclusively with colors. The functionality of the Colors section, which allows you to set both stroke and fill color, is duplicated in the Stroke and Fill controls in the Property Inspector. Don't worry about how you can use the tools in the Colors section just yet; we'll cover the use of color in Flash in Chapter 4.

Options Section

The Options section of the Toolbox, unlike the previous three sections discussed, doesn't contain a set of static tools. Instead, it contains modifiers for tools selected in any of the other three sections. For example, when you select the Rectangle tool from the Tools section of the Toolbox, the Round Rectangle Radius button appears in the Options section.

At this point, don't worry too much about figuring out how each of the modifiers work, as they'll all be covered in subsequent chapters.

Discovering the Stage and Work Area

Much like in a play, the Stage is where it all happens in Flash. This is where you craft your eye candy, where all your animations do their thing, and all your creations come to life. Ultimately, what happens on the Stage is what your audience sees after you've exported your movie.

The work area is the gray expanse that surrounds the Stage. You can think of the work area as "backstage," if you want to continue the theatrical metaphor. You can actually place elements in the work area as you would place them on the Stage. The difference is that they won't be visible in the Flash movie itself when it's exported or tested. The great thing is that all the elements placed in the work area behave in exactly the same way as if they were on the Stage. As a result, you could create an animation where a small sphere begins its journey in the work area and ends its journey on the Stage. Figure 3.3 shows the Stage and the work area.

Figure 3.3

The Stage and work area

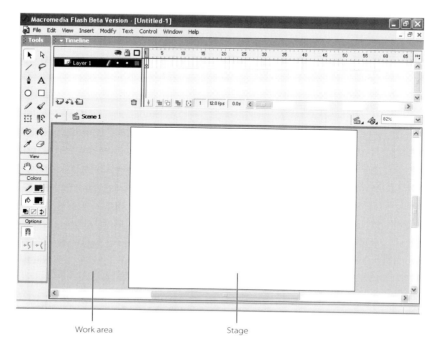

Work area   Stage

You can toggle the visibility of the work area by going to View → Work Area. Alternatively, you can use the shortcut Cmd+Shift+W (Mac)/Ctrl+Shift+W (Win).

> Like many of the "toggleable" features in Flash, a check mark next to its command in the View menu indicates the work area is visible.

Located just above the Stage proper and the work area, the Scene and Symbol bar not only gives you an indication of the scene in which you are currently working or the symbol which you are currently editing, but it also allows you to jump from scene to scene or from symbol to symbol using either the Edit Scene or Edit Symbol drop-down menu.

You'll also notice that in at the extreme right of the Scene and Symbol bar there is a drop-down menu that lets you dynamically change the Stage's magnification.

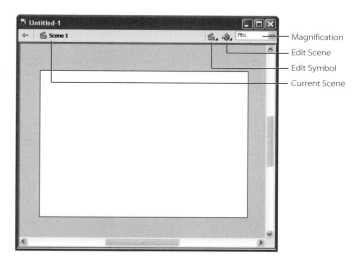

Customizing the Stage's Size

The Stage starts out as a blank slate upon which you create and choreograph your handi-work. As one would expect, the Stage certainly wouldn't be good to anyone if you couldn't mold it to look exactly how you wanted. Flash wouldn't be that exciting if everyone's movie had to be the same size or color. Never fear, Macromedia has built in the ability to change the Stage's size and color.

To change the Stage's size:

1. Go to Modify → Document or use the shortcut Cmd/Ctrl+J to open the Document Properties dialog box.

2. Enter pixel values into the Width and Height fields, and then hit OK. The dimensions of the Stage will immediately change.

Customizing the Stage's Color

Now, to change the background color of the Stage (and as a result, the background color of the movie), you follow almost the same steps. But, instead of entering a value into the Width and Height fields, click the Background Color swatch and choose a color from the Color Picker.

Alternatively, you can use the Property Inspector to change the look of the Stage. To do this, follow these steps:

1. If it isn't already, open the Property Inspector by going to Window → Properties or using the shortcut Cmd/Ctrl+F3.

2. If you don't have any other object selected on the Stage, the Property Inspector will display the Stage's properties.

3. To change the Stage's background color, just click the Background Color swatch in the Property Inspector. When the color palette opens, select the color you want.

4. Click the Size button to open the Document Properties dialog box. From there, you'll be able to change the dimensions of the Stage by entering a pixel value into the Width and Height fields.

If you want the changes you've made be the default for all the Flash movies you create, click the Make Default button in the Document Properties dialog box.

Exploring the Timeline

If the Stage is where "it all happens," the Timeline is what "makes it happen." The Timeline, which is discussed in-depth in Chapter 9, is the tool you employ when you add any kind of change over time to your Flash movie (see Figure 3.4).

Figure 3.4

The Flash Timeline

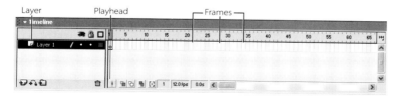

Without going into too much depth, the Timeline occupies the uppermost portion of the Flash interface and is broken up into three primary elements: the playhead, frames, and layers.

The Timeline, like many other interface elements within Flash MX, can be both minimized and docked/undocked. For more information on how to dock, undock, and minimize the Timeline, see the "Customizing Panels" section later in this chapter (the Timeline isn't a panel *per se*, but the same principles apply).

Playhead

When you play your Flash animation, the playhead travels through the Timeline (horizontally) at a consistent rate. As the playhead moves through each of the individual frames, the contents are displayed on the Stage, thereby creating the animation.

> Although Chapter 9 covers the ins and outs of the Timeline and the playhead, it's important to know you can move the playhead manually. You can either click the frame's location on the Timeline header (the strip on the top of the Timeline where the frame numbers—in increments of five—are located), or drag the playhead to the desired location.

Frames

Frames are pretty much the heart and soul of the Timeline. Each frame represents a moment of time in an animation. In addition, each frame contains unique content that changes from frame to frame. As the playhead moves through the Timeline, the content of each of the frames appears on the Stage.

> Your animation's frame rate determines the actual speed at which the animation plays. For more information on frame rate, see Chapter 9.

Layers

Flash animations are not just constructed horizontally (with frames) but also vertically with layers. Each layer contains a single element or animation. As a result, you can have many layers with many different elements and animations, thereby creating a complex movie.

> Layers give you the ability to separate content. For especially complex Flash movies, this is a good way to keep track of your work. To learn more about layers and how you can alter their appearance, see Chapter 8.

Understanding the Property Inspector

The Property Inspector, which is new to Flash MX, is a tool you'll undoubtedly find yourself using quite frequently during the creative process. Essentially, it serves as a doorway to the properties of any given object (be it some text, a shape, a button, or a Movie Clip).

Like many other interface elements within Flash MX, the Property Inspector can be both collapsed/expanded and docked/undocked. For more information on how to dock, undock, and minimize the Property Inspector, see the "Customizing Panels" section later in this chapter (the Property Inspector isn't a panel *per se*, but the same principles apply).

Its power is that it's a dynamic tool. By *dynamic*, I mean that the options displayed change depending on what sort of object you select. For example, if you select a string of text, you'll be able to change its font, color, and size. On the other hand, when you click a shape, you'll be able to change its stroke, fill, and dimensions. So, you see, it's a pretty powerful and useful tool. To access the Property Inspector, all you need to do is select Window → Properties or use the shortcut Cmd/Ctrl+F3.

To access less common attributes of a given object, all you need to do is click the expander arrow (the Down arrow in the bottom-right corner of the Property Inspector).

Working with Panels

Panels are arguably one of the most important aspects of the Flash MX interface. With them, you can access a whole bevy of incredibly powerful tools that work with any number of elements within Flash MX.

One of the coolest things about panels in Flash MX is that they can be integrated into the overall interface (opposed to *floating* around the workspace). *Docking*, as the process is called, makes it considerably easier for you to access tools and information while maximizing your workspace (see Figure 3.5).

To learn more about docking panels (as well as their many other workspace-streamlining features), see the "Customizing Panels" section later in this chapter.

On top of this, you can easily open, close, move, and resize panels to streamline your work environment (and therefore your creative process).

Each panel, regardless of its purpose, has an Options drop-down menu accessible by clicking the icon in its upper-right corner. Although some panels won't have many options in this menu, there will be some that have many options.

At this point, it's a good time to explore each of the panels available in Flash.

When you initially open Flash, you'll see the default organization of preset docked panels. If you open any new panels, they won't appear docked, but instead they will be free floating. Don't worry, you can easily dock them if you so desire.

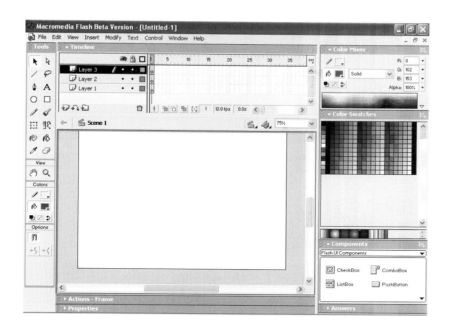

Figure 3.5

The default Flash MX interface complete with docked panels

Answers Panel

The Answers panel, accessible by going to Window → Answers, provides you a centralized location for accessing Flash MX's assorted support and help documents (Tutorials, What's New, Readme, and so on).

Align Panel

The Align panel, which you can open by going to Window → Align (Cmd/Ctrl+K), enables you to align objects (or groups of selected objects) according to a series of preset criteria—each of which is represented by a button. For more information on using the aligning objects with the Align panel, see Chapter 6.

Color Mixer Panel

The Color Mixer panel, accessible by selecting Window → Color Mixer (Shift+F2), gives you the ability to create colors, using RGB, HSB, or Hexadecimal Code, and save them as a swatch to the Color Swatches panel. The Color Mixer panel also enables you to assign colors to either the stroke or fill. For more information, see Chapter 4.

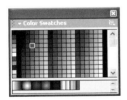

Color Swatches Panel

The Color Swatches panel, accessible by choosing Window → Color Swatches (Shift+F3), helps you organize, load, save, and remove individual colors from the currently used color palette. For more information on using the Color Swatches panel, see Chapter 4.

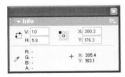

Info Panel

The Info panel, which is accessible by going to Window → Info (or by using the shortcut Cmd/Ctrl+I), gives you the ability to numerically change the dimensions (in the Width and Height fields) and the position (in the X and Y fields) of a given selected object. The bottom portion of the Info panel contains information (in RGB format) about the currently selected object's color. Finally, the lower-right corner of the panel provides information (in X/Y coordinates) as to the exact current position of the mouse.

Scene Panel

The Scene panel, accessible by going to Window → Scene, gives you the ability to navigate between, rename, add new, and delete scenes. To learn more about scenes and the Scene panel, see Chapter 11.

Transform Panel

Similar to the Info panel, the Transform panel gives you the ability to numerically manipulate a selected object. The top portion of the panel includes two fields that allow you to scale an object horizontally or vertically. You can open the Transform panel by selecting Window → Transform or by using the shortcut Cmd/Ctrl+T.

> When scaling an object with the Transform panel, you can constrain the proportions by clicking the Constrain check box.

The bottom portion of the Transform panel allows you to either rotate or skew, in degrees, the currently selected object.

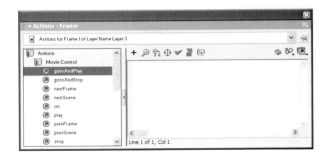

Actions Panel

The Actions panel, which can be opened by going to Window → Actions or by using the shortcut F9, is where you attach ActionScripts to either objects or frames. The Actions panel enables you to either choose from a preset list of ActionScripts or author your own in Normal or Expert mode. For more information on the Actions panel, see Chapter 12.

ActionScript Debugger

Because ActionScript is a scripting language, it's natural that Macromedia would include a debugger. The Action-Script Debugger, which was introduced in Flash 5 and is accessible by going to Window → Debugger, lets you troubleshoot troublesome ActionScript. Chapter 18 explores the ActionScript Debugger in detail.

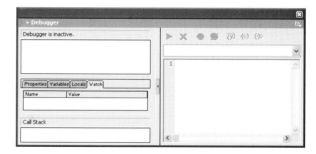

Movie Explorer

The Movie Explorer is a handy little tool introduced in Flash 5. Accessible by going to Window → Movie Explorer or by using the shortcut Option/Alt+F3, the Movie Explorer provides central access to all your movie's assets. From this central location, you can search for an object or element by name, display and alter the properties of a given element, and replace all instances of a font with another font. For a better look at the Movie Explorer, see Chapter 7.

Reference Panel

Let's face it, ActionScript (Flash's scripting language) is getting more complicated by the second. To help Flash developers cope, Macromedia has introduced the Reference panel (Window → Reference), an integrated repository in which individual listings (that include Flash version compatibility, parameters, a description, and an example) for each ActionScript element reside.

Output Window

The Output window, which cannot be docked with other panels, is a snazzy little tool that, once you've exported your Flash movie, provides you with a readout of the file size for all scenes, objects, text, symbols, and instances. You can open the Output window by going to Window → Output.

Accessibility Panel

A new addition to Flash MX, the Accessibility panel is an incredible step forward in making Flash content accessible to audiences with a variety of disabilities (who use a range of different technologies to access the Web). You can open the Accessibility panel by going to Window → Accessibility. The Accessibility panel will be discussed in Chapter 27.

Components Panel

 The Components panel, accessible by going to Window → Components, is the central repository for Flash MX's new Components feature—specialized, premade, complex Movie Clips with already defined parameters. Components are extremely handy if you want to create relatively complex user interface components (such as scrollable windows or drop-down menus) with a minimum of muss and fuss.

Component Parameters Panel

The Component Parameters panel, accessible by going to Window → Component Parameters, is the tool by which you edit the parameters of Components you've added to your movie using the Components panel.

Library

The Library, which can be opened by going to Window → Library (or by using the shortcut F11), is a repository of all of the symbols you create or use for your Flash movie. Whether a Movie Clip, Button, or Graphic symbol, the Library has it all. For more information on the Library, see Chapter 7.

Common Libraries

The Common Libraries, which are accessible though Window → Common Libraries, are slightly different from the Library itself. Where the Library contains only those symbols associated with the currently open Flash movie, the Common Libraries contain a series of symbol groups (Buttons, Learning Interactions, and Sounds). Each symbol group has a bunch of premade symbols that come with Flash. The Common Libraries give you lots of symbols so that you don't have to create them yourself.

Sitespring Panel

Sitespring is Macromedia's new groupware tool. Designed as a tool with which multiple design team members can track digital assets, communicate, maintain versioning, and create project schedules, Sitespring runs off a central server as opposed to the user's machine. The Sitespring panel, which is accessible by going to Window → Sitespring, lets you log in directly to a Sitespring server from within Flash.

Customizing Panels

One of the great things about the new Flash MX user interface is that it has evolved to such a point that all elements fit seamlessly and efficiently together to create an extremely usable work environment. This is no great surprise because, with the increasing complexity of the Flash itself, screen real estate has become increasingly precious.

One of the most obvious features of Flash MX's new-and-improved interface is its panels that, as mentioned before, are dockable and collapsible/expandable.

In the following section, you are going to learn how to make the most of the new panel paradigm. You'll learn how to dock panels, expand/collapse panels, choose from preset panel layouts, and create a custom panel layout.

Docking Panels

When you dock a panel, you physically combine it with another element of the interface. If you dock two floating panels, you create a floating "mega" panel (see Figure 3.6).

On the other hand, as illustrated in Figure 3.7, you can also dock a panel with a section of the underlying interface (underlying in the sense of what is below a floating panel) to create an area where all of your commonly used panels reside.

Ultimately, docking panels makes it considerably easier for you to access tools and information while maximizing your workspace.

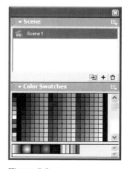

Figure 3.6

The Scene panel and Color Swatches panel have been combined to form a floating "mega" panel.

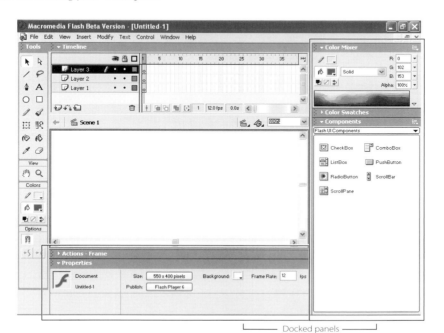

└─── Docked panels ───┘

Figure 3.7

Flash MX interface with docked panels

To dock two panels, follow these steps:

1. Open any two panels by using the Window menu.

2. Click the gripper region of the panel's title bar (represented by the small dots on the left side of the title bar) and drag it toward the target panel. Notice that a ghost image of the panel appears as you drag your mouse.

You'll notice that your cursor will change when it moves over the gripper region of the panel's title bar.

3. Move your cursor over the target panel.

4. When a black highlight appears around the target panel, release the mouse button.

To dock a panel with the underlying interface, follow these steps:

1. Open the panel you'd like to dock with the underlying interface by using the Window menu.

2. Click the gripper region of the panel's title bar and drag it over the area of the interface to which you'd like to dock it.

Flash MX lets you dock a panel to the left, bottom, and right side of the interface.

3. When the black highlight appears your mouse button and the panel will automatically dock.

Collapsing and Expanding Panels

As mentioned, the Flash MX interface has become a little crowded. As a result, Macromedia has provided users with the ability to expand and collapse panels, thereby economizing on space while still keeping the necessary tools at their fingertips (see Figure 3.8).

To expand a collapsed panel (or collapse an expanded panel), all you need to do is click the panel's name in the title bar.

Choosing Preset Panel Layouts

Because of the malleability of the Flash MX's working environment, there is any number of permutations for interface elements. You can certainly experiment and develop an interface layout that best suits your needs. If you aren't inclined to do so, you can also choose from a list of preset panel layouts that Macromedia has provided.

Go to Window → Panel Sets and choose one of the seven options. Each preset panel layout contains a specific set of panels arranged for a specific screen resolution (the higher the resolution, the more panels in the layout).

Creating Custom Panel Layouts

After working with Flash MX for a while, you'll get to the point where you develop a panel layout most conducive to your working style. If so, you don't want to have to constantly re-create the layout every time you fire up the program. Flash MX lets you take your layout and save it so it will be accessible from the same location as Flash MX's preset panel layouts. Let's take a look at how:

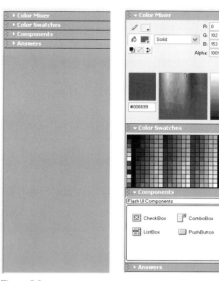

Figure 3.8

The left screen shows a series of panels that have been collapsed, and the right one shows the same panels expanded.

1. Go to Window → Save Panel Layout.
2. When the Save Panel Layout dialog box appears, enter a name for your custom layout into the field.
3. When you've finished, click OK.
4. From here, your custom panel layout will be accessible by going to Window → Panel Sets.

Customizing Shortcuts

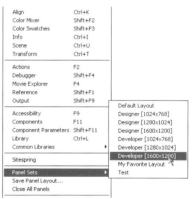

Keyboard shortcuts are a quick and easy way to access a program's functions. Up until now, however, most programs offered the user only an immutable set of shortcuts. But Flash MX, as well as many of the other Macromedia programs, offers a Keyboard Shortcuts editor that lets you use existing shortcuts, create your own shortcuts, and edit existing shortcuts. To access the Keyboard Shortcuts editor, select Edit → Keyboard Shortcuts (see Figure 3.9).

To learn more about customizing keyboard shortcuts, see Hands On 1: "Customizing Keyboard Shortcuts," which follows this chapter.

Figure 3.9

The Keyboard Shortcuts editor

Using Flash Help

Macromedia has provided Flash users with a pantheon of resources when you're in a jam and can't quite figure something out. Beyond the Macromedia Dashboard, you can access many help options through the Help menu, including:

Using Flash (Help → Using Flash) Provides a manual whose content is accessible through a content list, an index, or a search engine.

ActionScript Dictionary (Help → ActionScript Dictionary) Provides a syntactical reference (organized alphabetically) to the ActionScript language.

Lessons (Help → Lessons) Provides Flash-based tutorials, delivered in the program environment, covering topics that range from introducing Flash to using Flash with Freehand and Illustrator.

Samples (Help → Samples) Provides some interesting examples of Flash techniques that you can play with and pick apart.

Flash Support Center (Help → Flash Support Center) Provides up-to-date information on the latest Flash developments and technical issues. (It's sometimes referred to as the *Developers Resource Center.*)

Flash Tutorials (Help → Tutorials) Provides you with a whole series of project-based tutorials whose source files are installed on your hard drive (in the `Tutorials` directory) when you install Flash MX.

Summary

In this chapter you spent time getting familiar with the Flash interface. You explored the main menu, the toolbar, the Toolbox, the Property Inspector, the Stage, the work area, and the Timeline. Then, you moved on to a brief, but thorough, look at all the panels available to you when working with Flash. From there, you explored how to manipulate Flash MX's interface to maximize your efficiency and creativity. Finally, you explored the Flash help options.

Understanding the Flash interface is fundamentally important to continued success with the program. Remember, the better you understand your working environment, the better you can use it to produce amazing results!

Customizing Keyboard Shortcuts

As mentioned earlier, Flash offers you a way to customize the keyboard shortcuts you use. Not happy with the default setup for keyboard shortcuts? The Keyboard Shortcuts editor lets you change it to suit your fancy. Let's take a step-by step look at how to take advantage of the Keyboard Shortcuts editor.

Changing a Command's Shortcut

To redefine a command's shortcut:

1. Go to Edit → Keyboard Shortcuts to open up the Keyboard Shortcuts editor.

2. If it isn't already selected, choose Flash MX from the Current Set drop-down menu at the top of the Keyboard Shortcuts editor.

3. Click the Duplicate Set button 🔳 just to the right of the Current Set drop-down menu.

> You cannot manipulate the default keyboard shortcuts for Flash MX. Instead, you create a duplicate set and then make any changes you want.

4. When the Duplicate dialog box appears, enter a name into the Duplicate Name field, and click OK. Notice that the name of the duplicate set you've just created appears in the Current Set drop-down menu.

5. Now, choose the specific group of commands you'd like to work with from the Commands drop-down menu.

6. If you've chosen Drawing Menu Commands or Test Movie Menu Commands, click the plus sign to expand the command category (File, Edit, View, Insert, and so on) with which you want to work.

If you've chosen Drawing Tools or Actions Panel Commands, skip to step 9.

7. Select the specific command you want. Notice that the existing shortcuts attached to that command appear to the right of the command (the shortcut will also appear in the Shortcuts text box just below).

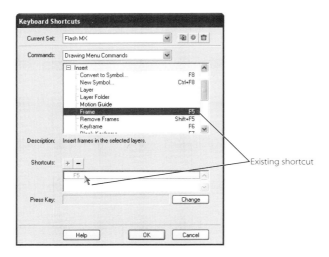

8. Select the command's existing shortcut in the Shortcuts text box.

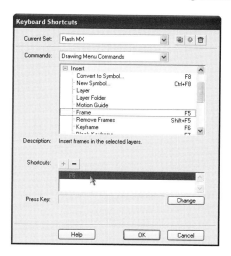

9. Click the Remove Shortcut (-) button 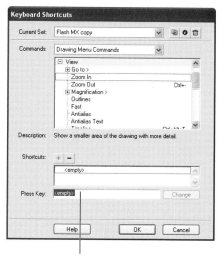 to strip the command's existing shortcut.

10. Press the Add Shortcut (+) button ; the Press Key field will automatically go live.

The Press Key field goes live.

11. Press the key combination you want to add; the key combination appears in the Press Key field.

12. Click the Change button to assign the new shortcut to the command.

> If your key combination is already assigned to another command, Flash will alert you and let you either reassign the shortcut or simply cancel it.

13. When you've finished, click OK and the new keyboard shortcut will be assigned.

PART II

Creating and Manipulating Visual Content

As you learned in Chapter 1, Flash MX is capable of creating an incredible array of exciting interactive products. Be it traditional websites, webtoons, kiosks, or other, more adventurous applications, the common thread is that the overwhelming majority are visually based. This is no great surprise as one of the greatest aspects of Flash MX is that it is vector based opposed to bitmap based, thereby allowing you to create some truly stunning visual imagery.

Ultimately, this means that you'll be spending a fair amount of your creative energy focusing on crafting the visual aspects of your beautiful Flash MX creation. As a result, Macromedia has included an extremely wide variety of tools designed to create, manage, and manipulate all visual aspects of your visual assets.

CHAPTER 4

Painting and Drawing

The good people at Macromedia have molded Flash into a topnotch animation program, as well as a graphics program of surprising power. The program boasts a whole host of powerful and usable tools for creating both vector and bitmap graphics. This chapter explores these tools. You'll start off by looking at the various selections tools available. Then, you'll learn about the line and shape drawing tools: the Pencil tool, the Brush tool, the Pen tool, the Ink Bottle tool, the Paint Bucket tool, and the Dropper tool. You'll close the chapter off by looking at the Eraser tool and learning how to manipulate stroke and fill with the Property Inspector.

- **Selecting items for manipulation**
- **Drawing lines**
- **Drawing basic shapes**
- **Using the Pencil, Brush, Pen, Subselection, Ink Bottle, and Paint Bucket tools**
- **Sampling with the Dropper tool**
- **Using the Eraser tool**
- **Changing an object's stroke with the Property Inspector**
- **Altering an object's fill with the Property Inspector**
- **Working with digital color**

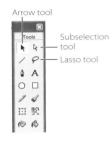

Arrow tool
Subselection tool
Lasso tool

Selecting Items for Manipulation

Flash MX prides itself on having a fairly extensive list of tools with which you can select lines, shapes, text, groups, symbols, buttons, and a multitude of other items you place on the Stage. Every item you place on the Stage has a tool with which to select it (or parts of it). In this section, you're going to quickly explore each of the various selection tools available, including the Arrow tool, the Subselection tool, and the Lasso tool.

> Because the Pen tool and the Subselection tool are intrinsically connected, it is difficult to separate them in a discussion such as this. A more in-depth discussion of the Subselection tool's functionality (especially in conjunction with the Pen tool) is provided in the "Drawing with the Pen Tool" section later in this chapter.

Selecting with the Arrow Tool

Located in the top-left corner of the Toolbox, the Arrow tool lets you select and move single or multiple items about the Stage. The Arrow tool also allows you to change the shape of an unselected line, stroke, or object.

> Selecting an object with the Arrow tool is the first step in editing an object's properties with the Property Inspector.

Selecting an Object

Selecting an object with the Arrow tool is actually quite simple—just point and click. However, a few tips and tricks will help you better take advantage of its functionality. First, when you select an ungrouped object, a checkered pattern appears over it to indicate it is currently selected.

> If you are interested in learning more about the difference between a grouped and an ungrouped object, as well as how you group and ungroup objects, see Chapter 6.

Figure 4.1

The left two are ungrouped objects selected with the Arrow tool, and the right two are grouped objects selected with the Arrow tool.

On the other hand, a grouped object that has been selected has a thin rectangular box around it. Figure 4.1 illustrates the difference between grouped objects that have been selected with the Arrow tool and ungrouped objects selected with the Arrow tool.

Many objects, especially if they have been drawn with one of the shape tools, usually have both a fill and a stroke. Therefore, if you want to select the entire object, you'll need to select both the fill and stroke separately. You can also double-click an object's fill to select both the fill and stroke. Alternatively, you can select both the stroke and fill, and then group them together by selecting Modify → Group. After grouping them, you'll only need to click the object to select the group.

To deselect an item that you've selected with the Arrow tool, click anywhere else on the Stage, go to Edit → Deselect All, hit your Esc key, or use the keyboard shortcut Cmd+Shift+A (Mac)/Ctrl+Shift+A (Win).

Moving an Object

To move an object with the Arrow tool, just click and drag it to the desired location, and release your mouse button. If you have grouped a series of objects, the process works the same way when you want to move the group.

Many objects are made up of both a stroke and fill. If you don't select both and attempt to move the object, the unselected portion of the object will be left behind.

Changing the Shape of an Object

Although you are able to alter the shapes of objects more easily with other Flash tools, the Arrow tool is a quick way to fiddle with the form of an unselected line, stroke, or shape:

1. Select the Arrow tool from the Toolbox. Make sure you have an ungrouped object on the Stage (this example shows a simple circle). Make sure the object itself is unselected.

2. Move the Arrow tool close to the edge of the circle and notice the cursor changes slightly (see Figure 4.2).

3. When the cursor changes, click and drag the line to where you want it. Notice that you get a ghost-like preview of the line's position (see Figure 4.3).

4. When the line, edge, or shape is altered the way in which you want, release your mouse button.

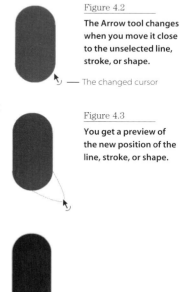

Figure 4.2

The Arrow tool changes when you move it close to the unselected line, stroke, or shape.

— The changed cursor

Figure 4.3

You get a preview of the new position of the line, stroke, or shape.

Using the Snap to Objects Option

When you toggle Snap to Objects, which is located in Toolbox's Options section when the Arrow tool is selected, you cause the selected objects to snap to other objects on the Stage. You can snap selected objects to just about anything: lines, freeform paths, shapes, and so on. In addition, you can even snap objects to the Stage's grid. Using the Snap to Objects option is useful when you want to make sure the objects on the Stage line up or arrange them in a consistent manner.

> To view the grid, select View → Grid → Show Grid. To snap objects to the grid, just choose View → Grid → Snap to Grid. Finally, if you want to edit the grid properties, just go to View → Grid → Edit Grid.

When you've got the Snap to Objects option toggled, you'll notice that a small circle appears in the center of the selected object when you move it with the Arrow tool. This small circle is called the *registration point* in Flash (see Figure 4.4).

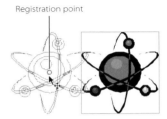

Registration point

Figure 4.4

A small circle appears in the center of the selected object when you move it with the Arrow tool.

The registration point, and not the object itself, is the thing that's doing the snapping. However, as the registration point and the object are one and the same thing, the point is pretty much moot. When you move the registration point of one object (and therefore the object itself) over another object (a straight line drawn with the line tool, for instance), it turns bold/black and snaps to it.

Although it isn't that vital to have a full understanding of registration points yet, your curiosity might be piqued. If this is the case, see Chapter 6 for an in-depth discussion of registration points and how you manipulate them.

> Snap to Objects is most useful when you are creating a tweened animation along a path. For more information on tweening along a path, see Chapter 9.

Snapping to Pixels

In addition to employing the Snap to Objects options, you can also use the Snap to Pixels option. Although it's not accessible in the Options section of the Toolbox when the Arrow tool is selected, the Snap to Pixels option is best explored at this stage of the discussion.

Essentially, when the Snap to Pixels option is turned on (View → Snap to Pixels), a pixel grid (visible only if the Stage is magnified to at least 400 percent) appears to which all objects will snap.

To temporarily make the pixels grid invisible, press X. When you hold down the X key, the grid will disappear, reappearing when you release the button.

Using the Smooth Option

The Arrow tool's Smooth option ➜$, which is located in the Toolbox's Options portion when you've got the Arrow tool selected, reduces the number of bumps in a selected curve. The result is a smoother curve than you had previously.

To use the Smooth option, simply select a curve with the Arrow tool, and click the Smooth button. Alternatively, you can select the curve with the Arrow tool, and go to Modify → Smooth.

Using the Straighten Option

The Arrow tool's Straighten option ➜⟨ , located in the Toolbox's Options portion next to the Smooth option button, takes the curve out of relatively straight lines—thereby making them perfectly straight.

To use the Straighten option, select a line with the Arrow tool, and click the Straighten button. Alternatively, you can select the curve with the Arrow tool, and go to Modify → Straighten.

Selecting with the Lasso Tool

While the Arrow tool selects individual objects, the Lasso tool ℘ selects all the objects (or parts of objects) in a specific area.

You can select portions of individual ungrouped objects (say, the corner of a large square) with the Lasso tool. That area will be selected independently from the rest of the object and can therefore be moved with the Arrow tool—creating the illusion you took a pair of scissors, cut off the corner, and then moved it away from the square.

The Lasso tool contains three options in the Toolbox's Options section: Magic Wand, Magic Wand Properties, and Polygon mode. Much like the Arrow tool, the Lasso tool is amazingly easy to use. All you need to do is click and drag the tool to draw a line around the area you want to select.

For selection purposes, the Lasso tool automatically closes an area that you don't close yourself.

Using Polygon Mode

Polygon mode 🔲 lets you assert a great deal more control over selection than you'd get if you were simply using the Lasso tool.

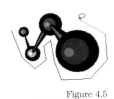

Figure 4.5

Polygon mode in action

Essentially, Polygon mode lets you select an area by drawing multiple connected straight edges. Make sense? In Polygon mode, the Lasso tool draws a straight line. Every time you hit your mouse button, a selection point is created. You can then draw another straight line (which is attached to the selection point you just created). The process is repeated until you encircle the entire selection area. When you double-click your mouse button, the area is selected. Figure 4.5 illustrates Polygon mode in action.

> Just like with the Lasso tool when it isn't in Polygon mode, an unclosed area is automatically closed when you finish your making your selection.

Working with the Magic Wand Option

The Lasso tool's Magic Wand option ✳ selects similar colors in a bitmap image that has been broken apart.

> When you break apart a bitmap (which isn't the same as tracing a bitmap), you are simply telling Flash to regard the image as a collection of individual color areas. For more information on how to work with bitmaps in Flash MX, refer to Chapter 6.

After the bitmap image has been broken apart (which is accomplished by selecting the image and then going to Modify → Break Apart), you can then click individual colors with the Magic Wand to select them.

> A color area selected with the Magic Wand is overlain by a checkerboard pattern to note its selection.

Setting Magic Wand Properties

The Magic Wand Properties button ✳…, which is located in the Toolbox's Options portion when you have the Lasso tool selected, allows you to set the properties of the Magic Wand. When you click the Magic Wand Properties button, the Magic Wand Settings dialog box opens and you can make the appropriate adjustments to the Magic Wand. The options are as follows:

Threshold Defines the degree to which the Magic Wand will select similar (but not identical) colors. Choices range from 0 to 200. For example, if you use a threshold setting of 0, only similar identical colors will be selected. As you increase the threshold setting, the amount of colors that are selected will increase.

Smoothing Determines how edges of a selection should be smoothed. The choices include Normal, Pixels, Rough, and Smooth.

Drawing Visual Elements

Now that you've looked at how to use Flash's various selection tools, it's time to create something that can be selected. Flash boasts a whole of host of great tools that allow you to draw anything you imagine. Want to create a Picasso-like portrait of yourself (remember, both eyes on one side of your face) or a drawing of your favorite flower? In this section, you'll look at the tools you'll need to draw these types of images.

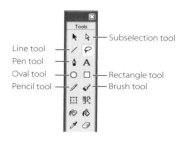

As with the previous tools discussed in this chapter, all the tools you'll need are located in the Toolbox.

> When you select one of the following drawing tools from the Toolbox, you can manipulate the drawn object's stroke and fill using the Property Inspector before you draw it.

Drawing with the Line Tool

Unlike the freeform Pencil tool, which will be discussed shortly, the Line tool ∕ creates single straight lines.

To use the Line tool, click where you want the line to begin, drag until it is the desired length, and release your mouse button. You can set the thickness and style of the Line tool using the Property Inspector. To learn more about manipulating an object's stroke, see the "Changing an Object's Stroke with the Property Inspector" section later in this chapter.

> Holding the Shift key down while you're using the Line tool will constrain the line to multiples of 45 degrees.

Drawing Basic Shapes

Flash provides you with two tools, the Oval tool and the Rectangle tool, for drawing basic shapes. Although fairly similar, each has particular characteristics you should explore.

Using the Oval Tool

Located in the Toolbox's Tools section, the Oval tool ◯ helps you draw ellipses and circles. To use the Oval tool, simple click your mouse where you want the shape to start and then drag until you have created the desired shape and size. When you are finished, release your mouse button. An oval is composed of both a stroke and a fill. To find out more about how you can adjust an oval's stroke and fill properties, see the "Changing an Object's Stroke with the Property Inspector" and "Altering an Object's Fill with the Property Inspector" sections later in this chapter.

> Holding down the Shift key while drawing your oval creates perfectly round circles.

Drawing a Rectangle

Located in the Toolbox's Tools section, the Rectangle tool ☐ lets you draw rectangles and squares. Much like the Oval tool, you can create a rectangle by selecting the Rectangle tool from the Toolbox, clicking your cursor on the Stage where you want the shape to start, and then dragging until you have created the desired shape and size. When you are finished, release your mouse button. A rectangle, like an oval, is composed of both a stroke and a fill. To find out more about how you can adjust a rectangle's stroke and fill, see the "Changing an Object's Stroke with the Property Inspector" and "Altering an Object's Fill with the Property Inspector" sections.

Holding down the Shift key while drawing your rectangle creates a perfect square.

CHANGING RECTANGLE CORNER RADIUS

The Rectangle tool has one available option in the Toolbox's Options portion—Rounded Rectangle Radius ⌐ . There will certainly be instances when you'll want to round the corners of the rectangle or square you create. This is where the Rounded Rectangle Corner Radius option comes in.

When you click the Rounded Rectangle Radius button, the Rectangle Settings dialog box opens.

From here, you can enter a value (from 0 to 100) in the Corner Radius field. The higher the value, the more rounded the corners of your rectangle become—give it a try and see what kind of results you get.

Drawing with the Pencil Tool

The Pencil tool ✎ creates single lines. Unlike the Line tool, however, the Pencil is a freehand tool. With it you can draw shapes that range from straight lines to incredibly squiggly doodles.

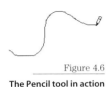

Figure 4.6

The Pencil tool in action

Using the Pencil tool is almost as simple as using an actual pencil. All you need to do is select the Pencil tool from the Toolbox, click the area of the Stage where you want your line to begin, hold down the mouse button, and draw the shape you want. When you're finished, just release the mouse button. Figure 4.6 illustrates the Pencil tool.

Setting Pencil Mode

The Pencil mode ↳ , which is the Pencil tool's only option, contains three options: Straighten, Smooth, or Ink. The specific Pencil mode you choose is applied to the line you draw *as you draw it*. However, you can straighten or smooth an already drawn line by selecting the target line and then going to Modify → Smooth or Modify → Straighten. Alternatively, you can also simply click either the Smooth or Straighten button after having selected the already drawn line. The Pencil modes include the following options:

Straighten Straightens all curves in a line. This creates a line angular in nature.

Smooth Smooths out any angularities in a line. Unfortunately, you have no real control over the degree to which Flash smooths out your lines.

Ink Ensures your line is displayed exactly how you've drawn it—no smoothing and no straightening.

Drawing with the Brush Tool

The Brush tool 🖌 , much like the Pencil tool, creates single freeform lines. Unlike the Pencil tool, however, the shapes created with the Brush tool are all fill. As a result, to change the color of the brush stroke, you'll need to use the Property Inspector (discussed in the "Altering an Object's Fill with the Property Inspector" section later in this chapter).

> The cool thing about the Brush tool is that, like the Pencil tool, you can smooth or straighten a stroke that you create. To do this, select the already created stroke with the Arrow tool and hit the Straighten or Smooth button. Alternatively, you can go to Modify → Smooth or Modify → Straighten.

Using the Brush tool is as easy as using the Pencil tool. Just select the Brush tool from the Toolbox, click the area of the Stage where you want your line to begin, hold down the mouse button, and draw the shape you want. When you're finished, just release the mouse button.

> Another cool thing about the Brush tool is that if you are using a graphics tablet, such as those produced by Wacom, you can dynamically vary the weight of the stroke. Toggle the Use Pressure button in the Options section of the Toolbox when you've got the Brush tool selected and alter the pressure of the stylus on the tablet.

Selecting Brush Size

The Brush tool certainly wouldn't be that useful if you were stuck with one size. Well, fear not, Macromedia has provided you with a series of different brush sizes ● , all of which are accessible through the Options portion of the Toolbox when you've got the Brush tool selected.

Brushes ranging from tiny to huge are accessible through the drop-down menu. To change the brush size, just make your choice from the drop-down menu *before* you draw your line—you can't dynamically change a line's size by choosing a different brush size after you've drawn it.

Setting Brush Shape

Flash also allows you to set your brush's shape ▮●▾▮ . Much like setting brush size, you need to choose a brush shape, all of which are accessible from the Brush Shape drop-down menu, *before* you draw your line.

> Unfortunately, Flash still doesn't give you the ability to create your own custom brush shapes, so you'll have to make do with what is available.

Setting Brush Mode

Brush mode ◉ , which is accessible through a drop-down menu in the Toolbox's Options section, is perhaps one of the most interesting aspects of the Brush tool.

Essentially, Brush mode lets you specify exactly how your brush stroke affects an existing drawn or painted element.

Paint Normal   Paint Fill   Paint Behind   Paint Selection   Paint Inside

There are five Brush mode options:

Paint Normal Applies a stroke from the Brush tool over the top of existing elements—just like if you were to take a can of spray paint to the (yikes!) Mona Lisa.

Paint Fill Applies your brush stroke to all areas made up of fills.

> The Paint Fill option leaves lines (like those created with the Pencil tool) unaltered.

Paint Behind Applies the strokes from your Brush tool behind any existing element.

Paint Selection Applies your brush stroke to areas of fill that have been previously selected.

Paint Inside Is interesting in that it applies brush strokes in only the same area in which it was initiated. Paint Inside mode will not paint over existing elements.

Drawing with the Pen Tool

The Pen tool ✒ is the primary tool for creating freeform vector art within Flash. Granted, the vast majority of the drawing tools in Flash (like the Line or the Pencil) create vector graphics. However, the Pen tool is by far the most useful and powerful.

> The Pen tool works closely with the Subselection tool, which is covered later in this chapter starting with the "Modifying a Point's Position with the Subselection Tool" section.

For those among you who are more familiar with illustration programs such as Macromedia FreeHand or Adobe Illustrator, you'll certainly recognize the Pen tool. Designed to build precision paths, the Pen tool works by creating points that are connected by paths to form a segment. The line segments can be either straight as an arrow or curved as a mountain path. One of the many joys of the Pen tool is that the points (which are created each time you click the mouse button) act as anchors that can be moved around to alter the characteristics of any of the line segments (see Figure 4.7). It's powerful!

Figure 4.7

Any complicated line (which is more than one segment long) is composed of paths linked by a series of points.

Setting Pen Tool Preferences

Before you tear off and start learning how to put the Pen tool to work, you need to become familiar with its preferences—accessible by going to Edit → Preferences and clicking the Editing tab. From here, you have three choices (all located in the upper-left corner of the Editing tab):

Show Pen Preview Lets you preview line segments as you draw. A preview of the line segment is displayed as you move the pointer around the Stage.

Show Solid Points Specifies that unselected anchor points appear as solid dots and selected anchor points appear as hollow dots.

Show Precise Cursors Specifies that the Pen tool pointer appears as a crosshair cursor, rather than the default Pen tool icon.

Drawing a Straight Line with the Pen Tool

Drawing a straight line is quite easy with the Pen tool. All you need to do is select the Pen tool from the Toolbox, click a place on the Stage where you want to begin the line (which creates a point), and then move your mouse and click to define the endpoint of the line. Whammo, you've just created a straight line with the Pen tool. Figure 4.8 shows a simple one-segment line drawn with the Pen tool.

Figure 4.8

A simple, one-segment line drawn with the Pen tool; notice that it ends and begins with a point.

Drawing a Curved Line with the Pen Tool

Drawing a curved line is where the Pen tool really begins to shine! Drawing a straight line is easy (and can be accomplished with many other drawing tools in Flash), but creating (and manipulating) curved segments is what the Pen tool is really good at.

> When you draw a curve with the Pen tool, you create curve points. When you draw a straight-line segment, you create corner points. When selected, curve points appear as hollow circles, and selected corner points appear as hollow squares.

To create a curved line with the Pen tool, follow these steps:

1. Select the Pen tool from the Toolbox.

Figure 4.9

The resulting curve that is created as you move the selected tangent handle away from the original end point. Note that the tangent handle stretches out the farther you drag it away.

2. Click anywhere on the Stage where you want your curve to begin.

3. Move the cursor to the location where you want the curve to end.

4. Click to add the end point in the segment. However, instead of releasing your mouse button, keep it pressed down and move the mouse a little bit in any direction. You'll notice that as you move your mouse away (with the button still held down), two things happen:

   - First, your cursor is actually dragging one of two tangent handles that are linked to the final point in the segment.

   - Second, the farther away you drag one of the tangent handles away from the original point, the more extreme your curve gets (see Figure 4.9).

5. To adjust the characteristics of the curve, simply move the selected tangent handle.

6. When the curve is exactly how you want it, release the mouse button. Notice that the tangent handles disappear.

Figure 4.10 illustrates the resulting curved segment.

Figure 4.10

The resulting curve

Adding a Point to a Line

Each time you click your mouse button when you use the Pen tool, you add a point to a path. When you are finished, you have a series of points and the segments that run between them. The points themselves really determine the way in which the line looks. As you'll see later in this section, you can move points around to alter the shape of the line. Given this, it's pretty obvious that the Pen tool wouldn't be all that useful unless you could add more points along the path *after* you've drawn it.

Follow these steps to add points to a path:

1. Make sure a curved path already exists on the Stage and that you have the Pen tool selected. (If you have difficulty remembering how to make a curved path, just refer to the "Drawing a Curved Line with the Pen Tool" section.)

2. Move the Pen tool over the area of the path you want to add the point. Notice that the cursor changes from a pen with a small x to its right (which is the default cursor when you are pointing anywhere on the Stage) to a pen with a small plus (+) to its right (see Figure 4.11).

3. Click to add the point.

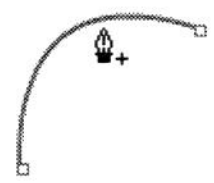

Figure 4.11

When you move the cursor over a curved path, the icon changes to a pen with a plus (+) next to it. This indicates that you can add a point.

Removing a Point from a Stroke

Removing a point from a stroke is as easy as adding one; follow these steps:

1. Make sure a multipoint path already exists on the Stage and you have the Pen tool selected.

Removing a curve point is a two-step process. First, you actually convert the curve point to a corner point and then you remove the corner point. If you want to remove a corner point, it's simply a one-step process.

2. Move the Pen tool over the point you want to remove. Notice that the cursor changes from a pen with a small x to its right (which is the default cursor when you are pointing anywhere on the Stage) to a pen with a small v shape to its right (see Figure 4.12).

3. Click once. This converts the curve point to a corner point. Once you do this, you'll notice that your cursor changes to a pen with a small minus (-) to its right (see Figure 4.13).

4. Click the point once again to remove it entirely.

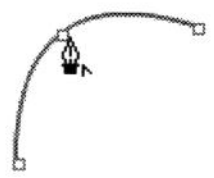

Figure 4.12

When you move the cursor over a path, the icon changes to a pen with a small v next to it.

Modifying a Point's Position with the Subselection Tool

Because the points in a path act as a sort of skeleton, moving any of the given points alters the structure of the path itself. To move a point with the Subselection tool, follow these steps:

1. Make sure you've got a multisegmented path on the Stage. Also, make sure you select the Subselection tool, which is located just to the right of the Arrow tool in the Toolbox's Tools section.

2. Click the path with the point you want to move to select it (notice that the path will turn a light blue).

3. Move your cursor over the point you want to move. Notice the cursor turns from an arrow with a small black box to its right, which is the default for the Subselection tool, to an arrow with a small empty box to its right, which indicates you are over an editable point.

4. Click and drag the point to the desired location.

5. When the point is at the desired location, simply release your mouse button.

Figure 4.13

Once you convert the curve point to a corner point, you'll notice that your cursor changes to a pen with a small minus (-) to its right.

If the point you've selected is a curve point, the tangent handles appear when you select it with the Subselection tool.

Editing a Curved Segment with the Subselection Tool

As discussed previously, it's pretty painless to create a curved segment with the Pen tool. But what happens if you want to edit the curviness, for example, of the curve after you've created it? Well, this is where the Subselection tool comes in. To alter a curve with the Subselection tool, follow these steps:

1. Make sure you've got a curved path on the Stage. Also, make sure you select the Subselection tool, which is located to the right of the Arrow tool in the Toolbox's Tools section.

Figure 4.14

After clicking the desired curve point with the Subselection tool, either one or two tangent handles will appear—depending on whether the point is at the end or in the middle of the path.

2. Click the path with the point you want to move to select it (notice that the path will turn a light blue).

3. Click the curve point once (remember that the curve point is usually the second point in the curved segment because that was the one whose tangent handles were used to modify the curve's shape). Depending on whether the curve point is at the end or in the middle of the path, either one or two tangent handles will appear (see Figure 4.14).

4. Click the point at the end of the tangent handle and drag it to adjust the curve's shape.

Converting a Corner Point to a Curve Point

Corner points are all well and good when you're drawing angular paths with the Pen tool. However, they are limited in that they can't be fiddled with to produce (or adjust) a curve. This is a little annoying if you have spent a couple of hours creating a perfect image only to find you need to make a slight curve in a straight line. Fortunately, Flash has the ability to turn a corner point into a curve point:

1. With the Subselection tool, select the corner point you want to convert. When it's selected, the corner point will turn from a hollow square to a filled square.

2. Once it has been selected, hold down the Option/Alt key.

3. Click the corner point you want to convert, and then and drag it slightly. Notice that two tangent handles immediately appear.

4. You can then click and drag either tangent handler to adjust the shape of the curve.

Using the Ink Bottle Tool

Located in the Tools section of the Toolbox, the Ink Bottle changes a stroke's color, width, and style. The benefit of using the Ink Bottle, opposed to just selecting the individual stroke and then using the Property Inspector, is that you can use it to make it easier to change the stroke attributes of multiple objects simultaneously.

> Using the Ink Bottle involves becoming familiar with the workings of the Property Inspector—something that hasn't been covered yet. For more information, see the "Changing an Object's Stroke with the Property Inspector" section later in this chapter.

To use the Ink Bottle, follow these steps:

1. Without anything selected on the Stage, select the Ink Bottle tool from the Tools section of the Toolbox.

2. If it isn't already, open the Property Inspector by going to Window → Properties. Notice that the Property Inspector displays the Ink Bottle options.

3. Choose a stroke color, stroke height, and stroke style.

> To learn how you go about creating a custom stroke, see the "Changing an Object's Stroke with the Property Inspector" section later in this chapter.

4. Now, move your cursor (which has changed into an ink bottle) over any stroke you want to change and click once. The target stroke will automatically change to reflect the options you chose in the Property Inspector.

> Once you've set the properties of the Ink Bottle tool, it remains "filled." This means that you could continue clicking other strokes on the Stage and they would all change to reflect the options you set in the Property Inspector.

Manipulating an Object's Fill with the Paint Bucket

While the Ink Bottle tool changes the character of an object's stroke, the Paint Bucket tool fills an area with color. It can both fill empty areas as well as change the color of already filled areas. You can paint with solid colors, gradient fills, and bitmap fills. One of the neat things about the Paint Bucket tool is that it can fill areas that are not entirely closed.

> Much like in the case of the Ink Bottle tool, using the Paint Bucket tool requires at least a basic understanding of how the Property Inspector works—something that hasn't been covered yet. As a result, see the "Altering an Object's Fill with the Property Inspector" section later in this chapter.

To use the Paint Bucket, follow these steps:

1. Without anything selected on the Stage, select the Paint Bucket tool from the Tools section of the Toolbox.

2. If it isn't already, open the Property Inspector by going to Window → Properties. Notice that the Property Inspector displays the Ink Bottle options.

3. Choose a fill color.

4. Now, move your cursor (which has changed into a paint bucket) over the inside of an empty shape or an existing fill and click once. The target area will automatically "fill up" with the new color you set using the Property Inspector.

Setting the Paint Bucket Gap Size Option

As mentioned previously, the Paint Bucket tool can actually fill objects that aren't entirely closed. The Gap Size option ⬤, which is accessible through the Toolbox's Options section, gives you the ability to set the gap size at which the Paint Bucket will still fill an open shape.

To set the gap size, just choose from one of these options in the drop-down menu: Don't Close Gaps, Close Small Gaps, Close Medium Gaps, or Close Large Gaps.

Using the Paint Bucket Lock Fill Option

The Paint Bucket's Lock Fill option 🔒 comes into play when you're using gradients as fill (something that's covered later in the "Working with the Color Mixer Panel" section). Located in the Toolbox's Options section when you've got the Paint Bucket selected, this

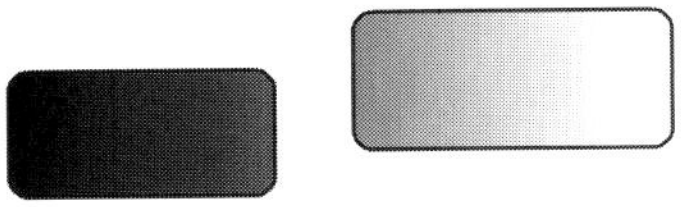

Figure 4.15

When used in conjunction with a gradient fill, the Lock Fill option creates the illusion that filled objects are part of the same, continuous gradient.

creates the illusion that all filled areas (regardless of whether they are side by side or far apart) are part of the same, continuous gradient. Figure 4.15 illustrates the Lock Fill option.

To use the Lock Fill option, just follow these steps:

1. Select or create a gradient fill using the Color Mixer panel.

> To learn about how you go about creating and manipulating gradient fills, see the "Working with the Color Mixer Panel" section later in this chapter.

2. Select the Paint Bucket tool.

3. Select the Lock Fill option.

4. Move your cursor (which has changed into an paint bucket with a small padlock icon to its right) over the inside of an empty shape or an existing fill and click once. The target area will automatically "fill up" with the gradient you mixed.

5. Repeat the process in step 4 to fill additional areas—by doing this, you'll get the illusion that the filled areas are part of the same, continuous gradient.

Using the Fill Transform Tool

The Fill Transform tool 🖌 , which used to be the Paint Bucket option but has been turned into a tool in its own right in Flash MX, lets you adjust the visual properties of a gradient or bitmap fill.

> This discussion hinges on at least a basic understanding of how you use the Color Mixer panel to create gradient and bitmap fills. As a result, you might want to read the "Working with the Color Mixer Panel" section later in this chapter before continuing.

Let's take a look at how you can use the Fill Transform tool:

1. Select the Fill Transform tool.

2. Click an area filled with a gradient or bitmap fill. Notice that when you select a fill for editing, a bounding box with handles and a center point appears. You'll find that, depending on whether you are working with a linear gradient, a radial gradient, or a bitmap fill, you'll get different handles.

- In the case of a linear gradient fill, the bounding box that appears is rectangular with a center point, a circular handle in the upper-right corner, and a square handle on the right.

- However, if you are working with a bitmap fill, the bounding box appears with two separate sets of handles: three circular ones (one on top, one in the top-right corner, and one in the right) and three square ones (one in the left, one in the bottom-left corner, and one in the bottom).

- On the other hand, if you are working with a radial gradient fill, the bounding box is oval in shape, with a square handle, and two circular handles.

When your pointer is over any of these handles, it changes to indicate the handle's specific function.

3. From here, you can perform several distinct actions:

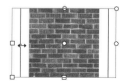

- **Reposition the center point of a gradient (either radial or linear)**: Simply click and drag the center point to a desired location within the bounding box.

- **Change the width of the linear gradient or bitmap fill**: Click and drag the square handle on the side of the bounding box.

Changing the width of the gradient or bitmap fill resizes only the fill and not the object itself.

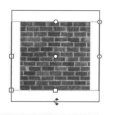

- **Change the height of a bitmap fill**: Click and drag the square handles at the bottom of the bounding box.

- **Rotate the linear gradient, radial gradient, or bitmap fill**: When you're working with a linear gradient or bitmap fill, drag the circular rotation handle at the corner.

As with adjusting the width, when you adjust the height of a gradient or bitmap fill, you are not adjusting the height of the actual filled object.

On the other hand, if you are working with a radial gradient, drag the bottom circular rotation handle.

- **Stretch or compact a linear gradient or a fill**: Drag the square handle at the center of the bounding box.

  However, if you are working with radial gradient, click and drag the first circular handle (just below the square handle).

- **Skew or slant a bitmap fill**: Drag one of the circular handles on the top or right side of the bounding box.

Sampling with the Dropper Tool

The Dropper tool , which is located in the Toolbox's Tools section, lets you sample the fill or stroke from one object and then apply it to another.

To sample the stroke of an object:

1. Make sure you have the Dropper tool selected and you have an object with a stroke on the Stage.

2. Move the Dropper over the stroke. You'll notice that the cursor changes from a simple dropper to a dropper with a small pencil to its right.

3. Click your mouse button once—notice that the Dropper instantly changes to the Ink Bottle tool. This means you are ready to apply the sampled stroke color to the stroke of another object.

4. Move the Ink Bottle cursor over another stroke and click once—voila! The stroke of the second object is changed to that of the first.

To sample the fill of an object:

1. Make sure you have the Dropper tool selected and you have an object with a fill on the Stage.

2. Move the Dropper over the fill. You'll notice that the cursor changes from a simple dropper to a dropper with a small brush to its right.

3. Click your mouse button once—notice that the Dropper instantly changes to the Paint Bucket tool. This means you are ready to apply the sampled fill color to the fill of another object.

4. Move the Paint Bucket cursor over another fill and click once.

If you hold down the Shift key when you click an object with the Dropper tool, both the fill and stroke are sampled and can be applied to another object.

Using the Eraser Tool

To use the Eraser tool , which is a heck of a lot easier than using a real eraser (no little rubber shavings), select it from the Toolbox, move it to the location on the Stage you want to erase, and click and drag until you've erased to your heart's content. Yup, it's that easy.

Selecting Eraser Mode

Much like with the Brush tool, the Eraser has several different modes, all of which are accessible through the Toolbox's Options section when you've got the Eraser selected.

Essentially, the five Eraser modes let you specify exactly how your Eraser affects an existing drawn or painted element:

Erase Normal Erases any fills or strokes over which you drag the Eraser tool.

Erase Fills Constrains the Eraser so it erases only fills and empty areas without erasing any strokes over which it passes.

Erase Lines Erases only strokes and lines. Any fills your cursor passes over will not be affected.

Erase Inside Erases within the constraints of a shape. When this mode is selected and you start your stroke in a filled area, only the section inside of that area is erased.

Erase Selected Fills Affects only fills that are selected.

Working with the Faucet Option

The Faucet option, which is located in the Toolbox's Options section when you've got the Eraser selected, automatically deletes any fill or stroke that you click. Just select the Faucet option and point and click—and say "bye bye" to the offending fill or stroke.

Selecting the Eraser Shape

As with the Brush Size mode, you can specify the size and shape of your Eraser. The available Eraser shapes and sizes range from small to large and are accessible through a drop-down menu in the Options section of the Toolbox when the Eraser is selected.

To change the Eraser shape and size, make your choice from the drop-down menu *before* you use the Eraser.

Changing an Object's Stroke with the Property Inspector

As mentioned in Chapter 3, stroke is the character of the line formed when you draw an object. Whether you want to change the character of a line drawn with the Pencil tool or the border of a rounded rectangle, you are going to need to use the Property Inspector.

As already discussed, you can use the Color Mixer panel to manipulate stroke color. However, if you want to fiddle with other stroke attributes, such as height and style, you need to use the Property Inspector.

With it, you can change the height, style, and color of an object's stroke. Let's take a look at how:

1. If it isn't already, open the Property Inspector by going to Window → Properties.

2. Now, select the object whose stroke you want to manipulate.

If you want to change the stroke of an ungrouped object, make sure you don't just select its fill. The easiest way to avoid this is to select the Arrow tool and click and drag so that the selection box encompasses the entire object.

3. Click the Stroke Color swatch. When the color palette opens, select the color you want to use for the object's stroke.

Stroke color swatch

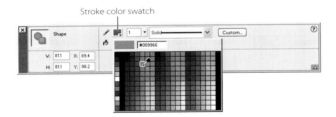

4. From here, you can set the stroke's height (thickness) by either adjusting the slider (accessible by clicking the little down arrow to the right of the Stroke Height field) or by simply typing in a numerical value into the Stroke Height field.

The minimum stroke height is 0.1, and the maximum is 10.

Stroke field —   — Stroke slider

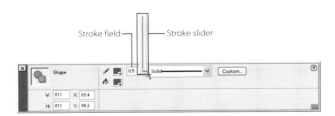

5. Now, you can set the stroke's style by choosing one of the options from the Stroke Style drop-down menu.

6. If you aren't happy with the preset stroke styles that Flash offers, you can create your own by clicking the Custom button to the right of the Stroke Style drop-down menu. The Stroke Style dialog box that appears initially lets you set the type and thickness of the custom stroke.

Stroke Style drop-down menu

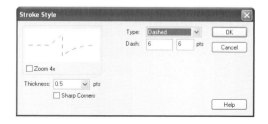

Your choices are automatically shown in the preview window in the left portion of the dialog box. To get a good feel how this dialog box works, experiment with the various options and see what kinds of results you get. Depending on the stroke type you've chosen, you will have access to a far wider range of unique options in the Stroke Style dialog box.

> You can also set an object's stroke color through the Stroke Color well in the Toolbox—represented by the color swatch just to the right of the Pencil icon. Just toggle the Stroke Color button, click the color swatch, and then choose the color you want.

Altering an Object's Fill with the Property Inspector

You have two ways of setting fill color. The first, which will be discussed in the "Working with the Color Mixer Panel" section later in this chapter. The second way, discussed in this section, involves using the Property Inspector. In all honesty, using the Property Inspector is a little limiting because you only have access to solid color—with the Color Mixer panel you've also got access to gradient and bitmap fill.

To set an object's fill using the Property Inspector, just follow these steps:

1. If it isn't already, open the Property Inspector by going to Window → Properties.

Fill color swatch

2. Now, select the object whose fill you want to manipulate.

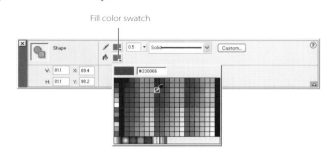

3. Click the Fill Color swatch. When the color palette opens, select the color you want to use for the object's stroke.

> Using the Fill Color well in the Toolbox works exactly the same as if you were to use the Color Mixer panel or the Property Inspector; it's just accessed from a different location. All you need to do is toggle the Fill Color button, click the color swatch, and then choose the color you want.

Creating with Digital Color

Like any other visual medium (such as painting, photography, film, or 3D modeling), color is an extremely important factor in crafting a creation with impact in Flash. Unless you are targeting your work toward an audience of visually impaired individuals (a process that involves a great deal of specialized knowledge and experience), you need to spend a great deal of time thinking about how you are going to effectively maximize color in Flash. In this section, you're going to explore some specific color-oriented topics.

Until the Web came along, all computer-oriented graphic designers created images and artwork specifically for print. When it comes to print, color is composed using a system designed to make sure that the color displayed on a computer monitor translated accurately into the ink in a printer. Called CMYK (Cyan/Magenta/Yellow/Black), the system defines individual colors as a percentage of each of these four colors. For example, the CMYK abbreviation for the color black would be 0-0-0-100.

When it comes to designing specifically for the screen, CMYK has no real place. Instead, color is composed using the RGB (Red/Green/Blue) system, which defines an individual color in terms of a combination of three colors.

When it comes to the Web, there is an additional color system of which you need to be aware. *Hexadecimal notation* (sometimes just referred to as *Hex*) is less of a real color system and more of a way to describe RGB color in an alternative format. Used by HTML, Hex notation is composed of six characters (00DDFF, for example). The first two characters represent the red color channel (R), the middle two the green channel (G), and the last two the blue channel (B). Each of the numeric characters (0–9) and each of the letters (A–F) represent an integer from 0–16. As a result, the Hex notation translates neatly into an RGB value.

Working with Web-Safe Color

When it comes to using color in conjunction with web-oriented media (HTML, Flash, digital video, and so on), there are some things you need to know.

Most computers can display at least 256 colors (most can display millions). The problem, however, is that you can't be exactly sure *which* 256 colors. This would normally cause some rather frustrating problems for web designers. Fortunately, the majority of web browsers (Netscape Navigator and Microsoft Internet Explorer are the most popular) all share a fixed-color palette—the *browser-safe palette* (or *web-safe palette* as it's sometimes called). So, if you choose a color from the browser-safe palette, you are guaranteed your design will look exactly the same (at least when it comes to color) from system to system.

If you use a color outside the web-safe color palette, the browser coverts the odd color to the closest color it can find in its system palette. As a result, you run the risk of having your colors look slightly different from machine to machine if you stray from the web-safe color palette.

Working with the Color Swatches Panel

Each Flash movie contains its own color palette, stored in the architecture of the file itself. Flash displays a file's palette as swatches (small squares of color) in the Color Swatches panel.

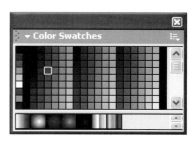

Although the Color Swatches panel (Window → Color Swatches) displays the web-safe palette by default, you can add, delete, edit, and duplicate colors as you need. You can also import and export custom-created palettes. You do all of these operations through the Color Swatches panel's Options pop-up menu—which, if you remember, is accessible by clicking the icon in the panel's top-right corner.

The options include the following:

Duplicate Swatch Automatically duplicates the currently selected swatch.

Delete Swatch Deletes the currently selected swatch.

Add Colors Lets you import color palettes that have been saved in the CLR (Flash Color Set) or ACT (Color Table) file format. After choosing the option from the drop-down menu, just navigate to the file on your hard drive and select it.

Replace Colors Lets you replace the current palette with an imported palette. Just choose the option from the drop-down menu, navigate to the CLR file, and select it.

Load Default Colors If you've manipulated your current palette, use the Load Default Colors option to revert back to the web-safe palette.

Save Colors To export a color palette, choose Save Colors from the drop-down menu. When the Export Color Swatch dialog box appears, navigate to the location where you want to save the palette, choose a desired file type from the Format menu (Mac) or Save as Type drop-down menu (Win), enter a desired name, and click Save.

Save as Default Designates the current palette as the default palette to be loaded when you use the Load Default Colors option in the drop-down menu.

Clear Colors Automatically removes all the colors from the current palette besides black and white.

Web 216 Switches the current palette to the web-safe palette.

Sort by Color Rearranges the color swatches by hue, allowing you to better locate a given color in the current palette.

Working with the Color Mixer Panel

Stroke Color icon
Fill Color icon

While the Color Swatches panel displays the individual colors in the current palette, the Color Mixer panel (Window → Color Mixer) creates and edits solid colors.

It is also used to create gradient and bitmap fills—something that we've already talked a bit about but haven't had the chance to go over in detail.

The primary purpose of the Color Mixer panel is to exert complete control over both fill and stroke color—to do this, just select either the Stroke Color icon (indicated by the pencil) or the Fill Color icon (indicated by the paint bucket) and follow the color-mixing procedures detailed next.

> Because you cannot create or edit gradient or bitmap fills using the Property Inspector, you'll find it's preferable to use the Color Mixer panel to do all of your fill work.

Mixing Solid Colors

You can use the Color Mixer panel to create solid RGB (Red, Green, Blue), HSB (Hue, Saturation, Brightness), or Hexadecimal notation colors using a series of different methods (all of which are explored in this section). Once you've created colors, you can add them to the current palette and displayed in the Color Swatches panel.

> One of the great things about using the Color Mixer panel is that you can dynamically apply fill. This means you can change and manipulate an object's fill either before or after it is created. If you want to change the fill of an existing object, make sure it has been selected (with the Arrow tool) and then make the desired changes in the Color Mixer panel.

Let's take a look at how you use the Color Mixer panel to create and mix solid colors.

> When you've mixed a color using any of the upcoming procedures, all you have to do is select the Add Swatch command from the Color Mixer panel's Options menu—the color will automatically be added to the Color Swatches panel.

MIXING AN RGB COLOR

To mix an RGB color, follow these steps:

1. If it isn't already, select Solid from the Fill Style drop-down menu.

2. Choose RGB from the Color Mixer panel's Options menu.

3. From here, simply enter numerical values into the R, G, and B fields. Alternatively, you can use the sliders to the right of the individual color channel fields.

   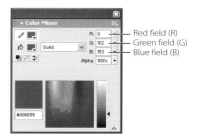

   You can also choose a color by clicking anywhere in the color box with your cursor. The appropriate RGB code automatically appears in the color channel fields.

4. If you want to manipulate the color's transparency, enter a value into the Alpha field (or adjust the slider) to specify the degree of transparency—

   0 for complete transparency to 100 for complete opacity.

MIXING AN HSB COLOR

The process for mixing an HSB color works exactly the same as mixing an RGB color. Simply choose HSB from the Color Mixer panel's Options menu (below left). From there, enter values (in percent) into the H, S, and B fields. You can also choose a color by clicking anywhere in the color box with your cursor. You can also enter a value into the Alpha field (or adjust the slider).

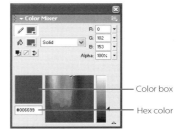

MIXING A HEX COLOR

Mixing a Hex color is just as easy as mixing either an RGB or an HSB color. Simply enter the appropriate Hex values into the Hex field.

> The Hex value of any color you create using RGB or HSB is automatically displayed in the Hex field.

You can also choose a color by clicking anywhere in the color bar with your cursor.

Using the None Fill Style

When you choose None from the Fill Style drop-down menu, any object you draw (oval, rectangle, and so on) won't have a fill.

Unlike the other choices in the Fill Style drop-down menu, you can't dynamically change an object's fill to None after it has been drawn. As a result, if you don't want an object to have a fill, select None from the Style drop-down menu before drawing it.

Creating a Linear Gradient

Figure 4.16

A linear gradient

A linear gradient is a fill that gradually changes from one color to another in a linear fashion—either vertically or horizontally (see Figure 4.16).

Let's take a step-by-step approach to creating and editing a linear gradient with the Color Mixer panel:

1. With the Color Mixer panel open and an object selected, choose Linear Gradient from the Fill Style drop-down menu.

> Alternatively, you can choose Linear Gradient from the Fill Style drop-down menu *before* you draw the object. By doing this, your object, when it's drawn, will be filled with the linear gradient you selected and edited beforehand.

2. To change a color in the selected gradient, first click one of the pointers below the gradient definition bar. As a gradient slowly changes from one color to another, the pointer you choose determines either the starting color or the ending color (below left).

3. Once you have one of the pointers selected, click the color swatch just above the gradient's definition bar. This will open the color palette from which you can choose a new color (below center).

4. To change the character of the gradient, click and drag either pointer. The farther apart the pointers are, the more gradual the gradient will appear. Conversely, the closer together the pointers are, the more abrupt the gradient will be (below center).

> As you move the pointers around or change the gradient colors, your changes will automatically preview in both the gradient definition bar and the gradient preview.

5. You can increase the complexity of the gradient by adding additional colors. To do this, click just below the gradient's color definition bar to add an additional pointer. Once it has been added, you can change the pointer's color by following the process outlined in step 4 (below right).

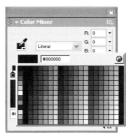

6. Once you've finished editing the gradient, you can add it to the Color Swatches panel (so it can be used whenever you want). To do this, select Add Swatch from the Color Mixer panel's Options drop-down menu.

> To transform a gradient fill of any kind (either linear or radial), you can use the Fill Transform tool described in the "Using the Fill Transform Tool" section earlier in this chapter.

Creating a Radial Gradient

A radial gradient is quite similar to a linear gradient. However, instead of the fill changing from one color to another in a linear pattern, it changes in a circular pattern (see Figure 4.17).

Beyond that detail, creating and editing a radial gradient is exactly the same as if you were working with a linear gradient.

Figure 4.17

A radial gradient

Creating a Bitmap Fill

You can use the Color Mixer panel to create a fill that is a bitmap image (opposed to a solid color or a gradient). Let's take a look at how:

1. With the Color Mixer panel open and an object selected, choose Bitmap from the Fill Style drop-down menu.

> Alternatively, you can choose Bitmap from the Fill Style drop-down menu *before* you draw the object. By doing this, your object, when it's drawn, will be filled with the bitmap you selected and edited beforehand.

2. If you haven't already imported another bitmap into your movie, the Import to Library dialog box will open. Navigate to where the bitmap you want to use as fill is located, select it, and then click Open.

3. If you've already imported a bitmap (or bitmaps), they will appear in the Bitmap Fill window.

4. Select the bitmap you want to use as fill from the thumbnails displayed in the Bitmap Fill window.

5. To manipulate the way in which the bitmap fill is displayed, use the Fill Transform tool, discussed in the "Using the Fill Transform Tool" section earlier in this chapter.

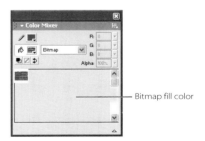

Bitmap fill color

Inspirational Design Model

Any successful Flash creation requires total control over all of the application's painting, drawing, and color tools. Although many examples of Flash movies exemplify this, arguably one of the coolest is the Peter Grafik Retro Experience site (`www.petergrafik.dk/dubonet_ retro_experience/`), shown in Figure 4.18. Designed as a self-promotional site by Peter Holm, one of the principals of Titoonic (the Inspirational Design Model for Chapter 26), this site is a tour de force of color, design, and illustration. (This version is actually the first generation of the site—the new version is visible at `www.petergrafik.dk`). His comfortable, cartoony style of illustration is incredibly well integrated into the overall interface. Ultimately, the site creates a certain feeling of groovy playfulness.

Figure 4.18

The overall use of color, design, and illustration in the Peter Grafik Retro Experience site creates a sense of playfulness.

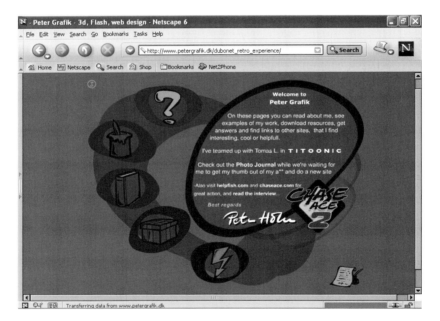

Summary

In this chapter, you spent a fair amount of time going over the various drawing and painting tools at your fingertips in Flash. You explored all of the various selection tools, which included the Arrow tool, the Subselection tool, and the Lasso tool. You looked at how to create shapes using the Oval and Rectangle tools. You also spent a great deal of time discussing the Pencil tool, the Pen tool, the Brush tool, and the Line tool—all of which create freeform paths. You then spent time looking at the Dropper tool, the Paint Bucket tool, the Ink Bottle tool, the Transform Fill tool, and the Eraser tool. You rounded out the chapter by exploring how you adjust an object's stroke and fill by using either the Property Inspector or the Color Mixer panel.

CHAPTER 5

Working with Text

When Edward Lytton said that the pen is mightier than the sword in his play *Richelieu,* he probably had no idea this phrase would be just as meaningful in the digital age. Even though the Web is becoming an increasingly more visual medium by the second, the majority of the information is still textual.

Beyond the textual content you can transmit, however, the type itself is an extremely powerful tool for giving your digital creation extra life and meaning. Because of Flash's vector animation tools, text—especially if it's properly crafted—can have an incredible impact on your visitors. Taking the time to choose the right type for your textual content can turn a good Flash site into a great Flash site.

In this chapter, you'll explore the following topics:

- **Understanding text, type, and fonts**
- **Working with Flash's font limitations**
- **Creating type with the Text tool**
- **Manipulating text with the Property Inspector**
- **Breaking text apart**
- **Manipulating text shape**
- **Creating a Font symbol**

Understanding Text, Type, and Fonts

When you work with text in Flash (or any other graphics program for that matter), you'll find that the words *text, font,* and *typeface* are often used interchangeably. Don't be fooled, however; there is a big difference among the three.

Text refers to any combination of characters that make up a written document of some sort (whether a word, a sentence, or a book). A *font*, on the other hand, is a complete set of characters in a particular size and style. This includes the letters, the numbers, and all of the special characters you get by pressing the Shift, Option, or Cmd/Ctrl keys. A *typeface,* on the other hand, contains a series of fonts. For example, the typeface Arial contains the fonts Arial, Arial Bold, Arial Italic, and Arial Bold Italic.

For more information about the art of text, type, fonts, and just about anything else typographic, try these great resources: www.typereview.com, www.rsub.com/typographic/, and http://counterspace.motivo.com/.

Working with Flash's Font Limitations

Although Flash has some font-related issues that need to be discussed, they are nowhere near as complicated (and limiting) as those related to fonts and HTML-based design. However, they are important and ultimately will impact your Flash creations.

Flash movies can use Type 1 PostScript fonts, TrueType fonts, and bitmap fonts (on the Macintosh only). To use PostScript fonts, you must have Adobe Type Manager (ATM) installed on your system.

If you're using Windows 2000, you don't need to install ATM to use Type 1 PostScript fonts.

For the most part, when you publish your final product, Flash embeds the necessary information about fonts, thereby allowing your audience's computers to display them properly. However, in some cases, fonts may still appear incorrectly in your Flash creation when your audience views it because they many not have that font installed on their machine.

You can avoid this problem in two ways. First, if you are not picky about the actual font you use, employ the _sans, _serif, or _typewriter fonts available in the Font drop-down menu of the Property Inspector (see the "Manipulating Text with the Property Inspector" section). Essentially, when you use these fonts (which are called *device fonts*), you are telling the Flash movie to use the equivalent fonts installed on your audience's computers. This way, you'll always know your text will appear correctly. Essentially, device fonts are the fonts that your operating system employs to display its textual information.

Second, to keep your fonts from displaying incorrectly when your Flash creation is viewed, you can break apart the given text and turn it into shapes instead of text. The process for breaking apart text will be covered later in this chapter in the "Breaking Apart Text" section.

Besides the problem of users not having a certain font installed, there are some other specific font issues of which you should be aware. When it comes to Windows machines, PostScript fonts are prone to display incorrectly. As a result, it is strongly suggested Windows users limit themselves to TrueType fonts.

Mac users need to be cautious when employing Adobe PostScript fonts. For the most part, PostScript fonts function properly, but there are situations where they cause problems. Sometimes, PostScript fonts will display properly while you are creating your Flash movie but will display incorrectly when the movie is actually published.

Creating Type with the Text Tool

Now that you've explored the limitations of Flash-based text, you can explore the process of creating text by using the Text tool **A** , which is located in the Tools section of the Toolbox.

Although the vast majority of your text editing in Flash will be facilitated with the Property Inspector (which you'll explore later in this chapter), you always need to start off by actually creating some text—a process made possible by the Text tool.

> You can antialias text by going to View → Antialias Text.

To use the Text tool, select it from the Toolbox, click anywhere on the Stage, and begin typing. Don't worry too much about how the text appears at this early stage of creation; you'll learn how you can get it to look exactly how you want in the "Manipulating Text with the Property Inspector" section later in this chapter.

> To edit text, simply click a text block with the Text tool (or double-click it with the Arrow tool) and make the changes you want. When finished, click anywhere outside of the text box.

Understanding Text Boxes

Flash creates text in blocks called *text boxes* (see Figure 5.1). The text blocks themselves become editable objects that you can move about the Stage at will.

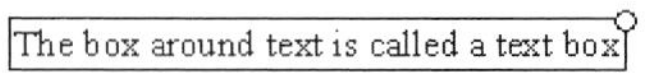

The box around text is called a text box

There are actually three distinct types of text boxes, all with a particular function within the process of creating and manipulating text in Flash.

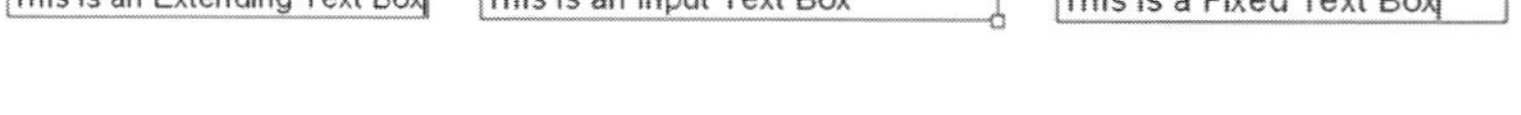

Figure 5.1

As you're typing the text, you'll notice it is contained in a rectangle with a small circle in the upper-right corner. This is a text box.

This is an Extending Text Box   This is an Input Text Box   This is a Fixed Text Box

An Extending text box extends as you type. You can easily recognize these by a small circle in the upper-right corner. The Extending text box is the default type of text box in Flash.

A Ffixed text box doesn't increase horizontally. To create a Fixed text box, which is recognizable by a small square in its upper-right corner, choose the Text tool from the Toolbox, click anywhere on the Stage, and drag the text block to the desired size. Notice that you can only drag horizontally. When you type, your text will automatically wrap, extending the size of the text block vertically, but not horizontally.

A Input text box contains Dynamic Text that can be changed by anyone viewing your Flash movie.

> For more information and how to create and work with Dynamic Text, see the "Working with Dynamic Text" section later in this chapter.

Say, for instance, you wanted to create a field where someone types a password to access a restricted area of your site. You would accomplish this (at least in part) by creating an Input text block. Unlike the other two types of text blocks already discussed, the Input text box, which is recognizable by a small square in the lower-right corner of the text box, is not created with the Text tool. Instead, you need to choose Dynamic Text or Input Text from the Text Type drop-down menu in the Property Inspector (see "Manipulating Text with the Property Inspector").

Manipulating Text with the Property Inspector

The Text tool is the prime method for *creating* text, and the Property Inspector is the prime tool for *editing* and *manipulating* it. Unlike previous versions of Flash, which used several different panels to control various aspects of Flash text, Flash MX uses the all-powerful Property Inspector to manipulate text. You can access it using Window → Properties.

Before learning how to manipulate text with the Property Inspector, however, there is a single detail that needs to be discussed. In Flash MX, there are three distinct types of text: Static Text, Dynamic Text, and Input Text. Each type, which will be discussed in the following sections, has its own place and function within a Flash creation.

Let's take a look at the process you need to follow to create and edit each of the three types using the Property Inspector:

1. If you haven't already, insert some text onto the Stage using the Text tool.

2. If the text box you've just created is still "live" (or, still editable), select the text using your cursor. If you've deselected the text box, simply reselect it with the Arrow tool (a light blue box will appear around the selected text block).

3. If it isn't already, open the Property Inspector by going to Window → Properties.

4. Select the specific type of text you want to create from the Text Type drop-down menu.

From here, the Property Inspector will change to reflect that text type's specific properties—all of which are described in the following sections.

Text Type drop-down menu

This step-by-step process describes how you can manipulate text *after* it's already been created. If you want to create some text with the Text tool whose properties have already been set, just select the Text tool from the Toolbox, open the Property Inspector, set the text properties (all of which are described next), and then insert the text onto the Stage. The inserted text will automatically have all the properties (font, color, size, and so on) that you set with the Property Inspector.

Working with Static Text

Although you are going to spend time exploring and discussing Dynamic Text and Input Text a little later in this section, it's important to recognize that Static Text, which is automatically created when you insert text using the Text tool, is the default type of text in Flash. In other words, when you create text with the Text tool, it is automatically Static Text.

When you want to work with Static Text, you really don't have to follow the steps in the previous section because Static Text is already chosen in the Text Type drop-down menu.

Beyond its innate ability to convey textual information, Static Text doesn't do anything special. As a result, you'll find that you'll probably use it the most. As a result, it's good that you become intimately familiar with all the following Static Text options accessible through the Property Inspector.

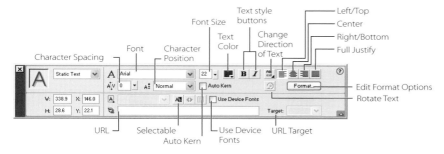

The options are as follows:

Font drop-down menu Displays the current font when the Text tool is active. The list shows every font currently installed on your computer. You can either choose a font with the Font drop-down menu before you begin typing or select existing text within a text block (or the text block itself) and change its font with the Font drop-down menu.

> You can also change the font of selected text by choosing Text → Font and then picking from the list of fonts installed on your machine.

Font Size field Sets a font's size. You can either enter a value (in point size) into the Font Size field or use the Font Size slider (which is accessible by clicking the small Down arrow to the right of the field).

> You can also change the font size by choosing Text → Size and picking from the list of sizes available.

Text style buttons Sets the text to either bold or italic. As with the rest of the options in the Property Inspector, you either select a block of text with the Arrow tool or use the Text tool to select the text when the text block is "live." Then click one of the style buttons. You can also click either of the style buttons before you create a new string of text.

> Unfortunately, the Property Inspector offers a limited array of style options. For more (though not much more), select Text → Style and choose a style from the list.

Text Color swatch Opens the Text Color palette so you can set your text's color. If you are unhappy with the available color choices, mix your own using the Color Picker (accessible by clicking the small color wheel in the top-right corner of the Text Color palette).

Character Spacing value Represents the distance between characters in a string of text. The higher the Character Spacing value, the farther apart the characters will be. Figure 5.2 illustrates different Character Spacing values, also referred to as *tracking*.

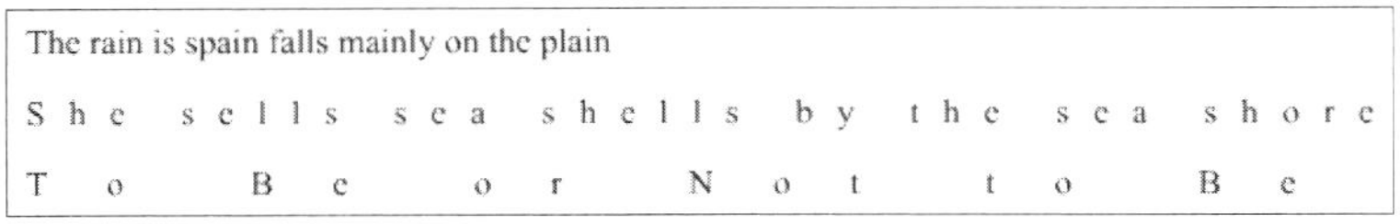

Figure 5.2

The top line of text has a character spacing of 0, the middle line has a tracking of 10, and the bottom line has a tracking of 25.

The rain is spain falls mainly on the plain
S h e   s e l l s   s e a   s h e l l s   b y   t h e   s e a   s h o r e
T o   B e   o r   N o t   t o   B e

The Property Inspector lets you set the Character Spacing for any given text block (either before or after it has been created). If the text has already been created, all you need to do is select the text block or the actual text and enter a value in the Character Spacing field. Alternatively, you can use the Tracking slider, which is accessible by clicking the small Down arrow just to the right of the Tracking field, to adjust the amount of tracking.

As with all of the other options in the Property Inspector, you can also set the tracking *before* you create text with the Text tool.

Character Position value Character Position, which is also referred to as *baseline shift* in graphic design, refers to how closely the text sits above or below its natural baseline (the bottom of the letters). By changing a text block's Character Position value, you can create superscript or subscript characters. Unlike most graphic design programs that allow you to set an exact baseline shift value, Flash gives you only three default settings: Normal, Superscript, and Subscript (see Figure 5.3).

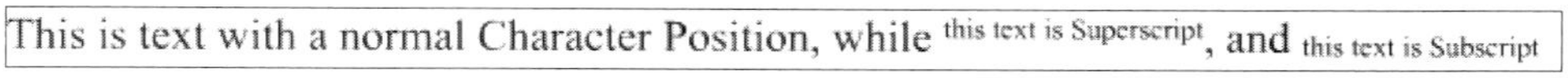

This is text with a normal Character Position, while ^{this text is Superscript}, and _{this text is Subscript}

Figure 5.3

The three baseline shift presets

To set the character position, select a string of already created text, and choose one of the three baseline shift options from the Character Position drop-down menu. As with all of the other options in the Property Inspector, you can also set the baseline shift *before* you create text with the Text tool.

> In addition to changing some text's Character Position value, you can also create superscript or subscript by going to Text → Style → Superscript or Subscript.

Auto Kern option Evens out the spacing between individual characters in a string of text. When you select the Auto Kern option, you activate the built-in kerning option of many (but not all) fonts.

> If you want to apply the Auto Kerning feature, a font must have kerning information built into the file—this is why some fonts will auto kern and others won't.

Change Direction of Text button Accesses a drop-down menu with a series of options that change the direction of the selected text. The default Horizontal option makes the text flow from left to right horizontally. The two remaining options—Vertical, Left to Right and Vertical, Right to Left—make the text flow vertically. The difference between the two is that if you apply the Vertical, Left to Right option to a block of text with more than one line, the first line will remain the first vertical line. However, if you choose the Vertical, Right to Left option, the last line in a text block with more than one line of text will be the first vertical line.

Rotate Text button Changes the text's orientation (only on vertical text). With rotation turned off, individual characters will face to the right.

On the other hand, if you turn the rotate option on, the individual characters will face downward.

URL field Flash offers several different ways in which to link to a URL. The easiest method uses the URL field in the Property Inspector.

Rotate Turned off

Rotate Turned on

Any Flash text to which you've attached a URL will appear on the Stage with a dotted underline.

Simply select a string of text you want to turn into a link, and type in a URL into the URL field.

You can only add a URL to horizontal text.

URL Target field Because it's entirely possible that your Flash movie be delivered in a framed HTML document, the Target drop-down menu lets you set the location in which the URL loads. There are four default options:

- Choosing `_blank` loads the link in a new browser window, maintaining the window in which the hyperlink was located just below the newly opened window.

- If you choose `_parent`, the document, when loaded, will occupy the entire area of the frameset document in which the link resides.

- Choosing `_self` (which is the default link target) simply opens the document in the frame where the link resides.

- If you choose `_top`, the document will be loaded into the uppermost (hierarchically speaking) frameset—wiping out all frames and nested framesets.

You can also manually enter a frame name into the Target drop-down menu/field if you want to target a specific named frame in the HTML document.

Selectable button Under normal circumstances, Static Text is part of the Flash movie and is therefore not selectable as text would be in an HTML document, for example. However, if you want your audience to be able to select the Static Text in your movie (and therefore copy and paste it), make sure the Selectable button is toggled.

Use Device Fonts option By selecting the Use Device Fonts option, you tell Flash not to embed the font used in a given text block. Instead, Flash will look at the user's computer and employ the most appropriate font on their system to display the text. Ultimately, because the font information is not embedded, the SWF file's size will be slightly smaller.

You can only evoke the Use Device Fonts option when you're working with horizontal text.

Alignment buttons The right side of the Property Inspector offers you four alignment options: Left/Top, Center, Right/Bottom, and Full Justify (see Figure 5.4). To align text, select a text block (or a string of text within a text block) and click one of the alignment buttons.

Figure 5.4

The results of the four alignment options from left to right: Left/Top, Center, Right/Bottom, and Full Justify.

This text is Left Justified	This text is Centered	This text is Right Justified	This text is full Justified

Formatting options By clicking the Edit Format Options button, you get access to a Format Options dialog box, which contains a series of options that affect the way in which an entire text block looks (opposed to individual characters within the text block).

When you set the left margin of a text block, you set the distance, in pixels, between the left side of the text box and the text itself. Enter a value numerically into the Left Margin field or use the Left Margin slider (accessible by clicking the small Down arrow to the right of the Left Margin field).

When you manipulate the right margin, you set the distance, in pixels, between the right side of the text box and the text itself. Enter a numerical value into the Right Margin field or use the Right Margin slider (accessible by clicking the Down arrow to the right of the Right Margin field).

The Indent setting changes the distance, in pixels, between the left side of the text box and the first line of text.

The Line Spacing setting represents the vertical distance, in points, between lines in a text block. To set the line spacing, enter a value numerically into the Line Spacing field, or use the Line Spacing slider.

Working with Dynamic Text

When you create Dynamic Text, you produce a text box with content dynamically updated from another source—say, a database or text file on your server. So, Dynamic Text is not really fixed or unchanging *per se*, even though it's created in the same way as Static Text. Instead, it is sort of like a text container whose contents can change. With this in mind, one can easily come up with some genuinely interesting uses. You could create a constantly changing list of your favorite jokes or your daily itinerary—the possibilities are endless.

If you are interested in using Dynamic Text to create dynamic content, see Chapter 17.

If you want to create and manipulate Dynamic Text, you have to go through an extra step that you wouldn't normally have to go through if you were working with Static Text—you'll need to manually select Dynamic Text from the Property Inspector's Text Type dropdown menu.

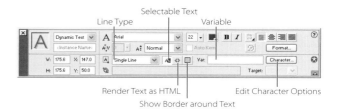

From there, you'll get access to the specific Dynamic Text properties in the lower-right corner of the expanded Property Inspector—each of which is described next:

Line Type drop-down menu   Displays three choices: Single Line, Multiline, and Multiline No Wrap. Single Line displays the text as one line, and both Multiline and Multiline No Wrap display it as more than one line. The difference between the two Multiline options is that Multiline No Wrap will only break a single line into more that one line if the last character is a breaking character—such as Return/Enter.

Variable field   Contains the name of the text block so that dynamic content intended for that specific text block will know exactly where it needs to go.

> Make sure the name you enter into the Variable field is unique.

Selectable Text button   Allows your audience to select the text within the Dynamic Text box, much like in the case of the Static Text option.

Render Text as HTML button   Tells Flash to retain certain HTML text formatting styles. Now, don't get all wild and crazy, thinking you can retain every HTML tag under the sun. Unfortunately, there are only a limited number of HTML tags (including bold, italic, underline, font face, font color, paragraph break, and font size) that are supported.

Show Border around Text button   Tells Flash you want the text box to be surrounded by a visible border.

> By default, when you've got the Show Border around Text option turned off, the Dynamic Text is always surrounded by a dotted border—which is not visible when the movie is published.

Edit Character Options button   When you click the Edit Character Options button (shown as Character), the Character Options dialog box opens.

From here you can determine exactly how many characters of the font are embedded in the file. From top to bottom, the radio buttons let you embed none of the characters, all of the characters, or specific characters in the font (uppercase characters, lowercase characters, numbers, and punctuation). By typing specific characters into the field at the bottom of the dialog box (which goes live when you select the Only option), you can customize which characters you'd like to embed.

> The fewer characters of a font you embed, the smaller the file will be.

Working with Input Text

Input Text is almost exactly the same as Dynamic Text. The only real difference lies in the fact that data is traveling in the other direction—from the user's computer to a server, rather than from server to computer.

As a result, most of the options available once you select Input Text from the Text Type drop-down menu in the Property Inspector are exactly the same as described previously.

There are, however, two additional options:

Password option Beyond the Single Line, Multiline, and Multiline No Wrap options in the Line Type drop-down menu, you have a fourth option: Password. Use the Password option to display the onscreen text as asterisks to maintain password security.

> Selecting the Password option only affects the display of the text entered by the user. To make the password work, you are going to have to use ActionScript to pass the information to a server-side application. For more information about integrating database-driven applications and Flash, see Chapter 17.

Maximum Characters field Entering a numerical value into the Maximum Characters field limits the number of characters that a user can enter into a given text field.

Breaking Apart Text

As you've probably noticed, when you create text, it's inserted onto the Stage as a block. Whether a letter, a word, or an entire Shakespearean soliloquy, you can't independently manipulate (scale, skew, move, and so on) one portion of the text block.

> You need to be aware of two problems when you break apart text and turn it into shapes. First, broken-apart text increases your Flash creation's file size considerably. Second, once text is broken apart, you can no longer edit it as you would other text.

Although this is especially irksome, there is a rather easy way around the problem. Essentially, you break the text block down into its parts—let's take a look at how:

1. Select a text block with the Arrow tool.

2. Go to Modify → Break Apart.

3. The result will be that the text block will be broken into its individual characters, each of which can be edited, moved, and manipulated independently of the others (see Figure 5.5).

Figure 5.5

The same block of text as it appears normally (left) and as it appears after it has been broken apart (right)

Breaking text apart is especially handy if you want to animate individual characters of a larger text block.

Manipulating Text Shape

One of the really neat things you can do with Flash is manipulate the shape of the individual characters of a given font. If you don't like how the *G* looks in Arial, you can change it to look exactly how you want. The process involves taking the text and breaking it apart several times—to accomplish this, follow these steps:

1. Make sure the Stage has some already created text.

2. Select the text box with the Arrow tool.

3. Go to Modify → Break Apart. At this point, the text should break down into multiple groups—each of which is composed of one character.

4. Again, go to Modify → Break Apart.

5. Deselect the shape by clicking anywhere else on the Stage or by going to Edit → Deselect All.

6. By doing this, you convert the text into a shape like any other. From here, you can use the Arrow tool to manipulate the shape of the character(s).

One of the coolest things about text that has been broken apart is that you can use the Ink Bottle to add an outline around the individual characters.

When you use the Break Apart command, you can really only affect TrueType fonts. Bitmap fonts disappear when you break them apart. PostScript fonts can be broken apart only on Mac systems running ATM.

Creating a Font Symbol

If you are planning on creating and using a Shared Library (discussed in Chapter 7), you would do well to become familiar with *Font symbols*. Essentially, a Font symbol allows you to stick any font into a Shared Library—which sits on a server somewhere. From there, any number of Flash movies can link to the Shared Library and use the font without it having to be embedded in their files, thereby reducing their overall sizes.

To create a Font symbol, follow these steps:

1. Open the movie that you want to house the Shared Library.
2. If it isn't already, open the Library by going to Window → Library.
3. Choose New Font from the Library Options menu.
4. When the Font Symbol Properties dialog box pops up, enter the name for the font that will appear in the Library into the Name field.

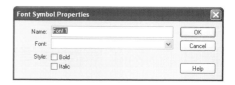

> The name you give isn't the official name of the font itself, just an identifier you assign for your own purposes.

5. Select the actual font from the Font drop-down menu.
6. Select whether you want the Font symbol to be either bold or italic.
7. When you are finished, click OK.

> For more information on Shared Libraries, see Chapter 7.

Inspirational Design Model

There is little doubt that sound digital typography gives a well-designed site that extra creative punch. Let's face it, folks: Type is power! Because of its foundation in vector technology, Flash gives you the opportunity to leverage typographic power. No site illustrates this more than typographic (www.typographic.com). Designed by Jimmy Chen, an astounding visual designer who lives in Los Angeles, typographic takes web design beyond the realm of the commercial, the corporate, and the everyday into something far more potent (see Figure 5.6). Every square centimeter is packed with beautiful digital typographic design. The visual subtleties of typographic are quite stunning and create a visual space that easily holds your attention for long periods of time.

Figure 5.6

Jimmy Chen's typographic

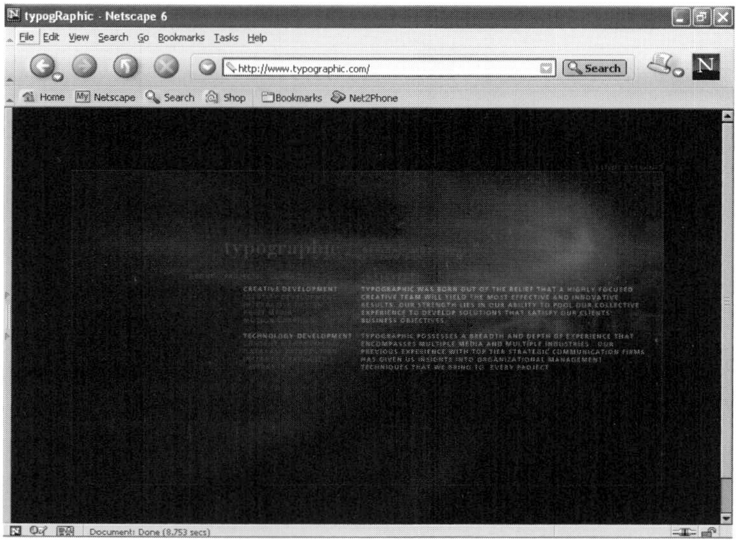

Summary

In this chapter, you received a tour of Flash's text-oriented tools. You started off with a short but vital look at the nature of text, type, and fonts. You continued by exploring the limitations that might be encountered when you are working with text in Flash. If you are planning to create an especially text-heavy site (or are just want to make absolutely sure your text appears exactly as you want it), understanding these limitations is particularly important. You then moved on to look at how you use the Text tool to create text, including the nature of text boxes. You then got into the meat of manipulating all aspects of text with a look at the Property Inspector. The chapter finished off with a short exploration of how you can reshape individual characters by breaking apart text.

CHAPTER 6

Working with Objects

In the previous chapters, you learned how to create various elements in Flash. Whether shapes, text, or color, you've spent a fair amount of time wading into the process of visual creation. To a certain degree, you've also learned how to manipulate the elements you've created.

The success of your Flash creation depends, at least partly, on your ability to exert complete control over the way in which your objects look. So, what exactly is an object? Well, simply put, an *object* is another word for anything visual you either create or import in Flash. This means that, for example, blocks of text, imported bitmaps, and shapes drawn in Flash are all referred to as *objects*.

The great thing about working with objects is that Flash offers a whole host of tools with which to manipulate and modify them. Whether you want to modify their shape, move them about the Stage, or group them with other objects, this chapter explores all the ways in which you can exert control over the look of the objects in your Flash creation.

In this chapter, you'll explore the following topics:

- **Understanding objects**
- **Working with external bitmaps**
- **Grouping and ungrouping objects**
- **Moving, manipulating, and arranging objects**
- **Transforming objects**
- **Working with transformation points**

Understanding Objects

Objects are the heart and soul of Flash. Anything you draw, paint, or import onto the Stage is considered an object. So, an object can range from an imported JPEG of your dog Zippy to an illustration of the solar system you created with the painting and drawing tools (and everything in between).

In the following sections, you're going to explore the plethora of tools and procedures that let you manipulate the appearance of individual objects.

> The term *object* is also used in ActionScripts. However, don't be fooled; an ActionScript object and the kind of object discussed in this chapter are totally different. For more information on ActionScript objects, see Chapter 14.

Working with External Bitmaps

Although Flash is designed to work primarily with vector-based art, it also handles bitmaps relatively well. The program boasts a virtual plethora of tools designed to import and manipulate bitmaps. Beyond getting acquainted with these tools, however, it's vitally important to understand the nature of bitmaps and how Flash deals with them. In Chapter 3, you learned how to use bitmaps as fill. Now you're going to learn how bitmaps integrate into the greater pantheon of Flash objects.

Bitmaps, which are also sometimes called *raster graphics*, are images composed of individual pixels that have a fixed size and take up a set amount of computer memory. The quality of a bitmap image is determined by its resolution. For the most part, resolution is expressed as dots per inch (dpi). A bitmap with a higher resolution (say, 300dpi) will be better quality than one with a lower resolution (say, 72dpi).

One of the other characteristics of a bitmap image is that it is resolution dependent. When the resolution and size is set, its quality is fixed. As a result, changing a bitmap's dimensions can drastically affect its quality. One of the most obvious manifestations of this quality change is something called *jaggies*. If you take a bitmap image and enlarge it, you'll be able to see its individual pixels. The edges of the image will have a jaggy appearance because the number of pixels per inch cannot change. A similar vector image, on the other hand, would simply recalculate the mathematical equations that define its shape and preserve a smooth edge at any size. Figure 6.1 illustrates bitmap jaggies and the lack thereof in vector images.

All of these characteristics make bitmaps larger and more memory intensive than vectors. As a result, it behooves you to use vector-based art as much as possible when orchestrating your Flash creation.

Figure 6.1

The individual pixels of the bitmap (on the left) are visible, and the edge of the vector image (on the right) is smooth.

However, sometimes bitmaps have a distinct advantage over vectors. Although vectors are smaller in file size, they are generally unable to efficiently display complex photorealistic images or images with continuous color tones.

As everything you create in Flash with the painting and drawing tools is vector-based, Flash doesn't have the ability to actually create bitmaps. However, Flash can easily import many different types of bitmap files. After imported, they can then be manipulated to minimize the amount of memory they'll consume in your Flash creation.

Importing Bitmaps

You can import bitmaps into Flash in two ways: by using the Import command or by simply pasting an image onto the Stage.

> Flash can import the following raster/bitmap files: Windows Bitmaps (BMP/DIB), GIF (GIF), JPEG (JPG/JPEG), PNG (PNG), and PICT (PCT/PIC). Flash can import the following bitmap/raster files *only* if you've got QuickTime 4 or above installed: MacPaint (PNTG), Quick-Time Image (QTIF), Photoshop (PSD), Silicon Graphics Images (.SGI), TGA (TGA), and TIFF (TIF).

A copy of QuickTime 5 has been included on this book's CD-ROM.

To import a bitmap:

1. Go to File → Import or use the shortcut Cmd/Ctrl+R.

2. When the Import dialog box opens, navigate the file you want to import, select it, and click on the Open button.

> Use the Files of Type drop-down menu at the bottom of the Import dialog box to choose the exact file type you are trying to import.

3. When the bitmap is imported into Flash, it is automatically placed both on the Stage and in the Library (as a symbol).

> If you want your imported bitmap to be placed only in the Library, and not on the Stage, select File → Import to Library.

Importing a TIFF file requires QuickTime. If you have QuickTime on your system, and you are trying to import a file called `image.tiff`, for example, you will get a rather odd prompt: "Flash doesn't recognize the file format of `image.tiff`. Would you like to try importing via QuickTime?" The prompt isn't much to worry about. If you select Yes, your imported image won't be adversely affected. On the other hand, if you do not have QuickTime on your system, you will get the message: "One or more files were not imported because there were problems reading them."

> Although Flash will import a PNG created in any program, if you're importing a Fireworks PNG, you get the Fireworks PNG Import Settings dialog box. From here, you can set a series of options, including whether you want the various layer in your image to be flattened into a single layer.

To copy a bitmap from another application:

1. Copy the intended bitmap from the other application by going to Edit → Copy or using the shortcut Cmd/Ctrl+C.

2. Return to Flash, and paste the bitmap onto the Stage by going to Edit → Paste or using the shortcut Cmd/Ctrl+V.

Tracing Bitmaps

The Trace Bitmap command lets you take a bitmap and convert it into a native Flash vector file format with discreet areas of color. This is a definite advantage if you want to manipulate the bitmap image as you would a vector image. Under most circumstances, tracing a bitmap and turning it into a vector image also decreases its file size.

> When you trace a bitmap, the link between the image and the symbol in the Library is severed. If you want to place the traced bitmap back into the Library, simply convert it to a symbol—a process discussed thoroughly in Chapter 7.

Don't get too excited, however, because when you trace a bitmap, the results are not necessarily what you would expect. It is nearly impossible to convert an image into a vector so that it looks that same as it did when it was a bitmap. This having been said, let's explore how you go about tracing an image:

1. With the Arrow tool, select a bitmap image on the Stage.

2. Go to Modify → Trace Bitmap to open the Trace Bitmap dialog box.

   From here, you can set the various Trace Bitmap properties:

   Color Threshold Determines the number of colors in the bitmap after it has been traced and turned into a vector image. When you trace a bitmap, the colors of adjacent pixels in the bitmap are compared. If the difference between the RGB color values of the adjacent pixels is lower than that entered in the Color Threshold field (which can be a number from 1 to 500) , then the adjacent pixels' col-

Figure 6.2

The image on the left is the original bitmap image. The other three images have a Color Threshold value of 25, 50, and 75, respectively.

ors are considered the same. By doing this, the process averages out the colors in the bitmap. The higher the color threshold, the fewer colors will be in the traced bitmap. On the other hand, if you enter a lower value into the Color Threshold field, the traced image will have more colors. Figure 6.2 illustrates the results of different Color Threshold values.

Minimum Area Sets the radius (from 1 to 1,000) at which the Color Threshold compares adjacent pixels. A higher Minimum Area means that more pixels will be compared. Alternatively, a lower Minimum Area means that less adjacent pixels will be compared.

Curve Fit Determines how the outlines of the traced bitmap are drawn. Options include Pixels, Very Tight, Tight, Normal, Smooth, and Very Smooth. If your image has many curves that you want to maintain, select Tight or Very Tight. On the other hand, if you aren't that worried about preserving the curves in your image, select Smooth or Very Smooth from the Curve Fit drop-down menu.

Corner Threshold Determines how the tracing process deals with corners in your bitmap image. Choosing Many Corners from the drop-down menu preserves the corners in the image, and choosing Few Corners smoothes them out.

Setting Bitmap Properties

Each bitmap you import into Flash has a series of properties you can manipulate.

When you set bitmap properties, you have to work with the Library. Don't worry too much about the intricacies of the Library yet because it will be covered in detail in Chapter 7.

To manipulate a bitmap, follow these steps:

1. Open the Library by going to Window → Library or use the shortcut F11.

2. To open the Bitmap Properties dialog box, select the bitmap in the Library, and do one of the following:

   • Click the Properties icon, which is the third icon from the left at the bottom of the Library (the small blue circle with an *i* in it).

   • Ctrl+click (Mac) or right-click (Windows) and choose Properties from the context menu.

   • Choose Properties from the Library's Options drop-down menu.

3. When open, the Bitmap Properties dialog box has several options:

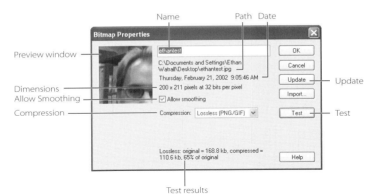

Preview window Gives you a preview of the selected bitmap. If the bitmap itself is larger than the preview window, a hand icon (which appears when you move your cursor over the preview window) lets you pan the image.

Name field Displays the name of the bitmap and lets you change it if you want.

When you change the name of the bitmap in the Bitmap Properties dialog box, you aren't actually changing the filename, just the name given to the bitmap in the Library.

Path, Date, and Dimensions areas Display the bitmap's path, date of creation, and dimensions.

Allow Smoothing option Instructs Flash to *dither* (or smooth) the image when checked.

Compression drop-down menu Gives you two choices:

- By choosing Photo (JPEG), you compress the image in JPEG format. To use the image's default compression quality, click the Use Document Default Quality check box. To choose a new quality compression setting, deselect Use Document Default Quality and enter a value between 1 and 100 in the Quality field. A higher value preserves greater image quality but results in a larger file size.

- By choosing Lossless (GIF/PNG), you maintains the image "as is" by not discarding any of its data. Although Lossless compression maintains image quality, it results in a far larger image size.

Use Document Default Quality option Ensures that the image maintains its original quality. (This option is only available if you haven't clicked the Test button.)

Test button Allows you to check the file's compression. The results, which include the file sizes of the original and the compressed images, are displayed at the bottom of the Bitmap Properties dialog box.

Update button Checks to see if any changes have been made to the original file. If there have been changes, the imported file will update to reflect the changes to its parent.

Once you've set the bitmap's properties, click OK.

Editing Bitmaps

Flash gives you the ability to launch an external image-editing program. From here, you can make any changes you want to a given bitmap and then have Flash reflect the changes.

> If you are editing a Fireworks PNG file that's been imported as a flattened image (by choosing the Flatten Image option from the Fireworks PNG Import Settings dialog box), you can choose to edit the PNG source file for the bitmap. If you've imported a PNG as an editable object, you won't be able to edit it with an alternate image-editing program.

To edit a PNG with Macromedia Fireworks 3 or later:

> If you don't have a version of Macromedia Fireworks installed, you won't have access to the Edit with Fireworks option.

1. Open the Library by going to Window → Library or use the shortcut F11.
2. Ctrl+click (Mac) or right-click (Windows) and choose Edit with Fireworks 4 from the context menu.
3. When the Edit Image dialog box appears, specify whether the PNG source file or the bitmap file is to be opened.
4. When Fireworks opens, make the desired changes to the file.
5. When finished, choose Select → Update, and Fireworks automatically updates the file. If you are using Fireworks 4 or later, simply click on the Done button in the upper-left corner of the Document window, and the file will automatically be updated in Flash.

If you want to edit a bitmap with an image-editing program other than Fireworks:

1. Open the Library by going to Window → Library or use the shortcut F11.
2. Ctrl+click (Mac) or right-click (Windows) and choose Edit With.
3. When the Select External Editor dialog box appears, navigate to the program file of the external editor you want to use, and select it.
4. After the external editor opens, make the desired changes to the image and save it.

5. To automatically update the file in Flash, do one of the following:

- Select the bitmap's icon in the Library and choose Update from the Library Options menu.

- Ctrl+click (Mac) or right-click (Windows) the bitmap in the Library and select Update from the context menu.

Grouping and Ungrouping Objects

When you combine multiple objects as one unit, it's called *grouping*. The process itself is useful for a number of reasons. Say you wanted to create a flower to use in your Flash movie. You can get a lot more visual detail and control over the way the flower looks if you draw the individual parts separately. So, you could draw the petals, the stem, the leaves, and then combine them on the Stage exactly how you want. However, what happens when you want to move the *whole* flower? Well, you could select each of the elements and then move them with the Arrow tool. However, what if you accidentally forgot to include a vital part of the flower (say, the stem) in the selection? When you moved the flower, the stem would stay behind, putting your beautiful creation out of whack.

Don't laugh; this kind of thing happens all the time to even the most accomplished Flashers. How could you avoid this potentially calamitous situation? This is where grouping comes in. When you group a series of objects, they are treated as one unit. So, in our silly flower example, if you had grouped all the elements, you'd be able to move them all as one unit, leaving no part behind.

As discussed in Chapter 4, you can also group the stroke and fill of a given object to avoid moving one independently of the other.

To group objects, follow these steps:

1. With the Arrow tool, select any objects on the Stage you want to include in the group. Remember, you can select anything on the Stage: text, shapes, bitmaps, and so on.

To select multiple objects, hold down the Shift key and click any items you want included in the selection.

2. With the various objects selected, select Modify → Group or use the shortcut Cmd/Ctrl+G. Figure 6.3 illustrates a series of grouped objects.

The Property Inspector will identify an object (or objects) as being grouped.

Ungrouping objects is just as easy as grouping them:

1. Select the grouped objects with the Arrow tool.

2. Go to Modify → Ungroup or use the shortcut Cmd/Ctrl+Shift+G.

One of the great things about the way Flash deals with grouped objects is that you can edit individual elements (for instance, the petals in our flower example) without having to ungroup them. This is quite helpful if you've created a particularly detailed image with which you don't want to go through the entire grouping process again. Let's take a look at how:

1. Select a group with the Arrow tool.

2. Go to Edit → Edit Selected. Alternatively, you can also simply double-click on an object in an already selected group. Notice that everything else on the Stage that isn't part of the group changes color slightly; this signals their temporary inaccessibility. Also, notice that the Scene and Symbol Bar, which is located along the top of the Stage, indicates you are currently editing the group (usually represented by the default name of Group).

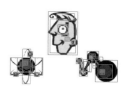

Figure 6.3

On the top is a series of ungrouped objects. On the bottom, the same objects have been grouped. Notice the line that surrounds the entire group as if they are one object.

3. From here make any changes you want to any of the objects within the group.

4. When finished, simply go to Edit → Edit All, double-click anywhere outside the group with the Arrow tool, or click the scene name in the Scene and Symbol bar.

Moving Objects

When it comes to working with objects, you'll need to move them around the Stage. You can move objects in four ways: with the Arrow tool, with the arrow keys, through the Property Inspector, or with the Info panel.

To move an object with the Arrow tool, just follow these steps:

1. Select an object. To select a series of objects, hold down the Shift key and click.

2. With the Arrow tool, click and drag the object (or series of objects) to the desired position on the Stage. If you want to constrain its movement vertically or horizontally, hold down the Shift key while moving the object(s).

If you hold down the Option/Alt key while dragging, Flash creates a copy of the object(s) and moves it instead of the original.

To move an object with the arrow keys on your keyboard:

1. Select an object, or group of objects, you want to move.

2. Use the arrow keys on your keyboard to move the selected object 1 pixel at a time in any direction. If you want to move the selected object 8 pixels at a time, hold down your Shift key while using the arrow keys.

To move an object, or objects, with the Property Inspector or the Info panel, follow these steps:

1. Open the Property Inspector by going to Window → Properties or open the Info panel by going to Window → Info.

2. Select the object or objects you want to move. Notice that there is an X field and a Y field in the lower-left corner of the Property Inspector or at the right side of the Info

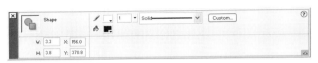

panel. These represent the vertical (Y) and horizontal (X) coordinates of the currently selected object. The X/Y coordinate system is relative to the upper-left corner of the Stage—the location of which is 0/0.

3. Type a value into each of the fields to change the position of the selected object.

The units used in the Info panel's X/Y coordinate system are determined by what you specified in the Ruler Units you set in the Document Properties dialog box. To change them, just go to Modify → Document (or use the shortcut Cmd/Ctrl+J) and choose an alternate one from the Ruler Units drop-down menu.

Manipulating Objects with the Align Panel

The Align panel, which is accessible by selecting Window → Align (or by using the shortcut Cmd/Ctrl+K), is a handy tool that lets you do all manner of interesting things. Figure 6.4 illustrates the Align panel and all of its options.

Figure 6.4

The Align panel has four sets of buttons: Align, Distribute, Match Size, and Space.

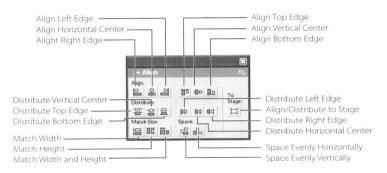

Align Left Edge
Align Horizontal Center
Alight Right Edge

Align Top Edge
Align Vertical Center
Align Bottom Edge

Distribute Vertical Center
Distribute Top Edge
Distribute Bottom Edge

Match Width
Match Height
Match Width and Height

Distribute Left Edge
Align/Distribute to Stage
Distribute Right Edge
Distribute Horizontal Center

Space Evenly Horizontally
Space Evenly Vertically

Beyond aligning objects on the Stage, the Align panel also lets you distribute, match size, and space objects. In the following section you'll look at each of these options separately.

> If you want to align objects to the Stage (opposed to other objects), click the Align/Distribute to Stage button in the right portion of the Align panel.

Aligning Objects

The top section of the Align panel contains a series of buttons that lets you align selected objects horizontally or vertically. From left to right, the buttons let you align objects by their left edges, horizontally by their center points, and by their right edges. The second set of buttons, from left to right, lets you align objects by their top edges, vertically by their center points, and by their bottom edges.

> Flash aligns objects according to their bounding boxes, not any feature of the object itself.

To align a series of objects, follow these steps:

1. With the Align panel open, select the objects you want to align. Remember, you can select multiple objects by clicking and dragging with the Arrow tool and surrounding them with the bounding box or selecting them individually with the Arrow tool (remember to hold down the Shift key to select multiple objects).

2. Select one of the alignment options from the Align panel. Figure 6.5 illustrates the effects that the various alignment options have on images.

> When aligning to the left, Flash uses the left edge of the leftmost object in the selection for the alignment. The same applies when you are aligning to the top, to the bottom, or to the right—Flash uses the edge of the topmost, bottommost, or rightmost object for the alignment.

Distributing Objects

Beyond alignment, the Align panel gives you the ability to distribute selected objects. This comes in handy if you want to evenly space three or more selected objects. From left to right, the buttons in the Distribute section of the Align panel let you distribute objects to their top edges, to their center points vertically, and to their bottom edges. The second set of the distribute buttons, from left to right, let you distribute objects to their left edge, to their center point horizontally, and to their right edge.

Figure 6.5

The first row is an illustration of three unaligned images. The bottom row illustrates the three same images that have been aligned horizontally to the top edge.

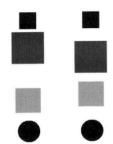

Figure 6.6

The left row of images is undistributed. The right row, however, contains the same images after they've been distributed vertically to their center points.

Figure 6.7

The top two images are unaltered. The bottom two are examples of the same images after their heights have been matched. As the one on the left was the larger of the two, it has remained unchanged. The right image, however, has been stretched.

To distribute a series of objects, follow these directions:

1. Select a series of objects (distributing less than two won't have any visible effect, so remember to select three or more).

2. Click on one of the distribute buttons in the Align panel. Figure 6.6 provides an example of the Distribute option's effects.

Matching Object Size

When you use the Match Size buttons in the Align panel, you can resize a series of selected objects so that their horizontal or vertical dimensions match those of the largest in the selection. From left to right, the Match Size buttons in the Align panel let you match two objects' width, height, or width and height.

To match object size, follow these steps:

1. Select two or more objects on the Stage.

2. Click on one of the Match Size buttons in the Align panel. Figure 6.7 illustrates the Match Size option's effects.

Spacing Objects

The Space buttons in the Align panel allows you to space selected objects vertically or horizontally. So, what exactly is the difference between the Space options and the Distribute options? Although you won't see much difference between two similarly sized images if they were either spaced or distributed, the difference is obvious when you're working with differently sized images.

When you use the Space Evenly Horizontally or the Space Evenly Vertically buttons, you are guaranteed that there will be a fixed number of pixels between each image. When you distribute images of varied sizes, you'll find that the larger the image is, the less space there will be between it and the next one. This is primarily because the Distribute options use a central reference point to arrange the images. As a result, you might want to use the Space option in the Align panel instead.

To space objects, follow these steps:

1. Select two or more objects on the Stage.

2. Click on one of the Space buttons in the Align panel. In Figure 6.8, you'll see an example of the Space Evenly Horizontally option.

Arranging Objects

Although you can use layers (something we'll talk about in depth in Chapter 8) to position objects in your Flash creation horizontally, you can also stack them within a single layer using the Arrange command. The result of both methods is that some objects appear to be either behind or in front of other objects.

So, what exactly is the difference between using layers to stack items and using the Arrange command? Well, as you'll come to learn in Chapter 8, layers provide you a great deal more control over the Z organization of your movie. However, in cases where all the elements in your movie exist within a single layer, the Arrange command is your best bet for manipulating the stacking order of your objects.

The Arrange commands, which are accessible by selecting Modify → Arrange, allow you to change the position of any selected object in the stack, thereby moving them in front of or behind other objects. The

Figure 6.8

The top three images are unaltered. The bottom three images, however, show what happens when you use the Space Evenly Horizontally option in the Align panel.

commands in the Arrange menu are pretty straightforward; let's take a look at each:

Bring to Front Moves the selected object to the absolute top/front of the stack in the currently selected layer.

Bring Forward Moves the currently selected object one increment forward/up in the stack of the currently selected layer.

Send Backward Moves the currently selected object backward/downward one increment in the stack of the currently selected layer.

Send to Back Moves the currently selected object to the absolute bottom/back of the stack of the currently selected layer.

Lock Locks the position of all the objects in the stack of a given layer.

Unlock All Unlocks the stack of the currently selected layer.

Transforming Objects

In previous versions of Flash, the tools with which you could manipulate an object's shape, size, and orientation were all accessible in the Options section of the Toolbox when the Arrow tool was selected. However, in Flash MX, Macromedia has introduced a discreet tool, called the Free Transform tool, with which you can manipulate all aspects of a given object.

Located in the Tools section of the Toolbox, the Free Transform tool ⬚ has a series of *modifiers* that let you transform a selected object. These modifiers are accessible in the Options section of the Toolbox when the Free Transform tool is selected.

Although you can specify the action you want to take on an object by selecting a specific transform modifier, the Free Transform tool also lets you manipulate an object without selecting one of the options. All you need to do is select the Free Transform tool, click the object you want to manipulate, and then move your cursor over any of the handles on the object's bounding box. Depending on the transform you can perform on that specific handle, your cursor will change accordingly.

The following sections will discuss the use of the Free Transform tool in conjunction with its various modifier options.

Never content to provide you with only one way to perform an action, Flash MX also allows you to do many of the same types of transformations with the Transform panel (which is accessible by going to Window → Transform).

In the following sections, you'll explore how to scale, rotate, flip, skew, distort, and edit the envelope of a selected object. You'll also learn how to restore a transformed object.

Scaling an Object

By scaling an object, you change its size (either horizontally, vertically, or uniformly). You can scale an object either with the Free Transform tool or the Transform panel.

To scale an object with the Free Transform tool, follow these steps:

1. Select the desired object with the Arrow tool, then choose the Free Transform tool ⊞ from the Toolbox. Alternatively, click the desired object with the Free Transform tool to select it.

2. From here, you'll notice that a bounding box with handles appears around the selected object.

3. Select the Scale button ⊡ in the Toolbox's Options section (accessible when you've selected the Free Transform tool). Alternatively, you can select Modify → Transform → Scale.

Remember, because of the nature of the Free Transform tool, you can bypass step 3 if you want and go straight on to step 4.

4. To scale horizontally, click on one of the transform handles on the left or right of the bounding box and drag until the object is the desired size.

5. To scale vertically, click on one of the transform handle on the top or the bottom of the bounding box and drag until the object is the desired size.

6. To scale vertically and horizontally at the same time, click on one of the corner trans-form handles and drag until the object is the desired size. By doing this, you'll also main-tain the object's proportions.

7. When you've finished, click anywhere off the object to hide the transform handles.

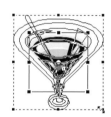

You can also scale an object with the Transform panel:

1. Select the object you want to scale.

2. Choose Window → Transform to open the Transform panel.

3. To scale the object horizontally, enter a value (in percent) into the Width field.

4. To scale the object vertically, enter a value (in percent) into the Height field.

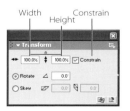

5. To scale the object both horizontally and vertically, click on the Constrain button and then enter a value (in percent) into either the Width or Height field.

> The value you enter into the Width or Height field can range from 1 to 1000.

6. When you've finished, click anywhere off the object to hide the transform handles.

Rotating an Object

When you rotate an object, it turns around its registration point. Don't worry too much about registration points yet because they're covered in the "Working with Transformation Points" section. For the time being, just recognize that they are a central point that acts as a pivot for rotation.

As with many of the transformation operations, you can rotate an object with the Free Transform tool or the Transform panel. To rotate an object with the Free Transform tool, fol-low these steps:

1. Select the desired object with the Arrow tool, then choose the Free Transform tool ⊞ from the Toolbox. Alternatively, click the desired object with the Free Transform tool to select it.

2. From here, you'll notice that a bounding box with handles appears around the selected object.

3. Select the Rotate and Skew button ↻ in the Toolbox's Options section (accessible when you've selected the Free Transform tool). Alternatively, you can go to Modify → Transform → Rotate and Skew.

> Remember, because of the nature of the Free Transform tool, you can bypass step 3 if you want and go straight on to step 4.

4. Move your cursor over one of the *corner* handles. Notice how your cursor changes to an icon with arrows that form a circle.

5. From here, click and drag in a circular motion to rotate your object.

6. When you are finished, click anywhere off the object to hide the transform handles.

To rotate an object with the Transform panel, follow these steps:

1. Select the object you want to rotate.

2. Go to Window → Transform to open the Transform panel.

3. Click on the Rotate radio button.

4. Enter a value (in degrees) into the Rotate field.

5. Click Return/Enter to apply the rotation to the selected object.

> You can also rotate a selected object 90° clockwise or counterclockwise by going to Modify → Transform → Rotate 90° CW or Rotate 90° CCW.

Flipping an Object

Flash lets you flip a selected object horizontally or vertically without changing its relative position on the Stage.

1. Use the Arrow tool to select the object you want to flip.

2. Select Modify → Transform → Flip Horizontal or Flip Vertical. Figure 6.9 illustrates the effects of the Flip Horizontal and Flip Vertical commands.

Skewing an Object

Skewing slants an object along its vertical or horizontal axis. As with many of the operations discussed in this chapter, you can slant an object in two ways.

To slant an object with the Free Transform tool:

1. Select the desired object with the Arrow tool, then choose the Free Transform tool ⌗ from the Toolbox. Alternatively, click the desired object with the Free Transform tool to select it.

2. Click on the Rotate and Skew button ↻ in the Toolbox's Options section (when you have the Free Transform tool selected).

> Remember, because of the nature of the Free Transform tool, you can bypass step 2 if you want and go straight on to step 4.

Figure 6.9

Three copies of the same image. The one on the top shows the original position. The middle illustrates the image after it has been flipped horizontally. The one on the bottom illustrates the same image after it has been flipped vertically.

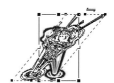

3. When the handles appear, move your cursor over one of handles in the *middle* of the side of the bounding box. Notice how your cursor changes to be to opposite pointing arrows oriented vertically or horizontally (depending on which handles you moved your cursor over)

4. Click and drag horizontally or vertically (depending on which handles you are manipulating).

5. To finish, click anywhere off the object to hide the transform handles.

To skew an object with the Transform panel, follow these steps:

1. Select the object you want to skew.

2. Go to Window → Transform to open the Transform panel.

3. Click on the Skew radio button.

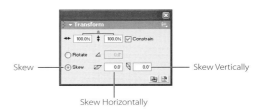

4. To skew the object vertically, enter a value (in degrees) into the Skew Vertically field.

5. To skew an object horizontally, enter a value (in degrees) into the Skew Horizontally field.

6. When you are finished, press Return/Enter.

Distorting an Object

When you apply a distort transformation, you can change the position of either the corner or side handles of an object's bounding box. This process not only changes the position of the selected handles (and therefore the shape of the object itself), but it also changes its adjoining edges.

> It's worth noting that while the Distort transformation won't work on a group (Modify → Group), but it works just fine on a group of individually selected objects.

If you hold down the Shift key while applying a distort transformation, the object will be tapered.

Unlike the previous transformations discussed, you can only distort an object using the Free Transform tool. Here's how:

1. Select the object you want to distort with the Arrow tool.

2. Select the Free Transform tool ⊡ .

3. Click on the Distort button ◰ in the Toolbox's Options section (when you have the Free Transform tool selected). Alternatively, you can also go to Modify → Transform → Distort.

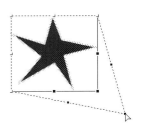

4. When the bounding box appears, move your cursor over any of the handles. Notice how your cursor changes to a larger white pointer.

5. Click and drag the handle. When you've reached the location on the Stage where you would like the handle to be moved, simply release your mouse button. Your object will distort accordingly.

Manipulating an Object's Envelope

An *envelope* is the bounding box that surrounds one or more *ungrouped* objects. With the Edit Envelope transform, you can effectively manipulate this envelope and thereby warp an object with a fair amount of precision.

> The Edit Envelope transformation does not work on grouped objects, symbols, bitmaps, gradients, or text.

To manipulate an object's envelope, follow these steps:

1. Select the object (or objects) whose envelope you want to edit with the Arrow tool.

> Although the Edit Envelope transformation won't work on a group (Modify → Group), but it works just fine on a group of individually selected objects.

2. Select the Free Transform tool 🔲 .

3. Click on the Envelope button 🔳 in the Toolbox's Options section (when you have the Free Transform tool selected). Alternatively, you can also go to Modify → Transform → Envelope.

> Remember, if the object is grouped, you won't have access to the Distort button.

4. When the bounding box appears, move your cursor over any of the handles. Notice how your cursor changes to a larger white pointer.

> You'll note that there are two types of handles: square and circular. The square handles are the points along the object's bounding box that you can directly manipulate, and the circular handles are tangent handles.

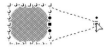

5. Click and drag the handle. When you've reached the location on the Stage where you would like the handle to be moved, simply release your mouse button. Your object will warp accordingly.

6. Notice that when you click and drag one of the envelope handles, tangent handles will appear. Much like in the case of path created with the Pen tool, you can manipulate the tangents (by clicking and dragging the handle at the end of the tangent) to further warp the object's envelope.

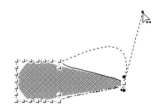

7. When you've finished distorting the object's envelope, just deselect it by clicking anywhere else on the Stage.

Restoring Transformed Objects

As you can see, you can apply a number of transformations to any given object. It would be quite easy to go wild and transform an object beyond all hope of returning it to its previous state. You'd be surprised how far away an object can wander from its initial appearance, leaving you totally stumped as to how it originally looked. But there is an easy way to restore objects to their pre-transformed state:

1. Select the object you want to restore.

2. Go to Modify → Transform → Remove Transform. Alternatively, you can click on the Reset button in the bottom-right corner of the Transform panel.

Working with Transformation Points

A *registration point* is a reference that Flash uses when it carries out all of the previously mentioned transformations. When you rotate an object, you rotate it around the registration point. When you align or distribute objects, the registration point acts as a reference for the procedure.

Unfortunately, you can't directly manipulate an object's registration point. However, you can change the position of an object's *transformation point*—which is like a temporary registration point that appears when an object is being transformed. Ultimately, by moving the position of the transformation point, you can get better control over the result of any given transformation. Say, for instance, you want an object to rotate not around its center but instead around its upper-right corner. Well, all you would need to do is move the object's transformation point from the center to the desired location in the upper-right corner.

When you move an object's transformation point, its new location is merely temporary. As soon as you apply a new transformation, the transformation point will reset to its default location, which is in the center of an object.

Let's take a look at how you go about moving an object's transformation point:

1. Select the object whose transformation point you want to manipulate.

2. Initiate any transform (either with the Free Transform tool or with the Modify → Transform menu). This will cause the bounding box to appear around the selected object.

3. Click and drag the transformation point (which appears in the center of the object as a white circle) and drag it to the desired location.

4. When the transformation point is in the desired location, carry out the desired transformation.

To reset the transformation point to its default location manually, simply double-click on it.

Inspirational Design Model

Working with objects is all about exerting control over your visual design so that it conveys the exact message you want. This chapter's Inspirational Design Model is Atomic Cartoons (`www.atomiccartoons.com`), which exemplifies the peak of visual control.

Based in the great city of Vancouver, in the wonderful province of British Columbia, in the beautiful country of Canada, Atomic Cartoons specializes in creating offbeat and hilarious Flash-animated shorts for distribution over the Web. Entertaining the masses, the Atomic Cartoons website features incredibly well-engineered graphics with stylish simplicity that scream creative talent (see Figure 6.10).

The beautifully constructed visual elements used in the site indicate that the good folks at Atomic Cartoons have a keen understanding of the tools used to manipulate objects in Flash.

Figure 6.10

Atomic Cartoons

Summary

In this chapter, you explored the wonderful world of objects. The chapter began by providing a brief introduction to the nature of objects themselves and then moved on to an extensive look at bitmaps. From there, you learned how objects are grouped and ungrouped. You then learned how you go about aligning and arranging objects. From there you looked at the various transformations you can apply to objects, including scaling, rotating, flipping, skewing, distorting, envelope editing, and restoring. The chapter finished off with an investigation of registration points, including a look at how you move an object's transformation point.

CHAPTER 7

Creating and Manipulating Reusable Content

Imagine if you created a Flash movie in which all the elements were variations on the same theme. Up until now, you would have to spend a great deal of time painstakingly creating each element individually. However, with the help of *symbols*, you will never have to toil in vain, oppressed under the weight of backbreaking digital labor. You will be able to create one master image and then base all subsequent images upon it, making specific changes to each as you go. Symbols help streamline the creative process and maximize your artistic juices. The purpose of this chapter, therefore, is to first explore symbols and then look at Flash MX's other cool reusable content and asset management tools.

The chapter covers the following topics:

- ■ **Understanding symbols and symbol types**
- ■ **Creating a symbol from scratch**
- ■ **Converting existing graphics to symbols**
- ■ **Importing symbols**
- ■ **Using the Library**
- ■ **Working with symbol instances**
- ■ **Using the Movie Explorer**

Understanding Symbols

Essentially, symbols are reusable elements that reside in the Library. You can use them repeatedly in either the same Flash creation or another one entirely. Whenever you create a symbol, it is automatically placed in the Library, where it is stored for future use. When you drag a symbol out of the Library (discussed later in the "Adding a Symbol to the Stage" section) onto the Stage, the symbol itself is not placed on the Stage. Instead, Flash creates a copy, called an *instance*, and places it on the Stage. You can change instances as many times or in as many different ways as you'd like without altering the original symbol. There will always be a copy of the original symbol residing in the Library.

Animation of any significant complexity can only be accomplished with symbols. As a result, it's important that most, if not all, of the graphical elements you create in Flash MX should either be converted to symbols or be created as symbols right off the bat. Don't worry too much about how symbols are animated with the Timeline—that will be covered in Part III of the book. For now, it's only important to understand the differences between the various types of symbols.

Symbols can fall into one of two categories: native Flash symbols and imported symbols. Native Flash symbols are those created directly within Flash, while imported Flash symbols are those created in another program and imported into Flash.

In Flash MX, native symbols are also referred to as *symbol behaviors*. This is due to the fact that, as you'll soon discover, there are three types of native Flash symbols, all of which behave and have different purposes within your movie.

Symbols are beneficial for a couple of reasons. The first, which has already been discussed briefly, is that they allow you to streamline the creative process. When it comes to native Flash symbols, all you need to do is create one object and then manipulate its instance on the Stage to create multiple variations without having to re-create the object from scratch every time. The second reason that symbols are so powerful is that they help you reduce the overall file size of your Flash creation. Each time a symbol is used, Flash simply refers to the profile of the original in the Library. If you are using multiple instances based on a single symbol, Flash only needs to save the information about their differences. If you were to use a one symbol for each of the various objects, each would be included in the Flash file, thereby increasing the overall file size.

Introducing Native Flash Symbols

Let's explore the three different types of native Flash symbols:

Graphic symbols   Graphic symbols 🖼 are static graphic objects created with the various Flash drawing and painting tools. They work in conjunction with the main movie and as such are most commonly used as elements in Timeline animations.

Button symbols   While the Graphic symbols are static elements, Button symbols 🔘 are dynamic, altering their appearance when clicked. Buttons are one of the most popular inter-active elements you can create in Flash. Although you'll get the chance to explore Button symbols (and how you make them) in Chapter 13, it's important to know they are made up of four different static images (referred to as *states*). Each state is visible based on how the user interacts with the button—when the button is up (the *up* state), when the user's mouse is over the button (the *over* state), and when the user clicks the button (the *down* state). The fourth button state, the *hit* state, is not a visible element in the button. Instead, it acts more like a hotspot that determines the active area of the button.

One of the most important things about Button symbols, at least in terms of creating interac-tivity, is that they can be tightly integrated with ActionScript.

Movie Clip symbols   It's no exaggeration to say that Movie Clips 🎬 are probably one of the most important aspects of Flash itself. Movie Clips are smaller, self-contained movies that you can place within another movie. They are infinitely nestable. Therefore, you could have a Movie Clip within a Movie Clip within a Movie Clip, and so on.

Movie Clips, which are in no way limited in their composition, run *independently* of the Timeline. They can also be placed within other symbols. So, you could insert a Movie Clip into one of the previously mentioned Button symbol states, thereby creating an animated button.

> If you are really interested in finding out how you can create and manipulate Movie Clips, see Chapter 10.

Introducing Imported Flash Symbols

Now that you've looked at the three native Flash symbols, you can move on to look at the various types of imported symbols:

Bitmaps   You've already looked at how you go about importing a bitmap into Flash. What you haven't learned is that all imported bitmaps are automatically inserted into the Library and converted into symbols for your use when they are imported into Flash.

Audio   Unlike graphical elements, audio files can't be seen. As a result, when they are imported, they are only placed in the Library (and not also on the Stage like imported bitmaps.) Because discussing audio at this point would be opening up a Pandora's box, there is little more you need to know at the moment other than they're one of the many types of nonnative Flash symbols.

For more about audio and Flash, see Part VI.

Digital Video One of the great things about Flash is that it lets you import and use a series of different digital video formats. If you have QuickTime 4 (or above) installed on your computer, you can import QuickTime files, Audio Video Interlace (AVI) files, Digital Video (DV) files, and Motion Picture Experts Group (MPEG) files.

You can also import sound-only QuickTime movie files and place them in the Library as symbols.

If you are working on a Windows machine, and you have DirectX 7 (or above) installed, you'll be able to import AVI, MPEG, or Window Media Files (WMV/ASF).

When imported, all digital video files are automatically placed in the Library to be used as symbols.

Creating Symbols

There is little doubt that symbols are one of the most important elements of Flash MX. Mastering their creation and manipulation will open up a world of incredible creative possibilities for you. In this section, you'll look at the two primary ways to create Graphic symbols: creating from scratch and converting from existing graphics.

Button and Movie Clip symbols are discussed in future chapters, so this section deals exclusively with creating Graphic symbols.

Creating a Symbol from Scratch

When it comes to Graphic symbols, it's more than likely that you'll create most within Flash with the painting and drawing tools:

1. Make sure you don't already have an object selected on the Stage.
2. Go to Insert → New Symbol or use the shortcut Cmd/Ctrl+F8. The Create New Symbol dialog box will appear.

You can switch between basic and advanced options in the Create New Symbol dialog box by clicking the Basic/Advanced button. The options available in the Advanced section relate to creating a Shared Library—something discussed in the "Working with Shared Symbol Libraries" section.

3. When the Create New Symbol dialog box appears, make sure the Graphic radio button is selected, enter a name for your symbol into the Name field, and click OK.

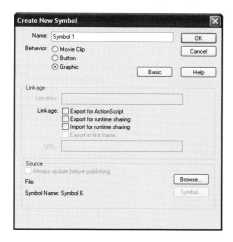

If your Flash creation is going to use a great deal of graphics, it's a good strategy to give each symbol a distinct name so that you won't get confused. By default, if you don't name the symbol, Flash MX will use the name Symbol X, where X is a sequential number.

4. From here, Flash adds the symbol to the Library and switches you to Symbol Editing mode (see Figure 7.1). The name of the symbol appears in the Scene and Symbol bar, just to the right of the name of the scene in which you are currently working. For reference, the symbol's registration point is represented by the crosshairs in the middle of the Symbol Editor.

The Symbol Editor is a little tricky in that it looks almost exactly like the regular Flash environment. Don't get confused, though; you can tell the difference because the symbol's name is displayed in the Scene and Symbol bar just to the right of the actual scene's name and a small cross, representing the symbol's eventual registration point, appears on the Stage.

Figure 7.1

Symbol Editing mode enables you to create your symbol with the same painting and drawing tools as when you're working in the Stage.

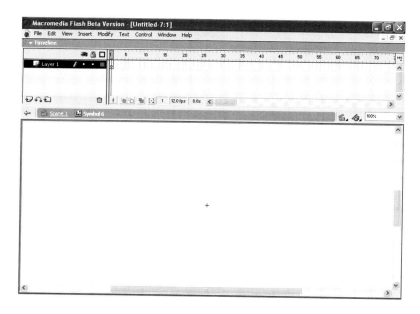

5. Use the skills you mastered in Chapter 3 to create the desired symbol.

6. When you are finished, you need to exit Symbol Editing mode. To do this, either go to Edit → Edit Document or click the scene name in the Scene and Symbol bar.

> Scenes are a way to break your Flash creation into manageable chunks. If you are interested in finding out more, see Chapter 11.

Converting an Existing Graphic to a Symbol

Although many of your Graphic symbols are going to be made from scratch in the Symbol Editor, you might come upon a situation where you need to convert an existing graphic (something you didn't create in the Symbol Editor) into a symbol:

Registration point diagram

1. On the Stage, select the object you want to turn into a Graphic symbol.

2. Go to Insert → Convert to Symbol.

3. When the Convert to Symbol dialog box pops up, make sure you select the radio button appropriate for the type of symbol you want to create.

4. Enter a name for your symbol into the Name field.

5. From here, you can set the location of your symbol's registration point. To do this, click one of the nine small boxes in the registration point diagram—each box represents the location of the symbol's registration point within its square bounding box.

6. When you're finished, click OK, and the symbol is automatically added to the Library.

7. The original object that you converted on the Stage is switched into an instance whose parent symbol now resides in the Library.

Leveraging the Power of the Library

The Library, accessible by going to Window → Library (or by using the shortcut F11), is the repository for all symbols in a given Flash project. Whether you are using Graphic symbols, Button symbols, Movie Clips, or any of the various imported symbols in your Flash project, the Library is where they'll be. The Library also offers you the ability to preview animations and sound files quickly and easily.

The Library has a second cousin called the Common Library, which is accessibly by going to Window → Common Libraries. There you'll find three groups of premade symbols—Buttons, Learning Interactions, and Sounds—that you can use in your own movie. With this basic introduction to the Library, you can begin to take advantage of its power and versatility.

Exploring the Library

The Library is packed with information and tools designed to make managing and manipulating symbols considerably easier (see Figure 7.2). The only way to get a handle on them is to explore each individually.

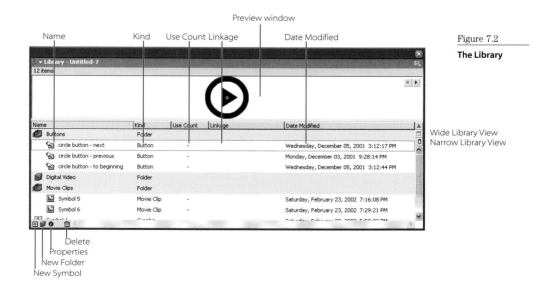

Figure 7.2

The Library

The Sort Window Columns

The Sort window displays information about each symbol in the Library in columns. Under normal circumstances, you can make all the columns visible only if you resize the Library horizontally (by clicking its left edge and dragging). Alternatively, you can also click the Wide Library View button in the right portion of the Library (just below the vertical scroll bar).

Clicking any aspect of a symbol (name, icon, linkage, date modified, and so on) will display a preview of it.

The Sort window contains the following columns:

Name Shows the name you assigned each symbol. The Name column also displays the filename for imported files such as audio files and bitmaps. The Name column is sorted alphabetically. To reverse the sort order, click the Sort Order button to the right of the Library window.

Kind Indicates whether the symbol is a Button, Bitmap, Graphic, Movie Clip, or Sound. To group items in the library by the type, click the Kind column header.

The type of symbol is also indicated by the small icon to the left of the name.

Use Count Tracks exactly how many times each symbol has been used. This is especially useful if you are working on a particularly large project, and you want to determine which symbols have actually been used in the final movie.

Linkage Indicates whether a symbol is being shared with another movie or imported from another movie.

Date Modified Indicates the last time a symbol or imported file was updated.

Library Panel Buttons

In addition to the Sort window columns, the bottom portion of the Library features several important buttons:

New Symbol Opens the Create New Symbol dialog box, thereby allowing you to create new symbols directly from within the Library.

New Folder Allows you to set up folders in the Library so you can better organize your content. This feature is amazingly useful when working with large, complex movies that need to be well organized. To add an item to a folder, click the item and drag it to the folder. To expand a folder, double-click it.

Properties Opens up the Symbol Properties dialog box. From there, you can change any of the selected symbol's properties.

Delete Lets you delete symbols from the Library. Just click the symbol you want to delete, and click the Delete button to remove it from the Library.

The Library Options Menu

The Library Options menu, accessible by clicking the menu icon in the upper-right corner of the Library, allows you to manage all aspects of the Library. A subset of these options is also available by Ctrl+clicking (Mac) or right-clicking (Win) a Library item.

> The New Symbol and New Folder options were discussed in the previous section.

The following settings are available in the Options menu:

New Font Lets you create font symbols that are stored in a shared Library. This is beneficial because you no longer have to embed a font directly in your Flash movie.

> If you are interested in learning more about Font symbols, see Chapter 5.

New Video Inserts an empty Video symbol into the Library. To fill the symbol, double-click the Video symbol's icon. When the Embedded Video Symbol dialog box opens, click the Import button. From there, navigate to where the desired video file is located, select it, and click OK.

Rename Allows you to rename a symbol directly within your Library. Simply select the symbol whose name you want to change, choose the Rename option from the Options menu, and type in a new name into the Sort window.

> You can also double-click the symbol's name in the Sort window to change it.

Move to a New Folder Automatically creates a new folder on the Sort window into which it will move the currently selected symbol.

Duplicate Makes an exact duplicate of the currently selected symbol. Simply select a symbol in the Sort window, choose Duplicate from the Options menu, and make any adjustments when the Duplicate Symbol dialog box opens.

Delete Works exactly the same as the Delete button at the bottom of the Library. Just select the unwanted Library item and select Delete from the Options menu.

Edit Opens the currently selected Graphic, Movie Clip, or Button in Symbol Editing mode. From there, you can make any changes you want, and the symbol in the Library will change accordingly.

Edit With The Edit With option opens the currently selected bitmap or sound with an external application. If you have Fireworks installed on your machine, Flash launches Fireworks for bitmap editing. Changes made using Fireworks do not affect the original bitmap; they appear only within Flash. When it comes to audio files in the Library, a dialog box appears, prompting you to choose a sound editor.

Properties Opens the Symbol Properties dialog box for the selected symbol. From there, you can change the symbol's type, edit its name, and manipulate its Linkage properties.

Linkage Lets you set several options needed to create a Shared Library. For more information on creating Shared Libraries, see the "Working with Shared Symbol Libraries" section later in this chapter.

Component Definition Lets you control the parameters of a Flash MX UI Component through the Component Definition dialog box.

For more information about Components, see Chapter 16.

Select Unused Items Automatically selects any symbols not currently used in the Flash project.

Update Automatically updates a bitmap or audio file you've altered in an external program rather than having to re-import it.

If you choose the Edit With option in conjunction with Macromedia Fireworks to make a change to artwork, you do not have to update it.

Play Plays any selected Movie Clip, Sound, or Button symbol.

You can also play a Movie Clip, Sound, or Button symbol by clicking the Play button in the upper-right corner of the preview window.

Expand Folder Automatically expands any selected folder so that all of its contents are visible.

Collapse Folder Collapses the currently selected folder so that none of its contents are visible—the opposite effect as the Expand Folder.

Expand All Folder Expands all of the folders in the current Library so all of their content is visible.

Shared Library Properties Opens the Shared Library Properties dialog box, allowing you to assign a URL for a given shared Library.

Keep Use Counts Updated Tells Flash to continuously update the use counts.

> Evoking the Keep Use Counts Updated option eats up a lot of your computers processing power, often resulting in a drastic slowdown.

Update Use Counts Now Lets you manually update the use counts.

Using the Library with Symbols

Now you are going to take your knowledge about symbols and put the Library to work. In this section, you'll start off by looking at how you add symbols to the Stage. You'll also explore how to use various Library options to manage and manipulate your symbols.

Adding a Symbol to the Stage

The Library is a two-way street—you can place symbols on the Stage just as easily as you can add them to the Library.

> Remember that when you place a symbol onto the Stage, you are creating an *instance*. An instance is a copy of the parent symbol that can you change and manipulate without altering the original symbol.

To add a symbol to the Stage, follow these steps:

1. Make sure the Library is open. If it isn't, go to Window → Library or use the shortcut F11.
2. Click and drag the desired symbol onto the Stage.

Renaming a Symbol

When you initially create a symbol, you give it a name. There are actually a number of different quick and easy ways to change that name:

1. Make sure the Library is open.
2. Select the symbol whose name you want to change.
3. Do one of the following:
   - Cmd+click (Mac) or right-click (Win) and choose Rename. When the current name is highlighted in the Sort window, simply type a new one.
   - Choose Rename from the Options menu. When the current name is highlighted, just type a new one.

- Choose Properties from the Options menu (or click the Properties button in the bottom of the Library) to open the Symbol Properties dialog box. From here, type in a new name into the Name field.
- Double-click the symbol name and type in a new name.

Duplicating Symbols

Flash gives you the ability to duplicate symbols in the Library with a minimum of trouble. You might find this handy if you had created a complex symbol that you wanted to copy, alter, and then subsequently add to the Library. Instead of jumping through a series of convoluted hoops, you can simply duplicate the symbol and then edit the copy in whatever way you want. Also, duplicating a symbol allows you to create a new symbol (to which you can make any changes) without actually changing any of that symbol's instances on the Stage.

To duplicate a symbol, follow these steps:

1. Make sure you have the Library open.

2. Select the symbol you want to duplicate.

3. Do one of the following:

    - Cmd+click (Mac) or right-click (Win) and choose Duplicate.
    - Choose Duplicate from the Options menu.

4. When the Duplicate Symbol dialog box appears, enter a new name. If you want to retain its original format, make sure to select the appropriate radio button. If you want to turn the duplicate symbol into an alternate format, click the desired radio button.

5. Click OK. The duplicated symbol is automatically placed in the Library.

6. From here, you can edit the duplicate symbol and make any changes you want.

Editing a Symbol

You may find yourself in a situation where you want to make more significant changes to a symbol that go beyond changing its name. All you need to do is follow these steps:

1. Make sure you have the Library open.

2. Select the symbol you want to edit.

3. Do one of the following:

    - Double-click the symbol's icon (to the left of the symbol name in the Sort window).
    - Cmd+click (Mac) or right-click (Win) and choose Edit.
    - Choose Edit from the Library's Options.
    - If the symbol you want to edit is a bitmap or audio file, select Edit With to open the appropriate external editor.

4. When Flash switches to the Symbol Editor, make any changes you want.

5. When you are finished, you need to exit Symbol Editing mode. To do this, either go to Edit → Edit Document or click the Scene button in the Scene and Symbol bar.

When you change a symbol, all of its associated instances will automatically change as well.

Organizing Your Library

As your experience with Flash develops, you will find find that many of your projects will use a large number of symbols. This can certainly lead to some workflow and organizational problems. To avoid this problem, you can do several things.

Figure 7.3

You can organize your Library by creating various folders in which you place common or similar symbols.

The first solution involves creating various folders in which similar symbols are placed (see Figure 7.3). Just as you can create folders in a website to better organize your files, you can make folders in a Flash Library to better organize your symbols, bitmaps, and sounds.

To create a folder, click the New Folder button in the bottom-left corner of the Library window. You can also choose New Folder from the Library Options menu. From here, simply click and drag the various symbols into their intended folders. Alternatively, you can also select a symbol and choose Move to New Folder from the Library's Options menu.

The second way to organize your Library, which has decidedly less of an impact on the Library's overall organization (but is nonetheless useful), involves using the Sort window columns. By clicking the name of either the Date Modified or Name column, the contents of the Library will be reorganized in a descending order.

Opening External Flash Libraries

One of the great things about Flash is that you aren't limited to the Library being used in your current Flash project—you can also open other Flash movie Libraries by using the Open as Library command.

External Libraries aren't really unique elements in Flash. Essentially, they are just regular FLA files, the contents of whose Library you've taken and shoved into your Library. Because of this, there is no special procedure for creating an external Library—you just need to create a Flash movie like any other.

Follow these steps:

1. Make sure you have the Library open.

2. Go to File → Open as Library.

3. When the Open as Library dialog box opens, navigate to the file whose Library you want to access, and open it (see Figure 7.4).

If you have not moved your original Library window, the new Library window might open directly on top of the old one. Drag the new Library window until you can see both windows.

4. From here, click and drag any symbol from the newly opened Library to the current project's Library. This automatically copies the desired symbol into the Library of your current project—to be used as any other symbol would.

Working with Shared Symbol Libraries

As Flash development teams become larger and projects become more complex, sharing assets becomes important. With Shared Symbol Libraries, also referred to as *Shared Library Assets* or *Shared Libraries,* you can use graphics, buttons, movies, audio files, and other assets in your movie by linking to the Library of a centrally located SWF file (on a web server, for example). The result is that a Flash movie no longer has to have its own individual Library.

The beauty of Shared Symbol Libraries is that teams can share standard set of symbols across multiple movies. You can make any final modification to a symbol in the Shared Library. After the Shared Library has been published, any other movies that use the Library are updated automatically. In addition, when you draw your symbols from a Shared Symbol Library, your final movie doesn't need any embedded symbols and therefore will be smaller.

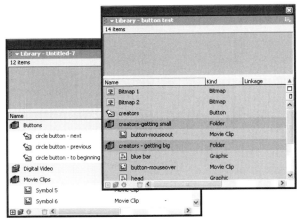

Figure 7.4

The original Library is on the left, and the Library on the right has been opened from an external Flash file.

Although Shared Symbol Libraries are beneficial to large projects, they have, unfortunately, proven to be somewhat unreliable and unpredictable. This having been said, it is strongly suggested that if you find the need to use Shared Libraries, you should limit their use to storage of relatively small (in terms of file size) elements.

Before you learn how to create and work with Shared Symbol Libraries, you need to realize there are two models for Shared Libraries: *runtime* and *author-time*.

- In a runtime Shared Symbol Library, assets are loaded into the destination movie from a source movie when the movie actually plays. Although the source movie (the movie from which you are drawing the symbols) doesn't have to be accessible when you initially author the movie, it must be posted to a web server and be accessible for the destination movie to draw the symbols at runtime. Using a runtime Shared Symbol Library is really only appropriate when you're distributing your Flash movie on the Web—this way, it will have access to the actual Shared Symbol Library.

- In an author-time Shared Symbol Library, you can replace any symbol in the movie upon which you are currently working with a symbol from another movie. Although the symbol in the destination movie retains its original name and properties, its contents are replaced. For example, you could use an author-time Shared Symbol Library when you want to integrate symbols into your movie that were created by someone else. The primary difference between an author-time Shared Symbol Library and a runtime Shared Symbol Library is that the movie being used as the source must be accessible on your local network (or on your own hard drive). Because you integrate symbols from a Shared Symbol Library into your own movie when it's being created, author-time Shared Symbol Libraries can be used whether you are distributing your movie over the Web or by some other means.

Creating a Runtime Shared Symbol Library

Creating and using a runtime Shared Symbol Library involves two discreet steps. The first involves creating the source movie (in which the Shared Symbol Library resides) and identifying symbols (through the use of unique names) within the source movie. The assignment of unique identifiers for symbols in the Shared Symbol Library is vital so the destination movie can successfully locate and acquire the symbols it needs to run properly.

> If you are planning on using runtime Shared Symbol Libraries, get into the habit of using the same name for the unique identifier as you did for the symbol's actual name—this might avoid some confusion in the long run.

The second part, which you do when you create the destination movie, involves telling Flash that the symbols being used will be drawn from a source movie at runtime.

Let's start off by looking at how you create a runtime Shared Symbol Library:

1. Create a new Flash file by going to File → New (or by using the shortcut Cmd/Ctrl+N).

2. Create or import all the elements you want to include in the final runtime Shared Symbol Library and add them to the currently active project's Library. If you are having trouble

remembering how to create either native Flash symbols or imported Flash symbols, see "Understanding Symbols."

3. If you want to include an entire font in your Shared Symbol Library, choose New Font from the Library Options menu. When the Font Symbol Properties dialog box opens, type a name for the font you want to include, locate the font in the Font menu, and select the style you want to be included.

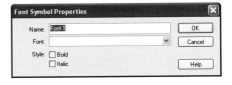

4. Delete all objects from your Stage that will be included in the final Shared Symbol Library.

Now that you've included all the symbols that will ultimately reside in the final runtime Shared Symbol Library, you need to assign a unique identifier to each so that they can be successfully located and used by the destination movie:

1. Select one of the symbols in the Library on which you're working.

2. From here, you've got a couple of different options:

   - Choose Linkage from the Library Options menu or from the Ctrl+click (Mac) or right-click (Win) context menu.

   - Select Properties from the Library Options menu or from the Ctrl+click (Mac) or right-click (Win) context menu. In the Symbol Properties dialog box that appears, click the Advanced button to access to the Shared Symbol Library options.

> If the item you've selected is not a native Flash symbol (Button, Movie Clip, or Graphic), you won't have access to the properties.

3. Select the Export for Runtime Sharing option.

4. Type in a unique name (without any spaces) into the Identifier field.

5. Enter the URL for the place where the source movie will be located into the URL field.

6. Repeat the process for each symbol that will ultimately be included in the final Shared Symbol Library.

7. When you've finished identifying all the desired symbols as assets within the runtime Shared Symbol Library, click OK.

The URL you enter into the URL field must be absolute (for example, `http://someURL.com/movies/mymovie.swf` not `/movies/mymovie.swf`). If you don't place the source movie in the location you set or enter the correct URL, the destination movie will not be able to locate and draw upon the necessary symbols.

Although the process of tagging each symbol with a unique identifier is tedious (especially if you've got a lot of symbols), it is necessary. Any of the symbols that aren't assigned a unique identifier will not work properly in the final Shared Symbol Library.

Now that you've set up all the properties of the source movie (which will act as the runtime Shared Symbol Library), save and publish it by following these steps:

1. Save the currently open Flash file (that contains the Library you've been working on) by going to File → Save. Alternatively, you can use the shortcut Cmd/Ctrl+S. So you don't get confused, make sure you give the file a distinct name that will identify it specifically as containing a runtime Shared Symbol Library.

2. From here, publish the FLA file as an SWF file (Flash's web format). All you need to do it go to File → Publish Settings. Make sure that Flash is the only format chosen in the Formats tab. Beyond that, you don't need to set any of the other options.

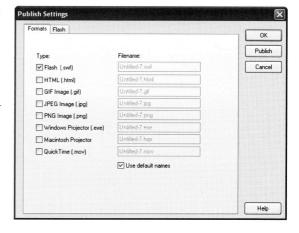

3. Once you've finished adjusting the necessary Publish Settings, click the Publish button. Then go to File → Publish (or use the shortcut Shift+F12). The SWF file will be saved to the same directory where you saved the original FLA file on which you were working.

4. At this point, you'll have to take the SWF file (which includes the tagged symbols) and upload it to the server whose URL corresponds to what you entered into the URL field.

For a far more detailed and thorough look at publishing your Flash movie, see Chapter 27.

Linking to a Runtime Shared Symbol Library

Now that you've gone through the process of creating a runtime Shared Symbol Library (the source movie), you can use its assets in another Flash movie (the destination movie).

The effect of linking to a runtime Shared Symbol Library is something like opening external Flash Libraries. The most important difference is that when you change a symbol in your runtime Shared Symbol Library (source movie), it changes all of the linked symbols in the destination movies that use it.

Unless you've got a copy of the symbol you want to draw from the runtime Shared Symbol Library (source movie) in the destination movie's Library, you aren't going to be able to do any linking at all. Although this seems a little counterproductive (what's the point of drawing the symbol from a runtime Shared Symbol Library if it's already in the destination movie?), it's important to realize that the symbol won't actually get exported if it has been linked to a runtime Shared Symbol Library. It really just acts as a placeholder in your movie.

Now follow these steps to link to a Library:

1. Create a new Flash movie (or open an existing one)—this will act as the destination movie.
2. Open the movie's Library by going to Window → Library.
3. Select the Graphic, Movie Clip, or Button symbol, and open the Symbol Properties dialog box by choosing Properties from the Library's Options menu. If the Symbol Properties dialog box isn't expanded, click the Advanced button.
4. Select the Import for Runtime Sharing option.
5. Enter the unique identifier for the symbol you are drawing from the runtime Shared Symbol Library (source movie) into the Identifier field.

If you don't put the exact identifier into the field, the destination movie will not be able to successfully locate the symbol you want to use.

6. Enter the exact location for where the runtime Shared Symbol Library (source movie) is posted into the URL field.

If you don't put the exact URL, the destination movie won't be able to locate the source movie and will therefore not be able to access the required symbol.

7. When you've finished, click OK.

Severing the Link to a Runtime Shared Symbol Library

Although linking to a runtime Shared Symbol Library is definitely a handy technique, you might find yourself in a position where you want to sever the link between your destination movie and the source movie—here's how:

1. Open the destination movie that contains the symbol you want to "de-link."

2. Open the Library by going to Window → Library.

3. Select the Movie Clip, Button, or Graphic symbol you want to de-link.

4. Open the Symbol Properties dialog box by selecting Properties from the Library Options menu.

5. De-select the Import for Runtime Sharing option.

6. Click OK.

Linking to an Author-Time Shared Symbol Library

As mentioned before, when you employ an author-time Shared Symbol Library, you can replace any symbol in the movie you are currently working on with a symbol from another movie entirely.

> When you're working with an author-time Shared Symbol Library, the source movie must be directly accessible—either over a local network or on your own computer.

Remember that although the symbol in the destination movie retains its original name and properties, its contents are replaced by that of the symbol you are drawing from the source movie.

> Any asset that the symbol from the source movie uses (such as an audio file in a Movie Clip) is also copied over to the destination movie.

To replace a symbol in a destination movie with one drawn from an author-time Shared Symbol Library, just follow these steps:

1. Open the movie that has the symbol you want to replace.

2. Open the Library by going to Window → Library.

3. Select the symbol you want to replace.

4. Open the Symbol Properties dialog box by selecting Properties from the Library Options menu.

5. Click the Browse button located at the bottom of the Symbol Properties dialog box.

6. When the Locate Macromedia Flash Document File dialog box pops up, navigate to where the FLA file containing the symbol you want to use as the replacement is located, select it, and click Open.

7. When the Select Source Symbol dialog box appears (which lists all the symbols in the FLA file you picked), select the symbol that you want to use as the replacement.

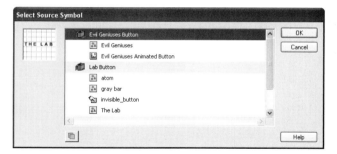

8. Click OK.

9. When you are returned to the Symbol Properties dialog box, click OK again. Note that the contents of the symbol have been replaced.

> To replace one symbol for another in the same movie, just click the Symbol button in the Source section of the Symbol Properties dialog box to access the Select Source Symbol dialog box.

Working with Symbol Instances

You've already learned that when you drag a symbol from the Library to the Stage, you are not really adding the symbol *per se*. Instead, you are creating a copy (called an *instance*) that you can alter without changing the parent symbol (which remains in the Library). As such, an instance can be changed to look quite different than its parent symbol. Although editing the symbol in the Library updates all of its instances, editing an instance of a symbol updates only that instance.

In the next section you'll investigate how you can manipulate the various visual characteristics of symbol instances.

Modifying the Appearance of Instances with the Property Inspector

Instances have a series of properties that you can manipulate to change the instance's visual character. You'll find that many, if not all, of these instance properties are particularly important when it comes to animation. You can animate each property—including transparency, brightness, and color—to create a change in the instance's visual appearance over time. For example, you could animate an instance's transparency so it appears to fade-in over time.

> For more information on how to animate an instance's visual properties, see Chapter 9.

This section of the chapter will get you familiar with the tools to change the overall appearance of any given symbol instance.

When it comes to the visual character of an instance property, you'll rely exclusively on the Color Style drop-down menu in the Property Inspector to make any changes:

1. Select the symbol instance whose visual properties you want to manipulate.

2. If the Property Inspector isn't already open, go to Window → Properties.

Color Style drop-down menu

3. Select one of the options from the Color Style drop-down menu (each of which has unique properties).

> The alterations you make to a symbol instance's visual properties in the Property Inspector will be dynamically applied to the selected symbol instance.

Let's take a look at each option individually:

None Leaves the symbol instance unaltered. Applying the None effect is a good way to revert a symbol instance back to its original form after you've fiddled with its visual properties.

Brightness Input a value (in percent) into the Brightness field (or use the Brightness slider) to change the relative brightness of the selected symbol instance. The value can range from 100 percent (white) to –100 percent (black).

> Setting the Brightness to 0 percent retains the original color of the symbol instance.

Brightness field Brightness slider

Tint Offers several ways to alter the color of the selected symbol instance. First, you can click the Tint swatch (which opens up the Color Picker) and choose a color. Alternatively you could mix your own RGB color by entering a value into the R, G, and B fields.

Tint color swatch
Tint amount

Blue color channel
Green color channel
Red color channel

> Remember, you can also use the sliders (accessible by clicking the small Down arrow just to the right of each field) to adjust the value of the individual RGB channels.

Finally, you can adjust the amount of tint by entering a value (in percent) between 0 and 100 into the Tint field.

Like the R, G, and B fields, the Tint amount can be manipulated by adjusting the slider (accessible by clicking the small Down arrow just to the right of the field).

Alpha Lets you adjust the transparency of a selected symbol instance. Enter a value into the Alpha field or use the slider (accessible by clicking the Down arrow to the right of the field) to adjust the value. The value can range from 0 (totally transparent) to 100 (no transparency).

Alpha field   Alpha slider

Advanced When you select Advanced from the Color Style drop-down menu, and click the Settings button in the Property Inspector, you open the Advanced Effect dialog box—where you can change the color and transparency of an object simultaneously.

Settings button

In the Advanced Effect dialog box, you'll notice that there are two sets of Tint and Alpha controls. The four controls on the right (R, G, B, and Alpha) change the color and transparency of a selected symbol instance by an absolute value. The four controls on the left change a symbol instance's Tint and Alpha value by a relative amount (percent).

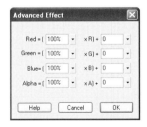

Replacing One Instance with Another

You might find yourself in a situation where you want to swap one instance for another. This is particularly useful when you have a complex scene where you want to swap one symbol instance with another but want to make sure the new one is placed in the exact same location as the old one. To do this, follow these steps:

1. Select the symbol instance you want to replace.

2. Go to Window → Properties.

3. Click the Swap button.

Swap

4. When the Swap Symbol dialog box opens, select the symbol you want to swap, and click OK.

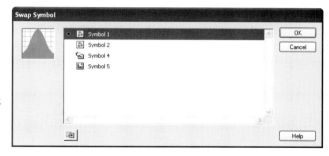

Editing an Instance on the Stage

Symbol instances are exact copies of their parent symbols in the Library. You can alter and edit them without changing the parent. As such, you are probably going to edit symbol instances on a regular basis. To do this, follow these steps:

1. Select the symbol instance you'd like to edit.

2. From here, use any of Flash's painting, drawing, or transformation tools to manipulate the symbol instance.

> To manipulate every aspect of the symbol instance, you will probably have to break it down into its parts—a process accomplished by selecting the symbol instance and then going to Modify → Break Apart.

If you want to edit the parent symbol of a given instance, you can open the Library, select the symbol, and choose Edit from the Library Options menu. Alternatively, you can double-click the symbol, which opens the Symbol Editor where you can make any changes you want.

> Remember, when you change the parent symbol, all of its associated symbol instances will also change.

Using the Movie Explorer

In the earlier versions of Flash, it was quite difficult to keep track of the structure of your Flash creation—especially if you were using Action-Scripts, nested symbols, or complex Movie Clips. Then, much to the joy of much of the Flash community, along came the Movie Explorer.

Essentially, the Movie Explorer displays the contents of your movie hierarchically (see Figure 7.5). The Movie Explorer lets you search your entire movie for any symbol or symbol instance. In addition, you can replace text and fonts with a few easy steps. You can also copy the contents of the Movie Explorer as text to the Clipboard or print the display list in the Movie Explorer. To activate the Movie Explorer, simply go to Window → Movie Explorer (or use the shortcut Option/Alt+F3).

In the next sections, you'll explore the various Movie Explorer options. You'll also look at how you filter the categories displayed in the

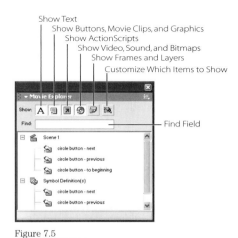

Figure 7.5

The Movie Explorer

Movie Explorer and how you search for items with the Find field. Finally, you'll learn how to edit symbol properties and replace fonts from within the Movie Explorer.

Understanding the Movie Explorer Options

As with many of Flash's panels, the Movie Explorer has an Options drop-down menu (accessible by clicking the icon in the panel's right corner). It contains the following options:

Go to Location   Jumps to the selected layer, scene, or frame in the movie. You can accomplish the same thing by simply double-clicking the item in the Movie Explorer.

Go to Symbol Definition   Automatically selects all files associated with the selected symbol. The Go to Symbol Definition option only works if you have the Show Buttons, Movie Clips, and Graphics button toggled, and it's only active when you're working in the Movie Elements section of the display list.

Select Symbol Instances   Automatically jumps to the scene in the Movie Elements section of the display list that contains the selected symbol's instance. This option is only accessible when the Show Buttons, Movie Clips, and Graphics button is toggled.

Find in Library   Opens the Library (if it is not already open) and jumps to the selected symbol.

Rename   Lets you rename the currently selected symbol.

Edit in Place   Allows you to edit the currently selected symbol on the Stage without entering into Symbol Editing mode.

Edit in New Window   Opens up a new window in which you can make changes to the selected symbol.

Show Movie Elements   Automatically displays all elements in the Flash movie, organized by scene.

Show Symbol Definitions   Displays all the files associated with the currently selected element (by toggling on and off).

Show All Scenes   Displays all the scenes in your movie (by toggling on and off).

Copy All Text to Clipboard   Copies selected text to your Clipboard so that you can paste it into another program (a word processor, for example).

Cut   Cuts selected text.

Copy   Copies selected text (but does not place it in the Clipboard like the Copy All Text to Clipboard option).

Paste   Allows you to paste text that has been copied either from within Flash or from another application.

Clear   Clears selected text.

Expand Branch Expands the currently selected branch of the hierarchical tree. You can accomplish the same result by clicking the small plus (+) sign to the right of any given section of the hierarchy.

Collapse Branch Collapses the currently selected branch of the hierarchy. You can accomplish the same effect by clicking the minus (-) symbol to the right of any given section of the hierarchy. This is the opposite of the Expand Branch option.

Collapse Others Automatically collapses all sections of the hierarchy except for the one currently selected.

Print Automatically prints all the contents of the Movie Explorer (with all sections of the hierarchy expanded). This is a good way to create a hard copy version of your Flash movie's structure.

Leveraging the Power of the Movie Explorer

Now that you've had a chance to fully explore all of the Movie Explorer options, you can learn how to manipulate the way your Flash movie's content is displayed and how you can manipulate that content.

Filtering the Displayed Categories

Several buttons allow you to customize which category of items are displayed in the Movie Explorer. By clicking any of the buttons (or a combination thereof), the Movie Explorer displays only those elements in your file.

From left to right, the buttons are Show Text; Show Buttons, Movie Clips, and Graphics; Show ActionScripts; Show Video, Sounds, and Bitmaps; and Show Frames and Layers. The final button, Customize Which Items to Show, brings up the Movie Explorer Settings dialog box so you can set the items you want visible.

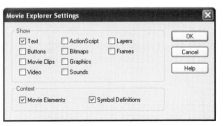

Searching for Items

When you are working with a particularly large movie with many discreet elements, you may become overwhelmed and have difficulty locating a given symbol or instance. In that case, the Movie Explorer provides you with a search tool. All you have to do is enter the name of a symbol, instance, font, ActionScript string, or frame number into the Find field, and the Movie Explorer automatically jumps to the location in the hierarchy where the item is located.

Editing Symbols

You will probably find yourself in the situation where you'd like to alter a given symbol instance from within the Movie Explorer:

1. Make sure the Movie Explorer is open.

2. Locate the symbol instance you want to edit. You can either navigate to its location in the hierarchy manually, or use the Movie Explorer's search tool to find it.

3. Ctrl+click (Mac) or right-click (Win) and choose Edit in Place or Edit in New Window from the pop-up menu. Alternatively, you can choose either of these options from the Movie Explorer's option menu (accessible by clicking the small right-pointing arrow in the top-right corner of the Movie Explorer).

You can also double-click the symbol instance in the Movie Explorer to enter into Symbol Editing mode.

4. Make any changes you want to the symbol instance and then return to working on your movie.

Replacing Fonts

The Movie Explorer lets you search for and replace any specific font you've used in your movie. This is particularly useful if you have many different instances of a given font that you want to change and don't want to switch each by hand:

1. Make sure the Movie Explorer is open.

2. Type the name of the font into the Find field.

3. After the Movie Explorer has jumped to the location in the hierarchy where the font in question resides, select it. If you've used the same font several times, it will display all occurrences.

If there is more than one use of the specific font, all occurrences will be displayed. To select them all, use Cmd/Ctrl+click.

4. Open the Property Inspector.

5. After the Property Inspector opens, make any changes you want—including font, style, color, size, and so on.

6. When you make your changes, your movie is automatically updated.

Inspirational Design Model

When it comes to reusable content, any Inspirational Design Model would have to feature a wide range of media types (vectors, bitmaps, sound, and so on) as well as consistency across the design. This kind of approach to design is easily recognizable in the website of Doug Chiang Studio (www.dchiang.com).

Founded by Doug Chiang, the design director for the *Star Wars* prequels, Doug Chiang Studio is currently working on a film/book project called *Robata: Reign of Machines*. The

160-page "film-format" illustrated book is to be published in 2002 and explores the relationship between technology and nature against the backdrop of a futuristic society. The website is intended to cater to those fascinated by the incredible work of Chiang, as well as publicize and explore the studio's current project.

Designed by Red Industries (`www.redindustries.com`) using a combination of Dreamweaver, Fireworks, and Flash, the website combines Chiang's compelling style of illustration with a highly intuitive navigational scheme to create an exceptionally immersive experience (see Figure 7.6). The site's design masterfully combines incredibly beautiful bitmap art and audio with consistently predictable and repeating interface elements, easily making it worthy as this chapter's Inspirational Design Model. Prepare to be inspired!

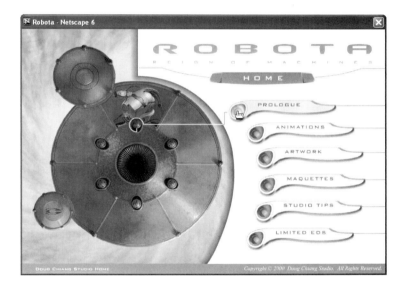

Figure 7.6

Doug Chiang Studio

Summary

In this chapter, you learned about reusable content. You looked at the nature of symbols and the different symbol types. You learned how to create a new symbol, import an existing symbol, and convert an existing graphic to a symbol. From there, you used your knowledge about symbols as a stepping-stone to investigate the Library. You learned how to add symbols to the Stage from the Library, how to duplicate symbols, how to rename a symbol, and how to edit symbols. You also learned about organizing your Library, opening external Flash Libraries, and creating Shared Symbol Libraries. From there, you explored how to use the Property Inspector to change the visual character of a symbol instance. You finished off the chapter with a thorough look at the Movie Explore—an extremely useful tool for managing and manipulating the assets in your movie.

CHAPTER 8

Adding Depth to Flash Graphics with Layers

Up until this point, all of the painting, drawing, and manipulating of visual elements you've done has taken place on one layer. Well, prepare yourself for the third dimension! Don't get too excited, you're not going to look at creating 3D images in Flash until Chapter 26. However, now is a perfect time to start exploring how you can create 2D visual content in discreet planes stacked one upon another.

Like many other graphics programs, Flash lets you create any number of individual layers in your movie. If you are confused as to what layers are, it's easiest to think of them as invisible levels where you can create and place objects. Layers let you partition your artwork when you're building complicated or composite images and animations so that you can focus on each element independently of the others. Layers are also extremely important when it comes to animation—a topic covered in Chapter 9. In this chapter, you're going to explore all aspects of layers.

Topics covered include:

- **Leveraging the power of layers**
- **Creating a new layer**
- **Creating and editing layer folders**
- **Adding content to a layer**
- **Working with layer properties**
- **Editing layers**
- **Distributing objects to layers**
- **Creating guide layers**
- **Creating mask layers**

Leveraging the Power of Layers

Each layer in a Flash movie acts like a transparent sheet upon which any number of individual objects reside. Ultimately, your final Flash movie will consist of a stack of layers. Although individual layers are not really recognizable on the Stage, they are displayed horizontally across (and accessible from) the Timeline.

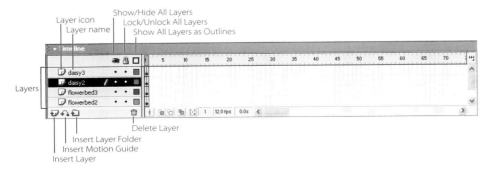

The way in which each layer is displayed in relation to other layers in the Timeline is important. Because the layers (and therefore the content on the layers) are stacked, the topmost ones appear in the foreground of the movie, and the bottommost ones appear in the background of the movie. Although this may be a little difficult to grasp in the abstract, look at it this way: Say you had two different images in two separate layers that occupied the same space on the Stage. The image in the top layer of the Timeline would appear in front of the image in the bottom layer.

Layers come in a number of different "flavors," all of which play distinct roles in Flash. Don't worry too much about the types of layers right now, as you'll learn all about them later in this chapter (see "Creating Guide Layers" and "Creating Mask Layers"). In addition, each layer has a series of different options accessible through the Timeline. You'll get a chance to explore these options shortly (see "Working with Layer Properties").

Selecting a layer is as simple as clicking its name in the Timeline. You'll notice that when it is selected, the layer is highlighted and a small pencil appears to the right of its name. This indicates the layer is active, and any objects you add to the Stage will be assigned to it.

Although layers play in integral part in static image creation, they become even more important when you start learning about animation, covered in Chapter 9. For the time being, however, it's important to familiarize yourself with creating and manipulating layers.

Creating a New Layer

When you start Flash, one layer appears in the Timeline. You certainly don't *have* to add more layers to your movie. However, once you are creating extensive (and, of course, amazingly brilliant) Flash movies, you'll find that working in one layer is not only confusing, but it may result in some functionality problems.

Without getting too much ahead of things, let's take a look at a short example. When you get into ActionScripts in Chapter 12, you'll learn it is possible create scripts that are activated when the playhead passes over a given frame. These are called *frame actions*. If your movie comprises only one layer, a frame action affects all the content of the layer, which could easily be far from what you intended. Instead, it would be better to create multiple layers. Then, you could include the frame action in a specific layer, thereby restricting the scripts to that layer. In addition, when it comes to creating complex animations, you'll find that you are going to want to create one layer for each discreet object or symbol. By doing this, you can exert greater control over each object (moving, manipulating, and so on) and therefore your overall animation. The bottom line, for a number of different reasons, is that it's wise to use many layers for each distinct object (or group of objects). The number of layers you can create is only limited by the amount of available memory on your computer.

> Because Flash flattens all of the layers upon export, you don't have to worry about increasing the file's size resulting from many different layers.

Do one of the following to create a new layer:

- Click the Insert Layer button ⏻ in the bottom-left corner of the Timeline.
- Go to Insert → Layer.
- Cmd+click (Mac) or right-click (Win) any layer in the Timeline and choose Insert Layer from the pop-up context menu.

When you carry out any of these procedures, Flash automatically adds the new layer above the existing one.

> If you have more than one layer, Flash inserts the new layer above the currently selected one.

Adding Content to a Layer

You'll find that through the course of creating your Flash masterpiece you will add layers as you need them. Adding new layers is all well and good, but what about adding content to those layers? The process itself is quite simple—all you need to do is select the layer by clicking it and insert any content you want onto the Stage (by using the painting and drawing tools or dragging a symbol instance from the Library). As long as that particular layer stays active, all content you add will automatically be placed in it.

As you add content to a layer, you'll notice that the small black outline of a circle (which always occupies the first frame of a newly created layer and is called a *blank keyframe*) will fill up and become a small solid black circle—this is called a *keyframe*.

You are going to learn all about frames, keyframes, and blank keyframes in Chapter 9, so all you need to know right now is that when a keyframe appears, it means that content has been added or manually changed in that frame.

Working with Layer Properties

Now that you've learned how to create and add content to layers, you can learn how to work with layer properties. Each layer has a series of properties represented and accessible through the icons to the right of the layer's name.

In this section, you'll explore how to turn layer visibility on/off, view layer objects as outlines, change the layer outline color, and lock/unlock a layer.

Turning Layer Visibility On/Off

One of the great things about layers in Flash is that they can be "turned off." By doing this, you make the content of any given layer invisible. Ultimately, this helps to unclutter the Stage and allows you to focus better on the objects on a particular layer. When you're done with whatever you were doing, you simply "turn the layer back on," and it becomes visible again. To change a layer's visibility, perform one of the following tasks:

- Click the small dot in the layer's eye column. A red X automatically appears, denoting the layer's hidden state. To turn the layer visibility back on, click the red X.

- To hide all the layers at the same time, click the eye icon. To reverse this process, click the eye icon again, or Cmd+click (Mac) or right-click (Win) and choose Show All from the pop-up context menu.

- To hide all the layers except one, Option/Alt+click the small dot in the layer's eye column that you want to stay visible. Alternatively, you can Cmd+click (Mac) or right-click (Win) and choose Hide Others from the pop-up context menu.

Viewing Layer Objects as Outlines

Viewing layer objects as outlines allows you to alter all of the layer's objects so they appear as colored outlines.

This is particularly useful if you want to speed up the display of your movie when editing or testing animations.

To view layer objects as outlines, you have three options:

- Click the layer's outline icon (represented by a colored box). The box icon will become hollow, indicating that the layer's objects are currently displayed only as outlines. To turn the option off, click the hollow box icon. Figure 8.1 shows both states of the layer's outline icon.

Figure 8.1

The left image displays the outline icon as it appears when you have the view layer objects as outlines option turned off. The right image shows the outline icon as it appears when you have the option activated.

- To display the content of all layers as outlines, click the Timeline's box icon (located above the layers themselves). To reverse the process, click the icon again.

- To view all layer objects as outlines except one, just Option/Alt+click the layer's outline icon whose objects you want to remain "solid."

Changing the Layer Outline Color

You'll notice that each of your layer's outline box icon is a different color—each of which represents the color of the layer's objects if they were to be reduced to outlines using one of the procedures described in the previous section. So, if your outline box icon is red, your objects are represented as red outlines. You certainly aren't stuck with the default color, though:

1. First, to open the Layer Properties dialog box, do one of the following:

   - Double-click the layer icon (to the left of the layer name).

   - Cmd+click (Mac) or right-click (Win) the layer and choose Properties from the pop-up context menu.

   - Select the layer whose outline color you want to change, and go to Modify → Layer.

2. When the Layer Properties dialog box opens, click the Outline Color swatch and choose the color you want.

3. When you've finished, click OK.

Locking/Unlocking Layers

When you first create a layer in Flash MX, it is automatically unlocked; otherwise, you wouldn't be able to add to or edit the layer. However, the tricky thing about layers is that you don't need to have them selected to actually manipulate their contents. As a result, you could inadvertently modify the content of one layer while working on the content of another. This can be particularly frustrating if the movie on which you're working took a great deal of time to create, and the mistaken displacement of any given object would result in lost work hours. To avoid

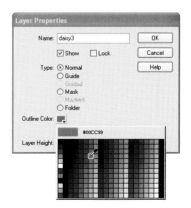

this sort of unfortunate situation, Flash lets you lock layers. You have a few ways to lock/unlock a layer:

- Click the small dot in the layer's lock column (represented by a padlock). A little padlock automatically appears, denoting the layer's locked state. To unlock the layer, click the padlock.

- To lock all layers at the same time, click the Timeline's padlock icon. To reverse this process, click the padlock icon again.

- To lock all the layers except one, just Option/Alt+click the small dot in the layer's eye column that you want to remain visible. Alternatively, you can Cmd+click (Mac) or right-click (Win) and choose Lock Others from the pop-up context menu.

Creating and Editing Layer Folders

One of the exciting features of Flash MX, at least in terms of layers, is the ability to create what are called *layer folders*. Essentially, layer folders are folders in the Timeline into which you can place multiple layers—thereby organizing your Timeline.

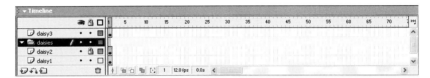

For instance, say you had an animation with a series of cartoon characters. If you've planned your movie correctly, each discreet part of the characters (arm, head, leg, floppy ears, and so on) occupies an individual layer. To cut down on the confusion in your Timeline, you could organize the body parts for each character into a layer folder—a Goofy folder, a Daffy folder, and so on.

One of the cool things about layer folders is that you can expand and collapse them, thereby hiding all of the associated layers in the Timeline without affecting what is visible on the Stage.

Although layer folders don't manifest themselves in the Timeline like layers do, they have many of the same properties (lock/unlock, visibility, name, and outline color)—all of which you can manipulate in the same way as you would if you were working with a regular layer.

In the following sections, you are going to learn everything you need to know about layer folders. You'll explore how to create them, edit them, add layers to layer folders, and expand and collapse them.

You can change the position of a layer folder in the same way that you can move a layer—a procedure we'll talk about shortly.

Creating a Layer Folder

The process by which you create a layer folder is really quite easy—just do one of the following:

- Click the Insert Layer Folder button in the bottom-left corner of the Timeline.
- Go to Insert → Layer Folder.
- Cmd+click (Mac) or right-click (Win) any layer in the Timeline and choose Insert Folder from the pop-up context menu.

When you carry out any of these procedures, Flash automatically adds the new layer folder above the selected layer.

> You can also convert a selected layer to a layer folder by changing its type from Normal to Folder in the Layer Properties dialog box (accessible by selecting the layer and then going to Modify → Layer).

Adding a Layer to a Layer Folder

The purpose of layer folders is to contain layers. As a result, you need to learn how to add layers to layer folders:

1. Make sure you've already created a layer folder using the procedure described in the previous section.

2. Click and drag the desired layer to the layer folder's icon (notice that the folder icon will be highlighted when your cursor is directly over it).

3. Release your mouse button.

4. The layer will move so that it's just below the layer folder. It will also be indented slightly, indicating its position within the layer folder.

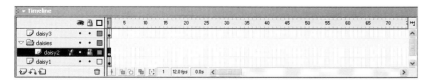

Expanding and Collapsing a Layer Folder

As mentioned previously, one of the benefits of a layer folder is that it can be expanded to show its contents and collapsed to hide them. Ultimately, this lets you unclutter your Timeline without actually removing the collapsed layer folder's associated objects/symbols from the Stage.

To either collapse or expand a layer folder, just click the small arrow to the left of the layer folder name. When the arrow is pointing down and the layer folder's associated layers are visible, you know that it is expanded.

On the other hand, if the arrow is pointing to the right, and the layer folder's associated layers aren't visible, you know it has been collapsed.

Editing Layers

Now that you've looked at how to manipulate a layer's properties, it's time to explore how to edit layers. You've already mastered the finer points of creating layers, adding content, and setting properties. In this section, you'll learn how to move a layer, copy layers, delete layers, rename a layer, and change a layer's height.

Moving a Layer

As you've already learned, the position of a layer within the stack determines whether its associated objects or symbols either overlay other layer content or are overlayed by the content from other layers. Because of this, you are going to want to be able to change the position of a layer within the stack, thereby changing the way in which objects and symbols on the Stage interact visually with one another. Here's how:

1. Select the layer you want to move.

2. Click and drag the layer to its intended place within the Timeline's layer stack. Notice that a thin black bar will appear, highlighting the projected position of the layer.

3. When the highlighted line reaches the location where you want to move the layer, simply release your mouse button.

Copying a Layer

You might find yourself in a situation where, instead of inserting a new layer, you want to copy an existing layer (along with all of its content). This process is a little cumbersome. You really don't copy the layer itself; you copy its content (frame by frame) and then paste it into a newly created layer. Follow these steps:

1. Select the layer you want to copy by clicking its name—this selects the entire layer.

2. Go to Edit → Copy Frames or use the shortcut Cmd/Ctrl+Option/Alt+C—this copies all the content in each of the layers' frames.

3. Create a new layer. If you are having trouble remembering how to insert a new layer, see the "Creating a New Layer" section.

4. Select the newly created layer by clicking its name.

5. Go to Edit → Paste Frames or use the shortcut Cmd/Ctrl+Option/Alt+V.

Deleting a Layer

Deleting a layer is just as simple as creating one:

1. Select the layer you'd like to delete by clicking its name.

2. Do one of the following:

   - Click the Delete button 🗑 .
   - Click and drag the layer to the Delete button.
   - Ctrl+click (Mac) or right-click (Win) and choose Delete Layer from the pop-up context menu.

> When you delete a layer, you also delete all of its content from the Stage. Therefore, make sure you want to do this because Flash doesn't ask you whether you *really* want to go ahead with the procedure.

Renaming a Layer

As you've already seen, each layer is created with a distinct name. Granted, the name *Layer 1* isn't all that imaginative, but Flash lets you change the layer name to anything you want.

> When renaming a layer, it's a good idea to give it a name that describes its content. This makes it easier for you to identify the layer's content as your Flash creation gets more complex.

You have a few ways to rename a layer:

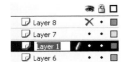

- Double-click the layer's name (not its icon) and then enter a new name when the editable field appears.

- Double-click the layer's icon (located to the left of its name). When the Layer Properties dialog box opens, enter a new name into the Name field. Alternately, you can go to Modify → Layer to open the Layer Properties dialog box.

If the entire layer name isn't visible, simply click and drag the bar that separates the area of the left part of the Timeline (where the layer name is) and the right part of the Timeline (where the frames are).

Altering Layer Dimensions

When layers are created, they are a default height. However, you might find yourself in a position where you want to change the height of the layer. For instance, when it comes to working with audio in Flash (covered in Part VI), you can add sounds to the Timeline. Unlike other objects that you work with in conjunction with the Timeline, the audio files are represented by the sound's waveform, which is easier to see when the layer's size is larger.

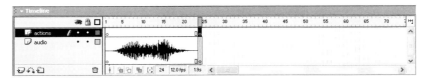

Although this section discusses how you can change a layer's height, you are going to learn how to manipulate the appearance of the frames within the layer (and thereby the layer itself) in Chapter 9.

To increase the height of a layer, follow these steps:

1. Open the Layer Properties dialog box. If you are having trouble remembering how, see "Working with Layer Properties."

2. Choose one of the options from the Layer Height drop-down menu (100%, 200%, 300%).

3. When you are finished, click OK.

You might find that the number or size of your layers inhibits the number of layers you can see simultaneously in the Timeline. There are a few ways to work around this. First, you can use the Timeline's scroll bar to scroll down to lower layers. Alternatively, you can click and drag the bar that separates the Timeline from the Stage to increase the amount of visible layers.

Distributing Objects to Layers

As mentioned previously, it's wise to limit a single object or symbol to a single layer when you are working with complex composite images or animations. However, you might find yourself in a situation where you end up with multiple objects or symbols on a single layer.

When you import many types of vector files (such as those from Adobe Illustrator or Macromedia FreeHand), the image will comprise many different ungrouped objects.

As a result, Flash MX has a handy command that allows you to select multiple objects and distribute them so that they each occupy their own discreet layer.

Flash MX will give all the newly created layers a unique name. In the case of letters in a string of text that has been broken apart (discussed in Chapter 5), each layer will be named with the particular character (F, L, A, S, or H, for example). In the case of a layer that contains a Library object (such as a symbol, bitmap, or video clip), Flash MX will give the layer the same name as the object itself. In the case of a layer containing a symbol instance, Flash MX will give the layer the same name as the instance. Finally, in the case of a layer containing a graphical object created using Flash's painting and drawing tools, Flash will give the layer a default name of Layer 1—which will increase sequentially (Layer 2, Layer 3, Layer 4, and so on).

To distribute objects to layers, follow these steps:

1. Select the objects on the Stage that you want to distribute to layers. Remember, you can select objects across multiple layers.

2. From here, either choose Modify → Distribute to Layers or use Ctrl+click (Mac) or right-click (Win) and select Distribute to Layers.

Creating Guide Layers

As mentioned, layers come in several different flavors. A *guide layer* is one of the various types in which a layer comes, and there are two different kinds of guide layers: regular guide layers and *motion guide layers*. You can fill a regular guide layer with content (lines, shapes, and so on) that help with layout and positioning (kind of like customizable, irregular graph paper). You can use a motion guide layer, on the other hand, to help create the complex motion path of an animation.

This section teaches you how to designate an existing layer as a guide layer and how to create a motion guide (without actually creating the animation proper). You'll get into how to create the animations in Chapter 9.

The cool thing about guide layers, whether you are using them for layout or to create a path for complex animation, is that they don't appear in the final Flash movie after it has been published.

To create a guide layer, follow these steps:

1. Select the layer you want to designate as a guide layer.

2. From here, you have several choices:

   - To create a regular guide layer (not a motion guide), Cmd+click (Mac) or right-click (Windows) and choose Guide from the pop-up context menu—the Guide Layer icon will then appear to the left of the layer's name.

   - To add a motion guide layer, you have three choices: Click the Add Motion Guide icon ⚓ in the lower portion of the Timeline, go to Insert → Motion Guide, or Ctrl+click (Mac) or right-click (Win) and choose Add Motion Guide from the pop-up context menu. An additional layer is created just above the current layer. You can identify the motion guide layer by the special symbol (which looks like an arc with a circle on top of it) just to the left of the layer's name.

Guide Layer icon

Motion Guide Layer icon
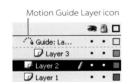

You can also create guide layers or motion guide layers by clicking the appropriate option in the Layer Properties dialog box.

After their creation, both types are immediately usable. When it comes to the regular guide layer, you can create any visual element (by painting and drawing or importing) to aid in your layout. When it comes to a motion guide layer, you can create a motion path for an animation. As mentioned before, the next step in using motion guide layers is beyond the scope of this chapter. If you are eager to learn about creating animation paths with a motion guide layer, see Chapter 9.

Creating Mask Layers

Mask layers are the second type of layer you'll look at in this chapter. Essentially, you use mask layers to create a hole through which the contents of one underlying layer are visible. Imagine looking through a keyhole at a complex scene. Because of the shape of the keyhole, you can only see a limited portion of the scene itself. This is essentially how a mask layer works. In Flash, you create the size and shape of the "hole" through which the scene beyond (or, because of the nature of layers, *below*) is visible. Figure 8.2 illustrates a mask layer in action.

One of the neat things about mask layers is that you can group a series of them together to create a single unit resulting in a complex effect. You can animate the mask so that it moves. Mask layers are useful for creating all sorts of effects such as a scene viewed through a telescope or a landscape revealed by a spotlight—the possibilities are endless.

Figure 8.2

The image on the left illustrates a non-masked imaged. The image on the right illustrates the same image with a circular mask.

Unfortunately, you cannot mask layers inside Button symbols.

Because you'll be exploring the process of animating mask layers in Chapter 9, you'll spend time in this chapter simply learning how to create a static mask layer.

Let's take a look at how you go about creating a mask layer:

1. Select the layer with the content that will be visible through the mask you create.

Remember that a mask layer only works on the layer immediately below it.

2. Insert a new layer by clicking the Insert Layer button in the Timeline or by selecting Insert → Layer.

3. In the newly created layer, which is placed above of the layer with the content you want the mask applied to, draw the "hole" through which the other layer will be visible. Although the hole doesn't have to circular (it can be any shape), it *must* be filled. When the layer is converted into a mask layer, all areas composed of a solid fill will be transparent. On the other hand, all areas not composed of a solid fill will become opaque.

4. Ctrl+click (Mac) or right-click (Win) the layer's name and choose Mask from the pop-up context menu.

5. The layer is automatically turned into a mask layer. Note that both the mask layer's and the masked layer's icons change.

Mask layer

Masked layer

Inspirational Design Model

Any complex Flash creation needs to leverage the power of layers to effectively and efficiently deliver its content. As a result, any Inspirational Design Model presented would need to exhibit an incredibly high level of design, interactivity, and animation that would only be made possible by layers. With this in mind, one needs to look no further than Blitz Digital Studios (`www.blitzds.com`).

Based in Valencia, California, Blitz Digital Studios produces innovative information and interactive entertainment for the traditional television markets, as well as emerging web and wireless markets.

Blitz Digital Studios' corporate website is an incredibly stylish and sophisticated interactive experience that, although somewhat bandwidth intensive, is a feast for the eyes (see Figure 8.3).

Figure 8.3

Blitz Digital Studios

Summary

In this chapter, you topped off your exploration of Flash's visual content creation tools with a look at layers. Essentially, layers are invisible levels (stacked one upon the other) where you can place all manner of content. You started the chapter off by looking at how to create a new layer. You then explored how to add content to layers. From there, you learned how to set the layer's various properties. You then mastered the ins and outs of creating layer folders and editing layers. Finally, you spent time looking at two different types of layers: guide layers and mask layers.

Creating a Garden with Objects and Layers

Throughout Part II, you explored the Flash tools for painting, drawing, and manipulating objects. In this tutorial, you're going to put all of your hard-earned knowledge to work by creating a garden scene. As you have yet to learn how to animate objects in Flash, the garden itself will be static. The tutorial will help you create a basic garden scene that you can later spruce up—no green thumb required.

 This tutorial's files are on the companion CD-ROM. Look for `garden.fla` in the Hands On 2 folder. In this file, you'll find a copy of the finished garden scene. Although you can certainly use the objects in the file's Library to create your own garden scene, it's strongly encouraged that you create and use your own graphics. The value of this assignment is based more on the process itself than on working with the actual graphics and duplicating each step.

Creating the Background

The first step in the tutorial is to create the background:

1. Create a new document by going to File → New or using the shortcut Cmd/Ctrl+N.
2. Go to Modify → Document or use Cmd/Ctrl+J to open the Movie Properties dialog box.
3. At this point, you want to see the color for the garden's sky. Click the Background Color swatch and choose a nice sky blue color from the Color Picker.
4. After you've chosen a color for the sky, click OK.

Creating the Ground

From here, you'll want to create the ground from which will spring your digital flowers:

1. First, double-click the existing layer's icon to open the Layer Properties dialog box.
2. Enter **Ground** into the Name field.
3. Click OK.
4. Select the Rectangle tool and choose a green color by clicking the Fill Color swatch in the Colors section of the Toolbox.

5. Because you don't want the ground to have an outline, you'll need to turn the stroke color off. To do this, click the Stroke Color swatch in the Toolbox and click the No Color button in the upper-right corner of the Color Picker (just to the left of the color wheel).

6. Now, you're ready to actually create the ground. With the Rectangle tool, draw a rectangle that occupies about half of the height of the Stage.

> Remember, the Rectangle tool can go beyond the Stage itself. However, anything in the work area (the gray area outside the Stage) will not be included when you publish the final scene.

7. From here, you need to take the rectangle you created and turn it into a symbol. To do this, select the ground/rectangle and go to Insert → Convert to Symbol or use the shortcut F8.

8. When the Convert to Symbol dialog box opens, make sure the Graphic radio button is checked and enter **Ground** into the Name field.

9. Click OK.

10. After you've done this, your scene will look roughly like this:

Setting Up the Flowerbeds

Now that you've created the sky and the ground that will serve as a background for your garden scene, it's time to create several flowerbeds:

1. The first step is to create several new layers into which you'll place a number of flowerbeds. Click the Insert Layer button in the bottom-left corner of the Timeline or go to Insert → Layer to create a new layer.

2. Double-click the new layer's icon, and enter the name **flowerbed1** into the Name field.

3. Repeat the process until you have a total of three new layers, each with a unique name (you can use **flowerbed1**, **flowerbed2**, and **flowerbed3** or another naming system entirely).

4. At this point, your Timeline should look something like this:

Creating the Flowerbeds

Now, to create the actual flowerbeds, follow these steps:

1. Select the Rectangle tool from the Toolbox.

2. Select a nice brown color for the dirt by clicking the Fill Color swatch in the Toolbox's Colors section.

3. As you don't want the flowerbed to have an outline, click the Stroke Color swatch in the Toolbox and click the No Color button in the upper-right corner of the Color Picker (just to the left of the color wheel).

4. To give the flowerbed a more organic look, click the Round Rectangle Radius button (accessible in the Toolbox's Options section when the Rectangle tool is selected), and enter a value of **5** in the Corner Radius field when the Rectangle Settings dialog box opens.

5. Select the flowerbed1 layer, and draw a vertical rectangle in the green area of the scene. Your scene now should look something like this:

6. Now, select the rectangle and convert it to a symbol by going to Insert → Convert to Symbol or by using the shortcut F8. When the Convert to Symbol dialog box opens, make sure the Graphic radio button is selected and enter **flowerbed1** into the Name field.

Adding Perspective

From here, you are going to want to add a little perspective to your scene by transforming the shape of the rectangle:

1. Select the rectangle, click the Free Transform tool in the Toolbox, and select the Rotate and Skew button from the Toolbox's Options section.

2. When the rotate handles appear around the rectangle, move your cursor over the top handle (not one of the ones in the two upper corners). When your cursor changes to two opposite-pointing arrows, click and drag to the right to skew the rectangle. Your scene should now look something like this:

3. To create a second bed, click the flowerbed2 layer.

4. Open the Library by going to Window → Library or by using the shortcut F11.

5. Select the flowerbed1 symbol, and Ctrl+click (Mac) or right-click (Win) and choose Duplicate from the pop-up context menu.

6. When the Duplicate Symbol dialog box opens, type **flowerbed2** in the Name field. Make sure the Graphic radio button is selected.

7. Click OK.

8. With the flowerbed2 layer still selected, drag the flowerbed2 symbol from the Library to the Stage.

9. From here, you'll need to skew the flowerbed "preform" that you just dragged into the flowerbed2 layer so that it's pointing in the opposite direction of the flowerbed1 symbol. To do this, select the rectangle, click the Free Transform tool in the Toolbox, and click the Rotate and Skew button in the Toolbox's Options section. When the rotate handles appear around the rectangle, move your cursor over the top handle (not one of the ones in the two upper corners). When your cursor changes to two opposite-pointing arrows, click and drag to the left to skew the rectangle.

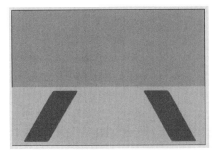

10. After you've skewed the symbol to the left, click and drag it to the right side of the Stage. Your scene should now look something like this:

Completing the Flowerbeds

Now that you you've created a flowerbed on both sides of the scene, you can then add a third one in the middle. As you are trying to give your scene some visual perspective, the middle flowerbed will need to have a different shape than the previous two:

1. If it isn't, open the Library by going to Window → Library.

2. Select the flowerbed1 symbol, and then Ctrl+click (Mac) or right-click (Win) and choose Duplicate from the pop-up context menu.

3   When the Duplicate Symbol dialog box opens, type **flowerbed3** in the Name field. Make sure the Graphic radio button is selected.

4. Click OK.

5. With the Library still open, double-click the flowerbed3 symbol to enter into Symbol Editing mode.

6. When the flowerbed3 symbol opens in the Symbol Editor, select it with the Arrow tool.

7. Select the Free Transform tool from the Toolbox and select the Distort button from the Options section of the Toolbox.

8. Hold down your Shift key, click either the top-left or top-right handle of the object's bounding box, and drag inward so that the top of the flowerbed becomes tapered. When you've finished tapering the object, release your mouse button.

9. Now, with the Shift button still held down, click either the bottom-left or bottom-right handle of the object's bounding box, and drag outward so that the bottom of the flowerbed becomes wider than the top. When you've finished, release your mouse button.

10. At this point, the flowerbed3 symbol should look something like this:

11. Click the Scene 1 link in the Scene and Symbol bar to return to the Stage.

12. Now, select the flowerbed3 layer.

13. Click and drag the flowerbed3 symbol from the Library onto the Stage. Position it so that it is between the two other flowerbeds. The scene should look something like this:

Creating the Flowers

Now that you've created the beds from which your digital flowers sprout, it's time to create the flowers themselves. In this section, you'll actually only create one flower (a daisy) that you'll then manipulate and transform to give it the appearance of many different flowers:

1. Because the scene is getting quite full already, start off by creating a symbol from scratch in Symbol Editing mode. Go to Insert → New Symbol or use the shortcut Cmd/Ctrl+F8 to enter Symbol Editing mode. When the New Symbol dialog box pops up, enter **daisy** into the Name field. Remember to make sure that the Graphic radio button is selected.

2. When the Symbol Editor opens, start by naming the existing layer **stem**.

3. From here, create four additional layers named **leaf 1**, **leaf 2**, **petals**, and **center**.

4. At this point, the Timeline in the Symbol Editor should look like this:

5. Now, click the Brush tool. Choose a dark green color by clicking the Fill Color swatch in the Toolbox's Colors section. From the Brush Size drop-down menu (located in the Toolbox's Options section when the Brush tool is selected), choose one of the smaller diameter brush sizes.

If you are using a graphics tablet (such as Wacom Intuos2), you can select the Use Pressure button in the Options section of the Toolbox (when the Brush tool is selected) to take advantage of your graphic tablet's variable pressure stylus.

6. Now, after selected the stem layer, draw a single vertical line about 2.5 centimeters (1 inch) long. It should look something like this:

7. From here, select the Pencil tool.

8. Click the leaf 1 layer and draw a leaf-shaped object. Make sure the shape is closed. When the outline of the leaf is drawn, choose a green color by clicking the Fill Color swatch in the Toolbox (if it isn't still selected), and fill the leaf outline using the Paint Bucket. Your leaf should look something like this:

> If you want your leaf to look a little smoother, choose Smooth from the Pencil Mode drop-down menu (which is accessible in the Toolbox's Options section when you've got the Pencil tool selected).

9. Select the entire leaf you just created (both stroke and fill), and go to Modify → Group.

10. Now that you've created the first leaf, you want to create the second. Select the leaf you've just created and copy it by going to Edit → Copy.

11. Now, select the leaf 2 layer and paste the copied leaf by going to Edit → Paste.

12. Select the newly pasted leaf and go to Modify → Transform → Flip Horizontal.

13. Now, position the two leaves on either side of the stem. Your image so far should look something like this:

14. Now, on to the central part of the flower. Select the center layer in the Timeline. Draw a small circle with the Oval tool in the area just above the stem (if it isn't exactly where you want it, just select and move it). Set whatever color you want (for both the stroke and fill) by clicking the appropriate color swatches in the Toolbox. It should look something like this in relation to the stem and leaves:

> Remember that all of the objects thus far consist of both a stroke and fill. It would be wise to group the two (select both and then go to Modify → Group) to avoid any problems.

15. From here, all you have to do is draw the flower's petals. Click the petals layer in the Timeline.

16. With the Pencil tool, draw a single shape for the petal. Make sure it's a closed shape.

> To avoid creating the shape with jaggy edges, you might want to select Smooth from the Pencil Mode drop-down menu in the Options section of the Toolbox when the Pencil tool is selected.

17. Set whatever color you want for the stroke using the Toolbox or the Property Inspector. Fill the leaf shape with any color you want using the Paint Bucket. It should look something like this in relation to the rest of the flower:

18. Now you need to "clone" the single petal into the remainder of the necessary petals. Select the petal, copy it by going to Edit → Copy, and then paste it (on the same layer as the original petal) by going to Edit → Paste.

19. Click and drag the new petal so that it's sticking out from the center, right next to the previous petal.

20. From there, select the petal with the Arrow tool (if it isn't already), select the Free Transform tool, and click the Rotate and Skew button (in the Options section of the Toolbox).

21. Move your cursor over one of the *corner* handles. When your cursor changes, click and drag your cursor so that the base of the petal aligns with the central part of the flower. After you've done this, the flower should look something like this:

22. Now, repeat steps 18–21 until petals surround the entire circumference of the central portion of the flower. When finished, it should look something like this:

Adding the Flowers to the Scene

Now, you're ready to go back to your original scene and start adding flowers:

1. Click the Scene 1 button in the Scene and Symbol bar to return to the original scene on which you were working.

2. Add an additional layer and call it **daisy1**.

3. Select the newly created daisy1 layer, and drag the daisy symbol from the Library onto one of the flowerbeds. So far, your scene should look something like image on bottom left.

4. Now, to add some variation to the scene, create an additional layer and call it **daisy2**.

5. Select the newly created daisy2 layer, and drag another symbol instance of the daisy from the Library onto the Stage.

6. Make sure it's selected and go to Modify → Transform → Flip Horizontal. After the daisy has been flipped, position it on one of the other flowerbeds. So far, your scene should look something like image on bottom right.

Now, to finish up this tutorial, you need to place one of the flowers farther away from the viewer, thereby preserving the scene's perspective:

1. Create an additional layer and call it **daisy3**.

2. Select the newly created layer, and drag the daisy symbol anywhere onto the Stage.

3. Select the newly placed daisy symbol with the Arrow tool.

4. Select the Free Transform tool from the Toolbox, and select the Scale options.

5. With the Shift key held down, click and drag inward on one of symbol's bounding box's four corner handles until it's about half of its original size.

6. After you've resized the daisy symbol, move it up (in relation to the Stage) toward the sky. Place it in one of the flowerbeds. By doing this, you will maintain the scene's perspective. Your final scene should look something like this:

Now that you've created a relatively simple garden (with only three flowers), you can use the processes described in this tutorial to make the scene more complex. Interested in adding a sun? Well, that's really just a yellow circle. How about some more flowers—or even some different types of flower? Take some time to experiment, and you're sure to get great results!

PART III

Animating with Flash

While Flash MX has evolved into a full fledged interactive design tool suitable for creating a whole range of groovy media, it is, at its heart, still an animation program. Flash's fundamental feature, vector based graphics, really shines when it comes to animation. As a result, it behooves you to become intimately familiar with all the ways in which you can infuse your beautiful Flash creation with movement.

In this section of the book, you are going to learn almost everything you need to know about the fundamentals of animating in Flash. You'll start off by looking at how to use the Timeline to make your creation zip, bounce, zing, and jump. From there, you'll explore one of the most important aspects of animating in Flash: Movie Clips (a topic which is vital to your future adventures in ActionScripting.) Finally, you'll explore one of the most useful tools with which you can control, manage, and manipulate your animation: Scenes.

CHAPTER 9

Animating with the Timeline

FutureSplash (later to become Flash) was a simple vector animation program when Macromedia acquired it from FutureWave in 1997. Though the most recent version of Flash has about 100 times the bells and whistles that FutureSplash did, it is still, at its core, an animation program. Although you can do much more than animate objects, much of Flash MX's power lies in its ability to create movies with content that changes over time.

Up until this point, you haven't created anything that *moves.* If you had wanted to just create static images, you could have easily turned to Macromedia Fireworks or Adobe Photoshop. But, no, you want to make things that move and spin and bounce! Whether it's a character that walks across the screen and promptly gets hit by a falling anvil or a button that spins around when users move their cursors over it, you want to create animations. In this chapter, you'll explore the primary tool with which you construct and manipulate animations in Flash MX: the Timeline.

Topics include the following:

- **Understanding animation**

- **Creating frame-by-frame animations**

- **Creating motion-tweened animations**

- **Animating changes in object shape**

- **Using a motion guide to animate an object along a path**

- **Animating a mask**

- **Extending a still image through time**

- **Creating animated special effects with the Property Inspector**

Understanding Animation

Animation is the process by which an object's size, position, color, or shape changes over time. In Flash, you have two animation methods, each with their own unique development process and strengths: frame by frame and tweening. Before you start learning about using these two methods to infuse your static creations with movement, you need to grasp some fundamental animation concepts, including frames, keyframes, and frame rate.

Understanding Frames and Keyframes

Any animation, whether the latest Hollywood 3D animated blockbuster, Walt Disney's original *Fantasia*, or your humble Flash creation, contains *frames*. Each frame contains one static image that, when displayed in succession with other images in other frames, creates the illusion of movement. In Flash MX, frames are displayed horizontally in the Timeline as small boxes.

> The small boxes in the Timeline are called *cells*. You can convert any cell into a frame, a keyframe, or an empty keyframe by using the commands in the Insert menu.

Each frame's content is displayed as the playhead passes through it, thereby creating something of a digital "flipbook."

In Flash, any frame populated by content (of any kind) that you've directly manipulated (opposed to being placed there by Flash in a tweened animation, for example) is represented in the Timeline by a small black circle—this is called a *keyframe*. A keyframe represents a point on the Timeline where a change occurs in the animation. For the time being, know that any time you want to change your animation in any way (add content, subtract content, start the motion of an object, and so on), you'll use a keyframe.

So what exactly is the difference between content in frames and content in keyframes? Well, it's pretty simple. Although a keyframe and a frame can have exactly the same content, you can only directly manipulate that content if it resides in a keyframe. If it resides within a frame, there is no way, short of turning the frame into a keyframe (which is a perfectly functional solution), to directly manipulate its content.

Beyond frames and keyframes, there is a third type of frame of which you should be aware. Somewhere between an ordinary frame and a keyframe, an *empty keyframe* is essentially a keyframe that has yet to be "filled" with content. An outline of a small circle represents an empty keyframe.

> By default, Flash designates the first frame of any animation as an empty keyframe. The remaining frames in any given layer are little more than placeholders for future empty keyframes or keyframes (which you need to create).

Empty Keyframes

Frames   Keyframes

Changing the Appearance of Frames in the Timeline

Up until now, the only way you could actually change the appearance of a frame was to change the height of an entire layer (discussed in Chapter 8). The problem with this is that you weren't really changing the appearance of the frames themselves, but the layer itself. And besides, as you've already discovered, there are only three options for layer height, making it a pretty limited solution.

However, in Flash MX, you have the ability to change the appearance of the frames themselves by using the Frame View button, located in the top-right corner of the Timeline. When clicked, the Frame View button opens a drop-down menu.

Frame View button

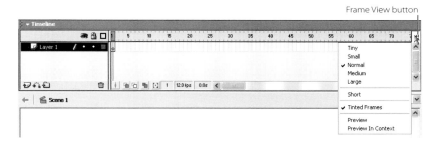

Unfortunately, the option you choose applies to all layers within the Timeline. You can't change the frame appearance for a single layer.

When clicked the Frame View button opens a drop-down menu containing the following options:

- **Tiny** makes the frames extremely small—thereby allowing more frames to be displayed at any given time in the Timeline.

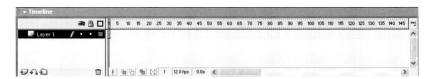

- **Small** changes the size of the frames so that they are between the Tiny option and the default, Normal.

- **Normal** is the default frame size.

- **Medium** changes the size of the frame so that they are slightly larger than the default Normal size.

- **Large** increases the Timeline's frames to their maximum sizes.

- **Short** reduces the height of the frames in the Timeline.

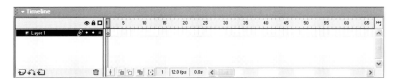

- The **Tinted Frames** option, which can be toggled on and off, controls whether every sequential frame in an animation is gray or unshaded.

- By selecting **Preview** in Context, Flash creates a thumbnail of each keyframe's contents that are a direct proportional reflection of what is on the Stage—including all the empty space as well.

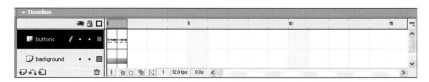

- When you choose **Preview**, you get a thumbnail of each keyframe's contents that fills the entire cell (opposed to being a proportional representation of the entire Stage). Don't be fooled—even though the results of Preview and Preview in Context might be similar, the difference usually asserts itself in the amount of white space that is displayed.

> Ultimately, because you are displaying extra information in the Timeline, using either Preview or Preview in Context will consume more processing power—thereby possibly causing your computer to slow down.

How the Timeline Represents Animation

The Timeline represents different kinds of animation (and Timeline elements) differently. As a result, it's in your best interest to become familiar with each so that when you get into animating with the Timeline, you won't be caught off guard by the way an animation looks.

- A frame-by-frame animation is usually represented by a layer with a series of sequential keyframes.

- A motion tween is denoted by a keyframe at the beginning and end, between which a black arrow (representing the actual tween) runs. In addition, a motion tween has a light blue background.

- Like a motion tween, a shape tween is denoted by a keyframe at the beginning and end, between which a black arrow (representing the actual tween) runs. The difference is that the intervening frames are light green instead of light blue.

- When a keyframe is followed by a dashed line, motion tween is incomplete (usually the result of the final keyframe being removed or not added).

- When a series of gray frames begins with a keyframe and ends with a hollow rectangle, all frames after the keyframe have exactly the same content.

- A frame or keyframe with a small lowercase *a* represents a point in the animation where a frame action has been added. (For more information on actions and ActionScripting, see Part IV and Part V.)

Frame action

- A frame or keyframe with a red flag indicates the presence of a frame label.

Frame labels are extremely useful for identifying and targeting specific frames (instead of using frame numbers) when you are using actions. You can also use them in the development process to add comments or notes to specific frames. To insert a frame label, select the frame, open the Property Inspector, and enter the label into the Frame Label field.

Understanding Frame Rate

Frame rate determines the rate at which an animation plays. Represented in frames per second (fps), an animation's frame rate is related both to the speed at which the animation plays as well as its overall quality. Think of it this way: If you have a high frame rate, more frames will be displayed in the space of a second, thereby increasing the animation's quality. The lower your frame rate, the fewer frames will be displayed in a given second, thereby increasing the animation's choppiness and decreasing its quality.

You're probably thinking, well, that's all great, but if a higher frame rate means a better quality animation, then why would anyone ever set a low frame rate? Well, there are some pretty important reasons why you shouldn't always set a high frame rate, the most important of which concern memory and bandwidth. When you set a high frame rate, you are forcing the user's computer to display more information in the span of a second. As a result, a higher frame rate might cause some slower computers (or slower Internet connections) to "choke" on the higher rate of information, thereby causing the animation to hang, skip, or crash entirely.

To set your animation's frame rate:

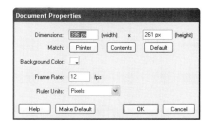

1. Go to Modify → Document or use the shortcut Cmd/Ctrl+J to open the Document Properties dialog box. Alternatively, you can double-click the frame rate indicator at the bottom of the Timeline.

2. Enter a value into the Frame Rate field.

> Although 12fps is Flash's default frame rate, you're certainly safe if you use a higher frame rate. However, it's wise, for the reasons already discussed, to set a frame rate no higher than 20 unless you are absolutely confident your users' systems can cope with more information.

Creating Frame-by-Frame Animations

Way back in the dark ages of animation (*before* computers), animators had to painstakingly create the individual images in each frame, varying each slightly to get the illusion of movement.

In Flash, the most basic form of animation, *frame-by-frame animation*, works the same way. Essentially, frame-by-frame animation works by creating a unique image in each frame. Each frame then becomes a keyframe (because it has content in it that alters the animation). As the playhead passes through each of the frames, the frame's content displays, thereby creating the illusion of changing over time. Frame-by-frame animations are great if you want to exert direct control over the details in your animation.

There is, however, one problem with creating a frame-by-frame animation. Because each frame needs to be "filled" with content unique from the previous frame, you end up creating a *lot* of art. Imagine if your movie contained an animation that was 300-frames long. You would have to create at least 300 static images—an altogether laborious undertaking. Granted, using the Library, symbols, and symbol instances to recycle some of your material could help reduce the workload. However, whichever way you look at it, you'd be spending a great deal of time creating art assets for your animation.

Now, let's create a frame-by-frame animation. You'll start with something particularly mundane, a sphere moving across the Stage, to help you grasp the basics of frame-by-frame animation:

1. Start with a new file (File → New or Cmd/Ctrl+N).

2. Go to Insert → New Symbol. When the Create New Symbol dialog box opens, enter **sphere** in the Name field, make sure the Graphic radio button is selected, and click OK. When the Symbol Editor opens, draw a sphere about 3 centimeters (1 inch) in diameter. When you're finished, return to the Stage by clicking the Scene 1 link in the Scene and Symbol bar. (See Chapter 7 if you have trouble remembering how to work with symbols.)

3. Now that you have a sphere in the Library, click the first frame of the Timeline's single layer (which, if you remember, is an empty keyframe by default), open the Library (Window → Library), and drag the sphere onto the left side of the Stage. Notice that the first frame automatically becomes a keyframe (denoted by the small black circle).

Remember, Flash automatically designates the first frame of any layer as an empty keyframe. As a result, you don't have to go through the process of inserting a keyframe. However, for the remainder of the layer, you'll have to insert each keyframe yourself.

4. Now that you've populated the first keyframe with content, you can create the remainder of the sequence. Click the second frame in the Timeline (just to the right of the keyframe you created) and go to Insert → Keyframe (or use F6). This inserts a second keyframe. You'll notice that Flash has automatically populated the keyframe with the content of the previous keyframe. You could keep on adding successive keyframes, and Flash would continue to populate them with the contents of the first one.

If, for some reason, you don't want the same content in the second frame, just insert a blank keyframe (Insert → Blank Keyframe). To add content to the blank keyframe, simply select it, and then add something to the Stage. When you do this, the blank keyframe will become a keyframe.

5. Make sure you have the second keyframe selected. Select the sphere with the Arrow tool, and move it to the right slightly.

6. Select the third frame in the Timeline, and insert a new keyframe.

7. Make sure you have the third keyframe selected. From here, select the sphere and move it slightly to the right.

8. Continue adding successive keyframes and moving the sphere to the right in each one until it has reached the right side of the Stage. Depending on how much you moved the sphere each time (the less you moved it, the more keyframes it will take to move it to the right side of the screen), your Timeline should be filled with several keyframes.

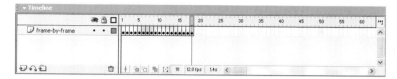

Congratulations, you've created your first frame-by-frame animation. To test it, you can do any of the following:

- Drag the playhead through the Timeline to view the animation.
- Go to Control → Play or hit Return/Enter.
- Go to Control → Test Scene or Control → Test Movie (which opens a new window where the animation will continue to loop).

Working with the Onion Skinning Option

When you were creating a frame-by-frame animation in the previous section, you moved the sphere in each successive keyframe without having real reference as to its position in the preceding frame. This probably proved to be a little frustrating because, without a way to get the sphere exactly in line with the one in the previous frame, your animation looked a little jumpy. Granted, you could simply click the previous frame, check the position of the sphere, and then click back and adjust the position of the next one. However, this process is a little time consuming and frustrating. This is where *onion skinning* comes in.

Basically, onion skinning lets you see the contents of frames preceding and following the currently selected frame. The concept comes from the traditional pen-and-paper animation technique of using tracing paper to view a sequence of animation frames. With onion skinning, you can do away with all the guesswork inherent in flipping back and forth to see the contents of previous frames and smoothly animate a moving object.

You have several options when using onion skinning:

Turning onion skinning on   To turn onion skinning on, click the Onion Skin button located at the bottom of the Timeline. By doing this, two things happen: First, the Onion Skin marker appears in the Timeline header. The Onion Skin marker displays the content of the frames included in the onion skinning. To increase, decrease, or change the number of frames included, click one of the handles on either side of the Onion Skin marker and drag it accordingly.

Second, the frames' content within the Onion Skin marker displays as partially transparent. In addition, the contents of the currently selected frame display normally.

If you've got any locked layers in your animation, they won't be displayed when you have onion skinning turned on.

Turning onion skinning outlines on By clicking the Onion Skin Outlines button, which is located at the bottom of the Timeline, you can display the content of multiple frames as outlines (instead of simply transparent). Note that the currently selected frame appears normally when you've got Onion Skin Outlines activated.

The particular layer's outline color determines the color of the onion skin outlines.

Editing multiple frames When you have onion skinning turned on, you can't actually edit the contents of a frame unless you've selected it in the Timeline. This can prove a little frustrating, as you will constantly have to switch to a given frame to edit its content. One of the great things about onion skinning is the Edit Multiple Frames button.

Located to the right of the Onion Skin Outlines button, the Edit Multiple Frames button lets you edit the contents of all frames without having to move from frame to frame. Unlike with simple onion skinning, the Edit Multiple Frames button displays all the contents without any transparency.

Modifying onion markers The Modify Onion Markers drop-down menu is accessible by clicking the Modify Onion Markers button ⟦·⟧ , which is located to the right of the Edit Multiple Frames button at the bottom of the Timeline. Each of the options contained in the menu affect the position of the Onion Skin marker and therefore the frames that are displayed:

- Always Show Markers displays the Onion Skin markers in the Timeline header regardless of whether onion skinning is turned on.

- Under normal circumstances, the Onion Skin range is relative to the current frame pointer and the Onion Skin markers. By selecting Anchor Onion, you lock the Onion Skin markers to their current position in the Timeline header.

- Onion 2 displays two frames on either side of the currently selected frame.

- Onion 5 displays five frames on either side of the currently selected frame.

- Onion All displays all the frames on either side of the currently selected frame.

Understanding Tweening

Now that you've created a frame-by-frame animation, let's take the next step and look at a far more efficient and less time-consuming way to create an animation: *tweening*. Essentially, tweening is the process by which you define a starting point/form and ending point/form for an object and then tell Flash to fill in all the in-be*tween* frames—hence the name *tween*ing.

Two types of tweening are available depending on what you want your animation to do. The first, *motion tweening*, is covered next. The second, *shape tweening*, is covered later in the "Creating a Shape-Tweened Animation" section. After having looked at motion-tweened animation and shape-tweened animation, you'll look at how you create a motion-tweened animation that follows a path in the "Creating a Motion-Tweened Animation That Follows a Path" section.

Creating a Motion-Tweened Animation

In the previous section, you learned how to create a frame-by-frame animation by filling each frame with content. All in all, the process is pretty clunky. This is where *motion tweening* comes it. Motion tweening is a quantum leap beyond frame-by-frame animation—no more working with frame after frame, painstakingly crafting each image in your animation so it is just right. With motion tweening, you merely create the first and last keyframes in your animation—from there, Flash completes the in-between frames. And because Flash only has to save the contents of the first and last keyframes (along with numerical values concerning how the object changes), tweened animations generally result in smaller file sizes than frame-by-frame animations.

Although you use tweening primarily for animating motion, you can also animate size, color, and orientation. In short, any transformation that can be applied to an object can be animated with tweening.

> You can use motion tweening on text as well as groups of objects.

In this section, you're going to create the same sort of animation you created using the frame-by-frame technique (a square moving across the Stage), but you'll do it instead with tweening:

1. Start with a new file (File → New or Cmd/Ctrl+N).

2. Go to Insert → New Symbol. When the Create New Symbol dialog box opens, enter **square** in the Name field, make sure the Graphic radio button is selected, and click OK. When the Symbol Editor opens, draw a square about 3 centimeters (1 inch) in diameter. When you're finished, return to the Stage.

3. Now that you have a square ready and waiting in the Library, click the first frame of the Timeline's single layer, open the Library (Window → Library), and drag the square onto the left side of the Stage. Notice that the default blank keyframe automatically becomes a keyframe (denoted by the small black circle).

4. Now that you've created the first keyframe in the animation, you can create the last one. Click frame 25, and insert a keyframe by going to Insert → Keyframe. At this point, your Timeline should look like this:

> The frames between the two keyframes are just that—frames. They really don't do much except contain the content that is automatically generated by Flash. If you want them to become more, you must insert a keyframe.

Much like in the case of frame-by-frame animation, Flash populated the second keyframe you created with the content of the first. As a result, you are going to want to move the square in the last keyframe to the location on the Stage where you want it to be at the end of the animation:

1. Select the final keyframe.

2. Click and drag the square to the right side of the Stage. By doing this, you tell Flash that in the first keyframe the square is at the left side of the Stage, and in the last keyframe it's in the right side of the Stage. Now comes the tweening.

3. Select the first keyframe.

4. Go to Insert → Create Motion Tween. Alternatively, you can select the first keyframe, open the Property Inspector (Window → Properties), and select Motion from the Tween drop-down menu.

5. Flash fills all the in-between frames, thereby creating the animation. You'll also notice that the Timeline itself changes. The change in the frames' colors as well as an addition of an arrow indicates the presence of a tween.

Congratulations, you've created your first tweened animation. To test it, do one of the following:

• Drag the playhead through the Timeline to view the animation.

• Go to Control → Play or hit Return/Enter.

• Go to Control → Test Scene/Test Movie (which opens up a new window in which the animation will continue to loop).

Even though the motion tween you've just created is amazingly simple, don't be fooled into believing that motion tweening creates simple animations. Quite the contrary! You can create some amazingly complex and varied animation with tweening. As an experiment, take the animation you just created, insert a keyframe in the middle, and alter the square's location. When you play the animation, Flash moves the square to the new location defined in the keyframe you just added and then to the position you set in the final keyframe.

You also don't have to merely move your square across the Stage. Try increasing the object's size in the final keyframe using the Transform panel or the Free Transform tool. When played, the square slowly grows until it reaches the defined size in the final keyframe.

You can also change the visual properties of a tweened symbol using the Property Inspector—something you'll learn how to do later in the "Creating Animated Special Effects with the Property Inspector" section.

Editing a Tweened Animation with the Property Inspector

Although you can create a motion-tweened animation with Flash's drop-down menu, you can't do much to edit the animation's characteristics this way. Instead, you use the Property Inspector (Window → Properties or Cmd/Ctrl+F3) to manipulate all manner of the tweened animation's characteristics, including those specific to motion tweening.

Some of the options in the Property Inspector apply to other types of tweening, such as shape and motion-path tweening. You'll get to them in "Creating a Shape-Tweening Animation" and "Creating an Animation That Follows a Path," respectively; for now, let's look at the motion-tweening options.

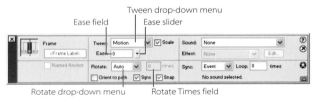

Easing Your Motion Tween

You probably noticed that your tweened square traveled at a constant rate across the Stage. If you want, you can use the Property Inspector to ease the object in or out of the animation. In other words, it starts off slower, gaining speed through the process of the animation. On the other hand, if you ease the object out of the animation, it slows down near the end.

To ease your motion tween, follow these steps:

1. Select the first frame in the motion tween.

2. Open the Property Inspector by going to Window → Properties or by using the shortcut Cmd/Ctrl+F3.

3. Enter a value into the Ease field. A positive number eases the object out of the animation, and a negative number eases it into the animation. A higher value (either negative or positive) increases the effect. Alternatively, you can use the Ease slider to adjust the value.

You can enter values from –100 to 100 in the Easing field.

Rotating an Object in a Motion Tween

Follow these steps to get an object to rotate through the tweening:

1. Select the first frame in the motion tween.

2. Open the Property Inspector by going to Window → Properties or by using the shortcut Cmd/Ctrl+F3.

3. Choose one of the options from the Rotate drop-down menu.

    None Applies no rotation to the object.

    Auto Rotates the object once in the direction that requires the least amount of movement.

    CW Rotates the object clockwise. You define the number of rotations by entering a value into the Times field (which is to the right of the Rotate drop-down menu).

    CCW Rotates the object counterclockwise. You define the number of rotations by entering a value into the Times field (which is to the right of the Rotate drop-down menu).

Creating a Shape-Tweened Animation

While motion tweening moves an object from one point of the Stage to another (or changes its characteristics, such as size or orientation), *shape tweening* morphs an object from one shape to another. You can create some decidedly interesting effects by using shape tweening.

One of the most fundamental things you need to remember about shape tweening is that it only works on shapes drawn on the Stage. You can't shape tween symbol instances, bitmaps, text, or groups of objects. You must break apart these elements (Modify → Break Apart) before you can shape tween them.

To create a shape tween:

1. Create a new document.

2. Select the first frame, which is a blank keyframe by default.

3. Use the drawing tools to create the image with which you want to start. Notice that the first frame automatically becomes a filled keyframe (denoted by the small black circle).

4. Click the frame where you want the shape tween to terminate, and insert a keyframe. As usual, Flash populates the last keyframe with the first keyframe's contents. From here, manipulate the existing image (using one of the various transform tools) so it looks like what you want for the final product of the shape tween. (Alternately, delete the image and create an entirely new one.)

If you place the last keyframe's shape in another location, Flash automatically motion tweens the animation as well. Not only will your object "morph," but it will do so as it is moving from one location to another on the Stage.

5. Now, select the first frame and then open the Properties Inspector (Window → Properties).

6. Choose Shape from the Tweening drop-down menu.

7. From here, you can set the shape tween's characteristics:

   • Enter a value into the Ease field to ease the tween in or out. Remember, a positive number makes the tween faster at the beginning, and a negative number makes it faster at the end. Alternatively, use the Ease slider to adjust the value.

   • Choose a blend option from the Blend drop-down menu. Choosing Distributive creates an animation in which the edges of the intermediate shapes are smoother. Alternatively, choosing Angular creates an animation in which straight edges are preserved in the intervening frames.

8. When you've finished, test your animation by moving the playhead, hitting Return/ Enter, selecting Control → Play, or choosing Control → Test Scene/Test Movie.

Creating a Motion-Tweened Animation That Follows a Path

When it comes to motion tweening, you've explored how to move an object along a straight line. Granted, you can vary the course of the object's motion by adding more keyframes to the animation (as discussed earlier), thereby creating a zigzag pattern. However, what if you wanted to make an object move along a circle? Well, *motion paths* let you move objects along a specific path.

You learned how to create motion guide layers in Chapter 8; in this section, you are going to take what you learned in Chapter 8 and combine it with what you've learned about motion tweening in this chapter to craft an animation that has an object traveling along a complex path.

To create an animation that follows a path, use these steps:

1. Create a simple motion-tweened animation with two keyframes, one at the beginning and one at the end. (If you want, you can use the square animation you created earlier in this chapter.) If you are having trouble remembering how to create a simple motion tween, see "Creating a Motion-Tweened Animation."

2. Select the layer with the tweened animation and go to Insert → Motion Guide. Alternatively, you can 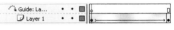 Ctrl+click (Mac) or right-click (Win) the layer's name and choose Add Motion Guide from the pop-up context menu or click the Add Motion Guide button in the bottom-left corner of the Timeline. This creates a motion guide layer just above the layer containing the animation.

3. Now, with the first frame (the empty keyframe) in the motion guide layer selected, draw the path you want the object to follow (as illustrated in Figure 9.1). You can use the Pencil tool, the Oval tool, the Rectangle tool, the Brush tool, the Pen tool, or the Line tool.

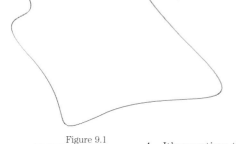

Figure 9.1

The motion path can take any form you desire—this one was drawn with the Pen tool.

4. It's now time to attach your object to the motion path you've created. Select the first keyframe of your tweened animation, go to Window → Properties, and make sure the Snap check box is selected. This makes sure your object's registration point will snap to the motion path.

Snap check box

5. Click and drag the object so the registration point snaps onto the beginning of the path you've drawn.

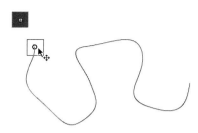

6. Now, click the final keyframe in the animation, and click and drag the object so the registration point snaps onto the end of the path you've drawn.

   If the registration point doesn't appear when you initially click and drag, click and hold down your mouse button for a few seconds before you move the object to the end of the path.

> If the registration point doesn't appear when you click the object, release it, click the central portion of the object (represented by a set of crosshairs), hold your mouse button down for a few seconds, and then drag it to the beginning of the path.

7. If you want the object to point in the direction of the path that it's moving along, make sure the Orient to Path check box is selected in the Property Inspector.

Orient to Path check box

8. From here, test your animation by hitting Return/Enter, going to Control → Play, or selecting Control → Test Scene/Test Movie.

> You can "unlink" a layer from a motion guide by selecting the layer and either clicking and dragging the layer above the motion guide layer in the Timeline or going to Modify → Layer and choosing Normal.

Animating a Mask

As explained in Chapter 8, mask layers create a hole through which the contents of one layer is visible. Better yet, you can animate mask layers to create any number of interesting effects—from the view through a telescope to the view through a keyhole. In this section, you're going to look at how to create a spotlight effect that moves across the Stage, revealing a stationary object as it passes over it:

1. First, create a new document.

2. Go to File → Import. When the Import dialog box pops up, navigate to the Chapter 9 directory on this book's CD-ROM, choose All Files from the Import dialog box's Files of Type drop-down menu, select the `flying_saucer.swf` file, and click OK.

3. Now, click frame 25, and go to Insert → Frame. This populates the frames from 2 to 25 with the content of the first keyframe.

4. From here, you're going to create the object that will serve as the mask. Go to Insert → New Symbol. When the Create New Symbol dialog box appears, make sure the Graphic radio button is checked, and enter **circle** into the Name field.

5. When the Symbol Editor opens, draw a single sphere of about 3 centimeters (1 inch) in diameter. Remember, the circle needs to be filled for the mask to work. Beyond that, the color of the fill makes no difference whatsoever.

6. Exit the Symbol Editor by clicking the Scene 1 link in the Scene and Symbol bar.

7. Now, create a new layer by clicking the Insert Layer button in the Timeline. Alternatively, you can Ctrl+click (Mac) or right-click (Win) and choose Insert Layer from the pop-up context menu or go to Insert → Layer. This layer will ultimately be converted into the mask layer.

8. Now, select the first blank keyframe in the new layer and drag the Circle symbol from the Library (Window → Library) to the left part of the Stage.

9. Click frame 25 (in the newly created layer), and go to Insert → Keyframe. With the last keyframe selected (the one you just created), click and drag the circle to the right side of the Stage.

10. Select the first keyframe and go to Insert → Create Motion Tween. This animates the sphere so that it moves across the Stage and passes over the flying saucer image you imported earlier.

11. Now, it's time to turn the tweened circle into a mask. Ctrl+click (Mac) or right-click (Win) the layer with the circle symbol, and choose Mask from the pop-up context menu. By doing this, you turn the layer with the circle into a mask layer. Notice that the appearance of both layers changes to reflect the relationship. Also, this process locks both the mask and masked layers. They must remain locked for the animation to work.

> Don't worry if the flying saucer disappears from the Stage—this is supposed to happen. If you want to view both the flying saucer image and the circle symbol, unlock all the layers.

12. From here, test your animation by hitting Return/Enter, going to Control → Play, or selecting Control → Test Scene/Test Movie.

Extending a Still Image through Time

Up until this point, you've explored how to do all sorts of cool animations with the Timeline. There is, however, an additional animation trick that, although straightforward, is incredibly useful. Specifically, you can integrate an image into your Flash movie that occupies a span of time (a series of frames) but doesn't actually move. Here's how you do it:

1. Create a new document.

2. Select the first blank keyframe in the single layer.

3. Place the desired image onto the Stage.

4. Click the last keyframe on which you would like the image to be visible.

5. Go to Insert → Frame or use the shortcut F5. Alternatively, you can Ctrl+click (Mac) or right-click (Win) and choose Insert Frame from the pop-up context menu.

6. Notice that all the intermediate frames are gray, and a small outline of a rectangle is placed in the final frame. This means that the content from the first keyframe has been carried over to all the frames.

Creating Animated Special Effects with the Property Inspector

One of the great things about tweening is that you are not limited to position, size, and shape. You can also tween more complicated changes to an object's appearance. You can animate a fade-in/fade-out or color change by taking what you've learned about tweening thus far and combining it with the tools in the Property Inspector (Window → Properties). You manipulated a symbol's visual properties with the Property Inspector in Chapter 6, so its options should be familiar to you. In the following sections you'll now learn how to animate changes in an object's transparency, brightness, and tint.

> You can carry out the following processes only on symbols—not on shapes or groups of shapes created with Flash's painting and drawing tools directly on the stage.

Animating Symbol's Transparency

By animating an object's Alpha effect (or transparency), you can create the illusion of a fade-in/fade-out:

1. Create a new document.

2. Create a tweened animation of some sort using symbols.

3. Now, click the first keyframe in the animation and select the object that you want to fade-in with the Arrow tool.

4. If it isn't already, open the Property Inspector by going to Window → Properties.

5. Choose Alpha from the Color drop-down menu.

6. Enter **0** into the Alpha Value field. By doing this, you are making the object in the first keyframe transparent.

7. Click the last keyframe in the animation, and select the object with which you're working with the Arrow tool.

8. With the Property Inspector open and Alpha selected from the Color drop-down menu, enter **100** into the Alpha Value field. This makes the object opaque (solid) in the final keyframe.

9. Now, test your animation by hitting Return/Enter, going to Control → Play, or select Control → Test Scene/Test Movie. Your object will now fade-in.

To have an item fade-out, do the opposite. Set the Alpha Value in the first keyframe to 100 and that of the last keyframe to 0.

Animating an Object's Brightness

Animating an object's brightness is almost identical to the process of animating an object's transparency:

1. Create a new document.

2. Create a tweened animation using a symbol.

3. Now, click the first keyframe in the animation, and select the object whose brightness you want to change.

4. If it isn't already, open the Property Inspector by going to Window → Properties.

5. Choose Brightness from the Color drop-down menu.

6. Enter a value into the Brightness Value field (or use the Brightness slider).

7. Click the last keyframe in the animation, and select the object with which you're working.

8. With the Property Inspector open, enter a different value into the Brightness Value field.

9. Now, test your animation by hitting Return/Enter, choosing Control → Play, or selecting Control → Test Scene/Test Movie.

Because you can't simulate the same sort of brightness experienced in the real world, altering the brightness of an object actually does more to change the intensity of its color.

Animating Color Change

Like the previous two procedures, animating a color change is just a matter of using a different area of the Property Inspector:

1. Create a new document.

2. Create a tweened animation of some sort using a symbol.

3. Now, click the first keyframe in the animation and select the object whose color you want to change.

4. If it isn't already, open the Property Inspector by going to Window → Properties.

5. Choose Tint from the Color drop-down menu.

6. From here, click the Tint color swatch to open up the Color Picker. From here, choose one of the colors. Alternatively, you can mix a custom RGB color by inputting values into the R, G, and B fields.

7. Click the last keyframe in the animation, and select the object with which you're working.

8. With the Property Inspector open, choose another color.

9. Now, test your animation by hitting Return/Enter, going to Control → Play, or selecting Control → Test Scene/Test Movie. Your object will change from the color set in the first keyframe to the color set in the last keyframe.

Inspirational Design Model

Creating effective and well-designed animations is tricky. Because much of Flash's power is derived from its ability to generate complex animations, the types of animations that one can experience range from simple moving text to full-blown professionally designed web-based animated shorts. As a result, this chapter's Inspirational Design Model should provide an example of smooth, stylish animation that leverages the power of Flash's entire animation repertoire. With this in mind, one needs look no further than Djojo Studios (www.djojostudios.com).

A one-man design studio based in the Netherlands (operated by the artistic powerhouse Joost van Schaik), Djojo Studios' mandate is to create rich visual interactive web-based multimedia. The website features smooth, stylish, and amazingly well-designed animation (see Figure 9.2). One of the most wonderful features is the spinning astronaut that was designed using a combination of 3D and 2D methods.

For animated eye candy, Djojo Studios can't be beat.

Figure 9.2

Djojo Studios

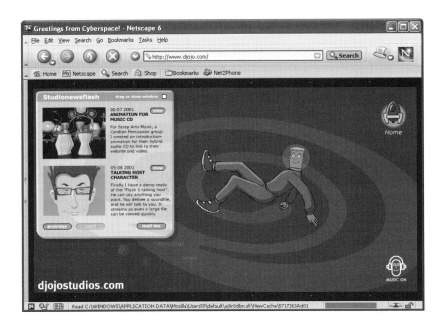

Summary

In this chapter, you were exposed the heart and soul of Flash: animation. You began by exploring some fundamental animation concepts such as frames, keyframes, and frame rate. From there, you jumped straight into the mighty world of moving pictures by mastering how to create a frame-by-frame animation. Moving on, you learned how to create a motion-tweened animation, a definite improvement to the frame-by-frame technique. Then, you explored the process of forging shape-tweened animations. Building on what you had learned previously, you looked at how to create a motion path that a tweened object would follow. You closed the chapter by exploring animated masks and creating animated special effects with the Property Inspector.

CHAPTER 10

Working with Movie Clips

One of the types of symbols discussed in Chapter 7 (but not focused on) was Movie Clips. Probably one of the most fundamentally important aspects of Flash, Movie Clips are fully functional, self-contained movies that can be placed on the Stage and run independently of the Timeline. In addition, you can control Movie Clips using ActionScript, which makes them incredibly powerful.

Because you've already mastered the basic skills necessary to create animations with the Timeline, you'll start this chapter off by exploring the nature of Movie Clips. You'll then learn how to create Movie Clips from scratch as well as from existing animations. Finally, you'll learn how to insert Movie Clips into the main Timeline.

Topics in this chapter include the following:

- **Understanding Movie Clips**
- **Creating Movie Clips from scratch**
- **Turning existing animations into Movie Clips**
- **Inserting Movie Clips into the Timeline**
- **Editing Movie Clips with the Property Inspector**
- **Seeing Movie Clips in action**

Understanding Movie Clips

It wouldn't be an exaggeration to say that Movie Clips are probably one of the most useful objects in Flash. However, unlike Button and Graphic symbols, Movie Clips are far better discussed in conjunction with animation. Why? Well, Movie Clips are essentially self-contained movies that you can nest within your primary movie. Because they are self-contained, their Timelines run independently of the main Timeline. In other words, you can think of a Movie Clip as a movie within a movie.

You can use Movie Clips in conjunction with other symbols or alone on the Stage. For instance, you could place a Movie Clip in one of the states of a Button symbol to create an animated button—a process discussed in Chapter 13. One of the great things about Movie Clips is that, unlike regular Timeline animations that use a great deal of frames and keyframes, Movie Clips need only one keyframe in the main Timeline to run.

Because Movie Clips run independently of the main Timeline, they are often quite detached from your main movie. Say, for instance, you've got an animation in which several birds (each of which is a Movie Clip) fly across the sky. Under normal circumstances, the Movie Clips will either loop or play once and stop—both of which are pretty limiting when it comes to intricate animations. This, however, is where ActionScript comes into the picture.

Flash's scripting language, ActionScript, allows you to exert a great deal of control over how a given Movie Clip behaves within the main Timeline. Essentially, you can write simple (or complex) scripts that control the independent behavior of an individual Movie Clip. For example, going back to the "flock" of birds example, you could write a script that would make sure none of the Movie Clips ever come in contact with one another. If you were really ambitious, you could write a script that would force the bird Movie Clips to emulate flocking behavior. (See Chapter 16 for more information on how you can use ActionScripts to control Movie Clips.)

Creating Movie Clips from Scratch

Creating a Movie Clip from scratch builds on the skills you've already mastered in Chapters 7 and 9:

1. Open a new document by going to File → New.

2. Go to Insert → New Symbol.

3. When the Create New Symbol dialog box opens, make sure the Movie Clip radio button is selected, enter a name into the Name field, and click OK. (If you're having trouble remembering your way around the Create New Symbol dialog box, refer to Chapter 7.)

4. This opens the Symbol Editor. From here, use the Timeline in the Symbol Editor to create an animation. Remember, a Movie Clip is exactly the same as a regular Timeline ani-

mation. As a result, you can use any of the techniques (tweening, frame by frame, special effects, and so on) that you've already learned. You also aren't limited to a single animated object in a single layer—you could have multiple layers with multiple animated objects.

> Because Movie Clips can contain complex animations, you will probably use Graphic symbols. You can create them directly from within the Movie Clip much as you would from the main Timeline, and they're automatically placed in the main movie's Library for future use.

5. When you've finished crafting the animation in your Movie Clip, click the scene link in the Scene and Symbol bar to return to the main Timeline.

6. Once you've returned to the main Timeline, you can view and test your Movie Clip by opening the Library (Window → Library), selecting the Movie Clip, and clicking the Play button in the preview window's top-right corner.

> You can also test the Movie Clip's animation directly from within Symbol Editing mode—just hit the Return/Enter button.

Turning Existing Animations into Movie Clips

It's more than likely that the majority of Movie Clips you create will be fashioned from scratch. However, you'll probably find yourself in the situation where you'll want to turn an existing animation into a Movie Clip. In that case, follow these steps:

1. In the main Timeline, select every frame in every layer that you want to turn into a Movie Clip.

2. Copy the frames you've selected by going to Edit → Copy Frames or by Ctrl+clicking (Mac) or right-clicking (Win) and choosing Copy Frames from the pop-up context menu.

3. Go to Insert → New Symbol or use Cmd/Ctrl+F8.

> Make sure nothing on the Stage is selected before you insert a new symbol.

4. When the Create New Symbol dialog box opens, enter a name into the Name field, select the Movie Clip radio button, and click OK.

5. When the Symbol Editor opens, select the first frame in the Timeline and go to Edit → Paste Frames or Ctrl+click (Mac) or right-click (Win) and choose Paste Frames from the pop-up context menu. This pastes all the copied frames into the Movie Clip.

6   To return to the main Timeline, go to Edit → Edit Movie or click the scene link in the Scene and Symbol bar.

7. Now that you've returned to the main movie, you can remove the animation you copied to create the Movie Clip (if you so desire). Just reselect all the frames you previously selected and then delete them by going to Edit → Cut Frames. Alternatively, you can Ctrl+click (Mac) or right-click (Win) and choose Cut Frames from the pop-up context menu.

Inserting Movie Clips into the Main Timeline

Now that you've learned how to create Movie Clips, either from scratch or an existing animation, insert them into your main movie:

1. If it isn't already, open the Library by going to Window → Library.

2. Click the exact location in the Timeline where you want to insert the Movie Clip. Remember, you'll need to insert a keyframe if one hasn't already been inserted.

3. Click and drag the Movie Clip from the Library onto the Stage. Even though a Movie Clip could run for hundreds of frames, when it's inserted into the main Timeline, it only occupies a single keyframe.

4. To see how your Movie Clip runs within your main movie, you'll need to go to Control → Test Movie or Control → Test Scene.

Manipulating Movie Clips

Once you have inserted a Movie Clip into the main Timeline, you can manipulate it—as you can all symbols—by using the Property Inspector (Window → Properties). You can also accomplish a series of important operations by using the Library. You'll take a look at each option in the next several sections.

Naming a Movie Clip Instance

As you leaned in Chapter 6, when you drag a symbol from the Library onto the Stage, you are creating a symbol instance—a copy of the parent symbol in the Library. This is no difference when creating Movie Clips (they are symbols, after all). What you haven't learned, however, is that you can easily assign a unique name to a symbol instance using the Property Inspector. So, the big question becomes, why exactly would you want to assign a name to a symbol instance? Well, you can use ActionScript to control and manipulate Movie Clips that reside on the main Timeline. To do this, however, you need to identify each Movie Clip symbol instance with a unique name so that you can appropriately target the ActionScript. So, although the process by which you name a Movie Clip symbol instance is really quite easy (as you'll find out shortly), it is absolutely vital to the creation of any moderately complex Flash creation that fully leverages the phenomenal power of Movie Clips.

To name a Movie Clip symbol instance, follow these steps:

1. With a new document open, drag a Movie Clip from the Library onto the Stage.

2. Select the Movie Clip symbol instance using the Arrow tool.

3. If it isn't already, open the Property Inspector by going to Window → Properties.

4. Enter a unique name into the Instance Name field.

Instance Name field

When entering a name into the Instance Name field, avoid using spaces. If you want a two-word name, use a hyphen (-) or an underscore (_).

Swapping One Movie Clip for Another

You might find yourself in a situation where you want to swap one instance for another. To do this, you use the Swap symbol in the Property Inspector:

Swap button

1. In the main Timeline, select the Movie Clip you want to swap out.

2. If it isn't already, open the Property Inspector by going to Window → Properties.

3. Click the Swap button.

4. When the Swap Symbol dialog box opens, select the symbol you want to swap in, and click OK.

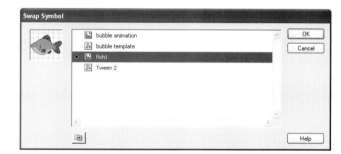

You don't have to swap a Movie Clip for a Movie Clip. You could easily swap a Movie Clip for a Graphic symbol, for example. However, the swapped symbol will retain the behavior (Movie Clip, Button, Graphic) of the symbol it's replacing.

Editing a Movie Clip

If you want to edit the parent symbol of a given Movie Clip, you can open the Library, select the Movie Clip, and choose Edit from the Library Options menu. Alternatively, you can double-click the Movie Clip instance on the Stage and then make any changes you want. Remember, when you've finished up in the Symbol Editor, just click the scene link in the Scene and Symbol bar to return to the main Timeline.

Duplicating a Movie Clip

You can use the Library to duplicate a Movie Clip, which is useful if you want to replace one symbol with an edited version of another. You just duplicate the symbol, edit it using the Edit command in the Library's Options drop-down menu, and then use it to replace the target symbol instance on the Stage. Let's take a look at the process for duplicating:

1. Open the Flash movie that contains the Movie Clip you want to duplicate.

2. If it isn't already, open the Library by going to Window → Library.

3. Select the Movie Clip you want to duplicate.

4. Select Duplicate from the Library's Options drop-down menu.

5. When the Duplicate Symbol dialog box appears, enter the name for the duplicated symbol into the Name field, make sure the Movie Clip radio button is selected, and click OK.

The duplicate Movie Clip is automatically added to the Library, and you can then manipulate it however you'd want.

Seeing Movie Clips in Action

Now that you've explored the basics of creating and manipulating Movie Clips, you can put all of your hard-earned knowledge to work. Even though you've yet to explore the Action-Script-related aspects of Movie Clips (discussed in Chapter 16), there is no better way to experiment with their power and versatility than by using them to create a scene that, under normal circumstances, would prove complex enough to be somewhat overwhelming if it were constructed using the main Timeline alone.

 All of the images (in SWF format) in this tutorial are located in the Chapter 10 folder of the companion CD-ROM. In addition, the files `under_the_sea.swf` and `under_the_sea.fla` provide an example of how the final product should look.

In this tutorial, you're going to create a simple 2D undersea scene in which a single fish swims by the camera. You will create all of the moving objects in the scene using Movie Clips.

Creating the Ocean

To start off, you'll need to create the ocean:

1. Create a new document by going to File → New.

2. Go to Modify → Document. When the Document Properties dialog box opens, change the Width to **500** and the Height to **400**.

3. Choose a light blue for the document's background color.

4. Click OK to exit the Document Properties dialog box.

5. Now, go to File → Import.

6. When the Import dialog box opens, navigate to the Chapter 10 directory on the CD-ROM, locate `water.swf`, and click Open. This imports the premade water (complete with gentle rolling waves) onto the Stage and into your Library. The file is nothing spectacular, so you might want to create your own.

> If you can't locate the file, you might have to select the All Files option from the Import dialog box's Files of Type drop-down menu.

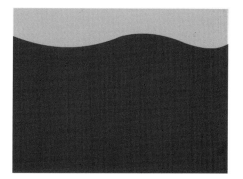

7. Position the water so that it lines up with the edges of the movie.

8. Because you are going to have a number of different layers in your scene, it's wise to name each. Double-click on your only layer's icon. When the Layer Properties dialog box opens, enter **Water** into the Name field. Click OK.

Creating the Fish

Now that you've got the ocean occupying a single keyframe of a single layer, it's time to create some fish:

1. Go to Insert → New Symbol (or use the shortcut Cmd/Ctrl+F8).

2. When the Create New Symbol dialog box opens, click the Movie Clip radio button, enter **fish1** into the name field, and click OK.

3. When the Symbol Editor opens, go to File → Import, navigate to the `Chapter 10` directory on your CD-ROM, and choose the file `fish.swf`. This imports the image you'll use to create your fish Movie Clip.

> If the image doesn't appear, it's possible that Flash placed it out of view. Scroll down until it's visible, and drag it up. Remember, the crosshairs represent the symbol's registration point.

4. Now it's time to create the animation where the fish "swims" horizontally from the right to the left. First, select the fish with the Arrow tool.

5. If it isn't already, open the Property Inspector by going to Window → Properties.

6. Enter **470** into the X field and **-78.5** into the Y field.

7. Click frame 90, and go to Insert → Keyframe.

8. With the newly created keyframe selected, select the fish with the Arrow tool.

9. Enter **–400** into the X field and **–78.5** into the Y field.

10. Select the first keyframe, and go to Insert → Create Motion Tween.

The whole point of creating an animation that covers this amount of distance is to ensure that you can place the Movie Clip on one side of the Stage in the work area, have it pass through the ocean scene, and then have it pass into the work area on the other side of the Stage before it loops. This gives the illusion that the fish is simply passing by your line of sight.

11. If you want to add a little more life to your scene, you can have the fish follow a wavy path—opposed to the straight one it currently follows. To add a motion guide, follow the steps described in Chapter 9.

12. Now that you've created the Movie Clip of the fish, you can insert it into the water. Return to the main scene by going to Edit → Document or by clicking on the scene link in the Scene and Symbol bar.

13. Create a new layer by going to Insert → Layer or clicking on the Insert Layer button in the bottom-left corner of the Timeline.

14. Now, rename the new layer **fish.**

15. If it isn't already, make sure the fish layer is above the ocean layer in the Timeline.

16. Select the first keyframe of the fish layer.

17. Open the Library (Window → Library) and click and drag the fish Movie Clip onto the Stage. You should position the Movie Clip in the work area to the right of the Stage. So far, your scene should look something like this:

Now that you've created a basic ocean scene, you can test it—simply go to Control → Test Movie or Control → Test Scene.

Adding Some Bubbles

You'll finish off this tutorial by adding some floating bubbles to the ocean:

1. Go to Insert → New Symbol.

2. When the Create New Symbol dialog box opens, click the Graphic radio button, type **bubble template** into the Name field, and click OK.

3. When the Symbol Editor opens, click on the first keyframe of the only layer in the Time-line and draw a small circle with the Oval tool in the lower portion of the screen. As this will be the template for your floating bubbles, you should choose a sufficiently bubble-like color for the stroke and fill.

4. From here, you are going to want to take the bubble template Graphic symbol you created, and use it in a Movie Clip to create an animation of a rising bubble. Go to Insert → New Symbol.

5. When the Create New Symbol dialog box pops up, enter **bubble** into the Name field, select the Movie Clip radio button, and click OK.

6. When you enter the Symbol Editor, select the first blank keyframe in the only layer, and drag the bubble template graphic symbol from the Library onto the Stage.

7. With the bubble template still selected, open the Info panel. Change the X value to **14.7** and the Y value to **76.3**.

8. Click on frame 30 and go to Insert → Keyframe.

9. With the second keyframe selected, change the bubble template's X value to **–9.8** and its Y value to **–202.7**.

10. Reselect the first keyframe in the layer and go to Insert → Create Motion Tween. This creates the animation of the rising bubble.

11. To add a little character to the rising bubble, click somewhere in the middle of the tween (say, frame 15 or so).

Even though the entire tween gets selected, don't be fooled into believing that you aren't selecting a specific frame. The playhead indicates the actual frame you've selected.

12. Go to Insert → Keyframe. By doing this, you've added another keyframe to the middle of the tween you created. Your Timeline should look something like this:

13. With the newly created middle keyframe selected, use either the Transform panel (Window → Transform) or the Scale tool (located in the Toolbox's Options section when the Free Transform tool is selected) to increase the size of the bubble slightly. By doing this, you've created a tween in which the bubble starts off small, gradually gets bigger, and then goes back to its previous size. All of this happens when the bubble is moving.

14. Now, you're going to add a little more subtlety to your rising bubble by making it disappear as it nears the top of its tween. First, select the final keyframe in the tween.

15. Using the Arrow tool, select the bubble.

16. If it isn't already, open the Property Inspector by going to Window → Properties.

17. Choose Alpha from the Color drop-down menu and enter **0** into the Alpha Value field. This makes the bubble appear transparent by the end of the tween.

Adding More Complexity to the Bubbles

Now that you've created the animation of one rising bubble, you can then add several more that rise at staggered intervals:

1. With the bubble Movie Clip still open in the Symbol Editor, add an additional layer (give it a unique name if you want) by going to Insert → Layer or by clicking the Insert Layer button in the bottom-left corner of the Timeline.

2. Click on frame 5 and go to Insert → Keyframe or use the shortcut F6. This guarantees that the second bubble won't appear and start rising until the playhead reaches frame 5. As a result, the two bubbles will be staggered.

3. Drag the bubble template Graphic symbol from the Library onto the Stage. With the Info panel, set the new bubble's X value to **–51.5** and its Y value to **91.5**.

4. Click on frame 35 and go to Insert → Keyframe.

5. From here, repeat the process described in the previous section—the only difference is that you set the bubble's X value to **–48.5** and its Y value to **–120.5** using the Info panel to create the second rising bubble.

6. Now that you've created two rising bubbles, you can continue adding rising bubbles. The only thing you have to vary is the frame at which the specific animation starts. You can also vary the size of each bubble instance to add variety.

Adding the Bubbles to the Main Scene

Now, you can add your rising bubble Movie Clip to the main scene:

1. Return to the main scene by going to Edit → Document or by clicking on the Scene button in Scene and Symbol bar.

2. Create a new layer by going to Insert → Layer or clicking on the Insert Layer button in the bottom-left corner of the Timeline.

3. Now, rename the new layer as **bubbles**.

4. Select the first keyframe of the bubbles layer.

5. Open the Library (Window → Library) and click and drag the bubbles Movie Clip onto the Stage. You should position the Movie Clip in the work area just below the Stage. By doing this, you'll get the illusion that the bubbles are passing into view from the bottom of the scene. Your scene should look something like this:

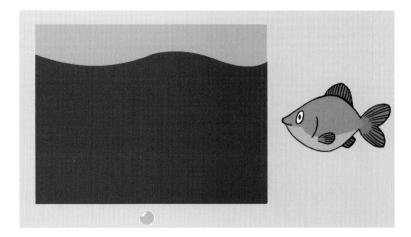

6. Now that you've created a basic ocean scene, you can test it. Simply go to Control → Test Movie or Control → Test Scene.

Congratulations, you've created your first scene using Movie Clips. Experiment with them by adding more objects to the scene. For example, try adding other fish or swaying sea plants.

Inspirational Design Model

Any good Flash creation will leverage Movie Clips to enhance the user experience. However, because of their sheer power and versatility, there exists an obvious gap between those who simply use Movie Clips and those who exploit Movie Clips to their maximum potential. A great example of an effective use of Movie Clips is Neostream (`www.neostream.com`)

Based in Sydney, Australia, Neostream is a topnotch multimedia company that specializes in CD-ROMs, the Web, and corporate identity. Its website is a fast-paced, beautiful example of clean Flash design (see Figure 10.1). The animation is extremely smooth, employing Movie Clips for all manner of elements—including its preloader screen and interface elements (specifically, its animated buttons). Log on and prepare to be dazzled with some serious animation.

Figure 10.1

Neostream

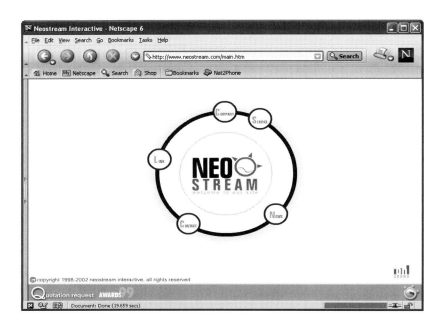

Summary

In this chapter, you extended your mastery of Flash animation with a solid introduction to Movie Clips. As mentioned in the onset of the chapter, you'll get into ActionScript-related aspects of Movie Clips (of which there are many) in Chapter 16. This chapter prepared the foundation upon which advanced Movie Clips will ultimately be based. You began the chapter with a look at the nature of Movie Clips. You continued by learning how to create Movie Clips from scratch and from existing Timeline animations. From there, you looked at inserting Movie Clips into the main Timeline and editing Movie Clips with tools such as the Property Inspector. Finally, in a hands-on exploration of Movie Clips, you created an animated seascape.

CHAPTER 11

Using Scenes to Organize Animated Content

By now you've probably figured out that Flash movies can be quite complex. A movie of even moderate size and intricacy can contain many discreet areas of action (interactivity, animation, and so on). As a result, it's fairly straightforward to create a Flash movie that, although compelling and beautiful, is an unorganized, chaotic nightmare. Whether you are creating a stand-alone animation, a web-based animated short, or a complete Flash site, you're going to have to develop and maintain a method of keeping your Flash creation well organized.

Now, imagine being able to break your creation into any number of manageable chunks, each containing a specific series of events (such as an animation, an interface, or some interactivity)—this is where Flash *scenes* come in. Like in theater, you can think of scenes as self-contained chunks that logically break up your movie's content. Each scene is something akin to a mini-movie that is strung together with other mini-movies to create the overall Flash movie. When it comes to movies of any significant complexity, scenes save you a great deal of time and trouble.

In this chapter, you'll explore the following topics:

- **Familiarizing yourself with scenes**

- **Creating and manipulating scenes**

- **Navigating between scenes**

- **Playing scenes**

- **How ActionScripting relates to scenes**

Familiarizing Yourself with Scenes

Scenes are wondrous little tools that segment the overall content in your movie into self-contained, manageable chunks. Each scene acts as a mini-movie that plays one after the other. Although they appear to be somewhat separated from one another within the Flash authoring environment, they really aren't. When you play the overall movie (either from within Flash or after it has been exported), the scenes string together as if they were one movie and play according to the sequence listed in the Scene panel. There is never any perceptible lag or flicker between scenes.

The number of scenes you can have is limited only by the amount of memory in your computer.

The possibilities for scenes are endless. Say, for instance, you are creating an entire Flash site. You could use a scene for each individual section and subsection of the site. Another possibility is along the lines of traditional film or theater. Web-based Flash animated shorts are becoming increasingly popular these days. You could use scenes to partition a Flash animated short you created into...well, scenes!

Introducing the Scene Panel

For the most part, you access the majority of scene functionality through the Scene panel. Opened by going to Window → Scene, the Scene panel displays the number and organization of your movie's scenes. In addition, it lets you duplicate, add, delete, and move scenes.

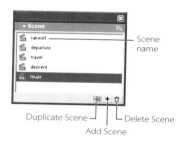

Unlike many other Flash panels, the Scene panel doesn't have any additional options beyond the default Maximize Panel, Close Panel, and Help options.

Introducing the Scene and Symbol Bar

Nestled above the Timeline and below the main program menu is the Scene and Symbol bar (see Figure 11.1). You used the Scene and Symbol bar in Chapter 7 when you were working with the Symbol Editor (more specifically, moving back to the main Timeline from the Symbol Editor). However, you didn't get a chance to explore its functionality in relation to scenes.

Figure 11.1

The Edit Scene button in the Scene and Symbol bar gives you access to all the scenes in the currently open movie.

Essentially, the Scene and Symbol bar displays the current scene (which is finale in Figure 11.1). When you move to another scene, the Scene and Symbol bar changes its display accordingly. Also, the Edit Scene button in the right portion of the Scene and Symbol bar displays a drop-down list that lets you switch the currently displayed scene. (For more information about this button, see the "Navigating Between Scenes" section.)

Creating and Manipulating Scenes

As mentioned previously, you'll use the Scene panel (Window → Scene) to work with scenes. In this section of the chapter, you're going to explore how to use the Scene panel to add, duplicate, rename, and rearrange scenes.

Adding Scenes

As your movie increases in size and complexity, you are going to want to add more scenes to keep a firm grip on its organization. By using the Scene panel, you can add as many scenes as you want by following these steps:

1. Make sure you have a document open.

2. Go to Window → Scene to open the Scene panel.

3. From here, click the Add Scene button ➕ located in the bottom-right corner of the Scene panel. Alternatively, besides using the Scene panel to add a new scene, you can also go to Insert → Scene.

4. You'll notice that Flash has added an additional scene to the movie. By default, Flash always adds the new scene below the currently selected one. The default naming convention for a new scene is numerical—for instance, Scene 1, Scene 2, and so on.

5. From here, all you have to do is select the newly added scene in the Scene panel and start creating.

When you create a new scene, Flash automatically switches to the newly created scene.

Deleting Scenes

If you want to delete a scene, follow these steps:

1. Open the Scene panel by going to Window → Scene.

2. Select the scene you'd like to delete.

3. Click the Delete Scene button 🗑 located in the bottom-right corner of the Scene panel.

4. When the prompt appears, click OK.

    As indicated in the prompt, you cannot undo a scene deletion. Alternatively, you can also go to Insert → Remove Scene to delete a scene.

Duplicating Scenes

In previous chapters, you looked at how to copy and duplicate various elements such as objects and animations (mostly for the purpose of converting them to symbols). The process, especially when it comes to copying entire animations, is fairly unwieldy. Imagine, then, having to duplicate an entire scene! The prospect is pretty daunting, especially if your movie (and its respective scenes) has become fairly complicated.

Macromedia has integrated a simple duplicate function that lets you create exact copies of any given scene with a click of a button:

1. With the Scene panel open (Window → Scene), select the scene you want to duplicate.

2. Click the Duplicate Scene button in the bottom-right section of the Scene panel.

3. You'll notice that a duplicate of your selected scene, with the word *copy* tagged onto the original name, appears in the Scene panel.

Renaming Scenes

The default names Flash assigns to new or duplicate scenes are not very original. Although logically numbered, the names aren't particularly useful when it comes to identifying the content of individual scenes in a large movie. To rename a scene, follow these steps:

1. With the Scene panel open, double-click the scene whose name you want to change. By doing this, the scene's name becomes editable.

2. From here, type a new name and click Return/Enter (or click anywhere off the Scene panel).

Rearranging Scenes

As mentioned, scenes play sequentially based on their positions in the Scene panel. But you certainly aren't stuck with the order in which the scenes were created (and therefore the sequence that they play). To change the arrangement of scenes, follow these steps:

1. Open the Scene panel (Window → Scene).

2. Click and drag the scene to the location you want. You'll notice that as long as you keep your mouse button down, your cursor changes and a blue line appears in the scene's projected location.

3. To move the scene, release the mouse button.

Navigating Between Scenes

Because you are going to want to switch back and forth between various scenes as you work on them, Flash has provided several scene navigation tools:

Scene panel To navigate between the various scenes in your movie, all you need to do is click the desired scene in the Scene panel. Remember, your current scene is displayed in the Scene and Symbol bar.

Edit Scene button Two buttons dominate the right portion of the Scene and Symbol bar. The leftmost one, when clicked (as illustrated in Figure 11.1), provides a menu of all the current scenes in your movie. All you need to do is select one and Flash automatically switches to that scene.

Movie Explorer As discussed in Chapter 7, the Movie Explorer (Window → Movie Explorer) displays the contents of your movie hierarchically, lets you search your entire movie for any symbol or symbol instance, and replaces text and fonts.

Because scenes are part of the overall movie, they are displayed in the Movie Explorer as top-level items in the organizational hierarchy.

Simply locate the scene by its name, and click it. Flash automatically switches you to the selected scene.

> Under normal circumstances, the Movie Explorer only displays the contents of the currently selected scene. To display all scenes (and their content), choose Show All Scenes from the Movie Explorer's drop-down Options menu.

Testing Scenes

So far, you've looked at a couple of different ways to test the movie you've created. When it comes to scenes, you should be aware that if you were to simply hit Return/Enter to play your movie within the Flash authoring environment, you would only be able to preview the currently selected scene. Although, when exported, the movie plays all the scenes sequentially, it does not do so from within Flash. As a result, you need to do one of the following:

• To test a scene other than the current one, use the Scene panel to select it, and then hit Return/Enter. Alternatively, you can go to Control → Test Scene.

• Now, if you want to test the movie in its entirety, go to Control → Test Movie or use the shortcut Cmd/Ctrl+Return/Enter. This opens the movie in a new window and plays all the scenes according to their sequence within the Scene panel.

> You can also play all the scenes in your movie by going to Control → Play All Scenes.

ActionScripting and Scenes

Although scenes are great for organizing animated content, they do tend to create a fairly linear product. Granted, there isn't much you can do about the linearity of scenes; you certainly can't have two scenes playing at the same time. However, what if you wanted to play your first scene, followed by your third scene, your second scene, and finally your fourth scene? Alternatively, what if you wanted your scenes to play from last to first, instead of first to last? Under normal circumstances, this defies the natural laws of Flash. However, with the use of ActionScript (specifically frame actions), you can be your own Einstein, shattering the conventions of the known Flash universe! But seriously, as is the case in many aspects of Flash, ActionScripting greatly extends scene functionality.

However, at this point it would be a little premature to get into ActionScript. Instead, this section will focus on what is *possible* when you use ActionScript to extend the usability of scenes. If you want to explore the step-by-step specifics of ActionScripting in general and frame actions in particular, see Chapter 12. For now, these frame actions can increase the versatility of scenes:

- `gotoAndPlay()` determines the specific scene and frame that the playhead jumps to when it evokes the action.

- `gotoAndStop()` goes to a specific scene or frame and stops the movie. This is a variation of the `gotoAndPlay()` action that you set by deselecting the GotoAndPlay check box at the bottom of the Actions panel.

- `play()` restarts a movie that has been previously stopped.

- `stop()` ends the movie from playing any further.

Inspirational Design Model

When it comes down to it, scenes let you partition your content (as well as the authoring process) into manageable chunks. Any good Flash creation leverages scenes in any number of interesting and creative ways. As a result, it is extremely difficult to single out one upon which the honor of Inspirational Design Model can be bestowed. However, a decidedly superior example of using scenes effectively is Mondo Media (www.mondomedia.com).

Mondo Media was founded to capitalize on a model of Internet syndication to develop and distribute animated entertainment. With such irreverent and hilarious online Flash animated shorts such as *Thugs on Film*, *The God and Devil Show*, and *Heavy Metal Guy*, Mondo Media has grown into an unstoppable powerhouse of online entertainment.

Mondo Media's website harnesses the power of scenes to partition content into discreet chunks for easy consumption (see Figure 11.2). The site's subsections (especially those pertaining to the animated shorts, called *Mondo Mini Shows*) are mini-sites unto themselves. In short, the Mondo Media website is an excellent example of how to effectively use scenes to get the most out of your content.

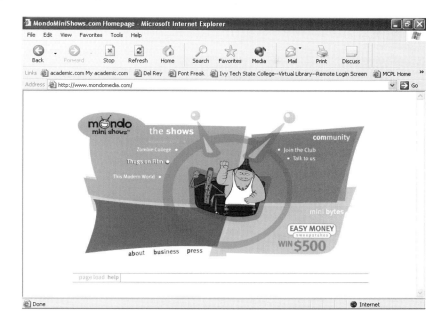

Figure 11.2

Mondo Media

Summary

In this chapter, you explored the power and versatility of scenes as a method to partition your content—both for the audience and for your own personal organizational purposes. You began the chapter by looking at how scenes work in the overall framework of a Flash movie. From there, you moved on to more practical topics such as how to use the Scene panel to create and manipulate scenes, how to navigate between scenes, and how to play scenes. You finished the chapter by looking at how ActionScript can control the default behavior of scenes in your Flash creation.

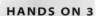

Animating a Space Scene

In this tutorial you're going to take all that (somewhat) abstract knowledge you've amassed about animating in Flash and put it to good use.

Ever wanted to travel into space? Well, here's your chance. You aren't really going to travel into space but, with the mighty power of Flash at your disposal, you'll create the next best thing—an animation of a voyage through the cosmos. The animation will draw on all of the techniques you've learned throughout Part III, including Timeline animations, Movie Clips, and scenes. The project itself will be broken up into five scenes. The first will be an animation of a rocket taking off from Earth. From there, you'll create three outer space scenes: one with the rocket blasting away from Earth, one with the rocket traveling through deep space, and one with the rocket heading toward a planet. The last scene you create will add a little "Hollywood" to the animation.

 You can find all of the images and files used in this tutorial in the Hands On 3 directory on this book's CD-ROM. You will also find a copy of the finished movie (`space_flight.swf` and `space_flight.fla`), so you can get an idea of what it might look like. However, as with all the tutorials in this book, the process is far more important than the final product.

Creating the Rocket Ship

Start off this tutorial by creating the first scene in the animation—your rocket ship blasting off from Earth:

1. Create a new file (File → New).

2. Open the Document Properties dialog box (Modify → Document). From here, change the frame rate to 15 and make the document's background color a light blue (suitable for the sky).

3. Click OK.

4. Select the Rectangle tool from the Toolbox.

5. Click the Stroke Color swatch in the Toolbox and hit the No Color button—which is the box with a red line through it just to the left of the color wheel. This guarantees the shape you draw won't have any stroke.

6. Now, click the Fill Color swatch and choose a brown or green color (the rectangle will serve as the ground, so pick an appropriate color).

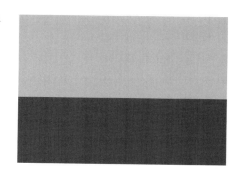

7. Use the Rectangle tool to draw a rectangle that occupies about one third of the bottom of the Stage. So far, things should look something like this:

8. Change the existing layer's name to **ground**.

> This step-by-step tutorial focuses almost no energy on creating a landscape in the first scene that is anything less than dull. To spruce up you movie, you might want to add additional elements (buildings and so on)—it's up to you.

9. Now, to keep things tidy, you need to name your scene. Open the Scene panel (Window → Scene), double-click Scene 1 (the only scene in your movie thus far), and type the name **takeoff**.

10. Now, you'll need to import all of the graphics you'll use in the scene. Go to Insert → New Symbol. When the Create New Symbol dialog box appears, make sure the Graphic radio button is selected, type **rocket ship** into the Name field, and click OK.

11. Now, when the Symbol Editor opens, go to File → Import. When the Import dialog box opens, navigate to the Hands On 3 folder of the book's CD-ROM, select `rocketship.swf`, and click Open. By doing this, you'll place the rocket ship graphic into the Symbol Editor. (Sometimes, when you import complex graphics, they'll appear as discreet parts— as opposed to one graphic. As a result, you'll need to group all of its elements. However, in the case of the rocket ship graphic, everything has already been grouped.)

> If you don't see the image in the Symbol Editor, scroll down. Sometimes Flash doesn't place the imported graphic in the center of the Symbol Editor. All you need to do is click and drag the rocket ship to the center of the Symbol Editor. Remember, where you put the image in relation to the small crosshairs determines where its registration point is.

12. From here, you're going to turn the static rocket ship graphic into a Movie Clip where flames shoot from its exhaust ports. First, select the rocket ship graphic in the Library and select Properties from the Library Options pop-up menu. Alternatively, you can simply click the Properties icon at the bottom of the Library.

13. When the Symbol Properties dialog box opens, select the Movie Clip radio button, and click OK. Now the static rocket ship graphic is a Movie Clip. From here, it's time to add some flames.

14. Name the existing layer **rocket ship** (remember, you're still working on the Movie Clip within the Symbol Editor).

15. Create a new layer and call it **flames**.

16. Move the flames layer so that it is below the rocket ship layer.

17. Now, select frame 5 in the rocket ship layer and go to Insert → Frame.

18. Now, select the second frame in the flames layer, and go to Insert → Keyframe.

The first keyframe will be left blank to simulate the rocket ship without any flames. The reason for this will become far more apparent when you put the scene together.

19. With the second keyframe selected (the one you just added), draw some flames coming from the exhaust of the rocket ship with the Pen tool. Use the Paint Bucket tool to fill the outline you've created with a red color. So far, your flames should look something like this:

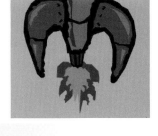

20. Now, click the third frame in the flames layer and go to Insert → Keyframe.

21. Click the fourth frame in the flames layer, go to Insert → Blank Keyframe.

If you are having trouble remembering how to use the Pen tool or the Paint Bucket, see Chapter 4.

22. With the newly created blank keyframe selected, draw another set of flames coming from the rocket ship's exhaust. Make sure they are similar, but not identical, to the first set of the flames you drew, and fill them with an orange color using the Paint Bucket. They should look something like this:

23. Now, click the fifth frame in the flames layer, and go to Insert → Keyframe. By doing this, you've created a Movie Clip in which the flames you've drawn will alternate. Because the Movie Clip will loop indefinitely when it's used in the main Timeline, you'll get a simple (but effective) moving flame effect.

24. Now it's time to insert the rocket ship Movie Clip into the launch scene. If you are still in the Symbol Editor, switch back to the main Timeline.

25. Insert a new layer and call it **rocket ship**.

26. With the first keyframe of the rocket ship layer selected, click and drag the rocket ship Movie Clip from the Library onto the Stage. Position it so that it is in the middle of the scene. So far, the scene should look something like this:

27. Now, it's time to do some animating. Select frame 30 in the background layer and go to Insert → Keyframe.

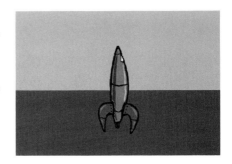

Remember back when you were creating the rocket ship Movie Clip you left the first keyframe in the flames layer blank? Well, here is where that amazing foresight comes in. If you hadn't left that first keyframe blank, you would have had flames coming out of the rocket ship while it was simply sitting there. The blank keyframe gives the illusion of the rocket ship starting up.

28. Select frame 30 in the ground layer and go to Insert → Frame or use the shortcut F5.

29. Select frame 30 in the rocket ship layer and go to Insert → Keyframe.

30. Now, with frame 30 in the rocket ship layer selected, move the rocket ship Movie Clip up until it's outside the Stage.

31. Select the first keyframe in the rocket ship layer and go to Insert → Create Motion Tween. This creates a tweened animation in which the rocket ship flies up into the sky.

32. To add a little more detail, select the first keyframe in the rocket ship tween, open the Property Inspector (Window → Properties), and set the Ease to **-100**. This gives the illusion that the rocket ship starts off slow but then picks up speed as it rises.

33. Now, save the file by going to File → Save. When the Save dialog box opens, navigate to the location of your hard drive where you want save the file, enter **rocket_animation** into the File Name field, and click Save.

You can test your movie by hitting Return/Enter. If you want the rocket ship Movie Clip to play, select Control → Test Movie.

Speeding Away from Earth

Now that you've created the first scene in your animation, you can create the second one. You'll be continuing your space voyage by creating a scene in which the rocket ship speeds into space with Earth receding in the background. As it will add another dimension to the scene, you're going to engineer a little visual trickery to simulate the illusion of depth and distance:

 1. Make sure you have the `rocket_animation` file open.

2. Open the Scene panel, if it isn't already open (Window → Scene), and add a second scene by clicking the Add Scene button (at the bottom of the Scene panel) or by going to Insert → Scene.

3. Double-click the name of the scene you've just created, and enter **departure** into the field.

4. If it isn't already, select the departure scene.

5. To create the blackness of space, select Modify → Document, click the Background Color swatch to open the Color Picker, and choose black.

6. Now, you're going to start off by creating the stars that will be scattered throughout the space portions of your animation. Go to Insert → New Symbol. When the Create New Symbol dialog box appears, enter **star** into the Name filed, select the Graphic radio button, and click OK.

7. When the Symbol Editor appears, use the Ellipse tool to draw a small yellow circle. Make sure the circle's stroke is also yellow. As with much of this tutorial, you are certainly welcome to create something a little more fancy for your stars. However, given the fact that the stars are meant to be in the background, it might be wiser to rely on something understated.

8. When you've finished creating your star (which you'll use repeatedly in the space scene), return to the main Timeline.

9. Now, import the graphic you'll be using for Earth. Go to Insert → New Symbol. When the Create New Symbol dialog box opens, enter **earth** into the Name field, select the Graphic radio button, and click OK.

10. When the Symbol Editor Opens, go to File → Import. When the Import dialog box opens, navigate to the Hands On 3 directory on the book's CD-ROM, locate the `earth.swf` file, and click Open.

11. Now, you're set to start adding assets to your scene. Use the Edit Scene button (in the right portion of the Symbol and Scene bar) to select the departure scene.

12. Change the single existing layer's name to **stars**.

13. Open the Library (Window → Library), select the first keyframe in the stars layer, and repeatedly drag the star symbol onto the Stage. The number of stars you place on the Stage is up to you.

14. Now, add an additional layer to the main Timeline by going to Insert → Layer or by clicking the Insert Layer button in the bottom-right corner of the Timeline. Double-click the layer's name and type **earth**. Alternatively, you can double-click the layer's icon (just to the left of the name itself) to open the Layer Properties dialog box and enter **earth** into the Name field.

15. Now, with the Library open (Window →
    Library), drag the earth symbol onto the
    Stage. Position it so that's it's located in the
    bottom-left corner of the Stage. So far, your
    scene should look something like this:

16. Now, create a third layer and call it **rocket
    ship**.

17. Select the first keyframe in the rocket ship
    layer, open the Library (Window → Library),
    and drag the rocket ship Movie Clip (which you created in the previous section of the
    Tutorial) onto the Stage.

18. The rocket ship Movie Clip's current size and orientation isn't appropriate for the cur-
    rent scene. As a result, you'll have to fiddle with it a bit. First, select it and go to Modify
    → Transform → Flip Horizontal.

19. Now, select Free Transform tool from the Toolbox, click the rocket ship Movie Clip, and
    select the Rotate and Skew button in the Options section of the Toolbox.

20. Rotate the rocket ship Movie Clip roughly 45° clockwise. This gives your rocket ship a
    decent trajectory as it speeds away from Earth.

Alternatively, you can simply use the Transform panel (Window → Panels → Transform). Just
click the Rotate radio button, and enter **45** into the Rotate Value field.

21. Now, with the first keyframe still selected, use either the Free Transform tool or the
    Transform panel to shrink the rocket ship symbol so it's small. By doing this, you create
    the illusion that the rocket ship is far away at the start of the animation. Later, you'll add
    to the illusion of depth and distance by having the rocket ship fly "toward" the viewer.

22. Select the rocket ship symbol with the
    Arrow tool and position it so that it's some-
    where over the middle of the earth symbol.
    So far, your scene should look something
    like this:

23. Now that you've placed all the elements you
    are going to use in the scene, it's time to do
    some animating. Select frame 35 in the stars
    layer, and go to Insert → Frame.

24. Select frame 35 in the earth layer and go to Insert → Frame.

25. Select frame 35 in the rocket ship layer, and go to Insert → Keyframe.

26. Select the keyframe you just created in the rocket ship layer. Click and drag the rocket ship symbol to a location just outside the top-right corner of the Stage.

27. With the Free Transform tool or the Transform panel, increase the rocket ship symbol to larger than its original size. Once you've scaled the symbol, make sure that all of it is off the Stage. Once animated, this will create the illusion that the rocket ship flies from Earth past your point of view. At this point, frame 35 should look some thing like this:

28. Select the first keyframe in the rocket ship layer, and go to Insert → Create Motion Tween. This creates a tweened animation of the rocket ship increasing in size as it "flies" past the camera. However, depending on where the rocket ship is in the final keyframe, the animation could look a little bit funny—like the rocket ship is flying without its nose pointed exactly forward. You'll remedy this by adding a straight path along which the rocket ship will move.

29. Select the first keyframe in the rocket ship layer, and click the Add Motion Guide button at the bottom-right corner of the main Timeline.

30. Select the first keyframe in the motion guide layer (which appears directly above the rocket ship layer), and use the Line tool to draw a trajectory from the middle of the earth symbol to a few centimeters past where your rocket ship ends up in the final keyframe.

Because the scene's background is black, you will have some problems with the line (whose default color is also black) getting lost. To avoid this, either change the stroke color before you draw the line (by using the Stroke Color Picker in the Toolbox's Colors section) or change the background color of your movie temporarily by going to Modify → Document and clicking the Background Color swatch.

31. With the first keyframe in the rocket ship layer selected, click and drag the small rocket ship symbol so that it snaps to the start of the linear motion path. Because the rocket ship symbol is small, you might want to use the Zoom tool to get a better look at the area with which you're working.

32. Now, click the last keyframe in the layer, and click and drag the larger rocket ship symbol so that it snaps onto the end of the motion path.

> If you have trouble snapping the rocket ship's registration point to the path, make sure Snap to Objects is turned on (View → Snap to Objects). Also, you might have to click the registration point and then hold your mouse down for a second before dragging to make the snapping registration point appear.

33. Select the first keyframe in the layer, and open the Property Inspector (Window → Properties).

34. Click the Orient to Path check box and set Easing to **-100**. By doing this, the rocket ship will always point in the direction of the path. By changing the Easing, the rocket ship will start off slowly and gain speed as it travels along the path, thereby furthering the illusion of depth and distance.

35. It's time to animate Earth receding into the distance. Click Keyframe 35 in the earth layer, and go to Insert → Keyframe.

36. With the newly created keyframe selected, click and drag the earth symbol into the work area, just outside the bottom-left corner of the Stage. With Keyframe 35 still selected, use the Free Transform tool or the Transform panel to shrink the earth symbol to about 25 percent of its former size. When animated, this creates the impression that Earth is moving off into the distance.

37. With the first keyframe of the earth layer selected, go to Insert → Create Motion Tween.

You've just finished the second scene in the animation! To test it, simply hit Return/Enter. If you want the rocket ship Movie Clip to work properly, select Control → Test Scene. If you want to view the entire animation thus far (including Scene 1), go to Control → Test Movie.

Zipping through Space

Now that you've created the scene in which the rocket ship zips away from Earth, you can start on the third scene in the animation, the rocket ship careening through space:

1. Make sure you have the `rocket_animation` file open.

2. Open the Scene panel, if it isn't already open (Window → Scene), and add a third scene by clicking the Add Scene button (at the bottom of the Scene panel) or by going to Insert → Scene.

3. Double-click the name of the scene you've just created, and enter **travel** into the field.

4. Select the single layer in the Timeline, and change its name to **stars**. Now, with the stars layer still selected, click frame 30 and go to Insert → Frame.

5. Select the first blank keyframe in the stars layer, open the Library, and click and drag as many instances of the star symbol as you want onto the Stage.

6. From here, you'll need to add some "texture" to the scene by including a planet for the rocket ship to pass by. Go to Insert → New Symbol. When the Create New Symbol dialog box opens, enter **planet1** into the Name field, click the Graphic radio button, and click OK.

7. When the Symbol Editor opens, go to File → Import. When the Import dialog box opens, navigate to the Hands On 3 directory on the book's CD-ROM, and select `planet1.swf`.

8. Remember to click and drag the graphic to the registration point marker in the middle of the Symbol Editor.

9. Return to the main Timeline. From there, create a new layer by clicking the Insert Layer button in the bottom-left corner of the Timeline or by going to Insert → Layer, and name it **planet**.

10. With the first keyframe of the planet layer selected, click and drag the planet1 symbol from the Library onto the right portion of the Stage. At this point, your scene should look something like this:

11. Now, to add some movement to the planet. With the planet layer selected, click frame 30 and go to Insert → Keyframe.

12. Select the final keyframe in the planet layer (the one you just created), and click and drag the planet1 symbol about four centimeters (1.5 inches) to the left. Now, select the first keyframe in the planet layer, and go to Insert → Create Motion Tween. By adding a little motion to the planet, you'll create the illusion that the rocket ship is traveling at high speed.

13. Now for the actual rocket ship. Create a new layer in the main Timeline and call it **rocket ship**.

14. Select the first keyframe in the rocket ship layer, and drag the rocket ship Movie Clip from the Library into the work area just to the left of the Stage. Use the Free Transform tool or the Transform panel to orient the rocket ship horizontally. So far, your scene should look something like this:

15. Now, with the rocket ship layer selected, click frame 30 and go to Insert → Keyframe.

16. Click the final keyframe in the rocket ship layer (the one you just created), and click and drag the rocket ship Movie Clip to the other side of the Stage into the work area.

17. Select the first keyframe in the rocket ship layer, and go to Insert → Create Motion Tween.

You've just completed the animation of the rocket ship hurtling though space. To test it, simply hit Return/Enter. If you want the rocket ship Movie Clip to work properly, you're going to have to go to Control → Test Scene. If you want to view the entire animation thus far (including Scene 1 and 2), select Control → Test Movie.

Approaching the Planet

Now it's time to create the sequence in the animation in which your little rocket ship flies toward its intended destination, the mysterious planet X:

1. Make sure you have the `rocket_animation` file open.

2. Open the Scene panel, if it isn't already open (Window → Panels → Scene), and add a fourth scene by clicking the Add Scene button (at the bottom of the Scene panel) or by going to Insert → Scene.

3. Double-click the name of the scene you've just created, and enter **descent** into the field.

4. Select the single layer in the Timeline, and change its name to **stars**. Now, with the stars layer still selected, click frame 30 and go to Insert → Frame.

5. Select the first blank keyframe in the stars layer, open the Library, and click and drag as many instances of the star symbol as you want onto the Stage.

6. From here, you'll need to add the planet to the scene. Go to Insert → New Symbol. When the Create New Symbol dialog box opens, enter **planet2** into the Name field, click the Graphic radio button, and click OK.

7. When the Symbol Editor opens, go to File → Import. When the Import dialog box opens, navigate to the Hands On 3 directory on the book's CD-ROM, and select `planet2.swf`.

8. Remember to click and drag the graphic to the registration point marker in the middle of the Symbol Editor.

9. Return to the main Timeline. From there, create a new layer by clicking the Insert Layer button in the bottom-right corner of the Timeline or by going to Insert → Layer, and name it **planet x**.

10. With the first keyframe of the planet x layer selected, drag the planet2 symbol from the Library to the lower-right portion of the Stage. As the symbol is fairly large, use the Free Transform tool or the Transform panel to shrink it to about 3 centimeters (1 inch) across—or about 123×123 pixels. So far, your scene should look something like this:

11. Select frame 30 in the stars layer and go to Insert → Frame or use the shortcut F5.

12. Now, click frame 30 in the planet x layer and go to Insert → Keyframe.

13. With the last keyframe selected in the planet x layer, select the planet2 symbol and increase its size (either with the Free Transform tool or the Transform panel) to the point where it dominates much of the Stage. At this point, the scene should look something like this:

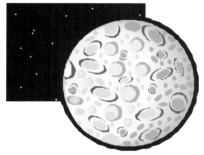

14. Now, with the first keyframe in the planet x layer selected, go to Insert → Create Motion Tween.

15. At this point, you can start working on the rocket ship itself. Create a new layer and call it **rocket ship**.

16. Select the first keyframe in the rocket ship layer, and drag the rocket ship Movie Clip from the Library onto the Stage. Position it so that it's in the work area just outside the top-left corner of the Stage.

17. Use either the Rotate tool or the Transform panel to rotate the rocket ship Movie Clip so that it's pointing toward the planet2 symbol. The result should be something like this:

18. Now, with the rocket ship layer still selected, click frame 30, and go to Insert → Keyframe.

19. Select the keyframe you've just created, and move the rocket ship Movie Clip over the middle of the planet. Then, use the Scale tool or the Transform panel to reduce its size substantially. The result should be something like this:

20. Select the first frame in the rocket ship layer, and go to Insert → Create Motion Tween.

21. Much like in the case when you created the first scene, your rocket ship's movement might look a little off. To correct this, you'll create a straight motion path for it to follow.

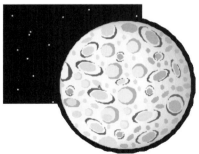

22. Select the first keyframe in the rocket ship layer, and click the Add Motion Guide button at the bottom-left of the main Timeline.

23. Select the first keyframe in the motion guide layer (which appears directly above the rocket ship layer), and use the Line tool to draw a trajectory from where the rocket ship starts to where it ends in the final keyframe—remember, you could run into problems if the Line tool draws a black line along the black background.

24. With the first keyframe in the rocket ship layer selected, click and drag the small rocket ship symbol so that it snaps to the start of the linear motion path.

25. Now, click the last keyframe in the layer, and click and drag the larger rocket ship symbol so that it snaps onto the end of the motion path—you'll probably need to zoom in because the rocket ship is so small.

26. Select the first keyframe in the layer, and open the Property Inspector (Window → Properties).

27. Click the Orient to Path check box, and set Easing to 100. By doing this, the rocket ship with always point in the direction of the path. By changing the Easing, the rocket ship will start off fast and slow down as it travels along the path, thereby furthering the illusion of depth and distance.

You've just finished the animation in which your rocket ship approaches planet X. To test it, hit Return/Enter. If you want the rocket ship Movie Clip to work properly, you're going to have to go to Control → Test Scene. If you want to view the entire animation thus far (including the other scenes), go to Control → Test Movie.

Adding Some Hollywood Glamour

You're just about there! You've finished the first four scenes in your animation. In the final scene, you're going to add a bit of cheesy "Hollywood" to cap it all off:

1. Make sure you have the `rocket_animation` file open.

2. Open the Scene panel, if it isn't already open (Window → Panels → Scene), and add a fifth scene by clicking the Add Scene button (at the bottom of the Scene panel) or by going to Insert → Scene.

3. Double-click the name of the scene you've just created, and enter **finale** into the field.

4. Go to Insert → New Symbol.

5. When the Create New Symbol dialog box opens, type **To Be Continued** into the Name field, click the Graphic radio button, and click OK.

6. Select the Text tool from the Toolbox.

7. *Before* you add any text, open the Property Inspector (Window → Properties).

8. When the Property Inspector opens, choose a font from the Font drop-down menu. (To preserve the effect, choose something big and blocky.) Then, enter a size (make it large) into the Size field.

9. Because the background of your movie is black, choose a light color for the text such as white.

10. Now, without clicking your cursor anywhere else, type **To Be Continued...** into the text box.

11. When you've finished, click your cursor anywhere outside the text box. Click and drag the text to the center of the Symbol Editor (if it isn't already there).

    If the edges of your text are jaggy, select the text, and go to View → Antialias Text.

12. Now, to create a "dramatic" fade-in text effect, switch back to the main Timeline and select the first keyframe in the scene's single layer. (If you want, you can name the layer something distinct. However, as it will be the only one in the scene, it's not necessary.)

13. Drag the To Be Continued symbol from the Library onto the middle of the Stage.

14. Click frame 15, and go to Insert → Keyframe.

15. Select the keyframe you just created, and open the Property Inspector (Window → Properties).

16. Choose Alpha from the Color drop-down menu, and enter **0** into the Alpha Value field.

17. Now, click the first keyframe in the layer and go to Insert → Create Motion Tween. This creates the fade-in text effect.

Congratulations, you've completed the final scene in the animation! To view the entire animation, select Control → Test Movie.

    If you want to have the animation stop at the end (instead of simply looping over and over), add a stop( ) frame action. To learn more about frame actions, see Chapter 12.

PART IV

Scripting for Interactivity with ActionScript

One of the more elusive *terms we hear as developers of digital media is* interactivity. *This word appears frequently in books, tutorials, and articles, and is usually used to qualify or categorize the media we produce. It has become a sort of buzzword, such that in many circles,* interactive *equals* cool. *In its defense, though, many things (digital and otherwise) are interactive and require this cyber-savvy stamp of approval. One fear, however, is that the word is used so often that either it has lost its meaning or its meaning has been diluted.*

So what exactly is interactivity? *Merriam-Webster's Collegiate Dictionary defines* interactive *as "of, relating to, or being a two-way electronic communication system…that involves a user's orders (as for information or merchandise) or responses…" Well, that gets us started—a two-way communication between a person and a machine, but how does this relate to Flash? That's where you come in. As a developer of Flash movies, you are the "ghost in the machine"; you're the person responsible for determining the nature of communication between your movies and your audience. Flash movies can respond to audience input in whatever manner you define; your task is to decide how that response will be delivered. This section of the book opens the floodgates to the vast world of interactivity. Here you will begin to understand the myriad techniques that afford communication between your audience and your Flash creations.*

CHAPTER 12

Adding Interactivity with Basic Actions

Up to this point, you have used Flash as a tool for creating low-bandwidth graphics and animation. But you can also use Flash to transform these elements into dynamic components of games, nonlinear stories, and interactive interfaces. It's not difficult to add this kind of functionality to your Flash movie, and it's all done with the help of actions.

Actions are sets of commands written in ActionScript, Flash's object-oriented programming language. In the most basic sense, actions tell a Flash movie how to perform. They can range from simple ones (for example, to tell Flash to skip ahead and play a particular frame) to complex ones (for example, to perform a computation and then do something based on the result).

This chapter focuses on the simple side of actions and includes these topics:

- What ActionScript is
- Normal scripting mode
- Object and frame actions
- Mouse and clip events
- Actions for interactivity and navigation

Understanding Actions

Actions are one of the more dynamic features that Flash offers its users; they allow you to add interactivity to your Flash movie. Actions can enable your audience to control the playback of your movie with mouse clicks, keystrokes, and custom menus. They also allow you as the designer to build a movie that plays in precisely the manner you desire.

To use actions in Flash, you don't have to be a programmer. It can be helpful to understand programming concepts if you plan to get into advanced actions, but it's not essential. Flash provides a simple, intuitive interface called the Actions panel, which allows you to create actions and place them in your movie. This scheme gives you access to an entire Library of ActionScript commands and involves a minimum of typing or "hand coding."

So, what is ActionScript? It's an object-oriented programming language that is native to the Flash environment. *Object-oriented* means that scripts are attached to "objects" or elements of your movie. When those objects encounter a particular event while the movie is running, their script (or action) is executed. For example:

```
on(press){
    gotoAndPlay("nextStop")
}
```

In this script, the `press` mouse event will cause the movie to jump ahead to a frame label named `"nextStop"` and continue playing from that position. Or, in more general terms, the event cues an action that changes the playback of the movie.

The relationship between events and actions is a fundamental concept of object-oriented programming. If you are new to scripting languages or have never seen any kind of programming, this may look a little weird, but don't be discouraged. As you become more familiar with actions, the syntax and structure of ActionScript will seem less cryptic.

In order to write actions for your Flash movie, you must first become familiar with the Actions panel.

Navigating the Actions Panel

The *Actions panel* is your interface for creating scripts that will be executed in a Flash movie. The panel offers two modes for composing ActionScript: Normal and Expert. *Normal mode* offers several automated features and is recommended for beginners. It allows you to add actions to a movie through a process of menu selections and drag-and-drop options. *Expert mode* is generally more appropriate for advanced users. This mode makes the Actions panel similar to a text editor and offers a great deal of flexibility when you are writing scripts.

To display the Actions panel, select Window → Actions or press the F9 key.

Many of the enhancements to Flash MX can be found in the Actions panel (see Figure 12.1). It is now equipped with several new features that make writing and editing scripts easier than ever before.

Figure 12.1

The Actions panel

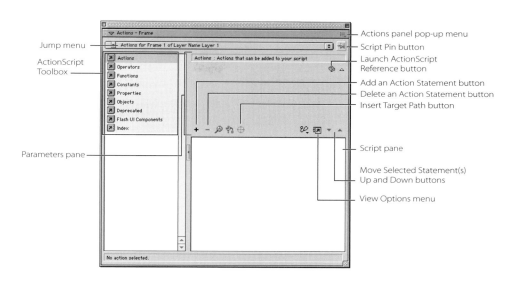

Following are descriptions of the Actions panel's features:

ActionScript Toolbox This menu is one location where you can access an ActionScript Library. Actions can be selected in this area of the panel and dragged into the Script pane.

Script pane Scripts are displayed in their entirety here. In Expert mode, this is the area where you compose ActionScript.

Parameters pane This area allows you to enter specific information (such as frame numbers or scene names) that will be plugged into a script. This option is available only while working in Normal mode. You can use the small triangle at the top right of the Actions panel to either expand or collapse the information area of the Parameters pane.

Add/Delete an Action Statement buttons Use these buttons to add or remove a statement of ActionScript. The Add button opens to a cascading series of ActionScript menus. When an item is selected, it will appear in the text box. The Delete button removes all highlighted statement(s).

Move Selected Action Statement(s) buttons Use the Up and Down buttons to change the order of statements within a script from top to bottom.

Insert Target Path button This button is used to launch the Insert Target Path dialog box. Use this option when referencing a button or Movie Clip instance along its target path.

The following Actions panel features are new in Flash MX:

Jump menu The Actions panel is context sensitive. When a scriptable element of your movie is selected, the panel's Jump menu will update its information to reflect that element. For instance, if you have a frame selected, the menu will show the frame number and both the name and number of the layer that holds the frame. If a button or Movie Clip is selected, the Jump menu will show the name of the button or Movie Clip.

View Options menu The View Options menu allows you to toggle between Normal and Expert modes and to enable the line numbering feature of the Actions panel. To read more about line numbering, see Chapter 14.

Launch ActionScript Reference button This handy button gives you access to Flash MX's built-in ActionScript reference. Click it, and the Reference panel will appear. To read more about the features of the Reference panel, see Chapter 14.

Script Pin button In previous versions of Flash, the Actions panel displayed only the script for the currently selected frame or symbol. Now, with the Script Pin button, you can "stick" a script to the panel. This is the digital equivalent of a pushpin cork board: Once you pin a script to the panel, it will remain there. This feature allows you to make one script viewable at all times while selecting other objects in your movie.

Scripting in Normal Mode

As mentioned earlier, the Actions panel offers two modes for writing ActionScript: Normal and Expert. Depending on your personal preference and level of comfort with the language, you may decide that one works better for you and your way of working in Flash. Table 12.1 shows the basic differences between the two modes of operation.

Table 12.1

Capabilities of Normal and Expert Modes

CAPABILITIES	NORMAL MODE	EXPERT MODE
Supports drag-and-drop from the ActionScript Toolbox.	Yes	Yes
Use the Parameters pane to enter script information.	Yes	No
Add/Delete a Statement buttons are fully functional.	Yes	Add Statement button only
Move Selected Statements buttons are fully functional.	Yes	No
Insert Target Path button is available.	Yes	Yes
Jump menu is fully functional.	Yes	Yes
Script Pin button is fully functional.	Yes	Yes

Generally, Expert mode puts more of the responsibility in the hands of the designer. There are fewer features, but there is also greater flexibility to write scripts in exactly the way you wish. For more information on Expert mode, see Chapter 14.

Normal mode is comparatively limiting because everything is done through menu selections. It offers a more automated approach, however. Normal mode requires less knowledge of the ActionScript language and involves a minimal amount of typing. If you are new to Action-Script, it's probably best that you begin your career as an "actionscripter" in Normal mode.

Feeling undecided? If so, you are in luck. Provided that your scripts are free of errors, Flash enables you to switch between modes whenever necessary.

To set the Actions panel so that you are working in Normal mode:

1. Select Window → Actions to display the Actions panel.

2. Do one of the following:

   - Click the Actions panel pop-up menu in the upper-right corner of the panel to display the menu, and select Normal Mode from the menu.

   - Press Cmd+Shift+N (Mac) or Ctrl+Shift+N (Windows).

   - Click the View Options menu above the Script pane and choose Normal Mode.

Working with Object Actions

Actions can be attached to two kinds of objects in Flash: buttons and Movie Clips. The attached action will be executed when the object receives an event message. For buttons, these messages generally come in the form of mouse interaction or other kinds of user input. Movie Clip event messages revolve around any changes or interactions that happen to the clip itself. When you attach an action and write an ActionScript, you specify the event trigger for each object.

Actions are attached to buttons and Movie Clips because they are the interactive components of your Flash movie. As objects, they can receive mouse clicks, data, and other kinds of information while the movie is running. The structure that you create with objects and their attached actions will determine the way your audience interacts with your movie.

It's important to remember that in Flash, button and MovieClip objects are stored in the Library as *symbols*. As symbols, they are unique. Each time they are used in your movie, they stand alone as an individual occurrence, or *instance,* of the symbol. (For details about symbols and instances, see Chapter 7.)

You can think of an instance as a copy of a symbol. Any changes made to an instance will not affect the original symbol or any other instances of that symbol. This characteristic remains true when you attach actions to a symbol instance. Any actions applied to an instance are available only at the time the instance occurs in a movie. This means that actions remain exclusive to the instance where they are attached.

However, in order for any actions to be executed, they must first be triggered by some kind of event in the movie. In ActionScript (and many other object-oriented languages), these events are called *handlers*.

Event Handlers

Object-oriented languages work in a cause-and-effect manner, where an action is the "effect" or the result that a script produces, and an event handler is the "cause" that pulls the trigger. For example, consider the following script:

```
on(thisEvent){
    doAnAction( );
}
```

Anyone who has had even the slightest exposure to ActionScript knows immediately that this code is object-oriented fiction. There is no handler named `thisEvent`, and there is certainly no action called `doAnAction`. But what this bit of imaginary code provides is a simple constructor for the sequence of events and actions. The event handler is almost always the first statement. The name of the handler is preceded by the word *on,* which can be interpreted as "when the following event occurs…" The handler creates the first part of a sentence that will tell your Flash movie to do something. That something is filled in by the action. The entire script can be better understood in sentence form: "When the following event occurs, `doAnAction`." There are many different kinds of event handlers in ActionScript, and we will discuss the specifics of each later in this chapter.

You should now know what a handler is, but it's also important to understand the event itself, and when and how it occurs in the context of the movie. As a designer or developer of interactive media, you need to know how each handler will affect the way your audience will experience your movie. If you were creating an interactive music mixer in Flash, what mouse-event handler would you want to use for buttons to turn the tracks off and on—a mouse button press or a mouse button release? Our vote would be for a press event. Why? Well, because we are talking about a music mixer. And when you deal with a music mixer, you want to be sure that the person playing it can sync the audio tracks and maintain a steady beat the entire time. The press event is easier to time because it's similar to tapping your hands on a tabletop or hitting a drum. The press event is more like actually playing an instrument.

With thoughtful planning and consideration, it's simple to choose the event handlers that will allow your actions to execute in the best way possible.

Working with Frame Actions

As you've probably guessed, frame actions are actions that are attached to a frame in your Flash movie. Specifically, frame actions are attached to a special kind of frame called a *keyframe.* Keyframes are used to signify important changes in the Flash movie, for both animation and actions. (To read more about keyframe concepts and animation, see Chapter 9.)

When an action is attached to a keyframe, the frame shows a small letter *a* in the Timeline (see Figure 12.2).

You attach actions to frames to cause your movie to play back in a particular manner. Take, for example, the following action:

```
gotoAndPlay(1);
```

If you attached this action to frame 10 of a Flash movie, it would create a playback loop. When the movie reached frame 10, it would immediately be sent back to frame 1

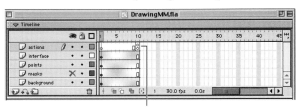

Figure 12.2

Frame action in the Timeline

Keyframe with an attached icon in frame 10

and told to continue playing. The cycle would persist until another action told the movie to either stop playing or do something else.

The greatest difference you will notice between object actions and frame actions is the absence of an event handler. With frame actions, the event handler is assumed. These actions require no specific handler because they are executed when the frame is played in the Flash movie.

Using Actions

Now that we have discussed the basic concepts involving actions, we can move on to the good part: implementing them in your Flash movie. To use actions in your movie, you must attach them to either an object or a frame. This is done through a simple process of selecting the object or frame, choosing the action you want to use, and then defining any parameters that the action requires. Any actions that you attach will affect only the instance of an object symbol or the single frame containing the action.

You use actions to control your movie so that it behaves exactly as you want. Actions can be used to control interactivity, to "listen" for user input, and to control the flow and direction of movie playback—just about anything that affects the way your movie is presented to the audience. Actions make Flash less of an animation program and more of an authoring environment for interactive media applications. Here are just a few possibilities that actions can offer your Flash movie:

- Create complex, interactive navigation
- Change the quality of movie playback
- Link to HTML pages on the Internet and communicate with server-side applications
- Communicate with host applications or other Flash movies
- Play additional movies within the host movie

Attaching Object Actions

Attaching an action to either a button object or a MovieClip object is a fairly simple and straightforward process. Here are just a few things to keep in mind along the way:

- You must first select an object in the Timeline (or on the Stage) before you can attach an action to it. If you call upon the Actions panel and have no object selected, all the actions will be unavailable.
- Actions are attached to an instance of a button or Movie Clip symbol; all other instances of the object will be left untouched.
- It's important to test an action after it has been attached. In editing mode, only simple frame actions (like `gotoAndPlay`) will work properly. To test an action, you must test your movie. Select Control → Test Movie and try out the newly applied action. (For more information on testing movies, see Chapter 28.)

Here are the basic steps for attaching an action to an object in Normal mode:

1. Select the object in the Timeline or on the Stage.

2. Choose Window → Actions from the menu bar or press F9.

3. The Actions panel appears. Select the following:

    An action   Choose from the list of actions in the ActionScript Toolbox.

    Action parameters   Select any information needed for the action in the Parameters pane.

An event handler   Each action will have a default handler. If necessary, you can change it in the Parameters pane.

To learn how to attach specific actions and define their parameters, skip ahead in this chapter to the section titled "Using Actions for Basic Movie Navigation and Interactivity."

Mouse Events

When you attach an action to a button object in Normal scripting mode, Flash automatically assigns a mouse-event handler to the action. This handler determines what event within the movie will execute the action(s) contained in the script. In most cases, the default handler provided by Flash will do the trick, but there may be times when you must change the mouse event to accommodate a particular kind of interaction.

To set or change the mouse-event handler for an action:

1. Select the button that either needs an action or needs to be changed.

2. Open the Actions panel and do either of the following:

    • If you need to set the mouse event, select the on action from the Actions → Movie Control category of the Actions panel.

    • If you need to change the mouse event for an action that already exists, click the event in the ActionScript text box.

There are four ways to choose actions while scripting in Normal mode. You can either double-click the desired action, grab the action from the ActionScript Toolbox and drag it to the text box, click the Add (+) button and select the action from the cascading menus, or type the action's key command. To display the key commands in the ActionScript Toolbox, select View Esc Shortcut Keys from the Actions panel pop-up menu.

3. The Parameters pane displays a list of the various Action-Script mouse-event handlers. Check the box next to your handler of choice, and your script will be updated. Notice in Figure 12.3 how the Parameters pane lists events when the handler is selected in the text box.

Following are the names and descriptions of the Action-Script mouse-event handlers:

Press The press event cues an action when the mouse button is pressed while the cursor is over the button object.

Release The release event cues an action when the mouse button is released while the cursor is over the button object. Release is the default mouse event.

Release Outside The releaseOutside event cues an action when the mouse button is released and the cursor is *not* over the button object.

Key Press The keyPress event doesn't involve the mouse at all. It is executed when the key listed in the adjacent field is pressed.

Roll Over The rollOver event cues an action when the cursor moves over (or within) the button object.

Roll Out The rollOut event cues an action when the cursor moves away from (or leaves) the button object.

Drag Over The dragOver event can be confusing at first. It involves a combination of two different mouse behaviors, a drag and a rollover. The sequence goes like this: The mouse is clicked over the button; the mouse is dragged outside of the button; the action is finally cued when the mouse is dragged back over the button.

Drag Out The dragOut event cues an action when the mouse is clicked over the button object and dragged outside of the button.

Remember that any of these event handlers can be used to cue multiple actions in a single script. Additionally, any one object can have more than one handler attached to it. For example:

```
on(press){
    gotoAndPlay(1);
}
on(release){
    gotoAndPlay(2);
}
```

Figure 12.3

An event handler selected in the Actions panel

In this script, a button tells a movie to play at frame 1 while the mouse is pressed, and then go to frame 2 when the mouse is released.

For a sample movie that demonstrates each handler in context, see the movie `HandlerMan` `.swf` on this book's companion CD-ROM.

Movie Clip Events

A Movie Clip is another kind of object that can have actions assigned to it. Because Movie Clips can behave differently from buttons in your Flash movie, they have their own unique handler to cue actions. The Movie Clip handler is called `onClipEvent`. When you select an action for a Movie Clip, Flash automatically inserts a default event handler to cue the action. But unlike the mouse-event handlers we saw earlier, the `onClipEvent` handler takes an argument that specifies what kind of clip event will trigger the action. The structure for `onClipEvent` is as follows:

```
onClipEvent(someMovieEvent){
    doAction(s);
}
```

In this example, `someMovieEvent` represents an argument to be filled by any of a number of Movie Clip–related events. The argument is there to more clearly define the handler. You may use any of the following possibilities to satisfy the `someMovieEvent` `argument:`

Load The `load` event is cued when the Movie Clip is first called to the Stage or is present in the current frame of the Timeline.

Unload The `unload` event is cued in the next possible frame after a Movie Clip is taken out of the Timeline or removed from the Stage.

EnterFrame The `enterFrame` event is cued as each frame of the Movie Clip is played.

MouseMove The `mouseMove` event is cued whenever the mouse is moved.

MouseDown The `mouseDown` event is cued when the mouse is pressed and the cursor is over any portion of the movie's Stage.

MouseUp The `mouseUp` event is cued when the mouse is released and the cursor is over any portion of the movie's Stage.

KeyDown The `keyDown` event is cued when a key is pressed. To monitor keystrokes, refer to the Key object and its methods in the ActionScript Reference section of this book.

KeyUp The `keyUp` event is cued when a key is released. To monitor keystrokes, refer to the Key object and its methods in the ActionScript Reference section.

Data The `data` event is executed whenever a Movie Clip receives data via the `loadVariables` or `loadMovie` action.

To set or change the event handler for a Movie Clip:

1. Select the clip to which you want to attach an action or that has an action that needs to be changed.

2. Open the Actions panel and do either of the following:

    • If you need to set the clip event, select the `onClipEvent` action from the Actions → Movie Clip Control category of the Actions panel.

    • If you need to change the clip event for an action that already exists, click the event in the ActionScript text box.

3. The Parameters pane displays a list of the various Movie Clip event handlers. Check the box next to your handler of choice, and your script will be updated.

Flash MX offers another way of assigning actions to buttons and Movie Clips. By using the events of the MovieClip and Button objects, you can assign action(s) in a single script, rather than attach multiple scripts to each instance individually. To read more about event handler methods for buttons and Movie Clips, see Chapter 16.

Attaching Frame Actions

Frame actions are another kind of ActionScript you can use in a Flash movie to control the way it plays back. When a keyframe with an attached action is encountered in the Timeline, that action is executed and the movie reacts accordingly. For more specifics on frame actions, refer to the section "Working with Frame Actions" earlier in this chapter.

Frame actions can be used within Movie Clips as well in the main Timeline. They are especially useful for creating internal Movie Clip loops.

To attach a frame action:

1. Select a keyframe where you wish to attach the action. If no keyframe is available, Flash will automatically attach the action to the first available keyframe to the left (earlier) in the Timeline. If you need to insert a keyframe, choose Insert → Keyframe.

2. With a keyframe selected, choose Window → Actions or press F9 to display the Actions panel.

3. To select an action, do one of the following:

    • Double-click an action from the Actions section of the Toolbox.

    • Drag an action from the Toolbox to the text box.

    • Select an action from the Add (+) menu.

    • Type a keystroke for the desired action. (For a list of Action keystrokes, see the ActionScript Reference section of this book.)

4. Make any necessary adjustments to the action by entering values in the Parameters pane. Not all actions require parameters; if the Parameters pane is collapsed, you can expand it by clicking the small triangle in the upper-right corner of the panel.

5. If necessary, repeat steps 3 and 4 to attach additional actions.

6. Frame actions require no event handler, since each action is executed when the frame is played in the Timeline. To test your actions, select Control → Test Movie.

Using Actions for Basic Movie Navigation and Interactivity

In the Actions category of the ActionScript Toolbox, you will find several subcategories of actions to control various aspects of movie playback. We have discussed the particulars of attaching an action to different elements of your movie; let's now focus on what some of those actions can do.

With the release of Flash MX, the organization of the Actions panel has changed significantly. The once-familiar Basic Actions category of previous Flash releases has been reorganized into a more comprehensive structure. Consequently, this may take a little getting used to if you have recently upgraded to Flash MX. This change may make the experience of learning how to script for a Flash MX movie a little more daunting at first, but take heart! With a little investigation, you will find that all the actions you require are still available and ready to go.

Due to the new organization of the Actions panel, it may be difficult to decide where to begin your ActionScript career, especially if you are a first-time Flash user. If you are in this situation, you have come to the right place. This section of the chapter aims to give you an overview of the most important and useful actions in the language. These "essential" actions are listed according to their subcategory in the Actions section of the Actions panel.

Movie Control

gotoAndPlay() Skips to a frame or movie scene and plays at that location.

gotoAndStop() Skips to a frame or movie scene and stops at that location.

on Defines the mouse handler that will trigger an action.

play() Plays a movie.

stop() Stops a movie.

stopAllSounds() Stops audio elements in a movie.

Browser/Network

fscommand() Controls the Flash player.

getURL() Links to a URL.

loadMovie() Loads other Flash movies.

unloadMovie() Unloads other Flash movies.

Movie Clip Control

setProperty() Sets the attributes of a Movie Clip: dimensions, position, and so on.

onClipEvent() Defines the clip event handler that will trigger an action.

Deprecated Actions

For now (and probably forever), the following actions have been relegated to the Action-Script scrap heap. *Deprecated* means that each term is no longer the preferred syntax and has been replaced or supplemented by a newer, more flexible, more powerful action that will accomplish the same goal. Deprecated terms are still functional, but they are not always the best or most efficient means of getting something done with ActionScript. For a more detailed description of each new term, see the ActionScript Reference section of this book.

tellTarget() Controlled Movie Clips and other movies. Now use the `with` action or a target path to control a specific Movie Clip or Timeline.

toggleHighQuality() Controlled the playback quality of a movie. Now use the `_quality` property.

ifFrameLoaded() Monitored whether a frame was loaded. Now use the `_framesloaded` property. The `ifFrameLoaded()` action was used to create preloaders, simple animated loops, or movies that managed the loading of movie assets. To learn how the `_framesloaded` property can be used to create preloaders, see the Appendix, "Cool Bells and Whistles."

Skip to a Frame or Movie Scene

The `goto` action is used for navigation and allows you to skip to a frame or scene in your movie. When your movie reaches the new scene, you can tell the movie to either stop or continue playing.

To attach a `goto` action:

1. Click the button, frame, or Movie Clip instance where you plan to attach the action.

2. Select Window → Actions or press F9 to open the Actions panel.

3. In the ActionScript Toolbox, open the Actions → Movie Control section and select the `goto` action by double-clicking it or dragging it to the text box.

4. The `goto` action now appears in the text box. In the Parameters pane, specify the following options:

   • If you want the movie to continue playing when it reaches its destination, leave the default Go to and Play radio button checked. If you wish to make the movie stop when it skips ahead, select Go to and Stop. The action is immediately updated and replaced with the `gotoAndStop()` action.

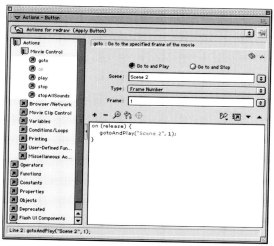

- Select the scene for your destination from the Scene pop-up menu. The Next and Previous options will take you to the first frame of either the next or previous scene. If you select either Current or a named scene in your movie, you must specify a destination frame in the scene.

- Use the Type pop-up menu to select the kind of destination. This can be either the next or previous frame, a frame number, a frame label, or an expression.

- If you select either Frame Number or Frame Label, you must enter the name of the label or the number of the frame in the Frame field. If you select Expression, you must enter a statement that can be evaluated. (For more about writing expressions, see Chapter 14.)

Set the Handler for a Mouse Event

In some cases, you may wish to declare your script's event handler first and then select the actions that will execute when it occurs. To set the event handler manually, you can use the `on` action. When you select this action, the default `on(release)` mouse-event handler appears in the text box. You can change the event and then select the actions you wish it to cue.

To attach the On Mouse Event action:

1. Click the button instance where you plan to attach the action.

2. Select Window → Actions or press F9 to open the Actions panel.

3. In the ActionScript Toolbox, open the Actions → Movie Control section and select the `on` action by double-clicking it or dragging it to the text box.

4. The default handler (`release`) can be changed in the Parameters pane. Initially, the action looks something like this:

```
on(release){
}
```

To change the handler, highlight the `on(release)` line and select from one of the handler options that appear in the Parameters pane. To read more about mouse-event handlers for buttons, see Chapter 13.

5. Once you have selected a handler, you must insert actions for it to execute. With the handler highlighted in the text box, select another action from the ActionScript Toolbox.

6. Enter any necessary values for the action in the Parameters pane.

7. To put other actions into the handler or attach additional actions, repeat steps 5 and 6. Actions can be reordered using the Up and Down arrows in the Actions panel.

Play or Stop a Movie

There are two actions to control whether or not a movie is playing. A Flash movie will play until it either runs out of frames in the Timeline or is halted by the `stop()` action. The `play()` action must be issued in order to restart the movie from wherever it was stopped. Both the `play()` and `stop()` actions can be used to control either the main Timeline or the Timeline of a Movie Clip. For more specifics on how you can control Movie Clips with ActionScript, see Chapter 16.

To attach either a `play()` or `stop()` action:

1. Click the button, frame, or Movie Clip instance where you plan to attach the action. Unless a target path is specified, an action will control only the Movie Clip or Timeline to which it is attached.

2. Select Window → Actions or press F9 to open the Actions panel.

3. In the ActionScript Toolbox, open the Actions → Movie Control section and select either the `play()` or `stop()` action.

4. If necessary, select the default event handler and change events in the Parameters pane. Frame actions to stop or play will be executed when the movie reaches the frame. If you were to create an action for an animation rewind button, it would resemble these statements:

```
on(release){
    gotoAndStop(1);
}
```

Stop Sounds

The `stopAllSounds()` action allows you to turn off the audio elements of your movie and leave any active Timeline animations untouched. This action will terminate the playback of all audible sounds when it is executed. Looping event sounds won't be heard until they are cued again. Stream sounds will play when they are encountered again in the Timeline. (For more information on cueing sounds, see Chapter 21.)

To attach the `stopAllSounds()` action:

1. Click the button, frame, or Movie Clip instance where you plan to attach the action.

2. Select Window → Actions or press F9 to open the Actions panel.

3. In the ActionScript Toolbox, open the Actions → Movie Control section and select the `stopAllSounds()` action. `stopAllSounds()` takes no arguments and will be executed when its event handler occurs or when its frame plays in the Timeline.

Link to a URL

It's possible to link to a URL from within your Flash movie using the `getURL()`action. Linking to a URL allows you to do two things. You can use Flash to hyperlink anywhere on the Web and load a URL into a browser window. You can also use the action to send variables to a source found at the particular URL, such as a Director movie, CGI script, or other kind of server-side script.

To attach the `getURL()`action:

1. Click the button, frame, or Movie Clip instance where you plan to attach the action.

2. Select Window → Actions or press F9 to open the Actions panel.

3. In the ActionScript Toolbox, open the Actions → Browser/Network section and select the `getURL()`action. This action has three parameters that must be specified: URL, Window, and Variables.

4. URL is a parameter that defines the URL to which you will link. You can enter either a relative path or an absolute path to the link. An absolute path includes the entire URL, such as `http://www.myflashlink.com/myfile.html`. A relative path tells the movie to link within the file structure where the Flash movie is saved—for example, `currentfolder/folder1/folder0`.

   It's also possible to use an expression that produces a value for the URL. To use an expression, check the box next to the URL field and enter the information. (For more specifics about writing expressions, see Chapter 14.)

5. Window tells the web browser where to load the URL. You can enter a specific frame or window name in the field, enter an expression that produces a value for the window, or choose a default from the pop-up menu:

   - `_self` targets the window and frame where the movie is currently sitting.

   - `_blank` targets a new browser window.

   - `_parent` targets the current window and replaces only the frameset where the movie is currently sitting. This option is best if you have nested framesets and you want to retain that structure.

   - `_top` targets the current window and replaces all framesets with the new URL. Use `_top` if your movie is in a frame and you want the URL to fill the entire browser window.

For example, to load a relative URL named `myinfo.html` in a new browser window when a button object is clicked, your script would look like this:

```
on(release){
    getURL("myinfo.html", "_blank");
}
```

6. Use the Variables pop-up menu to send variables to the URL to which you wish to link.

- *Don't Send* is the default and should be used for standard links where there is no transfer of data.

- *Send Using GET* will attach a few variables to the URL and is best for small transfers of information.

- *Send Using POST* is best for larger amounts of information.

Control the Flash Player

The `fscommand()` action is used to control the Flash Player when it's running as a stand-alone application or projector. `fscommand()` can also be used to pass information to an application that is hosting the movie, such as a web browser or a computer's operating system.

To control the stand-alone Flash Player:

1. Click the button, frame, or Movie Clip instance where you plan to attach the action.

2. Select Window → Actions or press F9 to open the Actions panel.

3. In the ActionScript Toolbox, open the Actions → Browser/Network section and select the `fscommand()` action.

4. In the Parameters pane, choose from the following options in the drop-down menu:

Fullscreen A setting of True will allow your projector to fill the entire screen and show no menu. False will play the projector in Normal mode in its own window.

Allowscale This controls the ability to scale the animation. True makes the animation scalable; False preserves it at the original size.

Showmenu The stand-alone Flash Player has a menu bar and offers Ctrl+click (Mac) and right-click (Win) menu options. When this value is set to True, these options are available; when it's False, they are not.

Quit This command causes the projector file to close.

Trapallkeys This feature, when set to True, disables any keyboard input. It's great for limiting all user input to the mouse-enabled controls you have created for the movie. If you plan to use this and set `showmenu` to False, be sure to include an element that issues a `quit` command.

Exec This opens and runs an application from within the projector. Enter a path to the application in the arguments field.

For more information about `fscommand()`, stand-alone projectors, and how they can be used for CD-ROM development, refer to Chapter 29.

Scripting for Multiple Movies

As a theater production brings different cast members onto the stage, you can call additional movies to play in a Flash production. To do this, you use two actions: Load Movie and Unload Movie. Through the process of loading and unloading movies, Flash can string together a series of movies, or layer one on top of another to create different playback permutations. Additionally, it allows you to play several movies in a single browser window. Rather than reload the browser when you need to link to a different movie, you can simply replace one movie with another. This technique produces a much smoother presentation of the content.

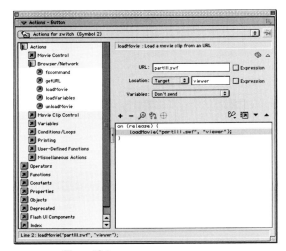

Figure 12.4

A loadMovie() action in the Actions panel

LOADING A MOVIE

To load additional movies in the Flash Player:

1. Click the button, frame, or Movie Clip instance where you plan to attach the action.

2. Select Window → Actions or press F9 to open the Actions panel.

3. In the ActionScript Toolbox, open the Actions → Browser/Network section and select the loadMovie() action (see Figure 12.4).

4. In the Parameters pane, use the URL field to enter the name of the SWF file you wish to load. It can be helpful to keep all movies (the main file and others to be loaded) in the same folder.

5. Choose either Level or Target from the Location pop-up menu.

6. If you chose Level, you must enter a level number:

   • 0 is the default level and the level of the movie that was loaded first. The level 0 movie sets the frame rate, background color, and size for all other loaded movies. If a new movie is loaded at level 0, it will replace the original movie and unload all other levels.

   • To load a new level, select the next available positive number that is greater than zero.

   • To replace a loaded movie, determine its level number and load a new movie at that same level.

7. If you chose Target in step 5, you must enter the name of a Movie Clip to be replaced by the loaded movie. The new movie will be positioned with its upper-left corner over the registration point of the Movie Clip. Newly loaded movies will also be given the attributes of the targeted Movie Clip instance (scale, rotation, and so on).

8. The Variables menu defaults to Don't Send. This will prohibit any variables from passing to the loaded movie. However, if you want to transfer variables, you can use either GET or POST. For a description of these methods, refer to the earlier discussion of the `getURL()` action.

UNLOADING A MOVIE

To unload a movie in the Flash Player:

1. Click the button, frame, or Movie Clip instance where you plan to attach the action.

2. Select Window → Actions or press F9 to open the Actions panel.

3. In the ActionScript Toolbox, open the Actions → Browser/Network section and select the `unloadMovie()` action.

4. In the Parameters pane, select either Level or Target from the Location pop-up menu.

5. If you selected Level, you must enter the level number containing the movie you wish to unload.

6. Target will unload the specified Movie Clip instance. Enter an instance name or target path to the instance you wish to unload.

> You may notice that the `loadMovie()` and `unloadMovie()` actions are sometimes listed as `loadMovieNum()` and `unloadMovieNum()`. In Normal mode, the Actions panel makes these changes for you automatically. Each action performs basically the same job but uses a different syntax, or structure, to do it. `loadMovie()` passes arguments as a string, while `loadMovieNum()` uses a number to specify a load level for the new movie. In Normal mode, `loadMovie()` is used as the default for loading movies into Movie Clip instances, and `loadMovieNum` is used for loading movies into levels. (To learn more about working with multiple Timelines, see Chapter 16.)

Set the Handler for a Movie Clip Event

In some cases, you may wish to declare a script's event handler first and then select the actions that will execute when it occurs. To set a Movie Clip event handler manually, you can use the `onClipEvent` action. When you select this action, the default `onClipEvent(load)` handler appears in the text box. You can change the event and then select the actions you wish it to cue.

To attach the `onClipEvent` event handler:

1. Select the Movie Clip instance where you plan to attach the action.

2. Select Window → Actions or press F9 to open the Actions panel.

3. In the ActionScript Toolbox, open the Actions → Movie Clip Control section and select the `onClipEvent` action.

4. The default handler (`load`) can be changed in the Parameters pane. Initially, the action looks something like this:

   ```
   onClipEvent(load){
   }
   ```

5. Once you have selected a handler, you must insert actions for it to execute. With the handler (usually the first line) highlighted in the text box, select another action from the ActionScript Toolbox.

6. Enter any necessary values for the action in the Parameters pane.

7. To put other actions into the handler or attach additional actions, repeat steps 5 and 6. Actions can be reordered using the Up and Down arrows in the Actions panel.

Control Movie Clips and Other Movies

You can control the playback of Movie Clips in your Flash movie by using the `tellTarget()` action. Although it is technically considered a deprecated term, `tellTarget()` is still very useful for controlling Movie Clips while working in Normal mode. This action can be attached to both objects and frames. For example, a button can be used to stop playing a clip, or a frame action can cue a Movie Clip to start playing.

You need to set a few things in your movie before using this action. First, you must have a Movie Clip in the movie to target. Additionally, the clip must have a unique instance name. To assign a name to a clip instance, select the instance in your movie and then choose Window → Properties to open the Properties inspector. Enter a name in the Instance Name field. You can use letters or a combination of letters and numbers. It's best to give instances meaningful names so that you can remember which Movie Clip they identify. The last condition is that a Movie Clip must be in the same frame as the element (either a frame or object) that will target it. A button in frame 1 cannot control a Movie Clip in frame 2.

To attach a `tellTarget()`action:

1. Click the button, frame, or Movie Clip instance where you plan to attach the action.

2. Select Window → Actions or press F9 to open the Actions panel.

3. In the ActionScript Toolbox, open the Actions → Deprecated section and select the `tellTarget()` action.

4. To specify the clip you wish to target, click the Insert Target Path button ⊕ in the Parameters pane. If the button is grayed out, click inside the Target field, and the button should become available.

5. The Insert Target Path dialog box appears and displays an outline of the Movie Clips in your movie.

6. For Notation, select the Dots radio button. This will define your target path using the more current dot syntax. The slash syntax is available if you are more comfortable with the older Flash 4 style.

7. The Mode setting allows you to choose which Movie Clips are displayed:

- *Relative* will show you only Movie Clips that are in the current scene. `this`, at the top of the outline, refers to the current Timeline or Movie Clip.

- *Absolute* will show every clip in the entire movie. In this mode, `_root` (at the top of the outline) shows the path to the clip from the main Timeline.

Although either mode will work, you will find that relative paths are more concise and can sometimes be easier to understand.

8. Select the clip you wish to target, and the instance name appears in the Target field. Click OK to return to the Actions panel.

9. Now that you have targeted a clip, you can insert an action that will control it. First, be sure that the `tellTarget()` action is highlighted in the text box. Then return to the Actions Toolbox and select the action(s) you would like `tellTarget()` to apply to the targeted clip. The final script for an action that stops a clip instance named "icon" would look like this:

```
on(release){
    tellTarget("icon") {
        stop();
    }
}
```

As we mentioned, the `tellTarget()` action is now deprecated but is still very useful while working in Normal mode. If you are interested in finding an alternative to this term, see "Writing ActionScript for Multiple-Timeline Movies" in Chapter 16, and the `with` action in the ActionScript Reference section.

Assign Properties to a Movie Clip

Using the `setProperty()`action, you can write scripts to manipulate the attributes or properties of a Movie Clip instance. Of course, it's possible to set the properties of a clip when you first create it, but it's more interesting (and fun for your audience) to change the clip dynamically using interactive controls such as mouse clicks or keystrokes. Remember, before you can control a Movie Clip with ActionScript, it must first have a unique instance name.

To attach the `setProperty()`action:

1. Click the button, frame, or Movie Clip instance where you plan to attach the action.

2. Select Window → Actions or press F9 to open the Actions panel.

3. In the ActionScript Toolbox, open the Actions → Movie Clip Control section and select the `setProperty()`action by double-clicking it or dragging it to the Script pane. This action has three parameters that must be specified:

   - For *Property,* choose one of the properties that is available in the drop-down menu.

   - For *Target,* enter the name of the Movie Clip instance you would like to affect. Alternately, you can use the Insert Target Path button to target the clip specifically. To learn about the Insert Target Path button, refer to steps 4 through 8 in the preceding section on the `tellTarget()` action.

   - For *Value,* assign a value that is consistent with the parameters of the property. Since most values are numeric, be sure to check the Expression box next to the Value field. To read more about the value ranges for Movie Clip properties, see the ActionScript Reference section.

Rather than using the `setProperty()` action, you can use dot syntax to target a Movie Clip directly. To learn how this is done, see Chapter 16.

Inspirational Design Model

Because there are so many excellent uses of actions on the Web today, choosing a site for an Inspirational Design Model is particularly difficult for this chapter. Actions are a cornerstone of interactive design with Flash and are an essential part of every interactive movie, animation, or game. Actions allow Flash designers to control the playback of their movie with great precision. This is an advantage in both the authoring stage and the final delivery of the movie.

For the Michael Schuster Associates site, Core Five Creative (`www.corefive.com`) built an intro animation that is run almost entirely with actions and Movie Clips. Although this technique is transparent in the final presentation of the animation (see Figure 12.5), it makes the creation of the animation much easier and increases flexibility by allowing several members of the design team to add their own Movie Clips to the piece. You can see the final animation at `www.msaarch.com`.

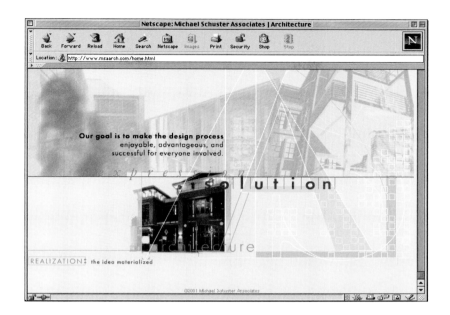

Figure 12.5

The Michael Schuster Associates intro animation by Core Five Creative

Summary

This chapter introduced you to ActionScript. You can now see how this powerful object-oriented language is a valuable asset to Flash. Not only is it useful for controlling movie playback, but it can also communicate with other movies and the Flash Player, open browser windows on the Web, and define the way your audience interacts with the movie. As you become more comfortable with actions and ActionScript, you will be able to create complex interactive environments and experiences.

CHAPTER 13

Creating Interactive Controls

At this point, you should know what actions are and should understand some of the basic components of the ActionScript language. What is missing is something to put all of this knowledge to use. Actions allow your audience to control the movie—but control it with what? Your movie needs some kind of switch or button to unlock its interactive potential.

Building controls in Flash is an essential step toward creating a movie that is both great to look at and easy to experience or play. At the most basic level, you can create simple buttons to turn a movie on or off and to skip to different sections. Flash controls can be as simple as those found on a VCR. They can also become an integral part of the overall design of your movie. As you progress to a more advanced stage, you will be able to create robust interfaces with flexible navigation options and a savvy look and feel.

In this chapter, you will learn about:

- **Button controls that are built into Flash**

- **Creating your own button controls**

- **Multilayered controllers**

- **Animated controllers**

- **Flash interfaces with multiple navigation buttons**

- **Integrated design and navigational elements**

Adding Interactivity with Simple Buttons

Flash is capable of managing complex and dynamic interactivity, but it's not always necessary to pull all the stops for your movie. Sometimes you may find that simple elements are just as effective as complex ones. Designing a movie for interactivity is no exception. For Flash developers or designers who are just learning the program or want to keep things easy, there are many options for adding interactive controls. The good news is that these options don't demand a lot of work or experience, and the results can be very satisfying.

Selecting Buttons from the Flash Common Library

Figure 13.1

The Common Library for buttons

Flash has several Common Libraries to offer its users. These Libraries include things like sounds, Movie Clips, and, yes, buttons. They are resources that are linked to the program and thus will be available every time you use Flash. The buttons in the Common Library are great for quick mock-ups or tests. Although some of the buttons in the Library may not fit your personal standards or design goals, all of them are very functional and can prove to be valuable assets in the Flash environment.

To open the button Library, select Window → Common Libraries → Buttons.fla (see Figure 13.1). This Library looks like any other in Flash. The only exception is its contents. It contains a wide assortment of buttons that are designed and ready for use in a movie.

For more information about working with Libraries and shared assets in Flash, see Chapter 7.

Figure 13.2

The Common Library folder structure

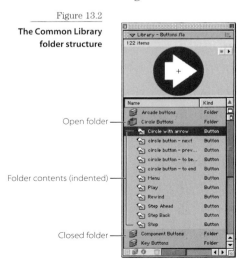

Open folder

Folder contents (indented)

Closed folder

The Library is organized with a series of individual folders that contain button *families*. Each family of buttons contains a group of graphics that originate from a common background and have a similar look and feel. This allows you to use the family as a set and maintain a consistent look for all navigational or interactive elements.

To use a Common Library button in your movie:

1. Select Window → Common Libraries → Buttons.fla to display the Library if it's not open already.

2. Open the folders within the Common Library panel to find the button you want. Folders in the panel can be opened and closed by double-clicking the folder icon (see Figure 13.2).

3. Do either of the following:

   • Drag a button from the Common Library to the main Library for your movie. If your movie Library isn't visible, you can display it by selecting Window → Library or pressing F11.

   • Drag a button from the Common Library directly to the Stage. It will automatically appear in your main movie Library.

At this point, the button is a symbol in your movie, either on the Stage or in your main Library, waiting to take the Stage.

From here, there are many different options for your button. If you put it directly onto the Stage, it becomes an instance in your movie and can have actions attached to it. To learn more about attaching actions to a button, see Chapter 12. If you would like to edit the button and customize it to better fit your movie, see the section "Editing Buttons in Your Movie" later in this chapter.

Creating Your Own Buttons

Although using buttons in the Common Library is convenient, you will likely want to create some of your own. After all, this is why we're here; working in Flash is fun! But beyond the fun factor, the process of creating your own buttons has some specific advantages as well. The greatest of these, of course, is that with some effort, you will get exactly what you want. A custom button can be built to your exact specifications so that it fits the specific design goals of your movie. Interactive controls are a big part of a Flash movie, and it's important to get them right.

So, in Flash, what exactly is a button? It is a short, interactive movie with only four frames. Each of the frames represents a different appearance, or "state," of the button that reflects user interaction. These different states are saved as separate images in keyframes along the Timeline of the button movie. As you move the mouse over the button and click it, it changes states accordingly by displaying the correct keyframe image.

By making a button change appearance while it's being manipulated, you show your audience that it is more than just a graphic. The simple animation lets them know that the button is "active" in the movie and that clicking it will produce a change in your movie.

Like Movie Clips, buttons are another kind of symbol. You can create a single button and use it repeatedly. Every instance of a button will be treated independently throughout an animation or interactive movie.

The four states of a button are as follows:

Up This first state represents the appearance of the button when the cursor is not over it. This can also be considered the "inactive" state.

Over The second keyframe of the button Timeline represents the Over state. This creates the appearance of the button when the cursor is positioned over it.

Down The third keyframe of the button Timeline shows the button graphic when it is clicked.

Hit The fourth and final keyframe defines the area of the button that will respond to a mouse click. Think of the Hit state as the button's hot spot. It defines the area that must be clicked in order for the button to execute any scripts attached to it.

Table 13.1 contains illustrations and descriptions of the four states of a typical button.

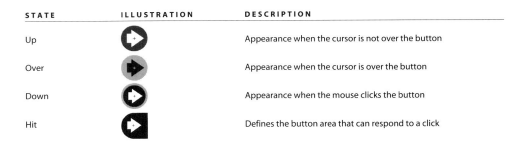

STATE	ILLUSTRATION	DESCRIPTION
Up		Appearance when the cursor is not over the button
Over		Appearance when the cursor is over the button
Down		Appearance when the mouse clicks the button
Hit		Defines the button area that can respond to a click

Table 13.1
The Four States of a Button

Now that you know a bit more about what goes into a button, you are ready to create your own. Just follow these steps:

1. Select Insert → New Symbol (Cmd/Ctrl+F8) to display the Create New Symbol dialog box.

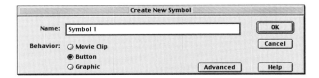

2. Choose Button as your Behavior and enter a name for the button in the Name field.

3. Click OK, and you are switched to Symbol Editing mode (see Figure 13.3). Notice that there are several changes to the appearance of Flash in this mode. The title of your symbol appears beside a button icon in the area between the Stage and the Timeline. The frames of the main Timeline disappear and are replaced by the new frames of your button. Also, the frames of the new Timeline are labeled to show the four states of your new button. The first frame for the Up state contains a blank keyframe.

Figure 13.3
The Timeline in Symbol Editing mode

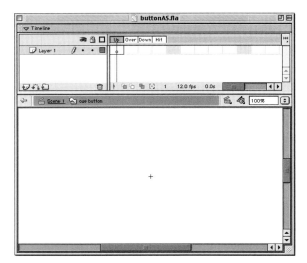

4. Create an Up state for the button by doing any one of the following:

   - Use the Flash drawing tools to create a graphic.

   - Import a graphic file and drag it onto the button's Stage.

   - Drag an instance of another graphic or Movie Clip symbol to the Stage to create an instance within a button.

   The crosshairs in the middle of the Stage represent the registration point of the button.

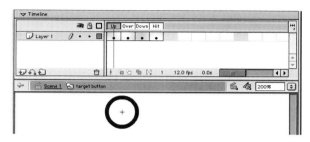

It's possible to use Movie Clips within button symbols, but you are not allowed to put a button within a button. Using a Movie Clip as part of a button creates an animated button. For more on this, see "Creating Animated Buttons" later in this chapter.

5. To create a new keyframe for the Over state, either click the Over state frame and then select Insert → Keyframe. Flash automatically duplicates the previous frame in the new keyframe.

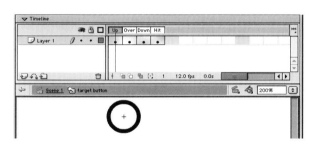

6. Make changes to the graphic in frame 2 or use any of the methods outlined above to alter the appearance of the Over state.

7. Repeat steps 5 and 6 for both the Down and Hit states.

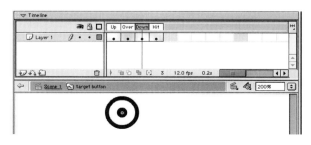

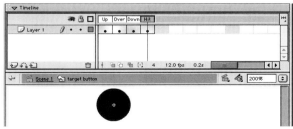

The Hit state is unique and constitutes a very important part of the button. It defines the area that will respond to any mouse clicks on the button. It's important that the Hit state has a solid graphic so that clicks don't "slip through the cracks" in the button. It's also important to be sure that the Hit state is large enough to be clicked. If it's too small, your audience may have a difficult time trying to click the right spot.

If you are creating a button that consists solely of text, the Hit state graphic is extremely important. Letters like o have "holes"; a mouse click in the middle of an o-shaped button will not be recognized if the Hit state is also shaped like an o. To avoid this potential problem, create a rectangular-shaped Hit state that is approximately the same size as the chunk of text that comprises your button. Since the button Hit state is invisible, this will not have an undesirable effect on the appearance of the button, and will make the button much easier for your audience to use.

8. With graphics for the four states in place, your button is ready to go. To leave Symbol Editing mode, either select Edit → Edit Document (Cmd/Ctrl+E) or simply click the Timeline icon for the current scene of your movie.

9. Drag your button from the Library to the Stage to create a button instance in your movie.

10. As needed, attach action(s) to the button so that it can be used to control various elements of your movie. For a discussion of basic actions, see Chapter 12. If you are interested in more advanced button actions, refer to Chapter 16.

These are the fundamental steps for creating a simple button for your Flash movie. From this point on, the possibilities are virtually limitless. For a discussion of how to add sound to a button in your movie, see Chapter 20. If you want to continue to work with your movie and explore the potential of buttons as interactive control sources, read on. In the next section, we will discuss the ins and outs of testing your buttons and making any changes or edits to their components.

Previewing, Testing, and Editing Buttons

Once you have created your buttons, it's a good idea to test them to be sure that they work properly and look the way you want. Flash offers two main techniques for testing buttons: You can work in the authoring environment or use the Test Movie command. Depending on your movie project, one technique may suit you better than the other. Whatever the case, it's a good idea to become familiar with both so that you are able to work smoothly and efficiently.

Previewing Buttons in the Flash Authoring Environment

It's possible to preview your buttons while you are working in Flash's authoring environment (also known as authoring mode). By default, Flash keeps all buttons in an inactive state while you are creating your movie. If necessary, you can activate your buttons and test them while you create the rest of the movie.

To test buttons in authoring mode, select Control → Enable Simple Buttons. A check next to the command appears, indicating that this option is turned on. To turn it off again, simply repeat the process, and buttons will be disabled.

> Working in Flash with buttons activated can sometimes be difficult. For example, it can be tricky to select a button on the Stage when it is enabled. If you need to select an activated button, you can click outside the button and drag a selection around it. Flash highlights the button with a rectangular marquee to let you know it is selected.

Testing Buttons

Previewing buttons in authoring mode gives you a rough idea of what they will look like in your final movie. However, Movie Clips won't be visible when you preview your buttons in authoring mode. Also, most actions attached to the button are disabled in this mode. To get a sneak peek at any animated buttons or actions, you must test your movie or scene. To preview animated buttons, select Control → Test Movie (Cmd/Ctrl+Return/Enter) or Control → Test Scene (Cmd/Ctrl+Option/Alt+Return/Enter). For more specifics on testing movies, see Chapter 27.

Editing Buttons in Your Movie

If a test or preview shows that a button needs some tweaking or fine-tuning, you will have to go back and edit the button. The good news is that if you have used a single button symbol over and over (meaning that you used multiple instances of the button), any changes you make to the button symbol will be updated in every instance. For more details on symbols and instances, see Chapter 7.

There are three ways to edit buttons in your Flash movie: You can edit a button on the Stage ("in place"), in Symbol Editing mode, or in a separate window. These options will achieve the same results, but you may find that one technique works better for you than the others.

To edit a button in place, do either of the following:

- Double-click the button instance.

- Ctrl+click (Mac) or right-click (Win) the instance and select Edit in Place from the context menu.

Items on the Stage will fade to the background, and the Timeline will change appearance to reveal the button Timeline and keyframes. This option allows you to edit the button and see how it changes in relation to other items around it on the Stage.

You can edit a button in Symbol Editing mode in one of four ways:

- Select the name of the button you would like to edit from the Edit Symbols menu 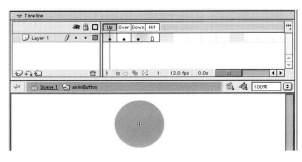 in the information bar between the Stage and the Timeline.

- Ctrl+click (Mac) or right-click (Win) the instance and select Edit from the context menu.

- Select the symbol instance on the Stage and choose Edit → Edit Symbols from the menu bar.

- In the Library panel, either double-click the symbol's button icon or highlight the symbol and choose Edit from the Library options menu.

To edit a button in a separate window, Ctrl+click (Mac) or right-click (Win) the instance and select Edit in New Window from the context menu. The new window will open directly over the window that contains your main Timeline.

All these options reveal basically the same thing: the button's Timeline and access to the four button states and keyframes. When you see this, you are free to make any necessary changes to the button. You can make changes using any of the tools available to you in Flash, by adding Movie Clip instances to the button and by importing bitmap graphics or other external files. Remember that any changes made here will affect all instances of the button in your movie.

When you are finished editing your button, do *one* of the following:

- Select Edit → Edit Document (Cmd/Ctrl+E).

- Click either the Scene button or the Back button (Figure 13.4) in the information bar between the Stage and the Timeline to return to the main Timeline of a particular scene.

For more information on moving around quickly and efficiently in the main Timeline, see Chapter 2.

Creating Complex Buttons

So far, we have covered all the basic steps for creating buttons and using them in your movie. With these essential skills, you are ready to move on to the next level: creating complex buttons and designing them to support the theme or concept of your movie. These buttons do more than serve as navigational icons. They allow you to give the audience a clear means of moving through your movie while offering visual interest and punch. Once you start to explore the possibilities outlined here, you will see the benefit that these techniques can bring to your Flash productions.

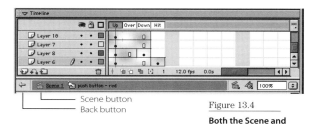

Scene button
Back button

Figure 13.4

Both the Scene and Back buttons will take you from Symbol Editing mode to the main Timeline.

Creating Multilayered Buttons

Buttons are not only controllers in your movie—they are graphics that have an impact on its overall look and feel. This presents you with several choices. On one hand, you can try to make the button as unobtrusive as possible, so that it is transparently woven into the fabric of your movie. On the other hand, you can play it up and allow the button to make a bold visual statement.

In the next example, you will see how to create a graphically dynamic button with components on several different layers. You can find the source files for this example on the companion CD-ROM. Look for the file named `multilayer.fla` in the Chapter 13 folder.

To create a multilayered button:

1. Select Insert → New Symbol or press Cmd/Ctrl+F8.

2. The Create New Symbol dialog box appears. Choose Button as the Behavior and give the symbol a name. Then click OK.

3. Flash automatically jumps into Symbol Editing mode. You will see the button Timeline and the Up, Over, Down, and Hit state keyframes.

4. The beauty of the multilayered button is that each graphic layer is independent. One layer can change without affecting the others. To add another layer to the button Timeline, select Insert → Layer or click the Insert Layer button ⟨⟩ in the Timeline. The new layer appears in the Timeline with an empty keyframe in the Up state frame.

5. Begin by drawing a graphic on Layer 1 to represent the Up state of the button. When you are finished, click Layer 2 and draw an additional portion of the graphic. Because each part is on its own layer, you have more flexibility to change the various states of the button.

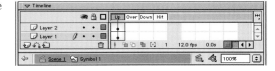

6. If necessary, repeat steps 4 and 5 to create additional layers for the button.

7. When the Up state is complete, click Layer 1 and either select Insert → Keyframe to add a keyframe for the Over state. When you do this, Flash automatically inserts a new frame in Layer 2 and duplicates the Up state graphics in the new frames (below left).

8. Draw a new graphic for the Over state of Layer 1 or make changes to the duplicated frame as needed. Then click frame 2 of Layer 2, insert a new keyframe, and adjust this image as needed.

9. Repeat the process outlined in steps 7 and 8 to create the appearance for the button's Down state (below right).

10. In this example, you can see that the button is a tomato. When it's rolled over, both the stem and the fruit change color. Then, when the tomato is clicked, it is squished and changed to a dark color. You can manipulate each element (stem and fruit) separately because each layer is autonomous and will not directly affect the other.

11. Insert a new keyframe in Layer 1 to complete the button and give it a Hit state. Because the Hit state isn't visible, it's necessary to put a Hit state keyframe in only one layer.

12. When you have finished creating the button, select Edit → Edit Document to return to the main Timeline. To preview your button, select Control → Enable Simple Buttons. This option will allow you to see how the multilayered button looks when manipulated by the cursor.

Creating Animated Buttons

You have seen how multilayered buttons provide a new graphic dimension to your button controls. With each element on a separate layer, you can edit and control them independently. This technique also opens the door to a variety of additional possibilities that can add yet another layer of interest to your button symbols.

Buttons are by default a kind of animation. When you roll over them, there is a graphic change. When you click them, there is another change. It's not a linear animation but rather one that demonstrates that the graphic is somehow significant; the animation begs you to click it. We can take this idea a step further by creating animated buttons. Such buttons use a Movie Clip or small animation to represent one of their states. Generally, this is done at the Over state, although it is certainly not a requirement. If a Movie Clip were used for the Up state, the animation could be distracting. If it were used as the Down state, there is a chance that the Movie Clip animation wouldn't be seen at the instant the button is clicked. The Over state presents the animation when the button is active (rolled over). It grabs your attention and adds more to the rollover effect than just a change of graphic.

In the next example, you will see how to create an animated button by using a Movie Clip. You can find this example on the CD-ROM. Look for the file named `animatedButton.fla` in the Chapter 13 folder.

To create an animated button:

1. Create a graphic on the Stage to use as your button. When it is complete, drag around it to select the entire graphic, and either choose Insert → Convert to Symbol or press F8. Select the Graphic Behavior and give the symbol a name in the Create New Symbol dialog box. Click OK.

2. The symbol appears in the Library. Delete the symbol from the main Timeline Stage.

   This graphic symbol will be used as the starting point for each component of our button. We use a symbol so that instances of the symbol can be used repeatedly in the button animation.

3. Select Insert → New Symbol or press Cmd/Ctrl+F8. This time, choose the Movie Clip Behavior, give the clip a name, and click OK when you are finished. Flash takes you immediately to Movie Clip Editing mode.

4. You can now create the animation that will be used as the Over state of your button. Drag the graphic symbol from the Library to the Stage while you are in Movie Clip mode. Use the arrow keys to nudge the symbol so that its registration point lines up with the registration point of the new Movie Clip.

Lining up the registration points is a good idea because you will use the graphic symbol several times in this process. This ensures that that each instance of the symbol is positioned in exactly the same place.

Alternatively, you can use the Align panel (Cmd/Ctrl+K) and have Flash handle the registration for you automatically. To learn more about working with the Align panel, see Chapter 6.

5. Create the animation using keyframes, tweening, and any other techniques that are available to you in Flash (see Figure 13.5). If you need to change the symbol, you can select Modify → Break Apart (Cmd/Ctrl+B) and edit its characteristics directly. For more information on keyframes and animation concepts, see Chapter 9.

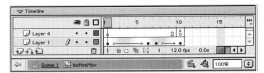

Figure 13.5

The Timeline for the Movie Clip in the file animatedButton .fla. Notice that there is a 40% Alpha effect at keyframe 7. Also, there is a stop() action in frame 10 to prevent the clip from looping when the cursor is over the button.

6. When you have finished creating your Movie Clip, select Edit → Edit Document and return to the main Timeline.

7. At this point, you are ready to create the button. You have a graphic and you have a Movie Clip; now is the time to bring it all together. Select Insert → New Symbol, and the Create New Symbol dialog box appears once again. This time, choose the Button Behavior and enter a name in the Name field.

8. Click OK, and Flash jumps into Button Editing mode.

9. Drag the graphic symbol to the Stage and use the arrow keys to nudge it into place so that the registration points line up. Notice that the symbol creates a keyframe for the Up state of the button.

> Nudging an object with the arrow keys moves it one pixel at a time. To move an object 10 pixels at a time, press the Shift key while nudging with the arrows.

10. After the Up state graphic is in place, you can move on to the Over state. Select Insert → Keyframe to insert a new keyframe. The keyframe appears in frame 2 as the 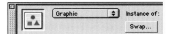 Over state graphic. Flash automatically copies the Up state graphic into the new keyframe. You will need to swap this with the Movie Clip you created in step 5. Select the graphic in the Over state frame and then click the Swap Symbols button on the Properties inspector.

    The Swap Symbol dialog box appears and allows you to exchange graphics for the Movie Clip symbol. Be sure that the Properties inspector displays Movie Clip in the Symbol Behavior menu after you have swapped symbols; otherwise, the clip will not animate. For specifics on swapping symbols, see Chapter 7.

> You may notice that the button in animatedButton.fla has multiple layers for both the Over and Down states. This was the choice for that particular button. Animated buttons may have just one layer or take advantage of several.

11. The bulk of the work is now over. You have an Up state and an animated Over state. The next step is to add a Down state to your button. Create a keyframe for the Down state in frame 3 of the button Timeline. Flash will duplicate the contents of the previous keyframe in the new frame. Using any of the previously described techniques, insert a graphic for the Down state in this keyframe.

12. Repeat the procedure in step 11 to insert a graphic for the Hit state of the button in frame 4. With keyframes and graphics for each of the four states, your animated button is now ready to go.

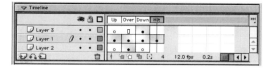

13. Select Edit → Edit Document (Cmd/Ctrl+E) to return to the main Timeline and save your movie. Since we used a Movie Clip, Flash won't give us a true preview of our animated button in authoring mode. To see the button in action, add an instance of the animated button to the movie; then select Control → Test Movie and give it a spin.

An animated button is a button like any other. Once it's in your Library as a button symbol, you are free to use it throughout your movie. You can attach actions to instances of the animated button and use it as a means of controlling other movie elements and playback.

Creating Multiple Button Interfaces

One thing you may have noticed with buttons in Flash is that after you click them, you can sometimes still see the Over state of the button symbol. At first, this can look like an error in your movie, but since your cursor is still over the button, Flash is technically doing what it should.

It's possible to create a button so that this doesn't happen. It's also possible to use the technique to create multiple button interfaces or navigation bars where any single button can take you to a new section of the movie and serve as a kind of "bookmark" when you arrive there.

In the next example, you will learn how to create a navigation bar with two buttons. Although it's a simple task, the concepts presented here can be used to build larger and more complicated interfaces. You can find the files for this example on the CD-ROM. Look for the file named navBar.fla in the Chapter 13 folder.

> Although this is a simple task, there are many steps to ensure consistency in the navigation bar. Be sure to follow the steps carefully!

To create a navigation bar with multiple buttons:

1. First, you must create a button. One button is enough for an entire navigation bar, although you may opt to use more in your own projects. Turn back in this chapter to revisit the process of making a simple button. Once it is complete, return to the main Timeline of your movie.

2. Now that you have a button, you can start to build a navigation bar. Use the Rectangle tool to draw a box that fills the width of your movie, making sure that the box is tall enough to accommodate your button.

3. You are ready to add your button now. Select Insert → Layer to add a layer to your movie Timeline. It isn't necessary to put items on different layers, but it can be helpful in keeping your movie organized. Name the new layer "buttons." For more details on organizing and working with layers, see Chapter 8.

4. Drag your button from the Library to the left corner of the navigation bar graphic and be sure that when you drop it into place, you are on the buttons layer (below left).

5. Repeat step 4 to create a second instance of the button, only this time, drop the button farther to the right of the first button instance. These two buttons will serve as the controls for the navigation bar.

6. Next, you need to enter some text so that you can distinguish which button will connect with which part of the movie. Create a new layer (select Insert → Layer) and name it "text." Then use the Text tool to enter text as follows(below right):

   - Beside the first button, create a text box and enter **Scene 1** in a small point size.

   - Enter **Scene 2** in a separate text box beside the second button.

   - In a large point size, type **Scene 1** somewhere near the middle of the Stage. This will serve as a temporary marker to help you when testing the navigation bar buttons.

   For more details about using the Text tool, see Chapter 5.

7. The final step in setting up the navigation bar involves adding a frame action so that the scenes will play correctly. Select Insert → Layer and name the new layer "actions." Click the keyframe in this new layer and select Window → Actions (F9) to display the Actions panel. Drag a `stop()`action from the Actions → Movie Control category to the text box.

8. All the basic elements for our scene and navigation bar are now set. With these in place, we can create an additional scene for the movie.

9. Select Window → Scene (Shift+F2) to display the Scene panel. Here you can duplicate the first scene so that you have two identical copies. Click the Duplicate Scene button at the bottom of the Scene panel (see Figure 13.6).

   Flash names the duplicate "Scene 1 copy." Double-click the name in the Scene panel and rename the scene "Scene 2."

Figure 13.6

The Scene panel

Duplicate Scene button

There is a definite advantage to duplicating scenes when you create a navigation bar. Because the new scene is a copy of the first, you can be sure that all of the navigation bar elements are in exactly the same position for every scene.

10. Use the Text tool to change the large text in Scene 2 so that it reads "Scene 2." We need to see some sort of contrast between one scene and the next so that we can test the movie later and determine whether or not it is working.

11. You are now ready to make your navigation bar jump to a new location in the movie. Make sure that you are working on Scene 1. Select the button on the right, choose Window → Actions (F9) or Ctrl+click (Mac) or right-click (Win), and select Actions from the context menu. Either way, the Actions panel appears.

12. Attach an action that will cause the movie to skip to frame 1 of Scene 2 when the button is clicked. The action should read:

```
on(release){
    gotoAndPlay("Scene 2",1);
}
```

For specifics on attaching actions to button objects, see Chapter 12.

13. Use the Scene panel to switch to the Timeline for Scene 2. Repeat steps 9 and 10 for the left button in Scene 2 (see Figure 13.7), except that when you attach actions to the button, they should read:

```
on(release){
    gotoAndPlay("Scene 1",1);
}
```

14. Your movie should now have buttons that will take you from one scene to another. To test that everything is working correctly, select Control → Test Movie.

15. Provided that there are no problems with your movie, you should be ready to finish the last feature of the navigation bar.

    One of the best qualities of a navigation bar is that it can serve as a kind of bookmark to let your audience know where they are in your movie at all times. To create this feature, all you need to do is manipulate a few of the graphics in your movie.

    Select Window → Library (F11) to display the Library.

16. Double-click the button icon in the Library to open the button in Symbol Editing mode. Click the third keyframe in the Timeline (the Down state) to select that portion of the button only.

17. Select Insert → Convert to Symbol (F8) to display the Create New Symbol dialog box. Choose the Graphic Behavior

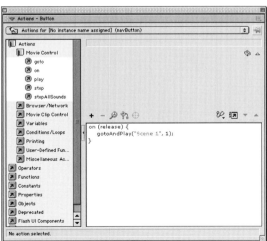

Figure 13.7

Whereas the right button in Scene 1 had an action that jumped to Scene 2, the left button in Scene 2 has an action that jumps to Scene 1.

and name the new symbol "bookmark." Click OK to return to Symbol Editing mode, and select Edit ➔ Edit Document to return to the main Timeline.

18. With the new graphic in the Library, you are ready to add the bookmark feature to your navigation bar. Make Scene 1 the current scene in your Timeline; then select the first button on the navigation bar.

19. Click the Swap Symbol button on the Properties inspector to display the Swap Symbol dialog box. Switch your Scene 1 button symbol with the bookmark symbol you just created. This puts the graphic symbol in place of the button and creates the effect of a bookmark in Scene 1 of your movie.

20. Switch to Scene 2 and repeat step 18, but be sure to select the button on the right before you swap symbols.

21. Your movie is complete! Or at least the navigation bar portion of it is. Select Control ➔ Test Movie to give your navigation bar a test drive. Notice how the bookmark symbol acts like a real bookmark. When you click a button to move to a particular scene, the graphic doesn't change after it has been clicked. This is like a "permanent Down state" to signify which section of the movie is currently playing.

Although the steps outlined here are for a movie with only two locations, it's possible to use this technique to build a navigation bar for an entire Flash website. Using these ideas, and with the help of additional graphics, scenes, and actions, you will be able to create a navigational tool that meets the demands of any Flash movie.

Flash MX increases the scripting possibilities for interactive controls by bringing you the Button object. It is a separate object class with its own set of ActionScript for controlling everything from movie navigation to button appearance. To learn more about the Button object and to see an alternative way to create a navigation bar using ActionScript, see "Scripting Button Behaviors with the Button Object" in Chapter 16.

Creating Non-Button Buttons

So what in the world are "non-button buttons"? Good question. Actually *non-button buttons* is a made-up term to describe any kind of interactive controller that functions as a button but doesn't look like a button. Let's clarify this a bit.

By nature, interactive media demands that there be some kind of control source. The audience should be able to shape the media content to fit their particular needs and desires. The control source is often presented to the audience as a button: Click here to do this, click there to do that. It is simple and direct, and it gets the job done.

One problem is that buttons can be disruptive to the presentation of the movie or message. In some forms, buttons work well. "Informational structures" are a good example of this (see Figure 13.8). Any time you have to present a large amount of information and you need for it to be clearly organized, a traditional button scheme can be useful, to both the designer and the audience. But what about something that is supposed to entertain or tell a story? Is it really in the best interest of your project to use the same kind of navigational structure as an online newspaper if you are trying to divert or amuse? This is where you say, "No! Interactive media deserve better than that!"

The whole idea behind non-button buttons is that you take advantage of the button convention but integrate it into the concept of your project. Buttons are established, and audiences know how they work. They are a sure way to help the audience navigate your movie. But if a button doesn't somehow tie into the theme of the movie, it can look tacked on and just plain awkward.

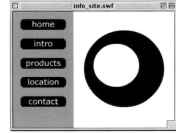

Figure 13.8

A traditional button scheme is clear to the audience and a good means of presenting organized information.

If you want to keep your audience engaged in your movie the entire time they are visiting it, non-button buttons can be a great strategy to use. By tying into the concept of your movie, non-button buttons provide a clear means of navigation that is seamless within the movie. They keep the audience's attention focused on the message of your movie but also allow for free navigation, or "surfing," within the piece.

Here are a few examples:

- An animated fairy tale or nursery rhyme where the buttons to advance the story are a book, magic wand, pixie dust, or other element from the genre

- A music player or mixer where the controls look like knobs on actual audio equipment or parts of a musical instrument

- A cartoon that uses character gestures or animated dialog bubbles to help move the story along

By using non-button buttons in your Flash movie (or any project, for that matter), you can help to keep the audience focused on the ideas you present in the movie. This approach also helps to push the artistic potential of your piece by setting some definite creative boundaries. You are forced to work within a set of self-imposed or story-imposed rules. The fewer the available resources, the more creative the solution. Try integrating non-button buttons into your next Flash project and see what kind of results they yield.

To witness a good example of this, see the Inspirational Design Model for Chapter 14, "Goodnight, Mr. Snoozleberg." This interactive game implements many different kinds of buttons to help get Mr. Snoozleberg safely along his journey. Notice how they are all elements that fit the environment that he is exploring. They function as buttons but look like something that is very much a part of the scenery.

Inspirational Design Model

Designing interactive media is so much more than just making "cool" stuff. Designers must take their audience into consideration so that their message is accessible and presented in the most effective manner. No matter how cool the animation or presentation of content, if an audience doesn't understand how to play or interact with the movie, you've lost them.

This is why intuitive interactive controls are so crucial to design. A naturally flowing design will be much more appealing to your viewers than a confusing display of technical fireworks and animation prowess. Remember, your audience is seeing a movie for the first time. Things that may seem obvious to you as the movie's creator can be potentially confusing if the design isn't clear. There are a few folks out there who are able to strike a unique balance between seamless presentation and technical moxie. Their art lies in creating something that is visually rich and immediately accessible to the audience. Check out San Francisco's THUNKdesign at `www.thunkdesign.com` (see Figure 13.9). In particular, follow the link to "Studio" and check out their 1999 website. Not only is this site gorgeous, but it's very cleverly written and fun to navigate.

Figure 13.9

THUNKdesign's 1999 website

Summary

In this chapter, you learned how to create buttons to control a Flash movie. Combined with your knowledge of basic actions, you are well on your way to creating a dynamic, interactive Flash production. In addition to using the built-in buttons of the Common Button Library, you learned how to design your own button from the ground up, test the button, and make any edits or changes to the button symbol. This chapter also covered several kinds of advanced button controllers for more sophisticated interaction. It's possible to use buttons as an integral part of your design scheme and to give each component of your movie a common link or bond to the movie concept.

Combining Basic Actions and Button Navigation to Create an Interactive Resume

This Hands On tutorial will help to cap off Part IV of this book and put some of your new Flash skills to work. Here we will put together all the techniques covered in this part: using basic actions to add interactivity and navigation, and working with buttons to provide sources for interactive control.

Part 1: Setting the Stage

The files for this tutorial are on the companion CD-ROM. Look for the file named `resume.fla` in the Hands On 4 folder. These files aren't essential for completing the exercise (see Figure H4.1). It's possible for you to complete it with your own graphics and visual design elements, and we strongly encourage you to do so. The value of this assignment is based more on the process that is presented than on working with the actual graphics and duplicating each step.

Figure H4.1

The finished interactive resume looks something like this. Use this image as a guide if you need to check on the layout of the resume.

The task is to create a simple, interactive resume that presents the essential information found in a typical resume. To complete this task, it will be helpful to have familiarity with basic actions, buttons, and type (working with text) and to have a good working knowledge of the Flash interface. Let's get to work!

1. Start by setting up a Stage size for your movie. Select Modify → Document (Cmd/Ctrl+J) to display the Document Properties dialog box. Enter a width and height of 480×480 pixels and choose the Background color swatch #666666 (charcoal gray). Click OK when you are finished.

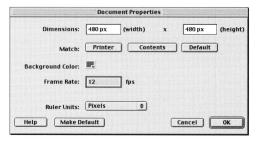

2. Select the Rectangle tool from the Toolbox and draw two rectangles to serve as header and footer graphics—one at the top of the Stage and one at the bottom. Be careful not to make them too large; 50 pixels is a good approximate height. A lot of information will be displayed in the movie, and you should leave a good amount of space free in the middle of the Stage. If it's helpful, select View → Rulers or use the Info panel (Cmd/Ctrl+I) so that you can see exactly how large the rectangles are.

3. Every resume needs a named title. Select the Text tool from the Toolbox. Use the Property inspector to choose a font, text color, and size for your title. Then use the Text tool to insert your name on the left side of the rectangle at the top of your Stage. (For more information about using the Text tool, see Chapter 5.)

4. Now you need to add an e-mail button so that readers of your resume can get in touch with you (to call for interviews and offer exorbitant sums of money for your Flash work). Use the steps outlined in Chapter 13 to create a button, and insert it in the top-right corner of your Stage. The file on the CD-ROM uses a button resembling an envelope. When the button is clicked (in the Down state), it reveals a stamped, addressed envelope.

5. Once the button is complete, you can attach an action so that when the button is clicked, your readers can send a message to you. Highlight the button on the Stage and then select Window → Actions (F9); the Actions panel appears.

6. In the Actions → Browser/Network category, select the getURL() action and either double-click it or drag it into the text box. In the URL line of the Parameters pane, enter mailto:*myAddress* *@myDomain*.com, where *myAddress* and *myDomain* are filled with your e-mail information.

When the button is clicked, the `getURL()` action uses the `mailto` protocol (part of HTML) and launches the e-mail application that has been assigned this responsibility on your audience's computer. This technique works well if your resume is displayed in a web browser or if you choose to distribute it as a stand-alone projector.

7. Save your movie and give it a name if you haven't done so already. You are now finished with the foundation of the resume and can move on to some of the more interesting features.

Part 2: Creating the Resume

8. This resume has four different sections: contact information, education, experience, and references. It's possible to take the groundwork laid in the previous seven steps and use it for each of the four sections. To do this, you can duplicate Scene 1 three times, as follows:

   - Select Window → Scene (Shift+F2) to display the Scene panel. Currently, it contains only one scene. To copy this scene, click its name in the Scene panel and then click the Duplicate Scene button at the bottom of the panel (see Figure H4.2).

   - A new scene titled "Scene 1 copy" appears in the panel. Double-click this new scene and rename it "Scene 2."

   - Repeat this process twice more and name the subsequent scenes "Scene 3" and "Scene 4." Using either the Scene panel or the Edit Scene button, you can navigate to each of the scenes and find that they are identical in every way.

   Now that you have a consistent template for the resume, you can start to build some of the interactive features.

9. The first interactive element you need is a button so that your readers can navigate to various sections of the resume. Select Insert → New Symbol (Cmd/Ctrl+F8). In the Create New Symbol dialog box, check the button behavior and give the new symbol a name. Click OK, and Flash jumps into Symbol Editing mode.

10. Let's create a new kind of rollover for this button. To do so, you are going to temporarily use other parts of your movie for layout and alignment purposes.

    Navigate to Scene 4 in your movie. In the empty rectangle at the bottom of the screen, create a button scheme with four "dummy" button graphics (placeholders) and a block of type that reads "contact." Make sure that the type is in a position that leaves enough room at the right side for words longer than "contact." The type will serve as a different kind of placeholder here as well. For an idea of what this looks like, refer to Figure H4.3.

Figure H4.2

Duplicate Scene button in the Scene panel

Duplicate Scene button

You may find it helpful to use the rulers (View → Rulers) and the Align panel (Cmd/Ctrl+K) to line up the dummy buttons.

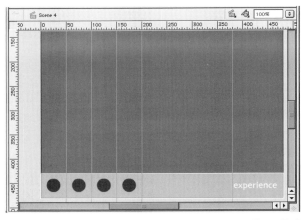

Figure H4.3

A dummy button layout. This will be used to help line up the buttons to create a rollover effect with two different elements.

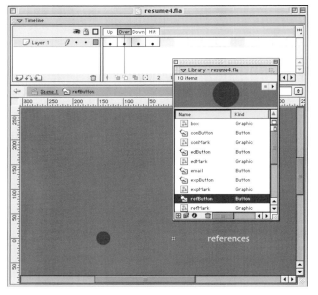

Figure H4.4

Each button position has a different line of text for the resume: "education," "experience," and "references." Name the graphics "edButton," "expButton," and "refButton," respectively.

11. You are now ready to create your first button. Use Shift+click to select the word *contact* and the button dummy 🔲 on the far-left side of the Stage; then choose Insert → Convert to Symbol (F8).

12. Make the new symbol a button, and name it "contactButton." Click OK. Next, you need to make some corrections to this new button. In the Edit Symbols menu, select contactButton, or double-click the contactButton symbol in the Library. Either way, Flash switches to Symbol Editing mode and reveals the new button's Timeline.

13. Select Insert → Keyframe three times. This will insert three new keyframes in the button Timeline that are duplicates of the first.

14. With your keyframes in place, you can edit the graphics to create the different button states. For now, leave the Up and Over states alone. You will need them to remain intact for alignment purposes later. For the Down state, change the color of the button but leave the type alone. For the Hit state, leave the button graphic alone but delete the type altogether. All you need for responding to mouse clicks is the main area of the button.

15. Now it's production time. Repeat steps 11–14 for the remaining three buttons. Figure H4.4 shows you which buttons match which text elements.

Part 3: Adding Navigational Elements

16. For this controller at the bottom of the resume, you are going to use the buttons in a navigation bar with a "bookmark" that tells the reader where they are in the resume at all times. (For specifics on creating a navigation bar, see Chapter 13.)

One of the most important features of the navigation bar is the bookmark. To create the bookmark, you need to use a portion of the button symbol created in steps 11–14.

17. Select Window → Library to open your movie's Library. Double-click the Contact button symbol to open it in Symbol Editing mode.

18. Click the Down state keyframe of this button to select both the graphic and the text elements of the button; then select Insert → Convert to Symbol (F8).

19. In the Create New Symbol box, name the symbol "conMark" and then choose the Graphic Behavior option. Click OK when you are finished.

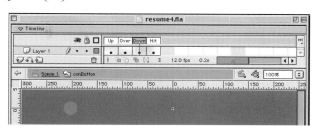

20. Repeat this procedure for the Down states of the other three buttons. Name the graphic symbols "edMark," "expMark," and "refMark," respectively. When you are finished, save your movie and return to the main Timeline of Scene 1.

21. Now that all the buttons and bookmarks have been created, you are ready to add them to your movie. Add a new layer to Scene 1 and name it "buttons." One by one, drag your buttons to the Stage so that they line up the same way as your dummy graphics. The text will overlap, but that's okay for now. Actually, the text is helpful for getting everything lined up properly.

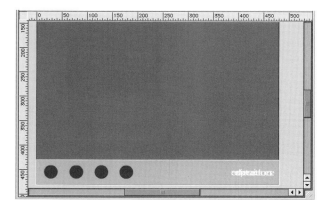

22. It's time now for some more production busy-work. Your buttons are in place in Scene 1, and they need to be copied into the other three scenes. Click the first keyframe of the "buttons" layer in Scene 1 and select Edit → Copy. Then, for the remaining scenes (Scenes 2–4), repeat these steps:

    • Insert a new layer and name it "buttons."

    • Select Edit → Paste in Place.

    Don't forget to remove the dummy buttons from Scene 4 before you paste the finished buttons in that scene.

23. With all the finished buttons in all the scenes, you can now insert the bookmark graphics that create the navigation bar. Jump to Scene 1 of your movie and select the conButton instance.

24. In the Properties inspector, click the Swap Symbols button. In the Swap Symbol dialog box, exchange the conButton symbol with the conMark graphic symbol. You will see the

change take place on the Stage as the symbols swap. Repeat this process with symbols in the following scenes:

- Scene 2: Swap edButton for edMark.
- Scene 3: Swap expButton for expMark.
- Scene 4: Swap refButton for refMark.

25. With all the bookmarks in place now, you can do some cleaning up and finish the button symbols that you started earlier in the movie. Right now, the buttons display their text component in the Up state. This is confusing and impossible to read! You left it like that so that you could use the text to help line things up; but now that the buttons are in order, you can delete the unnecessary text. Since you want the button to display the text only when the button is rolled over and clicked, all you have to do is delete the text from the Up state of each button symbol.

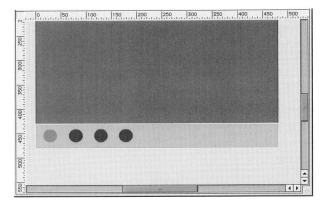

Open the Library panel and double-click the conButton symbol to open it in Symbol Editing mode. Be sure that the playback head is in frame 1 (the Up state) and delete the text that reads "contact" from the frame. Repeat this process with the other three buttons so that none of them have any text in their Up state frames.

Similarly, you must do the same with the text for the graphic symbol bookmarks. Now that everything is lined up, you are free to get rid of any extra text garbage. The process for these symbols is the same: Open the symbol in Symbol Editing mode and delete the text from the graphic. All instances of the symbol will be updated automatically.

26. Now that the buttons are cleaned up, the movie is finally starting to look like something! You should be able to see how each scene has its own bookmark to designate where you are in the movie. With all the button and bookmark graphics in order, you can attach the actions that are necessary to create the navigation.

> If you haven't done so in a while, save your movie. It might also be a good idea to do a Save As and give the movie a new name. That way, if there are any problems, you can come back to where you left off and not have to redo too much work.

Part 4: Scripting for Interactivity

27. For each scene, repeat these steps:

- Insert a new layer and name it "actions."
- Attach a `stop()` frame action to the first frame in this new layer.

28. For each scene in the movie, attach a `gotoAndPlay()` action that sends the movie to the correct scene when a button instance is clicked:

   - conButton instance goes to frame 1 of Scene 1.
   - edButton instance goes to frame 1 of Scene 2.
   - expButton instance goes to frame 1 of Scene 3.
   - refButton instance goes to frame 1 of Scene 4.

   For example, the script on the edButton instance in Scenes 1, 3, and 4 should read:

   ```
   on(release){
       gotoAndPlay("Scene 2",1);
   }
   ```

   No matter what scene is currently playing, the button instance will always point the movie to frame 1 of Scene 2.

   You must attach these actions to every instance in every scene of your movie. Happy scripting!

29. When you have finished attaching all your actions, select Control → Test Movie to test the button and action performance of your resume movie.

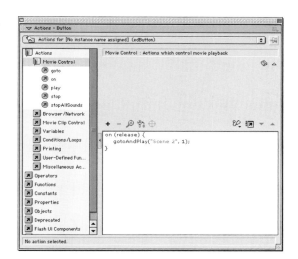

Part 5: Completing the Resume

30. Now that the controls work and you can navigate through the resume, it's time to create the rest of the design structure and content. To display the written information, you will need some kind of frame to put it in.

   In Scene 1, insert a new layer and name it "graphic box." On the new layer, create a box or frame in the middle of the Stage. When it looks the way you want, select the entire box and choose Insert → Convert to Symbol (F8). Give the box a name and a Graphic Behavior.

31. Click the box to select it and choose Edit → Copy. Then, for each scene in your movie, insert a new layer and name it "graphic box." When the layer is complete, select Edit → Paste in Place to paste the box in exactly the same location for every scene.

32. The next step is to add some simple animation to the box symbol. To add animation, you need to have additional frames in your Timeline. In Scene 1, click frame 1 of every layer, using the Shift+click technique to add to your selection. After each frame is selected, press the F5 key 11 times. This will leave you with a total of 12 frames in the Timeline for Scene 1. Repeat this process for scenes 2–4.

33. Next, you must move the stop() action that was attached to frame 1 of each scene back in step 27. This is easy to do by simply moving the action manually. Select the action's keyframe and position your mouse cursor over the action in the Timeline. Click the keyframe and drag it to frame 12 of the actions layer for each scene in your movie.

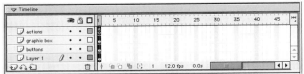

34. Now that the action is in frame 12, you have some room to create an animation before the Timeline is stopped. In this step, you will create an animation that tweens the Alpha, or opacity, of the instance. (For more details on tweening, refer to Chapter 9.)

    In the "graphic box" layer of Scene 1, click the last frame (frame 12) of the animation and select Insert → Keyframe to insert a new keyframe.

35. Select the graphic in the first keyframe (frame 1) and open the Properties inspector. Select Alpha from the Color drop-down menu. Then either enter a value of 0% in the text field or use the pop-up menu to access the Alpha slider and drag it down until the field reads 0%.

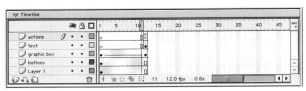

36. Your next step is to tween the animation so that the Alpha value slowly changes from 0% to 100%. Since the last keyframe at frame 12 was untouched, it still has the default Alpha setting of 100%, and the animation will fade up from 0% to 100%. To tween the animation, select keyframe 1. With the frame selected, choose Motion from the Tween menu in the Properties inspector. This step inserts an arrow pointing from one keyframe to the next. If you press Return/Enter on your keyboard, you will be able to see the animation play its first 12 frames.

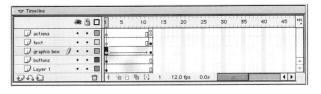

37. Repeat steps 34–36 to create identical animations for the other scenes in your movie.

38. You are ready now for the final step, which is to insert the text that will make up the informational content of your resume. You should put this text on a separate layer so that you can control and edit it independently. First, add the title text for each resume section. In Scene 1, insert another new layer and name it "text." Select Insert → Keyframe to insert a keyframe in frame 12 of the new text layer.

39. Use the Properties inspector to select a font, size, and style for the title text. Then, using the Text tool, insert text to serve as the title for this section of the resume. In the CD-ROM example, the title at the top is the same as the rollover graphic at the bottom.

40. Repeat steps 38 and 39 for the remaining scenes of your movie. Rather than trying to line up the text blocks from one scene to the next, you can use the Paste in Place command to ensure consistent placement of all items.

41. Use the Text tool to enter any additional text for your movie and to fill your resume with all the important information about you: your background, your experience, and other points of interest. (To learn more about working with text in Flash, see Chapter 5.)

42. After you have filled each scene of your resume movie with text, save the file and select Control → Test Movie to see how it works.

Congratulations! You have just completed one of your first large projects with Flash MX. Realize that this tutorial is only a point of departure. From the basic principles outlined here, you can build upon the techniques and strategies to create even more dynamic, interactive resumes and portfolios. Have fun, and keep up the good work.

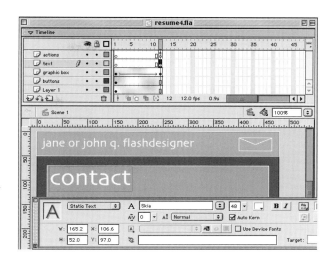

Adding Advanced Interactivity with ActionScript

Up to this point *in the book, you have worked with the elements of Flash that have helped the application build its reputation: clean vector graphics, smooth Timeline animation, and an intuitive user interface that streamlines your work flow. You have also learned how to make your movies interactive by adding simple scripts that direct a movie's playback and allow your audience to experience your content on their own terms.*

In recent years, Flash has become much more. Its scripting capabilities have grown considerably. ActionScript, once a simple "traffic cop" that controlled the flow of Time-lines, has become the "governor" of your Flash movie, with control over nearly every level of the movie. With this increased control comes the increased potential to make a simple Flash animation into an immersive multimedia experience.

In this part of the book, you will begin to dig deeper into the specifics of ActionScript and learn how to use the language as a tool for making your movies play and respond intelligently to the requests of your audience. Part V contains these topics:

CHAPTER 14

Understanding and Using ActionScript

So, you are ready to take the plunge into the world of ActionScript. Congratulations! This is one of the most exciting and rewarding aspects of working in Flash—but it can also be the most difficult and demanding.

This is not a warning to scare you off; it is a call to arms. Learning ActionScript and becoming comfortable with the language is a challenge. Getting to the point where you can use the language with fluidity can be even more tenuous. However, none of this is impossible. What is most important is that you practice diligently. Learning ActionScript (or any programming language, for that matter) is similar to learning to speak a foreign language: To use it fluently, you have to practice every day. Practice can be as basic as trying to create simple movies that perform tasks using capabilities of the ActionScript language. Repeated exposure to the language through this kind of routine will give you a good feel for the language in context. The more you practice, the more of the language you learn and the more comfortable you become with its elements.

This chapter covers fundamental ActionScript terms and concepts and gets you started with some advanced scripting techniques. It includes these topics:

- **ActionScript as an object-oriented language**
- **Components of a script in the context of a simple movie**
- **How scripts flow**
- **How to plan scripts before you create your movie**
- **Introduction to ActionScript terms**
- **The Actions panel in Expert mode**

Knowing and Applying the Anatomy of ActionScript

ActionScript is most similar to the programming language JavaScript. In fact, ActionScript is derived from the JavaScript specifications set forth by the European Computer Manufacturers Association (ECMA).

For more information about the history, role, and members of the ECMA, go to its website, www.ecma.ch.

As an object-oriented scripting language, ActionScript has components that follow a particular organization. Elements of a movie are organized into *classes*. Classes can then be expressed as individual or independent parts called *objects*. An object is an *instance* of a class.

A class has information that it passes on to each object it creates. This information comes in the form of *properties*, the qualities of an object, and *methods*, the actions an object can perform. In Flash, there are several predefined classes that create objects, such as Date objects and Sound objects. One of the most common predefined objects, the Movie Clip, has properties like _framesloaded and methods like play().

It's possible to create your own objects using ActionScript. For example, you could use a *constructor* function to create the class Dogs, with properties like _spotted and _scruffy, and the method fetch.

Breaking Down a Script

One way to understand how scripts work is to dissect a script that is working in the context of a movie. This approach is helpful because seeing a movie is the proof; you can witness the script running right before you. Once you grasp what is happening on the movie's Stage, you can take a look behind the scenes and see what kind of script is making the movie act a certain way or do a certain thing.

In the following example (tapGlass.fla in the Chapter 14 folder on this book's companion CD), the audience's standard pointer cursor is replaced with a custom hand cursor created in Flash. When someone clicks the glass (or "taps" it), the water in the glass ripples and a ping sound is heard. This movie takes place in a single frame (see Figure 14.1), although the ripple animation takes about 40 frames. However, this animation is part of a Movie Clip, and the glass is an instance of the Movie Clip.

The only scripts in the movie are a series of actions attached to the hand Movie Clip instance. These scripts are responsible for attaching the custom hand cursor, cueing the glass animation, and playing the sound.

Open and play the movie so that you can see exactly what it does. Also, select the hand instance and open the Actions panel (by pressing F9) to see the scripts that control the instance's behavior as a custom cursor. For a specific breakdown of the scripts in this movie, refer to Figure 14.2.

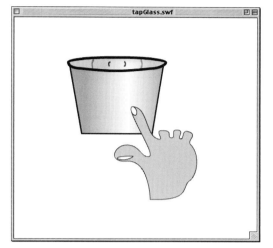

Figure 14.1

The tapGlass movie

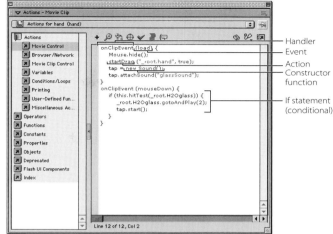

Figure 14.2

The Actions panel with attached scripts for the hand **instance**

In the actions, there are two main handlers; and since this movie deals with Movie Clips, each is an `onClipEvent` handler. The actions in the first handler execute only once, when the clip event loads. They are as follows:

```
mouse.hide();
startDrag("_root.hand",true);
tap=new Sound();
tap.attachSound("glassSound");
```

When the clip event loads, the Mouse object hides the cursor; then a `startDrag` action makes the Movie Clip draggable and replaces the cursor. The next two lines invoke a sound object using the `new Sound()` constructor function, and attach an instance named `tap` of the sound `glassSound`.

The next handler is also a clip-event handler, but it is executed only when the clip receives a `mouseDown`, or click, message. The `mouseDown` message is then run through a conditional:

```
if(this.hitTest(_root.H2Oglass)){
    _root.H2Oglass.gotoAndPlay(2);
    tap.start();
}
```

The conditional `if` statement asks if the hand clip (`this`) has collided with or is over the clip instance `H2Oglass` when the mouse is clicked. If it does intersect the other instance, the conditional returns a True value, and it sends the H2Oglass instance to play at frame 2 of its internal Timeline. After doing this, the script plays the sound object tap that was created when the clip first loaded into the movie. The conditional has no else statement. This means that if the two clips don't intersect when the mouse is clicked, the if statement returns a False value and nothing is done. Without the conditional statement to check whether the hand is over the glass, any mouseDown event would cause the animation and the sound to play. Try pulling this script apart and changing different parameters to see what different kinds of behavior you can create.

> There is one other script in this movie. In the glass Movie Clip, there is a stop()action at frame 1. This prevents the clip from playing until it receives a message that tells it to jump ahead to frame 2 and begin the animation.

How Scripts Flow

What is almost more important than understanding the elements of a language is understanding the *flow* of a language. Flow refers to the way that a script is read and processed while your movie is running. When scripts will not work properly, the cause is often a mistake in the flow, or order of the script, rather than a misuse of terms or incorrect syntax.

Like most programming languages, ActionScript follows a logical, step-by-step flow. This means that lines are executed in sequential order, starting at the top and working their way down through the script.

For example, in the following script, the playback head stops, sets the _alpha property, or transparency, of a Movie Clip named plane to 50%, and then continues playing at frame 11:

```
stop();
setProperty("_root.plane",_alpha,50);
gotoAndPlay(11);
```

The actions are carried out specifically in the order they are listed.

A script can take several diversions as it travels along in your movie. In ActionScript, there are statements known as *conditionals* that will reroute your script flow. This detour in the flow of the script is usually done to test a condition and then do something as a result of the test.

One of the most common conditionals is an if statement. Here is its basic structure:

```
if(thisStatementIsTrue){
    do thisStatement
}
```

The if statement tests a condition, which can be evaluated as either True or False; and if the evaluation is True, the statements in the body of the if statement are executed. The if statement can provide an else alternative. This way, if the condition tested is False, the

script will execute a separate action—the statements in the body of the `else` part of the
statement (see Figure 14.3). For example:

```
if(thisStatementIsTrue){
    do thisStatement
}else{
    do aDifferentStatement
}
```

In a script where the `if` statement evaluates False and there is no `else` alternative, the statements in the body of the `if` are skipped entirely.

These structures are very useful for testing different parameters in your movie and telling
Flash to act accordingly.

Related to the conditional script structure is the *loop* structure. The loop structure creates a repetition and performs a task or process repeatedly until a value is achieved to satisfy
the demands of the loop (see Figure 14.4).

For example:

```
i=100;
while(i>0){
    i=i-1;
    setProperty("_root.plane",_alpha,i);

}
gotoAndPlay (11);
```

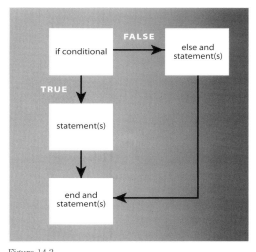

Figure 14.3

The flow of an `if…else` statement

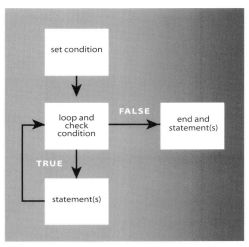

Figure 14.4

The flow of a `while` loop

This script is executed in the same step-by-step fashion as the `if...then` conditional. However, there is a slight delay before the script makes it to the last line. This script uses a `while` loop and detains the script flow while it runs the variable i through a decreasing series of values. Rather than simply set the Movie Clip to an `_alpha` value of 0%, this script methodically decreases the `_alpha` value by 1 as long as it is greater than 0. When the script has completed this task, it continues down the line and executes the last statement, sending the movie to play at frame 11. Loops like this are especially helpful for repetitive actions and information processing. For more information on loops and loop syntax, see both Chapter 15 and the ActionScript Reference section.

Planning and Assigning Scripts

Every designer or animator knows that one of the most essential parts of the development process is planning and storyboarding. Planning is crucial. It allows you to think things through before committing to a final version. It's also an opportunity to look at the big picture before zeroing in on the details during production. Planning answers the most important question: What am I creating?

Just as planning is common practice for design and animation, it should be so for scripting. Before writing a single line of ActionScript, you should know the purpose of every script and how it will work toward a goal in your movie.

To begin the process, you need to start at the top and decide what you need the movie to do. Then, break it down to the next level: What movie elements are needed to accomplish this? When the various movie components are clear, you should decide how they work and whether they interact. Once things have been reduced to this level, you should have a good start toward defining the purpose of ActionScript in your movie. The next step is, of course, to start writing scripts.

The best strategy for writing scripts is to start simple. Get one element of the movie working before you move on to the next one. This technique allows you to isolate problems as they occur. It's also good to get in the habit of saving your work often and saving multiple versions of a project. This way, if something goes horribly wrong, you can go back to the last working version and pick up where you left off, rather than build a movie from scratch.

If you are new to ActionScript, you are likely to spend a fair amount of time digging through ActionScript references looking for the components you need to build your scripts. Inevitably, you will encounter things that are not immediately helpful, but may be helpful in the future. In these occasions, it's a good idea to keep a list or journal of the terms you discover. That way, when the time comes and you need a term, you can reference your notes rather than dig through a book again.

Getting Familiar with ActionScript Terminology

As a powerful and flexible scripting language, ActionScript has many components within the language itself. It's important to understand these terms and how they fit together in the Action-Script family. The following list, organized alphabetically, is a breakdown of the key ActionScript terms and their general descriptions. For a more detailed account of these terms, see Chapter 16.

Actions are statements in ActionScript that tell a movie or one of its components to do something while the movie is running.

Arguments (or **parameters**) are containers that hold information and pass it on to actions or functions. For example, the custom function `newUser` has two arguments: `userName` and `userID`:

```
function newUser(userName,userID)
```

These arguments are stored and used later in the function. Similarly, ActionScript actions can take arguments. For example:

```
gotoAndStop(5);
```

The `gotoAndStop()` action requires an argument so that it knows where to stop the Timeline.

Classes are categories of information in your movie. Each object belongs to a class and is an individual *instance* of that class. To define a new object, you must create an instance of the object founded on a class. This is done with the help of a constructor function.

Constants are script elements that do not change. For example, an integer (whole number) is a constant and can be used to check the value of an expression. The key `SPACE` is a constant because it always refers to the spacebar.

Constructors are functions that are used to create objects based on classes. The function, in turn, has arguments that give the class properties.

Data types describe the kind of information that a variable or ActionScript element can communicate. In ActionScript, the data types are string, number, Boolean value (True and False), object, Movie Clip, and undefined or null (no data). For more information on data types, see Chapter 15.

Events happen while your movie is running. They are generated by such things as mouse clicks, the loading of Movie Clips, and keystrokes. Events are used to trigger scripts and actions.

An **expression** is any chunk of information that can produce a value. For example:

```
on(release){
    gotoAndPlay(_currentframe+1);
}
```

This script sends the movie to the frame number equal to the value of the expression `_currentframe+1.`

Functions are information processors. They can be passed information in the form of arguments and can return a value. Functions are great if you want to create a custom ActionScript routine or task that will be used repeatedly throughout a movie.

Handlers are used to perform actions in response to events. In ActionScript, there are handlers for both mouse and Movie Clip events.

Identifiers are unique names assigned to functions, methods, objects, properties, or variables. The first character of an identifier must be either a letter, dollar sign ($), or underscore (_). Every other character must be a number, letter, dollar sign ($), or underscore(_).

Instances are individual objects that belong to a class. For example, the `today` instance could belong to the `date` class.

An **instance name** is a unique name used to refer to a specific Movie Clip instance once it is in your main movie Timeline. For example, a Movie Clip symbol named `logoMovie` can be used repeatedly throughout a movie. You must give each instance a unique instance name, such as `logo1` or `logo2`. Each instance in the movie must be referred to by its unique instance name. This distinction allows ActionScript to control each instance of the one Movie Clip symbol independently.

Keywords are words with special meaning in the ActionScript language and are unavailable for use as variables, functions, and so on. Refer to Chapter 15 for a list of ActionScript keywords.

Methods are actions that can be performed by objects. For custom objects, you can create custom methods. In ActionScript, each predefined object (such as the Sound object or MovieClip object) has its own methods. For a list of object methods, see the ActionScript Reference section.

Objects are instances of a class. ActionScript has several built-in classes that are called objects; these include the Sound object, the Date object, and the MovieClip object.

Operators are elements that are used to calculate and compare values. For example, the forward-slash (/) operator is used to divide one number by another.

A **property** is any kind of quality that defines an object or instance of an object. For example, the `_x` property determines the X coordinate of a Movie Clip on the Stage.

Target paths are used to pass information along the chain of Movie Clip instance names, variables, and objects in a movie. For example:

```
menuBar.item1.selected
```

This is the target path to the variable `selected`, which is inside the Movie Clip `item1`, which is inside the Movie Clip `menuBar`. For more details on the hierarchy of Movie Clips, see Chapter 16.

Variables are storage locations that hold information and values. Variables can be used for permanent or temporary storage, and can be retrieved for use in scripts while a movie is playing.

Using the Actions Panel for Advanced Scripting

As you learned while working with some of ActionScript's basic actions, the Actions panel is your interface for adding actions to a Flash movie. It provides several window components that allow you to select ActionScript elements, arrange and order them as you see fit, and edit any individual parameters as needed.

Up to this point, your exposure to scripting in the Actions panel has occurred in Normal mode. This is the most user-friendly means of working with the panel, especially for beginners. However, as you become more comfortable with the language, you may find that it's helpful to have more control over the actions you write and how you write them. Absolute freedom and control over the Actions panel can come only through working in Expert scripting mode.

Scripting in Expert Mode

Working in Expert mode can be similar to working in Normal mode. The biggest difference is that in Expert mode, you are given complete control over the window and what can be entered in the text box. To set up the Actions panel so that you are working in Expert mode:

1. Select Window → Actions. The Actions panel appears (see Figure 14.5).

2. Do one of the following:

   - Click the Actions panel pop-up menu in the upper-right corner of the panel.

   - Choose Expert Mode ![icon] from the Actions panel's View Options menu.

   - Type Shift+Cmd+E (Mac)/ Shift+Ctrl+E (Win).

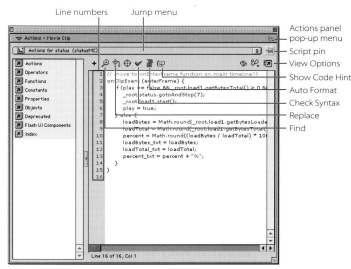

Figure 14.5

The Actions panel contains several unique and useful new features while running in Expert mode.

One of the immediate differences between modes is the absence of the Parameters pane in Expert mode. In Normal mode, you use the pane to enter parameters for the actions you select. In Expert mode, you type all of those parameters by hand.

You may remember from Chapter 12 that it's possible to switch from one mode to the other while you are writing scripts. This is true, but there are a few things to keep in mind:

- A script with errors can go from Normal mode to Expert mode but not from Expert to Normal. The script must be free of errors before switching back to Normal mode.

- Switching modes may cause some reformatting, so pay careful attention to any unwanted changes that appear when switching modes.

- With the release of Flash MX, the Actions panel can boast many new features. Many of these are available only while you are working in Expert mode. Keep reading to learn how the new additions to the Actions panel can help streamline your work flow and offer greater control over how actions are displayed in the text box.

Actions Panel Options

Besides enabling you to switch editing modes, the Actions panel offers several options to let you work with scripts more easily. You are able to search scripts and perform find and replace edits for ActionScript terms that appear more than once. It's also possible to write your scripts outside Flash and to include them in your movie from an external location. Additionally, the Actions panel allows you to print scripts and check for errors before testing your movie.

Script Display Options

In Flash MX, there are several new (and very welcome) additions to the Actions panel. Many of these features affect the way a script is displayed in the panel, offering greater control over the formatting, script font and color, and organization of information. To take advantage of these options, you need to run the panel in Expert scripting mode. Press Shift+Cmd+E (Mac)/Shift+Ctrl+E (Win) or use the View Options menu to switch to Expert mode.

LINE NUMBERING

The Actions panel's line-numbering feature allows you to better manage long scripts. Line numbering gives each line in your script an "address" of sorts, so that you can easily refer to each script component by number. To activate or deactivate line numbering:

1. Choose Window ➜ Actions or press F9 to open the Actions panel.

2. Select the View Options menu and do either of the following:

   - To display line numbering, select View Line Numbers or press Shift+Cmd+L (Mac)/Shift+Ctrl+L (Win). A check appears beside the menu option in the menu.

   - To hide line numbering, select View Line Numbers. The check beside the menu option disappears.

When line numbers are on, they appear in the vertical gray strip between the Actions Toolbox and the text box (see Figure 14.6). When the option is off, the gray strip is empty.

AUTO FORMAT

The ActionScript examples that you read in this book were specially prepared so that they were written as neatly and clearly as possible. In the real world, though, this isn't always the case. If you are "in the trenches" and under a tight deadline for preparing a script-intensive movie, the last thing on your mind is the tidiness of your script. A neat, orderly script isn't a necessity, but often a neat script makes it easier to find syntax errors or other glitches that prohibit a script from running properly or running at all.

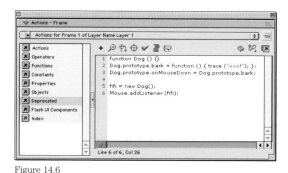

Figure 14.6

The Actions panel with the line numbering option turned on

Luckily, Flash MX offers a new auto-format feature that enables you to automatically clean up a messy script by using a single mouse click or keyboard shortcut. To apply auto-formatting to a script:

1. Select the object or frame that contains the script you wish to format.

2. Choose Window → Actions (F9) to open the Actions panel.

3. Do one of the following:

   • Press Shift+Cmd+F (Mac)/Shift+Ctrl+F (Win).

   • Choose Auto Format from the Actions panel pop-up menu.

   • Click the Auto Format button ▤ .

   Your script is automatically reformatted.

When you are using the auto-format feature, it's possible to control how Flash formats your scripts. To set the parameters for auto-formatting:

1. Click the Actions panel pop-up menu and select Auto Format Options.

2. The Auto Format Options dialog box appears. Use the check boxes to turn on or off the various formatting parameters. To see how a particular formatting option affects your script, look at the Preview window at the bottom of the dialog box. When finished, click OK to return to the Actions panel.

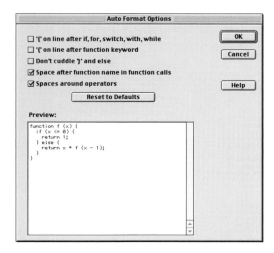

Once you have set the formatting options, they will be applied to the current script when-ever you use the Auto Format command.

ACTIONS PANEL TEXT DISPLAY

Flash MX allows you to have complete control over the display of actions in the Actions panel. This includes font, size, text color, and spacing. These options are controlled from the Action-

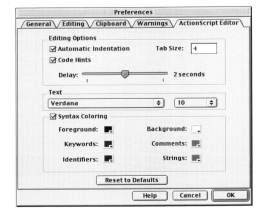

Script Editor tab of the Preferences menu. To open this menu, do either of the following:

- Select Edit → Preferences and choose the ActionScript Editor tab.
- Click the Actions panel pop-up menu and select Preferences. You can set several options on the ActionScript Editor tab:

Spacing Check the Automatic Indentation box, and Flash will auto-matically indent your scripts. To set the amount of indentation, type a number in the Tab Size field.

Text Use the Text menus to select a font and size for your actions. Because ActionScript must be entered with specific syntax, it's bet-ter to choose a legible screen font than your favorite deconstructed display typeface.

Color Flash allows several options for the display color of actions in your movie. When the Syntax Coloring box is checked, you can set a specific color for the following ActionScript elements: Foreground (text), Background (window color), Keywords, Comments, Identi-fiers, and Strings. Syntax coloring can make it easier to visually organize your scripts based on the color of individual script entries. Use the color swatch next to each element to choose a display color. If you prefer to view your scripts without the syntax coloration, deselect the Syntax Coloring option and choose appropriate foreground and background colors.

SYNTAX VERSION TRACKING

Although you are working with Flash MX, it's possible to publish your movie for older ver-sions of the Flash Player. Previous releases of Flash didn't contain all of the ActionScript that you now find in MX. As a result, you are unable to use those new terms when publishing for an older version. It can be hard to keep track of which terms are available in which versions, so the Actions panel makes it easy for you. Any terms that are unavailable in the version for which you are publishing will be highlighted in a bright yellow color. You cannot use these terms unless you switch your publish settings to a higher version number. You can read more about publishing movies in Chapter 28.

Automatic ActionScript Input Using Code Hints

Macromedia seems to be going out of its way to make it easier and easier to compose Action-Script in the Actions panel. Now in Flash MX, you can use *code hints,* an automated feature that provides yet another means of writing your scripts. Although the feature stems from a good idea, its actual implementation is a little cumbersome.

> Code hints are available only in Expert mode.

Code hints are intended to provide you with menu options so that rather than type an entire script, you can select pieces of it from a menu. Because code hints appear in the Actions panel alongside your script, it's easy to choose from the menu and build your script in a somewhat systematic fashion. You can use code hints to insert handler events, actions, and action parameters into a script. You can choose to have code hints displayed automatically or to call upon them as needed. When they are set to be automatic, Flash detects when you need a code hint and displays it in the Actions panel. To enable automatic code hints:

1. Choose Edit → Preferences and select the ActionScript Editor tab, or click the Actions panel pop-up menu and choose Preferences. The Preferences dialog box appears.

2. Check the Code Hints box to turn on automatic display of code hints. You can also use the Delay slider set the period of delay before a code hint appears; the minimum period is 0 seconds (no delay), and the maximum is 4 seconds.

3. Click OK to leave Preferences and return to your movie.

WRITING SCRIPTS WITH CODE HINTS

As mentioned earlier, code hints can be used for three ActionScript elements: event handlers, actions, and action parameters. In the steps that follow, you will learn how to use code hints to build a script with a minimum amount of typing.

Say, for example, you wanted to enter the following script:

```
on(press){
    menu.gotoAndPlay(5);
}
```

This button script will send the Movie Clip instance **menu** to play at frame 5. To enter this script using code hints:

1. Select a button object in your movie.

2. Choose Window → Actions (F9) to open the Actions panel.

3. Type **on(** in the Actions panel text box. If automatic code hints are enabled, a code hints menu of event handlers appears beside your script (see Figure 14.7).

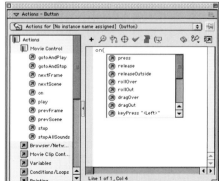

Figure 14.7

Code hints appear in the Actions panel text box along with your scripts.

If code hints are disabled, do one of the following to display the code hints menu:

- Press Cmd/Ctrl+spacebar.
- Click the Show Code Hint button 🖵 .
- Select Show Code Hint from the Actions panel pop-up menu.

4. Since you are writing a handler, the code hints menu knows to give you a list of handler events. Now you must choose the handler you want to use from the menu. There are two ways to do this:

- Use the arrow keys to navigate to the handler event, and press Return/Enter to make your selection.
- Choose and double-click an event from the menu.

Use either technique to select the **press** event. Flash enters the event into your script. Type **)**{ and press Return/Enter to start a new line. Your incomplete script should now look like this:

```
on(press){
```

5. Start the second line of your script by typing **menu**. This is the instance name of the Movie Clip you are scripting for in this example. If you are scripting for a clip with a different instance name or target path, insert that information here at the beginning of line two.

6. With the instance name (or target path) in place, you can use a code hint to enter an action. Flash doesn't always understand what action to display when you ask for a code hint. Here you are scripting to control a Movie Clip, but what if the menu instance were a Sound object or an Array? Flash has no way of knowing this. You must provide some additional information to give the code hint a little clue about your script. Type **_mc** after the word menu. Your script should now read like this:

```
on(press){
    menu_mc
```

The _mc class suffix lets Flash know that the menu instance is a Movie Clip. For a complete list of class suffixes, see Table 14.1 at the end of this section.

Using suffixes such as _mc is one of the "gotcha" features in Flash MX. By changing the script from *instanceName* to *instanceName*_mc, you are telling Flash to look for a completely different Movie Clip instance. The _mc suffix is interpreted as part of the full instance name. If you plan to use code hints when writing scripts for your movies, you will need to find a workaround solution. The best way to manage this situation is to name all of your instances with the appropriate code hint suffix. That way, there will be no confusion in your scripts.

7. After the _mc class suffix, type a period (.). If code hints are enabled, the code hints menu should appear. If not, use one of the techniques described in step 3 to display the menu.

8. Using one of the code hint selection techniques described in step 4, choose the `gotoAndPlay()` action from the code hints menu. Your incomplete script should now look like this:

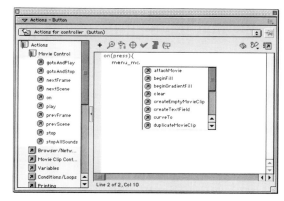

```
on(press){
    menu_mc.gotoAndPlay(
```

9. This next step may come as a bit of a surprise! After entering the `gotoAndPlay()` action via the code hints menu, you are automatically faced with another code hint choice—only this one is different from the others you have seen. This code hint appears in a yellow box and is called a tooltip-style code hint. Tooltip code hints are used to enter parameters for actions. The `gotoAndPlay()` action requires one parameter, a frame number. When the yellow tooltip code hint appears, you can type a value, and it will be inserted as the parameter for the current action. Type **5**; then type a closing parenthesis (`)`). This will hide the code hint. End the line with a semicolon (`;`).

> Some actions require more than one parameter. To enter multiple parameters when using code hints, simply type the parameters in the proper order, separating them with commas. Don't rely on Flash's tooltip-style code hints to give you the correct number or order of the parameters. To learn the correct parameter syntax for an action, see the ActionScript Reference section.

10. Press Return/Enter to start a new line, and type the closing curly-brace character (`}`) to end your script. The finished script should now read like this:

```
on(press){
    menu_mc.gotoAndPlay(5);
}
```

> Remember to update all your instance names in the Property Inspector so that your code hint suffixes will reference the correct instance names. In this example, you would need to change the instance menu to menu_mc.

Code hints are designed to make scripting a little less keyboard intensive. You should be the judge of whether or not they are helpful. One of the beauties of Flash MX is that the interface is completely customizable. Use the features you like, and ignore those you don't.

Table 14.1

Code Hint Class Suffixes

SUFFIX	OBJECT CLASS	SUFFIX	OBJECT CLASS
_array	Array	_so	SharedObject
_btn	Button	_sound	Sound
_camera	Camera	_str	String
_color	Color	_stream	NetStream
_connection	NetConnection	_txt	TextField
_date	Date	_video	Video
_fmt	TextFormat	_xml	XML
_mc	MovieClip	_xmlsocket	XMLSocket
_mic	Microphone		

To use code hints, enter the appropriate suffix after the name of the object you wish to control.

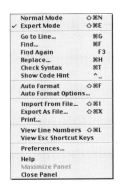

Navigating, Searching, and Replacing ActionScripts

To look for portions of an ActionScript, use the pop-up menu in the upper-right corner of the Actions panel:

Select **Go to Line** (Cmd+, (Mac), Ctrl+G (Win)) to skip to a particular line in a long script.

Select **Find** (Cmd/Ctrl+F) or click the Find button to locate a particular word or phrase. **Find Again** (Cmd+G (Mac), F3 (Win)) will locate the next occurrence of that text.

Select **Replace** (Cmd/Ctrl+Shift+H, (Mac), Cmd/Ctrl+H (Win)) or click the Replace button to find one set of text and replace it with another.

In Expert mode, Find and Replace will search the entire script body. In Normal mode, they will search only the information in the Parameters pane.

Find and Replace will search only the immediate script window. To do a movie-wide search, use the Movie Explorer. (For more information about the Movie Explorer, see Chapter 7.)

Getting Files in and out of the Actions Panel

There are several ways to move data in and out of the Actions panel. Use the pop-up menu in the upper-right corner of the panel to handle these tasks:

Import text Select Import from File or press Shift+Cmd+I (Mac)/Shift+Ctrl+I (Win), and browse to a text file composed of ActionScript. This option is particularly useful if you prefer to write scripts in a text- or script-editing program and want to integrate them directly into your movie.

Export your script Select Export as File or press Shift+Cmd+X (Mac)/Shift+Ctrl+X (Win), give the file a name, and click Save. Flash exports a text file containing your script.

Print Select Print, pick your print options, and click Print.

When you print scripts from the Actions panel, Flash doesn't include any information about the file that contains the script or the script's location in the movie. If you plan to print several scripts, it can be helpful to include comments that note where each script resides in your movie. (To learn more about working with comments, see Chapter 15.)

Checking Syntax and Errors

One advantage of Expert mode is that it gives you complete control over what is entered in the text box. The downside of this feature is that unlike Normal mode, it has no way to check automatically for errors as you input the actions. To ensure that your scripts are error-free before testing your movie, you can check the syntax in the Actions panel by doing one of the following:

- Click the Check Syntax button 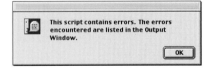 near the top of the Actions panel. This button looks like a check mark.

- In the pop-up menu in the upper-right corner of the Actions panel, select Check Syntax.

- Press Cmd/Ctrl+T while the Actions panel is active.

Whichever option you choose, if the script is free of mistakes, you will get a message that asks you to acknowledge this. If there are errors, you will be alerted, and any errors will be printed in the Output window. (For more specifics on using the Output window, see Chapter 18.)

Working with an External Script Editor

Although the Actions panel gives you total control while working in Expert mode, you may find it helpful to take advantage of an external editor and do your scripting outside Flash. If this is the case, all you need to do is replace any chunks of ActionScript with this line:

```
#include "actionScriptFile.as"
```

Here, `actionScriptFile.as` is a text file that contains all of the necessary code for the frame or object where the `#include` action is attached. The `#include` action imports the lines of Action-Script from the external AS file and runs it in the movie as though it were written directly in the Actions panel. To use this technique to import ActionScript from an external file:

1. Write your script in an external editor and save it with a `.as` extension.

2. Drag the `include` action from the ActionScript Toolbox or type `#include` in the text box.

3. In either the Parameters pane (when working in Normal mode) or in quotes after the `#include` action (when working in Expert mode), enter the path to the external script file. Use the forward-slash character (/) to delimit the path. For example, if `movie.fla` and `extScript.as` were in the same folder, the path would be `extScript.as`. If the script file were in a subfolder named Actions, the path would be `actions/extScript.as`.

Once you publish a movie that uses external scripts, those scripts become a permanent part of the movie. To make any changes to the script, you will have to change the Action-Script in the AS file and republish your movie.

Attaching Complex ActionScripts

Attaching complex scripts to objects and frames isn't very different than attaching basic actions. With advanced scripts, you will likely manage several scripts at a time. It's important to be aware of the impact one script will have on another while the movie is running. The Movie Explorer can be a valuable ally because it will allow you to see the hierarchy of movie elements and track which scripts are attached to which movie elements. (For more details on the Movie Explorer, see Chapter 7.)

The greatest difference between attaching simple and complex scripts is that most complex scripts are generally composed with the Actions panel in Expert mode. This is primarily because Expert mode offers more flexibility for creating scripts on your own terms, in the order you prefer.

When you attach scripts in Normal mode, you have to go through the process of dragging the actions from one side of the window to another. This is very convenient for just a few lines of code, but for complex scripts that go on and on, dragging scripts can become tedious. Moreover, to edit scripts in Normal mode, you have to make all your changes in the Parameters pane. This means that you have access to your script only through the options that the Parameters pane provides. In many cases, this is sufficient, but with Expert mode, it's never an obstacle; every element of your script is available for changes or modification.

The differences for creating scripts in this mode are few. Once you become familiar with Expert mode scripting, you will find that it is one of the most direct ways to attach scripts to your movie.

Attaching Scripts to Buttons and Movie Clips in Expert Mode

The objects in Flash that can have scripts attached to them are buttons and Movie Clips. With the right kind of script, buttons will respond to many kinds of mouse interaction, including clicks, rollovers, and drags. Movie Clips can also respond to events like loading into memory or playing through a frame. Additionally, both kinds of objects can monitor and record user keystrokes while a movie is running.

To attach an action to an object while working in Expert mode:

1. Click a button or MovieClip object and then either select Window → Actions or press F9.

2. Click the View Options menu and choose Expert Mode, or press Shift+Cmd+E (Mac)/Shift+Ctrl+E (Win).

3. Enter an action by doing one of the following:

    *   Select an action from a category of the ActionScript Toolbox and either double-click it or drag it to the text box.

    *   Use the Add Actions button (+) and select an action from the pop-up menu.

    *   Type ActionScript directly into the text box window.

> When you worked in Normal mode, event handlers were automatically inserted when you brought an action over from the Toolbox. In Expert mode, this isn't the case, so be sure to remember a handler. It assigns a trigger event that will set your script in motion. For a review of ActionScript event handlers, see Chapter 12.

4. When you are finished, it's a good idea to check the syntax of your script. Either select Check Syntax from the Actions panel pop-up menu, click the Check Syntax button, or press Cmd/Ctrl+T.

5. If the script is free of errors, select Control → Test Movie to see how it works in your movie.

    If you need to attach additional scripts, use the Jump menu to navigate to other objects in your movie and repeat steps 3 and 4. This allows you to write several scripts in your movie without ever having to leave the Actions panel. To keep an object script displayed in the Actions panel at all times, click the Script Pin button, and the script will remain in the text box. Even if you select other objects or frames in your movie, the "pinned" script won't disappear.

Attaching Actions to Frames in Expert Mode

Frame actions are a close relative of object actions. The biggest difference is that no handler is required. By default, when the movie playback head reaches a frame containing a script, that script is executed.

To attach a frame script in Expert mode:

1. Click a keyframe in the Timeline and select Window → Actions (F9). If there is no keyframe, click a frame and select Insert → Keyframe to insert one.

2. Click the View Options menu and choose Expert Mode, or press Shift+Cmd+E (Mac)/Shift+Ctrl+E (Win).

3. Enter an action by doing one of the following:

    *   Select an action from a category of the ActionScript Toolbox and then either double-click it or drag it to the text box.

    *   Use the Add Actions button (+) and select an action from the pop-up menu.

    *   Type ActionScript directly into the text box window.

4. When you are finished, it's a good idea to check the syntax of your script. Either select Check Syntax from the Actions panel pop-up menu, click the Check Syntax button, or press Cmd/Ctrl+T.

5. If the script is free of errors, select Control → Test Movie to see how it works in your movie.

   If you need to attach additional scripts, use the Jump menu to navigate to other keyframes in your movie and repeat steps 3 and 4. This allows you to write several scripts in your movie without ever having to leave the Actions panel. To keep a frame script displayed in the Actions panel at all times, click the Script Pin button, and the script will remain in the text box. Even if you select other frames or objects in your movie, the "pinned" script won't disappear.

Figure 14.8

"Goodnight Mr. Snoozleberg" by Sarbakan

Inspirational Design Model

ActionScript opens Flash to an enormous world of possibilities. With the help of ActionScript, Flash is no longer just a vector animation tool; it can be used to create rich multimedia websites, interactive forms, cartoon serials, and games.

"Goodnight Mr. Snoozleberg" is a combination game and cartoon developed by Sarbakan of Quebec (see Figure 14.8). Visit www.sarbakan.com/sybex/snooz for the latest information on where Mr.Snoozleberg is being hosted. It's an excellent example that shows Flash in its element—a perfect marriage of clean vector animation and programming to create a funny, entertaining, and very interactive web experience.

Summary

This chapter introduced you to some of the more advanced components of the ActionScript language. You saw how an advanced script can be broken down and reduced to its most basic elements. This is a helpful exercise because it allows you to see how the different parts of the language work together to create a meaningful script. You were also introduced to Expert scripting mode, which offers several alternatives to Normal scripting. With this new understanding, you should be ready to begin writing more complex and advanced ActionScripts of your own.

CHAPTER 15

Writing ActionScripts

The last chapter introduced the fundamental ActionScript terms and some of the concepts of using the ActionScript language. In this chapter, you will peel back another layer and delve deeper into the world of Flash-based scripting.

So far, you have seen the possibilities that ActionScript can offer to your movies: It transforms them from simple linear animations to complex interactive applications and experiences. What is missing right now is a framework for you to use when constructing your scripts. You need to learn the conventions and rules of the language. Without these, it's impossible to use ActionScript to communicate intelligently. This chapter covers these topics:

- **Elements of ActionScript syntax**

- **Key components of the ActionScript language**

- **The kind of information ActionScript handles**

- **Storing script elements for reuse**

- **Performing computations in ActionScript**

- **ActionScript commands**

- **Setting conditions for scripts**

- **Using functions and predefined objects**

Learning ActionScript Syntax

Like all spoken languages, computer languages such as ActionScript follow a particular set of rules, or *syntax*. It's crucial to understand the syntax of the language so that you can use it to say something meaningful. After all, the purpose of a language is to communicate, and ActionScript provides you with a communication link to Flash.

Knowing all of the ActionScript terms in this book can be helpful if you want to become an expert "ActionScripter." But it is even more important to know the rules that define how all the terms are used and how they work together as a language. Once you have grasped the rules of ActionScript syntax, you are well on your way to becoming a fluent script writer and an excellent communicator with your Flash movies.

Punctuation Marks in ActionScript

You will use several different punctuation marks when writing an ActionScript. You can use punctuation to issue a command or track the path to a movie or variable. It is also there to help annotate your scripts and provide both explanation and instruction. Mainly, the purpose of punctuation is to bring order to your scripts and organize their contents so that Flash can understand how the scripts should be executed.

ActionScript Dot Syntax

The ActionScript dot syntax was introduced when Flash evolved to version 5. The dot syntax makes ActionScript look similar to JavaScript. If you are comfortable with JavaScript, learning ActionScript will put you in familiar territory. The construction for the dot syntax is as follows:

The left side of the dot names either an object, instance, or Timeline reference in your movie. The right side of the dot can be either a property, target path, variable, or action that is directed at (or found within) the element on the left side. Here are three examples:

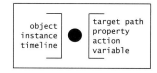

```
myClip._visible=0;
menuBar.menu1.item3;
_root.gotoAndPlay(5);
```

In the first example, a Movie Clip named `myClip` is made invisible by setting the `_visible` property to `0` with the dot syntax. The second example shows the path to the variable `item3` through `menu1`, a nested Movie Clip in the Movie Clip named `menuBar`. The third example uses the `_root` reference to command the main Timeline to jump to frame 5 and play. In each example, you can see how the left side of the dot names or references an object, while the right side contains some kind of instruction to define, or manipulate, that object.

The dot is also known as the *dot operator* because it can be used to issue commands and modify properties. For more information on other ActionScript operators, see the "Operators" section later in this chapter.

ActionScript Slash Syntax

The slash syntax was used in Flash 4 and has since been replaced by the dot syntax. Although slash syntax is still supported in Flash MX, it is deprecated, or no longer preferred. This syntax was used primarily in Flash 4 to delimit target paths. For example, the path to the nested Movie Clip `leg` through the clips `spider` and `body` was expressed like this:

```
"/spider/body/leg";
```

Now, using the dot syntax, the same path is written this way:

```
spider.body.leg;
```

The slash syntax was used to access variables belonging to other Timelines and was also used with the `tellTarget` action to target Movie Clips. Now that the `tellTarget` action has been deprecated, it's better to use the dot syntax and the `with` action.

Comments

It is a good idea to make notes as you write your scripts. Notes can provide guidance or instructions to someone who has to edit your scripts. They can also be helpful if you are forced to abandon a project for a period of time; when you come back to the code, your notes will remind you what each part of the script was doing.

To make notes in ActionScript, you have to insert them as *comments*. To insert comments in Normal scripting mode, simply drag or select the `comment` action from the Actions category of the script Toolbox and enter your notes in the text field of the Parameters pane. To enter comments in Expert mode, type two forward slashes (//) and enter your notes after them. For example:

```
// checks to see if all movie frames are loaded
if(_framesLoaded >=_totalFrames){
// if TRUE, then it starts the move at frame 6
    gotoAndPlay(6);
}else{
// if FALSE, it loops back to frame 1
    gotoAndPlay(1);
}
```

In ActionScript, anything that follows the double slash will be ignored by Flash. This means that you can type anything you like after the slashes because Flash will not interpret comments as ActionScript. Comments also allow you to "turn off" parts of a script. If there are one or more lines that are causing problems, you can comment them out and run the script without those lines. Flash will ignore the commented lines and run everything else in the script. To learn more about this technique, see Chapter 18.

> To insert large notes or blocks of text within your scripts, you can use the multiline comment operator (/*). This handy tool makes it easy to write long messages or explanations within the body of your ActionScripts. Simply begin the note with the opening operator (/*) and end with the closing operator (*/). All statements that are written between these markers will be ignored by the Flash Player.

When the ActionScript Editor Preferences are set to default, comments appear in the script window in a light gray color so that you can distinguish them from other parts of your script. To change this, select Edit → Preferences or choose Preferences from the Actions panel pop-up menu. Go to the ActionScript Editor tab and select a new color from the swatch menu next to the word *Comments*.

Curly Braces

ActionScript organizes the elements of a script by using the curly brace characters ({}). (These characters are also called *curly brackets*.) In the following script, all the statements between the pair of curly braces will be executed when the mouse is pressed:

```
on(press){
    with(fishClip){
        gotoAndStop(50);
    }
}
```

In this example, the curly braces organize the script into two parts. The on(press) handler executes the with action, and the with action targets the instance fishClip, sends it to frame 50, and stops it.

Parentheses

Parentheses are used in ActionScript to assign arguments for functions or to set the order of operations in an expression. For example, the setProperty action has three arguments: *target, property,* and *expression*. Here you use the parentheses to list the arguments after calling the action:

```
setProperty("testClip",_alpha,50);
```

This script sets the `_alpha` value (*property*) to 50% (*expression*) for the instance `testClip` (*target*).

You can also use parentheses to alter the order of operations. The expression 2 + 3 * 4 evaluates to 14, whereas the expression (2 + 3) * 4 evaluates to 20 because the parentheses force you to do the addition first.

Semicolon

In ActionScript, the semicolon (;) is used to mark the end of a statement. For example:

```
on(release){
    introClip._visible=0;
}
```

Here, the action that makes the instance `introClip` invisible is terminated with a semicolon. If you forget to use the semicolon, Flash will still compile the script correctly. However, it is good practice to follow correct syntax conventions and always terminate statements with the semicolon character.

Semicolons are also used to separate the parameters in a `for` loop structure. To learn more about this ActionScript convention, see the Conditionals section later in this chapter.

Other ActionScript Syntax Conventions

Aside from the mechanics of ActionScript, there are a few other conventions that are important to understand so that you can work flexibly with the language. Certain terms in the language are "protected" or reserved because they have a specific meaning in ActionScript. Other terms must follow a specific upper- or lowercase structure so that Flash will know how to interpret them.

Constants

Constants are terms or properties that retain a specific and unchanging value in ActionScript. In a script, they are written in all-capital letters. Constants are part of three ActionScript objects: the Key object, the Math object, and the Number object.

The following script uses the Key object to test whether the spacebar has been pressed:

```
if(Key.isdown(Key.SPACE)){
    laser.shoot(1);
}
```

The spacebar has a constant value, and it is a property of the Key object. When it is pressed, the statements below it execute.

In the next example, the Math object uses the constant value of `PI` to evaluate the area of a circle:

```
area=Math.PI*(radius*radius);
```

In the following example, the `MAX_VALUE` constant is used to set the variable `duration` to the highest possible value in ActionScript:

```
duration=Number.MAX_VALUE;
```

Keywords

Keywords are ActionScript terms that are reserved and have a specific purpose in the language. These terms are used only in a specific context and are not available as names of variables, functions, objects, or instances. See Table 15.1 for a list of ActionScript keywords.

Table 15.1

The ActionScript Keywords

break	else	instanceof	typeof
case	for	new	var
continue	function	return	void
default	if	switch	while
delete	in	this	with
do			

ActionScript Case Sensitivity

For the most part, ActionScript is fairly forgiving when it comes to upper- and lowercase letters. If you are scripting in Expert mode, you will notice that the color for a term will change if it isn't entered in the preferred upper- or lowercase syntax. For example, `stop()` is usually colored blue. If you were to enter it as `Stop()` (note the capital S), it would change to black. However, in most cases, Flash would still be able to interpret your script without error. To be safe, it is best to follow proper ActionScript syntax at all times; capitalize anything that should appear in uppercase, and keep all lowercase terms free of capital letters.

Learning ActionScript Language Elements

So far, you have learned the conventions of ActionScript and how the pieces of the language fit together to create scripts. Now it's time to look at those individual pieces and see exactly what ActionScript is made of. There are many components to the language, some of which will seem familiar based on what you already know. Luckily, most of the terms resemble a word in the English language that is near the term's meaning in ActionScript. This (hopefully) makes the terms easier to remember. The most important step toward learning to write ActionScript is understanding the *role* a particular term plays in the language. As the duties of these terms become clearer, you will begin to see how to fit pieces of the puzzle together to suit your needs.

Data Types

As you learned earlier, data types define the kind of information that can be represented by elements of ActionScript. There are six types of information used in a script: string, number, Boolean, object, Movie Clip, and undefined. We will discuss the specifics of each type.

Strings

Strings are literal chunks of information that hold no value. They are composed of any combination of letters, punctuation, and numbers. String data is enclosed in quotes (" " or ' ') and treated as a single piece of information. Because strings are literal, they are case sensitive, so, for instance, the strings `"one"` and `"One"` are different. In the following example, `Joe` is a string stored in `myName`:

```
myName="Joe";
```

Strings can be combined, or *concatenated*, to link string information together. For example:

```
fullName=myName+" Smith";
```

The addition operator (+) is used to concatenate string data. Note that in the preceding example, the string `" Smith"` contains a space. This is to prevent the two string elements from getting closed up when they are concatenated. When the strings are combined, you get this result:

```
fullName="Joe Smith";
```

Strings can also be organized alphabetically by using the comparison operators: `<`, `>`, `=<`, and `>=`. Flash uses the Latin 1 character set. When evaluating strings alphabetically, the letter *z* holds the highest value, while "A" holds the lowest. Note the following expression:

```
"alligator"<"zebra"=true
"alligator">"Zebra"=true
```

Here you can see how lowercase letters hold a higher value than uppercase ones. For more information on operators and comparisons, see the "Operators" section of this chapter.

Numbers

Numbers are characters that hold a specific numeric value. In ActionScript, number values can be manipulated in expressions using mathematical operators such as addition (+), subtraction (–), multiplication (*), division (/), modulo (%), increment (++), and decrement (– –). You can also use ActionScript's predefined Math object to evaluate numbers and expressions. For more information on this, see the "Operators" section of this chapter or the ActionScript Reference section.

Booleans

A *Boolean* is a value that is either True or False. Booleans are used in conditional statements to evaluate script elements and see if values have been met or initialized. The following statements evaluate whether or not all of a movie's frames have been loaded into memory:

```
_framesloaded=loaded;
if(loaded=true){
    introMovie.gotoAndPlay(2);
}
```

In most conditional statements, the Boolean value is assumed and not stated explicitly in the `if` statement. For more specifics on this, see the Conditionals section later in this chapter.

Objects

An *object* is a collection of information organized into properties. These properties have names and values that can be accessed in a Flash movie. The object data type allows you to manipulate the properties assigned to a particular object. In the following statement, the object `money` has a property named `myAccount`, which is assigned the value `5000`:

```
money.myAccount=5000;
```

Flash allows you to create your own objects or use one of the built-in objects such as Date, Array, and Color.

Movie Clips

Movie Clips are self-contained animations that run independently in a Flash movie. They are self-contained because they have their own Timeline. Movie Clips have properties such as `_alpha` or `_rotation` that can be assigned values in ActionScript. Here, a Movie Clip instance is rotated 180 degrees:

```
spinClip._rotation=180;
```

Movie Clips also have methods that you can use to control them. In this example, a clip is instructed to stop on the first frame of its Timeline:

```
audioClip.gotoAndStop(1);
```

Undefined

Undefined exists to represent a lack of data, or no data. A variable that has no value returns `undefined`. A variable with no value cannot be considered an "empty" variable. Without a value, it does not exist and is therefore undefined.

On a related note, if you want to create an empty variable, you can set the value of the variable to be `null`. Rather than not existing at all (undefined), the variable exists but is empty, or null. For example, the following statement returns nothing; as a nonexistent container, the variable is declared but has no value:

```
var one;
```

The next statement returns null; the variable is an empty but *existing* container:

```
var two=null;
```

To learn more about variables, see the next section.

Variables

Variables serve as storage locations for information that you need in a script. Variables are like pockets where you can put something, keep it there for a while, and then retrieve it when it's needed again later in your movie. To use a variable, you have to first *declare*, or state, the variable. Then you must *initialize* the variable to let Flash know that you are going to store something in it. Once you have initialized the variable with a starting value, it will hold that value until it is changed. To change the value of a variable, all you have to do is add to it, subtract from it, or reinitialize it.

Variables can be used to hold any type of data: string, number, Boolean, object, or Movie Clip. For example, the variable x can be initialized to either a numeric value or a set of string data:

```
x=24;
x="myName";
```

Variables can also be used in conditional loops to serve as the loop counter. For example:

```
j=2
while(j>0){
    duplicateMovieClip(_root.ship,"ship"+j,j);
    setProperty("ship"+j,_y,(_root.ship._y+50*j));
    trace("duplicated"+j);
    j=j-1;
}
```

In this example, the variable j is initialized to 2. Every time it passes through the while loop, it is reduced by 1, or reinitialized until it no longer meets the conditions of the loop. The variable j is also used to help name the duplicated Movie Clips and assign the level of each new clip in the duplicateMovieClip statement. Finally, in the setProperty statement, j is used in an expression to position the new Movie Clips at a location that is 50*j pixels away from the original clip. That's a lot of work for one variable! The important thing to realize is that you can use a variable over and over again in your scripts to help perform a variety of tasks.

When you use a variable, it's important to give it an appropriate name. There are a few rules concerning this. First, a variable must be an identifier—a combination of letters, numbers, underscore (_), or dollar sign character ($). See Chapter 14 for specifics on identifiers.

cond, a variable cannot be an ActionScript keyword, and it must be unique within your movie. It's good practice to name a variable something meaningful that relates to the job it will perform in your movie. If you use a variable to store the name of a visitor to your website, name the variable something like `siteVisitor` to keep things simple. For example, if visitors enter their names in an input text field, give the field the variable name `siteVisitor`. This way, any time you want to use a visitor's name, you can just call on the variable, and the name will be available immediately. If you wanted to print a farewell message in the text field `goodbye`, you would write:

```
goodbye="Thanks for visiting "+siteVisitor;
```

In the previous conditional loop script example, you may have noted the line that reads `trace("duplicated"+j);`. `trace` is a special function of ActionScript that allows you to monitor different elements of your script. In this line, the script will trace the word *duplicated* and concatenate it with the current value of j. It can be very helpful to use this function because it allows you to track the value of your variables as they change while your script executes.

To use the `trace()` function, all you have to do is enter the information you want to monitor in the parentheses following `trace`. When you test your movie, Flash will print all the information you asked it to trace in the Output window. Anything entered within quotes will be treated as a literal string and appear in the Output window exactly as it was entered. This can be helpful because it allows you to make a label for each item you need to trace. For the example `trace("duplicated"+j);`, the Output window will print:

```
duplicated2
duplicated1
```

This printout reflects the value of the variable j as it goes through the `while` loop twice, each time decreasing its value.

Variable Scope

One of the most important aspects of variables is their availability, or *scope*. A variable's scope determines how it is available to other portions of your movie. Because you use variables to store and retrieve information, having them available is very important. In ActionScript, variables have a scope that is either global, timeline-specific, or local.

If a variable is global, it is shared by all Timelines in your movie and is available at any time. Any script in any part of your movie can access or change the value of a global variable. You declare a global variable by using the reference `_global`. For example, this statement will create a global variable named `store1` and initialize its value to 1:

```
_global.store1=1;
```

The value of `store1` can be retrieved at any point in your movie with this statement:

```
trace(store1);
```

Because the variable is global, it is always available, by name.

A Timeline-specific variable is also available throughout your movie. However, you must always use a target path when working with the variable; otherwise, Flash won't know where to find the information the variable is storing. Declare a Timeline variable by giving it a name and assigning it a value. For example, to create a Timeline-specific variable named `store2`, you would enter the following statement on any Timeline (Movie Clip, main Timeline, and so on):

```
store2=2;
```

If you created this variable on the main Timeline, its value could be retrieved at any point in your movie with this statement:

```
_root.store2;
```

If you created `store2` on the Timeline of the Movie Clip instance `sprocket`, you would access it by using this target path:

```
_root.sprocket.store2
```

Because the variable is scoped to a particular Timeline, you must refer to it using a target path, or the "address" of the variable in your movie.

A local variable is different. Local variables are scoped to functions and can be changed only within the block of script or function where they reside. This can be helpful if you have a value that needs to exist for only a very brief period of time. To make a variable local, you must use the `var` action when you declare and initialize the variable. For example:

```
function init3(){
    var store3=3;
}
```

This script declares the variable `store3` as a local variable and initializes its value to 3. As a local variable, `store3` is available only within the curly braces (`{}`) of the function where it resides, and it will be "alive" (contain a value) only while the function is executing.

To create a global variable:

- In Normal mode, select Objects → Core → _global and assign a value in the Expression field.

- In Expert mode, type **_global=** and assign a value.

  To create a Timeline-specific variable:

- In Normal mode, select Actions → Variables → Set Variable. Enter a name in the Variable field and assign a value in the Value field. If the value is numeric, be sure to check the Expression box.

- In Expert mode, type the name of the variable and use the assignment operator (=) to assign a value.

To create a local variable inside a function:

- In Normal mode, select Actions → Variables → var and enter a name in the Variables field. Then, to assign it a value, follow the steps to create a Timeline variable.

- In Expert mode, type **var**, followed by the variable name, and use the assignment operator (=) to assign a value.

Operators

Operators are used to produce values. They are characters that instruct ActionScript how to combine, remove, or compare the values in an expression. On both sides of the operator, you have the values, known as the *operands*. The operator takes the operands, performs its function on them, and leaves a final value for the expression.

If there is more than one operator in an expression, they are executed in a specific order, which Macromedia calls *precedence*. Operators with the highest precedence are executed first, followed by others in order of highest to lowest precedence. For example:

```
total = 3 + 4 * 5
total = 23
```

According to the rules of precedence, the 4 and 5 are multiplied first, and then the 3 is added. Tables 15.2–15.5 list some of the ActionScript operators in order of precedence, from highest to lowest. Where operator precedence is equal, operations are performed from the left of an expression to the right.

Table 15.2

The Numeric Operators

OPERATOR	OPERATION
++	Increment by one
– –	Decrement by one
*	Multiplication
/	Division
%	Modulo
+	Addition
–	Subtraction

Numeric Operators

Numeric operators are used to add, subtract, multiply, and divide the operands of an expression. Table 15.2 lists the ActionScript numeric operators. Operators with the highest precedence are listed first; precedence decreases as you move down the table.

Table 15.3

The Comparison Operators

OPERATOR	OPERATION
<	Less than
<=	Less than or equal to
>	Greater than
>=	Greater than or equal to

Comparison Operators

The comparison operators are used to compare the value of two operands and return a Boolean (True or False) value based on the comparison. Table 15.3 lists the ActionScript comparison operators. Comparison operators have equal precedence and are read from left to right.

Logical Operators

Logical operators are used to compare two Boolean values and return a third Boolean value. LogicalAND will evaluate to `true` if both conditions are True. LogicalOR will evaluate to `true` if one of the

OPERATOR	OPERATION
!	LogicalNOT
&&	LogicalAND
||	LogicalOR

Table 15.4

The Logical Operators

conditions is True, and `false` if both conditions are False. LogicalNOT inverts the value of an expression—for example, `!false = true`. Table 15.4 lists the ActionScript logical operators. Operators with the highest precedence are listed first; precedence decreases as you move down the table.

Equality and Assignment Operators

The equality operators are used to test for equality between two operands. The operation will return a Boolean value based on the operands. The assignment operators make assignments and initialize variables. Table 15.5 lists the equality and assignment operators. Operators with the highest precedence are listed first; precedence decreases as you move down the table. All compound assignment operators (+=, −=, *=, and so on) have equal precedence and are read from left to right.

OPERATOR	OPERATION
==	Equality
===	Strict equality
!=	Inequality
!==	Strict inequality
=	Assignment
+=	Addition and assignment
−=	Subtraction and assignment
*=	Multiplication and assignment
/=	Division and assignment
%=	Modulo and assignment

Table 15.5

The Equality and Assignment Operators

ActionScript's bitwise operators, which are used to set and evaluate values at the bit level, are beyond the scope of this book and will not be covered. To learn more about them, refer to the documentation that ships with Flash.

Actions

Actions are statements in ActionScript that issue commands to a movie or one of its components, telling it to do something. For example:

```
gotoAndPlay(5);
```

This action tells the movie to go to frame 5 and continue playing when it gets there.

Here's another example:

```
duplicateMovieClip("myClip","myOtherClip",1);
```

This action makes a copy of the Movie Clip `myClip`, names the copy `myOtherClip`, and sets it at stacking level 1 above the original clip.

Actions are one of the largest portions of the ActionScript language. They can be found in the ActionScript Toolbox section of the Actions panel. Click the Actions icon to display a list of actions that are available to you.

Conditionals

In the preceding chapter, you learned about the flow of scripts. *Conditionals* are used to direct this flow. Conditionals present a script with a condition to be tested. The test returns a Boolean value, either `true` or `false`. Depending on this outcome, the script is routed in the appropriate direction by the conditional structure. In ActionScript, the main conditionals are `if`, `if...else`, `switch`, `while`, `do...while`, and `for`.

"if" and *"if...else"* Statements

Statements that test whether a condition evaluates to either `true` or `false` use the `if` action. ActionScript evaluates the condition in the first line of the script and then proceeds to execute the appropriate statements that follow, based on the condition's evaluation. For example:

```
if(y<_currentFrame){
    move=Math.PI*y;
    saucerClip._x=saucerClip._x+move;
}
```

In this script, if the statement `y<_currentFrame` evaluates to `true`, the following statements within the curly braces are executed. If it evaluates to `false`, the code in the `if` block is skipped and execution of the script skips to the first statement after the closing curly brace of the `if` action. `if` conditionals can have alternative statements as well. The preceding example could be expanded as follows:

```
if(y<_currentFrame){
    move=Math.PI*y;
    saucerClip._x=saucerClip._x+move;
}else{
    gotoAndPlay(1);
    y++;
}
```

This second script has an `else` component. This means that if the `y<_currentFrame` statement evaluates to `false`, the statements following `}else{` are executed as an alternative.

With the introduction of Flash MX, you are able to take advantage of a new conditional structure that provides an alternative to the `if...else` statements. This new structure, called `switch`, presents a script with a series of cases, each of which will be executed depending on the value of the condition to be tested. Consider the following statements:

```
num=1;
switch(num){
    case 1:
        trace("case 1 was true");
        break;
    case 2:
        trace("case 2 was true");
        break;
    case 3:
        trace("case 3 was true");
        break;
    default:
        trace("no case was true")
}
```

In the preceding switch statement, the value of num is tested over several conditions, or cases. If a case returns true, meaning that the value of the case equals that of the variable running through the conditional, its statements are executed. In this example, the Output window would print "case 1 was true" because the value of num happens to be 1. If the first line read num=3, you would see "case 3 was true" in the Output window. If no cases evaluated as true, the default case's statement(s) would be executed.

Notice that within each case statement, there is a break action. This ensures that only a single condition's statements are executed. If you ran this script but removed the break actions, it would print the following:

```
case 1 was true
case 2 was true
case 3 was true
no case was true
```

break causes a script to quit executing statements in the current block. This is defined by the pair of curly braces ({}) that contain the switch statement's case conditions. Without the break statement, the remaining conditions in the body of the switch statement will be evaluated as true.

Looping Scripts with Conditional Statements

ActionScript conditionals can also be used to loop repetitive tasks that perform an action or actions a certain number of times. A loop is created with either the while, do...while, or for action. Each of these loop structures has some kind of *counter* that monitors the number of times the loop should be executed. Generally, the counter is initialized as a variable at the outset of the loop and is either decremented or incremented (decreased or increased by one) with every loop cycle. The function of each loop structure is identical, but the way each performs its function is unique.

The `while` loop establishes a condition and then executes statements within the curly braces until the condition is no longer true. In the next example, the variable k is used as the loop counter and is decremented each time the loop statements are executed. This loop will execute three times:

```
k=3;
while(k>0){
    duplicatMovieClip("spotClip","spot"+k,k+1);
    k=k-1;
}
```

The `do...while` loop executes its statements first and then tests the condition to see whether the loop should continue. If the condition evaluates to `true`, the loop continues. With this kind of loop, the statements are always executed at least once, even if the condition is `false`. For example:

```
k=3;
do{
    duplicatMovieClip("spotClip","spot"+k,k+1);
    k=k-1;
} while(k>0);
```

The `for` loop puts all of the necessary loop information in the first statement: the counter initialization, the condition, and the count expression. For example:

```
for(k=3;k>0;k=k-1){
    duplicateMovieClip("spotClip","spot"+k,k+1);
}
```

Here you can see that the loop conditions and the count are the same as in the `while` and `do...while` examples. However, all of the information to establish and control the loop has been economically placed in the first line of the loop.

Another loop structure, `for...in`, is used to loop through the properties or nested objects of an object. This action can modify properties or use methods to control multiple nested Movie Clips or multiple objects. To learn more about `for...in` loops, see the ActionScript Reference section.

Functions

In the preceding chapter, functions were presented as information processors. You give them a set of arguments, and they perform a specific task using those arguments. The power of functions can be very useful if you have a series of tasks or operations that have to be performed over and over again in your movie. For example, if you need to frequently scale a Movie Clip to 50% of its original size, you can write a function. Rather than having to use both the _xscale and _yscale properties every time you do this, you can call on the function and it will do all the work for you.

First, you must define the function. The syntax for defining a function is as follows:

```
function functionName(arguments){
    statement(s);
}
```

Here is a function named `Half` that reduces the horizontal and vertical scale of a Movie Clip by 50% and moves it 100 pixels up and to the left:

```
function Half(myClip) {
    var x=myClip._x;
    var y=myClip._y;
    myClip._x=x-100;
    myClip._y=y-100;
    myClip._xscale=50;
    myClip._yscale=50;
}
```

In this function, the term `myClip` is used as an argument. When the function is called, the Movie Clip listed within the parentheses (an argument to the function) will be scaled down accordingly. When you create a function, it's best to put the constructor function script in a frame action at the beginning of your movie. If ActionScript hasn't read your function, it won't know what to do when you call it later.

When creating a function, it is essential to give it a unique name within your movie so that there is no confusion between functions, variables, and instances. For example, if you had a function named `Half` and a variable named `Half`, you would open the door to possible error and confusion with the ActionScript in your movie. If you can't use any other name, append the name with a prefix like `funHalf` for the function and `varHalf` for the variable.

Once you've created the function, you are free to call it whenever you need it in your movie. A function can be called in any script or in any handler, and from any level or Timeline of your movie. Here is an example where the `Half` function is called when a button is clicked and released:

```
on(release){
    _root.Half(invaders.rogue_1);
}
```

In this script, the clip `rogue_1` (nested inside the clip `invaders`) is moved and sized down by 50% using the `Half` function. The target path to `rogue_1` is passed as an argument to the function, and the clip is scaled. Because the `Half` function was created on the main Timeline, it is necessary to include the target reference `_root` when the function is called from a different Timeline.

Objects

Objects are one of the many data types in Flash, and as such, they can be referred to directly in an ActionScript statement. They are also an important element of the language because they hold chunks of information that affect different elements of your movie. Objects have properties that can be set and reset as needed within a movie. They also have methods, which are built-in functions that can be used to produce values or perform actions.

Following is a list of the predefined objects in ActionScript. Each object has a particular set of methods.

 Arguments object An array that is used to manage the arguments passed to a function.

Array object Used to get at and change the values and positions of elements in an array.

Boolean object Used to return a Boolean value (`true` or `false`) as either a primitive data type or a string representation of that data type—that is, either the string *true* or the string *false*.

 Button object Button symbols can now be controlled as objects, with their own set of methods and properties.

 Capabilities object Used to determine the technical abilities of the system and player running your movie.

Color object Allows you to transform, set, and retrieve the RGB colors of a Movie Clip.

Date object Allows you to get current date and time information relative to either Universal Coordinated Time or the operating system running the Flash Player.

Key object Used to capture keystrokes while your movie is playing.

 LoadVars object Used to pass variables between Flash movies and a server.

Math object Allows you to access mathematical constants and functions for crunching data in your movie.

Mouse object Used to show, hide, and script events for the cursor while your movie is running.

MovieClip object Allows you to control Movie Clip properties and playback.

Number object Used to calculate numeric values.

Object object The "generic" object is used in conjunction with the methods of other objects and for creating custom objects, properties, and methods.

Selection object Used to control editable text fields.

Sound object Used to manipulate the playback of sound in your movie.

Stage object Used to alter the size and position of your Flash movie.

String object Used to work with primitive string value types.

TextField object Used to control the behavior and properties of a text field instance.

TextFormat object Used to set and manipulate the formatting of text within text fields.

Video object Used to stream video from a camera into a Flash movie.

XML object Allows you to communicate with XML documents.

XML Socket object Allows the computer running the Flash Player to communicate directly with a server.

> The topics surrounding XML are beyond the scope of this book and will not be covered in detail. For an overview of the XML and XML Socket objects, see the ActionScript Reference section. For more specific information, choose Window → Reference or press Shift+F1 to consult Flash MX's built-in Reference panel.

Inspirational Design Model

For an example of the kind of interactive depth and interest that Flash can create, take a look at the Destroy Everything site designed by Nicola Stumpo at `www.abnormalbehaviorchild.com/nuovo/default.html` (Figure 15.1). This site features an interesting blend of music, text, imagery, animation, and interactivity. Little ActionScript "tricks," as Nico calls them, are used to make this project come to life. What is most compelling is the way visitors are drawn deeper into the site through its interactive animations and unique interface structure.

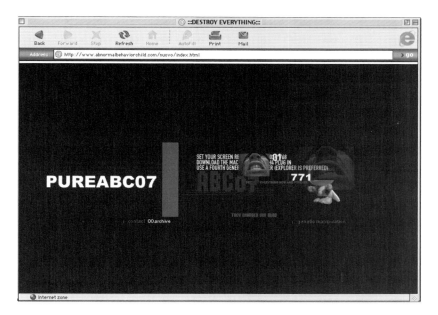

Figure 15.1

Destroy Everything by Nicola Stumpo

Summary

In this chapter, you learned two crucial parts of the ActionScript language: its syntax conventions and its elements. You saw how ActionScript uses punctuation to organize and issue commands in scripts, and how the language responds to upper- and lowercase letters. This chapter introduced you to the different kinds of information that can be included in an ActionScript element, as well as ways to store and evaluate information and to test conditions in a script.

With the details of the language behind you, the next chapter will put this information to use and show you how to control many different aspects of your movie using ActionScript.

CHAPTER 16

Creating Advanced Interaction

Okay, you can admit it: Learning all the technical ins and outs of ActionScript isn't a picnic. The language has many layers of detail, and understanding the relationships between them is a tough thing to wrap your brain around. If you are like most people, it will take months of mental pain and frustration to get a handle on how it all comes together. But be patient. As you progress, you will find that the moments of ActionScript success far outnumber the periods of frustration.

You have tackled the technical side of ActionScript, and you are now ready to put your newly acquired skills to use. As you can imagine, the possibilities that ActionScript offers are virtually unbounded; it can sometimes be stifling just trying to think about what you want to do with a particular movie, let alone how you will actually accomplish the task. The best approach to take is this: Think about *what* you would like to create rather than *how* you will create it. Let your artistic or design goals provide direction first; then figure out how they will be accomplished.

This chapter should provide the materials you need to help get you started. It would be impossible to cover all the features of both Flash and ActionScript in a single book. Here you will find examples that cover many of the Flash and ActionScript essentials. Think of these lessons as starter kits for your movies. Just add your own ideas, and you will be up and running in no time. As always, remember to work in small chunks, save often, and test your movie each time you add a new feature or change a script. If you follow this process, it will be much easier to pinpoint an error or problem if and when one occurs. Good luck, and have fun!

This chapter covers the following topics:

- **Button scripting beyond the basics**
- **Creating a slider to control movie elements**
- **How ActionScript watches and records keystrokes**
- **Managing multiple Timelines in your movie and targeting various movie layers**
- **ActionScript properties used to control Movie Clips**
- **Flash MX Components**
- **Using ActionScript to change graphic elements of your movie**

Scripting for User Input and Interactivity

Flash is a great application for creating vector animations, and with the help of ActionScript, it is also great for creating interactive games, interfaces, presentations, music players—the list goes on and on. When you are creating an interactive application, it is helpful to be able to monitor how your audience is interacting with your movie. That way, the movie can react appropriately and respond to the wishes and intentions of the audience. After all, this is what makes something interactive to begin with.

At the time of this writing, the main ways to communicate or interact with a computer program are through mouse and keyboard input. Someday (probably closer than we think), the mouse and keyboard will be under glass in museums around the world, and everyone will marvel that we actually used to *use* these things. Well, until that day comes, everyone is stuck in the Stone Age with two basic input devices. In keeping with the times, ActionScript provides a series of actions, properties, and methods that allow you to create your movies with mouse and keyboard input in mind.

Even though all of the ActionScript covered here can be entered in the Actions panel while working in Normal mode, all references will be made as though you were working in Expert mode. To learn about the ActionScript editing modes, see Chapter 12 for Normal scripting mode and Chapter 14 for Expert mode.

Advanced Button Scripting

Buttons are one of the most basic and intuitive kinds of interactive controls. Their role in an interactive movie is straightforward: You click them and something happens. Like a Movie Clip, a button can have actions attached to it. When the button is clicked, any attached actions are executed in accordance with the handler that is managing the action(s). To learn more about buttons and handlers, see Chapter 13.

At the most basic level, a button will have a single handler with a single action. For example:

```
on(release){
    gotoAndPlay(15);
}
```

When the mouse button is released, the action that sends the movie to play at frame 15 is executed. The handler event (`release`) sets the action in motion. For many buttons, this is all the complexity you will need, especially in the case of basic movie navigation. However, button scripts are capable of much more.

The mouse-event handlers used with button scripts, like any of the other handlers in ActionScript, can support multiple actions within a single handler. This means that you can make a button do all sorts of things when it is clicked: control the main Timeline, control other Timelines, play and stop sounds, perform functions or other computations, and send or modify variables—anything that is possible within ActionScript. When the mouse-event handler occurs, all actions within it are executed from top to bottom, and your movie is updated accordingly.

It's also possible to attach multiple handlers to a single button. This technique multiplies the performance of the button because it is no longer executing actions at the occurrence of a single event. For example:

```
on(rollOver){
    swish.start();
}
on(press){
    click.start();
}
on(release){
    ring.start();
}
```

This script sample plays three different sounds—swish, click, and ring—when you interact with the button. Swish is played when the mouse moves over the button, click is played when the mouse is pressed, and ring is heard when the mouse is released. All of this scripting creates a very musical and interactive button!

The technique of using multiple handlers and actions opens up the possibilities for the functionality of a button in your Flash movie. To explore this idea further, see both the listing for mouse-event handlers and the section on actions in the ActionScript Reference section of this book.

Scripting Button Behaviors with the Button Object

One of the exciting new features of Flash MX is the Button object. Buttons have always been objects of a Flash movie, but now they have their own object class. As a result, it's now possible to assign a unique instance name to a button and to control its behavior and properties via ActionScript. This feature will not significantly change the way you create Flash movies. It will, however, expand the possibilities of what you can do with a button in your interactive movies.

The Button object, like other objects, has a collection of associated methods, properties, and events. Methods work like actions to execute a particular task. Properties set the attributes of a Button object. Events are used like button-event handlers: They determine which button event must occur for an action (or actions) to be executed.

Like regular buttons, Button objects can be used as interactive controllers in your movie. The only differences, in fact, are that, to be an interactive controller, the Button object must have a unique instance name and a function assigned to it. When you assign a function to the Button object, you must specify which Button object event you would like to trigger the function. This makes Button object events one of the most important parts of this new feature.

The Button object events and their descriptions are as follows:

Button.onDragOut Occurs when the cursor is clicked over the button and dragged outside its bounds.

Button.onDragOver Occurs when the cursor is clicked over the button, dragged outside its bounds, and then dragged back inside.

Button.onKillFocus Occurs when the button loses keyboard focus.

Button.onPress Occurs when the cursor is pressed over the button.

Button.onRelease Occurs when the cursor is first pressed, then released over the button.

Button.onReleaseOutside Occurs when the cursor is first pressed over the button and then released outside the button's bounds.

Button.onRollOut Occurs when the cursor is moved outside the bounds of the button.

Button.onRollOver Occurs when the cursor is moved within the bounds of the button.

Button.onSetFocus Occurs when the button is given keyboard focus.

As you can see, there are many similarities between Button object events and regular button handlers.

Now that you are acquainted with the Button object events, you are ready to learn how to assign a function to a Button object. First, open a new Flash document and create a button symbol. For specifics on creating buttons, see Chapter 13. To assign an action to a Button object:

1. Select the button on the Stage. Choose Window → Properties or press Cmd/Ctrl+F3 to open the Property Inspector.

2. In the instance name field, type an instance name for the button. For the sake of this example, use the name **clicker**.

3. Insert a new layer in the Timeline and call it **actions**. Select the first keyframe of the actions layer and choose Window → Actions (F9) to open the Actions panel. Enter the following statements:

```
clicker.onRelease=function(){
    trace("clicked");
}
```

This script assigns a function to your `clicker` button instance. The function will print the phrase *clicked* in the Output window and will execute when the mouse is pressed and released over the `clicker` button instance.

4. Select Control → Test Movie to give your new function a try. When you click the button, the Output window should appear with the message *clicked.*

One advantage of this new scripting technique is that rather than having to attach actions to each button individually, you can assign them to each button from one location in your movie. If you have many buttons and button scripts, this can centralize the task of scripting for all of these elements. Be sure that for every Button object script you write, the object's corresponding button instance is on the Timeline at the same frame number. If a script is read on frame 1 but the button isn't encountered until frame 2, Flash won't know where to assign the function, and it will fail.

So far, what you have seen of the Button object is not tremendously different from what you saw in previous versions of Flash. Be not disappointed, for there are other techniques to explore that will show you the "coolness" of this new ActionScript feature. In Chapter 13, you learned how to use buttons to create a navigation bar. This was an important lesson because it showed you how to use buttons and graphic symbols together to create a navigational scheme that "bookmarked" where you were in the movie at all times. To do this, you had to work with a button, a graphic, and several movie scenes. However, by using the new Button object ActionScript, you can do this in a way that requires less work. And, best of all, it's a scalable technique. So, if your movie must be expanded, the task becomes a simple matter of changing some ActionScript and adding or subtracting elements from your Timeline as needed.

Check out the file `navBarButtons.fla` in the Chapter 16 folder on this book's companion CD-ROM. This file will allow you to see the finished scripts and techniques in context. To try the finished movie, open `navBarButtons.swf`, found in the same folder.

To make a navigation bar using Button object ActionScript:

1. Open the file `navBarLesson.fla` in the Chapter 16 folder. This file allows you to have some of the movie elements in place before you begin the lesson.

2. Use the Edit Symbols menu to open the `navMC` Timeline for editing. This is a Movie Clip, but in order to create the navigation bar, we will treat it as a button. In the `navMC` Timeline, select the first keyframe of the actions layer and open the Actions panel. Enter a `stop()` action. If this Movie Clip is going to act like a button, you cannot allow it to start playing right away.

3. With the first keyframe still selected, Choose Window → Properties to open the Property Inspector. In the Frame label field, enter the text **_up**. This causes this frame of the clip to behave like the Up state of a button Timeline.

4. For the remaining keyframes at frame 4 and frame 7, enter the frame labels **_over** and **_down**, respectively. The final Timeline should look like Figure 16.1.

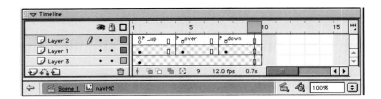

5. Return to the main Timeline. You will notice that at the lower left, there are two instances of navMC. For the clip on the left labeled "Section 1," assign the instance name **button_one** in the Property Inspector. For the clip labeled "Section 2," assign the name **button_two**. Now that both clips have instance names, you can control them with ActionScript.

6. Click the first keyframe of the actions layer in the main Timeline and open the Actions panel. Enter the following statements below the stop() action:

```
button_one.onRollOver=function(){
    button_one.gotoAndPlay("_over");
}
button_one.onPress=function(){
    marker.gotoAndStop(1);
    button_one.gotoAndStop("_down")
    button_two.gotoAndStop("_up")
}
button_one.onRollOut=function(){
    button_one.gotoAndStop("_over");
}
```

These statements create the navigation bar behavior for the first button:

- When the mouse moves over the button, the Movie Clip is sent to the _over frame.

- When the mouse is pressed, the marker clip instance is sent to its first Timeline frame, the button goes to its _down frame, and the other button is sent to its _up frame. This resets the appearance of the other button, so that it no longer looks like a bookmark.

- When the mouse moves outside the button, the clip instance goes to the _over frame to serve as a bookmark.

7. Copy the statements you just entered and paste them in the bottom of the Actions panel. In the copied statements, change every instance of button_one to button_two. This creates the behavior for the second button, which is the reverse of the first. The entire script should resemble Figure 16.2.

8. Select Control → Test Movie. Roll your mouse over the buttons and click to see the navigation bar in action. When you use the Section 2 button, you jump to Section 2 of the Movie Clip instance in the middle of the Stage. The Section 1 button takes you back to Section 1 of the clip instance. Also, while visiting each section, the button is locked in its Down state to create a bookmark that shows where you are in the movie.

So what's the deal? Why is this Movie Clip acting like a button? Well, that's just one of the ways the Button object works. You can script for buttons directly, or you can script for Movie Clips and make them behave like buttons. The only difference between this Movie Clip and a regular button is that the clip has no separate Hit state frame. It does, however, have a "simulated Hit state." Look closely at the navMC Timeline:

Figure 16.2

The final button behavior script

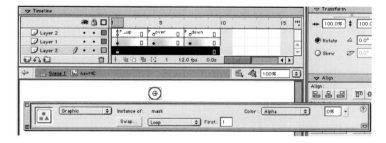

Notice the contents of layer 3: There is an invisible Graphic symbol. This works like the Hit state. When using Button object actions on a Movie Clip, the pixels of the actual clip make up the Hit state.

This lesson introduced you to the basics of scripting for Button objects using Movie Clips. Because Movie Clips are independent animations, there is a lot more you can do with this technique. Try taking advantage of the Movie Clip Timeline to create complex animated buttons and other kinds of interactive graphical changes.

Scripting for Custom Controllers

What is a *custom controller*? You can describe it as any kind of movie element, other than a button, that you create in order to direct the playback and display of your movie. Like most things you do in Flash, there is virtually no limit to the variety of controllers you can create: knobs that turn, rotary menus, virtual joysticks, and so on. The main thing that most custom controllers have in common is that you manipulate them with the mouse as though you were able to physically touch the controller. Even though actual contact is impossible in Flash, these objects attempt to simulate the experience. Custom controllers present the illusion that you can tweak some sort of physical object in your movie.

To create this illusion, it's necessary to be able to drag or move items around on the movie Stage. ActionScript allows you to create this kind of interaction with Movie Clips by providing two action statements: startDrag() and stopDrag(). These terms are fairly self-explanatory; startDrag() makes a specified clip draggable, while stopDrag() ends the action and keeps the clip locked in a stationary position. Each action has its own syntax. Whereas the stopDrag() action can be used on its own, the startDrag() action takes arguments, as shown in its syntax:

```
startDrag("target",lock,left,top,right,bottom)
```

The arguments of this action are as follows:

target represents the instance or path to the instance you wish to make draggable. If this argument is left blank (as an empty string ""), it refers to the clip that has the action attached.

lock is a Boolean value: true if the clip's registration point should lock to the mouse position, or false if the clip is locked to wherever it is first clicked. lock is an optional argument.

left, **top**, **right**, and **bottom** are optional arguments used to define the coordinate boundaries for the drag. All coordinates are relative to the Timeline where the clip is playing. If you plan to use these arguments, be sure to also enter a value for lock to ensure proper syntax.

Creating a Slider to Scroll a Timeline

One of the most common and useful kinds of custom controllers is the *slider*. A slider is simply a knob or lever that can be moved along a horizontal or vertical path. As the slider is moved, it changes some element or parameter in your movie. Sliders (also known as faders) are most often used as sound volume controllers, but they can also be used to create color changes, to position and scale objects on the Stage, to load additional Movie Clips, to navigate, and so on. When you create a slider, you start by creating the slider knob. Then you define the slider's bounds and put it on the Stage. Once it is in the movie, you can attach all kinds of ActionScript to make it perform the way you desire.

Here is a step-by-step example that shows you how to create a slider that scrolls a Timeline. You will find the file, named slider.fla, in the Chapter 16 folder on the companion CD-ROM. This example would be useful if you wanted your movie to present information from various periods of history. The process outlined here is fairly general, so any of the ideas presented should transfer to different kinds of sliders that you may need to create for your own movies.

To create a slider:

1. Create a button to use as the slider knob. It does not have to be a special kind of button, just something that works well in a draggable context. When you are finished, select Edit → Edit Document or click the Back button to return to the main Timeline.

2. Select Insert → New Symbol (Cmd/Ctrl+F8) to display the Create New Symbol dialog box. Enter the name **slider knob** and choose the Movie Clip behavior. Click OK, and Flash will jump into Symbol Editing mode.

3. Drag your button to the Stage of the `slider knob` Movie Clip. Click the button and choose Window → Actions (F9) to display the Actions panel. Here you can attach actions to the button *inside* the Movie Clip. This makes the scripts available for every instance where the slider knob is used.

4. Enter the following statements:

```
on(press){
    startDrag("",false,leftBounds,topBounds,rightBounds,bottomBounds);
    drag=true;
}
on(release){
    stopDrag();
    drag=false;
}
```

These actions turn on or off the ability to drag the slider knob when the button is pressed and released, respectively. Note that there are no specific values assigned to the `startDrag()`action that set the bounds for the drag. Instead, you use a set of variables that will be initialized later.

5. Close the Actions panel and return to your main movie Timeline. When working with a slider, it can be helpful to have some kind of graphic that shows its path. Use one of the painting tools to draw a line across the bottom of the Stage, leaving enough room for the slider knob. Then use the Oval tool to create a series of five dots along the line. Position each dot at the X (horizontal) values 100, 200, 300, 400, and 500.

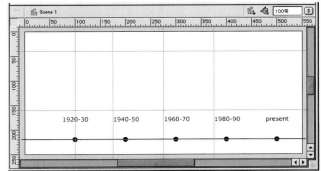

6. Drag an instance of the slider knob Movie Clip to the Stage and position it directly over the first dot. If necessary, select View → Rulers and drag a guide over to the 100-pixel mark to be sure the registration point of the clip is at exactly 100 pixels. You can confirm this in the Info panel.

7. Now that the clip is in your movie, you can assign the remaining actions that are needed to make the slider. Click the `slider knob` instance and choose Window → Actions (F9). Enter the following statements in the Actions panel:

    ```
    onClipEvent(load){
        topBounds=_y;
        leftBounds=_x;
        rightBounds=_x+400;
        bottomBounds=_y;
    }
    ```

    When the clip first appears on the Stage, these actions are executed. They initialize the variables that are used to set the boundaries for the drag. According to these actions, the drag is locked to the current vertical value of the Movie Clip (`_y`) and is allowed to move 400 pixels to the right of the current horizontal value (`_x`). Because these variables are initialized only once at the outset of the movie, the position of the slider knob is stored when the movie starts playing, and its drag boundaries are created relative to that position. Save your movie and select Control → Test Movie to see how it works.

8. At this point, your slider should be able to move around freely on the Stage and remain confined within 400 pixels of its initial horizontal location. However, the slider should not be able to move up or down.

    Next, you need something to control with the slider. Create a new Movie Clip symbol and name it `screen`. Make the `screen` Movie Clip a rectangle that is 1000×100 pixels. Be sure that the rectangle is positioned exactly in the center of the Stage. To do this, it will be helpful to use the Align panel (Window → Align, or Cmd/Ctrl+K).

9. The rectangle graphic should stretch 500 pixels to the left and right of the Movie Clip registration point. Create some kind of graphic that appears within the rectangle every 200 pixels. Because the `slider.fla` example is a Timeline, there are dates located at regular increments along the graphic.

10. When you have finished with the `screen` Movie Clip, return to the main Timeline. Drag an instance of the clip onto the Stage so that it is above the slider, and its left

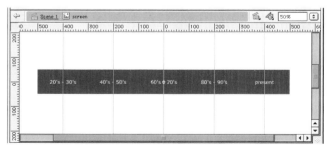

    edge is at 175 pixels. This should put the clip's registration point at 675 pixels. Use the Info panel to confirm this.

    Choose Window → Properties (Cmd/Ctrl+F3) to open the Property Inspector and enter the name **info** in the instance field to create a unique instance of the `screen` Movie Clip.

11. Now you can compose the actions that are needed to make the slider control the position of the info instance. Click the slider knob and open the Actions panel. Enter these additional statements in the window:

```
onClipEvent(enterFrame){
    if(drag==true){
    _root.info._x=(675-((root.slider._x-100)*2));
    }
}
```

These actions will control the _x position of the `info` instance relative to the _x position of the `slider` instance. Here is how it works: 675 is the total distance from the left edge of the Stage to the registration point of the `info` instance. As `slider` moves to the right 100 pixels, `info` should move left by 200 pixels, covering twice as much ground as `slider`. The expression `root.slider._x-100` "zeroes" the starting position of the slider knob, since its initial _x position is 100. This way, the clips can be manipulated from the _x values 0 and 675. Then, as it moves to the right, its _x location value is doubled and subtracted from 675. As `slider` moves farther from 0, `info` moves farther from 675 at twice the rate. The final value is used to set the _x position of the `info` instance. For a comparison of the values, see Table 16.1.

SLIDER._X	SLIDER._X-100	INFO._X
100	0	675
200	100	475
300	200	275
400	300	75
500	400	−125

Table 16.1

_X **Values for** slider.fla **Movie Clips**

So why are they moved at different "rates"? Both `slider` and `info` have five different sections of information to present. However, whereas `slider` has to move only 100 pixels to get to a new section, `info` has to move 200 pixels. As `slider` moves right in increments of 100 pixels, the value is doubled and subtracted from 675. This new value is assigned to the _x property of `info`, which moves `info` across the Stage to the left.

12. Your Timeline slider is now ready to go. Select Control → Test Movie to try it out. See Figure 16.3 for an illustration of the finished product.

The `slider.fla` movie has some additional features not covered in this example. There are a few text enhancements that help clarify the information it presents. Also, there is a layer mask that creates a window through which you can view the contents of the Timeline. To learn more about creating layer masks, see Chapter 8.

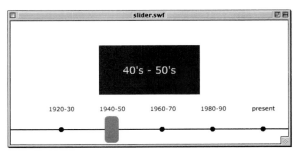

Figure 16.3

The final slider.fla **Timeline**

Recording and Monitoring Keystrokes

In addition to monitoring mouse-type interactions, ActionScript can be used to track keyboard input and interaction. This functionality enables you to create interactive controls, which in turn allows your audience to use their keyboard to interact with your movie. This kind of interaction can be particularly useful for creating games, interactive animators, quizzes, and easy-to-use presentations.

To take advantage of this feature, you can use one of ActionScript's predefined objects known as the Key object. The Key object and its methods allow you to track and set all parameters concerning keyboard input in your movie. Here is a partial list of Key object methods:

isDown(keyCode) Used to return a Boolean value: `true` if the key in the `keyCode` argument is pressed, and `false` if it is not.

getCode() Returns the key code of the last key pressed while the movie was running.

getAscii() Similar to `getCode()`, returns the ASCII value of the last key pressed.

In the preceding examples, the term `keyCode` was used as a placeholder for the argument where you would normally enter an ActionScript key code value. Key code values are ActionScript constants. They are numbers used to represent the keys on a standard keyboard. For example, the key code for the letter *A* is 65. For a complete listing of ActionScript key codes, see the Key Code Values table in the ActionScript Reference section.

> You may remember the on(keyPress) handler that is associated with buttons. This handler, when attached to a button, will also track keystrokes that occur while the movie is playing. To read more about on(keyPress) see Chapter 12.

Using Keystrokes to Track Answers in a Quiz

The keyboard can be a very useful alternative to the mouse when it comes to interacting with your movie. More than 90 different key codes are used to represent the keys on a standard keyboard. Not only does this present you with a lot of options for interaction, but it opens the door to creating movies that can be used by more than one person at a time. Use the Key object both to record keys that are pressed while the movie plays and to assign specific keys as hot keys or interactive controls.

> One thing to keep in mind when building interactive movies that use the keyboard is that a few keys have specific functions in Flash's Test Movie mode. These keys are Return/Enter, the comma (,) key, and the period (.) key. Try to avoid using these keys if possible. If you must use them, select Control → Disable Keyboard Shortcuts while you are in Test Movie mode. This will void their functions in Flash.

In the next example, you will learn how to set up a basic keyboard interface that serves as the input device for a Flash-based quiz. Open the file named `keyPress.fla` in the Chapter 16 folder on the companion CD-ROM to see these scripts in their specific context. You will find that this process is very simple once you become comfortable with the ActionScript terms used to create this kind of interaction.

To monitor keystrokes in your movie:

1. Drag a Movie Clip to the Stage. Select Window → Actions (F9) to display the Actions panel and then enter these statements:

   ```
   onClipEvent(keyDown){
       trace("the key was: "+Key.getCode());
   }
   ```

2. Select Control → Test Movie and try your movie by typing on the keyboard. When you type, you initiate a `keyDown` event that executes the statements in the script. The Output window returns the message you specified with the `trace()` function and gives you the key code for each key you pressed. The key code is provided by the Key object, using the `getCode()` method. This method retrieves the code, which is then concatenated in a string and printed in the Output window. If you don't have the ActionScript Reference section available, you can use this technique to get any key code values that you need.

3. Return to movie editing mode and open the Actions panel to display the script you just entered. Delete or comment out (//) the line that starts with `trace` and enter the following statements within the `onClipEvent` curly braces:

   ```
   if(Key.isDown(32)){
       _root.gotoAndPlay(1);
   }
   if(Key.isDown(65)){
       _root.gotoAndPlay(3);
   }
   if(Key.isDown(66)){
       _root.gotoAndPlay(2);
   }
   if(Key.isDown(67)){
       _root.gotoAndPlay(3);
   }
   ```

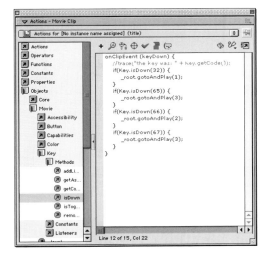

These statements monitor which keys have been pressed and then send the movie to a new location accordingly. Specifically, the script checks the answer to the first quiz question and sends the movie to a specific frame based on whether the answer is right or wrong. It also provides the opportunity to try the question again. If the spacebar is pressed (key code 32), the movie returns to frame 1. The other key codes are as follows: 65 = A, 66 = B, and 67 = C.

The Key object is not case sensitive. When using it to track keystrokes, there is no difference between *a* and *A*.

4. Press F5 to add two additional frames to the layer that contains your Movie Clip. Insert a new layer and insert three keyframes in the first three empty frames of the layer. Attach a `stop()` action to each. Then, use the Text tool to type the word **CORRECT!!** in the second frame and **SORRY, NO.** in the third frame.

5. Now you must write a multiple-choice question. It doesn't matter what it is, but it has to have at least three possible answers: A, B, and C. Based on the script you attached to the Movie Clip, make answer B the correct choice. Use the Text tool to write your question and put it on the first frame of another new layer (layer 3 if you started with a blank movie file).

6. Select Control → Test Movie and give your quiz a try. If you wrote your question correctly, pressing B should render a "CORRECT!!" answer, while A and C are incorrect. If this isn't working properly, you can either change the script or reorder the answers to your question.

Writing ActionScript for Multiple-Timeline Movies

One of the most important aspects of using ActionScript to create Flash content is understanding how Flash movies are constructed. In this case, *constructed* is not used in the hands-on sense, but in the compositional sense. It is essential to know what Flash movies are made of and how they are put together.

As an animation tool, Flash creates motion sequences using pictures and text. If this were all it could do, by today's standards the application would be simple indeed. However, Flash has the capability to layer and combine multiple animations. Additionally, you can use ActionScript to tell Flash how to assemble these animations and make them "talk" to one another. The simple behaviors and functions of individual animations can be used together in the same space, and as they interact with each other through ActionScript, rich and complex behaviors emerge.

To truly maximize the interactive potential of your movies, you must understand how to use Flash as a container or arena for animated content, and how many simple movies can synergize to create an interactive experience with great depth and potential.

How Flash Manages Multiple Movie Timelines

When a Flash movie plays, all of its elements appear (or are heard, in the case of sounds) on the movie Stage. This creates the illusion that all the movie components exist on an even playing field and share the same space within the Flash environment. Although they do share the common space of the Stage and its boundaries, there is a hierarchy to this space and to the elements that inhabit it.

Every Flash movie you create has a particular organization based on the animations it contains. This rule applies to animations in the form of both Movie Clips and additional Flash movies, or SWF files, that are loaded into a host Flash movie. When additional movies are loaded into a Flash movie, they are placed in a hierarchy and loaded onto a new movie level. In Flash, the main Timeline is the absolute bottom and is referred to as level 0. Subsequent movies that are loaded are stacked on top of it in succession: level 1, level 2, level 3, and so on. As each movie is loaded onto its own level, it maintains its autonomy and plays its Timeline independently of the other level Timelines.

Movie Clips also exhibit a similar kind of hierarchical relationship. One Movie Clip can contain another clip or clips. These, in turn, can contain additional Movie Clips. The stacking can go on and on. This stacking process is known as *nesting* Movie Clips. In the same way that movies can contain multiple independent Timelines on various levels, Movie Clips are able to hold other clips, and each clip is able to behave independently. The Movie Clip hierarchy has a different set of terms used to describe this relationship, though. A nested clip is known as a *child*, and the clip hosting it is referred to as the *parent*. It's possible for a clip to be both a child and a parent. If clip A contains clip B, and clip B contains clip C, then B is both a parent of C and a child of A. Ultimately, all Movie Clips are children of the Timeline where they are playing. In the preceding example, if clips A, B, and C all exist in the movie on level 2, then level 2 is the parent, and A, B, and C are all children. For an illustration of this, see Figure 16.4.

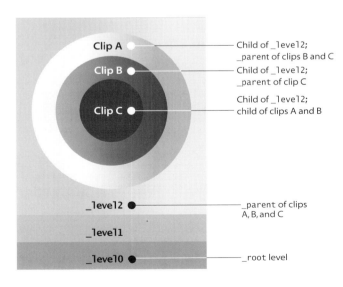

Figure 16.4

The hierarchical relationship of movie levels and Movie Clip parents and children. Here, the movie has three levels: 0, 1, and 2. Movie Clips A, B, and C exist on level 2 and are nested inside one another. Clip A is a parent of B and C, and B is a parent of C.

So, how would all of this apply in a Flash movie? Take, for example, a movie that contains an animated character named BubbleBody, or BB for short. If you wanted to create an animation of BB jumping straight up in the air, you would need to consider several things. As BB prepares for the jump, he crouches down, his head sinks a bit, and his arms widen. As he springs upward, he shoots his arms up over his head, and his fingers stretch to the sky. While this is happening, his legs push up, leaving the crouch stance and coming together as he rises above the ground.

Many things are going on in this animation. One of the greatest challenges is trying to make each event happen, and happen together, so that the animation looks as natural as possible. By making each part of BB's body a Movie Clip and nesting these clips inside a single BB clip, you can achieve this kind of synchronization and control. As the main BB clip rises, all the others (arms, legs, hands, and so on) rise with it. As the arm Movie Clips stretch to the sky, the hand instances are carried with it. This is accomplished because a nested clip sits on the Timeline of another clip. As the host clip is changed or moved, the nested clip is carried along with it.

In addition to keeping all the elements together, nested clips allow you to control each element independently. To create a "wave hello" animation with ActionScript, you would have to script the forearm Movie Clip to rotate 120 degrees, and also to tell the hand clip to rotate in some fashion. Creating the rotation with ActionScript is simple, and with independent control over each body part, you are able to manipulate the parts individually. In this case, since the hand clip is a child of the arm, the hand moves with the arm as it is raised. Then, because the arm is the parent clip, it is unaffected when the hand clip executes its "wave" rotation.

Creating Absolute Target Paths

To create this kind of animation, or to get the kind of control described in the preceding example, it's necessary to send ActionScript commands from one Timeline to another. In this case, a button or other control element has to send the commands along the hierarchy to tell the arm and hand clips to execute the appropriate actions.

The process of passing ActionScript commands and information to a Movie Clip is known as *targeting*. When you target a clip, you send a command through the Timeline chain so that it reaches the specific clip. This process can be compared to sending mail. To send a message to someone, you have to have their address so that your message will land in the right hands. Targeting a Movie Clip in ActionScript works the same way. If you don't enter the correct target path (or address) for the clip, the clip won't receive the message. In ActionScript, there are two ways to refer to a clip's target path: absolute and relative.

An *absolute path* is the ActionScript equivalent of a postal address for a Movie Clip instance. In the same way that your mailing address specifies country, state, zip code, street, building number, and so on, an absolute target path describes the location of the clip instance relative to the main Timeline. Going back to the BB animation presented earlier, the absolute path to BB's hand Movie Clip would be:

```
_root.BB.upperBody.armL.handL
```

This script example uses the **_root** reference to access the main Timeline. If, however, BB were in a movie on level 2, the target path to the hand would be:

```
_level2.BB.upperBody.armL.handL
```

You can use absolute target paths to send commands, variables, and any ActionScript information to Movie Clip instances and Timelines from any other location in your movie. Absolute paths are always a safe choice when the levels and nests of a movie start to get confusing or complicated. To get an idea of clip instances that make up BB, see Figure 16.5.

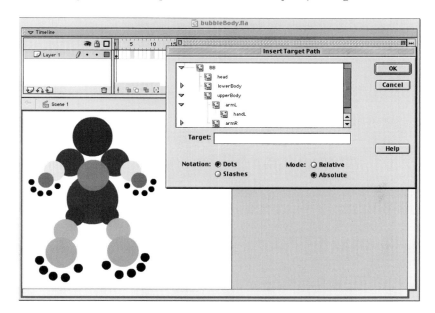

Figure 16.5

The BubbleBody Movie Clip is created from nine separate, nested Movie Clips. Notice how the Insert Target Path dialog box shows the hierarchical breakdown and structure of clip instances.

Targeting Timelines with Relative Paths

It is also possible to target clips with *relative paths*. These paths don't refer directly to the main Timeline, but rather the location of the clip you want to target relative to the location of the script that calls the action. Going back to the BB example, if you wanted to send an action from the handL clip to the armL clip, you could use the absolute target path

```
_root.BB.upperBody.armL._rotation=0;
```

Or you could use the relative path

```
_parent._rotation=0;
```

As you can see, in this case, the relative path is much shorter. Relative paths can use a different reference: _parent. This reference translates to "go back one nest level." Since the handL clip is a child nested inside armL, an action on the armL Timeline needs to go back only a single nest level. There is an additional relative target path reference called this, which refers to the current Timeline or the Timeline where the action is called. this is convenient because it allows you to access a clip directly from its own Timeline rather than enter a long, specific target path to the clip. To send a message to armR directly from the upperBody Timeline, you can use the this reference:

```
this.armR._rotation=-120;
```

The preceding script would rotate the armR instance to –120°. The this alias works to keep script actions relative to the Timeline where they are called: a child clip instance, a movie level number, or even the main Timeline (although the need for this is rare).

Controlling Multiple Movie Timelines with ActionScript

Now that you know how to properly refer to the various Timelines in your Flash movie, you should be able to apply what you know about ActionScript to control their playback and attributes. There are three main ActionScript components that you can use to do this:

Actions, or ActionScript commands, are used to control Timeline playback. These include statements like gotoAndPlay(), stop(), and nextFrame().

Methods that are specific to the MovieClip object can also be used in this context. There are several Movie Clip methods that don't have a counterpart in the Actions portion of the language and are unique to the MovieClip object, such as getBounds() and hitTest().

Properties, or the attributes of a Movie Clip, can be altered when you target a clip. Many of the Movie Clip properties are discussed in this chapter.

For complete listings of these components, see the ActionScript Reference section.

Depending on the type of Timeline that you have to control with ActionScript, you will use a different set of ActionScript statements and syntax to achieve the desired effect. The following example outlines the basic syntax used to load additional movie Timelines and to target a Movie Clip instance.

Loading Movie Levels

To load additional movies, you use the loadMovie() action. The syntax for loadMovie() is as follows:

```
loadMovie("URL","target",varMethod)
```

This action has three main arguments:

URL is the argument that specifies the location and name of the movie (SWF) file to be loaded. This URL can be either absolute or relative to the file loading the movie and should be specified as a string (in quotes).

target is a string argument used to specify where the new movie will be loaded. To load the movie on a new level, specify that level in this argument—for example, `"_level1"`. Alternatively, you can replace a Movie Clip instance with a newly loaded movie by specifying the target path to the clip you would like to replace.

varMethod is an optional argument that passes information to the new movie. For more on this, see the ActionScript Reference section.

The following statement loads the movie `levelOne.swf` into movie level 2:

```
loadMovie("levelOne.swf","_level2");
```

The next statement loads the movie `begin.swf` into a clip instance named `intro`, which is located on the main Timeline:

```
loadMovie("begin.swf","_root.intro");
```

Alternatively, you can use the `unloadMovie` action to reverse the process. The main difference with this action is that it takes only one argument—the location that gets unloaded:

```
unloadMovie("_level1");
```

This script removes the movie currently playing on level 1.

> Related to `loadMovie` and `unloadMovie` are the actions `loadMovieNum` and `unloadMovieNum`. Although the two sets of actions have identical purposes, each set takes a slightly different syntax. Depending on the application, you may find one set advantageous over the other. For specifics, see Chapter 12 or the ActionScript Reference section.

Targeting Movie Layers

To target the Timeline for a Movie Clip instance, you must use either a relative or absolute path to the clip you wish to target. After you specify that clip, you can use the dot operator to state the ActionScript property or action you would like to use to manipulate the instance. For example:

```
_root.upperBody.armL.handL._rotation=200;
```

This starts at the main Timeline, goes up a chain of nested instances, and sets a rotation value for the instance `handL`. It can be helpful to think of targeting with the dot operator as moving from the general to the specific.

This following script stops the parent of a nested Movie Clip at frame 1 on the parent's Timeline. When executed, the child clip that called this script would be able to continue playing independently.

```
_parent.gotoAndStop(1);
```

Adding Interface Elements with Components

Components are one of the most robust features implemented with the release of Flash MX. At the most basic level, Components are drag-and-drop interface widgets that add standard interactive controllers to your movie. Taken to an extreme, Components open the gateway to building completely customizable interface elements that can be used and reused by members of a development team. Think of them as "instant interfaces" that can be added to a movie by simply dragging them to the Stage.

If you were accustomed to Smart Clips, which were implemented in previous releases of Flash, you are going to love Components. Like Smart Clips, Components are meant to simplify the development process; but due to their modular nature, they can be customized to an entirely new degree.

> Components are like a separate authoring tool inside Flash MX. Their scope and complexity goes far beyond the reach of this book. In fact, Components and their related techniques could provide, on their own, enough information for an entirely separate book! This section of the chapter aims to give you an idea of what Components are and how to use them in your own Flash projects. To learn more about the nitty-gritty details of Components and how to create them from scratch with ActionScript, see the Reference panel (Shift+F1). For additional Components or updates, such as Components that create charts and graphs, visit www.macromedia.com/desdev/mx/flash.

Figure 16.6

The Components panel

Select Window → Components or press Cmd/Ctrl+F7 to see the Components panel (see Figure 16.6).

Components come in seven flavors:

CheckBox A laundry list of clickable options used for multiple selections.

ComboBox A single-selection drop-down list.

ListBox A scrollable menu box for single and multiple selections.

PushButton A standard, rectangular push button.

RadioButton An on/off toggle button. RadioButton components are grouped; they work as a team so that only one button in the group can be selected at a time.

ScrollBar A standard side-scroll controller for text boxes.

ScrollPane A standard side-scroll controller for large images and Movie Clips.

The seven Components cover just about every interface convention you find in contemporary computer software. The idea is that when your audience encounters a Component in your movie, it will be immediately recognizable and provide an intuitive solution for navigating and making selections.

Adding Components to your movie is a simple and straightforward process. In the following lesson, you will learn how to add a ScrollBar Component to a text field. Open the scroll-BarComponent.fla file, which you'll find in the Chapter 16 folder on the companion CD-ROM.

On the Stage, you'll see a dynamic text box containing the poem "Constantly Risking Absurdity" by Lawrence Ferlinghetti (see Figure 16.7).

As you can see, the poem is too long to fit into its text box. This is where your ScrollBar Component comes in. By adding it to the poem's text box, you will be able to scroll down and read the entire poem. To add a scroll bar to a text box:

1. Select the text box where you want to attach the Component. Choose Window → Properties (Cmd/Ctrl+F3) to open the Property Inspector. To attach a Component to a text field, that field must be either a dynamic or input text field. (To read about the specifics of text fields, see Chapters 5 and 17.) Use the drop-down menu in the Property Inspector to select one of these options and give the field an instance name. For this example, assign the instance name **poetry**.

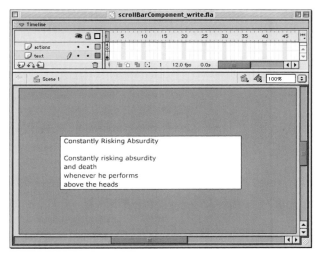

Figure 16.7

The scrollBarComponent.fla file contains a text box that is too small to display all the text it contains.

2. Now that the text box is prepared, you are ready to attach the ScrollBar Component. Choose Window → Components (Cmd/Ctrl+F7) to open the Components panel.

3. Grab the ScrollBar Component ⊟ ScrollBar and drag it to the Stage. When you release it, drop it over the text box, keeping it as close to the right edge of the box as possible. Flash is supposed to handle the alignment for you, although this doesn't always work. Use the arrow keys or mouse to move the scroll bar into the position you want.

4. Select the scroll bar (if it isn't already selected) and look at the Property Inspector. It should show you that the scroll bar has two parameters:

    Target TextField This option should read *poetry* since you dropped the component over the `poetry` field. If this parameter is blank, click the Target TextField option and enter the name **poetry**. This tells the scroll bar to control that particular text field instance.

    Horizontal This option determines whether the scroll bar is horizontal (`true`) or vertical (`false`). Be sure it is set to `false` for this example.

5. You can also see that the scroll bar is not quite the same height as the text box. Your `poetry` text box is 110 pixels tall, and the scroll bar only 100. This is easy to correct. Select the ScrollBar Component and look at the Property Inspector. To make the heights match, type **110** in the H field to make the scroll bar 10 pixels taller.

6. Select Control ➔ Test Movie to audition the scroll bar. Click the arrows, and the text box moves up and down; drag the shuttle box, and the field glides smoothly from top to bottom.

One of the most interesting features of Components is that you can change their appearance. Each Component is created from several Movie Clips called *skins*. Skins are literally the components of Components. By changing the color, shape, and overall appearance of a skin, you can transform the appearance of any Component. Editing skins is a tricky business, but here is one technique you can use to make some basic modifications. To edit a Component skin in the Library:

1. Open the Library for `scrollBarComponent.fla` by choosing Window ➔ Library (F11).

2. Open the following Library folder path: Flash UI Components ➔ Component Skins ➔ FScrollBar Skins.

3. To edit a skin, double-click its Movie Clip icon in the Library. For an illustration of this, see Figure 16.8.

4. Depending on the Component skin, you may need to dig deeper into the Movie Clip once it appears on the Stage for editing. Component skins are made up of clips nested several layers thick.

    Redraw, repaint, or change the clip as you see fit. Once you are finished, return to other layers of the skin by using the Back button or return to the main Timeline by selecting Edit ➔ Document. Any edits you make will not be visible until you test your movie.

There is a tremendous ActionScript vocabulary devoted to editing and changing the parameters of Components and their skins. Again, to see the specifics of these terms and concepts, refer to Flash MX's built-in help or the Reference panel.

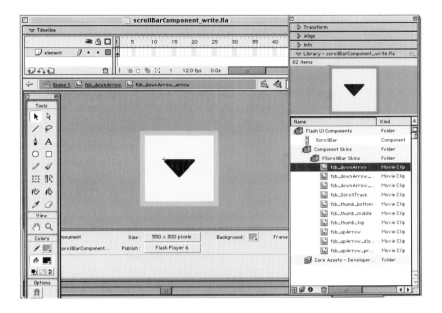

Figure 16.8

The arrow portion of the down-arrow button is prepared for editing on the Stage.

ActionScripting to Control Graphic Elements

One of the most important and unique aspects of Movie Clips is that they are the only member of the Flash Library that can have their appearance modified via ActionScript. This is an extremely important factor when it comes to creating interactive movies. In addition to navigational features in your movie, any kind of interactive control element can be scripted to move, scale, stretch, hide, spin, or perform any combination of these actions on a Movie Clip instance. Ultimately, this enables you to create interactive animation in your movie because you have access to all the parameters that affect the way graphics are positioned and displayed.

ActionScript provides a healthy dose of commands to manipulate visual content. Listed below are the properties you can use to alter the appearance of Movie Clip instances. You can find specifics of each in the ActionScript Reference section.

_alpha is used to change the transparency of a Movie Clip instance.

_height sets and returns the height of a Movie Clip instance.

_rotation sets the rotation of a Movie Clip. Values are specified in degrees.

_visible takes a Boolean argument. `true` makes a Movie Clip active and visible, while `false` hides the clip. Hidden clips remain active in your movie.

_width sets and returns the width of a Movie Clip instance.

_x and **_y** are two properties that set and return the X and Y coordinates of a Movie Clip. If a clip is on the main Timeline, its coordinates are relative to the point (0, 0) in the upper-left corner of the Stage. If a Movie Clip is nested inside another clip, its coordinates are relative to the registration point of the **_parent** clip.

_xscale and **_yscale** are two properties that set and return a percentage value that specifies the scaling of a Movie Clip instance.

In addition to these properties, there is a collection of methods associated with the predefined Color object. Using a small collection of methods, the Color object allows you to set and return RGB color values of a Movie Clip. To learn more about these methods, refer to the "Scripting Color Changes" section later in this chapter, or see the entry for the Color object in the ActionScript Reference section.

Scripting Animation

Many of the properties associated with Movie Clip appearance deal with the position of Movie Clips. By rapidly changing the position of a clip, you can create the illusion of smooth motion, or animation. ActionScript can also be used to modify the size or scale of a Movie Clip instance. Again, when done over a period of time, this creates an animated effect.

You can change these ActionScript properties in combination with one another to produce interesting graphic results. The results are not much different than those you get when creating a tweened animation. The main difference is that with ActionScript, the changes can be dynamically modified with scripting. And when you combine them with other Action-Script components, you are able to interactively control the appearance and movement of Movie Clips.

In the following examples, you will learn how to control and animate a Movie Clip using ActionScript. Two of the most basic graphic parameters are presented here: position and size. With the help of additional ActionScript commands and statements, you will be able to take a simple Movie Clip instance and either set it in motion or cause it to grow and expand.

Animating Graphic Elements with Motion and Custom Cursors

ActionScript provides a set of properties that allow you to track the position of the mouse cursor in your movie. Using X and Y coordinates, ActionScript will return the position of the cursor on the movie Stage. The properties are as follows:

_xmouse returns the X (horizontal) coordinate position of the mouse cursor.

_ymouse returns the Y (vertical) coordinate position of the mouse cursor.

All coordinates are returned relative to the movie origin, or coordinates (0, 0), located at the upper-left corner of the Stage. When you use these properties to get the mouse position, it's good practice to specify the Timeline you want to track. For example, to track the mouse on the main Timeline, you would write:

```
hPos=_root._xmouse;
vPos=_root._ymouse;
```

In this example, hPos and vPos are variables that store the current X and Y mouse coordinates.

This example also deals with the _x and _y properties for a Movie Clip. As mentioned earlier, these properties are used to monitor and set the X and Y coordinates of a Movie Clip instance, either on the Stage or within another clip instance. With the help of a few variables and some ActionScript number crunching, you will see how to create an ever-changing, organic animation. Also, you will learn how to take this animation and lock its position to that of the mouse cursor, providing an additional layer of animation.

The scripts presented here are in the flyCursor.fla file inside the Chapter 16 folder on the companion CD-ROM. You can also look at the finished version, flyCursor.swf, to get an idea of how the final animation looks and behaves.

To create a dynamic animation with ActionScript and attach it to a custom cursor:

1. Create a Movie Clip that you want to use for your animation. This example uses a Movie Clip of a fly, since the animation will randomly flutter around a single position on the Stage.

2. Drag this Movie Clip to the Stage to create an instance, and name it **fly**. Select the instance and choose Window → Actions to open the Actions panel.

3. Enter the following statements in the window:

```
onClipEvent(load){
    Mouse.hide();
}
onClipEvent(mouseMove){
    _x=_root._xmouse;
    _y=_root._ymouse;
}
```

Close the Actions panel and test your movie. The results are quite surprising! The first actions turn the Movie Clip instance into a custom cursor by using the Mouse object to conceal the mouse pointer. Then the onClipEvent(mouseMove) handler locks the position of the Movie Clip to the mouse cursor, creating the effect that the Movie Clip is the cursor. This works because the horizontal and vertical position of the clip (_x and _y properties) are set to the mouse cursor position, relative to its coordinates on the main Timeline Stage (_root).

4. Return to movie editing mode and reopen the Actions panel for the Movie Clip instance. Enter these additional actions in the window:

```
onClipEvent(enterFrame){
    v=_root.fly._x;
```

```
            h=_root.fly._y;
            posNeg=Math.round(Math.random()+1);
            if (posNeg>1){
                posNeg=1;
            }else{
                posNeg=-1;
            }
            moveV=Math.round(Math.random()*4*posNeg);
            moveH=Math.round(Math.random()*4*posNeg);
            _root.fly._x=v+moveV;
            _root.fly._x=h+moveH;
        }
```

To put it simply, this script does three things: It stores the current position of the instance, generates a random number between −4 and +4, and adds it to the original instance location, jumping it to a new position on the Stage.

In more specific terms, this is what is happening:

- The variables v and h are used to store the position of the instance on the enter-Frame event.

- The variable posNeg uses two methods of the Math object to randomly generate a value of either 1 or 2. The random() method randomly generates a value between 0.0 and 0.999…. This is then incremented by 1, and the sum is rounded to the nearest integer, 1 or 2.

- The new posNeg value is then passed through a conditional and reinitialized to −1 or +1.

It's necessary to use negative numbers to keep the clip from slowly drifting off to the lower-right corner of the Stage. If both the x and y values are always increasing positively, the clip will always move away (down and right) from the (0, 0) origin in the upper-left corner of the Stage.

- Next, a new set of variables, moveV and moveH, are initialized to a random number between−4 and 4 using a similar arithmetic technique. These values are added to the original position variables (v and h), and the sum is used to set the _x and _y properties of the Movie Clip instance. Because this script is rapidly executed on each exitFrame event, it creates the animated illusion of hovering.

5. Select Control → Test Movie to see the script in context and watch the fly buzz across the Stage.

Here are a few additional techniques you might want to try in addition to this script:

- Create separate variables to fill the role of the `posNeg` variable. Use one to control the horizontal change and another to control the vertical change. This creates a smoother hover effect.

- In this script example, the hover range was set to a maximum of 4. You can change this to create a more subtle or abrupt hover effect.

- Try creating tweened animations using this animated clip. Or use this technique to create dynamic, ever-changing background graphics that are constantly in motion.

Scaling Graphic Elements

Everyone knows the saying "there is always a bigger fish," which refers to the fact that everything is relative. Just when you think you have found something that is the absolute biggest or best, something better comes along. In Flash, you can use the `_xscale` and `_yscale` properties to create a bigger fish. And in the next example, that is exactly what you will do.

These properties are used to both set and retrieve the horizontal and vertical scale of a Movie Clip. Each property is entered and returned a percentage value. With the help of a few ActionScript actions, you can use scripting to change the size of an object by stretching its length and width to a percentage of the original size. The scripts in this example can be found on the companion CD-ROM in a file named `fishScaler.fla` inside the Chapter 16 folder.

To script changes to the scaling of a Movie Clip instance:

1. Open a new file and select Modify → Document to set the Stage dimensions to 400×400 pixels. Be sure the frame rate is at least 12 frames per second. Click OK.

2. Create a new Movie Clip symbol of a fish. Make it an animated clip that moves from right to left. Be sure that the clip both starts and ends slightly more than 200 pixels from its registration point (see Figure 16.9).

3. Return to the main Timeline and drag your fish Movie Clip to the center of the Stage; put its registration point at the coordinates (200, 200). Give it the instance name `fishy` in the Property Inspector. Test your movie to see the `fishy` instance in action.

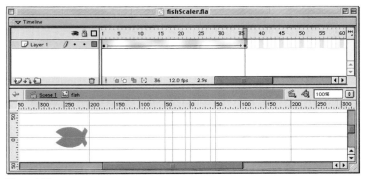

Figure 16.9

The fish Movie Clip starts at an _x value of 240 and ends at _x = –235.

4. Return to movie editing mode, select Insert → New Symbol, and create a new button symbol. The design of the button is left in your capable hands. The button in the `fishScaler.fla` example is made to look as though it is underwater. When you have finished with the button, return to the main Timeline and drag your button onto the Stage. Position it either above or below the fish Movie Clip animation.

5. You are now ready to enter the ActionScript that will scale (resize, not prepare for cooking) the `fishy` Movie Clip instance. Select the instance and choose Window → Actions (F9) to display the Actions panel. Enter these statements:

```
onClipEvent(load){
    count=0;
}
```

Next click the button and open the Actions panel once again. Enter the following statements in the window:

```
on(release){
    count+=1;
    duplicateMovieClip(_root.fishy,"fishy"+count,count);
    setProperty("fishy"+count,_xscale,count*200);
    setProperty("fishy"+count,_yscale,count*200);
}
```

6. Close the Actions panel and select Test → Movie. Each time you click the button, you will see a larger fish appear as it moves across the Stage. This effect is created through the combination of the `duplicateMovieclip` action and the `_xscale` and `_yscale` properties. The preceding script executes each time the button is clicked. When this happens, the `count` variable (initialized when the instance is first loaded) is incremented and used to perform two actions. The `fishy` instance, or *parent*, is duplicated. And each duplicate, or *child*, has the value of `count` appended to its name and is placed at the stacking level of `count` relative to its parent clip.

Each duplicate is still on the _root or _level0 Timeline, but it occupies a new layer above the original source clip. Duplicates are placed in an internal hierarchy called a *stacking level*. When a clip is duplicated, its duplicates are placed in a stacking level above it. Stacking levels work like layers in the Timeline, but they are generated via ActionScript when a clip is duplicated. Because a duplicate clip cannot exist in the same space as the original, each is placed in a unique location, or stacking level, above the last duplicate or source. In this example, `fishy` is duplicated and placed at stacking level count. The variable count is incremented each time the button is clicked, and the clips continue to stack above the original `fishy` instance.

Then, the _xscale and _yscale properties are used to scale each child to a value of count*200. Because count is incremented with each button click, the child clips are gradually scaled by increasing values, creating bigger and bigger fish.

> You may notice that each duplicate seems to move faster than those that came before it. This is because, as the duplicate clip is scaled, it has twice as far to travel as the clip that preceded it. All properties of the clip are scaled, including the width of the area it must travel. However, it must travel the new distance in the same number of frames. A clip that moves 400 frames in 3 seconds is not as fast as a clip that must move 1,600 frames in that same time span.

This example shows how the properties _xscale and _yscale can be used to dynamically change the size of a Movie Clip. You will also find that the _height and _width properties produce similar results when used in this fashion. To learn more about these properties, see their listings in the ActionScript Reference section.

Scripting Color Changes

In Chapter 9, you learned how to use the Effect panel to create animated color changes using Tint, Alpha, and some of the other color parameters. When combined with a motion tween, color animation effects can be created to change over a period of time, just like a regular motion animation. On a more advanced level, ActionScript is able to create the same kind of effects. Using the Color object and its methods, you are able to create dynamic color changes that will respond to controls or parameters you define in your scripts. The Color object is one of Flash's predefined objects. It allows you to read and write color changes and effects to Movie Clip instances in your movie.

To use the Color object, you must use a constructor function to create a new object instance; then you are able to set and return color information using the Color object methods:

getRGB() returns the numeric RGB value set by the last setRGB() command.

setRGB() sets a hexadecimal value for the specified Color object.

getTransform() returns the color transform value(s) set by the last setTransform() command.

setTransform() sets parameters to color-transform a Color object.

Once invoked, these methods can be used to create many kinds of color effects that change with your movie and the parameters you assign to the object that controls the color changes. For example, you could use the Color object to create a character that turns deeper shades of red as it is placed closer and closer to an image of the sun.

Using the Color Object to Create a Color Mixer

In this example, you will learn how to use the Color object to dynamically modify the color attributes of a Movie Clip. You will use a series of slider controllers to add and subtract color values to a Movie Clip instance. As the sliders are positioned and moved to different settings, the instance's color will change accordingly.

You will find two files for this example in the Chapter 16 folder on the companion CD-ROM. The finished file, `colorMixer.fla` (and `.swf`), has all the final components discussed here. If you would like to work through this example as you read, use the partially completed version, `colorMixerCD.fla`, to help you get started.

To create a set of slider controllers that modify the color of a Movie Clip:

1. Open the `colorMixerCD.fla` file and then select File → Save As to store it on your computer.

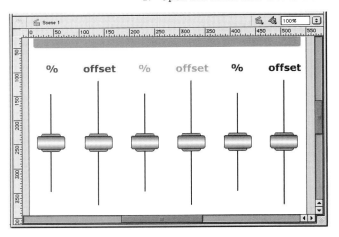

You will see that a lot of the grunt work has been done already, mainly to save time and allow you to focus on the important aspects of this lesson. All of the sliders have been created and are in position on the movie Stage. (To learn more about creating slider controls of your own, see the earlier section "Scripting for Custom Controllers.")

In this movie, there are two kinds of slider Movie Clips: one that controls values between –100 and 100, and another between –255 and 255. This is because when you work with the `setTransform()` method of the Color object, you must specify several parameters that range within either positive/negative 100 or positive/negative 255.

2. First, you must give each slider Movie Clip an instance name. Click the slider at the far left of the Stage and then select Window → Properties (Cmd/Ctrl+F3) to open the Property Inspector. Enter the name **ra** in the instance name field.

   Continue to do this with the remaining five Movie Clips. The remaining instances, from left to right, should be named **rb**, **ga**, **gb**, **ba**, and **bb**. When you have completed these tasks, save your movie.

3. Click the `ra` instance (far left) and then open the Actions panel. Enter the following statements in the window:

```
onClipEvent(enterFrame){
    raColor=new Color(_root.meter);
    raTransform=new Object();
    raTransform.ra=((this.knob100._y)*-1);
    trace("ra:"+raTransform.ra);
    raColor.setTransform(raTransform);
}
```

This script is executed as your movie plays through each frame. Since this movie exists in a single frame, Flash is simply looping frame 1 over and over. The second line of the script uses a constructor function to create a new Color object named `raColor` and targets the `meter` instance on the main Timeline. The next statement creates a new object named `raTransform`. This will be used later with the `setTransform()` method.

Now for the linchpin of the script: The `setTransform()` method can accept up to eight parameters defined here by the `raTransform` object. For this slider instance, you will use only one of these, `ra`, which represents the percentage of red in the transformation. This parameter is set to `((this.knob100._y)*-1)`, an expression that tracks the position of the slider knob and returns a numeric value. If you look at the script attached to the `knob100` instance, you will see that it is locked to the range of –100 to +100. In the preceding expression, its movement will return inverse values in this same range because each is multiplied by –1. This enables slider movement toward the top of the Stage to yield positive values.

The `trace()` function prints this value to the Output window. The final statement uses the `setTransform()` method; it takes the transform object `raTransform` as its argument to alter the red percentage value for the Color object `raColor` and applies it to the `meter` instance.

Here, where `ra` represents the percentage of red, other letter combinations will be used to specify additional color parameters. To learn about these in more detail, see the `setTransform()` method listing in the ActionScript Reference section.

4. Now that you have finished the hard work, you can copy and paste to attach the remaining actions. Select the actions you just entered and copy them to the clipboard (Cmd/Ctrl+C). Then, select the **ga** instance, open the Actions panel, and paste (Cmd/Ctrl+V) the actions into the window. Go through the script and change every iteration of the phrase **ra** to **ga**. Do the same for the **ba** instance.

You may find it helpful to use the Actions panel's Jump menu to move from script to script.

This process attaches the same script to each instance, but it changes the names of the objects so that each object is unique; also, each slider controls a different parameter for the object in the `setTransform()` method. To learn more about this, see the listing for this method in the ActionScript Reference section.

5. At this point, half of the sliders have their scripts attached. To script the remaining three, you will be able to cut and paste, but with a few additional modifications. The initial script should still be copied to your clipboard. Click the

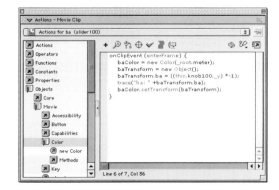

instance named `rb` and open the Actions panel. Paste your script into the window. First, change all iterations of the phrase `ra` to `rb`; then change the line that reads

```
raTransform.ra=((this.knob100._y)*-1);
```

to read

```
rbTransform.rb=((this.knob255._y)*-2);
```

This instance uses a different slider instance to generate a different numeric value when it is manipulated. This line of script targets the instance `knob255` and multiplies its vertical position (`_y`) by –2. The reasons for this are nearly the same as those encountered in the previous slider. Where `ra`, `ga`, and `ba` can accept a value between –100 and 100, `rb`, `gb`, and `bb` can hold a range of values between –255 and 255. The `knob255` instance is locked to a range between –127.5 and 127.5. As a result, values must be doubled in order to yield the full 255 possibilities in each direction.

Once you have completed this script, copy it to the clipboard and then close the Actions panel.

6. Select the instance named `gb`, open the Actions panel, and paste the script into the window. Be sure to update all iterations of `rb` to `gb` in the script statements. Do the same for the `bb` instance.

You have now completed all the scripting needed for this movie. Save the movie; then select Control → Test Movie. As you drag the sliders up and down, you will see the meter Movie Clip instance change color according to the parameters that each slider is feeding to the `setTransform()` method.

Inspirational Design Model

Great ideas defy genre and media boundaries. Many pieces of exceptional depth and quality have the ability to go beyond multimedia and become *transmedia* works—pieces that thrive in any format. The Inspirational Design Model for this chapter is one such piece.

"African Voices" was developed by the Smithsonian Institution to document the richness of Africa and its people. The exhibit "examines the diversity, dynamism, and global influence of Africa's peoples and cultures" across time, in the context of personal, family, and professional life. Although the exhibit is kept in Washington, D.C., at the National Museum of Natural History, it is also available via the Internet to those who cannot attend in person.

The African Voices website, at `www.mnh.si.edu/africanvoices/` (see Figure 16.10), was developed by both the Smithsonian Institution and Terra Incognita to bring portions of the live exhibit to a worldwide audience. Here you will find a comprehensive site where Flash and ActionScript are used to dynamically present vast amounts of information in an easily accessible format.

Figure 16.10

African Voices is a rich, dynamic site that explores the cultural intricacies of the African continent.

Summary

This chapter presented many of the most useful elements of the ActionScript language. You learned how to increase the interactivity of your movie through the use of alternative controllers and how to use the keyboard as another source for audience input. You also learned about the depth and versatility of movies that use multiple Timelines and Movie Clips, some of Flash's greatest assets.

You can use many different ActionScript properties and actions to control Movie Clips in a Flash animation or interactive movie. Some of these are used to affect playback directly, while others are primarily for changing appearance and creating interesting graphic effects. In the next chapter, you will learn additional ActionScript techniques for manipulating data and managing some of the less-visual components of a Flash movie.

CHAPTER 17

Managing Data Input and Output

One of Flash's powerful features is its ability to gather user data from within the client (the Flash movie within the browser) or display dynamic content that it has retrieved from the server. For instance, you can collect information from your audience through a form or display a constantly changing list of news headlines on your site. In these situations, Flash movies switch from being static to being dynamic, thereby becoming much more versatile and powerful.

To be fair, however, most of the time Flash only provides the dynamic *frontend* (what the user sees in the web browser) for these *web applications* (as they are called sometimes). The *backend* (the system used to parse, collect, and serve the information collected from the frontend) is made possible by a host of database-driven technologies. Any discussion about managing data input and output in Flash could easily go beyond the scope of this chapter. As a result, this chapter will be light on the backend technologies (though they won't be totally neglected) and heavy on the creation of the dynamic frontend. In any case, you'll be provided with enough information that you'll be in a great position to begin creating dynamic database-driven web applications.

Topics covered include the following:

- **Understanding databases and database-driven sites**
- **Creating the dynamic Flash frontend**
- **Introducing the dynamic backend**
- **Generating dynamic content from text files**

Understanding Databases and Database-Driven Sites

Up until a number of years ago, the Web was pretty static. People uploaded pages that contained a fixed, immutable amount of content that changed only when new HTML files were uploaded. Then, much to the collective applause of the development community, dynamic database-driven applications were developed. Rather than forcing people to be passive visitors, dynamic database-driven sites allowed users to change aspects of a page (whether content or design) in real time.

So what exactly is a dynamic database web application? Well, a web application consists of two parts: a frontend and a backend. The frontend consists of the portion of the application in the browser window with which the user interacts. Radio buttons, check boxes, text fields, drop-down menus, submit buttons, and the interface in which they all reside are all part of the frontend. The backend, on the other hand, is generally made up of three elements: a web server, a database, and a script that makes them all work together. The web server carries out a couple of functions: First, it delivers HTML documents to the user's computer when they are requested. Second, it processes the code that makes the web application work.

The database, which can range from Microsoft Access to Structured Query Language (SQL), contains all of the information dynamically delivered to the user based on their requests. For example, if you were creating a site where a user needed to register before getting access, you would use a database to store, manage, and manipulate username and password information.

> SQL is not really a database; it's a language used to format structured queries to databases.

> Databases are extremely complicated objects in their own right. If you are interested in learning more about databases, invest in alternate reference material. If you're using Microsoft Access (which is usually the database of choice for creating small- to medium-sized web applications), *Mastering Access 2002 Premium Edition* (Sybex, 2001) is a great place to start.

The script is the heart and soul of the dynamic database-driven application. There are many different solutions you can use to create the script that runs the application. In "Introducing the Dynamic Backend" later in this chapter, you'll get an introduction to many of the scripting solutions you can use.

Creating the Dynamic Flash Frontend

Where does Flash fit into all of this dynamic database-driven stuff? Well, used effectively, Flash is the perfect tool for building the frontend of a web application. By employing some fairly complicated ActionScript, Flash can easily hook up with a host of tools and technologies that provide the backend functionality in any given dynamic web application. In the following sections, you are going to go through three steps used to create the frontend of a dynamic Flash web application. The first involves creating the visual interface elements that will be used to either input or display data. The second and the third steps, which are somewhat inextricably entwined, involve sending data to the server and, if desired, dynamically displaying data within Flash.

Using Text Boxes to Gather and Display Dynamic Information

As covered in Chapter 5, there are three kinds of text in Flash: Static, Input, and Dynamic. You can access the options of each type through the Property Inspector (Window → Properties). The first type, Static Text, is the plain-Jane default text in Flash. However, the other two types, Input Text and Dynamic Text, are integral parts of any dynamic frontend. In this section, you're going to look at each type and explore how you can integrate them into your dynamic database-driven Flash application.

Gathering Data with Input Text Fields

The easiest way to think about an Input Text field is as a container into which the user enters information (their name, a favorite color, and so on). Any text entered into the field is assigned a variable (which you determine). Flash then sends the variable's value (the data entered by the user) to a server or uses it internally. For example, if you assign the variable userName to an Input Text field, anything the user types into that field (whether it's their name or not) becomes the value of userName.

Just like any other type of text within Flash, Input Text is created with the Text tool. Follow these steps:

1. Create a new document.
2. Select the Text tool from the Toolbox.
3. If it isn't already, open the Property Inspector by going to Window → Properties.
4. Choose Input Text from the Text Type drop-down menu. (If you are having trouble remembering how to work with the Input Text options in the Property Inspector, see Chapter 5.)
5. Click and drag to define a text box on the Stage.
6. From there, you have a series of options; the most pertinent to this discussion is the Var field. If you want the Input Text field to work properly, you *must* enter a variable into the Var field. If you want your field to be visible to the user, make sure you've checked Show Border around Text.

7. To test the Input Text field, save the document, and then view it by going to Control → Test Movie (or Control → Test Scene). Then type something into the field and go to Debug → List Variables. In the Output window, you'll get a display like this:

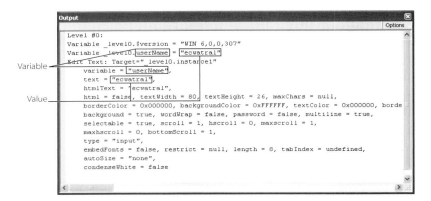

Taking the data the user has entered and sending it to Flash is part of a process (using the `getUrl()` and `loadVariables()` actions) that is covered shortly in "Moving Data to and from a Server."

Displaying Dynamic Data with Dynamic Text

Dynamic Text is almost the same as Input Text. The only difference, which is fairly significant, is that data is traveling in the other direction—from the server to the user's browser.

When you create a Dynamic Text field, you create a text box that has content dynamically generated from another source—say, a database or a text file on your server. With this in mind, one can easily come up with some interesting uses. For example, you could create a constantly changing list of your favorite jokes or your daily itinerary. The possibilities are definitely endless.

Let's take a look at how to create Dynamic Text:

1. Create a new document.

2. Select the Text tool from the Toolbox.

3. If it isn't already, open the Property Inspector by going to Window → Properties.

4. Click and drag to define a text box on the Stage—make sure the size of the text box is appropriate from the amount of text you want to display.

5. Choose Dynamic Text from the Text Type drop-down menu in the Property Inspector.

6. Enter a unique variable name for the Dynamic Text into the Var field. Like the Input Text, if you don't assign a variable, your Dynamic Text won't work.

Later in this chapter, you'll explore how to put Dynamic Text to work by creating a movie with content drawn from associated text files.

Moving Data to and from a Server

Now that you've explored the visual interface elements used to push data out of Flash and display data within Flash (Input Text and Dynamic Text), it's time to look at the Action-Script necessary to tell Flash where and how you want the data sent. In the next sections, you'll explore `getURL()`, `loadVariables()`, and `loadMovie()`.

Using *getURL()*

When it comes to creating dynamic Flash applications, the `getURL()` action lets you send variables to a given file and display the results in a new window, targeted frame, or existing window. The primary weakness of the `getURL()` action is that it won't return information to the actual Flash movie in the browser window. So, as a result, if you instruct Flash to return information to the currently open window, the Flash movie currently playing is replaced. The alternative is to instruct Flash to return the information to a new window by using the `_blank` target (something you'll learn how to do shortly). Granted, this is not a good solution if you want to limit your user's experience to within the Flash movie, but it is your only choice when it comes to the `getURL()` action.

In the following step-by-step example on how to use the `getURL()` action, you are going to send a variable to a fictional ASP file (called `name.asp`) sitting in the same directory of your movie:

1. Open a new document.
2. Select the Text tool from the Toolbox.
3. If it isn't already, open the Property Inspector by going to Window → Properties.
4. Click and drag to define a text box on the Stage.
5. Choose Input Text from the Text Type drop-down menu in the Property Inspector.
6. Click the Show Border around Text button to make sure the text box remains visible.
7. Type **userName** into the Var field.
8. Create a simple button (using the Symbol Editor) and place it on the Stage next to the Input Text. (If you are having difficulty remembering how to create a button symbol, see Chapter 13.)
9. Select the Button symbol, and go to Window → Actions.
10. If it isn't already, switch the Actions panel into Normal mode by clicking the View Options button, and selecting Normal Mode from the drop-down menu.

11. Click the Actions category in the ActionScript Toolbox (the left side of the Actions panel where all ActionScript elements are located).

12. When the Actions category opens, click the Browser/Network category.

13. Double-click the `getURL()` action to add it to the ActionScript text box.

14. Enter the filename into the URL field. In this case, type **name.asp**. If you were sending information to a web page, simply type in the full URL. If the file you are sending the information to is in another directory (as opposed to the one in which your Flash movie resides), you'll need to type in the exact path. Once you've entered the filename or URL into the URL field, you'll notice that it's added to the ActionScript in the ActionScript text box.

15. Now, it's time to tell Flash to which window you want the information returned. Open the Window drop-down menu (by clicking the small Down arrow to the right of the Window field), and choose one of the Window options:

    - `_blank` returns the information to a newly opened window (on top of the one in which the Flash movie resides).

    - `_self` returns the information to the current frame in the current window.

    - `_parent` returns the information into the parent frame of the current frame.

    - `_top` returns the information to the top frame of the current page.

16. Once you've set the window in which the information will be returned, you need to decide the method by which the information is sent. Just below the Window drop-down menu, there is a Variables drop-down menu:

    - The `GET` method sends the information in the form of a query string.

    - The `POST` method sends the information via a buffer—far more preferable if you are sending a great deal of information, as it isn't visible in the URL field of the browser.

When it's all said and done, the Actions panel should look something like this:

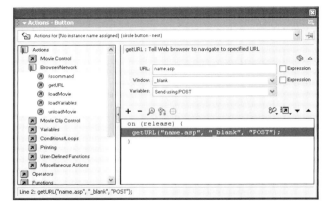

17. From there, your script is complete. Simply close down the Actions window.

Theoretically, when the button is clicked, the Flash movie will take the text that the user entered into the Input Text field, and send it to the `name.asp` file. From there, the ASP file will take the information (which is packaged as the variable/value combination) and do something with it—the *something* is determined by the ASP file itself (which you need to create).

The choice you made in the Window drop-down menu really only applies if the ASP file is created so that it spits some kind of data back to be displayed in the browser.

For example, you could construct the ASP file so that it takes the value of the variable userName, and sticks it in a database. Alternatively, instead of sticking it into a database, it could simply send the information to you in an e-mail.

Using *loadVariables()* or *loadVariablesNum()*

The getURL() action works well if you want to leave your Flash movie to return the desired information. But what if you wanted the desired information returned and displayed *within* the Flash movie? This is where the loadVariables() and loadVariablesNum() actions come in.

The two actions return information to either a targeted Movie Clip—loadVariables()—or a level within the main Timeline—loadVariablesNum()—within your Flash movie or update variables with new values inside the active movie.

At this point in the chapter, you aren't going to go into a step-by-step look at using either action like you did when you explored the getURL() action. After you've explored the backend of a dynamic web application (either Flash or regular HTML), you'll get a chance to create a movie that uses loadVariablesNum() to load dynamic content from a series of text files.

Using *loadMovie()* or *loadMovieNum()* to Dynamically Load JPEGs

As you've probably figured out, you use getUrl() and loadVariables()/loadVariablesNum() to either display or acquire textual information (at least in this context). So, what if you wanted to display something other than text? Well, that's where loadMovie() and loadMovieNum() (which are both actions of the Movie Clip object) enter the picture. With them, you can dynamically load JPEG images that reside on you web server—or another web server entirely—into a target Movie Clip (loadMovie()) or a level within the main Timeline (loadMovieNum()).

Although this section is going to focus on using loadMovie() or loadMovieNum() to dynamically display JPEGs within a Flash movie, you can also use them to load other SWF files into a movie.

To dynamically load a JPEG using either loadMovie() or loadMovieNum(), follow these steps:

1. Select the frame, Button, or Movie Clip that you want to activate the loadMovie() or loadMovieNum() action.

2. Open the Actions panel by going to Window → Actions.

3. If it isn't already, expand the Actions category in the ActionScript Toolbox by clicking it.

4. Expand the Browser/Network category in the ActionScript Toolbox.

5. Double-click the `loadMovie()` action to add it to the ActionScript text box.

6. Now, in the URL field of the Parameters pane, enter the location and name of the JPEG you want to load. Remember, if the image is in the same directory as the Flash movie, you really only have to enter the image name. However, if it isn't located in the same directory, you'll have to enter the exact path (either as an absolute or relative URL) so that the Flash movie can locate it.

7. Now, if you want to load the image into a document level or the main Timeline, choose Level from the Location drop-down menu, and then enter the level number into the field just to the right of the Location drop-down menu. On the other hand, if you want to load the image into a Movie Clip, select Target from the Location drop-down menu, and enter the name of the Movie Clip instance into which you are loading the JPEG in the field to the right of the Location drop-down menu.

8. When you've finished, close the Actions panel.

When you load directly into the main Timeline, the movie will automatically resize to fit the JPEG exactly. As a result, it's probably better to load into a Movie Clip that is the same size (or larger) as its JPEG images. The result will be that the Movie Clip will automatically resize to fit the image, and the overall movie won't be affected.

> If the Movie Clip into which you are loading the JPEG is not a direct child of the current Timeline, you'll need to enter the proper target path using dot syntax.

Although using `loadMovie()` or `loadMovieNum()` to dynamically load a JPEG is pretty easy, there are two things you need to realize. First, when it comes to using `loadMovie()`, all the contents of the target Movie Clip will be replaced by the loaded JPEG. Second, only one JPEG can occupy a given level in the Flash movie. As a result, if you load a second JPEG into `_level1`, the first one you loaded will be automatically replaced.

> For more information on levels in a Flash movie, see Chapter 16.

Introducing the Dynamic Backend

Earlier in this chapter, you learned about how dynamic database-driven applications work. Just to refresh your memory, dynamic database-driven web applications have two parts: a frontend and a backend. You explored how to create the frontend of a dynamic web application in Flash. The backend, on the other hand, includes three elements: a server, a database, and a script.

You've already learned how to send data to a web server. In the cases of both the `getUrl()` and `loadVariables()` actions, you target the script by entering the correct location into the URL field of the Actions window's Parameter section. Whether you are using an ASP file (like the fictional one you used when looking at the `getUrl()` action) or a CGI script, once you've told Flash where to send the data, the script takes care of the rest.

In the following sections, you'll be introduced to the various types of scripts and technologies available. The point of these sections is to adequately prepare you to choose the best solution for your needs and point you in the direction of learning more about that technology.

ASP

ASP (Active Server Pages) is a server-side scripting technology developed by Microsoft. ASP is based on an HTML-like syntax in which custom-made VBScript or Jscript (Microsoft's version of JavaScript) resides in specialized tags. Although the most common way to deploy ASP is with Microsoft's Internet Information Server, a number of other methods, mainly Sun's Chili!soft, can deploy ASP on other platforms such as Linux or Solaris.

One of the great joys of ASP is that it can store site information in a database. As users visit the site, the information is called from the database on a case-by-case basis. As a result, you can make all manner of changes to your layout (font, color, and so on) by changing the ASP code and not the actual HTML page. In addition, ASP, like many server-side technologies, can draw upon information within a database to continuously repopulate a web page or a Flash movie with dynamic data.

Although ASP can be written in any text program (such as Notepad or SimpleText), it tends to get a little complicated. As a result, a number of authoring environments are available that help you develop ASP. Most notably among these is Macromedia's Dreamweaver UltraDev. Built on the same authoring environment as Dreamweaver, UltraDev lets you create complicated ASP with minimum knowledge of the underlying code.

A demo copy of Macromedia's Dreamweaver UltraDev is included on the book's CD-ROM.

One of the other great things about ASP is that it can work with any Open Database Connection (ODBC)–compliant database. As a result, you can create your database in a wide range of programs.

ColdFusion

Originally developed by Allaire (which was acquired by Macromedia in 2001), ColdFusion is a dynamic database-driven application technology that uses a unique tag-based server scripting language (ColdFusion Markup Language, or CFML) in conjunction with a specialized server (ColdFusion Server) to deliver powerful dynamic web applications. Because ColdFusion's CFML scripting language is similar to HTML, it is fairly easy to learn and use.

When a user requests a ColdFusion document (which is called a *template* and has a `.cfm` extension), the web server passes the file first to the ColdFusion Server (which sits on the web server itself) before passing it to the user's browser. The ColdFusion Server looks at the template, interpreting any the embedded CFML. The ColdFusion Server then generates the output from the CFML in the template and returns the file to the web server to be passed back and displayed in the user's browser.

Let's take a look at a short example. Say, for instance, that you've created a ColdFusion template with all the necessary CFML to create a list of the current books you are reading. When a user tries to load that file (remember, it's called a *template*) into their browser, the server would notice `.cfm` extension and pass the request onto the ColdFusion Server. Now, when the ColdFusion Server received the request, it would pull the list of the current books you are reading from a database (which you keep constantly updated), stick the data in the appropriate places in the template (which are designated using CFML), and pass the file back to the web server. The web server would then send the file to the user's browser, letting them view the list of the books you are currently reading.

ColdFusion requires ColdFusion Server to work. Unlike ASP (which only requires a specific type of web server), ColdFusion actually needs this piece of software that sits on the web server to work properly.

> To learn more about ColdFusion, go to www.macromedia.com/coldfusion.

Just like with ASP, you can set a ColdFusion template as the target URL for either a `getUrl()` or a `loadVariables()` action. Once information (in the form of actual data or a request for data) is sent to a CFM document, ColdFusion will do its thing and then return the data back to Flash to be displayed in the manner you've defined (either in the Flash movie itself or in another window).

You can generate CFML a number of ways. You can simply write it from scratch as you would with HTML. You can also use either Macromedia Dreamweaver UltraDev or ColdFusion Studio (available from Macromedia).

PHP

Back in 1994, Rasmus Lerdorf developed a series of Perl (Practical Extraction and Reporting Language) scripts that allowed him to monitor the users who accessed his website. Word got around about Lerdorf's interesting invention, and people started asking to use his scripts on their pages. Shortly thereafter, Lerdorf released them as a package called Personal Home Page Tools (PHP).

By 1995, PHP—whose full name was changed from Personal Home Page Tools to Hypertext Preprocessor—had gained a large following. The popularity of PHP prompted Rasmus to release a scripting engine and additional scripts designed to process data from forms.

When the third incarnation of PHP (PHP3) was released, it included a far more efficient scripting engine. The syntax of PHP was changed so that it looked more like a cross between C/C++ and Perl, instead of just straight Perl (which isn't an object-oriented programming language). To allow third-party developers to further extend PHP by developing their own modules, PHP3 included an Application Programming Interface (API).

The current release of PHP (PHP4) has been completely reworked to give users far more control over their PHP creations. The API now more efficiently integrates third-party PHP modules.

PHP's benefits lie in several different areas. First, you can write PHP with a simple text utility such as Notepad, SimpleText, or Emacs. Like many server-side scripting technologies (including all those discussed in this chapter), PHP can draw information from any ODBC-compliant database on the server. PHP can be installed on most web servers (Windows- or Unix-based). Generally speaking, PHP is reported to be faster and more stable than both ASP and ColdFusion. All of these benefits are great, but the best is that it's free. You can use it for non-commercial or commercial applications, trade it with friends, hang it on your wall, use burn it on a CD, or use it to play fetch with your dog Oscar. Further, because PHP is open source, tens of thousands of developers are working hard to develop modules that do new things.

> Although Macromedia Dreamweaver UltraDev didn't feature integrated support for PHP at the time of this writing, a number of user-developed extensions add PHP functionality to UltraDev.

Like with any of the other technologies discussed so far, you can set a PHP file (which has a `.php` extension) as the target URL for either a `getUrl()` or `loadVariables()` action. Once information (in the form of actual data or a request for data) is sent to a PHP document, the PHP server will do its thing and return the data back to Flash to be displayed in the manner you've defined (either in the Flash movie itself or in another window).

> To find out more about PHP, go to www.php.net. You can also visit www.phpbuilder.com. If you are interested in open-source software, try www.opensource.org.

CGI

CGI (which stands for Common Gateway Interface) was around way before anyone ever thought of dynamic database-driven applications. To be honest, CGI isn't a programming language in itself. It's really a technology that allows the development of server-side programs that extend the functionality of HTML (and Flash for that matter).

Although Perl is by far the most popular programming language to develop CGI, there are certainly other options, including C/C++, Visual Basic, Applescript, Unix Shell, and Tcl.

As with all of the other technologies discussed, you can target a CGI file with the `getUrl()` or `loadVariables()` actions. Data passed out of Flash is processed by the particular CGI script and then returned and displayed in the method you determine.

For more information about CGI, visit www.`scriptsearch.com` or www.`cgi-resources.com`.

Generating Dynamic Content from Text Files

Now that you've looked at both the frontend and backend of dynamic database-driven web applications, it's time to create a Flash movie that displays dynamic information. In this section, you're going to take everything you've learned and create a Flash movie that displays information from text files. Granted, this is not particularly dynamic *per se* because the text files contain information that is static. The point of the exercise is that you'll be creating a Flash movie that draws and displays information from another source by using ActionScript (more specifically, the `loadVariablesNum()` action discussed earlier). To create something truly dynamic, you would have to use one of the previously mentioned technologies.

During this step-by-step example, you'll create four different buttons that, when clicked, will load the contents of four text files (each a quotation from a literary figure or orator) into the Flash movie.

 Although you certainly can use any text file you want, the Chapter 17 directory on the book's CD-ROM contains the four text files referred to in the following example. In addition, the `quotes.swf` file is an example of what the end result should be. As usual, however, the process is more important than the end result. So, let's get at it:

1. First, create a folder on your hard drive called Flash Quote Project. After you've done that, copy all of the text files in the Chapter 17 directory of the book's CD-ROM to the folder.

2. Now, create a new file by going to File → New. Before you create anything, save the file to the Flash Quote Project directory and call it **quotes**.

If you've copied the `quotes.fla` over from the Chapter 17 directory of the book's CD-ROM, the newly saved file will overwrite it. If you want to avoid this, either refrain from copying the finished `quotes.swf` from the CD-ROM or simply give your file another name.

3. First, name the existing layer **Dynamic Text**.

4. Select the Text tool from the Toolbox.

5. If it isn't already, open the Property Inspector by going to Window → Properties.

6. In the Property Inspector, select the Dynamic Text option from the Text Type drop-down menu.

7. Make sure Multiline is selected in the Line Type drop-down menu.

8. Now, select the first keyframe of the Dynamic Text layer and use the Text tool to draw an area roughly 10 centimeters (4 inches) wide and 7 centimeters (2.75 inches) high. This will serve as the "container" in which Flash will display the contents of each of the text files. Now, for the most important part, enter **quoteField** into the Property Inspector's Variable field.

   If you take a look at each of the text files, you'll notice the words *quoteField=* at the beginning of each text file. This string links each text file to the Dynamic box you've just created.

9. Now, you want to set the look of the text when it's displayed in the Dynamic Text field. So, with the field you created still selected, and the Property Inspector still open, set your font to Helvetica/Arial, the color to Black, the size to 12, and the style to Bold and Italic.

10. Now that you've created the Dynamic box in which Flash will place the text drawn from the text files, it's time to create the interactive controls that will call the content from each individual text file. From here, you can create four buttons (with the words *Homer*, *Plato*, *Frost*, and *Melville* on each respectively). Alternatively, you can just go to File → Open as Library, navigate to and select the `quotes.swf` file on the book's CD-ROM, and use the buttons that are included.

11. Create four additional layers and assign them the same names as the buttons (Homer, Plato, Frost, and Melville). Click and drag each individual button to their respective layer. Make sure the buttons are placed in an evenly spaced line below the Dynamic Text field. So far, your Stage should look something like this:

12. Now, you need to attach the ActionScript to each of the buttons so that when clicked, the appropriate text will be loaded into the Dynamic Text field. Select the first button in the row (Homer) and go to Window → Actions to open the Actions panel.

13. First, make sure you are in Normal mode. If the Actions category isn't already expanded in the ActionScript Toolbox (the left side of the Actions panel), do so by clicking it.

14. Then, expand the Browser/Network category.

15. Now, locate and double-click the `loadVariables()` action to add it to the ActionScript text box.

16. Next, you need to set the parameters for the `loadVariables()`. In the URL field, enter the name of the text file you want to load when the user clicks the button (in this case, `homer.txt`). If the text file is in the same directory as the Flash movie, you only need to type the filename. However, if the text file is sitting elsewhere, you have to enter the relative path.

17. In the Location drop-down menu, choose Level. Then, enter **0** into the field just to the right. By doing this, you are telling Flash to load the text file into the Dynamic box located in level 0 of the movie. You'll notice that when you choose Level, opposed to Target, from the Location drop-down menu, the action itself will switch from `load-Variables()` to `loadVariablesNum()`. Don't worry—you are loading the text files into the main Timeline (opposed to a Movie Clip), which is what is supposed to happen.

> Flash stores information in different hierarchical layers called *levels*. Movie Clips and scripts can easily access variables in the same level they occupy. If, however, a given variable occupies a different level, the Movie Clip or script must explicitly state in which level it's located.

At this point, your Actions panel should look like this:

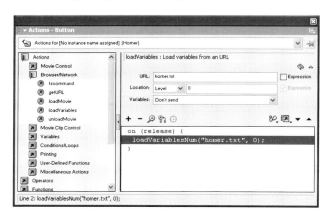

18. Repeat the process described in steps 12–17 to link each button to the appropriate text file.

19. Test your movie by going to Control → Test Movie or Control → Test Scene.

Inspirational Design Model

The world of dynamic Flash is an exciting one that is just starting to grow in popularity. Among the most interesting applications is real-time, web-based user feedback. One of the recognized leaders in the field is OpinionLab (`www.opinionlab.com`).

Their primary system, OpinionOnline, includes two tools (see Figure 17.1). The first tool, constructed using Dynamic HTML, facilitates the continuous collection of page-specific user feedback through an unobtrusive "rating system" menu widget. The second tool, which is facilitated with Macromedia Generator, consists of an amazingly varied toolset of statistical representations that display the feedback collected from users.

Working in tandem, these two tools provide a powerful system by which to get almost instantaneous marketing analysis—a process that traditionally took a great deal more time.

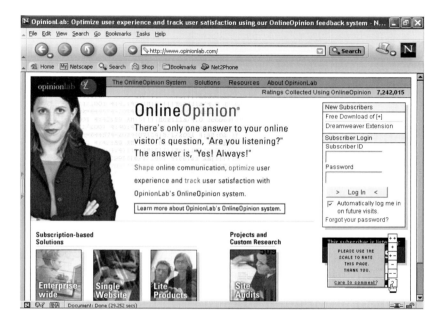

Figure 17.1

OpinionLab provides an amazing Generator-based system to collect and display real-time, page-specific user feedback.

Summary

In this chapter, you explored the ways that Flash can push data to server-side applications as well as receive and display data from server-side applications. You started off the chapter by looking at the basic mechanics of dynamic database-driven sites. From there, you created the dynamic frontend with Input Text and Dynamic Text. From there, you explored the dynamic backend. You started with a look at the two most important actions in your quest to create dynamic database-driven Flash sites: `getUrl()` and `loadVariables()`/`loadVariablesNum()`. Next, you investigated the various server-side technologies used to serve dynamic data to the Flash frontend, including ASP, ColdFusion, PHP, and CGI. To get some hands-on experience loading dynamic data into Flash, you worked through a step-by-step tutorial on how to create a Flash movie into which you load the contents of external text files.

CHAPTER 18

Troubleshooting ActionScript

In previous chapters, you have run the gamut as far as ActionScript is concerned. You have been bombarded with the terms, elements, techniques, concepts, technical and syntactical conventions, properties, methods, and commands of the language. You have probably been working and experimenting with ActionScript in your movies and run into a problem here and there.

Sometimes problems arise from unfamiliarity with the material you are using; other times they are caused by a simple typing error or misplaced character in your script. And, of course, there are times when an error or problem occurs and you have no idea whatsoever why something has gone wrong. These kinds of situations can be frustrating and sometimes even a little scary. The purpose of this chapter is to present a set of tools that you can use when the problems with the ActionScript in your movie are not immediately recognizable. The chapter covers these topics:

- **Authoring techniques to help avoid problems before they arise**
- **ActionScript conventions to aid in the troubleshooting process**
- **Using the Flash Debugger window**
- **Tracking script elements in the Output window**

Scripting and Working Smart: Some Suggestions

Even the most proficient and knowledgeable ActionScript gurus get stuck in technical ruts. One thing that separates them, though, is their ability to get out of these ruts. Experience has taught them how to step away from the problem, evaluate the situation, and dive in again with an appropriate solution. Often, technical problems are easily solved not through scripting wizardry but through a logical and methodical reevaluation of your code. Moreover, by practicing good, consistent habits while planning and writing your scripts, many problems can be avoided altogether. This section provides a set of useful tips and recommendations that should help you practice good scripting form and avoid many common technical stumbling blocks.

Although good *physical* form while typing (keeping your back straight, putting your feet on the floor, and so on) is critical in preventing repetitive stress injuries, good *scripting* form means good habits that minimize the possibility of errors. Good form ultimately means working smarter. It can also help you flush out problems and find their solutions when they do pop up. Following is a list of things you can do to help avoid problems while working on your Flash projects and writing ActionScript.

Use appropriate variable names. Variables are storage locations for many different kinds of information: values, properties, Movie Clip instances, frame labels—just about anything in a movie. When you initialize a variable, try to select a name that is meaningful—ideally a name that makes reference to the role or purpose of the variable. A variable name must be an identifier. For more on variables, see Chapter 15.

Use ActionScript terms correctly. Some elements of ActionScript are read-only, which means that they can be checked but not set. Many terms use a specific configuration or upper- and lowercase letters and punctuation. When in doubt about a particular term, consult this book's ActionScript Reference section or the built-in script help of the Reference panel (Shift+F1).

Work deliberately; test movies and scripts often. While you are creating a Flash movie, it's easy to be swept away by the pure joy of creativity and forget about the technical feasibility of what you are doing. Without compromising your work style, try to approach the creative process by taking small steps. With every little accomplishment or scripting victory, test the movie to ensure that *every* element is still working properly.

Save multiple versions, and back up your files. Everyone knows about frequent saves; but everyone forgets occasionally, too. Backup files are essential to ensure against disk errors, hard-drive crashes, and other anomalies that can plague the citizens of a digital world. Saving multiple versions of a file helps protect against major mistakes, lost data, corrupted files, and so on. If a newer version has problems or is altered beyond repair, it can be helpful to return to a previous version and start afresh.

Use the `trace` function to track variables and properties. The `trace` function is one of the most helpful parts of ActionScript. It allows you to get feedback from the Flash Player and tells you what is *really* going on in your movie with variables, loops, and other script elements. To learn more about this, see the section "Using `trace`" later in this chapter.

Use comments to mark up your code. Comments, created by typing a double forward slash (//), tell Flash to ignore whatever is written after the slashes. Use comments to leave notes to yourself or another member of your team, to make citations about the portions that work and the portions that don't, and so on. Comments can also help to keep script sections organized.

> For blocking out large chunks of code, also see the multiline comment operator (/* and */) in the ActionScript Reference section.

Storyboard a script to check the logic and flow. If you are going to tackle a large project involving a lot of ActionScript, it can be helpful to start by working on paper. You can plan and conceptualize your script outside of Flash, and then step into the program once you are ready to begin development. It can also be helpful to plan complex loop structures on paper, where you can do all the computations and logic in a medium that shows the flow of information.

Build your movie in small chunks. It can be advantageous to break a project into sections and tackle them one by one, a kind of divide-and-conquer approach. Get one portion of your movie working before moving on to the next.

Identify problems as they arise. If something seems to be amiss, chances are it is. It's always better to deal with problems right away than to let them linger. Also, as you troubleshoot and try different solutions, think about how temporary fixes may negatively impact other movie elements in the future.

This list of recommendations is not ActionScript dogma. Everyone has their own work style and must approach their projects in a way that encourages both creativity and productivity. The hope is that some of these techniques will help you avoid errors and focus on the more important aspects of a project.

Troubleshooting Tips

Try as you might, some problems simply cannot be avoided. When they occur, they are like sand in the gears of your scripting machine. Technical scripting errors can bring your productivity to a screeching halt and create frustration in the ranks of your development team. The good thing about technical errors is that you can overcome them. They are *errors,* and all you have to do is set things straight; change them and make them the way they ought to be.

Sound too easy to be true? Well, probably, but it surely does feel good to think about problems so confidently. Attitude can be a great asset when it comes to overcoming technical problems and errors. When you are calm and collected, it is easier to think with perspective and to examine the situation at hand logically. To do this, you must look at your scripts from every possible angle to try and discover what portion or component is causing the problem, and why.

Self-Help: Queries for Troubleshooting Common Mistakes

Following is a series of questions you can ask in order to get to the bottom of an Action-Script-related problem with your movie.

Is the syntax correct? There are many different ActionScript elements: actions, properties, methods, functions, and so on. It can be very easy to confuse one syntax for another, so be sure that you are using each term properly.

Make sure that you correctly spell each term and use the right upper- and lowercase characters where they are needed (for example, `onClipEvent`, not `onclipevent`).

Be sure to include a semicolon (`;`) at the end of statements, and be sure to use curly braces (`{}`) to enclose the statements of handlers and loops. ActionScript is often forgiving when it comes to missing semicolons, but a misplaced or forgotten curly brace will stop the Flash Player dead in its tracks when it is trying to read and process your scripts.

Watch your operators carefully! When evaluating a condition, 10<=10 evaluates as True because 10 is equal to 10, whereas 10<10 evaluates False (10 is not less than 10). Similarly, the assignment operator (=) and equality operator (==) have very different uses. The assignment operator is used to *assign* a value:

```
var i=0;
```

The equality operator is used to test whether two expressions are equal and will return a Boolean value:

```
if(this._x==bounds._x){
    //statement(s) if expressions are equal (returns True)
}
```

> If you're not sure of your syntax, Flash will tell you! While working in the Actions panel, simply click the Check Syntax button or press Cmd/Ctrl+T to verify the "correctness" of your Action-Script statements.

Did you specify the arguments correctly? On a related note, many ActionScript elements (actions and methods, in particular) can take arguments. Check to be sure that all arguments are entered properly. For example, if you entered a variable or identifier where there should be a string, your script will not function properly. The following statement will not execute properly because the `duplicateMovieClip` action dictates that the name of the new instance must be specified as a string:

```
duplicateMovieClip(bar,bar+i,1);
```

The correct syntax is:

```
duplicateMovieClip(bar,"bar"+i,1);
```

Here, using the right syntax, `"bar"` is specified as a string.

Is the handler getting executed? Every script is called from some kind of handler. However, if a handler does not get executed, the scripts it contains will not be called. Use the `trace` function to test for handler activity. For example, to test and see if a Movie Clip is responding to a mouse click event, you could write:

```
onClipEvent(release){
    trace("clicked");
    //other statement(s);
}
```

Did you use the correct target path? When you are creating a movie with multiple Movie Clip instances and Timelines, it can be easy to get confused and forget which clips and movies reside where. Check to see that you have correctly specified all of your target paths to functions, objects, Movie Clips, and their properties. For more specifics on this, see the section "Monitoring Scripts with the Output Window" later in this chapter.

What's the scope? While global (`_global`) variables are available at any time throughout an entire movie, others are not. Timeline-specific variables must be recalled using a target path to the Timeline where they were created. To read more about variables and their scope, see Chapter 15.

Does your math check out? How many expressions are you using in a script? Do they add up correctly to achieve the results you desire? If it is helpful, you can use the `trace` function to help with some in-context number crunching.

Are loops and conditionals executing properly? When you use a loop or conditional, you set the parameters to test a condition and then have ActionScript do something as a result of that condition. If a script is not behaving properly, check to see if loops and conditional statements are functioning correctly.

Are all Movie Clips and Button objects instances? Unless a Movie Clip or Button object is an instance, you will not be able to target (control) it with ActionScript. Consult the Property Inspector (choose Window → Properties or press Cmd/Ctrl+F3) to be sure that each Movie Clip or Button object you wish to target has a unique instance name.

Do all variables and functions have unique names? It is essential that all variables and functions are uniquely named so that they won't be confused with other elements in your movie.

Flash Troubleshooting Tools

Beyond the mental analysis of a technical problem, it's good to have additional resources that can help dig you out of trouble when problems do occur. It's good to be able to look at a script, walk through it slowly, step by step, and uncover the statements that are problematic. However, sometimes this can prove to be an enormous task! In the same way that it is helpful to create a movie in small, deliberate steps, it can be equally beneficial to troubleshoot in the same manner. You hunt for problems carefully, and make sure that one area of the movie is trouble free before moving on to the next area.

Flash provides a set of tools that can make this process easier. Using these as part of your troubleshooting strategy can help you break a problem down by isolating different parts of a script and testing them individually. Some of these tools are formalized; others are more like scripting techniques. All the tools will help you work through ActionScript problems and get your scripts running smoothly.

Comments were discussed earlier as a means of leaving notes and reminders within the body of a script. You are able to do this because Flash will ignore anything that follows the double slash (//). This feature makes comments the perfect tool for turning certain parts of a script on and off. For example, in the following script, part of the conditional statement is turned off so that the script will execute but not run the statements within the conditional.

```
onClipEvent(enterFrame){
    _root.Bbi._y-=j;
    i+=1;
    if(i>20){
        //_root.gotoAndPlay(1);
    }
}
```

The Debugger was introduced with Flash 5 and has since been improved for Flash MX. It offers a series of menus that allow you to monitor Movie Clip instances, variables, properties, and, in general, all of the technical happenings of your movie. To learn more about the Debugger, see the next section of this chapter.

The Output window can be used several different ways in your movie. It is involved any time you use the `trace` function. All items that you ask to trace will be printed in the Output window. Additionally, it can be used to provide information about any objects and variables that are active in your movie. To learn how to use this tool, see "Monitoring Scripts with the Output Window" later in this chapter.

Using the Debugger

The Debugger is your window to all the inner workings of your movie. It displays all the Movie Clip instances and levels in your movie, as well as the properties of each. The

Debugger will also track all the variables that are active within a given Timeline in your movie. It is an extremely useful and efficient tool because it presents all of the technical elements you need to monitor a movie within a single window. Use the Debugger to isolate errors in your scripts and look "under the hood." A close examination of your scripts and how they are executing can be invaluable when your movie isn't running properly.

In order to run, the Debugger requires additional software known as the Flash Debug Player. This is a special version of the Flash Player that automatically installs with the main Flash authoring application. The additional software is what allows Flash to load information about your movie into the Debugger window as you test a movie.

Activating the Debugger

When you select Window → Debugger or press Shift+F4, the Debugger window appears. However, it is in an inactive state and is nothing more than a shell waiting to receive information. To initiate debugging in your movie, you must *activate* the Debugger. This launches the Debug Player component and allows the Debug window to receive information.

To activate debugging in your movie, select Control → Debug Movie. Flash automatically jumps into Test Movie mode. The Debugger window opens and displays the contents of your movie. The Debugger is paused by default. To initiate debugging, click the green Continue button in the Code View menu.

Debugger Elements

While activated and running in Test Movie mode, the Debugger no longer looks like a dead window. It has several components, all of which are helpful in giving insight into the workings of your movie. Figure 18.1 shows the Debugger in an active state.

Status Bar

At the very top of the Debugger window is the status bar. It shows the following information:

- Debugging status—whether you're working in Test Movie mode from your local computer, or in Remote Flash Player while debugging from a remote location
- The movie's local file path or URL

Display List

When the Debugger is activated, the Display List shows you a breakdown of each movie level and Movie Clip instance, including a separate clip level for global variables (_global). This list is updated as movies are duplicated, removed, loaded, or unloaded from the main Timeline. The Display List shows these items in a format similar to the Movie Explorer so that you can see the hierarchical relationship between clip instances. If your movie contains lots of clips, you can resize the dimensions of the Display List so that it is taller, to show more information.

Figure 18.1

When the Debugger window is activated, it displays information about various components of your movie.

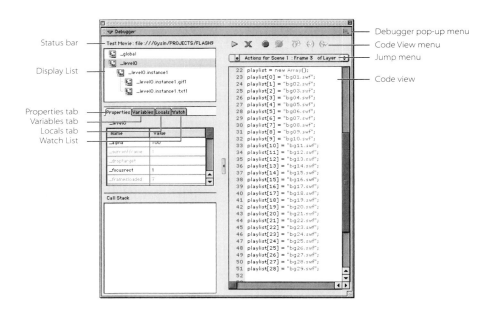

Status bar

Display List

Properties tab
Variables tab
Locals tab
Watch List

Debugger pop-up menu
Code View menu
Jump menu

Code view

Properties Tab

The Properties tab is used to monitor and change properties of a given Movie Clip instance. You can monitor a clip's properties while you test a movie and change them directly from the Debugger window. Any changes made in the Properties tab will not permanently affect your movie. They can only temporarily alter clip parameters while you test the movie.

To display the properties for a Movie Clip, select the clip in the Display List and then click the Properties tab. The tab will show a long list of clip properties. Depending on the clip and the way you use it in your movie, some properties may be constantly updating and changing in the Properties tab window.

To change the values for a property, select the clip instance you would like to modify from the Display List. Double-click the property value and then enter a new value in the field. Press Return/Enter, and your movie will update itself accordingly.

Variables Tab

The Variables tab gives you access to a live display of all the variables currently active on a given Timeline. You can select a Movie Clip instance in the Display List, and the Variables tab will list the current values of the variables that the instance contains. Selecting the _global clip in the Display List will show any global variables that your movie contains.

It is also possible to change variable values as you are testing your movie. Simply select the variable in the list, double-click its value, and enter a new value. Press Return/Enter, and your movie will respond accordingly.

Watch List Tab

The Watch List provides an easy way to monitor a set of variables from one location. For example, if you wanted to simultaneously monitor the variables in two different Movie Clips, you would have to jump back and forth between them in the Display List while watching the Variables tab. The Watch List allows you to select these variables and put them in one location so that they can be monitored easily within a single window. To do this, you must add the variables to the Watch List.

To create a Watch List, you can do one of two things:

- Select a variable in the Variables tab. Ctrl+click (Mac) or right-click (Win), and select Add from the context menu. Alternatively, you can select the variable and choose Add Watch from the Debugger pop-up menu. Any variables selected for a watch will be marked with a blue dot in the Variables tab.

- Ctrl+click (Mac) or right-click (Win) in the Watch List window. Double-click the new line and enter the target path to the variable you wish to watch.

It is not possible to directly assign an item from the Properties tab (like _alpha or _currentframe) to the Watch List. Flash allows you to watch variables only. As a workaround, initialize a variable to the property you would like to watch and then use the Debugger to set a watch for that variable. For example, if you need to constantly monitor the horizontal position of a Movie Clip, create a variable for the _x property:

```
onClipEvent(enterFrame){
    hPos=this._x;
}
```

Then use the Variables tab to set a watch for the variable hPos.

You can remove an item from the Watch List by Ctrl+clicking (Mac) or right-clicking (Win) the item and then selecting Remove from the context menu. You can also highlight the item and select Remove Watch from the Debugger pop-up menu.

Breakpoints

In Flash MX, it's now possible to set and remove breakpoints in your script. Breakpoints allow you to pause a script in your movie and walk through it step-by-step to more closely examine how and when each line effects changes in your movie.

To set and remove breakpoints in the Actions panel:

1. In the Actions panel text box, click on the line where you would like to set your breakpoint.

2. Do one of the following:

    *   Choose Set (or Remove) Breakpoint 🐾 from the Debug Options button menu.

    *   Control+click (Mac) or right-click (Win) and choose Set (or Remove) Breakpoint from the context menu.

    *   Type Cmd/Ctrl+Shift+B.

    To set and remove breakpoints in the Debugger:

1. In the Code View box, click the line where you would like to set your breakpoint.

2. Do one of the following:

Toggle Breakpoint

Remove All Breakpoints

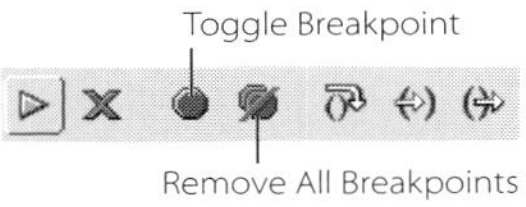

Figure 18.2

The Code View menu includes two options to set and remove breakpoints.

    *   Choose Toggle Breakpoint or Remove All Breakpoints from the Code View menu (see Figure 18.2).

    *   Control+click (Mac) or right-click (Win) and choose Set Breakpoint, Remove Breakpoint, or Remove All Breakpoints from the context menu.

    *   Type Cmd/Ctrl+Shift+B.

    Once you have set breakpoints, it's possible to move through your script line-by-line. This is done by using the Step In, Step Over, and Step Out buttons (see Figure 18.3).

Step In, Step Over, and Step Out work only within user-created functions.

Step Over   Step Out

Step In

Figure 18.3

The controls for moving through a script line-by-line are Step Over, Step In, and Step Out.

Step Over causes your script to skip a line within the function.

Step In advances your script flow into a function.

Step Out forces the debugger out of a user-defined function.

For troubleshooting custom functions and subroutines, this feature cannot be beat. And as you become more proficient with ActionScript, using Step In, Step Over, and Step Out is a topic you should be sure to investigate further. For more details on how to monitor the flow of your scripts, Choose Help → Using Flash. Then navigate to Testing a Movie → Using the Debugger → Stepping through Lines of Code.

Remote Debugging

Sometimes you may find it helpful to examine your scripts and do your debugging while your movie is running "live." For example, if you are working on a movie that involves heavy communication of variables to and from a server, it's essential to know that all the information is being exchanged properly. To activate remote debugging of a Flash movie, two steps are required: enable remote debugging for your movie, and activate the Debugger from a remote location.

ENABLE REMOTE DEBUGGING

To enable remote debugging for your movie:

1. Choose File → Publish Settings.

2. Select the Flash tab of the Publish Settings dialog box and check the Debugging Permitted option.

3. If you'd like to password-protect your movie so that only a select few can access the movie for debugging, enter a password in the Password box. If you don't enter a password, no password will be required to debug your movie.

4. When ready, publish your movie. In addition to the SWF file, Flash will also create a file with the `.swd` extension. This file is necessary for remote debugging. Upload it to the server along with your SWF file(s), HTML, and so on. Be sure that the SWD and SWF files are in the same directory on the server.

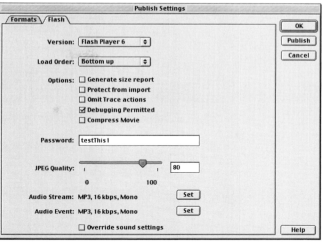

5. To prepare your movie for remote debugging, choose Window → Debugger (Shift+F4) to open the Debugger. Click the Debugger pop-up menu and select Enable Remote Debugging.

   Your movie is now ready for remote debugging.

ACTIVATE REMOTE DEBUGGING

Once you have made all the necessary settings in Flash, you are ready to do some remote debugging. To activate the remote debugger:

1. Launch Flash MX if it isn't already running.

2. Use either a web browser or the stand-alone Flash Player to open your finished movie from its remote location, by entering the movie's URL. The Remote Debug dialog box appears automatically.

3. Choose either Localhost or Other Machine. Select Localhost if the Debug Player and Flash MX are on the same computer; select Other Machine if they are on different computers. Enter the IP address of the computer running Flash MX. Click OK.

4. If you published your movie so that it requires a debugging password, you'll be asked to enter it. After doing so, click OK.

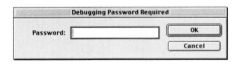

   Your computer switches to Flash MX, and the Debugger is now activated.

To read the latest information on debugging movies in Flash MX, consult the Macromedia website, `www.macromedia.com/support/flash`.

Monitoring Scripts with the Output Window

When Flash 5 introduced the Output window, it added a much-needed element to the ActionScript equation. The Output window is an essential part of building any movie that uses ActionScript. This is because the window allows you to ask specific questions of the Flash Player and get feedback.

What kinds of questions can you ask it? Anything that pertains to your movie. Unfortunately, you can't ask, "Why isn't this @#$%&!! thing working!" but you can ask for things like the values of variables and properties, the location of objects on the Stage, the path to a Movie Clip instance, or the name of the most recent frame label. The Output window will answer questions about any of the properties or parameters known in ActionScript. Additionally, the window is there to display any scripting errors as they arise. If you script something that Flash doesn't understand, it will tell you where the problem lies by printing a message in the Output window.

In some cases, it's possible to get the Output window to give you information without asking it a question directly. The List Objects and List Variables functions allow you to get information about the objects and variables in your movie by using simple menu commands.

In movie editing mode, the Output window is usually hidden and unnecessary. That's because its role deals more with the testing of movies than creating them. As you compose ActionScript and check its syntax, the window may pop open if there is an error to report.

When you're working in Test Movie mode, Flash will open the Output window whenever it has something to tell you; it will either report an error or respond to a question that you had asked it directly while using the `trace` function. (To learn more about `trace`, see its description later in this chapter.)

To open the Output window on your own, select Window → Output or press Shift+F9. The Output window will appear, and its contents will be blank. The Output window offers the following commands in its Options menu (see Figure 18.4):

Figure 18.4

The Options menu of the Output window

Copy (Cmd/Ctrl+C) Copies the contents of the Output window to your computer's Clipboard.

Clear Erases the contents of the Output window.

Find (Cmd/Ctrl+F) Searches the contents of the Output window.

Find Again (F3) Repeats the preceding search.

Save to File Saves all information in the window to a text file.

Print Prints all contents in the Output window.

Debug Level Sets the level of detail for information printed in the Output window.

List Objects Function

While working in Test Movie mode, you can call upon the Output window to give you specific information about all the objects in your movie. This information is delivered in a cascading, outline form to give you an idea of the hierarchy of objects as well. List Objects will tell you the level number, frame number, type of object (MovieClip, Button, or shape), and absolute target path to each Movie Clip instance. This feature can be especially handy when taking stock of a movie's "cast" or tracking down an errant target path.

Figure 18.5

The Output window will list all the objects in a movie while Flash is running in Test Movie mode.

To list the objects in a Flash movie:

1. Save your movie and then select Control → Test Movie to jump into Test Movie mode. (The List Objects feature isn't available in regular movie editing mode.)

2. Select Debug → List Objects (Cmd/Ctrl+L). The Output window appears and prints the information for all movie objects in the window. For an example, see Figure 18.5.

List Variables Function

List Variables is another function that is available only while Flash is running in Test Movie mode. Its purpose is somewhat self-explanatory. When selected, List Variables will cause the Output window to print all the variables in a movie, the target path to their location, and their value when the function is called.

To list the variables in a Flash movie:

1. Save your movie and then select Control → Test Movie to jump into Test Movie mode. (The List Variables feature isn't available in regular movie editing mode.)

2. Select Debug → List Variables (Cmd+Option+V [Mac]/Ctrl+Alt+V [Win]). The Output window will immediately print all the variables in your movie, their target path, and their value at the time they were printed.

Variables and objects are not tracked dynamically when you use the List Variables or List Objects command. Rather, when you select either List Variables or List Objects, the Output window prints the specified information at the instant it receives the command. To continuously monitor variables or objects in your movie, it's best to use either the Display List in the Debugger's Variables tab, or the trace function.

Using *trace*

The `trace` statement is every ActionScripter's best friend. It enables you to ask Flash to report specific bits of information about your movie. Flash answers your queries by printing information to the Output window each time you ask for it. This question-and-answer routine can allow you to gather all kinds of information about your movie and to track things like dead handlers, Movie Clip parameters, target paths, variable values, results of functions, and so on. Once you get started using `trace`, you will wonder how you ever created scripts without it.

Because it is an action, `trace` is entered in the Actions panel alongside all your other script statements. The syntax is as follows:

```
trace("literal info in quotes"+variablesOrProperties);
```

You can see that `trace` will accept several different kinds of information. It can be helpful to use literal statements when you use trace, especially if you are tracking multiple parameters, for example:

```
trace("loopcount: "+i);
trace("horizLoc: "+_root.ball._x);
trace("vertLoc: "+_root.ball._y);
trace("instance: "+_root.ball.newBall+i);
```

This example demonstrates the fundamental techniques involved in using `trace`. Place quotes around all information that you want to appear in the Output window exactly as it appears in the `trace` action statement (such as the name of the thing you want to trace). Flash interprets this as a literal string and prints it verbatim. This is extremely useful for creating labels for your information. For an illustration of this, see the preceding script example. The labels `loopcount:`, `horizLoc:`, `vertLoc:`, and `instance:` will appear in the Output window exactly as they appear in the `trace` statement because they were entered as strings.

Another common feature is the string operator (+). This character concatenates information so that it appears as one "thought" in the Output window. For example,

```
trace(":"+"-"+")");
```

would print to the Output window as simply

```
:-)
```

You can enter `trace` anywhere within a script, although you may find that some locations are better than others. For instance, to track a variable that increments while a loop is executed, you want to put the `trace` statement inside the loop so that it monitors the loop value each time it cycles through.

Inspirational Design Model

When we decided to present an inspirational example for each chapter, the idea was that each artist/site/game/movie/etc. we presented would be a shining example of the material covered in the chapter. This chapter is an exception. No one wants their work to be remembered as an example of debugging and troubleshooting! However, these tasks are something that everyone has to do at one point or another during the development process.

The example presented for this chapter is the Macromedia website or, more specifically, the Flash resources found at `www.macromedia.com/software/flash/`. This is an invaluable resource for Flash users and has many things to offer developers of all abilities. Here is a partial list of the Flash offerings at the Macromedia site:

- Training and tutorials
- Galleries of professional Flash work
- Application documentation and downloads
- Related software and products
- User forums, discussion groups, feature requests, and TechNotes

The Macromedia TechNotes and user forums are particularly helpful and can be a great source of information if you are stuck figuring something out. Remember, nothing is created in a bubble, and it can be good to get outside input. These resources are there to help members of the Flash community, so take advantage of them. Remember to use proper "netiquette" when interacting with any kind of user group, and be sure to read the FAQ sheet before posting any messages.

Do you have an idea for improving Flash? Submit a feature request to Macromedia to let them know what you think of the product.

Summary

This chapter concludes your initial lessons and introductions to ActionScript and brings the topic full circle. You learned many different approaches to help streamline the ActionScript writing process. Those tips are designed to help you work smarter and prevent script-related problems before they have a chance to occur. You were also presented with a list of troubleshooting questions to assist in more clearly defining a technical problem. The art of fixing scripting errors doesn't lie in one's knowledge of the language, but in the ability to understand the relationship and flow of ActionScript elements.

This chapter also introduced you to two essential problem-solving tools: the Debugger and the Output window. Even though these tools won't fix problems for you, they do provide a useful service by assembling all the script information contained in a movie. By organizing these details, the Debugger and the Output window enable you to take a broad view of the entire movie and the scripts it contains.

Using ActionScript to Create an Interactive, Multilayered Timeline

ActionScript makes it possible for you to create a Flash movie that performs any way you want it to. Although there are some technical limits to what Flash can and cannot do, ActionScript allows you to smash through the boundaries of Flash as an animation-only application. Once you progress to this level, Flash becomes a tool for authoring interactive experiences and creating robust, enveloping multimedia productions.

In this tutorial, you will expand some of the techniques you learned earlier. In Chapter 16, you learned how ActionScript can be used to create a simple slider controller. A button is placed within a Movie Clip, which is then locked to a set of coordinates on the Stage. When the Movie Clip is made draggable, it becomes a slider that you can move across the Stage by manipulating it with your mouse. As the slider moves, you can also track its position and use that information to effect other changes in your movie.

This tutorial takes some of these basic slider concepts and expands them to create a more advanced slider—one that "snaps" into place on the Stage when it reaches a hot spot. Also, when this slider reaches a hot spot, it loads another, new movie (an SWF file) into the original movie. In addition to all of this, you will learn how to write custom functions that can be used to control the loaded movies from the main movie Timeline.

This lesson assumes that you have already learned the specifics of creating a basic slider. If you have not yet done this or would like to review the steps, see the section on custom controllers in Chapter 16.

 To begin this tutorial, you will need to locate the Hands On 5 folder on the companion CD-ROM for this book. If you would like, you can also take a look at the finished file, `advSlider.fla`, which is in that folder.

> If you want to look at this movie, it is important that you either open the movie and run it from the CD-ROM drive, or copy the entire Hands On 5 folder to your computer's desktop. This movie uses external SWF files. If you separate the main movie from the additional files that it needs, it will be unable to perform correctly. If this is confusing, don't worry; it will all be covered in detail when you learn about the `loadMovieNum` action in this tutorial.

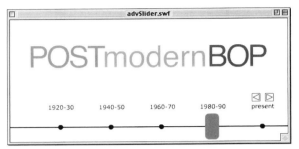

Figure H5.1

The finished movie has a Timeline slider that is used to load new movies into the main movie.

This movie (see Figure H5.1) is the finished version of what you will create in this tutorial. The specific content of this movie is not really finished; a discussion of all the possibilities of an interactive Timeline such as this would probably fill another book. What *is* included with this tutorial are all the components you need to get started and to master this idea; you can then tap your own creativity to add more visual content, additional external movies, and—the works!

Phase 1: Preparing the Movie

Are you ready to get started? Great! Launch Flash, copy the Hands On 5 folder to your computer's hard drive, and open the handsOn5.fla file—and you should be set to begin.

1. When you open the initial file, you should see a Timeline with dates, and a green slider knob sitting on top of the line in the left corner of the Stage. All of the ActionScript for the slider has been written so that you can focus on the more advanced topics of the tutorial. If you'd like, select Control → Test Movie to give the slider a try.

2. This slider will have a unique functionality. When it reaches one of the points (dates) on the Timeline, it will snap into position. To create this effect, you will need to add a few components to the movie. In the main Timeline window, click the Insert Layer button to create a new layer in your movie. Name it **targets**. Grab the layer and drag it *beneath* the layer named text; slider.

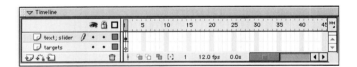

3. Select Window → Library to open this movie's Library panel. The Library contains several items, some of which are already in the movie. Drag the Movie Clip named dropTarget to the first keyframe of the targets layer. Position it so that it is beneath the first dot on the Timeline, under the phrase "1920–30."

    Select the Movie Clip (if it isn't highlighted already) and choose Window → Properties. In the Instance Name field, label the instance **drop1**.

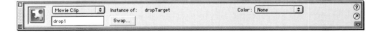

    Repeat this process for the remaining four dots of the Timeline. Drag the dropTarget clip to the Stage, position it under a dot, and give the instance a name. From left to

right, the remaining instances should be named
drop2, **drop3**, **drop4**, and **drop5** (see FigureH5.2).

4. The `dropTarget` instances are nearly complete.
Although the gray color creates a decent graphic look
to the Timeline, the instances should really not be a
part of this design. Click the `drop1` instance and go
to the Color menu of the Property Inspector. Choose
Alpha from the menu and enter a value of **0** in the
field. This makes the instance invisible (but still
functional) on the Stage. Repeat this process for the
remaining four `drop` instances.

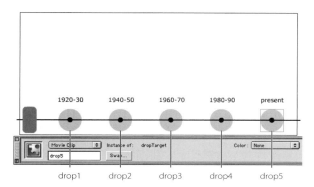

Figure H5.2

The `dropTarget`
instances are named
consecutively across
the stage.

Phase 2: Adding ActionScript

5. Now you are ready to enter some ActionScript to get the slider to function in a new way;
you will make the slider snap into position when it reaches one of the Timeline dots.
Click the Edit Symbols button 🖎 and select Slider Knob from the pop-up menu.

Flash switches to Symbol Editing mode, and the slider knob is centered on the screen.
Highlight the symbol and select Window → Actions to display the Actions panel. You
should see some existing ActionScript that helps the slider perform its basic duties.
You will add to these.

Click after the `stopDrag()` action and press Return/Enter to start a new line. Tab over
and enter these statements:

```
if(eval(_root.slider._dropTarget)==_root.drop1){
    _root.slider._x=100;
    lock.start();
}
```

All statements should fall within the curly braces ({}) for the on(release,releaseOutside)
handler. And what's with the double handler? Good question! It's there to help ensure that
the script fires, even if the mouse isn't over the slider button when it's released. This is a "pre-
cautionary" handler to help avoid potential buggy behavior.

These statements create the snapping behavior for the slider. The `if` statement evaluates an expression that uses the `_dropTarget` property. The expression checks to see if
the `slider` instance was dropped over the `drop1` instance. If it was, then the expression
evaluates **true** and the conditional statements are executed. In these conditional statements, the `slider` instance is set to a horizontal position of 100 (snapped into place),
and the sound `lock` is cued to play.

To read more about the `start()` method of the Sound object, see Chapter 22. It's important to reinforce the snap with audio; that's why it's included here. Try running the movie with the sound off. Its absence will show you that the sound is a helpful addition to any kind of drag-and-drop behavior.

6. Close the Actions panel and return to movie editing mode. Select Window → Test Movie and try the slider. Drag it over the first Timeline dot and watch it snap into place. Also, make sure that you have your system volume turned up so that you can hear the snap sound.

7. Leave Test Movie mode and return to your main Timeline. Again, click the Edit Symbols button and select Slider Knob from the pop-up menu. Open the Actions panel for the slider knob symbol. Enter this additional statement after the `lock.start()` line:

```
loadMovieNum("20.swf",1);
```

This statement provides a very important feature to your movie. It loads an additional Flash movie into the main movie. More accurately, it loads the new movie *above* the main Timeline into movie level 1. The `loadMovieNum()` action is used to load movies into levels above the main Timeline. In this statement, the movie `20.swf` is loaded into level 1. When you use this action, the new movie is loaded and positioned at the upper-left corner of the movie that is hosting it. `20.swf` was created so that it would fill the top half of the `handsOn5` Stage.

You may have noticed that when you copied the Hands On 5 folder to your hard drive, it contained several movies. The `loadMovieNum` action is the reason for this. When you load an external Flash movie, the main movie must be able to locate that movie before it can be loaded. The first parameter of this action asks you to specify a path to the external movie. The path can be either absolute (full URL) or relative to the movie where the action is called. This tutorial uses a relative URL. Since all the movies are in the same folder (Hands On 5), Flash is able to find `20.swf` and load it into `_level1`.

8. If you have not done so already, save your movie. Return to movie editing mode and select Control → Test Movie. Drag the slider over the first dot; it should snap into place and load the `20.swf` movie.

9. Return once again to movie editing mode. Now you will enter the additional actions to make the other **drop** instances work. This will make each dot of the Timeline a hot spot, so that when the slider is positioned over it, a new movie is loaded into level 1. Switch to Symbol Editing mode again and open the Actions panel for the slider knob symbol. Add the following actions so that the entire contents of the `on(release,releaseOutside)` handler look exactly like Listing H5.1.

Two movies cannot occupy the same movie level simultaneously. In this tutorial, each separate SWF file will be loaded into _level1. As a result, whatever SWF is currently sitting in that level will be replaced by the next movie loaded into that same position.

Listing H5.1

The on *(release, releaseOutside)* **Handler for the Slider Knob Movie Clip Symbol**

```
on(release, releaseOutside){
    stopDrag();
    if(eval(_root.slider._dropTarget)==_root.drop1){
        _root.slider._x=100;
        lock.start();
        loadMovieNum("20.swf",1);
    }else if(eval(_root.slider._dropTarget)==_root.drop2){
        _root.slider._x=200;
        lock.start();
        loadMovieNum("40.swf",1);
    }else if(eval(_root.slider._dropTarget)==_root.drop3){
        root.slider._x=300;
        lock.start();
        loadMovieNum("60.swf",1);
    }else if(eval(_root.slider._dropTarget)==_root.drop4){
        _root.slider._x=400;
        lock.start();
        loadMovieNum("80.swf",1);
    }else if(eval(_root.slider._dropTarget)==_root.drop5){
        _root.slider._x=500;
        lock.start();
        loadMovieNum("00.swf",1);
    }else{
        unloadMovie(1);
    }
}
```

The ActionScript in Listing H5.1 may look a little daunting, but it's really quite simple. In fact, you have already entered many of the basic components needed for this script. You can break it down by looking at each drop location as a series of four statements, like this:

```
conditional to check drop location;
position slider instance (snap effect);
play lock sound;
load external movie for the timeline location;
```

USING AN ALTERNATIVE SYNTAX FOR LONG CONDITIONAL STATEMENTS

Flash MX introduces a very welcome alternative to the if...else statement—it's called switch. It presents a series of separate conditions and allows a script to choose accordingly depending on which condition is true. The script in Listing H5.1 could be rewritten using the following much more elegant and easy-to-read syntax:

```
on(release,releaseOutside){
    stopDrag();
    dragging=false;
    switch(eval(_root.slider._dropTarget)){
    case eval(_root.drop1):
        _root.slider._x=100;
        lock.start();
        loadMovieNum("20.swf",1);
        break;
    case eval(_root.drop2):
        _root.slider._x=200;
        lock.start();
        loadMovieNum("40.swf",1);
        break;
    case eval(_root.drop3):
        _root.slider._x=300;
        lock.start();
        loadMovieNum("60.swf",1);
        break;
    case eval(_root.drop4):
        _root.slider._x=400;
        lock.start();
        loadMovieNum("80.swf",1);
        break;
    case eval(_root.drop5):
        _root.slider._x=500;
        lock.start();
        loadMovieNum("00.swf",1);
        break;
    default:
        unloadMovie(1);
    }
}
```

Each "chunk" of script is specific to an instance of `drop1` to `drop 5`. If the `slider` instance is dropped over one of these instances, the statements within the conditional are executed. Note that each set of statements is unique. Each locks the `slider` instance to a different location, and each loads a different external SWF file.

There is also a final `else` part of the condition. If the `slider` instance is not dropped over any of the `drop` instances, then whatever movie is playing at level 1 is unloaded.

> ActionScript does not require a URL to unload a movie; it requires only the level that you wish to remove.

10. Return to movie editing mode and save your movie. Then select Control → Test Movie and try out the new features of the Timeline. Each time you drag to a dot on the Timeline, a new movie is loaded. Conversely, each time the slider is left off of a dot, a movie is removed.

Phase 3: Adding Playback Controls

11. Your next step of the project is to include some buttons that allow you and your audience to control the loaded movies from the main Timeline. Drag the `navButton` button symbol from the Library panel to the Stage of the main Timeline. Position it somewhere below the 150-pixel mark.

> Each external movie that is loaded is 150 pixels tall. If your buttons were positioned above the 150-pixel mark, they would be covered by each external movie when it is loaded into the main movie. To check your button positioning, select View → Rulers to see exact pixel measurements.

Position the buttons so that one is to the left of the other. Highlight the leftmost button and select Window → Panels → Transform. In the Rotate field, enter a value of **180** to flip the button horizontally.

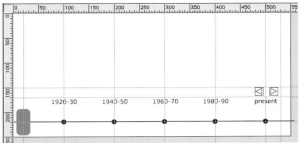

12. Rather than write specific scripts to control each movie, you will use functions to specify the scripts for each button. Functions are like preset routines that you can have your movie perform. Once Flash has executed the actions where you initialize your function, it acts as though it has "learned" the routine, and will be able to perform it whenever the routine is called.

Click frame 1 of the `targets` layer in your main Timeline. Select Window → Actions to display the Actions panel for this frame. Enter the following statements in the window:

```
function rewind(){
    _level1.gotoAndPlay(1);
}
function skip(){
    _level1.gotoAndStop("end");
}
```

These statements do something very important. They create two functions (or preset routines) for your movie. When you call the `rewind` routine, your movie knows to send the movie Timeline at `_level1` back to play at frame 1. The `skip` routine is similar; when called, it will tell the movie Timeline at `_level1` to go to a frame label named `end`, and stop there. A function has advantages: Rather than scripting specific actions each time you want to control an element of the movie, you can call the function. This saves time and space, especially if the routine will be used many times throughout a movie. To learn more about functions, see Chapter 15 or the ActionScript Reference section.

It is also very important to note where these scripts are placed in your movie. They are in frame 1, Scene 1, of the main Timeline. This means that when the movie starts playing, these scripts are among the first things to be read. Flash will not know how to perform a function routine unless you tell it what the routine involves. By putting this information at the start of your movie, you can be assured that Flash will know how to perform each function.

13. Constructing your functions is only the first part of the process. In order to use them in your movie, they have to be called by an ActionScript statement. Click the leftmost button (it should be pointing to the left side of the Stage). Select Window → Actions and enter the following statements in the window:

```
on(release){
    rewind();
}
```

This statement calls the `rewind` function when the mouse is released over the button. Now, open the Actions panel for the other button (pointing to the right side of the Stage) and enter these statements:

```
on(release){
    skip();
}
```

This script calls the `skip` function when the button is clicked. Because you wrote your functions with nonspecific ActionScript, they will work for any movie that is loaded into `_level1`. There is one catch, though: To perform the `skip` function, each external movie has to have a frame label in its last frame named `end`. Without this feature, Flash will not know how to interpret the function because it will be unable to find the label specified by the function.

In this example, it wasn't necessary to define a target path for the functions because they were declared *and* called from the _root level or main Timeline. If the functions were called from the movie in _level1 or from a Movie Clip, it would be necessary to include a target path for the function—for example, _root.rewind(). Functions, like Timeline-specific variables, have scope only within the Timeline on which they were created. In this tutorial, the rewind() function was created on the main Timeline. However, since it is also called from the main Timeline, no target path is needed.

14. Close the Actions panel and return to movie editing mode. Save your movie; then select Control → Test Movie. Experiment with your Timeline to see how it works. The buttons you just added should be able to rewind and jump to the end of each external movie.

Next Steps

This tutorial walked you through all the basic steps for creating an interactive Timeline that can load external SWF files. You also learned how to create functions that can control loaded movies from the main Timeline. This is just the beginning, however. With these basic elements of construction, you should be able to take this Timeline project to new heights. Here are just a few of the possibilities:

- Longer, more interactive external movies
- Additional navigational buttons that take your audience to different locations (not just the beginning and end) of the external movies
- Dynamic background graphics that change when the slider isn't over a Timeline dot

Working with Audio

Part VI begins one of the most interesting, important, and, we daresay, fun aspects of working with Flash—sound. Sound means all sorts of things: sound effects (BANG! KA-POW! CRUNCH!), music, dialog, and any other audible elements of your Flash movie. Sound adds life to your movies and animations. It provides extra impact for scenes that are funny or scary, gives your characters voices, and allows your audience to take a break from reading and to listen to your story or presentation.

Sound effects can offer feedback to your audience. For every button click or other interaction with your movie, sound can let your audience know that their request was received. And music…there are so many possibilities! Use music for theme songs, background ambience, and dramatic flair. Or harness the power of ActionScript to create interactive audio environments in which your movie's sound is dictated solely by the whims of the folks who are experiencing it. Whatever the audio demands and goals of your Flash movie, this part of the book will surely set you on the right path.

CHAPTER 19

Understanding Digital Audio in the Flash Environment

Sound is one of the most neglected yet potent components of contemporary multimedia. In this context, the word *sound* means many things: sound effects, music, narration, and dialog. Although all of these elements can lift a work of multimedia to new heights, designers rarely take advantage of the possibilities afforded by sound in their Flash productions. Sound in and of itself is a powerful medium; it communicates through channels that are unavailable to imagery and text. This characteristic doesn't make sound superior, but rather makes it uniquely suited to capturing and holding the attention of an audience through their sense of hearing.

There are many reasons why sound hasn't been a major player in the multimedia arena, particularly with web-based multimedia applications. Most of these are not germane to the topics surrounding Flash and will be saved for another time. What is very relevant, though, is the fact that Flash works well with audio components. It provides several options that allow you to include both sound and music in your movies. Every developer who opens or downloads a copy of the software should take advantage of the richness it can bring to their projects.

This chapter will introduce you to some of the possibilities that audio adds to the Flash equation. If you are new to working with sound on your computer, you will also learn some of the basic technical terms and theory surrounding digital audio. The topics in this chapter are as follows:

- Digital audio sample rate and bit depth
- Stereo and mono sound
- Flash-compatible digital audio file types
- How and where to acquire sounds for your work
- Preparing audio for the Flash environment
- Planning a movie with sound in mind
- Working with looped sounds

Digital Audio, Technically Speaking

To a Flash designer or developer, the technical specifics of digital audio may seem remote, abstract, and insignificant to the overall production of a Flash movie. Nothing could be further from the truth. In fact, the technical specifics of digital audio have a very important impact on your project, especially when it comes to publishing and delivering your final movie. A developer who knows the ins and outs of digital audio will be able to prepare and plan for a project while keeping sound in mind from the very beginning. Technical knowledge not only allows you to select the right options for your movie at the outset of a project, it enables you to troubleshoot problems when they arise. Plus, with a good understanding of how digital sound files work, it's much easier to bend them to your creative will in the context of your Flash projects and movies.

Sample Rate

It's likely that most of you reading this book have had some sound-recording experience using some form of magnetic tape. Whether it was with a toy tape recorder, Dictaphone, open-reel tape deck, or other recording device, magnetic tape has been accessible to people for both professional and hobbyist recording for many years. In this medium, sound waves are converted to magnetic impulses and stored on long strands of tape. When played back, these impulses are able to re-create sounds by imitating the pulsation of the original sound waves.

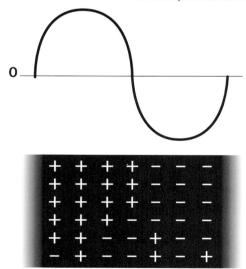

If you have worked with sound in this way, you have experience with *analog* sound recording. It's called analog because the magnetic information tries as closely as possible to remain true, or *analogous*, to the shape and amplitude of the original sound wave. Positive and negative curves in a sound wave are mimicked by the positive and negative magnetic charges on the recorded audio tape. For an illustration of this, see Figure 19.1.

In the world of interactive multimedia, analog recording has been supplanted by *digital* sound recording. In digital recording, positive and negative magnetic impulses have been replaced by the 1s and 0s of binary code. When making a digital recording, the digital recording device (a computer, for instance) examines the sound wave and takes snapshots of its amplitude. These snapshots are called *samples,* and the speed at which the snapshots are taken is called the *sample rate.* See Figure 19.2 for an illustration of sample rate.

Figure 19.1

Magnetic tape is used in analog sound recording. Charged particles are scattered on the tape to exactly represent the shape of the original sound wave.

For most consumer digital audio, the sampling rate is 44.1kHz, or 44,100 samples per second. This means that for every second of audio you wish to store digitally, there are over 44,000 pieces of information to represent that single second of sound. If you were to drop the sampling rate by half (22.05kHz), you would still be able to represent the original wave. However, because you would be trying to do it with half the amount of information, the quality of the sound would suffer. As samples are removed from a digital sound, it has fewer and fewer snapshots to re-create the original source sound.

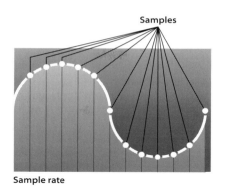

Samples

Sample rate

DIGITAL SAMPLING RATE AND THE NYQUIST THEOREM

The sample rate of 44.1kHz was neither selected whimsically nor plucked from a hat. It's actually rooted in scientific study into the transmission of data signals.

In the 1920s, Harry Nyquist developed many theories surrounding sound recording. One of these had an important impact on digital audio recording technology. The Nyquist theorem states that in order to accurately represent a sound, the sample rate must be at least twice the value of the highest frequency you wish to record. The reason for this is simple. A wave has two portions: positive and negative. To represent this accurately, you must have at least one snapshot from each of the extremes. Since human hearing tops out at around 20kHz, the Nyquist theorem proposes that the sample rate for recording should be at least 40kHz. This figure is twice as high, and can capture samples quickly enough to represent both the positive and negative slopes of a sound wave within the range of human hearing.

The sampling rate for a standard audio CD is 44.1kHz, which is 4,100Hz over the minimum value. This allows plenty of room to capture all the important frequencies and allows some extra room for others that make their way into the sound recording.

Bit-Depth Resolution

Bit depth is another important term in the world of digital sound recording. It is the number of values available to describe the amplitude of the wave for a given sample. Where sample rate is used to describe a sound along the X axis, bit depth is a measurement along the Y axis. For an illustration of this, see Figure 19.3.

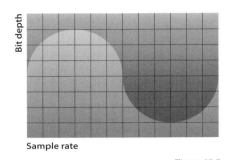

Sample rate

Figure 19.3

Bit depth measures the amplitude (Y axis value) of a wave for each sample (X axis) in the sound file.

Bit depth, like sample rate, has finite resolution. While most recording devices can sample sounds at only 44.1kHz or 48kHz, they are also generally limited to a bit depth of 8 or 16. Bit depth is represented by binary numbers. In an 8-bit system, there are 256 possible values ($2^8 = 256$), ranging from 00000000 to 11111111. With 16 bits, the values increase to a possible 65,536 ($2^{16} = 65,536$): 0000000000000000 to 1111111111111111. Clearly, you can see that 16-bit quality offers a much broader spectrum of values. At this resolution, it's less likely for samples to be rounded off to the nearest binary value. They will generally remain more true to the original wave shape than an 8-bit sound. To see the difference between the two possibilities, see Figure 19.4.

Stereo vs. Mono

If you have purchased any electronics during the last few decades, you have undoubtedly heard the term *stereo*. Whether or not you know it, you have probably been enjoying stereo sound recordings throughout most of your life. But what does it mean exactly? Most people usually answer that question by saying, "It sounds better!" Sure, in many cases, it does sound better, but that's not much of an answer. Stereo means that a sound is played through two simultaneous channels: left and right. As their names suggest, each channel has a unique position. A sound can be played back entirely in the right speaker channel, entirely in the left speaker channel, or any combination in between. This creates the aural illusion of space and position in an audio recording.

The process (and for many, the art) of assigning left and right channel information to a sound is known as *panning*. In a stereo sound recording, each element can have its own unique pan information. For instance, in a rock 'n' roll recording, you may hear drums and bass share the right and left channels equally, while the lead guitar is panned to the left and the rhythm guitar is panned to the right. There are no rules when it comes to stereo sounds; the best judge is your ears. Later in this chapter, you will learn about some of the considerations in using stereo sound from a sound design point of view.

The alternative to stereo sound is *monaural*, or mono, sound. The name is a bit of a giveaway. Monaural sounds have only a single channel and can be played through a single speaker. In the case of a two-speaker setup, mono sounds are shared equally between the left and right speakers. Because they contain no positional information, mono sounds are great for dialog, sound effects, and other elements in which position isn't crucial to the success of a sound, or in which the sound's position can be assigned later through another means, such as an ActionScript command.

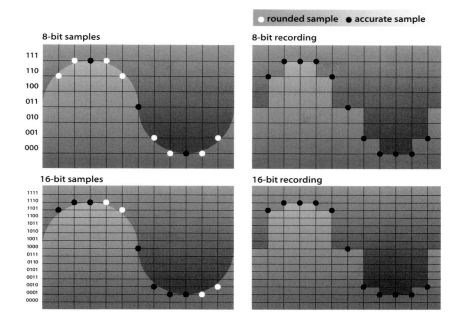

Figure 19.4

Eight-bit sounds have fewer values for each sample. Consequently, many samples are rounded to the nearest value, and the original wave shape is compromised in the digital recording. Because 16-bit sound offers a higher resolution with greater accuracy, there is less rounding, and a wave remains more true to the original (although still far from perfect).

Flash has several options that allow you to control stereo and mono parameters for a sound in your movie. To learn about the basic control options, see Chapter 20. To see some of the more advanced options provided by ActionScript, see Chapter 22.

Storing Sound: Digital Audio File Types

All of the technical specifics surrounding a sound have to be stored somewhere so that a sound can be played back and used in a Flash movie. As you can imagine, quite a lot of room is required to store a sound file. For a CD-quality sound recording, you have 44,100 sound samples per second, each with a 65,536-digit binary number to describe the sample value. If the sound is stereo, and thus has information for two channels, you have to double all of the sample and bit-depth information. For a 10-second, CD-quality, stereo sound, you need 1.7MB to store all of the necessary information. That amounts to around 30MB for your average 3-minute song!

If you are scared off by this, don't be. There are many techniques you will learn to curb the size of sound in your Flash movies. At this point, your major concern should be the *kinds* of sounds that you can use in the Flash authoring environment. You know that digital audio information is based on three things: sample rate, bit depth, and stereo/mono information.

All of this information is organized and packaged as a digital sound file that can be read by software on your computer, including Flash.

Flash is capable of handling most of the contemporary sound file formats that you will encounter. Each file format has its own particular idiosyncrasies. However, once the sound is in the Flash environment, it's available for use in your movie in a variety of ways. Following is a list of the different kinds of digital sound files that you can use with Flash. To learn more about how you can incorporate these files in your Flash movie, see Chapter 20.

AIFF: Audio Interchange File Format (`.aif`)   This format is for Macintosh import only, although most Windows-based computers should be able to read and play AIFF files with the help of QuickTime 4 or higher.

WAV: Windows Audio File Format (`.wav`)   This format is primarily for Windows, although Macintosh computers can import WAV files into Flash if QuickTime 4 or higher is present.

MP3: MPEG Layer 3 (`.mp3`)   This format can be imported on both the Macintosh and Windows platforms. This is the only compressed audio format that can be imported into Flash. To learn more about MP3 compression, see Chapter 20.

The following sound types require QuickTime 4 or higher:

Sound Designer II   Although Digidesign no longer manufactures the software, the Sound Designer II format is still used with Pro Tools audio-editing and audio-mixing software.

QuickTime movies (sound only)   QuickTime movies don't have to contain video information. These video-less files are called *sound-only* movies and can be used in Flash on either the Windows or Macintosh platform.

AU: Sun AU (`.au`)   This format is used primarily with Sun or Unix computers and can be used in Flash on either the Windows or Macintosh platform.

System 7 Sound   This is a Macintosh-only sound format that is used for the general system sounds of the Macintosh operating system.

Preparing Audio for Flash

Sound and music can add another dimension to your Flash movies. They can add the finishing touches to your animations and graphics by communicating tone. With the right sound components, a scene can be truly funny, dramatic, scary—whatever you like. Selecting or producing the right sound can make a huge difference in the success of a Flash production.

You are probably excited about getting some sounds into your movie so that you can see how all this works. However, it's important to be sure that your sounds are ready to be a part of a Flash movie before they hit the vector stage. After you have either created or found the right sounds, it's essential that you edit and prepare the files to fit your needs. This process demands an extra step before a sound is used in your movie, but it ensures that the sound is ready for the task.

Sound Resources

There are many, many sources where you can acquire audio for a Flash production. The first (and best) resource may be yourself. If you sing, play an instrument, or beat on pots and pans, you can create audio for a Flash production. Be creative! In many creative endeavors, the sincerity and originality of a work can far outshine its technical attributes. Something doesn't have to be "polished" to be good: It simply has to *work*. It must work in the context of your movie and fit the mood or message you wish to convey.

So, to all of you closet minstrels out there who are working with Flash, get offline for a few minutes and write some songs. Take a portable recording device outdoors someday and see what sounds you can record in your neighborhood. Are you doing a movie about the outdoors? Go for a hike and record everything: footsteps, birds, trees, water, and so on. You will be amazed at how the audio experience of the hike translates to your sound recordings. Do you need a sound effect of someone falling down? Record the sound of yourself kicking a cardboard box. Professional foley artists and sound designers (people who create sound effects for a living) don't always use a recording of an actual object or event to serve as the sound for that specific object or event. Do you think that's actually fire you hear? No, it's the sound of someone crumpling cellophane or a plastic shopping bag. The possibilities are vast when it comes to producing your own sound effects and music. Use your resources, be creative, and above all, follow your instincts over what you think is "right" or "expected."

As far as the technical side goes, when it comes to getting this done, you are on your own. The technical considerations of audio production are beyond the scope of this book. At the very least, you will need some kind of recording device, a cable to connect it to the computer, a sound card or audio input jack on the computer, and some audio software to record the sounds as digital files. If you have a laptop computer or a long audio cable, you can experiment with recording directly into the computer. For details on this, consult your owner's manual and the documentation for your sound card and audio software.

If you have tried and tried with no luck, or you simply don't have the time or resources, there are alternatives to creating your own sounds and music for a Flash movie. Here is a brief list of your options:

Sound effect CDs Sound effect libraries can be purchased for use in multimedia productions. Generally, you have to buy them from a company that distributes licensed music products and audio-sample libraries. There are too many to mention here; your best bet is to do a search for *sound effect libraries* on the Internet. Be sure to read and obey the licensing agreement for any library of this kind.

Royalty-free music and loop CDs These are also a fine source of music and loop material for your projects. Again, there are too many to mention, but a quick search on the Internet should give you plenty of options. As always, watch the licensing agreement to be sure that you use the product legally. When appropriate, give credit to the composer whose work you are using.

Flash and sound-effect resource websites Websites like `www.flashplanet.com`, `www.sonify.org`, and `www.flashkit.com` offer links to many different sound resources where you can go to find sound effects, music, and audio loops for your movies. Always be sure to read the legal agreement before using anything you get on the Web. Just because you downloaded something doesn't mean that you can use it any way you'd like.

DoReMedia Sound Families DoReMedia (`www.doremedia.com`) has developed a series of music "families" that are designed specifically to create multi-track audio in Flash. These can be licensed from the company directly at its website. To learn more about the techniques involved with using Sound Families, see Chapter 21.

Editing Sound Files

No matter where or how you acquire your sound files, it's important to edit them and make sure that they are ready for the Flash environment. Editing can accomplish several things. Because sound files demand a fair amount of storage space and add to the final size of a Flash production, it's important to make sure that any unneeded material is stripped from the sound file. Also, you want to ensure that the file is free of clicks, pops, and other strange noises that may have made their way into your recording.

If you can't hear a sound file, it is virtually useless unless you are going for an effect that requires an especially low sound volume. Before you bring any sounds into a Flash movie, you want to be sure that their output level is as healthy as possible. Once a sound is in Flash, you can always turn it down, but you can never turn it up.

The next two sections cover the most important and essential audio editing techniques for preparing a sound for a career in your Flash movie. While there are *many* other things you may want to do to ready a sound, these techniques are considered to be the most important and should be done to every single sound file before implementing it in a Flash movie.

Trimming and Cutting Sound Files

The name of this editing technique says it all, but why is it so important to trim your sound files? Well, because an extra second of CD-quality, mono sound can add between 80 and 90 kilobytes to your final movie before it is published. If you have lots of sound files with lots of extra space in them, this figure will really start to add up. The difference in file size between a 3-second drumbeat and 3 seconds of silence is … nothing. It takes exactly the same amount of space to store silence as it does a full symphony orchestra, so make your files count!

Any time you open a recorded sound file or music file, you are bound to have some dead space at the beginning and end of the sound. Your task is to make sure that this empty space is eliminated. Not only does this help keep your movie file size down, but it helps the file to play more quickly. If a sound has a quarter-second pause before anything is heard, it will always sound as though it is starting late—not because Flash is running slowly, but because it has to play through the silence or other junk before it gets to what is important (see Figure 19.5). Trimming sound files takes away the parts that are unnecessary and helps optimize their performance in a movie.

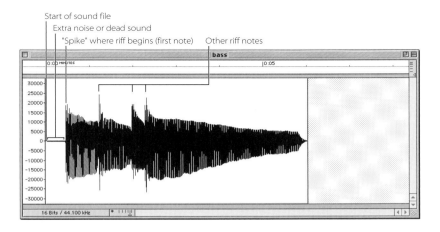

Start of sound file
Extra noise or dead sound
"Spike" where riff begins (first note)   Other riff notes

Figure 19.5

This sound file of a bass riff has unnecessary information at the beginning. Of course, listening is the key, but here you can tell where the musical information begins by the "spike" in the waveform. The wave is most active (tallest) where notes and other sounds are heard in the recording.

To trim a sound file:

1. Open the sound in your audio editor of choice. In a Windows environment, Sound Forge is a great choice. If you use a Mac, you can choose between SoundEdit 16 and Peak.

2. Navigate to the beginning of the sound file. Depending on the instrument or object that makes the sound, the wave will look very different. Play the sound and watch the playback head as you listen. You should be able to see and hear the point in the wave where the significant part of the sound begins. You may need to do this several times to pinpoint the spot.

3. Once you have found the "real" beginning of the sound, click that spot and drag a selection to the beginning of the sound file. You should see something like the picture in Figure 19.6.

4. Play back the selection and listen. Do you hear anything important to the sound? You shouldn't. Remember, you are trimming the *unwanted* material out of the file. When you play back the selection, you should be listening to all of the dead space that you want to trim off the file. If your audio editor supports this function, play back the

unselected portion of the sound file. In this case, playing the unselected portion should allow you to hear exactly what you want with no extra space or silence.

5. If your selection is correct and all of the extra material is selected, clear the unwanted material by either pressing Delete or selecting Delete from the Edit menu in your audio editor. If your selection is not quite right, you can always delete the unwanted material and go back for another pass to get the remaining portion of the wave. Or choose Edit → Undo and start the process again.

6. Remember that a sound file has two parts, a head and a tail. You just learned how to trim the head. To trim the tail, the steps are the same. The only exception, of course, is that you will make changes to the end of the file rather than the beginning.

Figure 19.6

To trim a sound file, you start by making a selection of the unneeded material at the beginning of the file.

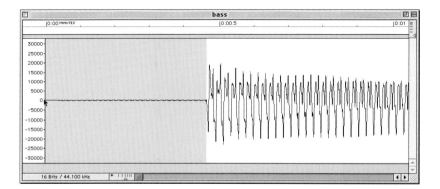

There are a few other considerations when it comes to trimming files. You should try as much as possible to trim them at points where the wave crosses the zero-amplitude center axis. There are many crossings in a single sound file, since a wave is constantly in flux between negative and positive amplitudes. By trimming at an axis point, you eliminate the possibility of a pop or click when the file plays back, because the wave is starting at a point of silence (see Figure 19.7). Alternately, after making your edit, you can fade out a tiny portion (a few samples or milliseconds) at the beginning of the sound to bring the wave down to zero amplitude.

Figure 19.7

When the selection is deleted, the wave will be trimmed at a zero point (shown here in Sound Forge as Infinity) to ensure a smooth start.

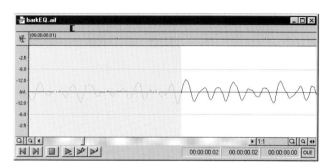

It can also be helpful to use fade-outs when trimming files, especially if you have a sound that sustains. If you select the beginning or end portion of a waveform and apply the fade-out effect, your audio editor will gradually decrease the sound's current volume to silence over the portion of the wave you selected (see Figure 19.8). A fade-out allows you to shorten the length of a sound that decays over a long time, like a gong or cymbal crash.

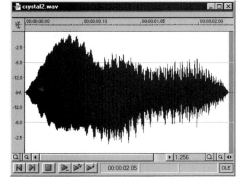
Before fade-out

Normalizing Audio Files

Volume is one of the most important aspects of sound. If a file doesn't have a strong volume, you will be unable to hear it. In general, it's better to have to turn something down because it's too loud than to crank it up because it's not loud enough. As the chief audio engineer for your Flash movie, you have the responsibility for ensuring that all your sounds are heard, and heard at the correct volume.

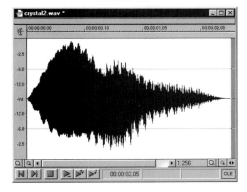
After fade-out

While assembling your audio, it can be difficult (if not impossible) to tell how loud a sound should be out of context. The good news is that with Flash, you can bring all your sounds into the program and then tweak the volume as you create your movie. This provides a great deal of flexibility and takes much of the pressure and guesswork out of the audio production.

Figure 19.8

Here you can see the difference in a sound file before and after a fade-out effect was applied.

Since Flash allows you to manipulate volume from within your movie, you want to be sure that all your sounds come into the movie at the strongest possible volume. Your audio editor can help you do this with a command called *Normalize*. Normalize looks at an entire waveform and boosts it proportionately within a volume range that you specify without clipping or distorting the sound. Basically, it ensures that a sound is as loud as it can be without going over its limit.

Clipping and/or distortion is what happens when a sound's level is pushed beyond the capabilities of the digital recording or playback device. Although in some analog applications, distortion is an interesting effect, digital audio distortion is especially harsh. Avoid it at all costs unless you are pursuing some wild, avant-garde effects.

To normalize audio for your Flash movie:

1. Open the sound file you wish to normalize. Choose Edit → Select All.

2. Depending on which editor you use, the Normalize command could be in a variety of locations. Generally, it's on a menu named something like Effects or Process. Choose Normalize from the menu where you find it.

3. A dialog box should appear, asking what settings you want to use for normalizing. For most multimedia work, a good rule of thumb is to normalize between 96% and 98%. This boosts the entire file proportionately to 96–98% of its maximum volume. After Normalize has been executed, save the sound file.

You can see the difference between files that have normalized and those that have not. In Figure 19.9, note the difference in the amplitudes of the various waveforms.

Figure 19.9

The sound on the left has been normalized, while the sound on the right has not.

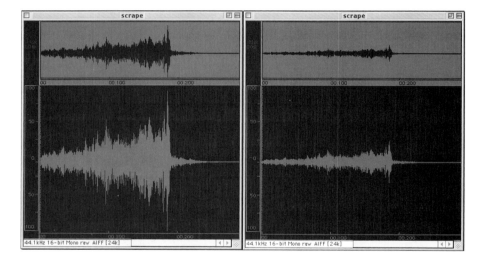

Planning for Audio Interactivity

When it comes to audio, sound, and music, one of the most common flaws in contemporary Flash work is a lack of planning and vision for the role of sound in the production. While developers spend more and more time pushing the visual and interactive envelopes with stunning graphics and ActionScript magic, there is a shortage of truly creative audio work. If you want to have an engaging Flash website or interactive animation, you should look beyond the visual possibilities Flash offers and explore some of its nonvisual aspects.

Sound is one of the keys to creating *immersion,* a sense of bathing in the content of a story or production. To make an audience feel as though they cannot leave your movie or website, you need to achieve this feeling of immersion. Sound helps create immersion because it draws an audience into an image, feeds them additional information about the image, and allows them to interpret its meaning within your story. Sound provides subtext to the dramatic flow and helps communicate a message that is left incomplete or vague by the visual elements alone. Sound can also create a sense of mood, and help to guide the audience on an emotional journey.

You can take advantage of these characteristics by adding sound and music to your Flash movies. This is not an "add audio and stir" recipe, however. To use audio to its fullest, you must plan how it will be used and decide which portions of your movie are best suited to audio components. You must select where sound will be used, and what sounds or music best convey the message you want to communicate.

Let's say, for example, that you are creating a movie that is like a fairy tale storybook—something that contains a collection of short stories and nursery rhymes. What kinds of sounds would you want to use, and what portions of the movie should use those sounds? There are no right or wrong answers to these questions. The important thing is that the sounds support the movie and make it a better, more immersive experience. You could consider using chimes, soft bells, mystical hums, and twinkle sounds for buttons or navigational elements. You could use soft classical music behind story narration and insert story-specific sound effects (such as knocks at the door) where appropriate. You could even add specific sounds to elements when they are clicked or moused over, like comments from Snow White's magic mirror.

The options for something like this go on forever; your creativity is the only limit. The important thing to remember is to *plan* for this. In the same way that you will choose color palettes, fonts, and other visual parameters, you will need to make some decisions about the content and use of audio in your movie. Not only does such planning provide you with direction, but it allows you to create the movie while knowing that sound will be a part of the final production. Your movie can be designed and scripted so that the audio is included and tested with all the other elements, rather than tacked on at the end.

Working with Sound Loops

Sound loops can be one of the most useful tools to a Flash developer. They can also be one of the most dreaded aspects of Flash content for your audience. Sound loops are musical phrases or rhythmic patterns that are played over and over and over ad nauseum. Sound loops often get a bad (and generally well-deserved) rap simply because they are not used well. Granted, listening to the same riff played repeatedly can grate on one's ears. However, there are different techniques that you can employ to create more musical interest with your loops and to get more mileage from them in a Flash movie.

First of all, loops are especially easy to use within Flash. The software supports looped sounds very well and does a good job of keeping the loop going without dropping beats or losing time. Because sound loops are somewhat "native" to the Flash environment, they can offer a certain amount of reliability over other kinds of sounds. Another advantage of loops is that they are compact. A loop may be only a few kilobytes large, but when it's played continuously over a long period of time, it stretches the length of a several-hundred-megabyte sound file. This is a definite advantage, and it can significantly affect the final size of your Flash movie.

One of the reasons that loops get a bad name is that they are too simple. The shorter the loop, the less it contains, and consequently, less musical contrast occurs within the looped phrase. Ultimately, this means that the loop sounds boring after a short listen because there is not as much music to hold your interest. Drum loops are probably the greatest offender in this case. This situation can be remedied, however: Simply use longer loops. The longer the loop sound file, the more you get to hear before it repeats itself. This helps make the loop less obvious and adds more contrast within the looped phrase.

You can take this technique a step further. Most loops tend to be broken into even chunks. Musically speaking, this means that the loops are in even bar or beat phrases: 4 beats, 8 beats, 2 bars, 4 bars, and so on. How you count the bars and beats is irrelevant. What is important, though, is that they are all *even*. The symmetrical structure makes it easy for your ears to organize the sound and detect the loop. The remedy is to create uneven loops: 7 beats, 3 bars, 5 bars, and so forth. Although this doesn't eliminate the loop altogether, it does help to mask the loop by placing the repeat point in an odd location within the musical phrase.

On the companion CD-ROM, open the file `loops.swf`, found in the Chapter 19 folder. It contains buttons that loop the playback of three sound files: `oneBar`, `fourBar`, and `fiveBar`. Click the green Play buttons and listen to these files carefully. You should be able to hear a distinct difference in the looped quality of these. Note how the one-bar phrase has an immediately detectable loop, while the longer, four-bar phrase holds your interest and is harder to spot. At the extreme end of things, there is a five-bar looping phrase. Hopefully, you can hear how it is the least easy to identify as a loop.

Creating sound loops can be simple, but it requires some time and patience if you really want to do it well. To create loops, all you really need is a digital audio editor that supports looped playback of a sound file. Software currently available that will allow you to create loops include Sound Forge and Cool Edit Pro for Windows computers, or SoundEdit 16 and Peak for the Mac. Most of these applications have a loop utility or feature that allows you to ensure a smooth loop that's free of clicks, pops, and other editing glitches. Additionally, Sonic Foundry manufactures a program called Acid, which is used specifically for creating sound loops and loop-based music. To learn more about working with these applications and preparing audio content for your Flash movie, see Chapter 26.

Inspirational Design Model

Nineteen Point Five Collective, at www.npfc.org, is a group of artists who focus their efforts on all forms of multimedia expression: sound, video, 3D imagery, and web/interactive media development. Their music is *transmedia*—it sounds at home whether heard on the Internet, in a multimedia application, or in a live-performance venue.

The NPFC website is designed entirely in Flash and does an excellent job of presenting the group's music in an accessible, easy-to-use fashion (see Figure 19.10). Note especially how their eclectic blend of musical sensibility meshes with the look and feel of their site to create a seamless, distinct impression of the group.

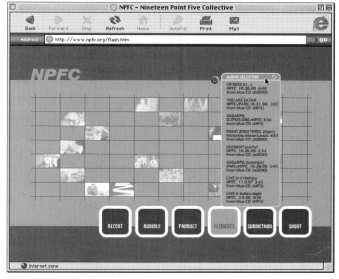

Figure 19.10

Nineteen Point Five Collective can be heard via Flash at www.npfc.org.

Summary

In this chapter, you learned how digital audio and sound elements can add a new level of interest to your Flash animations and movies. You saw all of the technical terms: sample rate, bit depth, and stereo/mono. These digital audio parameters both help to describe the information contained in a sound file and determine its overall quality. Also, once a file has been recorded, there are several different file formats in which it can be saved and brought into the Flash environment.

As a Flash developer, you have many resources available for either acquiring or creating sound content for your Flash movies. And, once you have the sounds you need, it's essential to prepare them for playback in a Flash production. This preparation should take place on both technical and conceptual levels. Select your sounds well, integrate them within your design or story, and use them to add potency to your message. This chapter has shown you how audio— both music and sound effects—can greatly enhance your projects and animations.

CHAPTER 20

Flash Audio Basics

Audio elements like music, sound effects, and narration can add greatly to the depth and interest of your Flash productions. Because sound is a unique, non-visual medium, it is capable of pushing your animations and interactive movies to a whole new level of creativity, expression, and fun. Now that you have read a general introduction to digital audio, you are ready to approach it specifically in the Flash environment.

Like most other interactive authoring applications, Flash has its own set of rules governing the way it handles audio. These rules are what you are about to learn. When approaching them, try not to think of them as rules, however, since *rules* carry a bad connotation. When one thinks of rules, it's too easy to focus on the limitations of what can and cannot be done. Don't think of this chapter's topic as rules for Flash audio, but as a set of techniques that you must implement to work with audio in Flash. More specifically, the rules are a set of techniques that can be mastered. And, when you are completely comfortable with them, your potential is limited only by the ability to use the techniques creatively to achieve your goals. Not only can Flash be a tool for dynamic animations and interactivity, but you can use it to deliver great audio, as well.

This chapter covers the following topics:

- **Bringing sounds into the Flash environment and implementing them in your movies**

- **Attaching sounds to buttons**

- **Controlling sound playback**

- **Using sound effects**

- **Understanding sound export options and compression**

Importing Sound Files

To begin the process of using audio in the Flash environment, you must first get the audio files into your movie Library. You do this by importing a sound or sounds. Your computer's operating system determines what kind of sounds you can import. In general, Flash can import WAV files with Windows, AIFF files with Macintosh, and MP3 files with both platforms. For more details on all the sound file types that are available to Flash, see Chapter19.

To import sound files in Flash:

1. Select File → Import or press Cmd/Ctrl+R. The Import dialog box appears.

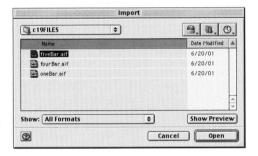

2. Choose the All Sound Formats option from the drop-down menu. This causes the Import dialog box to show you only sound files and makes it easier to find the files you need. Locate the folder containing the file(s) you wish to import. If you need to select multiple files, use Shift+click (Mac) or Ctrl+click (Win).

Sounds can be imported as a group (as discussed here) or individually, depending on your needs and work flow.

Figure 20.1

The Library panel displays sound files with a speaker icon beside the filenames.

3. When you're finished selecting all your sound files, click Open. All the selected files will be imported into your movie. You can confirm this by checking the contents of the Library. Select Window → Library (F11) to display the Library panel. All the sounds you just imported should appear there with the speaker icon beside the filenames (see Figure 20.1). When a sound is selected in the Library, its waveform appears in the top of the Library window. You can audition the sound by pressing the Play button in the upper-right corner of the panel.

4. Once the sound files are in your movie's Library, they will be available for unlimited use within your movie. Sounds can also be part of Libraries that are shared among several movies. To read more about Shared Libraries, see Chapter 7.

Adding Sound to a Movie

Importing sounds is the first part of the process. Once you have sounds in your Library, you must then place them in the movie Timeline so that they become a part of a movie's playback. To add sounds to a Timeline, you use the Property Inspector (see Figure 20.2). This multifaceted interface element is your window to many of the parameters affecting sound behavior in your movie.

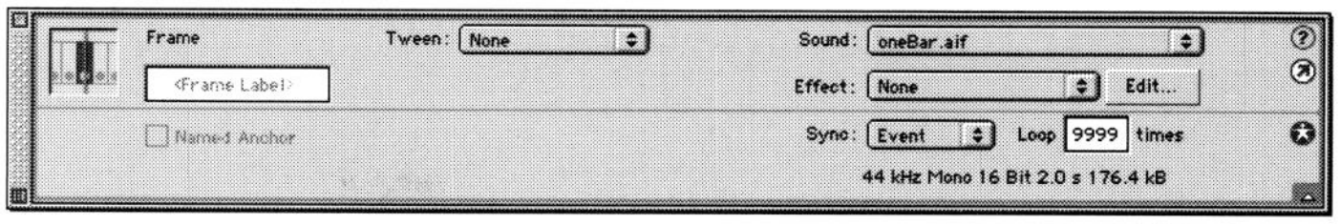

To add a sound to your movie:

1. Create a new layer and name it something like "sound." This isn't an essential step, but it can be helpful for keeping individual sounds on their own separate layers in your movie. Each layer can be named with a title that describes the sound it contains (introRiff, for example). And it's easier to manipulate the positioning of sounds when they are independent of other movie elements.

Figure 20.2

The Property Inspector serves as the interface for sound control in your movie.

> Although Flash can play only eight sounds simultaneously, there is virtually no limit to the number of sound layers you can have in a movie. On a very, *very* basic level, this feature makes Flash behave like a multi-track audio application, where you can stack many sounds on top of one another. To learn more about the possibilities of Flash and multi-track audio, see Hands On 6.

2. Click the frame where you would like the sound to start playing and then select Insert → Keyframe to insert a new keyframe.

3. Select Window → Properties to display the Property Inspector. Alternatively, you can Cmd+click (Mac) or right-click (Win) on the keyframe and select Properties from the context menu. The Property Inspector appears.

   At this point, you should already have imported sounds into your movie. If you haven't, see the preceding section to learn how this is done.

4. Choose a sound from the Sound drop-down menu. The Property Inspector will display the attributes of the file you select: its sample rate, bit depth, length in seconds, and file size. The sound you select will be the sound that is cued when Flash plays the current, selected keyframe.

5. If desired, select an option from the Effect drop-down menu. To learn more about Effect options, see "Working with Audio Effects" later in this chapter.

6. Select an option from the Sync drop-down menu.

   In general, use Event for shorter sounds that you wish to be played in time with a visual event in your movie—for example, a "thud" sound of a cartoon character falling down. Event sounds will play in their entirety until they are stopped or the sound is over. Use the Stream sync if you want Flash to force the movie animation to lock playback with a sound file.

Some Notes on Stream Sounds: Unlike event sounds, stream sounds will only play through the number of frames they occupy in the Timeline. You must add extra frames to accommodate the length of a stream sound. To learn more about these and other sound sync options, see Chapter 20. Also, if you plan to use an MP3 file as a stream sound, you must recompress the file within Flash before publishing your movie. To learn more about this, see "Exporting and Compressing Audio Files" later in this chapter.

7. Enter a value in the Loop field. Flash will play the sound back the number of times that you specify here. To loop a sound for the entire length of your movie, enter a very high number (9999 works well). When you are finished, you should have something that looks like Figure 20.3.

Figure 20.3

Here the sound drumGroove.aif is cued as an event sound with no effect and will be looped eight times.

Stopping Sounds

Once a sound starts playing in Flash, there are few things to interrupt it. In most cases, a sound will continue to play until either it runs out of frames (if it is a stream sound), it is finished, or it runs out of loops. These events depend largely on the length of the sound file and the parameters you assign the sound when it is first played in your movie. There are times, though, when it may be necessary for you to intervene and stop a sound or series of sounds explicitly.

To stop a specific sound from playing:

1. Click the frame in the sound layer where you would like to stop the sound.

2. Select Insert → Keyframe to insert a new keyframe.

3. Select Window → Properties to display the Property Inspector if it is not already visible.

4. In the Sound drop-down menu, select the name of the sound file you would like to stop playing. Choose the Stop option from the Sync drop-down menu. When the new keyframe is reached, the specified sound will stop playing.

To stop all sounds from playing:

1. Choose the frame where you would like to stop the playback of every sound in your movie. It is also common to have a button that can be used to stop your movie's sounds.

2. Open the Actions panel for either the frame or the button you want to use. In Normal scripting mode, drag the `stopAllSounds()` action from the Actions → Movie Control category into the script window. In Expert mode, you can simply enter this statement:

   `stopAllSounds();`

3. Depending on where you attached this action, when either the frame is played or the button is clicked, every sound that is currently playing in your movie will stop. Playback cannot resume until each sound is explicitly started once again.

This technique of stopping all sounds is particularly useful if you need to stop several sound files simultaneously to sync with an animation, or to create a "sound off" button for your movie.

Attaching Sound to a Button

It is common to use sounds in conjunction with a button. In the same way that the various button states offer visual indications of interaction, sounds can help add to the interactive experience by offering audible feedback. For example, if you wanted to create a button that looked and sounded like the door to a haunted house, you could add the sound of a low "creeeeak!" to the button's Over state. Then you could use the sound of a rusty latch or door-knob for the Down state. Ultimately, both of these sounds would make the door button much more interesting (and scary) in the context of your movie.

Adding sound(s) to a button is a very simple and effective way to add some audio interest to your movie. Here is how you do it:

1. Import into your movie any sounds you need for the button. To learn how to do this, see "Importing Sound Files" earlier in this chapter.

> Flash's built-in sound Library has a decent offering of general-purpose button sounds. Select Window → Common Libraries → Sounds.fla to display this Library. Grab any of the sounds you find there and either drag them to the Stage or into the Library panel for your movie.

2. Select the button on the Stage where you would like to attach the sound and choose Edit → Edit Symbols. Flash jumps into Symbol Editing mode for the button you selected. In this mode, you should be able to see the button's Timeline with the Up, Over, Down, and Hit keyframe states. To learn more about the various states of a button, see Chapter 13.

3. Insert a new layer in the button Timeline and name it "sounds."

4. Click the Over state frame in the new layer and then select Insert → Keyframe to insert a new keyframe.

5. Select Window → Properties to display the Property Inspector if it isn't already visible. In the same way that you added a sound to the main Timeline, you will add a sound to the button's Timeline (see Figure 20.4). Select a sound file from the panel's Sound drop-down

menu. Assign any effect you would like to use, and set the sync to Start. To learn more about Start sync and the other sound sync options, see Chapter 21.

6. Select Edit → Edit Document to return to the main Timeline. You can test the button sound in Movie Editing mode by selecting Control → Enable Simple Buttons. If you would like to test the sound in the context of the entire movie, select Control → Test Movie. Roll your mouse cursor over the button to hear the sound you just attached.

In the same way that you attached a sound to the Over state of a button, you can attach a sound the Down state as well. This helps to create a more realistic "click" effect. Simply follow the steps previously outlined in this section. Create a new keyframe for the Down state and attach the sound you wish to use. Because the two keyframes represent different button events, they will be cued separately—one when the cursor rolls over the button, and another when the button is clicked.

> When working with button sounds, it is important that the waveform is trimmed so that there is no dead space at the start of the audio file. If your sound has dead space, there will be a lag between when the sound is cued and when you actually hear it.

Working with Audio Effects

One of the most overlooked aspects of audio production and design in interactive media is the use of audio effects. Audio effects are accomplished by altering the volume level and pan position of a sound's playback. Dramatic or even subtle changes of volume and position can add a new dimension to even the most ordinary sounds. You can use audio effects to give a sound a particular kind of character; for example, make it sound near or far, or make it sound like it is on one side moving to another. Audio effects add depth to a sound by creating a sense of space and presence.

Using your audio editor, you can apply audio effects to a sound before you import it into the Flash environment. However, Flash allows you to set the audio effects for the sounds in your movies, and there are several advantages to this feature. First of all, effects are applied to a sound when it is placed in the Timeline, so each individual instance of a sound can have its own effect. This keeps you from having to import multiple versions of the same sound, each with a different effect. The other advantage of the Flash sound effects feature is that it helps minimize the file size for sounds that require pan effects. If you remember from Chapter 19, sounds that contain stereo information (left and right channels) require twice as much space in your movie's Library. But by using the Flash audio effects, you can apply panning to a mono sound and get the same results for half the number of audio file kilobytes. Not a bad deal!

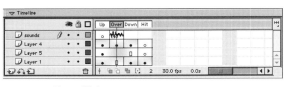

Figure 20.4

A button Timeline with a sound attached to the Over state keyframe

Pan effects are best for mono sound effects. For example, if you wanted a "swoooosh!" sound to start in the left speaker and end in the right one, you could use a mono file and have Flash take care of panning it for you. The alternative would be to create the pan effect in your audio editor. While it would sound the same, the stereo "swoooosh!" sound would be twice as large because it would contain the stereo information for left and right speaker channels.

To apply audio effects to a sound in your movie Timeline:

1. Click the sound's starting keyframe and then select Window → Properties to display the Property Inspector if it isn't already visible.

2. The Property Inspector will show you the name of the sound, its sync setting, and the number of loops. There is also an Effect drop-down menu that contains several effects options:

> **Left/Right Channel** plays the sound in only the left or right speaker.
>
> **Fade Left to Right** and **Fade Right to Left** pan a sound from one speaker to the other over the duration of the sound file.
>
> **Fade In** starts a sound at silence and gradually increases it to full volume.
>
> **Fade Out** starts a sound at full volume and gradually decreases it to silence.
>
> **Custom** opens the Edit Envelope dialog box, which can be used to create custom audio effects. To learn more about this, see the next section of this chapter.

If you apply effects to looped sounds, you may experience some inconsistencies in their playback. For instance, a Fade Left to Right effect will work for only the first iteration of the sound. All subsequent loops will play in the right channel because that is where this effect "leaves" the sound. To work around this, you can create a custom effect to control the entire looped sequence. You can learn more about this in the next section as well.

3. After you have applied an effect, select Control → Test Movie to listen to the effect in the context of your movie.

If your movie is a linear animation in the Timeline and doesn't require any special Action-Script to play properly, or if you are working with your sounds in a Movie Clip Timeline, you can listen to audio effects in Movie Editing mode. Select Control → Play (or press Return/Enter) to play the sounds in the Timeline.

Creating Custom Effects with Sound Envelopes

Depending on your audio design intentions, there are situations in which you will need to have precise control over the effects applied to a sound. This can be done by creating custom audio effects. Flash allows you to do this by manipulating the *envelope:* changes of volume over time. By creating different envelope combinations in the left and right channels, you can produce many different and interesting audio effects.

Technically speaking, in the world of audio engineering and acoustics, envelopes make changes to a sound over time. In Flash, the envelope happens to make changes in volume.

To create a custom audio effect:

1. Click the starting keyframe of the sound whose effect you would like to edit and then select Window → Properties to display the Property Inspector if it isn't already visible.

2. In the Property Inspector, either choose Custom from the Effect drop-down menu or click the Edit button. The Edit Envelope dialog box appears (see Figure 20.5).

Figure 20.5

The Edit Envelope dialog box offers many options for changing various sound parameters to create an audio effect.

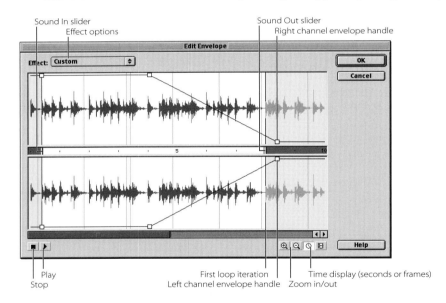

3. The most important thing to understand about this editing tool is that it is controlling the envelope (again, think volume) of each channel. Even if the sound is mono, you are still able to manipulate it to create stereo effects, because it will be routed to both the left and right channels, as defined by the envelope edits you make. By changing the envelope of each channel, you put more or less of the sound in a particular channel.

Click and drag the envelope handle for each channel to adjust the volume of the sound to be played in each channel. For example, to create an effect that pans from left to right and back again, click the left channel envelope line to create a new handle at the end of the sound's waveform. Click in the middle of the envelope line to create another handle, and drag it to the bottom of the envelope. Do this for the right channel, but make it a mirror image of the left envelope (see Figure 20.6). This way, whatever is happening in one channel, the opposite will take place in the other. As the left channel's envelope fades, the right channel becomes louder, and vice versa. When opposite channels carry different amounts of the sound, a pan effect is created.

4. After you finish tweaking the envelope, click OK to return to the main Timeline.

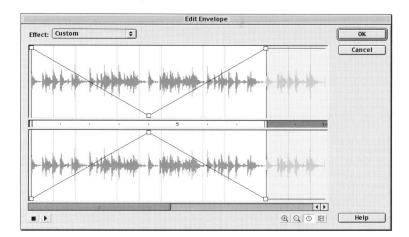

Figure 20.6

This envelope configuration will create a pan effect from left to right and then back again.

The Edit Envelope dialog box has a few other features that can help you create effects and edit a sound:

- Use the Play and Stop buttons to audition an effect.

- Use the Zoom buttons to see more or less of the sound wave. This is helpful if you are trying to create very precise envelope changes.

- Use the Sound In or Sound Out slider to trim the beginning or end of a sound file. This can be useful for last-minute tweaks to button sounds.

- If you apply an effect to a looped sound, the subsequent loops will be displayed in a hazy, gray color. You can use the envelope handles to create effects for the remaining cycles of the sound loop.

Exporting and Compressing Audio Files

When you finish creating a Flash movie, you must go through the process of *publishing* your movie, or finalizing it for presentation to your audience. When you publish a Flash movie, all of your audio content is *exported*, and included in the final movie. When a sound is exported, it is often changed from its original format to something that is more manageable in a bandwidth-sensitive environment. Because audio can greatly add to the size of a movie file, the process of exporting sounds generally involves *compression*.

Compression comes in many different forms and is used to shrink, or compress, the final size of a sound file. Compression takes the original file and squeezes it down to a more portable, compact file that is easier to use in situations where file size is a crucial part of development. Sound great? Not always. Compression can have an adverse affect on sound files. In general, file size and sound quality are directly related. As you add more compression, the file size drops, but so does the sound quality.

As a sound file is compressed, certain parts of the sound (usually those deemed least important by the compression codec) are removed. Although this works to create a more compact sound, it also takes away certain elements of the original. The more this is done, the fewer original elements remain, which can leave you with a sound of very marginal quality. Don't be too discouraged, though. Flash offers several different compression and resampling options that allow you to strike a happy balance between file size and sound quality.

Adjusting Individual Export Settings

You have a great deal of control when it comes to exporting sounds in Flash. In general, it is best to use individual settings for each sound in your movie, for a couple of reasons. First, all sounds are different. Some sounds may sound fine at a low quality level or under high levels of compression. Second, sounds that are short or not as important in your movie can be squeezed down even further with high-compression, minimum-quality settings.

To set the export settings for a sound in your movie:

1. Select Window → Library to display the Library panel.

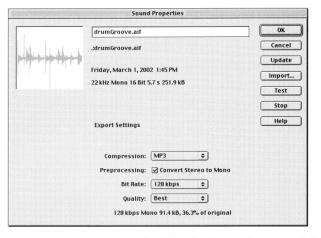

2. Highlight the sound name in the Library and then select Properties from the Options drop-down menu in the Library panel. Alternatively, you can double-click the sound's speaker icon. The Sound Properties dialog box appears.

3. If the sound has been changed outside of Flash since it was imported, click the Update button. This retrieves the most recent version of the file.

4. Choose an option from the Compression drop-down menu and select the settings you would like to use. To learn more about your options, see the next section of this chapter.

5. Click the Test button to audition the sound and readjust the compression settings as needed. When you are finished, click OK to return to your movie. Each sound you adjust in this fashion will be exported with the settings you specify.

Selecting a Compression Option

Flash offers several compression choices, which are suited to different applications depending on your needs. When you select one of these from the Compression drop-down menu, its options (sample rate, bit depth, and so on) appear at the bottom of the Sound Properties dialog box. Note that as you change these options, the dialog box updates information about the size of the compressed sound.

Default Compression

To use the Default compression options, leave the menu selection as Default. This will apply whatever options are set in the Publish Settings dialog box to the sound. To check the publish settings for your movie, select File → Publish Settings (see Figure 20.7). Here you can set the compression options for both stream and event sounds in your movie.

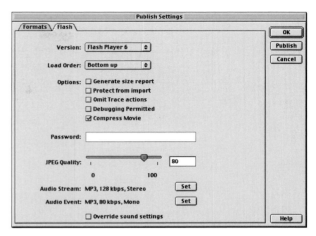

Figure 20.7

The Publish Settings dialog box enables you to define the default sound compression parameters for sounds in your movie.

To learn more about the export settings in the Publish Settings dialog box, see their individual listings later in this section.

If the Override Sound Settings box is checked, Flash will export all sounds, regardless of their settings in the Library, with the parameters defined in the Publish Settings dialog box. This produces the same results as setting all sounds to Default compression in the Library.

ADPCM Compression

ADPCM, which stands for adaptive differential pulse-code modulation, is best for short sounds that can work well at lower quality settings.

To use ADPCM compression:

1. Select ADPCM from the Compression drop-down menu.
2. Check the Convert Stereo to Mono box if you want to mix your stereo sounds into a single channel.
3. Select a sample rate between 44kHz and 5kHz. In general, the higher the sample rate, the better the sound quality you can expect.
4. Select ADPCM bits between 5 and 2. Again, a higher number of bits equals better quality.

MP3 Compression

MP3 compression is very popular for distributing CD-quality or near-CD-quality audio in a compact digital format. MP3 compression is probably the best choice for music, dialog, longer sound effects, and any kind of stream sync sound in your movie. It yields great results in terms of both final file size and sound quality. MP3 compression was not introduced until Flash evolved to version 4, so be sure that your audience has a Flash Player version that can support this feature.

To export with MP3 compression:

1. Select MP3 from the Compression drop-down menu.

2. Choose a bit rate between 160Kbps and 8Kbps (kilobits per second). You should get good results with MP3 settings at just about any quality; however, the general rule that higher settings equal better quality still applies. When in doubt, produce multiple versions and weigh the aesthetics of exported sound quality versus file size. Your ears should be the final judge. A setting of 56Kbps yields a happy medium between acceptable quality and manageable size; use 112Kbps or higher to achieve near-CD-quality sound.

3. If you select a bit rate of 20 or above, you have the option to mix stereo channels to a single mono channel by checking the Convert Stereo to Mono box.

4. Select a quality setting:

   Fast compresses files quickly but has the poorest quality. This option is not recommended for sounds that are predominant or significant in your movie.

   Medium takes longer to compress but renders the files at a better quality than Fast.

   Best is your best choice for music or files where quality is important. Although it takes longer to compress the files, it renders the highest quality MP3s for your movie.

Raw Compression

This option translates to no compression. Rather, the sound is either mixed to a single channel and/or sampled down to a lower sampling rate.

To use the Raw settings:

1. Select Raw from the Compression drop-down menu.

2. Check Convert Stereo to Mono if you want to mix your stereo sounds into a single channel.

3. Select a sample rate between 44kHz and 5kHz. In general, the higher the sample rate, the better the sound quality you can expect.

Speech Compression

New in Flash MX, the Speech compression option is designed specifically for spoken sounds. When used on narration and dialog, it produces decent-sounding results while maintaining a small file size.

To use Speech compression:

1. Select Speech from the Compression drop-down menu.

2. Select a sample rate between 44kHz and 5kHz. In general, the higher the sample rate, the better the sound quality you can expect. Be sure to test each sound before settling on a compression setting.

> Speech compression doesn't support stereo sounds. All sounds are automatically converted to mono.

QuickTime Compression Options

Flash allows you to publish your movie as a QuickTime Flash movie rather than Shockwave Flash. With this publish option, there are additional sound options that affect the quality of sound in the QuickTime movie. Note that the compression options presented here are available *only* if you plan to publish your movie as a QuickTime Flash movie.

When working with Flash movies that will be published as QuickTime, you have a good deal of flexibility in terms of what you can do with audio. There is no limit to the number of tracks, so feel free to use as much audio as you deem necessary. And, because QuickTime files are linear, all the sounds will be mixed to a single audio track (or a pair of tracks if you use stereo sounds).

To set QuickTime compression settings:

1. Select File → Publish Settings. In the Formats tab, check the box for QuickTime. A QuickTime tab appears; select it.

2. Check the box for Streaming Sound that reads "Use QuickTime Compression." This activates the Settings button.

3. Click the Settings button, and the Sound Settings dialog box appears. (There are several different dialog boxes that carry the name *Sound Settings*. In this step, the Sound Settings dialog box will affect QuickTime streaming sounds.)

   Here you can choose from a variety of QuickTime sound settings, each of which has its own individual options. See Table 20.1 for a complete listing of your choices. Since some compression schemes are better suited to certain tasks than others, try to find a codec that fits your specific needs. It can be helpful to experiment with several different options and test them back-to-back on several systems before making a final compression decision.

Table 20.1

**QuickTime Sound
Compression Options**

COMPRESSION CODEC	DESCRIPTION/APPLICATION
24-bit Integer, 32-bit Integer	Increases bit depth (sample size) to 24 and 32.
32-bit Floating Point 64-bit Floating Point	Increases bit depth (sample size) to 32 and 64. Most computers are incapable of playing sounds at this high bit depth and will convert back to 8- or 16-bit.
ALaw 2:1	Poor-quality compression; not recommended.
IMA 4:1	Decent compression ratios; must be 16-bit; fine for CD-ROM delivery.
MACE 3:1, MACE 6:1	Dated codecs; not worth the trouble.
Q Design Music 2	Superb compression ratios; great for streaming music.
Qualcomm PureVoice	Superb compression ratios; preferred format for streamed dialog and narration.
uLaw 2:1	Old codec; not worth the trouble.

For the latest information on QuickTime, visit the Apple website: `www.apple.com/quicktime/products/`.

4. After you have selected the right compression options, click OK in the Sound Settings dialog box. Then select the Flash tab. Click the Set button next to the Audio Stream label. The Sound Settings dialog box appears again, this time for Flash streaming sounds. Choose Disable from the Compression drop-down menu. This prevents extra streaming sound instances from getting into your final movie. Click OK.

   Repeat this process with the Set button beside the Audio Event label. This disables event sound compression in your Flash movie. Click OK in the Publish Settings dialog box when you have finished.

It is necessary to disable sound options in the Flash tab when exporting a QuickTime Flash movie; otherwise, sounds are doubled in the final QuickTime file.

With these options in place, your QuickTime compression settings will be applied to the *streaming* sounds of any movie you publish in QuickTime format. Event sounds will not be published with the QuickTime settings you have chosen. If you are using event sounds in your movie, use the Property Inspector and change their sync to Stream before publishing the final movie file.

Inspirational Design Model

Since the birth of MTV, music videos have become a major part of pop culture. Both the animation and sound capabilities of Flash make it an ideal tool for creating music videos of your own design, and Joe Sparks is one Flash developer who is taking full advantage of this. Sparks is responsible for the musically charged web serial "Radiskull & Devil Doll" (Figure 20.8), which can be found at `http://joesparks.com`.

Each episode features a music video in which Radiskull and his sidekick, Devil Doll, are "kickin' it"—singing and rapping about their adventures of mischief and mayhem. These animated musical numbers are a fantastic example of how you can use Flash to deliver exceptional audio and animation over the Web.

Figure 20.8

"Radiskull & Devil Doll" can be found online at `http://joesparks.com`, "kickin' it" for you and your listening pleasure.

Summary

This chapter outlined all the technical aspects of playing sounds in the Flash environment. The intention is that you master the techniques first and then apply them to creative ends in your projects. After all, once you understand how the application handles audio, creating movies with stunning music and sound effects is just a matter of infusing your own creativity and ingenuity.

You learned how to start and stop sounds on both animation and button Timelines. You were also presented with several options for adding effects to audio playback. Finally, you learned how Flash handles the delivery of sound in movies that can be distributed on either CD-ROM or over the Internet. With these essential techniques under your belt, you are well on your way to turning Flash into a delivery medium for creative and inspiring audio content.

CHAPTER 21

Synchronizing Audio with Animations

When one thinks of animation, it is hard not to be reminded of the classic Warner Brothers cartoons starring Bugs Bunny, Daffy Duck, the Road Runner, Wile E. Coyote, Elmer Fudd, and Marvin the Martian. And, when you think about these animated cartoons, it's impossible not to remember all the crazy sounds that were so much a part of the show: anvils clanking on heads, *zips, swooshes,* and nimble violin strings plucking out the sound of a character's tiptoe entrance onto the screen. All these sounds were crucial to the success of the animation; they communicated the things left unsaid by the visual track.

As you know by now, Flash is much more than an animation program. It can be used to create interactive menu systems, games, websites, and more. Are these animations? No, not really, but in the Flash environment, you have to think about everything as if it were an animation. Flash's Timeline structure applies to just about every element of the program, including buttons, Movie Clips, and scenes; even graphics are affected by this structure because they are *used* in Timelines. Whatever your design goals may be, try to think of every project as a kind of animation.

As in the classic Warner Brothers cartoons, you will get more out of your Flash movies through the creative use of sound, and one of the keys to this is synchronization. This chapter discusses how Flash deals with sound in the context of animations, and how you can get the best results through synchronization of audio and visual events. The chapter covers these topics:

- **Specifics of the Flash synchronization options: Event, Stream, Start, and Stop**
- **Lip-syncing and forcing the animation frame rate**
- **Creating complex animation and button sound events**
- **Syncing audio with Movie Clips**

Synchronization Options in Flash

Any time you attach a sound to a frame in the Timeline, you must assign a sync option in the Properties inspector (see Figure 21.1). The *sync options* (short for *synchronization*)— Event, Stream, Start, and Stop—tell Flash how to play a sound when it is encountered in your movie. Synchronization determines the relationship between the sound (music, sound effects, dialog, and so on) and animated components of your movie.

In Flash, a sound can be made to play and loop independently of the animation in the Timeline, resulting in loose synchronization. Or you can have the sound lock the movie's frame rate to keep tight sync between audio and visual tracks. Flash also considers the act of stopping a sound to be a kind of sync, and will allow you to halt playback to match a visual event. Learning how these choices affect your movie is an important part of fine-tuning an animation and getting the most out of your movie's sounds.

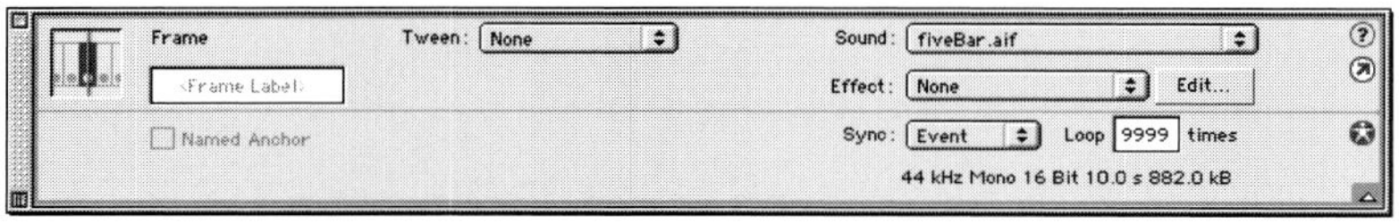

Figure 21.1

The Property Inspector has a pop-up menu where you can assign the type of sync you wish to use for each sound. Here the sync option is set to Event.

Using Event Sync

Event sync is one of the most commonly used means of audio synchronization in Flash. Its name is fairly self-explanatory; this option creates a sound event by responding to an animation event in your movie. When Flash plays a frame that contains an event-synced sound, that sound is cued to play in its entirety, independently of the Timeline. If the Timeline stops playing frames, an event sound will continue to play until it has finished or has run out of loops. Think of an event sound as a kind of cue that you can attach to a Timeline frame.

Event sounds offer a lot of flexibility with your movie because all you have to do is set them in motion and let the sound take it from there. Because event sounds play independently of your animation, you don't have to worry about having enough frames to accommodate the length of the sound. These characteristics make event sounds ideally suited to various applications in a Flash movie:

Buttons *Button sounds* are usually attached to the Over and Down states of a button animation. When the mouse cursor is moused over a button, a sound is played; when the button is clicked, another sound is played. Because these button events (Over and Down) can happen quickly, it is important to use a sync option that will respond quickly. If a button is moused over or clicked more than once, the Event sync option will cue the sound each time and will mix multiple instances of the sound together. Consequently, this allows you to create interesting layered sound or musical effects with multiple button sounds. To learn more about the specifics of this technique, see the section "Working with Event Sound Effects and Music" later in this chapter.

> If you are adding sound to a button and you specifically *don't* want sounds to layer and overlap, see the explanation of Start sync at the end of this section.

Sound effects If your movie calls for sound effects, the Event option is definitely the one to use. It allows you to perfectly sync an animation event, like a basketball going through the hoop, with the sound *swish!!* Create a new keyframe with an event sound on one of your movie's sound layers. The frame should line up with the correct moment in the animation. When your movie plays back, you will see the ball go through the hoop and hear a gratifying *swish!!* to make the animation complete. To learn more about the specifics of this technique, see "Working with Event Sound Effects and Music" later in this chapter.

Stingers In film scoring, sudden musical stabs that are played to add dramatic punch are called *stingers*. For instance, a woman is peacefully sleeping in her bed when the French doors to her chamber mysteriously open…you hear nothing. Then suddenly, as the vampire's face appears, you hear a high violin tremolo, and the hairs on the back of your neck stand up straight! This device has been used for years to enhance the dramatic tension of cinematic and cartoon scenes. In the same way that you add sound effects, you can use the Event sync option to cue dramatic musical stingers in your movie.

Using Stream Sync

Stream sync is quite a bit different than the other sync options available to you in Flash. Stream sync locks the movie's frame rate to the playback of the sound and will skip (or "drop") frames if the animation cannot keep the pace. This option makes Flash more like a video editing application, where the audio and video tracks are locked together to preserve their synchronization. The opposite of event sounds, stream sounds will play only if they have enough frames to accommodate their length. In many cases, you will have to add frames to enable long sounds to play completely. For an illustration of this, see Figure 21.2

Due to the nature of the Stream sync option, we recommend that you avoid looping stream sounds if possible. Audio data cannot be reused as efficiently when sounds are set to stream. Flash will add unnecessary

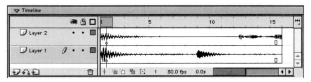

Figure 21.2

The top sound (Layer 2) does not have enough frames to play the entire file. You can tell because the waveform is cut off at the last frame. Notice that the bottom sound (Layer 1) *does* have enough frames. The waveform ends as a straight, horizontal line similar to what you would see in a digital audio editor.

extra information to your final movie and create a larger SWF file. The Stream sync option does, however, have some excellent uses:

Scored music If you have long sections of music that are supposed to sync precisely with an animation, the Stream sync option is your best bet. The Stream audio will force Flash to maintain a consistent frame rate and keep tight synchronization between audio and animation events.

Lip sync To create tightly synchronized talking or singing animations, use Stream sync. It allows Flash to maintain a consistent pace and keep the dialog or music in sync with the mouth animation. To learn more about the specifics of this technique, see the section "Creating Lip Sync Animations" later in this chapter.

Multitrack and component audio All sync options in Flash allow you to play up to eight different sounds simultaneously. If you place each sound on its own layer, you can create a multitrack sound movie. Using the Stream sync option, it is possible to do this in a way that keeps all the tracks (individual sound layers) synchronized perfectly. To learn more about this technique, see Hands On 6.

Using Start Sync

The *Start sync* option is very similar to Event sync. When the sound's frame is played, the Start option cues the sound and plays it in its entirety. The only difference is that if another instance of the sound is already playing, the new instance will not be heard. You can use Start sync as a kind of filter to prevent too many occurrences of a single sound.

Start sync is the best choice for buttons in situations where you do not want a button's sound to play more than once. For example, if you attach a sound to the button's Over state frame and use Event sync, the sound will be heard each time your mouse moves over the button. If the mouse crosses over the button frequently, this can cause too many simultaneous instances of the sound. Start sync prevents this because only one instance of the sound is allowed to play at a time.

 For an example of Event sync versus Start sync with buttons, open the file `buttonSync.swf` in the Chapter 21 folder of this book's companion CD-ROM. Quickly move your mouse over the button labeled "Event" several times. You will hear the sound repeated each time your mouse crosses over the button. (This particular sound is Visor Hum Loop from Window → Common Libraries → Sounds.fla.) The more you do this, the more confusing things can start to sound. Next, do the same with the button labeled "Start." This time, no matter how often your mouse crosses over the button, you will only hear one instance of the sound. Start sync helps to keep your button sounds tidy.

Syncing Sounds to Stop

The final sync option Flash offers is Stop, and, as you probably guessed, this is what you use to silence a sound's playback. *Stop sync* is used specifically to silence sounds that were cued via Event or Start sync. To sync the end of a sound:

1. Insert a new keyframe where you would like the sound to end. The keyframe should be positioned so that the sound will stop in sync with an animation event.

2. Select Window → Properties to display the Property Inspector. From the Sound pop-up menu, choose the name of the sound you wish to stop from the Sound pop-up menu and then select the Stop sync option. When the Timeline reaches this frame, the sound you have specified will stop.

The Stop sync option works for event and start sounds, but stream sounds must be handled differently. You must make the last frame of the stream sound exactly match the animation event. To stop a stream sound:

1. Find the animation event in the Timeline you wish to sync with the end of a stream sound. Remember the frame number where this event takes place.

2. Stream sounds will only play through the number of frames they occupy, so you must calculate the number of extra frames to be cleared. Find the last frame of the stream sound you wish to sync and subtract that from the frame number of the animation event. For example, if you have a sound that plays until frame 46 and you want to silence it in sync with an event at frame 20, you have the difference of 26 frames.

3. Click the first keyframe of the stream sound and press Shift+F5 once for every frame you wish to clear. In the example in step 2, you would press this key combination 26 times. For an illustration of a synced stream sound, see Figure 21.3.

> Another way to clear frames is by selecting a range and clearing them from the timeline. To do this, select the first frame you would like to remove and then Shift+click to extend your selection to the last frame you want to clear. Press Shift+F5 and the range of selected frames will disappear from the timeline.

4. After you have cleared the unnecessary frames, select Control → Test Movie to see and hear how the sync works. You can add or subtract additional frames to the sound if the sync needs some tweaking.

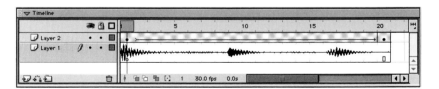

Figure 21.3

In this Timeline, the stream sound that starts at frame 1 is stopped to sync with an event in the animation at frame 20.

Flash Synchronization Techniques

Now that you know how Flash handles animation/sound synchronization, you are ready to dig deeper into the subject and see how these techniques work in the context of your movie. As with many things in Flash, the techniques are simple; the real magic comes through your ability to use them creatively and move beyond the capabilities of the software. The examples presented here should not be seen as absolute answers, but as points of departure for your own wild and creative uses of sound synchronization.

Creating Lip Sync Animations

Many different options are available to you for creating lip sync animations. Depending on the kind of animation you wish to create, Flash allows you to animate with either loose, stylish synchronization or with lifelike accuracy, or with anything in between. A good lip sync animation can make animated characters come to life in your movie.

This technique uses the Stream sync option to force the animation to keep pace with the audio track. Another advantage of this option is that with stream sounds, you can *scrub* the audio track. When you scrub a track, you use the mouse to move the playback head over the audio waveform and hear what part is synchronized with a particular frame. Scrubbing allows you to test certain sections manually to see how the audio and animation line up.

To create a lip sync animation, it is assumed that you have drawn a character, recorded some dialog, and imported it into your movie. The only quirk to this technique is that your character's mouth has to be on its own layer. The reason is that when you animate a lip sync, you don't have to use just one mouth graphic. Rather, you can use several mouth graphics that have different shapes representing the different mouth positions for the various words and letters in your character's language.

In this lesson, all of the media has been created for you. On the companion CD-ROM, open the file named `lipSync.fla` inside the Chapter 21 folder and save it to your hard drive.

lipSync.swf

If you would like to see what you are getting yourself into, open `lipSync.swf` to see and hear the finished file.

To create a lip sync animation:

1. Using the `lipSync.fla` file, insert two new layers; name one `dialog` and the other `mouth`.

2. Insert a new keyframe (select Insert → Keyframe) in the second frame of the `dialog` layer. Select Window → Properties and choose `woofwoofbark.aif` from the Sound pop-up menu. Select the Stream sync option. You want to use stream so that the animation will be forced to keep pace with the audio and maintain a tight synchronization.

3. You are now ready to create the animation for the phrase "woof woof, bark." Notice that the waveform looks chunky in some places and flat in others. The dense, chunky areas are where the sound is loudest (see Figure 21.4). If you click the playback head and drag it across the Timeline (scrub the sound), you will hear the audio track play back slowly. This should give you an idea of what "words" fall on which frames in the Timeline.

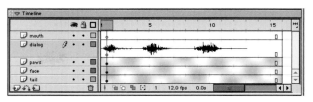

Figure 21.4

The peaks of the audio waveform show you which places are the loudest, and the valleys represent the quiet sections.

4. Select frame 1 of the `mouth` layer and insert a new keyframe. Drag the `closed` graphic symbol from the Library to the Stage and place it where the mouth should be. This will start the mouth animation in a closed position.

5. Create another new keyframe in frame 2 of the `mouth` layer and drag the `W` graphic symbol to the Stage, placing it where the mouth should be (roughly X = 275, Y = 300). To be sure your alignment is consistent, use either the Align panel or Info panel. The `W` graphic symbol creates a mouth position to say the letter *w* and starts the first part of your animation.

6. Create yet another new keyframe in frame 3 of the `mouth` layer and drag the `F` graphic symbol to the Stage. Add another keyframe to frame 4 and drag the `closed` graphic symbol to the Stage. This completes the first word, "woof."

7. Continue adding new keyframes and placing symbols on the Stage until the entire phrase is paired with mouth position graphics. It can be fun to experiment with this on your own, but if it becomes frustrating, you can refer to Table 21.1 for a listing of which symbols go in which frames.

8. When you have finished, select Control → Test Movie to hear and see what the dog has to say! This dialog is short, so the synchronization is not a great issue here. However, when you select the Stream sync option, you can start to work with longer lines of dialog, and the animation will keep the sync.

FRAME	GRAPHIC SYMBOL (MOUTH POSITION)
1	Closed
2	W
3	F
4	Closed
5	W
6	F
7, 8	Closed
9	B
10	A
11	K
12	Closed

Table 21.1

Frame and Graphic Symbol Combinations for the `lipSync.fla` Movie

Lip sync animation is a topic that can grow extremely complex. Although this simple example is just a glimpse of the big picture, all of the important concepts are addressed here. There are several additional steps you can take to become more proficient with this technique:

- Keep a hand mirror with you when you work so that you can speak the words and watch the position of your mouth as you speak.

- Don't lose sight of the entire phrase. Some letters and words don't always match with the mouth shapes you think they should.

- Use temporary `gotoAndPlay()` actions to isolate and loop specific parts where you need to focus on a word or words.

- Drawing good mouth shapes is critical! You can read about the art of drawing animation in *The Animator's Workbook* by Tony White (Watson-Guptill Publications, 1988) or *The Animation Book: A Complete Guide to Animated Filmmaking—From Flip-Books to Sound Cartoons to 3-D Animation* by Kit Laybourne (Three Rivers Press, 1998).

Working with Event Sound Effects and Music

Event sounds offer you the greatest amount of freedom and flexibility when cueing your sounds. As a result, it is also the loosest of all the sync options in Flash. This is not necessarily a bad thing. Even though "loose sync" may sound negative, there are actually times when it is especially useful.

Event sync is appropriately named because you pair the sound (music, effect, and so on) with an *event* in your movie or animation. When the visual event occurs, the sound is triggered. This is, of course, a very tight kind of sync, where both a visual event and a sound happen at exactly the same moment. However, after the initial sound cue, the sync becomes much less clear. Event sounds will play independently of the Timeline and continue to be heard until the entire sound has finished playing or has been stopped explicitly. For example, if you wanted to use the sound of a cymbal crash for a "falling down" animation, the cymbal would continue to reverberate long after the character's rear end hit the pavement.

Because Event sync sounds will continue to sustain depending on their specific length, you can achieve all sorts of interesting layering effects with multiple sounds in your movie. For example, if a waiter drops a tray full of dishes and glasses, you would hear not one *crash!* but a flurry of *cracks, shatters,* and *smashes*! Depending on how the scene is animated, you can pair a specific sound effect to each event where a bowl, plate, or glass hits the floor. All you need to do is create a separate sound layer for each effect you wish to use. Then, insert a new keyframe that lines up with the animated event you wish to sync, and attach a sound with the Event sync option. As the Timeline plays through the series of animated events, each sound will be cued at the appropriate time. See Figure 21.5 for an example of this in your movie's Timeline. Because each sound is left to play independently, each will continue to ring until the sound is over, creating a great, layered sound effect to enhance your animation. The advantage of this technique is this: Rather than have to create a long sound effect and guess when each element falls into place, you can build the entire effect in Flash and get much better synchronized results.

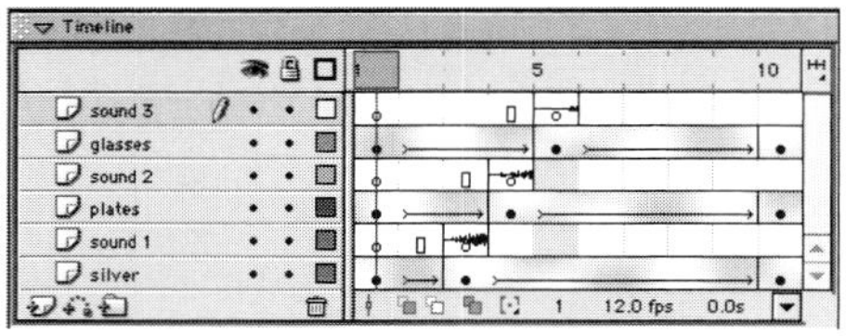

Figure 21.5

This Timeline shows how event sounds can be paired with animation keyframes to create a layered sound effect.

There are a few things to keep in mind when working with Event sound effects:

- Event sounds are heard when they are first encountered in the Timeline. To prevent latency, be sure that the sound is trimmed and has no dead space or silence at the start of the sound file. To learn more about trimming audio files, see Chapter 19.

- If you are layering several loud sounds, you may need to adjust their envelopes so that the sounds aren't distorted when played in your movie. To learn more about working with sound envelopes in Flash, see Chapter 20.

- Flash can play only eight sounds simultaneously. Look at your Timeline to see if there are any spots where eight different audio layers have active sounds at the same time. If you encounter this in your Timeline, try some re-adjustments to prevent too many overlaps.

- In the same way that this technique works for sound effects, it can also work for music, particularly sweeping flourishes, melismatic vocal cues, horn and guitar riffs, and so on. Experiment with this technique to see what kinds of interesting musical effects you can create with event sounds.

Syncing Audio with Movie Clips

Movie clips are one of the most important elements in any Flash movie. They can perform their own independent animations, apart from the activity taking place on the main Timeline. Consequently, they can be a great asset to the synchronization of sound in your movies. You can create Movie Clips that contain sound files attached to their various frames. Then, by targeting a clip, you are able to control the sound or sounds it holds in its frames. This technique takes you one step beyond playing sounds from your main Timeline and affords a great deal of audio playback control.

In this example, you will learn how to use Movie Clips to control sound playback. You can take a look at the finished files, which are in the Chapter 21 folder on the companion CD-ROM: `audioMC.fla` and `audioMC.swf`. To use Movie Clips to sync sounds, there are two steps you must take: create the sound Movie Clip and set up a means of controlling the clip.

To create a Movie Clip that can sync sounds:

1. If you have not done so already, import a sound into your movie. Then select Insert → New Symbol, name the clip `audio`, and check the Movie Clip radio button.

2. Click frame 2 of the `audio` Timeline and insert a new keyframe; then press F5 twice to insert two additional frames.

3. Create another new keyframe at frame 5 and add four new frames after it. Do the same thing at frame 10, extending four new frames through frame 14. Finally, add one last keyframe at frame 14. The finished frame construction should look like Figure 21.6.

Figure 21.6

The frame structure for the sound Movie Clip has keyframes at frames 2, 5, 10, and 14.

4. Now that the clip has its basic structure, you can start to fill in its components. Attach the following actions to keyframe 2:

```
stop();
stopAllSounds();
```

This stops the clip from playing any farther in the Timeline and silences any active sounds at frame 2.

5. Attach your sound to keyframe 5 and assign the Start sync option. Enter the number of loops and any effects you desire. Here you use the Start sync option so that if the sound is already playing, it will not be interrupted or overlapped.

6. Attach the following ActionScript statement to keyframe 14:

```
gotoAndPlay(10);
```

This line is the most important part of the Movie Clip because it creates a playback loop. The clip cues the sound at frame 5; then, as it continues through the Timeline, it reaches the playback loop action at frame 14. There the clip's playback head is sent to frame 10. Since there is nothing in frame 10, the clip will continue to play toward frame 14 once more. Again, it is sent back to frame 10, and on and on. This kind of loop allows the clip to play its sound once, and then go into an "idle" state while it awaits another command. Since the sound was cued with Start sync, it will play independently of any Timeline until it has either finished playing or exhausted its loops.

Now that you have completed the Movie Clip, you can create a means to control it in your movie. There are many different ways to do this. Here you will learn both how to make the controls part of the clip itself and how to control the clip from the main Timeline.

To put controls in the clip itself:

1. If you are not already in Symbol Editing mode, select the **audio** Movie Clip from the Edit Symbols menu or double-click it in the Library.

2. Insert a new layer in the clip and drag a button onto its Stage. This will serve as your Play button. Attach the following ActionScript statements to the button:

```
on(release){
    this.gotoAndPlay(5);
}
```

These actions should make perfect sense: Since the sound file is cued at frame 5, you have to send the Movie Clip to play at frame 5 in order to start the sound.

3. Drag a new button to the Stage once again to serve as your Stop button and attach the following statements:

```
on(release){
    this.gotoAndPlay(1);
}
```

The term this is not absolutely necessary in these examples. It is used to make an explicit reference to the current Timeline. A simple gotoAndPlay(5) or gotoAndPlay(1) would work just as well.

This sends the Movie Clip back to frame 1. When it gets there, it will play through to frame 2, where it will encounter both the stop() and stopAllSounds() actions. These will halt the clip's playback and stop any currently active sounds in the movie.

Let's recap what is happening in the clip. When it is first loaded into the movie, it is stopped at frame 2 and no sound is heard (remember, the sound is at frame 5). When it receives a message to go to frame 5, the sound is cued and the clip is told to loop in some inactive frames (10–14). Then, when you wish to stop the sound, the Stop button sends the clip to play at frame 1, where it soon encounters the stop() and stopAllSounds() actions in frame 2. This quiets the clip and prevents it from playing any further.

4. These statements complete the controls for your Movie Clip. Exit Symbol Editing mode and return to the main Timeline. Drag an instance of the audio Movie Clip to the Stage of the main Timeline. Select Control → Test Movie and experiment with switching the sound on and off.

It's great to be able to toggle the sounds on and off from the clip itself, but it's equally important to control the clip from the main Timeline. To do this, you will need to target the clip specifically so that you can send it to play at the correct frames:

1. Give your audio Movie Clip the instance name soundMC in the Property Inspector. Then, drag two buttons to the Stage of the main Timeline (if there are no buttons in your movie's Library, you'll need to create some). Use one for Play, and the other for Stop.

2. Attach the following statements to the Play button:

```
on(release){
    soundMC.gotoAndPlay(5);
}
```

3. Attach the following statements to the Stop button:

```
on(release){
    soundMC.gotoAndPlay(1);
}
```

Both sets of actions target the soundMC instance with an absolute pathname.

4. Select Control → Test Movie. You should now be able to toggle the sound with both sets of buttons—those in the Movie Clip and those on the main Timeline.

When you control a clip from the main Timeline, it's not necessary to have buttons built into the clip itself. If you want, take the buttons out of the clip and leave it in your movie as a sound-only Movie Clip. A Movie Clip does not have to have graphics to work, only frames. In this case, the clip's frames are filled with nothing but actions, keyframes, and a sound cue.

Inspirational Design Model

There are so many excellent movies and websites using Flash audio synchronization that it was really tough to pick one to speak for all the others. The solution was to pick one that, at the time of writing, was exceptionally original and unique. Sometimes the most interesting or memorable work is not the most technically dazzling but rather has a strong concept and is ingeniously presented to its audience. "Eugene, the marvelous crooning child," at `www.eugenemirman.com`, proves that even the simplest audio synchronization can render hilarious results when done well. (See Figure 21.7.)

Figure 21.7

"Eugene, the marvelous crooning child" was created by Eugene Mirman, with voice synchronization by Scott Bowers.

Summary

Audio in the form of music, dialog, and sound effects can add new levels of interest to your Flash movies. When including these kinds of elements, it is important to pair the audio with a visual component of your movie so that the two are linked in some kind of meaningful relationship. This is accomplished by setting the sync. Flash allows you to establish tight synchronization for things like spoken dialog and scored music. It also makes room for loose syncs for things like button sounds, short musical cues, and sound effects. This chapter presented the various sync options that Flash provides and walked through the specifics of each. You learned the best type of application for each synchronization option and put them into practice in three short examples.

Flash's sync options allow a fair amount of control over the way your movie will play the sounds it encounters in the Timeline. Your next step is to dive into the world of ActionScript, where you can tell Flash specifically how and when you wish to play sounds in your movie. Through scripting, you are able to achieve complete control over sound playback.

CHAPTER 22

Controlling Audio with ActionScript

Up to this point, your exposure to audio in the Flash environment has consisted mainly of sounds that are attached to your movie's Timeline and cued when their host frames are played. This technique works well for cueing music, sound effects, and dialog in such a way that they line up in sync with an animation. The only disadvantage to this approach is that all sounds are bound to frames, within either a Movie Clip or your main Timeline. As a result, if a Timeline has sounds you need but is not currently loaded, you are forced to call it to the Stage, adding an extra and often unwanted step to the process. Flash changes all of this with ActionScript.

When Flash evolved to version 5, it introduced the Sound object. The Sound object is an element of ActionScript that allows you to have complete control over every sound in your movie, whether the sound is in a Timeline or not. Flash MX continues the tradition by introducing additional terms that will allow you to load external sounds, manage sound playback, and track sound-related events. The Sound object opens the possibilities for interactive audio in Flash, and allows you to change every sound parameter dynamically through scripting rather than with keyframes and sync options. This chapter will show you how to:

- ■ **Create Sound objects**
- ■ **Play and stop sounds with ActionScript commands**
- ■ **Set and dynamically change a sound's volume**
- ■ **Set and dynamically change a sound's pan position**
- ■ **Apply stereo effects to sounds**
- ■ **Use interactive controls to manipulate sound in your movies**
- ■ **Load external MP3 sound files into a movie**

Working with the Sound Object

The Sound object is one of ActionScript's predefined objects. You use it to control the playback parameters of sounds in your movie. The Sound object allows you to play and stop sounds, set their volume level, and change their position and volume in the left and right speakers. The Sound object also makes it possible for you to monitor the volume, panning, and effects applied to a particular sound. To use this object, it's important to understand what it is and how it works as part of the ActionScript language.

Understanding the Sound Object

Like all other objects in ActionScript, the Sound object holds information about various components of your movie. Just as the MovieClip object holds information about the properties of a particular clip, and the Math object stores specifics of arithmetic, this Sound object stores information about a movie's sounds and their properties. More specifically, it stores information as to whether a sound is currently playing and, if so, how loud, in what speaker(s), and so on. To monitor or control a sound via ActionScript, you must create a new Sound object. Once a sound has an object associated with it, the object allows you to pass information to and from the sound.

Objects can encapsulate the specific attributes of an element in your movie and allow you to control them. They also serve as a medium of exchange. In the exchange, you must have currency—something common that can be understood and used by both your movie and its objects. ActionScript refers to this kind of currency as *methods*. Methods are used to send and retrieve information between your movie and its objects. Every object has a particular set of methods that it implements. The Sound object has methods that check and set volume and panning, play (start), and stop active sounds in your movie. When you need to communicate with an object, you must use its methods.

Using the Sound Object

The first step toward working with the Sound object is knowing how to create a Sound object instance. Without it, you will have no means of communicating with a particular sound. When you create a new Sound object, it can be used to control:

- All sounds currently available in the Flash Player (all SWF files loaded in at various levels)
- All sounds currently available in the movie
- The sounds in a specified Movie Clip instance
- A sound you specifically attach to the object

Depending on how you create the object, you will be able to use it for any of these applications. The generic constructor for a Sound object is as follows:

```
soundObjectName=new Sound("targetInstance");
```

Here, `soundObjectName` is a placeholder for whatever you wish to call the object. `tar-getInstance` is an optional argument (enclosed in quotes) for the function. If you plan to control the sounds in a particular Movie Clip, you must target the clip specifically.

To create an object for every movie currently available in the Flash Player, no target argument is necessary. Use this constructor:

```
globalMovieSound=new Sound();
```

Here, *globalMovieSound* is the name of a new object to control the sounds on all Timelines.

To create an object for all sounds in a Movie Clip or on a specific Timeline, you must create the object and specify a target argument:

```
monkeyClipSound=new Sound("bananas");
loadedSound=new Sound("_level1");
```

In the first example, an object named `monkeyClipSound` is created to control the attributes of sounds in the Movie Clip named `bananas`. The second statement creates an object named `loadedSound` for all sounds on the Timeline of the movie loaded at `_level1`.

When a Sound object targets a sound in another Timeline, the object can only be used to control the volume and panning of the sound. Play and stop don't work, because the sound is bound to the frames of the Timeline where it resides. However, Sound objects can control individual sounds that reside in a movie's Library. To facilitate this, you must attach the sound directly to the object. To learn how to do this, see the later section "Attaching Sounds with Linkage Identifiers."

Controlling Sound Playback

Creating a Sound object is an essential step to controlling your sounds dynamically with ActionScript. Without the object, you have no means of issuing commands to the sound. After you construct an object for a specific sound, you are free to invoke the methods of the Sound object to control their playback.

Controlling a sound via ActionScript offers several advantages over the conventional frame-based sound cues. First of all, if you only want to cue a particular sound, you don't have to target a Movie Clip or Timeline to play a specific frame. In many cases, the Sound object allows you to refer to a sound specifically, and you can cue it without having to play the frame where it resides in your movie. Conventional ActionScript has provisions for you to stop all sounds in your movie. In addition to providing this same stop feature, the Sound object allows you to start all the sounds in your movie with a single set of script commands.

The other advantage of controlling a sound through ActionScript is greater flexibility. Any element of your movie that uses scripting represents an opportunity to control sound playback. As graphic elements of your movie are dynamically manipulated or moved, you can echo these changes in your sound scripting.

Here are some of the Sound object methods used to control sound playback:

start(*secondsOffset,loops*) Used to cue sounds. start() can take two optional arguments. The secondsOffset argument can be used to start a sound from any point within the sound file. To start a 10-second sound at its halfway point, you would specify an offset of 5. The loops argument establishes the number of times a sound will play. If no loop is specified, the sound will play once (the default). To play it twice, enter a value of 2; enter 3 to play it three times, and so on.

> To cue a sound using the start() method of the Sound object, the sound must first be exported from the Library using the Linkage option. To learn more about this, see the later section "Attaching Sounds with Linkage Identifiers."

stop("*soundID*") Used to stop sounds. stop() will silence all sounds in the object it is used to control. The optional argument soundID is used to stop sounds that were attached to the Sound object directly with symbol linkage.

To see specific examples using these methods, see the section "Playing and Stopping Sounds" later in this chapter.

Setting Volume and Pan Parameters Dynamically

Without the help of ActionScript and the Sound object, you are forced to cue sounds by placing them in frames of your main Timeline or a Movie Clip. The same is true for the parameters that affect a sound's volume and panning. In order to change this kind of information for a sound placed in a keyframe, you must use the Edit Envelope dialog box and drag the envelope handles into position (Figure 22.1). Although this technique does give you a convenient graphical representation of the changes affecting a sound's envelope, the changes are permanent and cannot be altered after the movie is published. To make changes to an envelope effect, you have to go back to the keyframe where the sound is cued, open the Sound panel, and enter a new envelope shape.

ActionScript expands the possibilities tremendously by providing four methods for setting and monitoring the volume and pan parameters of a sound. And because this can all be accomplished via scripting, you have the potential to dynamically change volume and pan information at any time and from any location in your movie. Here are the methods:

setVolume(*volume*) Controls the volume of a sound's playback. Specify the argument volume between 0 (muted) and 100 (full volume). The default volume setting is 100.

getVolume() Monitors the volume of a Sound object. This method returns a value between 0 and 100, representing the current volume of the object.

setPan(*pan*) Sets the pan position for a Sound object. The argument `pan` determines where the sound is positioned. A value of 100 indicates that the sound is panned hard right (panned completely to the right speaker); –100 indicates that the sound is panned hard left (panned completely to the left speaker); and 0 indicates that the sound is centered (the default pan position). Once an object's panning has been set, it will remain in that position until it is changed.

getPan() Monitors the pan position of a Sound object. This method returns values ranging between –100 (hard left) and 100 (hard right), which represent the pan position of the object. The value 0 (the default) means that a sound is shared equally between the two speakers.

To see specific examples using these methods, see the section "Setting Volume and Pan Levels" later in this chapter.

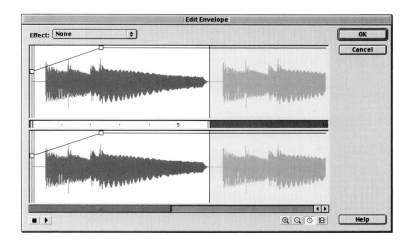

Figure 22.1

The Edit Envelope dialog box.

Creating Special Stereo Effects

ActionScript provides a special Sound object method that allows you to create unique effects with stereo sounds in your movie; it is called `setTransform()`. While the effects it creates are similar to those accomplished with panning, there is a bit more to this method. You may remember from Chapter 19 that stereo sounds are sounds that have been mixed with different components in the left and right speaker channels. For instance, a barbershop quartet may have the bass and lead voices mixed more heavily in the left channel, while the baritone and tenor voices are mixed more to the right. If you were to listen to only one channel of a stereo mix, you would hear an incomplete rendition of the audio because it would be missing about half of its components.

The `setTransform()` method doesn't affect sounds directly. To use it, you must create a generic object that applies the transform information to the sound object you wish to alter. The generic object (call it a *transformer*) allows you control each channel of a stereo mix and assign output values for each as percentages. For each channel of stereo sound, the `transformer` object has two properties, one that controls a channel's left output, and one for the right. This gives you a total of four properties that can be used to alter the stereo composition of a sound. See Table 22.1 for a rundown of the generic object (`transformer`) properties.

	PROPERTY	VALUE	DESCRIPTION
Table 22.1	ll	0–100	Percentage of left channel sound to play in the left speaker
Properties for the	lr	0–100	Percentage of right channel sound to play in the left speaker
`transformer` **Used with**	rr	0–100	Percentage of right channel sound to play in the right speaker
`setTransform()`	rl	0–100	Percentage of left channel sound to play in the right speaker

Confused? Take a look at two examples of property settings to see how they would work in context. The following properties play a stereo sound as true stereo; all of the left information is played in the left speaker, and all right information is played in the right speaker:

```
ll = 100
lr = 0
rr = 100
rl = 0
```

These next property settings swap the left and right channel information to create a reverse stereo effect; all left information is played right, and all right information is played left:

```
ll = 0
lr = 100
rr = 0
rl = 100
```

Of course, by changing the values assigned to each property, you can create many different kinds of interesting stereo effects.

Once the properties have been stored in the generic `transformer` object, it is passed to the sound object via the `setTransform()` method. Here is a breakdown of the method's syntax:

setTransform(*transformer*) Applies the properties stored in the `transformer` object to a sound object.

getTransform() Retrieves the properties applied to a sound object in the last `setTransform` command.

For specific examples of using the `setTransform()` method and creating a generic `transformer` object, see "Scripting Special Effects" later in this chapter.

Cueing Sounds with the Sound Object

The Sound object provides you with a great deal of flexibility in controlling sound playback. You will find that it offers substantial advantages over conventional frame-based sound cues because you can cue sounds at any time and manipulate their attributes dynamically. Now that you know what the Sound object is and how it works, you're ready to put it to use in the context of your Flash projects. This section shows you how to use the Sound object to export and attach a sound from your movie's Library and then cue it in your movie.

Attaching Sounds with Linkage Identifiers

One of the most useful functions of the Sound object is that it allows you to play sounds that are not directly inserted in a Timeline keyframe. However, before you can do this, you must attach the sound to the object you are using to cue the sound and control it. By attaching a sound, you are adding it to your movie while it is running. In some ways, this is the Action-Script equivalent of cueing a sound from a frame. The main difference is that when a sound is attached, it is done with ActionScript. Consequently, it can be paired with button clicks, keystrokes, and other types of user interaction.

To attach a sound to a Sound object, you must first export the sound from your movie's Library. Here are the steps:

1. In your movie's Library, highlight the name of the sound you wish to export.

2. In the Options pop-up menu, select Linkage. The Linkage Properties dialog box appears (see Figure 22.2).

3. Check the button next to Export for ActionScript and give it a unique name in the Identifier box. The Identifier is the name you will use to attach the sound to a Sound object. In Figure 22.2, the exported sound will be attached to an object as libSound.

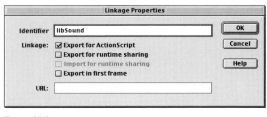

Figure 22.2

The Linkage Properties dialog box is used to export a sound from the Library so that it can be attached to a Sound object.

4. Click OK when you are finished. The sound is now ready to be attached to a Sound object.

> The Linkage Properties dialog box is also used to include sounds as a Shared Library asset. Shared Libraries allow you to exchange common files between several different Flash movies. To learn more about creating and working with Shared Libraries, see Chapter 7.

After you export the sound from the Library, you are able to attach it to a Sound object. This step officially associates the sound with an object, which in turn can be used to control the various parameters of the sound's playback. An object can have only one sound attached at a time. Attaching a new sound to an object will replace any sounds the object previously contained. To attach a sound, you use the `attachSound` method, which has this syntax:

```
sndObj.attachSound("idName")
```

Here, `sndObj` is a placeholder for the name of the object to which you will attach the sound. The argument `idName` (a string, entered in quotes) is used to declare the name of the identifier associated with the exported sound you wish to attach.

The following example creates a new Sound object called `movAudio` and attaches the sound exported from the Library as `libSound`:

```
movAudio=new Sound();
movAudio.attachSound("libSound");
```

After completing these steps, any methods applied to the `movAudio` object will affect the playback of the sound file exported as `libSound`.

Playing and Stopping Sounds

Two of the most important methods of the Sound object are those used to play and silence sounds. After all, a sound has to be cued (or stopped and recued) before you can make any audible changes to its panning, volume, or stereo composition. To cue a sound from scratch:

1. Go through the steps of exporting the sound from the Library and assigning it an identifier. To learn more about this, see the preceding section.

2. Once you have exported the sound, you can add the following script statements to the script of a button, frame, or other movie element:

```
mySound=new Sound();
mySound.attachSound("bkgdLoop");
mySound.start(0,999);
```

The script example just above does three things:

- It creates a new Sound object named `mySound`.

- It attaches the sound exported as `bkgdLoop` to the object.

- It cues the sound from its beginning and loops it 999 times.

Assume for the moment that this object controls a sound that is 4 seconds long. To loop the sound 999 times from its halfway point, you would enter:

```
mySound.start(2,999);
```

This statement uses the `secondsOffset` argument to start the 4-second sound 2 seconds (or halfway) into the file.

Another variation on this would be to use a variable to set the number of loops for a particular sound. For example:

```
loop=4
mySound.start(0,loop);
```

In this example, the variable loop is initialized to 4 and will cause the mySound object to loop four times. However, because loop is a variable, you are able to manipulate its value with ActionScript in other portions of your movie. You can create some sort of interactive controller (slider, button, keystroke, and so on) that will increase or decrease the number of times a sound will loop when it is cued.

When playing sounds via the Sound object, you'll find that you can also exert a fair amount of control in stopping sounds. Consider the following statements:

```
addASound=new Sound();
addASound.attachSound("ambient");
addASound.start();
addASound.stop();
```

This script example does the following:

- It creates a new global Sound object named addASound.

- It attaches the linked sound ambient to the object.

- It cues the sound.

- It stops all sounds in the movie (because the object is global). If the addASound object were targeted to a specific level or Movie Clip, this final statement would stop only the sounds in that target.

The stop() method will also accept an argument in its parentheses; this argument is known as soundID. The argument is available so that you can silence a specific sound by referring to its symbol identifier. Consider the following example:

```
addASound=new Sound();
addASound.attachSound("ambient");
addASound.start();
addASound.stop("ambient");
```

Here you see the same set of commands as before. The main difference is that the stop method uses an argument in its parentheses. In this case, even though addASound is a global Sound object, the only sound that will be stopped is "ambient". Because "ambient" is an attached sound, and because it is stopped explicitly, it will cease to play but leave other sounds in the movie alone.

Scripting to Control Volume and Panning

At this point, you have learned about the Sound object, how it is used, and how to cue sounds in your movie using ActionScript and the Sound object methods. The Sound object allows you to control all parameters of sound playback through scripting; this includes ActionScript techniques that can dynamically set the volume level and pan position of a sound in your movie. Using ActionScript to create different kinds of controllers or script calls, you are able to make changes to a movie's audio based on user interaction and various movie events. The best thing about this is that the changes can take place at runtime and be continually updated to match the interactive structure of your movie.

This section presents several key concepts that show you how to set volume and pan levels using ActionScript. Related to this, there are also techniques for creating audio fades and stereo effects. Like many of the examples presented in this book, these are *germ* ideas. The intention is that you grasp the basic concepts here and then take them to new heights in movies of your own. Dig in and, most of all, have fun! With the precise audio control that ActionScript adds to your movies, you will find an entirely new level of sound possibilities in Flash.

Setting Volume and Pan Levels

Volume and panning are two of the most important considerations when it comes to putting together an audio mix. By assigning each sound its proper level, you are able to create an ideal balance among all audio components of a movie: sound effects, music, dialog, and narration. Positioning a sound in the stereo field helps create an audio environment where each element has its own niche in the overall sound composition of your movie. With the help of ActionScript, this can all be done using a few simple lines of code that set the audio changes in motion.

When you manipulate volume and pan data in Flash, it is assumed that the sound you wish to affect is already playing. If a particular sound associated with the Sound object has not yet been cued, Flash will have nothing to control. However, once a sound *is* playing, you are free to use the methods of the Sound object to change its pan and volume attributes.

To set the volume level of a sound, you must use the `setVolume()` method. This method uses the dot operator to apply the volume information to the Sound object that you specify in your script. For example, to set the level of a sound to full volume, enter the following statement:

```
myObject.setVolume(100);
```

In this example, `myObject` is the name of the Sound object you will affect. This script example must be preceded by statements that create the Sound object `myObject`, attach a sound from the Library, and cue the sound using the `start()` method. Of course, these elements don't have to appear in the same script window as the `setVolume()` call, but they must be executed in the movie before you can manipulate the sound's volume.

The `setVolume()` method can also be used to control a frame-based sound in your movie once it has started playing. Sounds attached to the frames of Movie Clips or to loaded SWF files can have their volume manipulated by the Sound object as well. Consider the following example:

```
loaded=new Sound("_level1");
loaded.setVolume(50);
```

In this script, a new Sound object named `loaded` is created for the sound(s) of the SWF file playing on level 1. The `setVolume()` method lowers the level of these sounds to 50% of their total volume. Using this same syntax, the method can also target the volume of sounds in Movie Clip instances. Simply enter the target path to the clip, and the Sound object will be able to find it.

Controlling panning with ActionScript is very similar. The main difference is that the `set-Pan()` method takes both positive and negative numbers as arguments: –100 to pan hard left, and 100 to pan hard right. Consider the following script:

```
bass=new Sound();
bass.attachSound("fenderjazz");
guitar = new Sound();
guitar.attachSound ("strat");
bass.start(0,100);
bass.setPan(-75)
strat.start(0,50);
strat.setPan(75)
```

This example cues two sounds after creating objects for each and attaching sound files from the Library. After each cue, the `setPan` method is invoked to position each sound in an individual location: `bass` is panned mostly to the left, and `guitar` mostly to the right. I say *mostly* because each statement pans 75% of the sound to one speaker but leaves the remaining 25% in the opposite speaker. This pan configuration creates a fair amount of stereo separation for the sounds but still allows them to mingle and blend a bit.

> You can also use setPan() to manipulate the panning of sounds in a Movie Clip or loaded SWF file. Simply enter a target argument in the parentheses when you create the Sound object. Any methods that manipulate that Sound object will apply to the targeted Timeline.

When setting the pan position of sounds, there is no "golden rule" to follow. Your best bet is to use your ears and develop a scheme that sounds good and fits your sound design goals. Remember, to correctly hear the panned sound, you must have a two-speaker stereo setup for your computer. If you don't have access to a set of speakers, headphones are always a good way to hear the subtle details of an audio mix.

Scripting Volume Controls

Once you have mastered the basics of manipulating volume settings, it's possible to combine that knowledge with what you already know about ActionScript, and create controls for changing the volume of various sounds in a movie. In previous sections of this book, you used ActionScript to control many different parameters of graphic elements in your movie. The only difference here is that rather than use ActionScript to change the visual properties of

Movie Clips, you will use it with the Sound object methods to change the properties of audio playback.

You already know that the `setVolume()` method is the part of ActionScript used to create changes in audio level. Here you will incorporate that technique with a few basic actions inside a Movie Clip to create a simple, yet flexible and powerful, volume controller.

To get an idea of what you will be creating, open the `volumePanner.swf` file found in the Chapter 22 folder on the companion CD-ROM. Although this example doesn't cover the specifics of creating this movie's graphic component, you can take a look at the finished Timeline structure in the `volumePanner.fla` file to get an idea of how it was constructed.

To create a set of volume control buttons:

1. Prepare a couple of items before you begin working on this exercise:

   - First, you will need a sound to control. Import a sound to your movie's Library and export the sound symbol using the Linkage Properties dialog box. To learn more about importing sounds, see Chapter 20; to learn more about linking sounds, see "Attaching Sounds and Symbol Linkage" earlier in this chapter.

   - You will also need at least one button to serve as part of your volume controller. One button is sufficient because it can be used several times in the same Timeline. However, if you would like to create two buttons, you can. To learn more about creating buttons, see Chapter 13.

2. After you've set up your sound and button in step 1, begin by selecting Insert → New Symbol. Name the symbol **volume** and select Movie Clip as its behavior. Click OK, and Flash jumps into Symbol Editing mode.

3. Rename the first layer **actions** and enter seven new keyframes in the layer. Click the first keyframe and select Window → Actions (if the panel is not already visible). Enter the following statements:

```
cue=new Sound();
cue.attachSound("yourLinkedSound");
cue.start(0,100);
```

In this example, the reference `yourLinkedSound` is a placeholder based on whatever name you assigned to the sound you exported using Linkage Properties. Also, the name of the Sound object `cue` is arbitrary and can be changed if you like; just be sure to use the new name consistently throughout your scripts.

4. Click the second keyframe and display the Actions panel once again. Enter these statements:

```
cue.setVolume(100);
stop();
```

These statements set the initial volume and stop the playback head at frame 2.

5. In the remaining five keyframes, you will enter similar lines of ActionScript. See Table 22.2 for a listing of scripts and the keyframes they go in. When you have finished entering all of the statements in their various frames, you can close the Actions panel and return to the `volume` Movie Clip Timeline. The role of these statements will be explained shortly.

6. Grab a button from your movie's Library and drag it to the Stage of the `volume` Movie Clip. Drag another button to the Stage and position it near the first button. If you use different buttons, there is no need to change them once they are on the Stage. The buttons used in `volumePanner.fla` are identical, but one has been rotated 180° so that it looks different. It's not essential that the buttons look different, but it can be helpful to show which one raises the volume and which one lowers it.

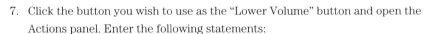

7. Click the button you wish to use as the "Lower Volume" button and open the Actions panel. Enter the following statements:

```
on(release){
    if(_currentFrame<7){
        nextFrame();
    }
}
```

When this button is clicked, the script checks to see the position of the playback head in the Movie Clip. If it is sitting at a frame number less than 7, the clip is told to advance a frame using the `nextFrame()` action. Your `volume` Movie Clip has seven frames. Once the clip is sitting in frame 7, it doesn't advance if the button is clicked, since 7 is not less than seven. Also, because each frame contains both a `stop()` action and a statement that sets a new volume level, every new frame that is encountered both halts the playback of the clip and updates the volume level of the Sound object.

KEYFRAME	ACTIONSCRIPT
3	`stop();` `cue.setVolume(80);`
4	`stop();` `cue.setVolume(60);`
5	`stop();` `cue.setVolume(40);`
6	`stop();` `cue.setVolume(20);`
7	`stop();` `cue.setVolume(0);`

Table 22.2

Keyframe Actions for the Volume Movie Clip

8. Click the button you wish to use as the "Raise Volume" button and open the Actions panel. Enter the following statements:

```
on(release){
    if(_currentFrame>2){
        prevFrame();
    }
}
```

This button works in a similar fashion to the Lower Volume button. Each time the button is clicked, the script checks the current frame where the clip is stopped. If it is a frame greater than 2, the playback head moves to the preceding frame number, or to the left across the Timeline. Because the `setVolume` statements increase in value from right to left, the Sound object volume is gradually raised as the head moves closer to frame 2.

9. Close the Actions panel and return to your movie's main Timeline. Grab an instance of the `volume` Movie Clip and drag it from the Library to the Stage. At this point, there is no need to assign an instance name to the clip. Select Control → Test Movie to give this controller a spin. As you click the Lower Volume button, you should hear the sound level drop; conversely, the Raise Volume button should increase the volume of the sound.

Creating Audio Fade-Ins and Fade-Outs

What exactly is a *fade-in* or *fade-out*? It's an audio effect that gradually raises or lowers the volume of a sound to either ease it up to full volume or taper it off to silence. As you've probably already guessed, fade-ins and -outs require you to manipulate the volume of a sound as you did to create a volume controller. This is true, but with one exception: Fades are gradual effects; once you set them in motion, they happen slowly over time. To create a fade, you must design a Movie Clip structure that can gradually take a sound from one volume extreme to another in a single step, rather than with the individual mouse clicks you used to create volume controls.

Open the file `fadeInOut.swf` or `fadeInOut.fla` from the Chapter 22 folder on the companion CD-ROM. Play around with the fade-in and fade-out buttons to see and hear exactly what happens with a fade controller. The process of creating a fade is simple, and, based on what you already know about volume controls, you should easily grasp the concepts behind a fade controller.

To create controls that fade a sound in and out:

1. Prepare a couple of items before you begin working on this exercise:

    • Here again, you need a sound to control. Import a sound to your movie's Library and export the sound symbol using the Linkage Properties dialog box. To learn more about importing sounds, see Chapter 20; to learn more about linking sounds, see "Attaching Sounds with Linkage Identifiers" earlier in this chapter.

    • You will need at least one button to serve as part of your fade controller. One button is sufficient because it can be used several times in the same Timeline. However, if you would like to create two buttons, you can. To learn more about creating buttons, see Chapter 13.

2. Begin by selecting Insert → New Symbol. Name the symbol **fader** and select Movie Clip as its behavior. Click OK, and Flash jumps into Symbol Editing mode.

3. Rename the first layer **actions** and enter 12 new keyframes in the layer (you should have a total of 13 in the entire clip). Click the first keyframe and select Window → Actions to display the Actions panel (if it is not already visible). Enter the following statements:

```
cue=new Sound();
cue.attachSound("yourLinkedSound");
cue.start(0,100);
cue.setVolume(100);
```

In this example, the reference yourLinkedSound is a placeholder based on whatever name you assigned to the sound you exported using Linkage Properties. Also, the name of the Sound object cue is arbitrary and can be changed if you like; just be sure to use the new name consistently throughout your scripts.

4. Click the keyframe at frame 2 and enter a stop() action in the Actions panel. The remaining 11 keyframes will need fairly repetitive and similar actions. See Table 22.3 for a listing of each keyframe and its corresponding action.

This step completes your work for the fader Movie Clip. If you looked at the fadeInOut.fla file on the CD, you will notice that there some graphic enhancements to the clip. These are optional, however, and won't influence the functionality of the Movie Clip in your movie. Close the Actions panel and switch back to Movie Editing mode and your main Timeline.

KEYFRAME	ACTIONSCRIPT
3	cue.setVolume(80);
4	cue.setVolume(60);
5	cue.setVolume(40);
6	cue.setVolume(20);
7	cue.setVolume(0);
8	stop();
9	cue.setVolume(20);
10	cue.setVolume(40);
11	cue.setVolume(60);
12	cue.setVolume(80);
13	cue.setVolume(100); gotoAndStop(2);

Table 22.3

Keyframe Actions for the Fader Movie Clip

5. Drag the fader Movie Clip to your Stage and assign it the instance name fade in the Property Inspector.

As it appears on the CD-ROM, fadeInOut.swf has a simple graphic element that represents an LED volume meter. This can be added if you desire but is not totally necessary. If you followed the preceding, the clip won't have any sort of significant graphical representation—only a hollow circle to serve as a placeholder for the clip. The fade instance (as described in this lesson) is what you call a *sound-only Movie Clip*, meaning that the clip has sound(s), frame(s), and, in most cases, some ActionScript. Sound-only clips can be targeted just like any other kind of clip; the only difference is that they don't have any kind of visual animated components.

6. Create a new layer in the main Timeline and name it **buttons**. Drag two buttons to this layer of the Stage to serve as your fade-in and fade-out controls. If necessary, change one of the two buttons graphically so that it is distinguishable from the other.

7. Select the fade-out button and open the Actions panel. Enter the following statements:

```
on(release){
    _root.fade.gotoAndPlay(3);
}
```

This script targets the clip instance `fade` when the button is clicked and sends it to play at frame 3. The clip is sent to frame 3 because this is the button used to fade a sound out. Frame 3 is the frame where the volume begins to decrease (see Table 22.3). Notice, however, that there is no `stop()` action until the clip reaches frame 8. Between frames 3 and 8, the `setVolume()` method gradually decreases the volume of the sound. Then, once it has been set to a level of 0, the clip is stopped.

8. Select the fade-in button and open the Actions panel. Enter the following statements:

```
on(release){
    _root.fade.gotoAndPlay(9);
}
```

This script targets the clip instance `fade` when the button is clicked and sends it to play at frame 9. The reason should be clear. At frame 9, the volume is set to a level of 20; at frame 10, a level of 40; and so on. When the volume finally reaches a level of 100 at frame 13, the clip is sent to frame 2 and told to stop. It will sit there until another button click executes a script that runs it through the fade-in or fade-out animation once again.

9. Select Control → Test Movie and give your fade controller a try.

After testing this Movie Clip, you may find that the fade is either too short or too long for your purposes. You can fix this easily because there are a couple of strategies for tweaking the length of a fade.

If your fade is too short, do one of the following:

• Create a longer animation. If you put a greater distance between the keyframes that set volume levels, it will take Flash longer to execute the animation.

• Adjust your volume levels in smaller increments. In this exercise, you adjusted the sound in increments of 20%. Adjusting the volume in chunks of 5% or 2% will create a longer, more gradual fade effect.

If you wish to *shorten* a fade (that is, decrease its length), simply reverse either of the techniques for lengthening the fade.

Scripting Pan Controls

Another important element of audio control is *panning.* By placing sounds in the stereo field, you can create a sense of space in the "world" of your movie. Panning assigns a source location to ambient sound effects and allows you to balance the positioning of multiple music tracks. And with the help of some additional ActionScript, the Sound object can be used to create controllers that dynamically adjust the pan position of a particular sound.

The finished file described in this exercise is the same that you used if you worked with the volume control buttons. If you haven't yet seen and heard this movie, open the `volumePanner.swf` or `volumePanner.fla` file found in the Chapter 22 folder on the companion CD-ROM. In addition to the volume button controls, there is a slider that, when moved left or right, adjusts the panning of the movie's sound accordingly. This exercise assumes that you are already familiar with the basics of creating a slider type of controller. If you would like to learn more about this topic, see Chapter 16.

To create a stereo pan controller:

1. Prepare a couple of items before you begin working on this exercise:

    * You need a sound to control; for this exercise, either a mono or stereo sound will do. However, since you will be manipulating the pan position, a mono sound really makes the most sense. Import a sound to your movie's Library and export the sound symbol using the Linkage Properties dialog box. To learn more about importing sounds, see Chapter 20; to learn more about linking sounds, see "Attaching Sounds with Linkage Identifiers" earlier in this chapter.

    * You will need one button to serve as the knob of your slider. To learn more about creating buttons, see Chapter 13.

2. Begin by selecting Insert ➜ New Symbol. Name the symbol **slider** and select Movie Clip as its behavior. Click OK, and Flash jumps into Symbol Editing mode.

3. Drag the button to the Stage of the `slider` Movie Clip and use the Align panel to position it in the exact middle of the Stage. Click the button and choose Window ➜ Actions to display the Actions panel (if it is not already visible). Enter the following statements in the window:

```
on(press){
    startDrag("",false,l,t,r,b);
    drag=true;
}
on(release,releaseOutside){
    stopDrag();
    drag=false;
}
```

These statements help to define the parameters of the slider. For a full explanation of what each line accomplishes, see Chapter16. Close the Actions panel and return to Movie Editing mode.

4. Now you are ready to begin putting together the components of the slider controller. Create a new layer in the main Timeline and name it **panner**. Then drag the `slider` Movie Clip to the Stage. Draw a horizontal line 100 pixels long on the layer beneath the `panner` layer. (You can use the Info panel to confirm the length.) This guide line is the other graphic component of the slider. Position it so that it is directly behind the `slider` clip, making sure that the two elements have their centers aligned (see Figure 22.3).

Pan information in Flash can have a maximum value of 100. By using a graphic that is 100 pixels long, you guarantee that it will always be positioned beneath the slider knob when it is moved, and the pan values will be updated accurately.

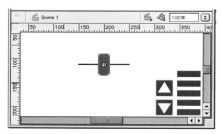

Figure 22.3

The pan slider knob (`slider` Movie Clip) should have its guide line positioned behind it with the centers aligned.

5. With the major graphic elements in place, you can now get to the sound elements of this movie. You will create a new Movie Clip that is a sound-only clip. It will have one purpose: to cue a sound to play in this movie.

Select Insert → New Symbol. Give the symbol a name and set its behavior to Movie Clip. In this new Movie Clip, insert two keyframes in the first layer. In frame 1, attach the following actions:

```
cue=new Sound();
cue.attachSound("yourLinkedSound");
cue.start(0, 100);
```

If you are looking at the `volumePanner.fla` file found on the CD-ROM, the Sound object is created in the `volume` Movie Clip.

Again, `"yourLinkedSound"` is a placeholder for the sound you exported from your movie's Library.

In the second keyframe, attach a `stop()` action. This series of ActionScript commands creates a Sound object, attaches a sound from the Library, and plays the sound (all in frame 1). When the clip finishes executing these statements and moves to frame 2, it is stopped but the sound continues to play.

Return to Movie Editing mode and drag the clip onto the Stage of the main Timeline. Use the Instance panel and assign the instance name **audio** for the clip. This will allow you to target the clip so that you can control the panning of the sound it contains.

6. Now that you have a sound set to play, you can write the ActionScript necessary to make the slider control the sound's pan position. Highlight the `slider` Movie Clip and open the Actions panel. Enter the following statements:

```
onClipEvent(load){
    t=_y;
    b=_y;
    l=_x-50;
    r=_x+50;
    mid=_x;
}
onClipEvent(enterFrame){
    if(drag==true){
        _root.audio.cue.setPan((_x-mid)*2);
    }
}
```

These statements do two things. In the first chunk, within the `onClipEvent(load)` handler, the bounds for the slider are set when it is first loaded into memory at runtime. To set the horizontal bounds of the slider, you use the `_x` property plus or minus 50. This allows the slider to move from the middle of the guide line to either the right or left edge. The variable `mid` stores the original horizontal location of the clip when it loads.

The second chunk of script is monitored on every `enterFrame` event. If the clip is being dragged, it executes a statement that pans the sound in your movie. This third line targets the sound using an absolute path from the main Timeline and uses the `setPan` method to control the sound's left or right speaker position. The expression `((_x-mid)*2)` returns a value between –100 and 100 based on the clip's current horizontal position in the movie. It subtracts the starting position (`mid`) from the current position (`_x`) and multiplies that by 2. Since the value for `_x` lies between –50 and 50, the expression will always return –100 to 100.

7. The pan slider is now complete! Select Control → Test Movie to give it a try.

The preceding script example contains one slight difference from the `volumePanner.fla` file. In that demo file, the instance name of the Movie Clip that cues the audio is `volumeControl`. Rather than target the clip instance named `audio`, it targets `volumeControl`. The two movies will perform the same, even with a difference in clip names.

Scripting Special Effects

The setTransform() method is your key to creating interesting stereo effects in Flash. Like the other techniques presented in this chapter, setTransform() can be combined with other ActionScript elements to create a dynamic means of controlling or creating the effect. This example presents the steps required to do just that.

On the companion CD-ROM, you will find three files in the Chapter 22 folder: set-Transformer.fla, setTransformer.swf, and stereoEffect.fla. You can open either of the setTransformer files to see how this all looks and sounds once it is completed. However, to go through the exercise presented here, you will need to open the stereoEffect.fla file and save it to your computer's hard drive so that you can work with it. Many of the details have already been completed so that you can focus on the more important scripting issues at hand. Open the file, save it locally, and let's get to work!

To create a dynamically controllable stereo effect:

1. Let's assume that you already have all of your movie components in place. In the case of this exercise, you do. There is a Movie Clip on the Stage that is draggable; you will create an effect such that moving the clip to the left or right will change the stereo composition of the movie's sound. The first thing you need to do is get some sounds going in your movie.

   In the main Timeline, create a new keyframe in the first frame of the layer named actions. Open the Actions panel and enter the following statements:

   ```
   1  sfx = new Sound();
   2  sfx.attachSound("stereo");
   3  sfx.start(0, 100);
   4  xfadr = new Object();
   5  xfadr.ll = 50;
   6  xfadr.lr = 25;
   7  xfadr.rr = 50;
   8  xfadr.rl = 25;
   9  sfx.setTransform(xfadr);
   ```

   Here is what is happening with this code: Statements 1 through 3 create a Sound object named sfx, attach a sound to it, and cue the sound. Note that a sound has already been exported for you under the name stereo. If you were creating this from scratch, you would have to go through the steps of exporting the sound from the Library yourself.

   Statement 4 creates a new generic object called xfadr. This object will be used as our transformer, and hold the effect information you wish to apply to the sound object sfx. Statements 5 through 8 initialize values for the properties of the transformer. The final statement applies the transformer object properties (stored in xfadr) to the sfx Sound object.

The stereo effect you will script here creates different balances between the contents of the left and right channels of a stereo sound file. When the clip is positioned at its extreme left, you will hear 100% of the sound's left channel. At the extreme right, you will hear 100% of the right channel. In the middle (where the settings were initialized), you will hear a 50/50 balance between left and right. You will also hear 25% of the right channel in the left speaker, and 25% of the left channel in the right speaker. As the Movie Clip is moved toward the extreme left or right, though, these values will slowly decrease to 0 so that there is no bleed across stereo channels. See Table 22.4 for a breakdown of channel levels relative to clip position.

CLIP _X POSITION	LL LEVEL	LR LEVEL	RR LEVEL	RL LEVEL
0	100	0	0	0
100	75	12.5	25	12.5
200	50	25	50	25
300	25	12.5	75	12.5
400	0	0	100	0

Table 22.4

Horizontal Position of Movie Clip Relative to Percentages of Stereo Channel Levels

2. Create another new keyframe in frame 2 of the **actions** layer and attach a **stop()** action to the frame. The ActionScript commands in these two frames will get the sound going and apply the initial stereo effect in frame 1, and will then stop the movie in frame 2 while the sound continues to play. With all of this in place, you can script the actions that will interactively manipulate the **setTransform()** effect.

3. Click the red sphere sitting in the middle of the Stage and select Window → Actions to display the Actions panel. You will see that some script has already been entered. It is there to set the drag parameters of the clip. Look at the script if you wish, but you will not need to make any changes for this exercise.

Enter the following statements in the window below the existing script:

```
1   onClipEvent(enterFrame){
2       if(drag==true){
3           _root.xfadr.ll=(400-_x)/4;
4           _root.xfadr.rr=_x/4;
5           if(_x>mid){
6               _root.xfadr.lr=Math.abs(((_x-mid)/8)-25);
7               _root.xfadr.rl=Math.abs(((_x-mid)/8)-25);
8           }else{
9           _root.xfadr.lr=_x/8;
10          _root.xfadr.rl=_x/8;
11          }
12      }
13      _root.sfx.setTransform(_root.xfadr);
14  }
```

Let's break this down bit by bit so that it doesn't look so abstract:

Line 1 The `enterFrame` handler continually monitors the position of the Movie Clip and updates values for the `sfx` (`transformer`) object.

Line 2 This `if` conditional executes statements only if the Movie Clip is being dragged across the Stage.

Lines 3–4 The Movie Clip has bounds of 400 pixels. These statements set values for the `ll` and `rr` properties using expressions to return a value based on the clip's current position. As the clip moves to the left, `ll` gets closer to a value of 100 and `rr` drops toward 0. As it moves right, `rr` is incremented toward 100 and `ll` decreases proportionately. Since the `xfadr` object was created on the main Timeline, it is necessary to use the `_root` reference to target the object and its properties correctly. The same holds true for references later in this script to the `sfx` object (also created at the `_root` level).

Line 5 The values of the `lr` and `rl` properties for creating this effect are a little strange. Both properties have values that start at 25 (see Table 22.4) and then drop to zero as the clip is moved 200 pixels in either direction from its starting point. Because the draggable clip in this movie starts at `_x` position 200 (stored in the variable `mid`), there is an `if` conditional to accommodate the math needed to create each value.

Lines 6–7 These expressions generate values for the `lr` and `rl` properties if the clip is past the `mid` variable point (200). Refer back to Table 22.4 to see the corresponding values between Movie Clip position and Stage pixel coordinates. Some values generate a negative number, so the `Math.abs()` method is used to convert all values to positive integers. You can read more about the Math object and its methods in the ActionScript Reference section.

Lines 9–10 In the `else` condition for the `if` statement, the expression `_x/8` produces a value for the `lr` and `rl` properties if they are *not* greater than `mid` (meaning less than 200).

Line 13 This statement, which makes it all happen, targets the `sfx` object on the main Timeline and applies the property information of the `xfadr` object via the `setTransform()` method.

4. Close the Actions panel and select Control ➔ Test Movie. Drag the sphere from side to side and listen to how it changes. As the clip moves to the left, you hear less of the right channel, and the left channel plays exclusively in the left speaker. The opposite is true when you drag the clip to the right.

So what happens next? How can this be used in a *real* movie? Let's say that you were creating a game in which a character could explore a world that is populated with ambient sounds and music. This technique would allow you to manipulate their playback so that, depending on the character's position in the world, the character would hear the nearest sounds clearly, while others would be slightly obscured.

This stereo technique could also be used to dynamically change the sound-effects track of an animation. Perhaps you are animating a propeller plane. As the plane gets "closer," the sound becomes louder; if it's on one side of the Stage or another, you can hear the sound in that channel at a higher volume. In this situation, you could script the sound controls so that the animation is autonomous and controls the sounds according to its playback. Or everything (both animation and sounds) could be controlled solely by audience input.

Loading External Sounds with ActionScript

One of the most compelling new features of Flash MX is its ability to load external MP3 sound files. Rather than include a sound or group of sounds in your movie, you may now leave them outside your movie and call them in as needed.

This approach presents several advantages. First, sounds always add to the size of your final SWF file. So keeping sounds outside the final movie allow it to be smaller and may help it load more quickly. Additionally, because using external files cuts down significantly on movie file size, you'll be able to use a Library of sounds from which your audience can pick and choose. If they want to browse your movie while listening to classical music, reggae, western swing…whatever, you can give them a host of files to choose from and then load the appropriate soundtrack for each visitor. External sounds can be loaded into a Flash MX movie from any location on the Internet. This means it's also possible to use Flash to create a forum for MP3 playback. Your audience can share the URLs of sounds they would like you and others to hear, making your movie a sort of MP3 jukebox.

The list of other possibilities goes on and on. As always, Flash is limited only by your time, budget, and creativity. To help you accomplish these new feats, ActionScript's Sound object has been given several new terms, including these:

Sound.loadSound("*url*",*stream*) Used to load external sounds into the specified Sound object. `loadSound()` takes two arguments. Enter the external sound's URL as a string, and enter a Boolean value for `stream`. A setting of `false` means that the sound must load entirely before it can begin playback; `true` makes the sound a streaming sound, and it will begin to play once a sufficient amount has been downloaded.

Sound.getBytesLoaded() Used to monitor the number of bytes in an external sound that have been loaded into the specified Sound object.

Sound.getBytesTotal() Returns the total number of bytes for the specified Sound object. You can use the methods `getBytesLoaded()` and `getBytesTotal()`to create preloaders for external sound files.

Now that you are familiar with some of the new Sound object terms, you can get down to business. To make the following introductory procedure as simple as possible, we have prepared a starter file for you on the companion CD-ROM. Go to the Chapter 22 folder and open the file loadMP3.fla; copy it to your computer's desktop. Several additional steps have already been completed so that you can focus on the most important aspects of this technique.

To load an external sound:

1. First, you must have a remote MP3 file that you can load. We recommend that you start with something small so that while you're testing this procedure, you don't waste a lot of time waiting for a large file to load. Upload an MP3 file to your web server and be sure to write down the file's URL.

If you don't have a web server or an MP3 file to use, we have provided one for you. Use the following URL to link to the file savvySound.mp3 at www.vonflashenstein.com/resources/savvySound.mp3.

2. In the loadMP3.fla file, select the first (and only) keyframe of Layer 1. Choose Window → Actions (F9) to open the Actions panel. You'll see something that resembles Figure 22.4.

3. In line 2, notice the phrase "enterYourURLHere." Replace that phrase with the absolute URL of the MP3 file you want to load into your movie. An absolute URL is written as http://www.*myDomain.com*/file.mp3, where *myDomain.com* is the name of your domain and *file.mp3* is the name of your MP3 file.

   Line 1 creates the Sound object load1. Line 2 uses the loadSound() method to load the external file you just specified. false, an argument to loadSound(), determines that the loaded sound will behave like an event sound and must be completely loaded into memory before it can begin its playback. Line 3 initializes the variable audio to False (this will be used later on).

4. Select the status Movie Clip on your movie's Stage (Figure 22.5). Open the Actions panel (if it is not already open). The ActionScript attached to the status instance, shown here, is responsible for monitoring the progress of the loading sound.

```
1  onClipEvent (enterFrame) {
2    if (_root.audio == false) {
3      if (_root.load1.getBytesTotal() > 0 && _root.load1.getBytesLoaded() == _root.load1.getBytesTotal()) {
4        _root.status.gotoAndStop(7);
5        _root.load1.start();
6        _root.audio = true;
7      } else {
8        loadBytes = Math.round(_root.load1.getBytesLoaded() / 1024);
9        loadTotal = Math.round(_root.load1.getBytesTotal() / 1024);
10       percent = Math.round((loadBytes / loadTotal) * 100);
11       loadBytes_txt = loadBytes;
12       loadTotal_txt = loadTotal;
13       percent_txt = percent + "%";
14     }
15   }
16 }
```

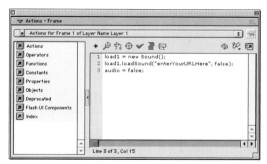

Figure 22.4

The actions for the first keyframe of the loadMP3.fla **file. You'll enter the URL for your external sound within the quotes of the** loadSound **statement.**

Figure 22.5

The status **Movie Clip**

Let's examine this script line by line:

Line 1 The handler onClipEvent(enterFrame) checks the statements in this script continually every time a frame is played.

Line 2 Because the variable audio was created on the main Timeline, it must be referenced using _root. This variable works as a sort of lynchpin. If it is False, the sound is still in the process of loading. Once the sound has been loaded, Line 6 resets the variable to True.

Line 3 This conditional statement checks the status of the sound while it's loading. It tests two things: whether the total byte count of the sound is greater than 0 and whether the bytes that have been loaded are equal to the total number of bytes. Only when both of these statements are true will the script proceed with lines 4–6.

It's good to check whether *Sound*.getBytesTotal() is greater than zero. This helps prevent a sound that's slow to load from jumping the gun. If the sound hasn't loaded at all, it contains 0 bytes. Because it has loaded 0 bytes and contains 0 bytes, the statement 0==0 will obviously return true, and Flash will think that the sound has loaded completely.

Lines 4–6 When the sound is completely loaded, these statements update the status instance by sending it to frame 7 for a change of appearance, cueing the load1 Sound object, and setting the audio variable to True to prevent the sound from being cued repeatedly, now that it has loaded into your movie.

Lines 8–13 If the sound hasn't loaded completely into load1, a series of alternative statements will execute to show the load progress:

loadBytes is a variable storing the number of loaded bytes.

> **loadTotal** is a variable storing the number of total bytes.
>
> **percent** stores the percentage of the sound that has loaded.
>
> **loadBytes_txt** is a text field variable that displays the current value of loadBytes.
>
> **loadTotal_txt** is a text field variable that displays the current value of loadTotal.
>
> **percent_txt** is a text field variable that displays the current value of percent.

Lines 8 and 9 use the `Math.round()` method to round the byte count to the nearest integer. Values are divided by 1,024 to give the kilobyte count.

5. Select Control → Test Movie to give the loaded sound a try. As the sound is loading, the gray and white wheel should spin, and the text fields should print a numeric display of the loading sound's progress. Once the sound has finished loading, the spinning wheel becomes a green dot, and the text display beside it changes to read "playing."

If your movie doesn't work properly right away, here are a few things to check:

- Be sure you are connected to the Internet.
- Check the speed of your connection. A busy network will slow the loading process.
- Be certain that your URL to the external sound is correct.

This section has given you just a glimpse of the possibilities offered by external sounds. To learn about additional ActionScript terms that can enhance your movies and their ability to work with external sounds, see the Sound object section of the ActionScript Reference section.

Inspirational Design Model

Creating a truly interactive audio experience is a very difficult thing to do, not so much from a technical angle but from a point of communication. The designer's greatest task is deciding how to make the sound interactive while ensuring that it still works synergistically with the movie's graphic components. Even for movies that offer very little graphic interest, there is still a need for some sort of control source that allows an audience to manipulate the interactive audio.

Visit `www.pianographique.com` (see Figure 22.6). This site features work by Jean-luc Lamarque and a group of other musicians and multimedia artists. You'll find a collection of intriguing interactive audio movies. Not only is the music engaging, but it works very, very well with the visual content to create an immersive, interactive experience that you may want to explore for hours.

Figure 22.6

"Angular entropy," with code by Jean-luc Lamarque and sound and graphics by Jean Pehuet and Xavier Pehuet. This piece was created in Flash and is an exceptional example of the possibilities of interactive sound and imagery.

Summary

You are sound savvy. This chapter completes the discussion of sound topics for now. With all the particulars covered in this part of the book, you have been introduced to basic digital audio concepts and have run through the steps of preparing audio files for the Flash environment. You learned how to work with sound in Flash, in terms of both getting sound into your movies and syncing it with different kinds of animations. In this chapter, you raised the bar a notch and started to explore the possibilities of sound control and manipulation using ActionScript.

You were introduced to the Sound object: its nature, its function, and the ActionScript terms or methods it understands. You learned how to cue and silence sounds, set their volume and pan information, and create interesting effects with stereo sound files. Also, using elements of ActionScript that are not sound related, you learned how to create several different kinds of audio controllers for manipulating volume, panning, creating fades, and adjusting stereo sound balance. In the next part of the book, you will put much of this knowledge together to create an interactive, multitrack audio movie that loads quickly in a low-bandwidth environment.

Flash MX Savvy Color Gallery

This section is a full-color gallery of the best and brightest creations in the wonderful world of Flash. Designed as a source of awe and inspiration, the gallery includes a wealth of examples from the most creative, cutting-edge Flash designers around. What you will see here is just a glimpse of the masterful work exhibited by a few select designers and developers. If you like what you see, visit the actual websites to experience these pieces firsthand.

Becoming Human (www.becominghuman.com)

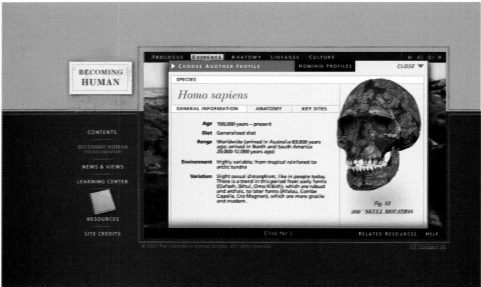

TOP: Developed jointly by **NeonSky Creative Media** (www.neonsky.com) and **Terra Incognita** (www.terraincognita.com) for the Arizona State Institute for Human Origins, Becoming Human is an original interactive Flash documentary that explores human evolution from our earliest ancestors to the emergence of *Homo sapiens*. **BOTTOM:** Becoming Human features a host of innovative and interactive tools (such as interactive exhibits) that allow you to go beyond the Flash documentary itself and pursue your personal exploration into the fascinating world of human evolution.

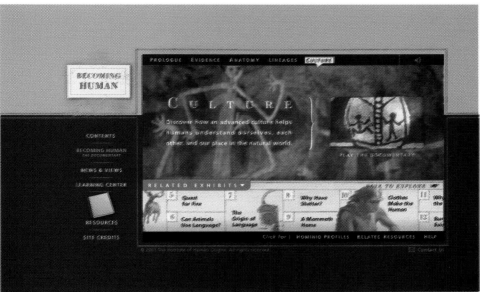

TOP: Becoming Human is partitioned into several sections that allow you to explore questions about culture, hominid anatomy, archaeological evidence, and lineage. Each section features not only a spectacular linear Flash documentary narrated by the prestigious paleoanthropologist Dr. Donald Johanson, but also topical discussions by many other prominent scholars in the field of human evolution. **BOTTOM:** The combination of the linear documentary and the interactive exploratory tools (both of which are created totally in Flash) makes Becoming Human one of the most interesting, innovative, and cutting-edge Flash creations out there.

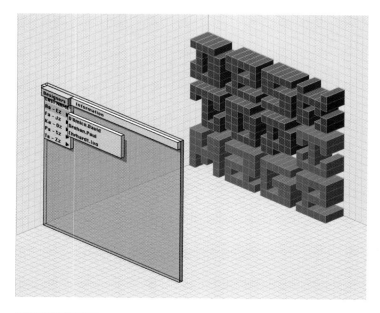

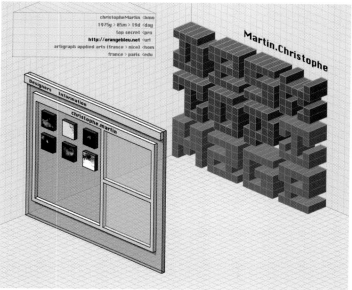

TOP: Conceived and designed by **Michael Sten** with programming help from **Otty Soemitro**, DesktopImage is dedicated solely to the free distribution of high-quality desktop images created by talented graphic designers and digital artists. **BOTTOM:** The DesktopImage site features a very innovative three-dimensional isometric interface that creatively emulates an early Macintosh graphic user interface.

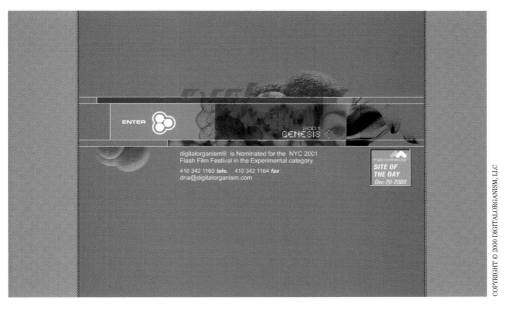

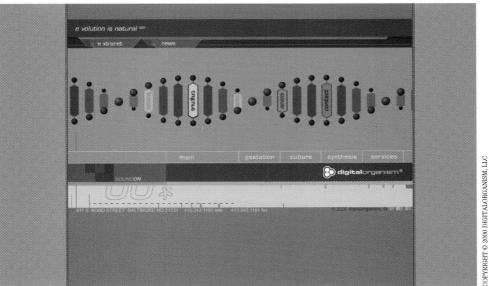

TOP: Through the use of inspirational digital content and innovative design, **digitalorganism**, a full-service multimedia and design studio based in Baltimore, strives to merge cutting-edge aesthetics with functionality to advance corporate identity and branding. **BOTTOM:** digital-organism's interface, the center of which is a stunning 3D DNA menu system, is remarkably stylish and sleek. Exploration is made easy and entertaining by the site's immersive, integrated navigation system.

Djojostudios (www.djojo.com)

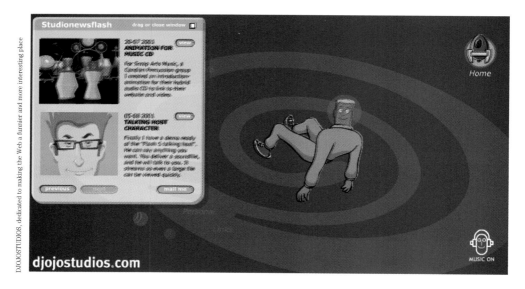

TOP: Many of Djojostudios's creations tend toward character animation. One of the most recent is a wonderfully conceived and illustrated Talking Host character that will "speak" any audio file uploaded by the user. **BOTTOM:** Taking the interactive, animated character one step farther, Djojostudios is in the process of creating an experimental online experience (www.djojo.com) that stars Djojo himself. Once completed, the new site will feature a dynamic environment that changes depending on the time of day and the mood of Djojo himself. Users will be able to interact with Djojo and enjoy regularly scheduled programs starring—you guessed it—Djojo himself.

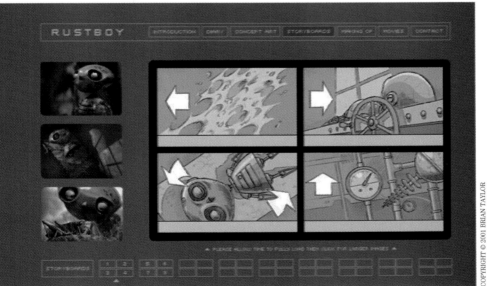

T O P : Created by the talented **Brian Taylor** (whose other work can be seen at www.15design.com), Rustboy is a promotional site for a short film of the same name that is currently being created and will ultimately be distributed online and on DVD. Rustboy (the primary character of the film) originally began life as a simple 2D creation but has since been thrust into the glorious world of 3D. **B O T T O M :** The site, which is a great example of simple but stylish design, features a constantly updated diary on the current Rustboy milestones, beautifully illustrated storyboards and concept art, short QuickTime teasers, and insights into the creation of the film. The site perfectly captures the slightly dark feeling of Rustboy (and the world in which he lives).

Moccu (www.moccu.com)

TOP: Located in Berlin, **Moccu**, which was founded in 2000, is a full-featured digital design studio that specializes in Flash- and Generator-based web design, interfaces, animation, applications, entertainment, and interactive storytelling. Their projects have included interface and animation design for a proposed touch-screen gas pump, an online recruiting game for Challenge Unlimited, and an online banking portal. **BOTTOM:** Beyond the stylish graphic design, Moccu's most interesting feature is its 3D environmental interface. While the vast majority of advanced Flash interface design conforms to a 2D computerlike GUI model, Moccu has created an innovative interface that emulates an integrated 3D space.

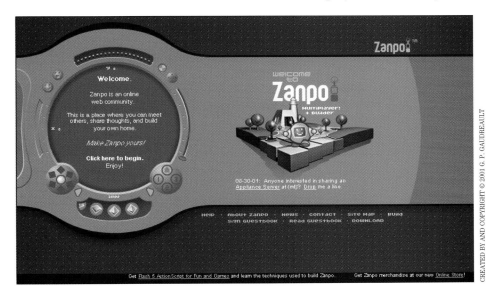

TOP: G. P. Gaudreault originally created Zanpo with the humble goal of putting his portfolio online. The results of his labor have yielded something quite spectacular: a multiuser, web-based world where inhabitants can share ideas and stories and build their own online home. As a result, the Zanpo community is a constantly evolving virtual society. **BOTTOM:** The Zanpo online community is built around a grid format. All pathways and structures conform to a set configuration of square tiles. On top of this framework, users can construct their own home that will be visible to the entire Zanpo community. It's also possible for citizens of Zanpo to leave messages, hyperlinks, and other bits of information they would like to share with the rest of the community.

Once Upon a Forest (www.once-upon-a-forest.com)

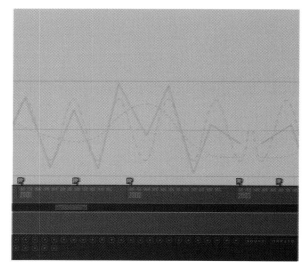

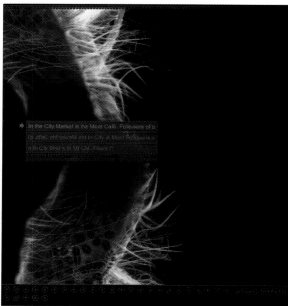

TOP: The website Once Upon a Forest hosts a collection of interesting and explorative inter-active work by **Joshua Davis**. Although the content ranges broadly, you are sure to find thought-provoking pieces of interactive art. This website changes and updates its content frequently; consequently, pieces that you see during one visit may not be available during your next visit. Many of Davis's works feature elegant, intuitive interfaces. This piece demonstrates a scrolling calendar or timeline. **BOTTOM:** This movie presents an interesting ambient music track and allows its audience to enter text into the work itself. Through the use of some clever ActionScript, the text is deconstructed and used as a kind of texture to enhance the mysteriously beautiful background graphic.

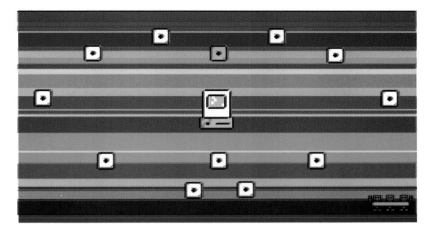

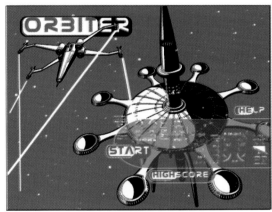

T O P : Hands down, this is one of the most inviting game sites on the Web. The folks at **Hui Hui** have really got something special going here. The funky interface and design have a very retro feel and are a welcome alternative to the cyberpunk stylings of so many sites. **B O T T O M :** You can use the drag-and-drop interface to "load" diskettes into the computer and launch the various games offered at this site. Featured here are the games "Orbiter" and "Squash."

Curious Media (www.curiousmedia.com)

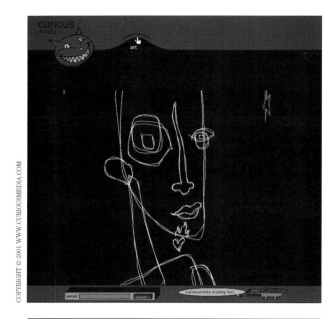

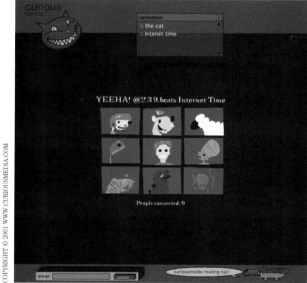

TOP: **Randy Jamison's** Curious Media website features one of the most interesting and playful interface concepts around. All menu items are found by "peeking" beneath the gray curtain. Notice in this image how the link to "art" is exposed. BOTTOM: The animated short "Internet Time" tells the story of nine Internet users from around the globe who enjoy spending time in their favorite chat room. Reference to a popular American sitcom makes this piece especially funny.

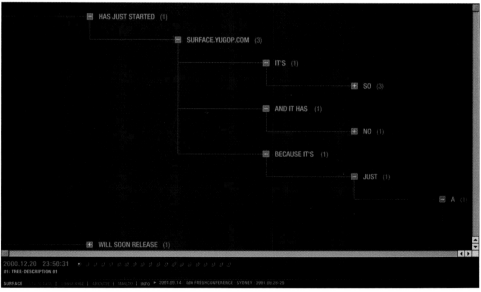

TOP: **Yugo Nakamura** is one of the most talked-about interactive designers currently on the scene. He maintains a site called "MONO*crafts" (www.yugop.com), where he showcases his interactive creations. The content of the site covers a wide range of interactive possibilities. All things considered, his work can be described as organic, malleable, and open to personalization by its audience. **BOTTOM:** Yugo's interface designs are fluid and intuitive; don't expect to see anything very similar to conventional buttons or navigational widgets. His site features interactive studies and experimental works of digital media and design.

Camp Chaos (www.campchaos.com)

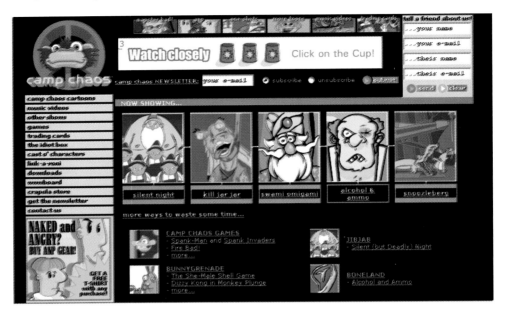

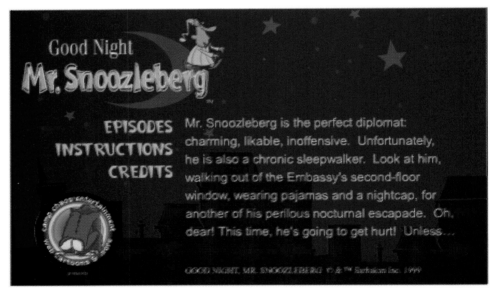

TOP: Are Flash-based interactive games and cartoons a blessing or a curse? It's just too easy to spend hours in front of your favorite web toon or game and forget all about tomorrow's deadlines. **Camp Chaos** offers a unique blend of edgy humor and biting social commentary that is sure to provide a welcome respite from the doldrums of your 9-to-5 gig. (Note this site is not for all ages or sensibilities.) **BOTTOM:** If you are especially interested in whiling away the afternoons in the blissful repose of Flash-based games, check out Camp Chaos's "Timekillers" via the "Games" link. Here you'll find Sarbakan's "Goodnight Mr. Snoozleberg" (see Chapter 14's "Inspirational Design Model") among other interactive delights.

TOP: The African Voices exhibit was developed by the Smithsonian Institution in Washington, D.C., to document the richness of Africa and its people. The African Voices website was created by both the **Smithsonian Institution** and **Terra Incognita** to bring portions of the live exhibit to the Web. Flash and ActionScript are used extensively to present information dynamically in an easily accessible format. **BOTTOM:** The site features a section on the history of the people of Africa, from the dawn of humankind to the present time. Timelines are employed throughout the site's interactive interface to help present a story that spans thousands of years.

African Voices (www.mnh.si.edu/africanvoices)

TOP: African living spaces are the foundations of family and community. Even in times of change and upheaval, they are places of history, warmth, and beauty that create connections among people and generations. The site focuses on the realities of living on one of the most diverse and complex continents in the world. **BOTTOM:** One of the most interesting interactive features of the African Voices site is the ability to tour an African marketplace and be introduced to the merchants and artisans who conduct business at the Makola market in Accra, Ghana. You can read about their trade and hear the sounds of the burgeoning marketplace.

Creating Dynamic Soundtracks with DoReMedia Sound Families

If you are a designer who wishes to make your Flash creations come alive with sound effects and music, the cards are certainly not stacked in your favor. This is not to say that it can't be done, but there are many obstacles that make the task difficult. If your Flash piece will be delivered on the Internet, you have to be concerned with the size of your files. Digital audio by nature takes up a good deal of storage space. File size alone is often prohibitive when it comes to adding sound to a Flash website or animation. Another factor in the equation is interactivity. This poses possibly an even greater challenge.

Sound is a time-based medium. In order to hear something, you have to wait for it to be cued and then wait for it to conclude. Oftentimes it needs to be heard in combination with another audio element. Lining up audio events becomes very difficult when there is nothing consistent on which to base them. The whole idea of interactivity opens the possibilities to events that cannot be scheduled; they are solely dependent on the whimsy of an audience who chooses what they want to see or hear at any given moment. This unpredictability makes things especially difficult for designers planning to use audio in their Flash animations; if sound timing is so crucial, but there is no way to predict the timing, how can one possibly design with it in mind?

The answer is creativity, ingenuity, and a good collection of useful sound files that have been developed for interactive applications. With the right kind of audio source material, you will find that it is actually possible to create dynamic soundtracks that can both hold an audience's musical interest and support the interactive features of your movies.

DoReMedia Sound Families have been professionally produced to provide seamless integration with Flash from a perspective of both tight synchronization and interactivity. In this tutorial, you will learn how to take a set of audio and music components and use them to create a rich, dynamic sound experience that supports interactive navigation.

Planning Your Movie for Audio Interactivity

If you were approaching this project for the first time (rather than taking a guided tour and learning as you go), you would find it helpful to decide roughly what your audio goals are before setting out to work. In other words, how do you want the piece to sound? It's best to plan *roughly,* because it is never a good idea to box yourself in creatively. By all means, don't eliminate ideas because they may not fit with the initial creative direction you decided on. The best way to begin the conceptual process is to close your eyes, imagine someone interacting with your movie, and listen: What do you think it should sound like? This technique will give birth to your ideas and help forge the path toward a finished piece.

Since this is a tutorial and your task is to learn a technique rather than create an original soundtrack, the creative work has been done for you already. After completing the steps outlined here, you should be able to apply the skills you have learned to create your own dynamic soundtrack.

First, open the file `whiskey100.swf` from the Hands On 6 folder on the companion CD-ROM to this book (or you can find the finished file, `whiskey100.fla`). Experiment with the simple navigation in this movie and listen to the ways the music changes as you navigate from one portion of the movie to another. You should be able to hear how the tightly integrated audio elements work together to create one coherent audio statement that fits in with the navigational structure of the movie.

DoReMedia Sound Families are divided into three main categories: layers, chunks, and SFX. *Layers* are the most basic element; they are individual musical phrases or components of a song. A song's bass line or a lead guitar riff are good examples of layers. *Chunks* are single files that contain entire sections of a song. Several layers can be combined to create a new chunk, or you can use them independently. *SFX,* as the name suggests, can be thought of as sound or musical effects. They are sound files that can be cued independently to enhance the overall musical direction or provide a transition without getting in the way. Cymbal crashes, electronic swishes, or any kind of loose rhythmic phrase can all work this way.

In this tutorial, you will learn to combine these components in a way that creates a soundtrack with shape and serves to support basic interactivity in a Flash movie. Let's get started!

Creating Your Soundtrack

To begin this tutorial, you will need to gather a few files. Inside the Hands On 6 folder on the companion CD-ROM, you will find a folder named DoReMedia. Open it and import the following files into a new Flash movie:

`SYNC_100.aif`	`Whiskey_crash.aif`
`Whiskey_A.aif`	`Whiskey_drums.aif`
`Whiskey_A_02.aif`	`Whiskey_fill_01.aif`
`Whiskey_B.aif`	`Whiskey_lead_01.aif`
`Whiskey_B_02.aif`	`Whiskey_lead_02.aif`
`Whiskey_break.aif`	`Whiskey_lead_03.aif`

Once you've successfully imported all the sound files into your movie's Library, you can begin to build your movie and an interactive soundtrack. This tutorial assumes a comfortable familiarity with the Flash environment and audio elements. To learn more about how Flash handles sound elements, see Chapter 20.

1. Set the frame rate of your movie. DoReMedia Sound Families use a sound file called a Sync Track to ensure that your sounds lock to a consistent tempo. You will learn more about this later, but for now, select Modify → Document and set the frame rate of your movie to 10 frames per second.

2. Select Insert → New Symbol and create a new Movie Clip symbol named **soundtrack**. You will create the entire soundtrack in this Movie Clip. Then, using ActionScript, you will be able to direct the playback of the music based on the interactive choices made in your movie. Rename Layer 1 **graphic** and create a simple graphic to visually represent the Movie Clip. Drag an instance of the Movie Clip to the Stage.

> From this point on, all changes you make concerning layers, frames, and so on, will be made to the soundtrack Movie Clip Timeline, so be sure that you are working with this clip in Symbol Editing mode.

3. Create 11 new layers in the Timeline (for a total of 12). From the bottom up, the layers should be named `graphic` (created in step 2), `markers`, `actions`, `sync`, `drum`, `fills`, `A section`, `A2 section`, `loop riffs`, `B section`, `B2 section`, and `breakdown`. (See Figure H6.1.)

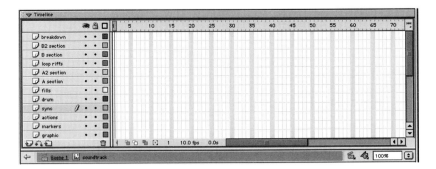

Figure H6.1

The layer names and Timeline for the soundtrack **Movie Clip**

4. Insert a keyframe on frame 1 of the `sync` layer. Attach the sound `SYNC_100.aif` to the keyframe, enter a loop value of 50, and set its sync to Stream. Scroll to frame 1200, select it, and press F5. (If Flash allows you to see only 500 or so frames in the Timeline initially, that's okay. Scroll as far as you can, select a frame and press F5, then scroll farther again and repeat the process. Flash will give you around 500 more empty frames. Continue to

scroll and press F5 until the looped Sync Track sound completes its loops at frame 1200.) You should see the repetitions of the sound file stretch along the length of the layer.

Then, click the Edit button on the Property Inspector to open the Edit Envelope dialog box. Select Custom from the Effect drop-down menu and drag the envelope handles to the bottom of each track to mute their playback. Click OK when you have finished.

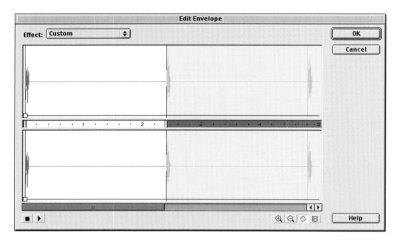

Even with its volume muted, the Sync Track is the most crucial component of the DoReMedia Sound Family. It is a low-quality sound file that has been optimized to match the tempo of your music. When you use it, you set the sync of the Sync Track to Stream so that Flash is forced to play back at a consistent frame rate. This consistency allows your music to stay in line, beat for beat. Earlier, you set the frame rate of your movie to 10 frames per second. The music you will use in this tutorial has a tempo of 100 beats per minute. The Sync Track is designed specifically to be sure that these tempos match and that every loop of the track lands within a new frame of the Timeline. If you visit the DoReMedia website, you can use its Frame Rate Calculator (`www.expectaudio.com/fmxsavvy/calculator2.html`) to decide which frame rate is best for your movie and the tempo of the Sound Family you use.

The Sync Track has another purpose as well. If you look at it closely in the Timeline, you will see that it has a large "spike" in the sound file. Use this spike as a visual reference to help line up the beats of the music. Each spike tells you where the first beat of each bar or measure begins. You set the loop count of this sound to 50. That means that you will have markers at each measure for the first 50 bars of the soundtrack.

5. With your Sync Track in place, you are free to assemble the musical components of your soundtrack. Scroll to frame 1200, and for each remaining layer, select the frame and press F5. This will insert more than enough frames needed to complete the soundtrack.

Now, note the second audio spike at frame 25 in the `sync` layer. This shows the start of a new measure in the music. Insert a new keyframe in the `drum` layer at frame 25 and attach the sound `Whiskey_drums.aif`. Set the sync to Event. For all remaining sounds, you will use Event sync. This is because Event requires much less memory for Flash. Once an event sound has been played, it is loaded into memory and can be looped or used over and over without adding to the size of the movie. Select Control → Play to hear the track in context.

6. Now you can add a percussive embellishment to this track. Insert a keyframe at frame 25 of the `fills` layer. Attach the sound `Whiskey_crash.aif` and set the sync to Event. Then, insert another new keyframe at frame 19 and attach the `Whiskey_fill_01.aif` file with Event sync. Notice how it ends just as the file at frame 25 is cued. If you play back the track, you should hear a short drum fill and crash that set up and punctuate the beginning of the drum groove.

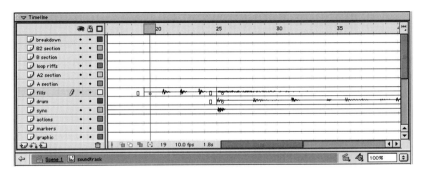

7. Scroll ahead in the Timeline. Insert a new keyframe at frame 73 in the `A section` layer. Attach the sound `Whiskey_A.aif`, set its sync to Event, and enter a loop value of 2. If you listen to this track, you will hear that it is the beginning of the song. You can add a drum fill that helps lead into the beginning guitar riff, giving the track a little more punch. Insert a keyframe at frame 67 of the `fills` layer. Attach the sound `Whiskey_fill_01.aif` and set its sync to Event. Now, play the tracks back. You can hear the drum intro, but when it gets to the drum fill, there is some disagreement between the different drum tracks as to where the beats fall. This can be easily fixed. Look at the two tracks and you'll see that at frame 68, there is a gap in the `drum` layer track, where the `fills` layer track shows its first spike. You can edit the volume of the `drum` track so that it drops out of the way and allows the `fills` track to take over. Select the keyframe at frame 25 where you cued the `Whiskey_drums.aif` file. Click Edit in the Property Inspector to open the Edit Envelope dialog box.

Click the Frames button ▦ in the Edit Envelope box so that you can see the sound in relation to the frames of the Timeline. Select Custom from the Effect drop-down menu and insert two handles so that the volume of the track drops out at frame 69. See Figure H6.2 for an illustration of the envelopes. Click OK when you have finished.

Figure H6.2

Use the Edit Envelope dialog box to drop the volume of the drum layer, clearing the way for the drum fill at frame 67.

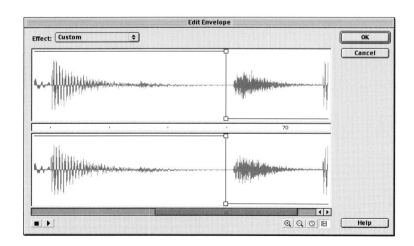

8. Now you can continue to build the A section of the soundtrack. Insert a new keyframe at frame 265 of the A2 section layer. Attach the sound Whiskey_A_02.aif, set its sync to Event, and enter a loop value of 2. This last sound completes the A section of the song. This part of the song will serve as the music for one section of your movie. This lasts a little over 45 seconds. Since someone is likely to spend more than 45 seconds looking at your movie, you need to make this section repeat so that the music doesn't just stop or drop out altogether.

9. You can repeat sections of music by sending the playback head back to the frame where the music was cued. However, when you do this, you will find that Flash is unable to maintain a consistent tempo. In the process of skipping back, it always misses a beat somewhere and disrupts the flow of the music. This is where the DoReMedia SFX tracks come in handy. You can use them to smooth over the transition and disguise the skip in the music.

   Scroll ahead in the Timeline and insert a new keyframe at frame 457 in the actions layer. Open the Actions panel and enter the following statement:

   ```
   gotoAndPlay(25);
   ```

   This action will send the playback head back to where the A section of your soundtrack starts. Now, you can smooth over this transition using a short sound. Insert another new keyframe at frame 457, this time in the loop riffs layer. Attach the sound Whiskey_lead_01.aif and set its sync to Event.

10. Select Control → Test Movie to hear what you have created so far. After the A section has finished, you will hear the slide guitar riff play and mix over the drum intro—a seamless transition!

11. With the entire A section in place, you can now create the other half, or the B section, of your soundtrack. Insert a new keyframe at frame 481 of the breakdown layer. Attach the sound Whiskey_break.aif, set the sync to Event, and enter a loop value of 2. Again, you can insert a cymbal crash to add punch to this chunk of music. Insert another new keyframe at frame 481 of the fills layer. Attach the sound Whiskey_crash.aif, and set the sync to Event.

12. The sound Whiskey_break.aif is a duet between the bass guitar and drums. In your soundtrack arrangement, this section is repeated twice. You can add contrast to the repetition by layering other sounds over this section of the song. Insert another new keyframe at frame 577 of the loop riffs layer. Attach the sound Whiskey_lead_01.aif, and set the sync to Event. In the same layer, attach the sound Whiskey_lead_03.aif to a keyframe at frame 625, and Whiskey_lead_02.aif to a keyframe at frame 649. Notice that all these keyframes are lining up with spikes in the Sync Track. The visual reference it provides is extremely valuable for lining up chunks of music! If you like, you can also add cymbal crashes to keyframes of the same number in the fills layer. See Figure H6.3 for an illustration of this in the Timeline.

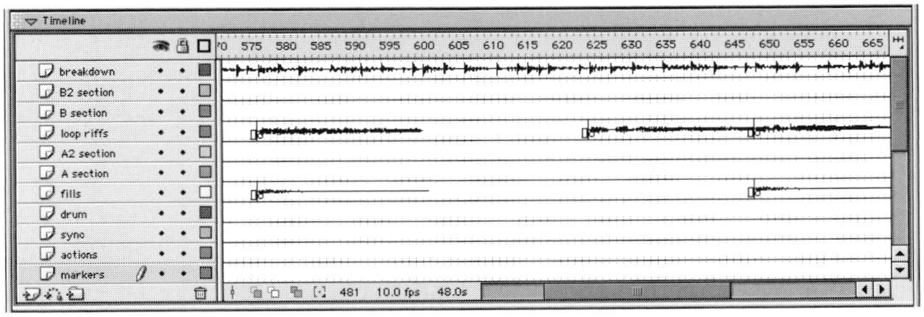

Figure H6.3

The B section of the soundtrack has slide guitar riffs and cymbal crashes (optional) that add musical contrast to the bass and drum breakdown.

13. Continue to build the B section by inserting a new keyframe at frame 673 of the B section layer. Attach the sound Whiskey_B.aif, set the sync to Event, and enter a loop value of 2. Then, to wrap up the section, attach the sound Whiskey_B_02.aif to a keyframe at frame 817 in the B2 section layer. Set its sync to Event as well.

14. You will notice that you have two tracks that overlap in the B section and B2 section layers. If you give your soundtrack a listen, it sounds like a confused mess! In this tutorial, the file Whiskey_B_02.aif is meant to be a two-bar concluding musical phrase. In order to remain consistent with the eight-bar structure of this song, you will mute the last two bars of Whiskey_B.aif (starting at frame 817) so that the concluding phrase can be heard clearly. The result will yield six bars of Whiskey_B.aif plus two bars of Whiskey_B_02.aif, for a total of eight bars.

Select keyframe 673 in the `B section` layer where `Whiskey_B.aif` is cued. Click Edit in the Sound panel to open the Edit Envelope dialog box. Click the Frames button and scroll the dialog box ahead to frame 817. Select Custom from the Effect drop-down menu and create an envelope so that the volume of this track drops out completely at frame 817. For an illustration, see Figure H6.4.

Figure H6.4

The Edit Envelope dialog box allows you to mute the B section track at frame 817.

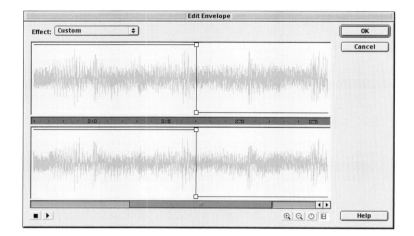

When you have finished creating the envelope, click OK. Now that the music of the B section is finished, you can work on making it repeat smoothly.

15. To repeat the B section, you will implement the same technique used to repeat the A section. Insert a new keyframe at frame 871 in the `actions` layer. Open the Actions panel and enter the following statement:

    ```
    gotoAndPlay(481);
    ```

    This will send the playback head back to the frame where the B section begins. Now you will attach two sounds to serve as transitions for the repeat. Insert new keyframes at frame 865 in both the `fills` and `loop riffs` layers. Attach `Whiskey_lead_03.aif` to the `loop riffs` keyframe, and `Whiskey_crash.aif` to the `fills` keyframe. This concludes the music tracks for the B section.

You may notice that the repeat action `gotoAndPlay(481)` and the transition sounds are in different frames. We did this intentionally. By setting the loop action later in the Timeline, you allow the transition sounds to be heard independently for a brief moment. This gives the transition more prominence and demonstrates that you have flexibility when creating these types of Timeline loops using an audio transition. We selected frame 871 because we felt that it provided the best-sounding result. Ultimately, the choice of positioning for the repeat action is left to your discretion.

16. If you wanted to test your movie so that you could hear the
B section in context, you would be unable to do so. This is
because the actions at frame 457 send the movie back to the
beginning of the A section. Your movie cannot currently make it
past that frame. To test your movie, open the actions at frame
457 and add two slashes (//) to comment out these actions.

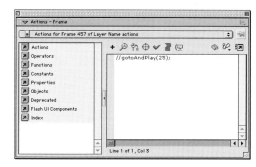

Select Control → Test Movie and give it a spin—now you should
be able to hear all of the A section and have it play right into
the B section. The only catch is that your B section will repeat!
This will be more controllable in a while. For now, just under-
stand that the movie is incomplete and you have to use this workaround to test its performance. When you are finished, be sure to uncomment (remove the slash characters)
for the actions at frame 457.

17. Musically, everything is working according to plan. You have two different sections of a
song to "score" two different sections of a Flash movie. The key now is to set everything
up so that the `soundtrack` Movie Clip can be controlled interactively. This takes you back
to the concept of time. You have no idea how long someone will spend looking at a particular section of your movie. And for this reason, you have constructed the soundtrack in
such a way that each section will repeat to accommodate visits of different lengths.

The catch is that you have used Event sync to cue all your sound files. Remember that
Event sync will start a file playing, and the file will continue until it is finished or has
run out of loops. If you were to skip between the A and B sections of your soundtrack
right now, the various event sounds would mix and create a whirl of musical confusion.
To make this soundtrack work so that you can switch between sections freely, you
have to stop each sound explicitly when you move to a new section. This means stopping all of the A section sounds at the start
of the B section, and vice versa. To do this,
attach the sound you wish to stop at a new
keyframe, and assign the Stop sync method
to each. See Table H6.1 for a listing of the
frame locations, layers, and sounds where
you will assign stops.

LAYER	KEYFRAME	SOUND
breakdown	25	Whiskey_break.aif
B2 section	25	Whiskey_B_02.aif
B section	25	Whiskey_B.aif
A2 section	481	Whiskey_A_02.aif
A section	481	Whiskey_A.aif
drum	481	Whiskey_drums.aif

Table H6.1

**Sound and Keyframe
Stop Sync Combinations**

When you assign the Stop sync to each sound, you will notice that the Stop sync
frames for one section correspond with the Event sync frames for the other. Any time
the movie jumps to frame 25 or 481 to play a new section of music, the old section will
be stopped as the new one begins.

This step concludes the soundtrack portion of your movie. You should have two independent sections of music that work together to make up a song. With this in place,
you can put the soundtrack Movie Clip to work and use it to play different song sections based on interactive choices made in your main movie.

Adding the Final Interactive Touches

To complete the tutorial, you will need to add a few items to your Library. You will need at least one button. The movie you create here has two buttons, each of which cues a different section of music. You can use the same button twice or have two buttons—the choice is yours. You may also wish to add some graphic components to your movie. Since this tutorial is geared toward creating a two-part soundtrack, you may want to include two distinctly different sets of graphics—one for each section. Again, it is up to you. The only graphic element required is a button to signal interactive choices.

1. Insert two new layers in the main Timeline. Name one layer **actions** and the other **buttons**. Then name the layer containing your soundtrack Movie Clip MC, and assign the clip an instance name. Highlight it and enter the name soundtrack in the Property Inspector.

2. Drag two buttons to the Stage, making sure they are on the buttons layer. Position them wherever you like. For purposes of this tutorial, consider one button the A section button and the other the B section button. Each button will eventually take you to the section of music having the same name.

3. Insert a new keyframe in both the buttons layer and the actions layer. Then, add a frame (F5) to the MC layer so that your clip stretches across two frames. When finished, your main Timeline should resemble Figure H6.5.

4. Highlight the first keyframe of the actions layer and open the Actions panel. Enter a single stop() statement. Do the same for the keyframe at frame 2. This isolates each frame of the movie and limits the playback to a single frame.

5. Highlight the B section button at frame 1 and open the Actions panel. Enter the following statements:

```
on(press){
    if(_root.soundtrack._currentframe<481){
        _root.soundtrack.gotoAndPlay(481);
        gotoAndStop(2);
    }
}
```

These statements create the behavior that allows you to switch from one section of music to another. In your soundtrack Movie Clip, the A section is contained in the frames before frame 481. The if statement in this script makes sure that this button will respond only if the clip is playing those frames (meaning you can't cue the B section unless the A section is currently playing). The next statement sends the instance soundtrack to play at frame 481 (the B section), and the third statement sends the main Timeline to frame 2.

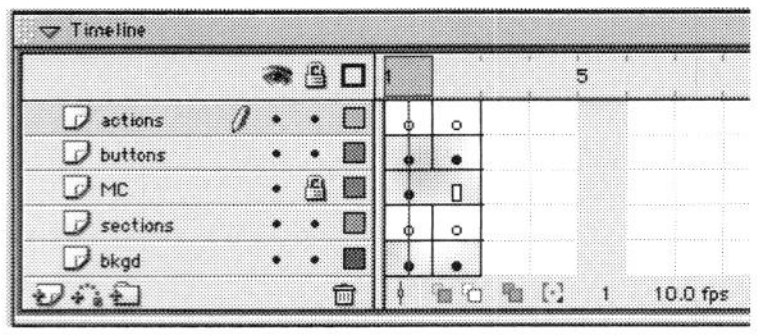

Figure H6.5

The main Timeline has two frames, one for each section of the soundtrack.

6. Now you can script the interactivity for the other section of the soundtrack. Highlight the A section button at frame 2 and open the Actions panel. Enter the following statements:

```
on(press){
    if(_root.soundtrack._currentframe>481){
        _root.soundtrack.gotoAndPlay(25);
        gotoAndStop(1);
    }
}
```

These statements do the opposite of the other button. If the B section is playing (frames greater than 481), the button will send the clip to frame 25, where the A section starts, and send the main Timeline to frame 1.

Select Control → Test Movie to see and hear how this works.

7. One more thing you can do to enhance the musical interactivity of the movie (as well as the soundtrack) is to add a sound to the button(s). When you click a button, not only will you launch a new section of music, but you'll have a transitional sound (DoReMedia SFX) to help bridge the gap.

Switch to Symbol Editing mode for one of your buttons. Add a new layer to the button and insert a new keyframe for the Down state of the button. Attach one of the slide guitar riff sounds to this keyframe and assign the Event sync option. For the `whiskey100.swf` example you listened to earlier, the sounds `Whiskey_lead_01.aif` and `Whiskey_lead_02.aif` were used as button sounds. These sounds were selected because they are not very rhythmic and they taper at the end, making them perfect candidates for layering over rhythmically strong tracks.

8. After you have finished with your buttons, select Control → Test Movie and give this a try. Your interactive soundtrack is complete!

Before publishing your interactive soundtrack movie, it's a good idea to check the sound options in the Publish Settings dialog box (File → Publish Settings). For Audio Event options, select whatever settings best match the requirements of your project, based on delivery medium, audience connection speed, and so on. Earlier, you dropped the volume of the Sync Track. Since this track will be inaudible, you can drop its quality settings. Select MP3, 8Kbps, and Mono for your Audio Stream options.

To conserve file size, it is necessary to remove the loops of the Sync Track in your soundtrack Movie Clip. According to the DoReMedia Sound Family specifications, Flash needs only one iteration of the Sync Track to lock in the frame rate. Because a looped stream sound adds greatly to the size of a published movie, it's best to use only as much of a stream sound as is necessary. However, to preserve the sync in the B section, you must attach another instance of the Sync Track sound (`SYNC_100.aif`) to a keyframe at frame 481. Select the frame, select Insert → Keyframe, and select the file `SYNC_100.aif` in the Sound panel. Set the sound's sync to Stream. This additional instance of the Sync Track will regulate the frame rate when your soundtrack is skipped ahead to the B section.

> In some cases, a Sync Track that starts at frame 1 will not properly lock in a movie's frame rate. To work around this technical glitch, move the Sync Track to frame 10. This gives Flash a little while to "get started" before it encounters the Sync Track and locks the movie's frame rate into place.

Closing Thoughts on the Interactive Soundtrack

You have just completed a very significant chunk of Flash-based interactive media. Congratulations! What you have learned here gives you exposure to all the basic techniques and a few advanced topics concerning DoReMedia Sound Families. Clearly, you can see the advantages that Sound Families provide, in terms of both musicality and compact file sizes in a low-bandwidth, interactive environment. Here are a few suggestions for things you may want to try on your own as you become more comfortable with these techniques:

- Experiment with different pan options for each chunk, layer, and SFX file you use. In the whiskey100.swf demo file, there are several instances where slide guitar fills are panned from one speaker to another. Also, a lot can be done by changing the volume (dynamics) of the music tracks. Fine-tune your tracks by tweaking their volume with the Edit Envelope dialog box.

- Try rearranging the chunks to create a third section of music for the soundtrack. Each Sound Family provides you with enough material to create several permutations of the same song.

- Experiment with the use of SFX sounds and buttons. It's possible to construct an entire soundtrack from mouse clicks alone.

- Sound Families can be licensed from DoReMedia. The company has a large Sound Family library containing a broad range of musical styles to choose from. Visit the DoReMedia website (www.doremedia.com) for updates on available Sound Families and additional discussions of the techniques described in this tutorial.

 If you enjoyed working with the *Whiskey* Sound Family you may also have fun with techno-flavored *Passive Aggression*. Go the companion CD-ROM → Hands On 6 → DoRe Media. Here you will find two folders labeled Passive Aggression, one containing AIFF files, the other WAVs. Use the techniques discussed here to create a soundtrack of your own using the Passive Aggression Sound Family files.

PART VII

Integrating Flash with Other Programs

Great bodies of work—art, music, literature, drama, and so on—are not created in a bubble. It's impossible to accomplish creative goals without some kind of outside input, and creating in Flash is certainly no exception. Up to this point in the book, you have read, studied, and practiced many different aspects of creative work you can do with Flash. Sometimes, however, it's important to step away and consider the bigger picture. Flash is an excellent and versatile application, yes. But it cannot do it all.

Depending on your creative goals, it's likely that you won't be able to do everything you want to do or dream of doing in Flash alone. The good news is that, as one of the more versatile applications available today, Flash shares common ground with plenty of other kinds of software. Not only can you bring your Flash creations into other authoring environments, but you can bring many foreign file types and media into Flash. This section explores the relationships between Flash and other digital media applications.

CHAPTER 23

Working with Flash and Director

In spite of the fact that Flash is a great multimedia authoring application, there are times when it may not be able to deliver all the functionality that you require. Even with the flexibility and speed of vector art and animation, and the interactive possibilities offered by ActionScript, neither Flash nor any other application, for that matter, can do it all. *Multimedia* by nature and definition is an enormous vein of expression; it embraces the synergy of various forms and makes them one. When your projects are open to this kind of crossover, you will find an entirely new realm of possibilities to satisfy your goals, whether they be rooted in art, entertainment, business, learning, or another form of communication.

Whereas Flash is uniquely suited for fast delivery on the Internet and in other bandwidth-conscious applications, Macromedia Director shines in the realm of CD and DVD-ROM development, as well as in the creation of Shockwave content for the Web. There is no doubt that Director is the multimedia authoring tool of choice for projects that are large in scope and require many different kinds of media. Director allows you to work with 2D bitmap graphics, 2D vector graphics, digital video, sound, true 3D graphics (introduced in Director 8.5), and most important to this discussion, Flash SWF files. In this chapter, you will learn how Director and Flash can be used together to create interactive movies that possess the best characteristics of each application. The chapter covers these topics:

- **Getting Flash movies into a Director movie**
- **The characteristics of Flash in the Director environment**
- **How Flash movies function as sprites**
- **Communicating with Director via ActionScript**
- **Communicating with Flash via Lingo**

Working with Flash in the Director Environment

Flash movies are supported in Director with the help of the Flash Asset Xtra. Currently, Director 8.5 ships with a Flash Asset Xtra that supports the functionality of Flash 5. At the time of this writing, Macromedia had not introduced a new Flash Asset Xtra to support the expanded functionality of Flash MX and the Flash 6 Player. Until this is rectified by Macromedia, any Flash movies you wish to run within Director should be targeted to the capabilities of Flash 5. Older versions of Director may support Flash, but often with limitations as to which versions. Table 23.1 provides a guide to Flash and Director version compatibility.

Table 23.1

Director/Flash Asset Xtra Compatibility

FLASH PLAYER VERSION	DIRECTOR VERSION
6 (Flash MX) and earlier	Unknown at time of publication
5 and earlier	8.5
4 and earlier	8.0, 7.02
3 and earlier	7.0
2	6.5, 6.02

Movies created in Flash MX can always be saved to a lower version if you don't have a version of Director that supports them. To learn how to do this, see Chapter 27. To read the most up-to-date information concerning Flash and Director version compatibility, see www.macromedia.com/support/director at the Macromedia website.

With the help of Lingo, Director's native scripting language, you are able to manipulate many of the parameters that control the playback of a Flash movie while it is contained in a Director movie. There are several advantages that this scheme can offer to your multimedia projects:

Graphics flexibility Director deals primarily with bitmap graphics. As a result, if any stretching or scaling of graphics is required in your movie, Director will probably not be able to do this very well (the graphics will be stretched into gigantic chunky blobs). Vector graphics change this because they can be scaled without losing resolution. Although vector graphics can be created in Director, the vector drawing tool it offers isn't nearly as sophisticated as those found in Flash. Flash is championed as an animation application, but it's also great for creating still images such as titles, credits, and interface elements.

Expanded control over animated elements Although Lingo gives you a great deal of control over the elements of a Director movie, there are some tasks that Flash can make easier, simply because of the way the application works. In Flash, the Movie Clip is an essential part of any Flash production. As an independent Timeline, a Movie Clip can maintain animated autonomy and keep a agenda that's separate from other elements of a Flash movie. In Director, this works largely to your advantage. Use Flash to create an SWF marionette, where each of the puppet's limbs is a separate Movie Clip. Then, in Director, you can use Lingo to target each clip individually to make your marionette perform a variety of animated routines. To read more about this technique, see "Manipulating Flash Sprites with Lingo" later in this chapter.

Best of both scripting worlds Where Flash has ActionScript, Director has Lingo. Chances are, if you know either of these languages or JavaScript, you have a good footing for picking up the one you don't currently know. Although ActionScript is much closer to JavaScript than Lingo, Lingo has changed over the years to adopt more conventions (mainly the dot syntax) that bring it closer to ActionScript or JavaScript in terms of syntax. When working with both Flash and Director, you can use ActionScript to control elements in Director, and Lingo to control elements of a Flash movie.

Clearly there are many advantages, many of which are bound only by your creative ingenuity for solving problems and combining or layering your work. Director can be used to create something as simple as a gallery of your favorite SWF creations, or something as complicated as a massive multiplayer world where users can create their own characters and interact with other members of the online community. The first step to any of this involves getting Flash into the Director environment and understanding how it behaves once it's there.

Importing Flash Movies

In order to incorporate Flash movies in your Director projects, you must first bring the Flash file into the Director authoring environment. Similar to Flash, this process is called *importing*. Once a file has been imported into Director, it is stored in the *cast*, and is ready to be used in the Director movie.

Director? Cast? Wait a second… Yes, you see a pattern emerging here. Macromedia uses the analogy of a theater or film production to describe the elements of the software. It is done very well, too, and makes learning the software a little easier. Any media elements that can be used in the movie are stored in the cast and called *cast members*, just like actresses and actors sitting in the wings of a theater (this is like the Library in Flash). As you probably guessed, all action in the movie takes place on the *Stage.*

Taking the analogy a step further (and closer to opera), the window that manages the placement of cast members on the Stage is called the *Score*. As soon as a cast member is placed in the Score, it is referred to as a *sprite*. The Score has horizontal rows for sprites (called *channels*), and vertical columns for frames. (This is similar to the Flash Timeline, which has layers and frames.) Additionally, the rows for sprite channels are numbered (see Figure 23.1). When you manipulate an element in Director, you often refer to it by its sprite number, such as *sprite(1)* or *sprite(13)*. There are many levels of complexity in the Director environment, depending on how much of the program you need to use. Consult the Director Help files (Help → Director Help) for specifics on the interface and its components.

Figure 23.1

The Score in Director
consists of sprite chan-
nels (rows) and Time-
line frames (columns).

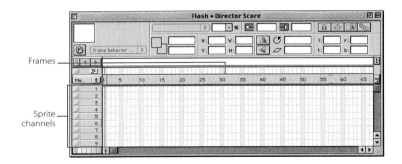

Frames

Sprite
channels

In order for a Flash movie to be part of a Director production, it has to be a sprite in the Score and on the Stage; in order for it to be a sprite, it has to be a cast member. And to be a cast member, it must first be imported into a Director movie. Whew! So many steps! It may sound confusing, but once you've grown accustomed to Director, it's very easy to understand how all the elements are interrelated.

To import a Flash movie into your Director project:

1. In Director, select File → Import (Cmd/Ctrl+R). The Import Files dialog box appears. It's similar to the one used in Flash, only larger and more detailed.

2. The window at the top allows you to browse for the files you need. Use the drop-down menu to locate the SWF files you want to import.

3. After you locate and select the file you need, click the Add button. This will place the file in the lower window, which is like an on-deck circle for files about to be imported. Continue to use the top window to browse for any additional files you need.

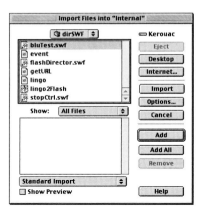

4. When you have finished, click the Import button. This will make all of the selected files part of your Director movie cast and a permanent part of the Director file.

In addition to the buttons and methods discussed here, Director offers a range of other import options that go beyond the scope of this section. Consult the Director Help files (Help → Director Help) for all the options available to you while importing media.

Understanding Flash Movie Properties

Once you have successfully imported a Flash movie into your Director project, it will appear as a cast member in the Internal Cast window (see Figure 23.2). Director automatically includes for you the Flash Asset Xtra that is needed to support the Flash cast member, so there is no need to retrieve it from your computer's hard drive. However, if you plan to create a stand-alone projector, be sure that the supporting Flash Asset Xtra and any other Xtras you need are available for the final projector file.

Figure 23.2

Director's Internal Cast window holds Flash movies and many other types of media for use in a Director production.

From here, you are free to use Director to work with the movie in any way you see fit. Flash cast members are somewhat unique in the Director environment because they are interactive multimedia movies *within* an interactive multimedia movie. As a result, there are many parameters that can be assigned to the Flash cast member to determine how it will perform as a cast member in Director. You can set these parameters using the Flash Asset Properties dialog box. In this window, you can control many characteristics of a Flash movie: its playback quality, scaling properties, sound options, and so on. Think of this dialog box as your interface for customizing the technical details of a Flash cast member.

To access the Flash Asset Properties dialog box and edit the parameters of a Flash member, double-click the cast member icon in the cast window. The Flash Asset Properties dialog box appears. The window offers you the following options for editing a cast member:

Media management If you use the Browse button to link to a Flash file, the field at the top of the window will show the path to that file, either on your computer's hard drive or on the Internet.

Flash movies can be either imported or linked. If you check the Linked box, the file will be handled from a remote location. When the movie is used in your Score, Director will go to the remote location and call that member to the Stage. Linked members will stream into memory unless Preload is checked. Preload requires that the entire Flash movie be loaded before playback begins.

Unless you are creating a Shockwave movie that will appear on the Internet, it is recommended that you leave the Linked option deselected so that a Flash member is imported to the cast and saved as a permanent part of your movie.

Playback There are several playback options that control how the Flash movie will be delivered in the Director movie:

> **Image** determines whether the image track of a movie is visible. If the box is checked, you will see the Flash movie; if it is unchecked, you will not. Deselect this option for sound-only or script-only SWF files.

> **Sound** toggles the audio track of a Flash member. If the box is checked, the movie will play with its sound on; if unchecked, the movie will play silently.

Paused determines how the movie will play when it is first encountered in the Score. If Paused is checked, the first frame of the Flash movie is displayed. After that, the movie will have to be prompted either by Lingo or by a control in the Flash movie itself to begin playback. If Paused is unchecked, the movie will play immediately when Director loads the movie onto the Stage.

Loop is an on/off option that determines how a movie will act when it has finished playing. If Loop is turned on (checked), the movie will resume playback at its first frame after it finishes playing. If Loop is unchecked, the movie will play once and then stop.

Direct to Stage controls the priority that Director assigns to a Flash cast member. If this option is checked, Director will devote resources to making the movie play back as smoothly as possible. This option disables sprite ink effects and will always place a Flash sprite on top of any others in the movie.

Quality Director has several quality options for Flash cast member playback. These options produce the same results as those found in the HTML tab of Flash's Publish Settings dialog box. The settings are High, Auto-High, Low, and Auto-Low. To read more about these options, see Chapter 27.

Scale This field allows you to enter a scale value for the cast member. This value will be used for the Flash movie each time it appears in your Director movie. Settings in this field are directly related to choices made in the Scale Mode drop-down menu.

Scale Mode This menu offers several options concerning the scaling of Flash cast members when they are manipulated either in the Score or by Lingo:

Auto-Size is the default setting. This option locks the scaling of the Flash movie to the scaling of a sprite in your Director movie. As a sprite is scaled, so will the Flash movie be scaled. This option defaults the value of the Scale field to 100% so that the Flash movie and the sprite maintain the same scale relationship. If you change this number to 50%, the Flash movie will retain the new scale value and always be one-half the size of the sprite that holds it. Change it to 200%, and the Flash movie will be twice the size of the sprite and appear cropped within its bounding box.

No Scale retains the size of the Flash cast member as it is set in the Scale field. No matter how a sprite is stretched or shrunk, this option leaves the Flash movie at the size set by the Scale option. If a sprite is scaled to a value less than that specified in the Scale field, the Flash movie will be cropped by the sprite bounding box.

The remaining options—**Show All**, **No Border**, and **Exact Fit**—are identical to those found in the HTML tab of Flash's Publish Settings dialog box. To read more about these options, see Chapter 27.

Rate This option allows you to control the speed of playback (frame rate) of a Flash movie cast member. This functionality is unavailable to you in Flash, and is thus another reason to combine Flash and Director. Rate has three settings:

Normal retains the original frame rate settings of the SWF file.

Lock-Step matches the playback of your Director movie with the Flash member, frame for frame. If the Director movie is set to play at 30 frames per second, so will a Flash cast member when Lock-Step is enabled.

Fixed activates the fps (frames per second) field and allows you to enter a custom value to set the frame rate of a Flash cast member. This setting is unique and will override tempo settings in both the original Flash movie and Director's Score. However, a Flash movie will not play faster than the frame rate that is set in the Director movie.

Besides the Flash Asset Properties dialog box, there is another means of changing the parameters of a Flash cast member. One of the more important windows in the Director interface is the Property Inspector (see Figure 23.3). It is very similar to the Property Inspector found in Flash's interface and provides a lot of the same kind of functionality. It allows you to access many commands and parameters that define a component of your movie: scaling, color, name, and other specifics that are unique to each element or cast member.

To display the Property Inspector for a Flash cast member, highlight that member in the cast window and then click the Property Inspector button ⓘ . This button, noticeable because it is an italic letter *i* within a blue circle, is present in many different locations of the Director interface but will always launch the Property Inspector. It will allow you to change the following attributes of a Flash cast member:

- Member name and path
- Scale mode
- Quality
- Rate
- Playback options

By clicking the More Options button, you can launch the Flash Asset Properties dialog box to change additional parameters not available in the Inspector. The Property Inspector is a quick alternative to using the dialog box and provides a way to edit the most common attributes of a Flash cast member.

Using Flash Movies as Sprites

To make a Flash cast member officially part of your movie, you must place that cast member on the Stage. Unless a cast member is brought to the Stage (either physically or through Lingo), it will not make an appearance in your movie. When you drag a cast member from the cast window to the Stage, it becomes a sprite and is automatically assigned a sprite number based on the next available sprite channel in the Score. For example, if you presently have six sprites in your movie and you drag a Flash member to the Stage, it will be referred to as *sprite(7)* throughout the Director movie. This number is very important, because it is how you identify the Flash member when you want to control it with Lingo scripts. For instance, `sprite(7).visible=0` makes your Flash movie, sprite(7), invisible. You can also create a sprite by dragging a cast member to the Score window directly. This allows you to place it in whichever sprite channel you desire, and automatically centers the sprite on the Stage.

Confused about the Score and the Stage? One of the greatest challenges in learning Director is understanding the role of each window and how its elements are used in a movie. If a cast member appears on the Stage, it is automatically also in the Score. While the Stage is the window in which your movie takes place, the Score is where all the technical elements of a movie are determined, such as a cast member's time on the Stage, script placement, and overall movie structure (frames, markers, and so on).

Once a Flash cast member has become a sprite in your Director movie, there are several behaviors that you can expect it to exhibit. Listed below are some of the capabilities and limitations of a Flash movie once it's part of a Director project:

Playback A Flash movie will play back in a Director movie as long as the Director movie has enough frames to accommodate its length. For instance, a Flash movie with 100 frames could play only halfway in a Director movie with 50 frames. One workaround for this characteristic is placing the Flash movie in a single Director frame and attaching the following Lingo statements to the frame script channel of the Score:

```
on exitFrame
    go to the frame
end
```

This creates a continuous playback loop and allows the Flash movie to play in its entirety while Director loops in a single frame. Additionally, if the Loop parameter of the Flash cast member is turned on, the movie will loop inside Director continuously. To learn more about working with Flash movies while Director is looping its playback, see the later section "Controlling Flash Playback with Lingo."

Vector format As a vector graphic, your Flash movie is excellent for applications where you need to stretch and resize graphics or text without distortion. With the help of Lingo, Director allows you to do this dynamically, based on audience interactivity in your movie.

Sprite manipulation In addition to its own built-in animated characteristics, a Flash movie member can be moved and repositioned on the Stage as a sprite to create another layer of animated interest. To learn more about this, see the next section of this chapter.

Presentation If the Flash movie has Direct to Stage turned on, it will always appear on top of other sprites, and Director will devote resources to ensuring the smooth playback of the movie. Use the Direct to Stage option for Flash movies that are featured and must play back with the highest priority. It is best to leave this option off for other kinds of movies, such as button interfaces, animated characters, and other elements that must be more flexible as sprites.

Ink effects Ink effects are settings that you can apply to sprites to change their appearance on the Stage. There are four Ink settings that apply to Flash members: Copy, Background Transparent, Transparent, and Blend.

> **Copy** displays a Flash movie exactly as it was created, pixel for pixel. Copy is the default option.

> **Background Transparent** makes the background color of a sprite invisible (transparent) and allows you to see through to the elements behind the sprite.

> **Transparent** allows some color bleed between a movie and the color of the elements behind it. This effect is more apparent with light colors than with dark.

> **Blend** is similar to the _alpha property in ActionScript. Think of it as an opacity setting for each sprite. Blend values and Ink effects can be set in the Sprite Toolbar area of the Score (see Figure 23.4).

Macromedia recommends using the Copy setting for most applications because it requires the least amount of memory to display. If possible, a good strategy is to create your movies with the same background color so that knocking out an unwanted background color is unnecessary.

Sound Working with simultaneous audio streams (from both the Flash movie and your Director movie) can be a bit tricky. The difficulty is that Flash and Director are forced to share sound channels. If you are using Windows, you can take advantage of the global property soundMixMedia. When set to true, this

Figure 23.4

The Sprite Toolbar area of the Score window allows access to Ink and Blend settings for the sprites in your movies. Ink settings can also be accessed by Cmd/Ctrl+clicking a sprite and choosing an option from the context menu.

property enables Director to mix Score channel sounds with those playing in a Flash cast member. If it is set to `false`, then Flash and Director sounds must be played at separate times.

> Mixing Flash audio into a Director movie can produce undesirable results throughout your production. We recommend that you implement and control all audio elements within Director and Lingo.

Communicating Across Movies with Lingo and ActionScript

Now that you are familiar with some of the more technical aspects of working with Flash movies as sprites and cast members, you are ready to begin working with the fun stuff: using one type of media to pass information and commands to the other. This is an essential part of authoring interactive movies. By combining Flash and Director, not only can you combine the best of both worlds, but you can allow them to communicate with one another. This relationship adds yet another layer of interactive possibilities and flexibility to your interactive media productions.

Lingo is an enormous scripting language. If ActionScript is a stream, Lingo is a river; and there are more Lingo topics related to Flash than could possibly be covered in a section of this book. Here, we present some of the more essential elements of Lingo as it pertains to Flash. For a complete listing of Flash-related Lingo, select Help → Lingo Dictionary from Director's main menu bar.

> This section assumes that you have basic familiarity with Director, Lingo, and the conventions of the Director authoring environment. To learn more about these topics, consult the help files that ship with Director.

Controlling Flash Playback with Lingo

One of the more common uses of Flash cast members is to use them with movies within movies. In the same way that Movie Clips in Flash are independent animations that can be manipulated via ActionScript, Flash movies can be controlled in Director with Lingo. The Lingo language reserves several special commands to do this. Plus, with a little Lingo know-how, you can create your own scripts for various kinds of custom control options. Start here with some of the basics and then take it from there.

Play Command

To play a Flash cast member, you can use Lingo's `play()` command. This statement tells a specified Flash member sprite to play. For example:

```
on mouseUp
    sprite(1).play()
end
```

This script, attached to some kind of button, will play sprite 1 when the mouse button is released.

> Remember to use the Paused option in the Property Inspector if you don't want a Flash movie to start playing when it's encountered on Director's Stage. Alternately, you can set this property in Lingo by using the pausedAtStart cast member property.

Stop Command

To stop a Flash cast member at its current location, you can use Lingo's `stop()` command. This statement tells a specified Flash member sprite to stop playing. For example:

```
on mouseUp
    sprite(1).stop()
end
```

This script, also attached to some kind of button, will stop sprite 1 when the mouse button is released.

Rewind Command

Use `rewind()` to send a Flash sprite back to its first frame, or, to use the tape metaphor, *rewind* it.

```
on mouseUp
    sprite(1).rewind()
end
```

This script would serve well attached to a rewind button cast member or as part of a rewind behavior script.

Unfortunately, there is no such thing as a fast-forward command for Flash movies in Lingo. However, it is possible to create one. Consider the following script:

```
on exitFrame
    if gFfwd=true then
        swfFrame=sprite(1).frame
        sprite(1).goToFrame(swfFrame+2)
    end if
end
```

This script stores the current frame of the Flash movie in the variable `swfFrame`. Then, using the `goToFrame()` command, it sends the movie ahead two frames. These statements are executed every frame if the variable `gFfwd` is `true`. In context, you can use a fast-forward button to toggle the variable off and on, which in turn will control this fast-forward function.

frame and *frameCount* **Properties**

You can use these properties to monitor the playback status of a Flash movie. `frameCount` will get the total length of a Flash movie in terms of frames. For example, this statement:

```
put sprite(1).member.frameCount
```

prints to Director's Message window the total number of frames for the Flash cast member that is sitting in sprite channel 1. If the Flash movie in sprite channel 1 had 19 frames, the Message window would reveal the following:

The `frame` property monitors the current frame number that a Flash cast member sprite is playing. In conjunction with the `frameCount` property, this can be used to create a script that tells your Director movie to perform an action (such as going to a new frame) when the Flash movie has finished playing. For example:

```
on exitFrame
    if sprite(1).frame<sprite(1).member.frameCount then
        go to the frame
    else
        go to "done"
    end if
end
```

This script checks a condition every time a frame loops. The condition uses the `frame` property and checks to see if the current frame playing (`sprite(1).frame`) is less than the total number of frames in the Flash movie member that occupies sprite channel 1 (see line 2). If it is, then the script loops in the current frame. If it is not, meaning that the current frame is probably equal to the total number of frames because it has finished playing, the script sends the Director movie to the marker named `done`.

Toggling ActionScript

Use the `actionsEnabled` property to have Lingo turn a Flash movie's actions off and on. Consider the following Lingo behavior:

```
on mouseDown
    if sprite(1).actionsEnabled=1 then
        sprite(1).actionsEnabled=0
```

```
    else
        sprite(1).actionsEnabled=1
    end if
end
```

This behavior script can be attached to a button to create a toggle switch for the actions of the Flash movie in sprite channel 1. Using a simple `if...then` conditional in line 2, this script checks the status of actions for sprite 1. If they are on, this turns them off; otherwise (if they are off), it turns them on. This property can be helpful if you have a Flash movie containing `gotoAndPlay()` loops. By setting `actionsEnabled=1`, you cause the Flash movie to ignore these scripts (and all others, for that matter) and to play through its frames without interruption.

Passing Information from Flash to Director

Depending on the way you use Flash within Director, there may be times when it's necessary to pass information directly from a Flash movie to the Director movie that is hosting it. This kind of functionality would be useful if you had created a Flash navigation bar with animated buttons to be used for controlling the playback of a Director movie. In this situation, it would be helpful to have a means of allowing each Flash button to pass an argument to Director, telling it to which frame it should jump. This can be accomplished using ActionScript's `getURL()` action. This action will pass a string of information from the Flash movie (where the action is called) to the Director movie that is hosting it.

To make a button in your Flash movie pass information to Director, select the button and open the Actions panel. Enter the following statements:

```
on (release){
    getURL("directorMarker");
}
```

In this example, `directorMarker` is a placeholder for the name of a Score marker where you would like to redirect Director's playback head when the Flash button is clicked. Flash will pass the URL information as a string to Director.

Before the button will work completely, however, you have to enter some Lingo that prepares Director to receive the string director Marker from Flash. In Director, create a behavior script and attach it to the Flash sprite that contains the button. The Lingo for the behavior should read like this:

```
on getURL me, flashStringInfo
    go to frame flashStringInfo
end
```

This Lingo enables the sprite to which it is attached to receive the URL string information and store it in the variable `flashStringInfo`. This variable can be used later in the script. Here, because this string is supposed to help with Director movie navigation, the string holds the name of a marker in your Director movie. If you have a Flash movie with several buttons, each with a different navigation-related string to pass, this behavior will be able to handle each string and route the Director movie accordingly.

The getURL() action also allows you to specify a specific event in Director. An event could be something like a custom handler that you write in Lingo to manage specific kinds of Flash interaction. Take navigation for instance. Moving around in an interactive movie is something that must be done repeatedly throughout the movie. You could write a custom handler to direct navigation so that every time a Flash button is clicked, it moves the Director movie to the proper location. To do this, you start by assigning the getURL() action to a Flash button. Only this time, you must specify an event and an argument:

```
on(release){
    getURL("event:flashButton \"start\"")
}
```

In this example, the event protocol specifies an event named flashButton. The argument for the event is "start".

> In this example, the argument "start" must include the quotation marks so that Director can interpret the string correctly as the name of a marker. To prevent the quotes from confusing and breaking the ActionScript string, each quote mark is escaped (ignored) by using the backslash character (\).

For this technique to work, the event called in Flash must have a counterpart in Director. Otherwise, the event will not be understood and will fail in your Director movie. You create a counterpart by writing a custom function in Lingo and saving it as a Movie script. For the preceding example, the custom function should be written like this:

```
on flashButton me, swfString
    go to frame swfString
end
```

Here, the name of the event specified in Flash is the name of the handler, flashButton. The argument it passes as a string is stored in swfString, then used later in the script to send the movie to a particular frame. In this example, the script would send the movie to a frame marker named start.

This approach is similar to the previous example that uses on getURL me. There is a difference that is important to understand, however. When using the event protocol, Flash relies on a custom function in your Director movie. The advantage of the function is that you needn't attach a Lingo script to every Flash sprite. Because your function is sitting in a Movie script in your Director cast, it is always available when your Flash movie calls for it.

ActionScript's getURL() function provides yet another way to pass information from Flash to Director. The lingo protocol is probably the most straightforward, but allows the least amount of flexibility because all statements are hard-coded. Using this technique, you specify specific Lingo statements in your Flash movie so that they can be passed directly to a Director host movie. For example:

```
on(release){
    getURL("lingo:go to frame 10")
}
```

This script, when attached to a button in Flash, will pass a message to Director telling it to jump to frame 10. Because the `lingo` protocol uses explicit Lingo statements, there is no need for any additional scripting in Director.

Manipulating Flash Sprites with Lingo

As sprites under the control of Lingo in a Director movie, Flash movies seem to lose some of their "Flash-ness," but you can still manipulate the sprites in much the same way as if they were inside a Flash movie. For basic navigation, you can use `tellTarget()`, `endTellTarget()`, and a handful of basic Timeline actions: `play()`, `stop()`, and `gotoFrame()`. To set and retrieve the attributes of a Flash movie within Director, use `setFlashProperty()` and `getFlashProperty()`. The `getFlashProperty()` function monitors the current attributes of a Flash movie sprite, and `setFlashProperty()` assigns a new value to a component of a Flash movie. For example, if a Flash movie sprite contained a Movie Clip, you could use these functions to monitor the clip's attributes and set them as needed. Their syntax is as follows:

```
sprite(spriteNum).setFlashProperty("targetName",#property,newValue)
sprite(spriteNum).getFlashProperty("targetName",#property,newValue)
```

In each, you must specify the sprite number of the Flash movie. Then you use the function you need and specify the name of the clip you wish to target, the property you need to set or retrieve, and a new value.See the following example:

```
on mouseUp
    if sprite(1).getFlashProperty("topleft",#alpha,"")=100
    then
        sprite(1).setFlashProperty("topleft",#alpha,50)
    else
        sprite(1).setFlashProperty("topleft",#alpha,100)
    end if
end
```

This script can be used to toggle the opacity (`#alpha` in Lingo, `_alpha` in ActionScript) of a Movie Clip instance named `topleft` of the Flash movie in sprite 1. If the `#alpha` value of the target equals 100, then it is set to one-half its value (50). If it is not 100, then it is set back to its full value (100). If you are using `getFlashProperty()` and don't need to set a new value, simply use an empty string (`""`) for that argument.

There are many properties that Lingo can use to manipulate targets and their values in a Flash sprite. See Table 23.2 for a complete listing and description of each.

Table 23.2

Lingo Terms for Manipulating Flash Movie Properties

NAME	TYPE	DESCRIPTION
#posX	R W	Pixel value for the X axis location of a target
#posY	R W	Pixel value for the Y axis location of a target
#scaleX	R W	Pixel value for the X scale of a target
#scaleY	R W	Pixel value for the Y scale of a target
#visible	R W	Determines whether a target is hidden or visible
#rotate	R W	Degree value for a target's rotation
#alpha	R W	Percent value of a target's opacity
#name	R W	Name assigned to a Movie Clip instance
#width	R	Pixel width of a target
#height	R	Pixel height of a target
#target	R	Full path in slash notation for a target relative to a movie's main Timeline
#url	R	Full path in HTTP syntax for a target
#dropTarget	R	Full path in slash notation for a target on which a draggable Movie Clip was dropped
#totalFrames	R	Total number of frames in a target
#currentFrame	R	Location of the playback head in a target's Timeline
#lastFrameLoaded	R	Last frame number to be loaded for a Flash sprite to be fully loaded into memory; see _framesLoaded property in ActionScript
#focusRect	R W G	Controls the visibility of the button focus rectangles in a Flash movie
#spriteSoundBufferTime	R W G	Determines how many seconds of sound should preload before playback begins

R = a property that can be read or retrieved; W = write, or a property that can be set; G = global property for an entire Flash movie.

In Table 23.2, there are two global properties that apply to an entire Flash movie. When working with these, enter an empty string (" ") as the target argument—for example, `sprite(1).getFlashProperty("", #focusRect, "")`.

To control the playback of the main Timeline and Movie Clip instances in your Flash movie, use the `tellTarget()` and `endTellTarget()`commands. Although these terms are deprecated in Flash, they work within Director to target individual clip instances. The Lingo syntax is as follows:

```
on mouseDown
    sprite(whichSprite).tellTarget("targetPath")
    --statements to target a clip or Timeline
    sprite(whichSprite).endTellTarget()
end
```

In this script "template," you use the `tellTarget()` and `endTellTarget()` statements like bookends; they enclose the statements that control a clip instance or movie Timeline. In the `tellTarget()` statement, you must specify, using slash syntax, the target path to the Timeline or clip you wish to control. Consider the following example:

```
on mouseDown
    sprite(1).tellTarget("/menu")
    sprite(1).play()
    sprite(1).endTellTarget()
end
```

This Lingo example tells the clip menu to start playing. The equivalent ActionScript would look like this:

```
on(press){
    _root.menu.play();
}
```

Here are a few other Lingo terms you can use to target clip instances and Timelines in your Flash movies:

play() Starts the playback of a Movie Clip or Timeline when the statement is called. Comparable to ActionScript's `play()` action.

stop() Halts the playback of a Movie Clip or Timeline when the statement is called. Comparable to ActionScript's `stop()` action.

gotoFrame(*frame*) Skips the playback head to the specified frame of a Movie Clip or Timeline when the statement is called. Comparable to ActionScript's `gotoAndStop()` action.

If you want `gotoFrame()`to skip to a particular frame *and* resume playback from that point (like a `gotoAndPlay()` action), you can use the following script, which combines these two terms. This script sends the Timeline of the menu instance ahead to frame 10 and resumes playback from that point.

```
on mouseDown
    sprite(1).tellTarget("/menu")
    sprite(1).gotoFrame(10)
    sprite(1).play()
    sprite(1).endtellTarget()
end
```

This simple technique is the building block of something quite powerful. Remember BubbleBody from Chapter 16? If not, skip back to "How Flash Manages Multiple Movie Timelines" in that chapter. Consider the idea of a Movie Clip that consists entirely of other nested Movie Clip instances, each of which is a body part of a digital puppet or marionette. Because each clip can be targeted as an individual instance, you can control the animation of any body part through scripting. Now, add this character to a Director movie. Not only can your puppet exist as a scalable, vector-based cast member; it is a cast member that you can control completely through Lingo scripting. You can use Lingo to skip your character ahead to frames and animated loops, to perform lip sync animations, to create facial expressions… the works!

Lingo can also be used to manipulate Flash sprites in the same way it does the other elements of Director movies. This means that Flash movies can be scaled, spun, flipped, restacked, and altered just like any other sprite. Lingo sprite properties present you with another option for customizing the performance of a Flash sprite in your Director production. There are many sprite properties that can be set and retrieved in Lingo. First, you should take a look at the basic syntax structure:

```
sprite(spriteNum).property=value
```

In Lingo, you must first identify the sprite that you wish to control. Then you state the property you would like to change, and assign a new value to that property. Consider the following Lingo example:

```
on mouseUp me
    spin=sprite(me.spriteNum).rotation
    sprite(me.spriteNum).rotation=spin+90
end
```

This script works as a behavior to rotate by 90° the sprite to which it is attached each time that sprite is clicked. This script stores the current rotation value in the variable **spin**. Then it reassigns the sprite's rotation to the current value plus 90°.

There are many Lingo properties that can be used to control the attributes of a sprite. See Table 23.3 for a partial listing and description of sprite properties that can be used to manipulate a Flash movie sprite.

	PROPERTY	DESCRIPTION
Table 23.3	rotation	Sets the rotation value for a sprite by degrees of rotation.
Lingo Properties	scale	Scales a sprite relative to its origin point.
for Manipulating	locH	The horizontal location of a sprite on the Stage in pixels, measured from the Stage's upper-left corner.
Flash Sprites	locV	The vertical location of a sprite on the Stage in pixels, measured from the Stage's upper-left corner.
	locZ	Controls the layering order of sprites in the Score.
	flipV	Determines whether a sprite has been flipped vertically on the Stage; if so, this returns **true**.
	flipH	Determines whether a sprite has been flipped horizontally on the Stage; if so, this returns **true**.
	skew	Sets the skew value for a sprite by degrees of tilt from an upright, vertical position.
	blend	Sets the opacity of a sprite; 100 = fully opaque, 0 = transparent.
	color	Determines the foreground color of a sprite.

For a complete listing and description of sprite properties, see the documentation that ships with Director and the Lingo Dictionary.

Inspirational Design Model

The possibilities given to you by Flash and Director—two very powerful authoring applications—are vast. For a glimpse of something that's on the entertaining side of this spectrum, visit www.lego.com/build. Here you can experience one of the more entertaining games on the Web today: Junkbot (see Figure 23.5). In this LEGO game, your goal is to help Junkbot through his daily task of emptying all the recycling bins at the local factory. The fun and creativity of the LEGO world make Junkbot more than just another digital puzzle game.

Developed by New York City's gameLab, Junkbot uses a combination of Director (Shockwave) and Flash elements. Although most of the game was created in Director, its introduction was animated in Flash to introduce players to Junkbot and provide the back story.

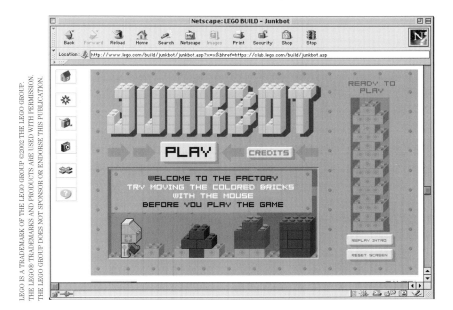

Figure 23.5

Junkbot is an online game that incorporates both Flash and Director.

Summary

This chapter discussed the issues and techniques inherent in combining two powerful multimedia creation tools: Macromedia Flash and Macromedia Director. Due to the strengths of each application, there are clear advantages to using one with the other. This chapter introduced Director "newbies" to some of the basic concepts behind Director's authoring environment and to how it's compatible with the SWF file type. You also learned how to import a Flash movie into the Director environment, or cast. Once in the cast, a Flash movie has many parameters that will determine how Director handles the movie. This chapter covered the specifics of these and other settings that affect how a Flash movie is displayed and treated as part of a Director production.

One of the best features of combining media is the expanded scripting possibilities. Like Flash, Director has its own scripting language, called Lingo. You learned that in the same way ActionScript controls the elements of a Flash movie, Lingo has great control over a Director movie. It's possible to use these languages to send information between movies as well. Action-Script can pass messages to Director, and Lingo can target different elements of a Flash movie. Together, the applications work to combine the flexibility of interactive vector graphic animations with the depth of multimedia authoring and scripting.

CHAPTER 24

Working with Flash and FreeHand

In Chapter 4 you explored all of the tools available for creating visual content in Flash. There is little doubt that you can produce some pretty cool stuff by using Flash's native painting and drawing tools. However, when it comes to creating multifaceted and precise works of art, Flash's drawing tools sometimes fall a little short—especially for those users with print vector illustration experience. The good thing is that Macromedia has provided some fairly powerful ways to integrate Macromedia FreeHand, one of the industry's leading vector illustration programs, into your grand creative process.

In this chapter, you're going to investigate the ways you can use FreeHand's vector illustration capabilities with Flash's phenomenal animation and interactivity tools to engineer some truly incredible creations.

In this chapter, you'll examine the following topics:

- Learning about FreeHand
- Creating multiframe Flash animations in FreeHand
- Simulating a shape-tweened animation in FreeHand
- Previewing Flash animations in FreeHand
- Using the Flash Anti-Alias mode
- Attaching actions in FreeHand
- Setting Flash movie properties in FreeHand
- Exporting FreeHand files to Flash

An Introduction to FreeHand

Before this whole digital media revolution hit big, print was king. It's not like print is now dead—quite the contrary! In fact, some of the most interesting, innovative, and exciting stuff in design is happening in print. However, many of the tools used exclusively for print design in the past have had to adapt to this digital world. As a result, you'll see traditional print programs such as QuarkXPress, Adobe Illustrator, and Adobe PageMaker boasting web features such as HTML export (to name just one).

The most recent version of Macromedia FreeHand is no different. A traditional vector-based print design program (quite similar to Adobe Illustrator), Macromedia FreeHand is geared toward illustration, productivity, and publishing. The difference between FreeHand and its print design competitors is that it takes full advantage of Macromedia's suite of other digital design tools. Early on, Macromedia astutely recognized the future of its company rested primarily in the realm of web design and publishing. This prompted a refocusing of the company's software development and resulted in the release of such industry-leading programs as Dreamweaver, Dreamweaver UltraDev, Fireworks, and Flash. So, where does this leave FreeHand? Well, unlike many other software developers (such as Adobe), Macromedia was able to use its powerful software packages as a lever with which to add a series of cool web features to FreeHand.

The most interesting of these features is Flash support. Because FreeHand produces vector-based art, it seemed only natural to link it closely with Flash. In the most recent versions of FreeHand (most notably, versions 9 and 10), Macromedia has added a series of powerful features that let you export vector artwork directly into Flash. Even more exciting is FreeHand's ability to create frame-by-frame animations and directly import them into Flash.

All in all, these additions make FreeHand a much more valuable tool to Flash developers as well as maintaining its reputation as a topnotch print design program.

 A demo copy of Macromedia FreeHand 10 has been included on this book's CD-ROM.

Creating Multiframe Animations in FreeHand

Exporting complex static vector artwork in a form easily importable by Flash is a great labor-saving feature. However, FreeHand's greatest strength, at least when it comes to Flash, is the ability to create animations that can then be seamlessly moved into Flash. This means you aren't forced to create detailed vector art that is exported to Flash for animation—you can actually take care of many of your animation needs from within FreeHand.

Unfortunately, FreeHand doesn't have the ability to tween. As a result, any animations you create within FreeHand that are destined for SWF export will be frame-by-frame animations.

Let's take a look at how you can create a frame-by-frame animation in FreeHand. For the purposes of this example, you're going to create an animation of a sphere moving across the screen—not a particularly difficult or impressive animation. However, it will give you the foundation to animate more complex images created in FreeHand. Follow these steps:

1. Open FreeHand, and create a new document by selecting File → New or by using Cmd/Ctrl+N.

2. Go to View → Fit All. By doing this, you'll ensure that FreeHand automatically sets the magnification so that your entire page is displayed. Because FreeHand is designed primarily for print design, the default size of any new document created is 8.5×11.

3. Before you create the object you're going to animate, you need to create a new layer. Open the Layers panel by going to Window → Panels → Layers. From here, choose New from the Layers panel's Options menu (accessible by clicking the small right-pointing arrow in the top-right corner of the panel).

When it comes to creating animations in FreeHand, each layer's content will be transformed into a discreet frame when imported into Flash.

4. Now create the object you're going to animate. With the Toolbox open (Window → Tools), select the Ellipse tool ○ .

5. Place your cursor at the top of the page. Click and drag to create a circle that is about 3 centimeters (1.25 inches) in diameter.

To show the ruler in FreeHand, select View → Page Rulers → Show. If you want to edit the units displayed on the ruler, go to View → Page Rulers → Edit. This opens the Edit Units dialog box, where you can choose which units are displayed on the ruler.

6. Now, to continue with the animation process, you need to turn the circle you've just drawn into a symbol. To do this, either go to Modify → Symbol → Convert to Symbol or use the shortcut F8. This will automatically insert the circle into FreeHand's Library (which is accessible by going to Window → Library).

7. Now, create a new layer using the procedure in step 3.

8. With the Library open (Window → Library) and the new layer selected, click and drag another circle symbol from the Library to a position just below the original circle.

9. Now that you've created the first two frames, simply repeat the process described in steps 3 through 8 (creating a new layer and dragging the circle symbol into it) until your circle has traversed the entire length of the page.

Congratulations, you've just created your first Flash-focused animation in FreeHand. Granted, the way it appears in the FreeHand document isn't particularly pretty, but don't worry about that too much right now. In "Previewing Flash Animations in FreeHand," you're going to see the animation you've just created.

Instead of using individual layers to simulate the frames in an animation, you can also use discreet *pages* to create the frames in your animation. However, if you use pages instead of layers, you won't be able to simulate a shape-tweened animation—a process described in the next section.

Simulating a Shape-Tweened Animation in FreeHand

In the previous section, you created a frame-by-frame animation using layers and symbols. Although you can't create a tweened animation like in Flash, you can get FreeHand to simulate one object changing into another—the result of which is similar to a shape tween. Let's take a look at how:

1. Create a new document by selecting File → New or by using Cmd/Ctrl+N.

2. Create a new layer by opening the Layers panel (Window → Panels → Layers) and choosing New from the Options pop-up menu.

3. With the new layer selected, draw a large circle (with the Ellipse tool) in the top-left corner of the document.

4. On the same layer, use Rectangle tool to draw a small square in the document's lower-right corner.

5. Select both shapes with the Pointer tool ⬉ (located in the top-left corner of the Toolbox). To do this, you can either click and drag so that the marquee surrounds both shapes or hold down the Shift key while you select each shape.

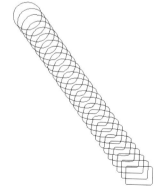

6. Now, go to Modify → Combine → Blend. When you do this, FreeHand creates a series of intervening shapes to create a blend from the first shape to the second shape.

7. Without clicking anywhere (which would deselect the blend you've just created), open the Object Inspector by going to Window → Inspectors → Object (if it is not already opened).

8. In the Object Inspector, enter a value into the Steps field—the default is 25, but you can enter any value you want. This essentially sets the number of images in the blend. The more steps you have, the smoother the animation will be. Remember, however, more steps mean a larger file size.

9. When you've set the number of steps in the blend, go to Xtras → Animate → Release to Layers. This opens the Release to Layers dialog box. Make sure Sequence is selected from the drop-down menu at the top of the dialog box. When you're finished, click OK. By doing this, you're telling FreeHand to take each of the shapes in the blend and stick them on individual layers.

> If you want your animation to play in reverse, select the Reverse Direction check box in the Release to Layers dialog box.

You've just simulated a motion tween with FreeHand. All that you need to do is preview your creation and then export it. You'll learn how to preview the animation in the next section.

Previewing Flash Animations in FreeHand

You've just created a frame-by-frame (or layer-by-layer) animation in FreeHand. This is all fine and good, but what if you want to find out how it's going to look when it's exported to SWF (covered later in "Exporting FreeHand Files to Flash")? To preview a Flash animation from within FreeHand, follow these steps:

1. Open the document that contains the layer-by-layer animation you want to preview.

2. Go to Control → Test Movie. From there, your animation will open and play in the Flash Player within FreeHand.

3. To control the movie while it's playing, you can use the Controller toolbar, which is accessible by going to Window → Toolbars → Controller. This opens up a set of VCR-like controls displayed at the top of the FreeHand environment.

Beyond the tools necessary to control the playback of your movie, the Controller tool-bar also contains buttons to preview the movie (which has the same effect as Control → Test Movie), set the movie properties (something we'll talk about later in the chapter), and export the movie.

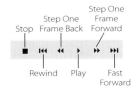

> You can't preview your movie from directly within the FreeHand environment—you need to open it in the Flash Player. As a result, unless you've told FreeHand to preview your movie (by either selecting Control → Test Movie or clicking the Test Movie button in the Controller tool-bar), the VCR-like controls in the Controller toolbar will not be accessible.

Using the Flash Anti-Alias Display Mode

If you look at the smooth, crisp appearance of the animations or static images you create in Flash and compare it to the objects you create in FreeHand, you'll notice a marked difference. Why do the vector images in FreeHand look different from the vector images in Flash? They're all just vector images, right? Well, yes and no. The display engines that run Flash and FreeHand are quite different. As a result, FreeHand, which is geared toward the creation of print design, displays its vector-based art much differently than Flash (whose products are ultimately destined for a computer screen). If you're creating artwork or animations in FreeHand for importing into Flash, the difference in display can be a bit annoying.

One solution is to preview your creations in the Flash Player (as discussed in the previous section). Unfortunately, this removes the artwork from the FreeHand authoring environment. When you preview vector art in the Flash Player from within FreeHand, you are no longer able to edit it. Switching back and forth between FreeHand and the Flash Player is a pretty grim prospect if you want to get your work done quickly. Don't sweat it—FreeHand offers you a great tool, the Anti-Alias display mode, for working on your artwork while viewing it as it would appear in Flash.

To access the Flash Anti-Alias display mode, you have two options. First, you can go to View → Flash Anti-Alias. Alternatively, you can choose Flash Anti-Alias from the Drawing Mode drop-down list in the status bar.

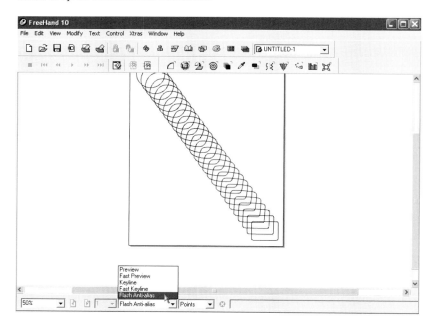

Once you've selected the mode, you'll see a marked difference between how FreeHand usually displays artwork and how Flash displays it. Figure 24.1 illustrates the difference between the two modes.

Figure 24.1

The image on the left illustrates how FreeHand normally displays artwork. The image on the right illustrates the same artwork in Flash Anti-Alias display mode.

Attaching Actions in FreeHand

Easily one of the most useful features in FreeHand is the ability to attach Flash actions to your artwork. Essentially, after creating your vector animations as static artwork in Free-Hand, you can integrate some limited ActionScript before even moving your creations into Flash. Granted, it's nowhere near as involved a process as in Flash itself. However, it does provide you with some genuinely interesting possibilities.

Follow these steps to attach a Flash action to your FreeHand image:

1. Select the object to which you want to attach the action.

2. Now, open the Navigation panel by selecting Window → Panels → Navigation.

3. Choose the action you want to assign to that object with the Action drop-down menu. (For an in-depth look at your choices, see Chapter 12.)

4. Now, choose the event that will trigger the action from the Event drop-down menu. (For an in-depth look at event handlers, see Chapter 12.)

5. If you've chosen Go To, Print, Load/Unload Movie, or Tell Target, you need to set the action's parameters. The Parameters drop-down menu allows you to designate different pages in your animation, and the Frame drop-down menu allows you to designate different layers.

6. When you've finished, close the Navigation panel.

Setting Flash Movie Properties in FreeHand

Whether you've fashioned a frame-by-frame animation, a simulated shape tween, or a single object to which an action is attached, your ultimate goal is to export your creation in SWF format. FreeHand features some fairly robust tools for setting the properties of the SWF file upon export.

FreeHand only exports in SWF format—and not FLA (Flash's native file type). As a result, you can't *open* images created in FreeHand in Flash. Instead, you need to *import* them into Flash.

Once you've crafted the animation or artwork you want to export as a SWF file, there are a couple of ways to access the Movie Settings dialog box, the tool with which you'll access your movie's various options:

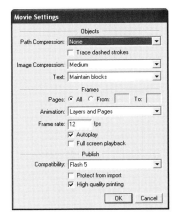

- Go to File → Export. When the Export Document dialog box opens, choose Macromedia Flash (SWF) from the Save as Type drop-down menu, and then click the Setup button (just below the Save and Cancel buttons).

- Click the Movie Settings button [icon] located in the Controller toolbar (accessible by going to Window → Toolbars → Controller).

The Export button is only accessible after you've clicked the Test Movie button in the Controller toolbar. Alternatively, you can also go to Control → Test Movie.

At this point, let's look at each option in the Movie Settings dialog box in detail:

Path Compression Determines how your artwork will be compressed upon export. The options range from None, which maintains the original number of points and results in the highest quality (but a larger file size), to Maximum, which results in the smallest number of points possible and the lowest file size (and lowest quality).

Trace Dashed Strokes Guarantees that any dashed strokes in your art will be converted to a discreet object upon export. As one would expect, the process increases the time it takes to export the image as well as the final file size.

Image Compression Determines the quality at which bitmaps are converted to JPEGs. The options range from None, which results in the largest file size with the greatest quality, to Maximum, which results in the smallest file size with the lowest image quality.

Text Determines how FreeHand exports any text in your artwork. If you choose Maintain Blocks, the text is exported as a text block, which is then editable in Flash. On the other hand, if you choose Convert to Paths, the text is converted to a vector path, thereby making it uneditable as text. If you choose None, all text is omitted from the exported file.

Pages Allows you to determine the range of pages that are exported (if you have more than one page in your document).

Animation Lets you specify the way in which FreeHand exports any animation you've created:

- Layers and Pages will export all the layers on the first page as a series of frames. Then, it will move on to all the subsequent pages (one after another) and export all the layers as frames.

- Layers will export all the layers in your document as a series of frames.

- Pages will export each page as a single frame in a single SWF file. If any of the pages have more than one layer, they'll all be squished into one for the purposes of export.

- None will export each page as an individual SWF file. Multiple layers will simply be compressed to comprise one frame in one SWF file.

Frame Rate Sets the frame rate of the animation in question in frames per second (fps). If you're having trouble remembering exactly how frame rate works, see Chapter 10.

Autoplay Makes sure the animation begins playing automatically when opened in the stand-alone Flash Player.

Full Screen Playback Makes the movie automatically take up the entire monitor (until the user presses Esc). It's important to note that this option will only work if the user opens the movie in the stand-alone Flash Player; it won't work if the movie is embedded in a web page viewed by a browser.

Compatibility Lets you choose the version of Flash to which your exported SWF files is targeted. Remember, the different versions of Flash have different levels of support (or total lack thereof, in some cases) for ActionScript.

> Unfortunately, because FreeHand 10 was a generation before Flash MX, the highest version of Flash you'll see in the Compatibility drop-down menu is Flash 5. Don't worry too much, though, because Flash MX can easily import Flash 5 SWF files.

Protect from Import Makes sure no one can import your exported SWF file.

High Quality Printing Lets the user print each frame in the animation at high resolution (regardless of whether they're viewing the movie with the stand-alone Flash Player or from within a browser). If the option is deselected, the user's computer will print at the screen resolution of 72dpi.

After you've set all the appropriate setting for your movie, click OK. From here, it's time to export the file—a process you'll explore in the following section.

Exporting FreeHand Files to Flash

Now that you've looked at how to set the various properties of your creation with the Movie Properties dialog box, you can export your artwork. After setting the movie's properties, you'll find that exporting your file is somewhat anticlimactic. Follow these steps:

1. Click the Test Movie button located in the Controller toolbar (or simply go to Control → Test Movie).

2. When the Movie Player opens, click the Export Movie button [image]. Alternatively, you can go to Control → Export Movie after the Movie Player opens.

3. When the Export Movie dialog box opens, enter a name in the Name field, navigate to the location on your hard drive where you want the movie exported, and click Save.

You can also select File → Export. When the Export Document dialog box opens, enter a name in the Name field, choose Macromedia Flash (SWF) from the Save as Type drop-down menu, navigate to the location where you want to export the file, and click Save.

Inspirational Design Model

Complex illustration has always featured fairly prominently in Flash creations. This is especially true for Flash-based web cartoons (or *webtoons*), which live or die by the quality of their illustrations. Although this book is full of great examples of Flash-based webtoons (hey, what can I say—we love 'em), arguably one of the grooviest comes courtesy of Renegade Cartoons (www.renegadecartoons.com), which is the digital arm of Renegade Animation (www.renegadeanimation.com).

A small animation house run by Darell Van Citters and Ashley Postlewaite, Renegade Cartoons produces all manner of incredibly stylish episodic webtoons—chief among them being the adventures of the lovable Elmo the Ardvaark. Figure 24.2 shows a sample of this terribly cool site.

Figure 24.2

Renegade Cartoons produces incredibly stylish Flash animations and webtoons.

Summary

In this chapter, you explored how you can integrate Flash with Macromedia FreeHand. You started off by getting a brief introduction to the nature of FreeHand itself. From there, you jumped into creating frame-by-frame animations in FreeHand with the layer-by-layer technique and the simulated shape-tweening technique. You continued by previewing your animation, using the Flash Anti-Alias display mode, and attaching Flash actions to artwork created in FreeHand. You finished the chapter off by setting movie properties and exporting files to Flash.

CHAPTER 25

Working with Flash and Digital Audio Applications

Of all the different types of applications that can be used in conjunction with Flash, digital audio programs are the least similar to Flash itself. In digital audio, there are no animated frames, no movie clips, and no scripting language. It is just you, a sound file or sample, and lots of tools to change the way something sounds. Additionally, audio applications demand a completely different kind of mind-set. You must make the shift from a visual time-based medium to an aural time-based medium. Your ears are most important!

You have learned quite a bit about digital audio in this book, particularly how to prepare sound files for the Flash environment and how to handle them once they get there. Now it's time to step back and look at some of the additional resources you can use outside of Flash to give your movies a great sonic punch. With the right tools and a little know-how, you will discover a world of creative possibilities.

This chapter contains the following topics:

- **Introduction to current multi-track, loop, and wave-editing audio applications**

- **Review of current MIDI sequencing applications**

- **Audio effects and digital processing techniques**

- **Creating your own seamless loops**

- **Flash techniques for adding interactive audio loops to your movies**

Digital Audio Tools

More digital audio applications are available today than ever before. The range of software is enormous: from robust, professional, multi-track systems to smaller, homemade sound gadgets and audio modifiers or creators. Whatever your budget, you are bound to find something that will help you create the music, vocal, or effects soundtrack that will accompany your Flash movie.

The overview of software presented here is by no means complete. There are many additional tools that will render excellent results in your Flash soundtrack. This collection is more or less a highlight list of reputable applications that are often used in conjunction with digital multimedia. Choosing the one (or two or three...) that works best for you can take some time. It helps to have a little experience working with audio on your computer so that you know the kinds of features that will be most helpful, based on your working style, your equipment, the size of a typical project, and so on. In most cases, the manufacturers make it easy for you to decide. Many software companies offer free trial downloads of their products. What better way to shop for an application than to test-drive it for free and be absolutely sure that it is right for you? For each entry in this section, you will find a list of online resources where you get additional information about the software, manufacturer, compatibility, and pricing.

This section of the chapter is meant both to inform you about the audio tools that are currently available and to offer some guidance based on the particular strengths and weaknesses of each application. Consequently, it is divided into four parts: multi-track applications, waveform editors, loop editors, and MIDI sequencers. If you are already familiar with these terms, you should have no problem locating the information you need. If this is all very new, then keep reading. With each description, you will find that it's easy to narrow things down based on the demands of your current projects.

Multi-Track Audio Editors

Multi-track applications are used primarily for three things: recording audio, cutting and editing, and mixing together the final song or piece. Because they have great depth and offer a wide range of possibilities, most of them are used for large-scale projects, or projects that require you to combine many different elements into a single song or composition. If you plan to produce your own original music, or assemble a track using narration, dialog, music, and sound effects, then a multi-track audio editor is for you.

Pro Tools

Pro Tools is currently the industry standard for professional-level recording, editing, and mixing of digital audio. Manufactured by Digidesign, this application is built for large audio projects involving many tracks, and it gives you complete control over the performance of each element in your mix. Additionally, Pro Tools offers support for video, MIDI, and both multi-channel and surround sound mixing.

Pro Tools has two types of systems. The primary one is known as TDM, which stands for *time division multiplexing*. With a Pro Tools TDM system, audio information is routed through additional hardware that's installed on your computer. The power of the TDM system lies in this additional hardware, because it manages most of the DSP (*digital signal processing*) and allows the computer to work with multiple simultaneous audio streams in real time. TDM systems provide the greatest amount of power and flexibility, but they demand a substantial financial investment and are recommended for serious users only.

The other kind of Pro Tools system is RTAS, or Real-Time AudioSuite. The main difference is this: RTAS systems use *host processing*, or the CPU of the computer running the software, rather than additional hardware. Consequently, the performance of the system is affected greatly by the speed and efficiency of the computer running the software. RTAS systems (Pro Tools LE) are great for smaller-scale projects and still offer all the editing capabilities of a TDM system. For an illustration of the Pro Tools LE environment, see Figure 25.1.

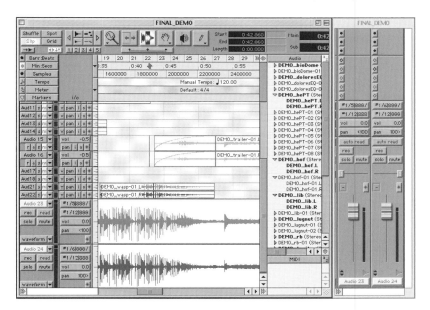

Figure 25.1

Pro Tools LE has all the editing features of regular Pro Tools but depends on the host computer to do any digital signal processing (DSP).

Currently, Pro Tools is supported on Macintosh, Windows 2000, Windows 98, and Windows Me computers. Consult Digidesign (`www.digidesign.com`) for up-to-date information on compatibility and system requirements. If interested, you can try Pro Tools for free. Visit the Digidesign website and follow the link for Pro Tools FREE. This software is a scaled-down but fully functional version of Pro Tools that will give you a taste of the application. Pro Tools FREE is also supported on both Macintosh and Windows platforms.

Vegas Audio

Vegas Audio is a Windows-only multi-track audio editing and mixing tool manufactured by Sonic Foundry (`www.sonicfoundry.com`). Unlike a Pro Tools TDM system, this software requires no additional hardware and will run on your computer using the host processor. Vegas boasts a simple drag-and-drop interface that allows you to combine and recombine your audio to create multifaceted soundtracks. See Figure 25.2 for an illustration of the Vegas Audio editing environment.

Figure 25.2

Sonic Foundry's Vegas Audio interface

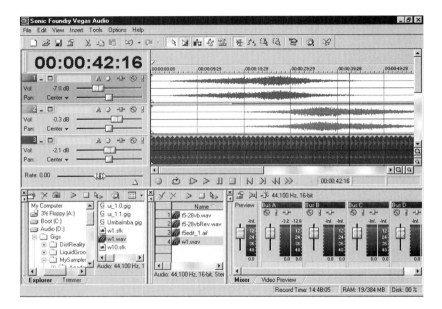

Vegas offers an unlimited number of audio tracks and supports up to 18 Sonic Foundry DirectX plug-in effects (XFX 1, 2, and 3). Additionally, it supports synchronization with QuickTime 4, and can be used to score Flash movies that you publish in QuickTime format. Sonic Foundry currently offers two versions of this application: Vegas Audio and Vegas Audio LE. The scaled-down LE version offers many of the same features as Vegas Audio but carries a few limitations, including a maximum of eight audio tracks. Both versions of Vegas will run on Windows 98SE, Me, 2000, and XP systems.

For complete information on Vegas Audio, system requirements, and trial download offers, consult the Sonic Foundry website.

Waveform Editors

Waveform editors are a step down from multi-track editors—not because they are less useful, but because they take a different approach to audio editing. In reality, most waveform editors have many of the features found in a multi-track system. The main difference is *size*. Waveform editors are generally geared to handle only one or two simultaneous tracks (mono and stereo files). While this may seem limiting, it has its advantages. It can be easier to work quickly when you have fewer options. Waveform editors may not have all the bells and whistles of a larger audio application, but they do provide a simple, streamlined environment for editing, tweaking, and preparing audio files. Depending on your profession or your role on a Flash development team, it's safe to say that a reliable waveform editor will be able to take care of 85% to 90 % of the audio work that is required to produce a Flash movie.

Sound Forge

Sound Forge has quickly become one of the staples of the digital media industry. This Windows-only waveform editor provides excellent support for cutting, pasting, trimming, creating fades, recording, doing signal processing, editing loop points, and much more. Sound Forge also includes three kinds of equalizers: graphic, parametric, and paragraphic. It can also be used to encode MP3 files for direct import into Flash. Additionally, Sound Forge offers several DirectX audio plug-ins: Amplitude Modulation, Chorus, Delay, Distortion, Flange, Gapper, Noise Gate, Pitch Bend, Reverb, Vibrato, Time Compression, Wave Hammer, and more. You can see an illustration of Sound Forge in Figure 25.3.

Sound Forge is manufactured by Sonic Foundry (`www.sonicfoundry.com`) and runs on the following systems: Windows 98SE, Me, 2000, and XP. Look for a demo version of SoundForge on this book's companion CD-ROM.

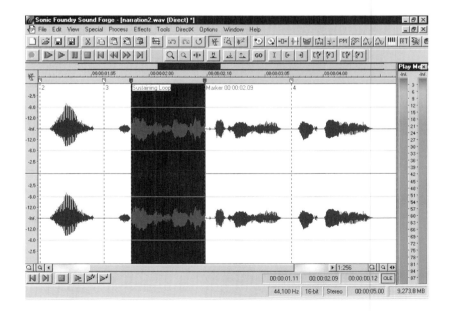

Figure 25.3

Sound Forge is a top-quality, intuitive waveform editor made by Sonic Foundry.

Peak 3

Peak is manufactured by BIAS, or Berkley Integrated Audio Software. Currently, it is one of the few professional-quality digital audio editing applications made expressly for the Macintosh operating system. As an audio editor, it has the kinds of tools that you would expect: You can cut, paste, fade, cross-fade, change pitch and duration, normalize, and perform stereo-to-mono conversions. Besides the main, detailed waveform display, Peak provides the useful "Audio Waveform Overview," a kind of panoramic display of the entire sound file. If your main window shows a detail of the wave, the Overview window will still display the entire file, along with an indicator of which area you are currently examining (see Figure 25.4).

Figure 25.4

The Peak interface provides two levels of navigation for a sound file, regular (detailed waveform) and Overview, shown in the topmost window.

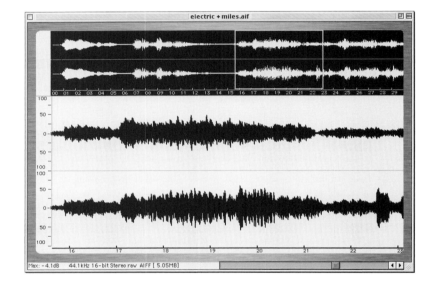

In addition to its editing features, Peak 3 supports Steinberg VST plug-ins. You can use these in a variety of ways to apply equalization, compression, reverb, and many other kinds of processing to a sound file. Additionally, BIAS, Inc., has recently released its own 10-band parametric equalizer called SuperFreq.

Peak 3 also offers a batch-processing feature. This asset comes as a huge relief if you have ever had to convert a large collection of files to a different sample rate, file type, and so on. Peak expands the possibilities of a batch processor by also providing an option to apply DSP (normalize, stereo/mono conversion, and so on) to the batch-processed files.

Peak will run on any PowerPC-equipped or G3/G4 Macintosh computer. Peak 3 has also been "carbonized" for users running Mac OS X. For additional system requirements and compatibility information, or to download a trial version of Peak, visit BIAS at www.bias-inc.com.

SoundEdit 16

SoundEdit 16 is a classic—or, if it isn't officially, it should be. It's very likely that anyone who develops multimedia or does video editing on a Macintosh owns a copy of SoundEdit 16. This is a unique audio application. At one time, it was manufactured by Macromedia. Today it is no longer in development, but is still supported at the Macromedia website (www.macromedia.com/software/sound) and is used throughout many circles of the digital media industry. As a typical waveform editor, SoundEdit 16 has many of the features that you would expect to see: copy, cut, paste, fade-in and out, normalize, pitch shift, backwards, tempo, and so on. SoundEdit 16 also provides support for creating and inserting loop points in an audio file or sample. Simply stated, SoundEdit (see Figure 25.5) is a great, compact, no-frills editor.

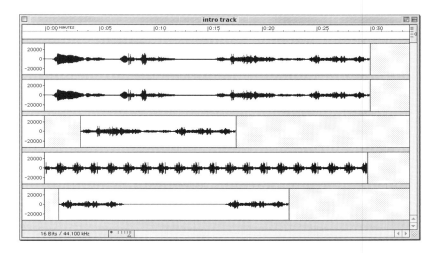

Figure 25.5

SoundEdit 16 is rare in that it's one of the few waveform editors that accommodates multi-track editing and mixing.

One big characteristic that makes SoundEdit 16 unique is that unlike most other wave editors, it supports multiple, simultaneous audio tracks. This makes it uniquely suited to create all sorts of strange and interesting layered sounds or to edit and mix a multicomponent soundtrack. It is not multi-track-savvy to the extent of Pro Tools or some of the other editors discussed here, but it can do much more with multi-track audio than both Sound Forge and Peak. Another trait that sets it apart is its ability to zoom into the sample level, allowing you to manipulate each sample individually as shown here:

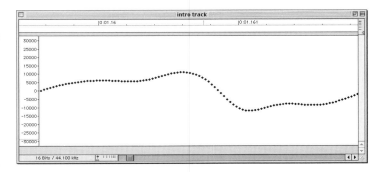

As an older application, SoundEdit 16 has minimal system requirements: Mac System 7.1

or higher; 68030 processor or faster. SoundEdit 16 is still available but is no longer evolving as a software package. Consult your favorite software dealer for pricing and availability information.

Loop Creation and Editing

If you are interested in putting together your own music but don't necessarily have the inclination to dive into full-blown composition or song writing, loop software may be a good choice for you. Working with loops is one part composing, one part editing, and features the best of both worlds. When you work with loops, much of the musical material is finished and has been prepared for you as repeatable audio segments known as *loops*. Audio loops can then be cut, layered, mixed, remixed, and combined to produce an entirely new piece of music. Or, using your own music, you can create your own loops and produce remixes or variations to create a different kind of interactive sound experience. Used tastefully, loop software is a great way to produce original music for your Flash movies. To read more about specific uses of looped audio in Flash, see "Creating Seamless Audio Loops" later in this chapter, as well as in Hands On 6.

ACID PRO

ACID PRO is Sonic Foundry's all-popular application for creating loops and loop-based music. To use it, you simply assemble the loops you would like to use, arrange them in ACID's timeline, click the Play button, and away you go! Because most loops you encounter are "finished" chunks of music, there is often little work required in terms of editing sound files. ACID PRO allows you to get right into the music and create your musical statements almost instantly (see Figure 25.6).

Figure 25.6

The ACID PRO editing environment allows you to compose and produce music using different combinations of looped sound files.

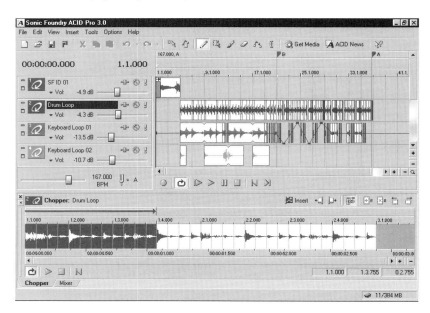

ACID PRO loop tracks can be manipulated in several ways. You are able to control overall tempo, panning, and volume (envelope), and to create track fades and transitions. And, like most other Sonic Foundry software, ACID PRO supports 18 Sonic Foundry DirectX plug-ins to add effects and apply processing to your looped creations. ACID PRO ships with a CD that contains a large loop library filled with musical gestures in a variety of styles. Additional audio loop libraries are available from Sonic Foundry as well as other third-party manufacturers. One of ACID's best features, though, is that it will allow you to bring in original loops (edited in Sound Forge and other applications) to add a personal flair to your project. ACID PRO will run on Windows 98SE, Me, 2000, and XP systems.

If you use Windows and want to try your hand (and ears) at creating music with ACID, check out the free ACID XPress 3.0 demo on this book's CD-ROM. This introductory version of ACID allows you to explore the possibilities of loop-based music at no cost whatsoever.

MIDI Sequencers

MIDI, or Musical Instrument Digital Interface, has been an important player in audio production for years. It is another one of those topics that could easily fill an entire book unto itself. In a nutshell, MIDI music has two main components: a sequence and a sound bank or module. A *sequence* is a computer file saved in a MIDI-compatible format that serves as a kind of digital piano roll. When it is played back by the computer, it communicates via MIDI with a sound module. The *sound module* reads the MIDI information that is sent by the sequence, provides the correct notes, sounds, and effects, and plays them back in real time. To create MIDI music, you need to have both of these components: a sound module or sampler, and a MIDI sequencer to create MIDI files and send musical information.

MIDI music is a topic more closely related to audio production than to Flash. However, MIDI music can certainly provide a valuable musical asset to any Flash movie. The important thing to remember, though, is that a MIDI sequence itself isn't music, but rather a list of instructions sent to a sound module or bank. When the sound device receives the instructions, it plays the notes accordingly. As a result, to capture MIDI music, you must record the sounds coming from the device playing your MIDI file as a digital audio file.

Whether you use Windows or a Macintosh, there is a MIDI sequencing application for you. Here is a brief list to check out:

Cakewalk Home Studio 2002 A Windows-based application for MIDI sequencing, recording, and a little bit of everything else (including multi-track digital audio) described in this chapter. See `www.cakewalk.com` for specific information, PC compatibility, and related products like Cakewalk Pro Audio and Sonar.

Cubase VST Manufactured by Steinberg Media Technologies AG, this application, like Cakewalk, can "do it all." The unique thing about Cubase is that Steinberg manufactures versions for both Windows and the Macintosh. Visit `www.steinberg.net` for details.

Digital Performer   A Macintosh native application for, you guessed it, MIDI sequencing and everything else musical under the sun. This application is made by Mark of the Unicorn (MOTU). For compatibility information, visit www.motu.com.

All the applications discussed here may seem to be very much the same, and to a certain extent, this is true. After all, they are all geared to do one thing: produce digital audio in some way, shape, or form. However, after experimenting with several of them, you will find that each has its own unique personality, just like Flash. The key is to settle on a tool that works for you and the demands of your Flash projects.

Digital Audio Techniques

So far, you have learned about the vast array of tools that are currently available for creating, editing, mixing, and producing audio for Flash movies and animations. However, selecting a tool for the job is only half the battle. Being able to use it to do the job creatively and professionally is the real trick. And to reach this level, it takes some time to learn how the features of audio editors affect the files they manipulate.

This section of the chapter focuses on different audio editing techniques that are particularly useful in preparing audio for Flash and other kinds of digital media. If you are unfamiliar with digital audio concepts, it may be helpful to refer to Chapter 19 and gain a basic understanding before proceeding with the ideas presented here. Because there are so many different audio applications, the instructions and steps described in this section are general. Each concept or technique is presented in a way that applies to all applications.

Audio Effects and Processing

When working with digital audio, any time you need to change the way something sounds you can apply digital processing or an effect. Depending on the effect, DSP will perform an operation on the audio waveform to change the way it sounds. Like cutting and pasting, this is part of the editing process.

In the world of digital audio, there are two kinds of editing: destructive and nondestructive. The names are rather self-explanatory. *Destructive* editing means that the wave will be forever changed, unless you undo the operation. *Nondestructive* means that the original will *not* be altered. Generally, a new file is created with the particular edit and used in place of the original. This applies to all kinds of edits, particularly edits that involve processing and effects. Depending on which application you use, you will be doing either destructive editing, nondestructive editing, or perhaps a bit of each. Be sure to check before you begin working so that you won't ruin an irreplaceable file by accident. When all else fails, you can usually undo (Cmd/Ctrl+Z) an operation to return to the last state of a file. Well, enough of the precautions; let's do some editing.

Normalize

In some respects, *normalization* is the single most important kind of processing you can apply to a digital audio file, especially if you are preparing the audio for computer-based multimedia. The reason is that you never know how loud someone will have their system volume or speakers set to play. And although you have no (or little) control over this, the one thing you can do is ensure that your sounds are set at their highest possible volume. Plus, to avoid possible audio distortion, it's always easier and better sounding to turn something down than to have to turn it up.

Normalization is used to increase the overall volume of a sound. It looks at a sound file and finds the loudest point. Then it boosts the loudest point to a specified value and brings everything else along with it, keeping the dynamics of the file in proportion.

To normalize a sound file or sample:

1. Select the portion of the file you would like to normalize. Generally, this is the entire sound file.

2. Choose Normalize from one of the application's menus (usually Process or Effects). A Normalize dialog box appears:

3. Enter a value for the loudest point, generally 96–98%. This will boost the loudest point of the file to 96–98% of its total possible volume and make the volume for the rest of the file change relative to that.

4. Click OK, and the editor will perform the edit. You should see a change in the amplitude of the sound file. For an example of this change, see Figure 19.9 in Chapter 19.

You should normalize all sounds before importing them to Flash to ensure the highest possible volume. Once they are in your movie, you can always tweak volume levels using either the envelope controls or methods of the Sound object.

USING THE LEVEL METER TO MONITOR CLIPPING

If you have spent any time at all with a digital audio application, you have undoubtedly encountered the word *clipping*. Clipping means that a sound's level has been boosted beyond the capabilities of the playback system. (To read more about this, see Chapter 19.) While working with a sound, you can monitor its level using the level meter in your digital audio application. These are usually designed to resemble the LEDs (light-emitting diodes) found on many professional mixing boards. The meter will track the level of a sound as it plays back, and give you a readout of a sound's dynamics. As a sound approaches the point of clipping, the meter will generally change from green to yellow to orange. If the sound goes over the limit, the meter will usually display a red "clip indicator" to let you know that the sound's dynamics are out of range, or the sound is distorting.

The accompanying graphic illustrates a typical level meter. This particular example (called Play Meters) is drawn from Sonic Foundry's Sound Forge.

Equalizer

An *equalizer* is a tool that is used to alter the frequency balance of a sound file. *Equalization* (also known by the slang term *EQ*) makes adjustments to the frequencies of a sound by either boosting or cutting them. For example, cutting the low frequencies of a sound will take out the "boominess" or "muddy" quality of a sound. Boosting the high range will make a sound "brighter"; too much of this can make a sound shrill or tinny.

Generally, an equalizer is used to make a sound clearer. As with most effects, your ears are the best judge. Work with the equalizer until the file sounds the way you think it should. And as always, monitor the levels of a sound so that you don't clip, or distort, the file. Too much EQ can send a sound flying off the meters!

To apply EQ to a sound file or sample:

1. Select the portion of the file you would like to equalize. This is usually the entire sound file.

2. Choose Equalizer from one of the application's menus (usually Process or Effects). A Equalizer dialog box appears (see Figure 25.7).

Figure 25.7

Sound Forge offers several kinds of EQ. This is the Graphic Equalizer.

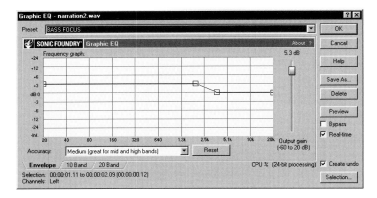

3. Using the equalizer's slider controls (this is typical in most interfaces), set values for the various frequencies of a sound.

Table 25.1

Bernie Mack's Subjective EQ Terms

FREQUENCY OF SOUND (IN HERTZ)	DESCRIPTION OF SOUND
60–80	Bass
200–250	Muddy
350	Pinched, nasal
450	Warm
5,000 (5kHz)	S's
7,000 (7kHz)	Attack
12,000 (12kHz)	High end, bright

As a general guide to frequency adjustment, see Table 25.1, "Bernie Mack's Subjective EQ Terms." Chicago-based recording engineer and instructor Bernie Mack developed this chart to help his students match sound characteristics or descriptions with frequency ranges. For example, you might hear a sound and realize that it's "muddy." *Muddy* is a great descriptive word, but it doesn't tell you how to make the sound clearer. Using the chart, you can see that frequencies described as muddy are usually in the range of 200–250Hz. By attenuating (reducing the level of) these frequencies, you can make a sound clearer, or less muddy. Similarly, to adjust the *bass* qualities of a sound you would add to or take away from the frequencies around 60–80Hz. To give a sound more *attack* you could add to the frequencies at 7,000Hz. Realize that these terms offer a general range for adjustment; every sound you work with will yield slightly different results.

4. Some equalizers allow you to preview the new settings. Click Preview to audition the sound. When you have the sound dialed in to where it sounds best, click OK to finalize the edit.

EQUALIZING AUDIO FILES FOR FLASH MP3 COMPRESSION

If you have exported sounds with Flash's internal MP3 compression, you have surely noticed a drop in sound quality of the exported files. Every sound responds to compression differently. For some, the changes rendered by the compression are minimal, while other sounds show a definite difference in their overall character and quality. In general, the lower you set the bit rate and encoding speed, the lower the quality of your sound file will be, and the more drastically a sound will be changed.

These changes in sound quality, however, don't have to be a permanent part of your movie. You can correct the effects of compression by using equalization to bring a sound to a point of equilibrium. By attenuating the frequencies that compression boosts, and boosting the frequencies that compression dampens, you will be able to retain more of a sound's original character after your movie is published.

These changes should be applied to the original sound file (or copy of the original file) *before* it is imported into Flash. By doing this, you will compensate ahead of time for the adverse effects MP3 compression has on the sound file. Ideally, when the Flash movie is published, all sounds will be brought back to their original character. A sound will probably never be exactly the same, but it will be a definite improvement over the unequalized alternative.

Use the following image as a guideline for your EQ:

This EQ setting boosts the low end, cuts the low-to-mid range, and slightly boosts the high-mids and the highs. All EQ settings affect different sounds in different ways, however. Use this example as a starting point. With a little tweaking and experimentation, you should be able to bring your compressed Flash sound files closer to the original.

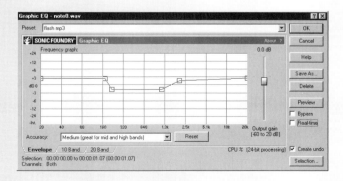

Compression

Compression is like normalization in that it affects the volume of a sound. However, there is more to it than just a change of volume. Whereas normalization boosts the peaks and valleys of a sound and keeps their relationships intact, compression alters the overall dynamics of a sound and can bring its peaks and valleys closer together. If you have a sound with very erratic volume levels, a compressor can level the playing field by cutting the loud parts, bringing them closer to the soft parts. Then, after bringing the levels closer together, a compressor can boost the overall volume of the entire sound file with the new, closer relationship of highs and lows.

To apply compression to a sound or sample:

1. Select the entire sound file or the portion of the file you need to compress.

2. Choose either Compressor or Dynamics from one of the application's menus (usually Process or Effects). A Dynamics dialog box appears. With most compressors, you are asked to specify five things: Threshold, Ratio, Attack, Release, and Output.

   Threshold determines at what point the compressor kicks in.

   Ratio sets the amount of compression. It is usually best to keep this between 2:1 and 6:1. For every 2dB of change, the compressor yields 1dB; for every 6dB of change, the compressor yields 1dB, and so on.

   Attack and **Release** set how quickly the compressor kicks in once it is beyond the threshold.

   Output allows you to boost the final volume of the compressed sound.

3. Once you have made your settings, you can click the Preview option to test the compressor. If the results meet your satisfaction, click OK to compress the sound.

Compression can be a big asset to the production of Flash projects. Use it to compress dialog and narration so that it sounds even and has no "dips" that obscure the meaning or clarity of the words.

Reverb

Reverb is an effect used to make a sound or sample seem like it is heard in a particular acoustic space. Reverb can make something sound like it is in a tiled bathroom, long hallway, or cathedral. It is often used to simulate the natural mixing of sounds that occurs in a room with reverberation.

When working with sounds for Flash movies, you can use reverb to create echo effects, sweeten the quality of a vocal line (spoken or sung), add authenticity to environmental sound effects, and much more. Although there are too many different kinds of reverb available today to discuss using them in any kind of detail, here are a few of the parameters you can expect to see:

Room size This causes the effect to simulate the natural acoustics of certain kinds of rooms.

High cut and low cut These are filters that dampen the high or low frequencies of the reverberated sound.

Decay This parameter controls how long the reverb effect persists.

Diffusion This parameter controls the density of the reverberation.

Amount/mix This option allows you to set how much of the effect is applied to the sound. The end result is a mixture of the original sound (referred to as "dry") and the reverberated sound ("wet"). See Figure 25.8 for an illustration of the options provided in a reverb feature.

If you like the results of reverb but want something that has more of a bounce or more clear repetitions, you can also try experimenting with echo and delay effects.

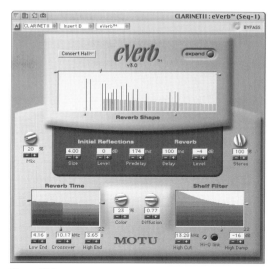

Figure 25.8

Digital Performer's eVerb plug-in has many options for fine-tuning the reverb setting parameters.

Pitch Shift

A *pitch shift* effect can produce wild and humorous results to sound samples, especially when used in the extreme ranges. Pitch shifting basically takes the pitch of a sound and transforms it to a lower or higher pitch; for example, it can make the human voice sound like that of a chipmunk. Pitch shifting is a fabulous technique for modifying sounds to create new and interesting sound effects.

Depending on the sophistication of the software you are using, pitch shifting can be done one of two ways. In many cases, pitch shifting changes the duration of the sound: Pitch shifting up (a higher pitch) makes a sound shorter, while pitch shifting down (a lower pitch) elongates a sound. With newer pitch shift effects, you may have the option to preserve the original duration of the sound or sample.

To apply pitch shifting:

1. Select the entire sample or portion of the sound that you would like to pitch-shift.

2. Choose Pitch Shift from the Effects (or similarly titled) menu. The Pitch Shift dialog box appears.

3. Set the pitch shift value and click OK to perform the shift. Figure 25.9 illustrates SoundEdit 16's pitch shift features.

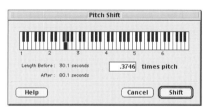

Figure 25.9

The Pitch Shift window in SoundEdit 16 uses a keyboard graphic to set changes in pitch based on the intervals of a keyboard.

Pitch shifting is a sound designer's best friend. With a little experimentation, you will be surprised at how typical, everyday sounds can be transformed into wild sonic oddities. Use this effect liberally in Flash cartoons to create crazy, over-the-top CLANKS!, BOINKS!, and KA-BOOMS!

Time Shift

Time shift and pitch shift are similar in nature, but they affect different aspects of a sound. Whereas pitch shift can raise or lower the pitch of a particular sound, the *time shift* effect will increase or decrease a sound's duration. And unlike some pitch shift effects that alter the duration of a sound, time shift will generally try to preserve the original pitch of the sound it is shifting.

To apply a time shift effect:

1. Select the portion of the file or sample you would like to time-shift.

2. Choose Time Shift (or Tempo, Stretch, etc.) from the audio application's Effects menu. The Time Shift dialog box appears.

3. Every interface varies; generally, you either use a slider to set the value, or type in a number for the length of the "shifted" file.

4. If the application provides a Preview option, select it to audition the sound. When you have created the right effect, click OK to apply the time shift.

Time shift effects are particularly good for making sound effects shorter or longer. For example, if you have an explosion sound that you want to sustain for an extended period of time, apply a time shift effect and stretch it to the length you desire.

Creating Seamless Audio Loops

Chapter 19 introduced you to loops, small chunks of music that can be repeated, or looped, continuously. And in Hands On 6, you learned how loops can be inserted accurately into a Flash movie Timeline to ensure accurate beat-timing between loops. When you combine loops in different ways throughout the movie, they can serve as the impetus for a highly interactive soundtrack. Yes, loops do carry a negative connotation, but hopefully these techniques illustrate how loops can produce pleasing, musical results. Remember that loops themselves are not always grating or annoying; rather, the unimaginative *application* of loops can make them so.

Whatever creative solution you may devise for working with loops, it is important that they are created in such a way that they sound clean and are free of pops, clicks, and bumps when played back. The best way to do this is to be sure that the loop file has one continuous waveform with no seams or gaps. If the line of the wave ever has to jump or skip, the break in the wave will be unpleasantly audible when you play back the looped file (see Figure 25.10).

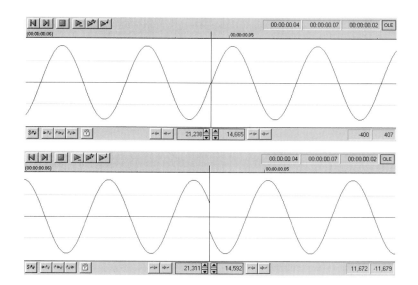

Figure 25.10

The image on top shows a sample with two loop points that meet smoothly; this sound will play back without glitches. The sample on the bottom will pop every time it loops, due to the gap in the waveform.

So, the key to a smooth-sounding loop is to have one continuous wave that never breaks. Because it's nearly impossible to find a natural sound that's like this, you must edit the file to create the loop. Many audio editing applications offer loop creation tools that assist you with this, and generally they have names like "Loop Tuner." Built-in loop editing tools such as these can be very helpful, but they don't always give you complete control over the file while you are defining its loop points. These tools work very well for rhythmic loops, where the beats of the music are clearly defined by the shape of the wave. For ambient, loosely rhythmic, or *rubato* music, though, using the tools can be difficult.

In the following steps, you will learn how to create ambient loops that work as a musical backdrop to your Flash movies. First, though, you should understand what is meant by an ambient loop. An *ambient loop* is a sound, often with no particular rhythm or pulse, which repeats continuously. It sounds boring by definition, but an ambient loop can sound absolutely beautiful. Think of such loops as textures—or, as LucasArts' Peter McConnell calls them, audio "wallpaper"—that create an environment without ever getting in the way. Ambient loops serve as excellent musical backdrops for websites and interactive interfaces, because they establish a mood without ever stepping in the way of the other design elements. In a sense, the sound is as integral to the design as the type, colors, and images.

To create a smooth loop for an ambient sound:

1. Open a sound that you think will be appropriate for your purpose, and listen to it. Are the beginning and the end drastically different? If so, you may need to do some creative editing to reorder the parts of the music or sound collage that make up the sound. To get the best results from this technique, work with a sound that has an ending that will

transition smoothly to the beginning without sounding strange or awkward. Additionally, the sound should be at least 30 seconds long. Looped sounds are most obvious when they are short, so work with the longest sound file your movie can afford in terms of file size.

2. Using your audio editor's selection tool, select the last few seconds of the sound file. (The portion that you select will ultimately have to blend with the audio at the beginning of the file. Try to make a generous selection so that you leave plenty of room to blend. Four to ten seconds is a good, flexible range with which to work.) Let's assume that the sound is stereo and you have selected both tracks. It's critical that your selection starts at a point where the sound wave is crossing the 0 amplitude line (see Figure 25.11). If you make the selection at any other point in the wave, you'll get a glitch when the file loops.

Figure 25.11

When making your loop selection, be sure that the selection begins at a point in the sound wave (or waves, if stereo) where there is a zero crossing.

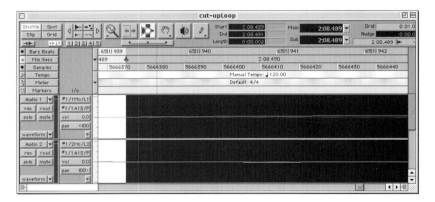

3. Select Edit → Cut (Cmd/Ctrl+X) to cut the audio chunk you selected. Then, create two new tracks (or one stereo pair) in the sound file. Make the new tracks active by dropping your cursor in the tracks. Make sure that the cursor is at the very beginning of the sound file, and then select Edit → Paste (Cmd/Ctrl+V) to insert the information you cut from the sound's tail end into the new tracks. Your file should now resemble something like Figure 25.12. Depending on the editor you use, you may need to set the pan position for each of the new tracks.

If you are using an editor like Sound Forge or Peak that doesn't support multiple tracks, you will still be able to use this technique but with less flexibility. Rather than create two new tracks, perform a crossfade or blend edit to paste the tail-end portion smoothly over the beginning of the file. Set the blend or crossfade so that the pasted information starts at full volume and fades to silence, and the original starts at silence and fades to full volume. Creating this effect with a multi-track editor is much easier and gives you greater control over the outcome.

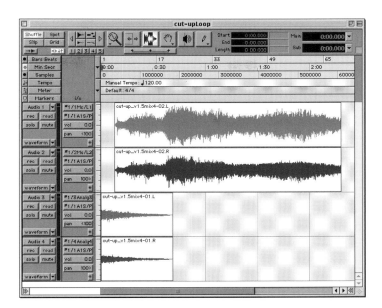

Figure 25.12

The original sound file after cutting the last few seconds and pasting it into two new tracks

4. Now you are ready to blend the newly pasted tracks (the old tail end of the sound) with the beginning of the sound. This can be done in one of two ways:

- Create a fade-in for the top stereo pair and a fade-out for the bottom pair. In effect, this is fading out the tail while fading in the head.

- Create a crossfade transition (if your audio editor supports this feature). Crossfade between the four tracks so that as two are fading in, the other two are fading out.

> In some situations, you may also find that it is helpful to move the original track slightly to the right to allow more room for the fades to take place.

Whichever method you choose, the idea is to create a seamless transition that blends the various tracks. This final step creates the smooth loop. Because the new beginning of the file *exactly* matches the tail (remember, one used to be attached to the other), there is no glitch or gap in the loop. And, because you were able to fade one chunk of the sound into another, there is no longer any differentiation between where the track starts and where it stops (see Figure 25.13).

5. To finalize the process, mix the edited file to a two-track (stereo) file. It's now ready to be imported into a Flash movie.

Ambient loops serve as nice background sounds and can loop whimsically due to their loose rhythmic nature. Because they have no one section that sticks out above the others, ambient loops provide a pleasant alternative to rhythmic loops. The absence of repetitive components like prominent drumbeats and bass or guitar riffs makes the cycles of the loop less obvious.

Figure 25.13

The final file has a fade-out to contour the tracks that were pasted in, and a gradual fade-in to raise the volume of the track's original beginning.

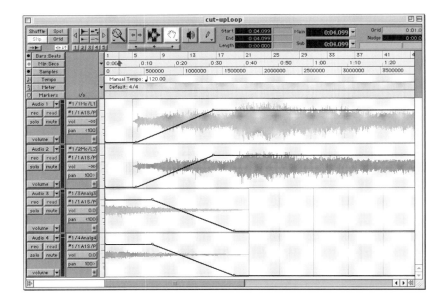

Ambient Loops in Context

On the companion CD-ROM for this book, there is a file that uses both the ambient loop technique and rhythmic loops. In the Chapter 25 folder, open the file named `loopDesign.html` in your web browser (be sure the Flash plug-in is installed). Here you can hear two different looping techniques in action.

The ambient loop is stored in a sound-only SWF file that is loaded onto `_level1` at the outset of the main movie. This loop is cued as an event sound and uses the techniques described earlier to create a seamless (and continuous) background loop.

Additionally, there are several rhythmic loops that are cued when you interact with the movie. Each of these loops was composed to fit musically with the ambient background and provide a different feel for each section of the movie. The visual and informational content of this movie is incomplete. What is there is intended solely to serve as a navigational structure so that the audio techniques can be tested. The idea is that the ambient piece provides a common thread for the entire movie, while the loops add special flavor to the individual movie sections.

Inspirational Design Model

An additional audio application not covered here but certainly deserving a mention is Beatnik. Beatnik is not just an audio application, though. We mention it here because, like Pro Tools and Sound Forge, it is a tool that can be used in the development of audio for websites, Director/Shockwave, and of course Flash movies. However, unlike Pro Tools and Sound Forge, Beatnik is neither an editing nor mixing environment. In a nutshell, it consists of four main elements: the Beatnik Player, a plug-in that hosts many of the Beatnik sounds; MIDI files that you create with a MIDI sequencing program to cue the Beatnik Player; and two elements of code: the Beatnik Music Object, and your code (JavaScript, Lingo, or ActionScript) that cues your music in the way you want. It is probably best to think of Beatnik as an *audio engine* for delivering low-bandwidth music and sound effects. Using Beatnik RMF (Rich Music format), Beatnik files are able to squeeze large amounts of audio information through small pipes with great success. To learn more about Beatnik or to download the plug-in and listen to Beatnik music, go to: `www.beatnik.com`.

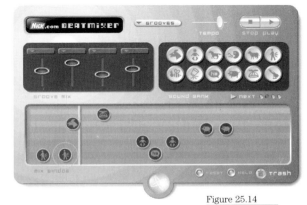

Figure 25.14

The Nick.com Beatmixer

For an additional example of Beatnik in action, check out the Nick.com Beatmixer at `www.nick.com/music/beatmixer/index.jhtml` (see Figure 25.14). This audio mixer was designed in Flash and uses Beatnik (a.k.a. Flashnik) to deliver interactive musical mixes for "children" of all ages.

Summary

This chapter is the final installment of sound and audio topics in this book. It introduced you to many of the applications that are currently available for editing, mixing, recording, and creating sound and audio elements for your Flash projects. Many applications are available, and it's important that you find one or two that will serve your creative needs. This chapter also provided some of the techniques that you can employ with applications of this kind. You learned about several kinds of effects that you can use to enhance the audio content of your movies: normalize, EQ, compression, reverb, pitch shift, and time shift. You were also introduced to some additional looping concepts, which expand the possibilities of looped sounds within interactive animations. With a little practice, you will find that these techniques can significantly improve the quality of audio in your Flash creations.

CHAPTER 26

Making Flash 3D

Up until this point, all of your visual creations have existed in two dimensions. You've simulated depth by using some nifty optical tricks—like creating perspective in Hands On 2, "Creating a Garden with Objects and Layers." But they were just that: tricks.

The universe exists in three dimensions: height, width, *and* depth. A whole subset of digital media specializes in creating 3D models and animations for games, television, and movies. Unfortunately, the technology as well as the skills needed to create 3D models and animations is *extremely* specialized. As a result, the worlds of 3D and Flash have remained separate—that is, until recently. As Flash grew in prominence as a tool for authoring 2D visual creations, developers inevitably started looking toward 3D as a new means by which to express their digital vision.

Unfortunately, on its own, Flash's inherently 2D-focused painting and drawing tools are not particularly suited for creating 3D models. But there are many techniques and third-party applications designed specifically to integrate 3D into your Flash creations.

In this chapter, you're going to explore the following topics:

■ **Simulating 3D in Flash**

■ **Using third-party 3D applications to export directly to SWF**

■ **Using Non-SWF-Exporting 3D Applications with Flash**

Simulating 3D in Flash

Although Flash is not particularly suited to creating 3D objects or animations, there are some tricks you can use to integrate the appearance of the third dimension—depth—into your Flash creation. For instance, in Hands On 2, "Creating a Garden with Objects and Layers," when you created the flowerbeds in the image, you manipulated them using the Transform tool so they looked like they receded off into the distance. This simulates depth; however, it's nothing more than sleight of hand. The objects are only a two-dimensional drawing that you've manipulated to fool the viewer's eye into believing they're three-dimensional.

> Although it is easy enough to create 3D sleight of hand in Flash, you can create "real" 3D using some fairly complicated and advanced ActionScript that employs pretty scary math—a process well beyond the scope of this book. To see some great examples of "real" Flash 3D, refer to the FLA section of www.ultrashock.com. Alternatively, you can see some wonderful Flash 3D creations at Wireframe Studio (www.wireframe.co.za).

Even though these tricks aren't designed to create real 3D, don't dismiss them immediately. They have their uses, and in using them, you take your first step on the grand adventure of Flash and 3D. In the following sections, you're going to take some of the skills you learned in Chapter 4 and create static 2D objects that look like they're 3D. You'll then create a simulated 3D animation.

Creating Simulated 3D Objects with the Painting and Drawing Tools

If you think back to your high school geometry class, you'll remember that the textbook featured a slew of diagrams that, although appearing to be 3D, were actually 2D. In this section you're going to look at how you can replicate this effect by using Flash's painting and drawing tools.

Creating a Pseudo-3D Sphere

You are going to start off by taking a step-by-step look at creating a pseudo-3D sphere:

1. Open a new document by going to File → New.

2. In the middle of the Stage, use the Ellipse tool to draw a circle about 3 centimeters (1.5 inches) in diameter. Make sure you hold down the Shift key while you are drawing the ellipse to ensure it's a perfect circle.

3. Make sure that the circle has a solid color fill by using the Fill Color picker in the Toolbox's Colors section.

4. Now, select the circle's fill with the Arrow tool.

5. Go to Window → Color Mixer to open the Color Mixer panel.

6. From the Fill Style drop-down menu, choose Radial. At this point, your soon-to-be 3D sphere should look something like this:

7. You'll notice that, by default, Flash makes the two colors in the gradient black and white—with the white on the outside and the black in the inside. The colors themselves need to be switched, with the light on the inside and the dark on the outside, so that it gives the impression that a light source is reflecting off the curved 3D surface of a sphere. First, select the sphere's fill with the Arrow tool.

8. Now, with the Color Mixer panel still open, select the right gradient handle (the white one). Next, click the color swatch to the left of the Fill Style drop-down menu and choose a dark color (in this example, it's black).

9. From here, click the left gradient handle (the black one). Next, click the color swatch to the left of the Fill Style drop-down menu and choose a very light color (in this example, it's white). From here, the sphere should look something like this:

10. Now, you need to manipulate the gradient so that it gives a more realistic impression that a light source is reflecting off the curved 3D surface of the sphere. With the Color Mixer panel still open, click and drag the right gradient handle toward the center of the Gradient Definition bar. By doing this, you restrict the size of the simulated reflection.

11. Now, you need to manipulate the shape and position of the gradient to enhance the look of the simulated reflection. First, make sure the sphere's fill is deselected.

> If you hadn't noticed, the simulated reflection created by the gradient is what changes the humdrum circle into a magnificent pseudo-3D sphere. As a result, you should spend some time getting it to look exactly how you want.

12. Select the Fill Transform tool from the Toolbox and then click the sphere's fill. By doing this, the gradient's bounding box and associated handles will appear. (If you are having trouble remembering how to manipulate a gradient fill using the Fill Transform tool, see Chapter 4.)

13. Now, to change the position of the simulated reflection, move your mouse over the handle in the center of the fill. Notice that your cursor changes. Click and drag to the upper-right area of your sphere. By doing this, you change the center of the circle gradient's position. At this point, your sphere should look something like this:

14. Next, to change the shape of the simulated reflection, move your cursor over the *square* handle on the circle's edge (notice your cursor changes). Click and drag toward the center of the circle slightly—this "squishes" the gradient, making it more linear.

> If, when you are editing the gradient, it snaps, then you'll need to turn the Snap to Objects feature off (View → Snap to Objects).

15. At this point, you want to rotate the simulated reflection so that it looks like light is hitting the sphere from the upper right. With the Transform Fill tool and the circle's fill selected, move your cursor over the bottommost circular handle. You'll notice that your cursor switches into four arrows arrayed in a circle. Click and drag so that your simulated reflection is slanted at a roughly 45 degree angle.

16. Now, click and drag the center handle to reposition your radial gradient's center near the upper-right corner of the sphere.

Congratulations, you've just created a pseudo-3D sphere using a simple circle and radial gradient.

As you'll employ a sphere such as the one you've just created in the "Animating Simulated 3D Objects" section later in this chapter, you might want to save this one.

> Fiddle around with the shape, size, and orientation of the gradient to get different looks for your pseudo-3D sphere.

Creating a Wireframe Cube

The next trick you are going to try is how to create a wireframe cube using Flash's drawing tools.

> The term *wireframe* is taken straight out of traditional 3D modeling. Essentially, it's a display mode in which objects are represented by lines—resulting in the object looking like it is made of a wire mesh.

Follow these steps:

1. Open a new document by going to File → New.

2. Draw a perfectly proportioned square with the Rectangle tool (remember to hold down the Shift key to maintain the proportions).

3. As the pseudo-3D cube you are drawing is wireframe, you need to make sure it doesn't have a fill. To do this, select the square's fill with the Arrow tool and delete it.

4. Now, select the square (which should simply be a black outline) with the Arrow tool and group it by going to Modify → Group.

5. Now that you've created the front face of the pseudo-3D cube, you can create the back face. Select the square, copy it (Edit → Copy), and then paste it (Edit → Paste).

6. Click and drag the newly pasted square so that it is located slightly up and to the right of the first square. Make sure each square's bottom-left corners line up diagonally lined. So far, the scene should look something like this:

7. Now that you've created the front and back face of the pseudo-3D cube, it's time to create all the other faces. To do this, you are going to link each of the two square's respective corners with the Line tool. First, you want to turn Snap to Objects on by going to View → Snap to Objects. By doing this, you'll make sure the lines you draw with the Line tool will snap exactly to the corners of the squares.

8. Now, select the Line tool from the Toolbox. Position your cursor over the bottom-left corner of the lower square (which will serve at the cube's front face). Click and drag to the bottom-left corner of the upper square (which will serve as the cube's back face). Notice that your line will snap exactly to the square's corner. At this point, the cube should look something like this:

9. Now, repeat the process for the two cubes' upper-right corners, their bottom-right corners, and their upper-left corners.

Congratulations, you've created a pseudo-wireframe 3D cube that should look something like this:

Animating Simulated 3D Objects

Now that you've learned how to create pseudo-3D objects using Flash's painting and drawing tools, you'll now learn how to simulate 3D animation with your pseudo-3D objects. The main goal in creating pseudo-3D animations with your pseudo-3D objects is, as you've probably guessed, to create and maintain the illusion of depth. To do this, you can use a couple of techniques. The most basic one involves creating an animation in which a single objects moves in front of and behind another object, thereby creating the necessary illusion.

In this section, you are going to take the animation skills you already mastered in Part III and create a simple animation in which a pseudo-3D sphere orbits around a second, larger pseudo-3D sphere. To accomplish this, you're going to use a little ActionScript trickery—in particular, you'll be leveraging the power of the setProperty() action.

A working version of this project has been included in the Chapter 26 folder of the book's CD-ROM (in both SWF and FLA formats).

If you are new to ActionScript, see Parts IV and V.

Follow these steps:

1. Open a new document by going to File → New. Open the Document Properties dialog box (Modify → Document) and set the width of the Stage to **600** and the height to **400**.

2. Start off by creating three pseudo-3D spheres using the process described earlier in this chapter. Make one of the spheres small, and make the other two (which *must* be exactly identical in size, shape, and color) larger. This is an example of what your three spheres might look like:

3. Now, convert each 3D sphere to a Movie Clip. Although the name of the small spheres (which will be doing the orbiting) doesn't really matter, make sure one of the large spheres is named **front**, and the other is named **back**.

The reason you are making these Movie Clips opposed to just plain Graphic symbols is that the ActionScript you are going to use later in the tutorial only works with Movie Clip symbols.

4. Now, because you've converted the three spheres to symbols, you can delete the original spheres from the Stage.

5. Next, create three additional layers (which would give you a total of four). Name each of the layers, from top to bottom: **actions**, **front**, **small ball**, and **back**.

6. Click the first keyframe in the front layer and drag the front symbol from the Library onto the Stage.

7. Open the Info panel (Window → Info) and enter **253.3** for the X value and **153.3** for the Y value.

Remember, you can also add the X and Y coordinates using the Property Inspector (Window → Properties).

8. Select frame 30 in the front layer and go to Insert → Frame (or use the shortcut F5).

9. Select frame 30 in the back layer, and go to Insert → Frame.

10. Click the first keyframe in the back layer and drag the back symbol onto the Stage.

11. With the back symbol still selected, open the Info panel (Window → Info) and enter **253.3** for the X value and **153.3** for the Y value. By doing this, you make it appear that there is only one large sphere on the Stage while there are actually two.

12. Now, select the small ball layer and insert a motion guide by clicking the Add Motion Guide button at the bottom left of the Timeline or by going to Insert → Motion Guide.

13. Select the first keyframe of the new motion guide layer (which appears just about the small ball layer), and use the Ellipse tool to draw a compressed ellipse. Make sure the newly created ellipse doesn't have any fill. Position the ellipse (which will serve as the motion path for the small orbiting ball) over the large sphere. The result should look something like this:

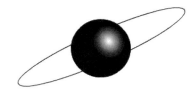

14. Now, it's time to fiddle with the motion path a bit so that it will function properly in relation to your intended product. Hide the back and front layers by clicking their Show/Hide buttons (represented by the little black dots below the eye icon in the Timeline).

    After you've manipulated the motion path, you can turn the back and front layers back on by clicking their Show/Hide buttons.

15. Use the Zoom tool to zoom into a section of the motion path that is behind the large sphere (make sure you are at the maximum magnification). With the Lasso tool, select a small section of the magnified motion path, and then delete it. (Once you've cut the small section out of the motion path, you can set the Stage's magnification back to 100 percent.)

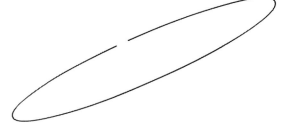

    By doing this, your motion path will no longer be closed but will have a small break. The result should look something like this:

16. Now, you need to attach the small orbiting sphere to the motion path. Click the first keyframe of the small ball layer, and drag the small sphere symbol onto the Stage. With the Library open (Window → Library), click and drag the small sphere symbol so that it snaps to one end of the motion path.

17. Select frame 30 in the small ball layer and go to Insert → Keyframe.

18. Select the final keyframe in the layer, and click and drag the small sphere so that it snaps to the other end of the motion path.

19. Now, to add the motion tween, select the first keyframe in the small ball layer and go to Window → Properties. Choose Motion from the Tween drop-down menu.

20. Test your motion tween by hitting the Return/Enter key or by going to Control → Test Movie. You'll notice that the motion of your small orbiting ball is partially hidden by the front symbol. In the next few steps, you're going to use some ActionScript to dynamically change the visibility of both large spheres to create the illusion that the small sphere is passing in front of and behind the same object.

21. Now, if you haven't already, you need to turn the visibility of the two large spheres back on.

22. Click the front layer and select the front symbol. Now, go to Window → Properties, and enter **front** into the Name field. Repeat the process for the back symbol in the back layer (but instead enter **back** into the Name field). By doing this, you are assigning a unique identifier to the instance; this is *absolutely* necessary if you want the Action-Script you'll write in the next few steps to work properly.

> To select each symbol (remember, they are placed one on top of the other), you could hide the back layer and then select the front symbol. Then, you could hide the front layer and select the back symbol.

23. Now onto the ActionScript that makes it all possible. Select the first keyframe in the actions layer and open the Actions panel by going to Window → Actions.

24. Expand the Actions category in the ActionScript Toolbox, expand the Movie Clip Control category, and double-click the `setProperty()` action to add it to the ActionScript text box.

25. Choose `_visible` from the Property drop-down menu, type **front** into the Target field, type **true** into the Value field, and make sure the Value field's Expression check box is selected. By doing this, you tell Flash to display the front symbol.

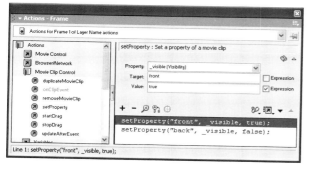

26. Now, repeat the process described in the previous step, but instead enter **back** into the Target field and **false** in the Value field. By doing this, you tell Flash to hide the back symbol. The resulting script in the ActionScript text box should look like the image shown here.

If you don't enter the exact same name into the Target field as you put in the Name field of the Property Inspector, the ActionScript simply won't work.

27. Now, you need to create the ActionScript that will hide the front symbol and display the back symbol, thereby giving the illusion that the orbiting ball is passing in front of the large sphere. First, select frame 10 in the actions layer (or the frame in which the sphere has reached the maximum extent of its orbit).

28. Go to Insert → Keyframe.

29. Repeat the process described in steps 24–26. However, switch the value of the front symbol to **false** and the value of the back symbol to **true** and change the appropriate values instead of building the script from scratch.

If you want, you can simply cut and paste the script created in steps 24 and 25.

30. Now that you've allowed the small sphere to pass in "front" of the large one, you'll create a script that will hide the back symbol and display the front symbol, thereby allowing the sphere to pass "behind" the large sphere and complete its orbit. First, click frame 28 (or the frame just before the small sphere touches the larger one).

31. Repeat the process described in steps 25 and 26. Use the exact same script. By doing this, you tell Flash to display the front symbol and hide the back symbol—allowing the sphere to pass "behind." In the end, your Timeline should look something like this:

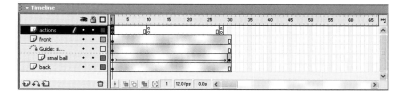

Congratulations, you've just created an animation in which a pseudo-3D sphere rotates around another pseudo-3D sphere. Test your movie by going to Control → Test Movie. Now that you've mastered the basics, you can play around with the effect. Try adding more orbiting spheres to create a molecule or create an animation that is more than just two spheres.

Using Third-Party 3D Applications to Export Directly to SWF

As the integration of Flash and 3D has become more popular, several astute 3D modeling software companies have caught on and have added the ability to export SWF files from their programs. This is a huge advancement for Flash and 3D. Now there is little need to resort to visual trickery (like that described earlier) to add the illusion of depth to your Flash creations. Now, you can simply create a 3D model or animation (which is exported to a SWF file) and import it directly into Flash.

In the following sections, you are going to explore some of the more prominent 3D modeling programs that feature SWF export, including Swift 3D, Amorphium Pro, Poser Pro Pack, Amapi 3D, and Vecta3D. In some cases, like in the discussion of Swift 3D (designed purely for creating 3D models destined for Flash export), you'll delve deeply into the program. In other cases, such as in the discussion of middle- to high-end 3D modelers such as Amapi 3D and Amorphium Pro (which do far more than create models for Flash export), you'll focus on the process by which models are exported as SWF files.

Swift 3D

Electric Rain's Swift 3D (www.erain.com) was one of the first stand-alone programs designed to create 3D models directly exportable to SWF. Although the program can't compare with most of the more robust 3D modeling programs, it does have a hefty set of features, including direct 3DS (3D Studio Max) import, EPS and AI import, complex lighting, and preset animation templates, which allow you to create and optimize 3D models for Flash. Many other programs lack these features. In addition, Swift 3D comes in both a Mac and a PC version. Although cross-platform support should be a given, 3D modeling has traditionally been the domain of the Windows and Unix operating systems. Up until fairly recently, Mac users have been pretty cut off from the world of 3D modeling. As a result, Swift 3D's cross-platform support is a welcome feature for all Mac users.

Despite Swift 3D's usefulness, you shouldn't mistake it for a full-featured 3D modeling program. Comparing it with 3D modeling programs such as Maya, 3ds max, LightWave 3D, or Cinema 4D would be inappropriate. Swift 3D's ability to create even marginally complex 3D models is limited. If you're interested in experimenting with the most basic of polygon modeling techniques, Swift 3D is probably not for you. However, this doesn't mean the program isn't useful; Swift 3D is quite easy to learn, which puts it in a category altogether different from most of the full-featured 3D modeling programs (some of which require years of study to learn and a small fortune to acquire). Those who have experience working with high-end 3D modeling programs can use Swift 3D as a filter of sorts to set Flash-specific properties of an imported 3ds max file before exporting it as an SWF file.

In the following sections, you're going to explore the Swift 3D creative process. Be aware, however, that although Swift 3D is on the "light" end of 3D modelers, it still has a fair amount of features. As a result, we won't cover Swift 3D in its entirety. To get an in-depth account of the program and all of its options and tools, refer to the documentation that accompanies the program.

A demo copy of Swift 3D has been included on this book's CD-ROM.

Starting a Swift 3D Project

You have a handful of options for starting a new Swift 3D project:

- Go to File → New.
- Click the New button ![3D] in the top-left corner of the program's interface.

- To open an existing document, click the Open button   in the top-left corner of the program's interface. When the Open File dialog box appears, navigate the location where the file you want to open is located, and select it.

- Go to File → Import to import Encapsulated Postscript (EPS) or Adobe Illustrator (AI) files. When the Import File dialog box appears, navigate to the location where the file you want to open is located, and select it.

> Any Encapsulated Postscript or Adobe Illustrator image imported into Swift 3D is converted into a three-dimensional object, while still retaining its original 2D shape. Any previously applied color will be lost when the file is imported.

- To start a new document based on an existing 3ds max file (`.3ds`), go to File → New from 3DS.

Working with the Swift 3D Property Toolbox

The Property Toolbox, which is located on the left side of the program's interface, is one of the most vital tools in Swift 3D. With it, you can access all the properties of the scene on which you're currently working. As you add objects to your scene, their properties become accessible by clicking the appropriate heading in the Property Toolbox's list box.

SETTING LAYOUT PROPERTIES

The Layout properties allow you to control various aspects of your scene in Swift 3D.

By clicking the Layout heading located in Property Toolbox's list box, you'll see three discreet groups of controls: Layout, Display, Keyboard Nudge.

Layout Lets you set the dimensions of your project. Simply choose a unit of measurement from the Units drop-down menu and then enter values into the Height and Width fields.

Display Lets you manipulate the way in which the objects are displayed in the program's viewport. You have the following options:

- The Shaded option displays your objects as closely as they would appear when exported to SWF—complete with materials and lighting.

- The Fast Shaded option displays the object shaded, but without smooth gradients.

- The Outline option displays your objects as wireframe models.

- The Box option displays each object as a three-dimensional bounding box.

- When checked, the Pivots option displays the object's pivot point—which is kind of like the registration point for a 3D object.

- When checked, the Paths option displays the motion paths in your scene as purple lines.

- The Grid option toggles the XYZ coordinate system on and off.

- The Hidden option lets you either hide or show objects in your scene.

Keyboard Nudge Lets you set the value (in pixels) of the distance a selected object will move when the user hits one of the arrow keys on their keyboard.

SETTING CAMERA PROPERTIES

The Camera properties, accessible by clicking the Camera header in the Property Toolbox, allow you to access the properties of any selected camera.

You have these options:

- The Name field displays the name of the currently selected camera. When selected, the field becomes live, thereby allowing you to change the camera's name.

- The Lens Length setting (expressed in millimeters) behaves exactly like the lens length of a camera. The longer the lens length, the more the camera will zoom in on your scene. The shorter the lens length, the more distant you appear to be from your scene.

Just like with a camera lens, if the length is shortened, your image will get distorted as the view becomes more panoramic in nature.

SETTING ENVIRONMENTAL PROPERTIES

The Environmental properties, accessible by clicking the Environment header in the Property Toolbox's list box, allow you to access two rather important properties: Background Color and Ambient Light Color.

The Background Color, as you may have already guessed, is the color of your final rendered image's background. To set the background color, simply click the Background Color swatch to open the Color Picker. From here, you can pick the color you want for the background or mix your own custom color. When you're finished, just click the Apply button.

Ambient light, theoretically speaking, is the cumulative effect of all the light bouncing off of all the objects in a given area. Practically speaking, the Ambient Light option equally illuminates all objects in a given scene. To set the Ambient Light color, simply click the Ambient Light Color swatch to open the Color Picker. From here, you can pick the color you want for the scene's ambient light or mix your own custom color. When you're finished, click the Apply button.

Adding Primitive Objects

A large part of the modeling you'll do in Swift 3D entails adding and manipulating a series of shape primitives. Once you insert the shape into your scene, you can then manipulate its properties (size, orientation, and so on).

To add a shape primitive to your scene, click the appropriate button. The corresponding shape will be inserted at the intersection of the X, Y, and Z axes.

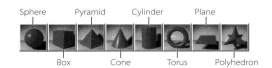

Using the Object Trackball

Now that you've added an object to your scene, you can manipulate its orientation. Located in the bottom-left corner of the program interface, the Object Trackball lets you adjust the orientation of objects in your scene.

The Object Trackball remains inactive until you select an object in the viewport. Once selected, the object appears within the Object Trackball. From there, you can click and drag the trackball to rotate the object itself.

You can also constrain the direction in which the trackball moves by clicking one of the Lock Axis (Lock Horizontal or Lock Vertical) buttons located to the left of the Object Trackball.

The Lock Horizontal button constrains the movement of the selected object along its horizontal axis.

The Lock Vertical button constrains the movement of the selected object along its vertical axis.

The Lock Spin button constrains the movement of the selected object so that is can only rotate in a clockwise or counterclockwise direction.

By clicking the Rotation Increment button $0°$, you can set the value (in degrees) that the trackball rotates.

Adding and Manipulating 3D Text

Text is a powerful tool in any medium, including 3D. In Swift 3D, text is considered an object just like any of the shape primitives you looked at previously. Let's take a look at a step-by-step approach to adding and manipulating text in Swift 3D:

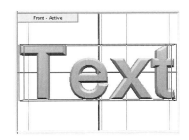

1. With a new document open, click the Create Text button . By doing this, the program inserts a default text object into your current scene.

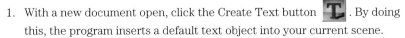

Remember that you can only access the properties of a currently selected object. As a result, make sure you select the text with which you're currently working by clicking it.

2. Click the Text heading in the Property Toolbox's list box.

3. Choose a font from the Font drop-down menu.

4. Enter the desired text into the Text field.

5. Choose one of the alignment options by clicking the appropriate alignment button.

6. Click the Apply button to apply your changes to the text in the viewport.

7. Now, click the Bevel heading in the Property Toolbox. From here, you'll be able to manipulate the bevel properties of the text.

8. Choose a bevel style for the Style drop-down menu (to get an idea of your options, experiment with each).

9. Enter a value into the depth field to set the depth of the bevel. The higher the value, the higher the bevel will be.

10. Choose a Face option. By choosing front, the bevel will only appear on the front of the text. Choosing back will only display the bevel on the back of the text. Choosing both will apply the bevel to both faces of the text.

11. Adjust the Smoothness slider to alter how Swift 3D draws the curves of the text. Moving the slider more toward Course makes the text more angular and block, and moving it more toward Smooth makes the curves smoother.

A higher level of Smoothness results in a higher file size, and less smoothness results in a smaller file size.

12. Adjust the Mesh Quality slider—which lets you exert some control over the quality of the 3D object's mesh.

13. Now, click the Sizing heading in the Property Toolbox's list box.

14. Enter a value into the Height, Width, and Depth fields to adjust the actual size of the 3D text.

15. Enter a value into the Inter Character field to adjust the space between characters.

16. Enter a value into the Inter Line field to adjust the space between lines.

Working with Preset Materials

Although delving too deeply into Swift 3D's limited ability to create and mix custom materials is beyond the scope of this chapter, you are going to apply materials from a preset library to the objects within your scene.

Unlike other 3D modeling programs where you've got access to all manner of tools and techniques for creating and mixing materials, Flash's inherent limitations (especially when it comes to bitmaps) limit the types of materials you can apply to objects in Swift 3D.

To apply preset materials to your objects, follow these steps:

1. Make sure the object with which you want to work is selected.

2. Click the Show Materials button 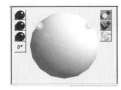 in the Gallery (located in the bottom-right corner of the program interface) to open the Materials palette.

3. Click one of the tabs in the Materials palette to access a particular subset of materials.

4. Simply click and drag the desired material from the Materials palette onto the currently selected object.

> When it comes to text (or complex models imported), you'll need to apply materials to each separate section of the object. For text, this means applying the material to both faces as well as the bevel.

Working with Lights

One of the most important aspects of any 3D creation is lighting. With proper lighting, you can turn a mediocre model into a great model. Don't get too excited, however; because of the Flash medium, your lighting options in Swift 3D are somewhat limited. But this doesn't mean you should spend any less time on lighting your 3D scene. When exported, a well-lit 3D Flash scene can be quite compelling.

Swift 3D gives you two types of lights to work with: Point Lights and Spot Lights—which can be added to a scene in two different ways (with the Lighting Trackball or directly into the scene). Point Lights act somewhat like a light bulb, casting illumination in a more diffuse area, and Spot Lights focus illumination on a specific area.

ADDING AND SUBTRACTING TRACKBALL LIGHTS

You can add any number of lights to your scene by clicking either the Create Trackball Point Light button or Create Trackball Spot Light button , both to the right of the Lighting Trackball at the bottom of the program interface.

As you add lights, they'll be displayed on the Lighting Trackball.

To delete a light from your scene, select the light on the Lighting Trackball (by clicking it), and click the Remove Light button .

ADDING AND SUBTRACTING SCENE LIGHTS

You can also add lights directly into the scene. To do so, just click one of the four light buttons (Create Free Point Light, Create Target Point Light, Create Free Spot Light, Create Target Spot Light).

Free Point Light   Free Spot Light

Target Point Light   Target Spot Light

> When you add a light, it will appear in the scene as a small yellow symbol.

A free light (Free Point Light or Free Spot Light) acts like any other object in your scene. As such, once you have added one, you can easily select and manipulate it using the Rotation Trackball (below left).

When you select a light in the scene (by clicking it), the symbol's color changes from yellow to red.

A target light (Target Point Light or Target Spot Light), on the other hand, always points at the pivot point of the object that was selected when it was inserted into the scene (below right).

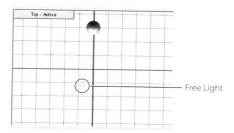
Free Light

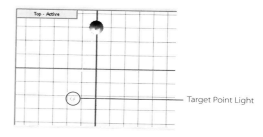
Target Point Light

MANIPULATING THE POSITION OF LIGHTS

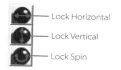
Lock Horizontal
Lock Vertical
Lock Spin

Manipulating the position of a light in your scene is extremely easy. In the case of a trackball light, all you need to do is select the light on the Lighting Trackball, and then drag the trackball itself.

Much like with the Object Trackball, you can use the Lock Axis buttons (located to the left of the Lighting Trackball) to constrain the movement of the light.

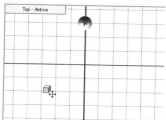

You'll notice that as you drag the Lighting Trackball, your scene will dynamically change to reflect the new lighting scheme.

In the case of a scene light, all you need to do is click and drag the light symbol in the scene (notice that your cursor changes), move it to its new position, and then release your mouse button.

If you are moving the position of a target light, you'll notice that the line that links the light symbol to the object's pivot point (which represents the direction in which the light itself is pointing) remains no matter where you move the light.

Using Drag-and-Drop Animations

Swift 3D not only functions as a limited modeling program, but also as an animation program. You can create true 3D animations (quite unlike those requiring the kind of visual trickery employed earlier in the chapter) and then export them as SWF.

Swift 3D's animation tools use frames and keyframes just like Flash. There are, however, some differences in the ways in which the two programs work. Much like with materials in Swift 3D, you've got a whole library of preset animations you can apply to any given object in your scene. These *drag-and-drop animations*, as they are called, are pretty useful for quickly adding moderately sophisticated animations. Follow these steps to put these drag-and-drop animations to work in your scene:

1. Make sure the object you want to work with is selected.

2. Click the Show Animations button  in the Gallery (located in the bottom-right corner of the program interface) to open the Animations palette.

3. From here, you see a single tab—Regular Spins—which gives you access to a series of animations you can apply to your objects to make them spin in place.

4. Simply click and drag the desired animation from the Animations palette onto the currently selected object.

5. To test your animation, click the Play button ▶| located just below the Timeline.

Exporting to SWF

Now that you've created your model, applied materials to it, and infused movement into it with animations, you can now output your creation as an SWF file:

1. Click the Preview and Export Editor tab at the top of the program interface.

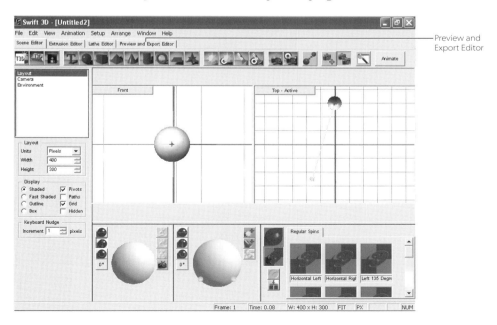

Preview and Export Editor

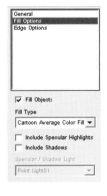

2. From here, you have quite a few different options you can set for the exported animation—all of which are accessible through the Property Toolbox. To start off with, click the General option in the Property Toolbox.

3. Select the file format to which you want to export your Swift 3D project from—in this case, Flash Player (SWF).

4. Choose the version of Flash for your exported SWF from the File Level drop-down menu.

5. Choose the level of detail for your exported SWF file from the Detail Level drop-down menu. Remember, a higher level of detail means a larger file size. Also, the lower the detail level, the faster your SWF file will render.

6. Adjust the Curve Fitting slider. When you adjust the slider toward the Curves end, the program will smooth out the irregular curves in your objects.

7. If you want, select the Combine Edges and Fills option. By doing this, your object will be rendered so that both the line and fill are part of the same object (kind of like being grouped together). If, on the other hand, you leave the option unchecked, the exported SWF file will contain an object (or objects) whose stroke and fill will be able to be manipulated independently without having to break the object apart.

8. Now, select Fill Options in the Property Toolbox.

9. If you want the object (or objects) in the exported SWF file to have fill, check the Fill Object option.

10. From here, select one of the options from the Fill Type drop-down menu. The more colors in an exported SWF, the larger the file will be. Each will affect the way in which your object's fill appears in the exported SWF:

   - When you choose Cartoon Single Color Fill, the diffuse color of an object is sampled and then applied to the entire object, thereby creating objects with solid color.

   - By selecting the Cartoon Average Color Fill, groups of individual polygons that occur on similar surfaces will have the same color in the exported file.

   - Like the Cartoon Average Color Fill, the Cartoon Two Color Fill option colors groups of individual polygons on similar surfaces. The difference is that the Cartoon Two Color Fill option applies two colors, instead of one, to the groups of polygons.

   - By selecting the Cartoon Four Color Fill, four colors, instead of two, will be applied to groups of polygons on similar surfaces.

   - When you choose Cartoon Full Color Fill, a separate color can be applied to each individual polygon.

Despite that the Cartoon Full Color Fill option results in a relatively detailed image, there is no shading between the color areas.

- When you select Area Gradient Shading, the program looks for groups of polygons that appear on similar surfaces and applies a radial gradient—thereby creating the appearance of a light reflecting off a surface.

- When you select the Area Gradient Shading, the Include Specular Highlights option becomes available. When checked, the program will search for surfaces perpendicular to the scene's light source and apply a lighter color to them. Be aware that turning this option on greatly increases the size of your exported file.

- The Mesh Gradient Shading option results in the highest quality image by fully merging all the colors in all the model's polygons.

11. If you want your exported scene to include shadows, select the Include Shadows option.

12. From here, choose the light source that you want to cast shadows in the exported file. Unfortunately, you can only select one light in your scene.

13. Select the Edge Options in the Property Toolbox.

14. If you want the object (or objects) in the exported SWF file to have a stroke, check the Include Edges option.

15. Select an option from the Edge Type drop-down menu:

- When you choose the Outlines option, the edges of all objects will be outlined with a solid line.

- By choosing the Entire Mesh option, the edges of all polygons in the 3D object (objects) will be outline with a solid line—thereby creating a wireframe-like result.

16. If you want the edges on the backside of a 3D object to be visible, select the Include Hidden Edges option.

17. Both the Include Detail Edges and Detail Edge Angle options affect the amount (and detail) of internal edges displayed in the final SWF exported file.

18. Select the width (thickness) of the line from the Line Weight drop-down menu.

19. To set the color of the line, double-click the color within the Line Color box. This opens the Color Picker—from which you can either choose a new color or mix your own.

20. From here, the animation needs to be rendered before it's exported. To render the entire animation, click the Generate Entire Animation button. To render a single frame, select the appropriate frame in the Render Preview bar, and then click the Generate Current Frame button.

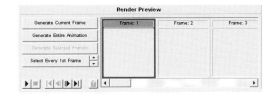

21. From here, Swift 3D will render each individual frame. The more frames, the longer it will take to render the animation.

22. When it's finished rendering, you can click the Export Entire Animation button to export the entire animation. To export an individual frame in the animation, select the desired frame in the Render Preview bar, and click the Export Current Frame button.

23. When the Export Vector File dialog box pops up, navigate to the location where you want the SWF file exported, enter a name into the File Name field, and click Save.

Poser and Poser Pro Pack

Creating believable and realistic characters is one of the most difficult undertakings in 3D modeling. Whether a human being, a dog, or a three-headed alien from the planet Xyzax, organic modeling is incredibly complex. Not only do you have to be exceedingly proficient with the 3D modeling program in which you are working, but you also have to be intimately familiar with principles of anatomy, biomechanics, and locomotion. Without these skills, character models usually turn out fairly unsophisticated. So, what's a moderately skilled 3D modeler to do? The discipline and skill necessary to create high-quality organic models is not something one comes by easily or quickly. Wouldn't it be nice if there were a program designed to provide an accessible and satisfying method to create high-quality character models without having to spend years mastering the skills to manually create them? Well, Curious Labs' Poser does exactly that.

Poser is one of those applications with a unique charm and usefulness all its own. With it, you can create static images, movies, and exportable 3D figures from a diverse collection of fully manipulatable, articulated human and animal models. Libraries of poses, facial expressions, hand gestures, clothing, props, and animations can be quickly applied to your model using Poser's unique interface (see Figure 26.1). A series of interactive controls exists for each part of the character's anatomy, allowing you to manipulate *morph targets*. By manipulating the model's morph targets, you can exert a great deal of control over the model's final appearance. You can also use morph targets to smoothly animate facial expressions and changes in body proportion. Aimed at novices and intermediate users alike, Poser offers a wealth of features and options for creating animations and images based on human (and not-so-human) figures.

Originally developed by MetaCreations (the folks responsible for such notable titles as Ray Dream, Infini-D, Bryce, and Painter), Poser was in danger of being left out in the cold when the company, in a rather unpredictable move, divested itself of all of its 3D and 2D graphics authoring programs. Lucky for the legions of Poser users who had sprung up over the years, the program's original design team wisely decided to continue development. As with many similar situations in the computer world, they scrambled to form their own company and simply bought Poser. The new company, called Curious Labs, was quick on its feet, releasing a free upgrade (version 4.03). Although the release was only a maintenance upgrade of sorts, it boasted some major bug cleaning and feature tweaking, making it far more usable and stable than before.

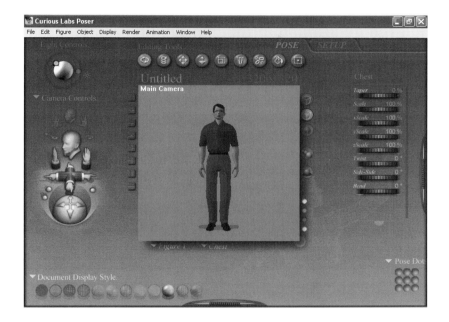

Figure 26.1

The unique Poser interface is designed to be extremely usable and ergonomic.

Early in 2001, in an effort to further push the boundaries of accessible 3D character modeling, Curious Labs (`www.curiouslabs.com`) announced the release of the Poser Pro Pack. Situated somewhere between a regular update and a new Poser release, the Pro Pack, which is sold separately from Poser 4, is a series of extensions, enhancements, plug-ins, and improvements that greatly enhance the power and usability of Poser. Among other serious enhancements, the Pro Pack includes an improved interface, a 3ds max integration plug-in, a LightWave integration plug-in, a Python-based scripting language, bones, and enhanced file compression. The most noteworthy feature of the Poser Pro Pack, at least in terms of this chapter's topic, is the ability to export models and animations as Flash files. When you think about it, this feature alone is a monumental development for Flash developers. With companies such as Mondo Media and Camp Chaos churning out extremely popular web shorts, Flash entertainment is gaining steam quickly. Poser Pro Pack provides an accessible way for Flash developers, who might not be that familiar with 3D, to create professional-looking Flash characters.

A demo copy of Poser 4 has been included on this book's CD-ROM.

To download a demo version of Poser Pro Pack, point your web browser to `www.curiouslabs` `.com/products/proPack/html/proPackDemoDownload.html`.

In short, Poser is a remarkably accessible 3D program. When you add the enhancements offered by the Pro Pack, you've got more program than can be covered in a single chapter (let alone a section of a chapter). As a result, this section focuses solely on the process by which you export a 3D character you've developed in Poser as an SWF file.

If you are eager to jump into Poser's character modeling features, there are a couple of good places to start. First, the 180-page user guide offers a decent walkthrough of the program's tools. Second, the Curious Labs' website (`www.curiouslabs.com`) features links to helpful tutorial sites.

Like in the case of many other 3D modeling programs that feature Flash export, outputting a file to SWF with Poser Pro Pack is fairly easy. There are, however, some export properties you need to be aware of so you can take full advantage of Flash output. To do this, follow this step-by-step approach to the process:

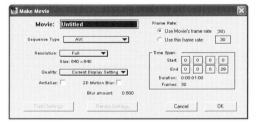

1. With the file you want to export to Flash open in Poser Pro Pack, go to Animations → Make Movie to open the Make Movie dialog box.

2. Enter a name for your movie into the Movie field.

3. Select Macromedia Flash (.swf) from the Sequencer Type drop-down menu.

4. From here, you've got a series of generic export options:

   • The Resolution drop-down menu provides you with a choice of four preset resolutions (Current, Full, Half, and Quarter). Notice that the actual size of each choice is displayed just below the actual menu.

   • The Quality drop-down menu provides you with two choices: Current Display Settings or Current Render Settings. To adjust the render settings, go to Render → Render Options.

   • The two frame rate options let you use either the movie's current frame rate (if it's an animation you're exporting) or set your own by entering a value (in frames per second) into the field.

   • By default, the Time Span section of the Make Movie dialog box displays the actual length of the movie. However, you can always change it by entering a new value in Hours:Minutes:Seconds:Frames. This feature is particularly useful if you only want to export a section of your animation (opposed to the entire thing).

5. Click the Flash Settings button in the lower-left corner of the Make Movie dialog box. This opens a second dialog box where you can set Flash specific properties.

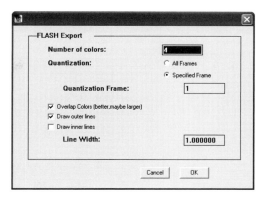

6. From here, you've got a series of additional options:

   - The Number of Colors field lets you specify the number of colors used in the exported SWF file. Your decision will be based on the desired quality of the exported file. More colors will add more visual variation but will increase the file size. Fewer colors will create a lower quality image (colorwise), but will result in a smaller file size.

   - The Quantization options let you determine the process by which a specific number of colors that best represent your model are selected.

   - Selecting the Overlap Colors check box forces Flash to take the color used the most to create a silhouette of the entire model. The next most-used color is placed on top of the first, and so on. When you select this option, your exported file will be larger, but will be better quality.

   - When you select the Draw Outer Lines option, your model will be exported with a line around its entire silhouette. The thickness of the line is set by entering a value (in pixels) into the Line Width field in the bottom-right corner of the dialog box.

   - By selecting the Draw Inner Lines option, Flash draws a line (whose width is set in the Line Width field) around each color layer.

7. Click OK to exit the Flash Export dialog box.

8. Click OK in the Make Movie dialog box.

9. When the Save File As dialog box opens, navigate to the location to which you want the file to be exported, and click Save.

Amapi 3D

Amapi has been unconventional since its inception. The program features a natural design interface that has the tool icons floating in an arc at the right corner of the screen (see Figure 26.2). Although its interesting interface makes it distinctly different than other 3D modelers, Amapi 3D, which is now developed by Eovia (www.eovia.com), shouldn't be mistaken for anything less than a topnotch professional 3D modeler. Placing it anywhere near Swift 3D in terms of functionality would be most inappropriate. Amapi 3D is used all around the world for 3D modeling in architecture, product design, marketing, engineering, illustration, interactive entertainment, television, and film.

Figure 26.2

The Amapi 3D interface is considerably different from the vast majority of other 3D modeling programs.

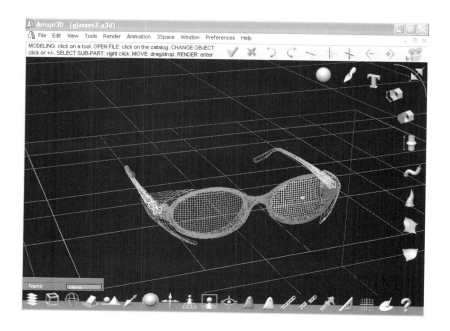

Amapi 3D's primary strength is that it employs a set of modeling tools based on a hybrid technology that allows users to work seamlessly on both Nonuniform Rational B-Splines (NURBS) and polygon models. NURBS is an amazingly powerful type of modeling in which a spline has control points residing on or away from the resulting curve. Amapi 3D's hybrid modeling technology allows the program's construction and modeling tools to naturally adapt themselves to the type of object being manipulated.

The program also boasts powerful modeling tools such as 2D and 3D primitives, advanced surface construction tools, global and local deformers, subdivision and smoothing tools, and unique 3D drawing assistants. Of course, Amapi 3D isn't just a modeling program. It features a complex rendering system (called *raytracing*) as well as a sophisticated material system that features a layered shader system. The most recent version of Amapi 3D (version 6.1) also offers SWF export.

 A demo copy of Amapi 3D 6.1 has been included on this book's CD-ROM.

A thorough exploration of Amapi 3D is beyond the scope of this chapter. You'd need an entire book to do justice all the intricacies of the program. As a result, this section will focus solely on the process of exporting a model in Amapi 3D as an SWF file.

If you are interesting in getting into Amapi 3D as a modeler, dig into the program's documentation or see the Tutorials section of the Eovia site (www.eovia.com).

Follow these steps to export a model or animation as a SWF file from within Amapi 3D:

1. Go to File → Export → Flash.
2. When the Flash Export Settings dialog box opens, there are several properties to set.

   - By selecting the Details check box and adjusting the slider, you can either increase or decrease the smoothness of the wireframe details.

   - Adjusting the Silhouette Thickness slider, you can increase or decrease the thickness of the object's silhouette.

   - Checking either the Low Quality or Better Quality check box determines the quality, and therefore the file size, of your exported SWF file.

   - By checking the Animation Loop check box, you ensure your Flash animation (if you are exporting an animation) loops.

> If you are exporting an animation, opposed to a static SWF file, you can go to Animation → Save Animation as Flash to open the Export Flash Settings dialog box.

3. Click OK.
4. When the Save As dialog box appears, enter a name into the File Name field, navigate to the location on your hard drive where you want the file saved, and click Save.

Vecta3D

Vecta3D is one of the earliest programs designed to take traditional 3D files and output them to Flash. Developed by Ideaworks3D (`www.ideaworks3D.com`), Vecta3D isn't a modeling program but is a filter into which 3D files go in one end and come out the other end as Flash files.

All in all, Vecta3D is a compact, handy program that doesn't have any pretensions toward being a 3D modeler (see Figure 26.3). It's content to take 3D files you've created in another program (exported as a 3ds max file or a DXF), fiddle with some export options, and then output them to Flash SWF. You can also use the program to turn EPS and AI files into 3D objects through a process called *extrusion*.

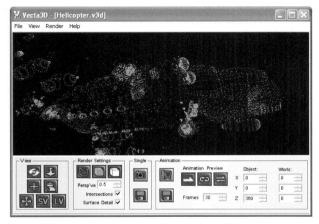

Figure 26.3

Vecta3D's interface is straightforward and uncomplicated, letting you convert 3D files with a minimum of fuss.

> Don't worry too much that Vecta3D only imports 3DS and DXF files. Most, if not all, good 3D modelers will export to 3DS or DXF.

Beyond simple import and export, Vecta3D lets you apply color to your model and define all aspects of line style and weight, geometry settings, and output quality. Also included are a series of tools that let you manipulate the position of the model when it's exported. Finally, Vecta3D features some basic tools for animating your model.

> Vecta3D's animation tools are amazingly simple. However, you can use an animation from your 3D modeler that you've exported as a sequence of files to create something far more complex.

In the following sections, you're going to explore some topics that, when put together, will allow you to take full advantage of Vecta3D's understated power.

Importing a 3D File

The first step in converting a 3D model into an SWF file with Vecta 3D is importing the model:

1. Go to File → Open.

2. When the Open dialog box appears, choose the appropriate file type from the Files of Type drop-down menu.

3. Navigate to the location on your hard drive where the intended file is located, and select it.

4. Click Open.

You've probably noticed there is also an Import command in the File menu (File → Import). The difference between this command and the Open command is that you use the Import command on EPS and AI files.

Importing a Sequence of 3D Files

Despite that Vecta3D's animation tools are amazingly simple, you can still use them to export high-quality, complex Flash animations. The process entails creating an animation in the 3D modeling program of your choice, exporting it as a sequence, and then using Vecta3D to string the files together into a Flash movie.

> Each imported file in the sequence is used as a single frame in the Flash animation.

To do this, follow these steps:

1. Go to File → Open.

2. When the Open dialog box pops up, navigate to the location on your hard drive where the file sequence is saved.

3. Select the first file in the sequence (`circle_00.3ds`, for example) and click Open.

4. When the dialog box opens, click Load Sequence.

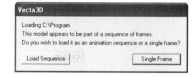

If you want to import a single file in a sequence, click Single Frame instead of Load Sequence.

Manipulating a 3D Model with the View Tools

After you've imported a single model or a sequence of models, you can use the View tools (located in the bottom left of the screen) to manipulate the position and orientation.

Spin The Spin tool rotates the model in all axes (opposed to being constrained to one axis). To use it, click the Spin button ⟳ from the View section of the interface, move your cursor over the model, and click and drag.

While you're in Spin mode, holding down the Ctrl button will activate Zoom mode.

Zoom The Zoom tool moves the camera toward or away from the model. To use it, click the Zoom button ⇳ in the View section of the interface, move your cursor over the model, and click and drag. Moving your cursor toward the top of the screen zooms out, and moving it toward the bottom of the screen zooms in.

While you're in Zoom mode, you can hold down the Ctrl key to temporarily activate Spin mode.

Edit Registration Center Much like objects in Flash, every model brought into Vecta3D has a center point around which it rotates. You can move this *registration center*, as it's called in Vecta3D, using the Edit Registration Center tool. To manipulate a model's registration center, click the Edit Registration Center button ✛ in the View section of the program's interface. You'll notice that a red arrow appears in the center of the mode—this is the registration center. From here, click and drag the model itself to another location, thereby changing its position relative to the registration center.

Reset Model Position You might find yourself in a situation where you want to return the model you're working with to its original position upon import. If this is the case, all you need to do is click the Reset Model Position button ✳ in the View section of the program's interface.

Save View You can use the Save View button SV to save the current scale and orientation of your model. The view information is saved in a V3D file.

Load View   When you click the Load View button 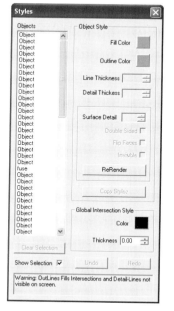, you can load a V3D file where you saved position, scale, and orientation information.

Working with the Styles Window

The Styles window, accessible by clicking the Toggle Styles Window button in the View section of the program's interface, allows you to manipulate the color and line style of your Flash file when it's exported.

Objects List   The Objects List, which takes up the entire left portion of the Styles window, provides you with a list of all the individual objects in the imported 3D model. These objects are named when the model is created in the original program. By clicking any of them, you can set their individual style characteristics.

Object Style Fill Color   You can change the fill color of the currently selected object by clicking the Fill Color swatch and choosing (or mixing) a new color.

Object Style Outline Color   By clicking the Outline Color swatch, you can choose (or mix) a new color for the object's outline.

Line Thickness   The thickness of the currently selected object's outline is set by entering a value (in pixels) into the Line Thickness field. You can also use the arrows just to the right of the field to adjust the value.

Detail Thickness   By entering a value (in pixels) into the Detail Thickness field, you can adjust the thickness of any internal details in the currently selected object.

Surface Detail   Any imported 3D model will have surface detail created by its geometry. By entering a value into the Surface Detail field, you can determine the amount of that detail rendered in the final Flash file. A value of 0 results in a file without any internal detail. On the other hand, a value of 100 results in the model to be rendered as a wireframe.

Double Sided   For the most part, 3D models are composed of single-sided polygons. Vecta3D can only render polygons that it is looking directly at. This can sometimes cause errors when the model is rendered to SWF. By selecting the Double Sided check box, you make both sides of the polygon visible. Be aware, however, that enabling the Double Sided option can result in a longer render time.

Flip Faces   By selecting the Flip Faces option, all outwardly facing surfaces on the currently selected object flip to face inwardly (and vice versa).

Invisible   When the Invisible option is turned on, the currently selected object will be invisible when the object is rendered to SWF.

ReRender Surface Detail, Flip Faces, and Invisible are all render effects. This means they will only take effect when the object is rendered (either by using the preview button or by exporting the file). If you want to view your changes while still in the Styles window, click the ReRender button.

Copy Styles By using the Copy Styles option, you can immediately copy the styles from one object to another. To use the option, simply select the object whose styles you want to use, hold down the Ctrl key and select the object to which you want the styles copied. Then, simply click the Copy Styles button. When the dialog box appears, select the style you want copied, and click Copy Styles.

Global Intersection Style Color In Vecta3D any two intersecting lines are given a single set of styles. To set their color, click the Global Intersection Style color swatch and choose (or mix) a new color.

Global Intersection Style Thickness Enter a value into the Thickness field to set the thickness of intersecting lines.

When you've finished working with the Styles window, close it. All of your changes are applied to the model immediately from within the Styles window, so there is no need to click an Apply button (there isn't one) before you exit.

Creating a Simple Animation

In the "Importing a Sequence of 3D Files" section, you created an animation by importing a sequence of 3D files. In addition to this method, Vecta3D offers some simple tools to create a simple rotating animation:

1. Make sure you've got a model open in the workspace.

2. In the Animation section of the interface, enter a value into any of the Object Rotation/World Rotation fields. By entering a value (in degrees) into any of the Object Rotation axes fields, your object will rotate around its own rotation center. If you enter a value into any of the World Rotation axes fields, the object rotates around the world rotation center (which is smack dab in the middle of the workspace).

3. Once you've set the direction and axis along which your object will spin, enter a value into the Frames field. The more frames there are in your animation, the slower the animation will run.

4. Select one of the Animation Preview buttons:

   - The Play Once button ![button] sets the animation so that it will only play once when it's previewed.

   - The Loop button ![button] sets the animation so that it loops indefinitely when it's previewed.

   - The Play Back and Fourth button ![button] sets the animation so that it plays from beginning to end and then from end to beginning when it's previewed.

To preview your animation inside the workspace, click the Preview Animation button [icon]. Please note that the animation will only preview in "dots" mode, not as it will look when it's rendered to SWF.

Working with Render Settings

To determine the way in which your animation or still is rendered, you need to manipulate some additional properties:

Render Outlines By clicking the Render Outlines button [icon], your model exports looking something like a line drawing.

Render fills When you click the Render button [icon], your model exports with only its fill.

Render lines and fills By clicking the Lines and Fills button [icon], your model exports with both lines and fills.

Perspective The Perspective field lets you adjust the perspective of your model when it's exported. By entering **1** into the field, you'll get a fish-eye perspective. On the other hand, if you enter **0** into the field, the exported file will have a default isometric perspective.

Intersections When you select the Intersections option, the lines of intersecting surfaces are visible when the model is rendered.

Surface Detail When you select the Surface Detail option, all of the model's surface detail is visible when rendered.

Rendering an Animation or Still Image

Now that you've imported your model, set its style, determined its render settings, and animated it (if that was your goal), you can now render it to SWF:

- To render the animation, click the Save Animation to Disk button [icon]. When the Save As dialog box appears, enter a name into the Name field, navigate to the location on the hard drive when you want the file saved, and click Save.

- To save a still image, click Save Still [icon]. When the Save As dialog box appears, enter a name into the Name field, navigate to the location on the hard drive when you want the file saved, and click Save.

If you want to preview your still in the workspace, click the Preview Still button (just above the Save Still button) in the Single Frame section of the interface.

Amorphium Pro

One of the major complaints of first-time 3D modelers is that the vast majority of programs are painfully counterintuitive. The first time a 3D novice opens any of the middle- to high-end modeling programs, they are often overwhelmed by the complexity of the authoring environment. On the whole, polygon modeling is a pretty esoteric skill whose concepts alone take a fair amount of time to get a handle on. 3D modeling programs just aren't designed for those who have experience in more traditional forms of art such as sculpting, printmaking, painting, or ceramics. You may be surprised to know that many traditional artists and graphic designers are looking to the world of 3D for a new way to express their creative vision. Heck, you might even *be* one of these traditional artists. So what's a person to do if they love the kind of intuitive, tactile creative process that comes with traditional art forms, but doesn't want to spend the time learning 3D modeling the "hard" way? Well, there is an alternative: Amorphium Pro.

Electric Image's Amorphium Pro (`www.electricimage.com`) isn't like most 3D modeling programs. The program's main focus is to provide a set of tools for sculpting and molding 3D objects as if they were lumps of clay sitting in front of you. The program allows you to manipulate 3D models by pushing, pulling, twisting, morphing, and painting them. Any changes you make happen in real-time! Amorphium Pro is a great tool in this respect because it introduces a whole different approach 3D modeling.

The program boasts a particularly interesting interface that is broken into separate "rooms" (see Figure 26.4). The rooms, which are accessible through the menu bar at the top of the program's authoring environment, features a set of tools designed to carry out specific operations.

Figure 26.4

Amorphium Pro's interface is partitioned into a series of rooms (or modes) in which you'll carry out specific tasks.

The main room, the Tools room, lets you to mold 3D objects by pushing and pulling on their surfaces with different brushes. Other rooms, such as the FX room, let you deform your 3D object by using special procedural deformers such as Bend and Twirl.

Aside from a good MetaBall-type modeling tool called Biospheres, which is great for modeling complex organic shapes with a minimum of fuss, Amorphium Pro also features a modeling technique called Wax that allows you to grow your 3D models.

> *Biospheres* are little blobby spheres of digital goo that interact with one another in interesting ways. Comparing Biospheres to liquid mercury is pretty apt.

Beyond its modeling tools, the program has a full material-editing system complete with infinitely stackable procedural textures that can be dragged about the surface of the model so their placement is just right. In addition, the program's animations tools are based on standard keyframe techniques that are easily picked by even the most inexperienced of users.

Amorphium Pro's rendering engine features full raytracing and radiosity. Finally, Amorphium Pro lets you export models and animations as Flash files.

 A demo copy of Amorphium Pro has been included on this book's CD-ROM.

Like many of the previous sections, you aren't going to spend any time going into Amorphium Pro's modeling tools. Instead, this section simply discusses the features you need to know to take advantage of the program's Flash export.

> If you're interested in getting into Amorphium Pro as a modeling tool, the first place to look is Electric Image's website (www.electricimage.com), which has some pretty useful tutorials. Also, Amorphium Pro's documentation is a good place to start.

After having created and animated an image destined for Flash export, you need to set the file's output options.

You accomplish this through the RaydioCity Options dialog box, which you can open by clicking the Radiosity button ▣ in the Composer Palette.

If you're going to output to Flash, you'll work with a number of the tabs in the RaydioCity Options dialog box. At this point, it's best to take a step-by-step approach to the process:

1. With the RaydioCity Options dialog box open, click the Render tab.

2. Choose a camera from which the project will be rendered from the Camera drop-down menu. Your choices include Top, Front, Right, and Isometric. You'll also be able to choose from any additional camera you created.

3. Choose Flash from the Output drop-down menu.

4. Choose the size of your exported file from the Size drop-down menu. You can choose from several preset sizes. Alternatively, you can enter a custom size into the Width and Height fields. Remember, the larger the dimensions, the larger your file will be.

5. Leave the Radiosity option unchecked. Radiosity, which is an advanced shading option that takes account for the energy of a light and how it falls off when hitting other objects, doesn't factor into a file exported in Flash format.

6. Check the Shadows option if you want the shadows in your scene to be visible in the final file.

7. Click the Antialiasing tab. From here, you'll be able to set the anti-aliasing properties of your final file.

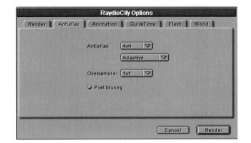

8. Choose either the Adaptive or Oversampling technique of the Antialias option. The Adaptive technique results in a sharper image, and the Oversampling technique results in a softer image.

9. If you want your image to be blurred slightly when it's exported, select the Postblurring option.

10. If you are exporting an animation, opposed to a still image, click the Animation tab. From here you'll be able to set the animation properties of your final file.

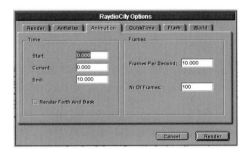

11. Enter value into the Start, Current, and End fields to determine the length of the exported animation. The values entered into the respective fields are numerical representations of the same information that is graphically displayed in the project window.

12. Enter a value into the Frames per Second field. Remember, a higher frame rate results in a larger, higher-quality movie. On the other hand, a lower frame rate results in a small, lower-quality movie.

> If you are having trouble remembering exactly how frame rate relates to Flash, see Chapter 9.

13. If you want a specific number of frames rendered, you can enter the exact value into the Nr of Frames field. Amorphium Pro automatically adjusts the frame rate by taking into account the Start Time and the End Time. For instance, if you set the Start Time to 0, the End Time to 10, and the Number of Frames to 200, the Frames per Second changes to 20.

14. Click the Flash tab.

15. Choose an option from the Lines drop-down menu:

- By choosing None, your final file will not include lines at the edges of polygons or where objects intersect.
- The Outlines option renders your final file with lines at intersections of objects.
- When you choose Wireframe, your final file is rendered as a wireframe.

16. The Polygons drop-down menu determines how Amorphium Pro renders the polygons of your object or objects:

- Selecting None causes your file to be rendered without filled polygons—as a wireframe.
- When you choose Cartoon, the polygons in your model are exported with solid colors opposed to gradients.
- The Gradients option simulates variable lighting across an object by using gradients when it's exported to Flash.

17. Click the Lines color swatch to choose a color for the lines in your final files.

18. Click the Global Ambient swatch to choose a color for the ambient light in your final exported scene. By setting this value to something other than black, areas hidden from lights appear dark, but not black.

19. By default, the color of any exported Flash file is black; by clicking the Background Color swatch you can choose an alternate color.

20. You can numerically set the quality of the exported Flash file by entering a value into the Sampling Quality field. A larger value means a higher quality, but a larger file size.

21. If you want to include specular highlights into the final Flash file, click the Separate Specular Polygons option.

22. When you're finished, click the Render button in the bottom-right corner of the RaydioCity Options dialog box.

23. When the Export dialog box opens, enter a name for your file into the Name field, navigate to the location of your hard drive when you want the file to be exported, and click Save.

Using Non-SWF-Exporting 3D Applications with Flash

Not all 3D modeling programs feature Flash export. In fact, the ones that don't may outnumber those that do. The world of 3D is a really big place. People have been using 3D in the television, game, film, architecture, and product-design industries well before Flash ever came along. As a result, you're going to find that many of the more widely used, higher-end 3D modeling programs will be far likelier *not* to feature built-in Flash export. Most of the programs that do feature Flash export, including those discussed in this chapter, are designed for less-experienced 3D modelers and therefore are nowhere near as versatile, powerful, or all-around cool as those high-end programs that have been around for a while.

This state of affairs places 3D Flash designers in a tough spot. If you are an experienced 3D modeler who thinks 3D Flash is the coolest thing to come out since those little plastic tables that keep the top of the pizza box from sticking to the top of the pizza, you certainly don't want to abandon your favorite 3D modeling program in favor of one of these lower-end Flash capable programs. Likewise, if you are a Flash designer who is willing to spend the time (and the brain cells) to learn a high-end 3D modeling program for the sake of your creations, you'll be disappointed by the lack of Flash export. However, you do have some other options. The most notable is Vecta3D—a program discussed previously that will take either 3ds max files (a fairly ubiquitous file type in the world of 3D) and export them to Flash. Also, a few companies produce plug-ins that give your favorite 3D modeling program the ability to export Flash. As a result, if you are thinking of becoming a dedicated 3D Flash guru, it's a good idea to get a good handle on the higher-end 3D modelers. The following sections cover many of these programs.

3ds max

3ds max, which is made by Canadian-based Discreet (a division of Autodesk), is one of the most widely used 3D modeling programs on the market. In the interactive entertainment industry, it is the leading 3D modeler. In fact, it's rare to find a game developer anywhere in the world who doesn't use 3ds max.

The newest version of the program, 3ds max 4 offers 3D professionals extremely advanced tools for character animation, next-generation game development, and visual effects production. Many new features and architectural enhancements complement these three major initiatives.

3ds max features all manner of modeling systems, including NURBS, Patch, polygon, spline, and primitive, as well as exceedingly powerful animation, effects, materials, lights, scripting, workflow, and rendering tools.

For those interested in 3D Flash, Electric Rain (the makers of Swift 3D) makes a plug-in for 3ds max called Swift 3D Max that allows direct Flash export.

In August of 2001, Macromedia announced a strategic partnership with Discreet to accelerate the deployment of interactive 3D content on the Web. By bundling a complete version of Macromedia Director 8.5 (the most recent version of the product has some powerful tools geared toward the creation of interactive 3D web multimedia) with 3ds max, Discreet expressed a decidedly solid commitment to 3D on the Web. Although the deal itself doesn't directly affect the topic at hand, it does have some interesting ramifications for the future of 3D Flash.

If you are interested in the mighty Director/3ds max one-two combination punch, visit `www.macromedia.com/director`.

Cinema 4D

Cinema 4D is probably one of the best-kept secrets in 3D. Made by Maxon Computer, Cinema 4D (www.cinema4d.com) is an astonishingly powerful 3D modeler and animator that can easily compete on the same footing as 3ds max and LightWave 3D.

Cinema 4D's interface is fully customizable so that you can create exactly the kind of working environment you are comfortable (see Figure 26.5). The program features numerous modeling systems, including HyperNURBS (a variant of NURBS), parametric primitive modeling, interactive symmetry objects, and MetaBalls.

Figure 26.5

Cinema 4D's interface is fully customizable, allowing you to tweak the working environment to maximize your creative potential.

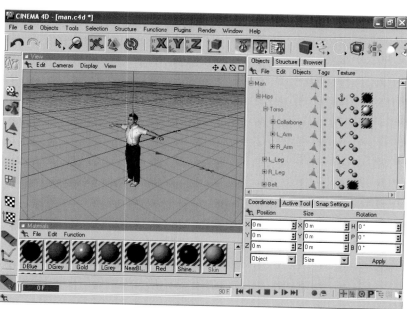

Cinema 4D features a complex shading and materials system, lighting systems, and animations tools. The program also integrated seamlessly with BodyPaint, a program designed to let you interactively paint directly on any 3D object.

LightWave 3D

LightWave 3D, which is produced by NewTek (www.newtek.com), is one of those programs that has an extremely dedicated and loyal following. The most recent version (version 7) incorporates real-time subdivision surfaces, extensive texturing tools, character animation tools, radiosity, caustics, HyperVoxels, and ray tracing, and an extremely powerful animation system.

On the topic of 3D Flash, Electric Rain, the makers of Swift 3D, have created a plug-in called Swift 3D LW that allows LightWave 3D users to export their models directly to Flash.

Carrara Studio

The origins of Carrara Studio are similar to those of Poser 4.03. Originally developed by MetaCreations, Carrara Studio (originally called Carrara) was in danger of disappearing into that great processor in the sky when the company divested itself of all its creative 3D and 2D software. Fortunately, the original development team got together, formed a company called Eovia, and snatched up Carrara. They released a minor bug-fix upgrade and then, in June of 2001, released Carrara Studio.

Carrara Studio is designed to be an accessible, middle-range, one-stop rendering and animation solution. Perhaps one of the most interesting features of the program is its highly unorthodox and intuitive interface, which is divided into "rooms," each with its own toolset. Carrara Studio has five such rooms: Assemble, Storyboard, Model, Texture, and Render, which are accessed via a set of icons located in the top-right corner of the screen. The setup allows you to flip between rooms, creating a model in one, adding texture in another, and then rendering in another.

The focus of the workflow is the Assemble room, where you place and animate models, lights, and cameras. The most interesting feature of the Assemble room is the 3D work area, where you'll find three intersecting planes (X, Y, and Z) forming an open box. Any models you import are displayed as solids with projections on the box "walls." These projections enable you to locate the object in 3D space and can also be used to select, reposition, and resize the object. This feature alone is quite interesting and diverges from the traditional 3D modeling workspace.

Carrara features several modeling systems, each of which allows you to create objects using splines, vertices, text, and MetaBall. The spline and vertex modelers are graphically enhanced versions of those found in MetaCreations old modeling package Infini-D, and the MetaBall modeler traces its origin back to Ray Dream. Boolean modeling is also fully supported in Carrara Studio. If you're mathematically inclined (or particularly masochistic), you can also create models with mathematical formulae. The program features a whole host of modifiers that you can apply to models to change their physical shape or movement.

For those who want a little more robust modeling experience, Carrara Studio ships with a fully functional version of Amapi 3D (version 5). So, Carrara Studio files can be exported into Amapi 3D format and then output to SWF using Amapi 3D's native Flash export. This minor miracle is courtesy of Eovia's new parent company, TGS, which was the original developer of Amapi 3D. Carrara Studio also exports files to 3DS so that you can open them in Vecta3D.

Maya

Maya is the granddaddy of all 3D modeling programs. If you are looking for the pinnacle of the 3D industry, Maya is it. You can't get any more powerful (or complicated and expensive, for that matter). Maya is the 500-pound gorilla of the 3D industry. Need I go on?

Published by the Canadian-based Alias|Wavefront (`www.aliaswavefront.com`), Maya is predominantly used in the film industry. It's not that individuals or groups outside the film industry consciously choose not to use Maya, it's just that the $16,000 price tag is somewhat inhibitive for average users. You can see Maya at work in such recent films as *How the Grinch Stole Christmas*, *The Mummy*, *The Mummy Returns*, *Star Wars: The Phantom Menace*, and *Enemy at the Gates*. At the hands of an extremely well-trained artist, Maya can produce some truly beautiful things.

Because it's so high end, it seems a little foolish to even mention it and Flash in the same sentence—right? Well, yes and no. Though the program doesn't feature a Flash export, Alias|Wavefront is now distributing an exporter that outputs files to Shockwave3D (the 3D format for Macromedia's Director 8.5 Shockwave Studio). This move has affirmed Alias|Wavefront's commitment to interactive web 3D. Given the geometric expansion of Flash as a creative medium, Maya is assuredly going to play a role in the undoubtedly bright future of 3D Flash.

Inspirational Design Model

Though 3D Flash is a relatively young creative enterprise, quite a few motivating examples exist. One of the most interesting is Titoonic (see Figure 26.6).

Figure 26.6

Titoonic's main focus is the creation of 3D characters and character animation for consumption over the Web.

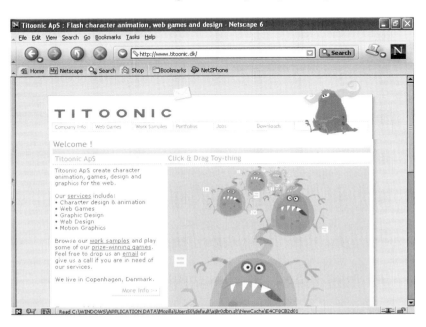

Founded in August 2000, Titoonic (`www.titoonic.dk`) is a creative web production company located in Copenhagen, Denmark. Although the company specializes in all manner of web-based multimedia, it is best known for its 3D character animation and design. It has been responsible for the design and implementation of numerous 3D Flash characters whose implementation includes visual guides on websites, character-based Flash games, greeting cards, and "webisodes."

Founded by a group of highly creative individuals whose backgrounds include classical animation and graphical storytelling, Titoonic is pushing the boundaries of the cutting-edge of 3D Flash development with its extremely stylish and compelling 3D character design.

Summary

In this chapter you explored creating 3D images in Flash. You started off with a basic, but vital, exploration of 3D fundamentals. From there, you used Flash's painting and drawing tools to simulate static 3D objects. Taking this knowledge to the next step, you explored how to use ActionScript in conjunction with simulated 3D objects to create a pseudo-3D animation.

Because Flash's 3D abilities are extremely limited, the chapter continued by looking at the various programs designed to export 3D models to Flash. These included Swift 3D, Amapi 3D, Vecta3D, Poser, and Amorphium Pro. The chapter closed by exploring other 3D modeling programs that, although not yet featuring Flash export, may well be the future of 3D Flash.

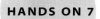

Creating an Animated 3D Flash Logo

Throughout Part VII, you looked at how you can integrate Flash with other programs. For this tutorial, you're going to take some of the skills you've mastered (as well as some new ones introduced here) and create an animated 3D Flash logo for the splash page of a fictional design studio called Retro Studios. You'll start off by taking the 3D model (which has already been created in Amorphium Pro) and export it as an SWF file that you'll then import into Flash and incorporate it with the other graphical elements of the logo. To finish up, you'll take the animated Flash/3D logo (which will be exported as an SWF) and place it in a Dreamweaver HTML document.

> Although it would be advantageous to go through the step-by-step process of creating the 3D logo, such an undertaking would be outside the scope of this tutorial. If you are interested in getting better acquainted with Amorphium Pro, you can download the entire manual in PDF (if you don't already own the program) from Electric Image's website. Simply point your browser to www.electricimage.com/amorphium/manual.html.

 You'll find demo copies of both Electric Image's Amorphium Pro and Macromedia's Dreamweaver on this book's CD-ROM. In addition, you can find all of the files used in this tutorial in the Hands On 7 directory on your book's CD-ROM. There, you will also find a copy of the finished files (so you can get an idea of what the final product might look like). However, as with all the tutorials in this book, the process is far more important than the final product.

Exporting the 3D Animation

You'll start off by working in Amorphium Pro:

1. Open Amorphium Pro. When the Save As dialog box opens, click Cancel.

2. Now, go to Project → Open Project. When the Open dialog box opens, navigate to the Hands On 7 directory on the book's CD-ROM, select the logo.cmf, and click Open.

If you had previously been working on a project in Amorphium Pro, the program automatically reopens that project when you start off. You must close this project before you can open a new one. To do this, go to Project → Close Project. From there, the program prompts you to save the project. After you've either saved or canceled out of the prompt, follow steps 1 and 2 to open the file with which you'll be working in this tutorial.

3. When the snazzy 3D logo animation opens, click the RaydioCity button , which is located at the bottom of the Composer palette.

4. Now, click anywhere in the Camera (Perspective) window to open the RaydioCity Options dialog box. From here, you'll set all of the properties of the animation when it's exported as an SWF file.

5. Select the Render tab, if it isn't already selected, and choose 128×128 from the Size drop-down menu.

6. Now, choose Camera from the Camera drop-down menu.

7. After you've done this, choose Flash Animation from the Output drop-down menu.

8. Now that you've set all the render options, select the Flash tab. First, choose Outlines from the Lines drop-down menu.

9. Choose Average from the Polygons drop-down menu.

10. Now, you can set the various color values of your exported SWF. First, click the (very) small color wheel icon located in the bottom-left corner of the Global Ambient color swatch (located in the bottom-right corner of the Flash section of the RaydioCity Options dialog box).

Global ambient color is the color of the light that uniformly lights all objects within the scene. Although it's customary in 3D modeling to turn off ambient lighting, doing so in a file destined for SWF export can create an image (or animation) in which all areas hidden by the scene's other sources of illumination are completely black. As a result, you'll want to choose a color that isn't too dark, but isn't too light.

11. When the Color Picker pops up, enter **128** into the Red field, **128** into the Green field, and **128** into the Blue field. When you've finished doing this, click OK.

12. Now you can set the background color of the exported SWF file. Click the (very) small color wheel icon located in the bottom-left corner of the Background Color swatch.

13. When the Color Picker opens, enter **255** into the Red field, **255** into the Green field, and **255** into the Blue field. Once you've done this, click OK.

> As you are going to leave the Line color black and the Line Width at 1 pixel, which is the default, don't worry about changing anything in the Lines section.

14. After you've finished setting all the Flash properties, click Render.

15. When the Save As dialog box pops up, navigate to the location on your hard drive where you want to save the SWF file (remember, as you are going to use it later, stick it somewhere where it won't get lost), enter **3D_object** into the File Name field, and click Save.

16. From there, your SWF file will render frame by frame. Depending on the speed of your computer, this could take a bit. Just sit back and relax while Amorphium Pro does its thing. When it's finished, the program lets you preview the exported animation.

17. From here, simply click the small square in the upper-left corner of the file's preview window to close it down. This returns you to the main program interface.

18. Go to Project → Quit. Amorphium Pro will prompt you to save the project. Either save the project (by hitting Save) or exit without saving (by hitting Don't Save).

Working with the Animation in Flash

Now that you've exported the snazzy 3D animation that you'll be using in the final product, it's time to pull it into Flash and add some more elements to the logo:

1. Start Flash.

2. Go to Modify → Document.

3. When the Document Properties dialog box opens, change the dimensions to 550×300 pixels. Then, click the Background Color swatch, and select the #999999 gray color (whose color square is located fourth from the top along the left side of the Color Picker).

4. Once you've modified the background color and dimensions of the movie, the first thing you are going to do is create the basic background shape of the logo. To do this, start off by going to Insert → New Symbol. When the Create New Symbol dialog box opens, select the Graphic radio button, enter **background** into the Name field, and click OK.

5. When the Symbol Editor opens, use Flash's painting and drawing tools to create a shape something like that shown here (make sure that the shape occupies only a single keyframe):

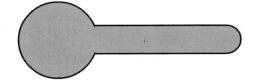

It doesn't really matter which tools you use to create the shape. You could draw a rounded rectangle and combine it with an ellipse. You could also use the Pen tool to draw the shape freehand. The important feature is that, when complete, the shape should have a fill of 255.152.0 (RGB). In addition, the shape's stroke should be black and 3-pixels wide. Finally, the shape itself should also be roughly the size of the one shown in the previous image.

If you want to cut a few corners, you could open the finished FLA file (called `retro_logo.fla`), located in the Hands On 7 directory on the book's CD-ROM, and copy and paste the background symbol into your own movie.

6. When you've finished creating the background portion of the logo, insert an additional layer called **text**.

7. Select the first keyframe in the text layer, select the Text tool, and insert the words **retro-labs**. (For the time being, you can place the text anywhere—you'll move it into position later.)

8. Select the text you just entered, and open the Property Inspector by going to Windows → Properties.

9. When the Property Inspector opens, choose Eight Track Program 3 from the Font drop-down menu.

Eight Track Program 3, created by Fontalicious (`www.fontalicious.com`), isn't your run-of-the-mill font. As a result, it's highly doubtful you'll have it installed on your machine, which is why we've included a copy of the font (which you can install) in the Hands On 7 directory on the book's CD-ROM.

10. Enter **35** into the Font Height field.

11. Enter **1** into the Character Spacing field.

12. If it isn't already, change the text's color to black.

13. Set the text's style to Italic and Bold.

14. Once you've finished manipulating the text, click your cursor anywhere off the text box to deselect it.

15. Select the Arrow tool, and use it to reposition the text relative to the background shape, as shown here:

16. Now that you've created the static elements in the project, it's time to take the SWF file you exported from Amorphium Pro, and integrate it into the logo. To do this, switch back to the main Timeline.

17. Go to Insert → New Symbol. When the Create New Symbol dialog box opens, select the Movie Clip radio button, enter **3D object** into the Name field, and click OK.

18. When you enter the Symbol Editor, go to File → Import.

19. When the Import dialog box opens, navigate to the location in which you saved the `3D_object.swf` file, select it, and click open. When you do this, the animated SWF file will be imported as a frame-by-frame animation in which each keyframe corresponds to a frame in the original Amorphium Pro file.

> It is more than likely that, when imported, the 3D animation you exported from Amorphium Pro will be placed slightly off center in the Symbol Editor. Because the file is imported as a frame-by-frame animation, it would be quite difficult to reposition it—you would need to move the contents of each keyframe individually (a difficult and timely process). However, the imported animation being off-center in the Symbol Editor won't affect your movie that much. It will just result in the Movie Clip's registration point not being in the center of the actual symbol when it is used in the main Timeline.

20. Now it's time to take the background symbol you created earlier and combine it with the actual 3D animation into a Movie Clip that you'll then place on the main Timeline to produce the finished logo movie. Start off by going to Insert → New Symbol.

21. When the Create New Symbol dialog box opens, select the Movie Clip radio button, enter **logo** into the Name field, and click OK.

22. When the Symbol Editor opens, rename the existing layer **background**.

23. Add an additional layer, and call it **3D Animation**.

24. If the Library isn't already open, open it by going to Window → Library.

25. Then, select the first keyframe of the background layer and drag the background symbol from the Library onto the Stage.

26. Now, select the first keyframe of the 3D Animation layer, and drag the 3D object Movie Clip from the Library onto the Stage. Position it relative to the background symbol as shown here:

27. From here, hop back to the main Timeline, select the first keyframe of the single existing layer, and drag the 3D animation from the Library onto the Stage. Position it so that the logo is in the center of the Stage.

28. Now, you can test out the logo by going to Control → Test Movie.

29. All that's left to do before you move into the final stage of the project (which involves placing your newly created 3D Flash animated logo into an HTML document using Dreamweaver) is exporting the movie as a SWF file. To do this, go to File → Export Movie.

> Although it may seem a little elementary, it's important to remember that the native Flash file format (FLA) is not readable by web browsers with the Flash plug-in. Instead, the SWF file format is the file type that you'll ultimately want to export.

30. When the Export Movie dialog box opens, type **retro_logo** into the Name field, navigate to the location on your hard drive when you want to save the SWF file, and click Save.

31. When the Export Flash Player dialog box pops up, leave everything at its default setting and click OK.

Inserting Your Animation into a Dreamweaver Document

Now that you've created your animated 3D Flash logo and exported is as a SWF file, you can use Dreamweaver to insert it into an HTML file.

We've included the `Dreamweaver.pdf` file, "Working with Flash and Dreamweaver," on this book's CD-ROM to help you with this section of the tutorial. You'll also find a demo copy of Dreamweaver 4 on the CD-ROM for your use.

1. Start off by opening Dreamweaver.

2. Go to Modify → Page Properties to open the Page Properties dialog box. From here, you'll change the color of the page so that it matches the background color of your animated Flash/3D logo, as well as the title of the web page.

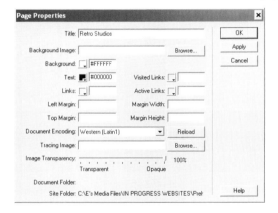

3. In the Title field, type **Retro Studios**.

4. Click the Background color swatch, and click the system Color Picker icon (the small color wheel in the upper-right corner of the color palette).

5. When the Color Picker opens, enter **160** into the Red field, **156** into the Green field, and **160** into the Blue field. When you've finished, click OK.

6. When you are returned to the Page Properties dialog box, click Apply and then OK.

7. Now insert the animated Flash logo into the Dreamweaver document. To do this, select Insert → Media → Flash.

Alternatively, you can also click the Insert Flash button located in the Common section of the Objects palette (accessible by going to Window → Objects).

8. When the Select File dialog box pops up, navigate to the location where you saved the `retro_logo.swf` file, select it, and hit Select.

9. Before Dreamweaver inserts the Flash movie into your page, you'll be faced with a series of prompts. For the first, which suggests you save your file to make the Flash file's path document relative, you can hit OK. For the second, which asks you whether you want to copy the Flash file to your local site, hit No.

Dreamweaver is as much a website creation and management tool as it is a web page creation tool. The program is designed to help you create, manipulate, and manage entire sites. All of these tools revolve around the initial creation of a local site, which will ultimately include all the files in your site and reside in a specific location (usually a single folder) on your hard drive. There are a couple of reasons for creating a local site, the most important of which is that when you get to the point where you want to upload your site to a web server, you'll just upload the entire site's folder. By doing this, you ensure that when you upload your local site to a remote web server, you won't be missing any components. When you set up your local site, you'll also be able to track and maintain your links.

When it's initially placed in the Dreamweaver document, the Flash file is represented by a gray box with a Flash icon in the center. Don't worry, as this is quite normal. You'll be able to preview the Flash movie from within Dreamweaver—something we'll explore a little later. After your SWF file has been inserted into the Dreamweaver document, it's time to position it so that the overall page is a little more aesthetically pleasing.

10. First, click your mouse just to the right of the Flash file (so that the file is no longer selected). From there, go to Window → Properties to open the Property Inspector.

11. Now, click the Align Center button ≣ , which is the center button in the group of three alignment buttons located in the top-right corner of the Property Inspector. This aligns the Flash file to the center of the page.

12. Now, click your mouse just to the left of the Flash file and hit the Enter/Return button three or four times. This simply moves the Flash movie down so that it is located more in the center of the page.

13. Now that you've positioned the Flash movie, it's time to use the Property Inspector to do some final tweaking. Select the Flash movie. If the Property Inspector isn't already open, go to Window → Property Inspector.

14. If it isn't already, expand the Property Inspector by clicking the small Down arrow located in its bottom-right corner.

15. If it isn't already, select High from the Quality drop-down menu.

16. Select the Autoplay check box located in the expanded section of the Property Inspector. This ensures that the Flash movie will automatically play when the page is located.

Although selecting the Loop check box might seem like a good idea, it really would have no effect on whether the movie actually loops. Because the animation you created in Flash was composed primarily of a Movie Clip (which automatically loops unless it includes some ActionScript that instructs it to do otherwise), your groovy animated 3D/Flash logo will automatically loop regardless of whether you select the Loop option.

17. Select Default (Show All) from the Scale drop-down menu.

18. To preview the Flash movie, click the Play button. ▷ Play

19. Now save the document by selecting File → Save. When the Save As dialog box appears, navigate to the location in which you want to save the HTML file (which should be in the same folder in which you saved the `retro_logo.swf` file), enter **retro_splash** into the Name field, and hit Save.

If you haven't saved the HTML document in the same location as the SWF file, you are going to have some problems. Essentially, when you try to view the HTML file, the browser won't be able to locate the SWF file and will therefore not display it.

20. Finally, to preview your creation in a browser, hit F12 or go to File → Preview in Browser.

If you haven't gone through the process of setting up a Target Browser, refer to Dreamweaver's Help files (Help → Using Dreamweaver).

PART VIII

Publishing and Distributing Your Flash Movies

So, you've spent hours creating your Flash masterpiece. You've created cool images, crafted groovy animation, and added amazing interactivity with ActionScript. What's next? Well, after a bit of a breather and a good pat on the back, its time to start thinking about what to do with this amazing piece of brain sweat? Yeah, that's right, it isn't finished yet. The whole point of creating interactive media of any kind is so that other people can enjoy, experience, and explore your creative vision.

In this section of the book, you are going to explore the various ways in which you can get your masterpiece "out there." First, you'll get a chnace to explore how you take your native Flash FLA file and convert it to a wide variety of differnt file formats (the chief among them being SWF) suitable for distribution. From there, you are going to delve into the world of integrating Flash with video. Finally, you are going to investigate all the issues surrounding taking your Flash movie and distributing it on a CD.

CHAPTER 27

Publishing Your Flash Movie

You've spent hours creating beautiful graphics, prodding your animation, and tweaking your ActionScript, so what's next? Well, all of your hard work is for naught if others weren't able to experience your beautiful creation.

The process of converting an FLA file (the native type of Flash) into a format that can be distributed over the Web or via another medium is called *publishing*. Although publishing your movie is pretty straightforward, you need to make sure the file's settings maximize your movie for its intended audience and file format. As a result, it behooves you to become familiar with the various file types available as well as their often copious publishing settings.

Through the course of this chapter, you'll explore the following topics:

- **Working with the Flash publishing settings**

- **Previewing your Flash movie**

- **Optimizing your Flash movie**

- **Publishing your Flash movie**

- **Publishing accessible content**

- **Creating printable movies**

Working with Flash Publishing Settings

The majority of the time, you are going to publish your movies as SWF files (the format viewable by browsers with the Flash plug-in). However, Macromedia has provided a series of other file formats for publishing your movie. This enables you to tailor your Flash creation so you can reach the maximum number of people. For instance, if you created a series of noninteractive animated shorts, you could publish them as both SWF and QuickTime files to take advantage of those two formats' wide installation base. Publishing your creation also allows you to output your FLA file to a number of other formats simultaneously. As you might have guessed, each of the various file types has quite a few settings that allow you to further manipulate a movie's ultimate look and behavior.

In the following sections you are going to explore each of these various file types. You'll then look at the individual publishing settings for each of the file types.

> Although the process of publishing your movie is relatively simple, it actually involves two separate tasks. The first task, inputting the publishing settings, will be discussed after you've thoroughly explored all the files types to which the Flash movie can be outputted. The second task, telling Flash to publish your creation based on the settings, will be discussed in "Publishing Your Flash Movie."

Publishing Formats

Flash offers a series of file types to which your creation can be published. Each has its own particular strengths and weaknesses; therefore, you should learn about each one so that you know which you to use.

Flash

Most of the time, you are going to publish your Flash creations as SWF files. The default publishing format, SWF is viewable only if your intended audience has installed the Flash plug-in on their computers. It's definitely important to know that, of all the possible file types, SWF is the only one that fully supports all ActionScript and animation; other formats such as QuickTime don't fully support these features. So, if you want to leverage the full power of Flash, use SWF.

> If you are planning on distributing your SWF movie over the web (opposed to creating a standalone SWF that is played by the Flash Player), you'll need to publish an HTML file as well—a process discussed in the "Manipulating HTML Settings" section later in this chapter.

HTML

Playing an SWF movie in a web browser requires an HTML document in which the Flash movie is embedded. The HTML file serves to activate the movie, specify browser settings, and, to a certain degree, determine how the SWF file appears. As a result, if your SWF file is destined for distribution on the Web, you must publish it with an HTML file.

The Flash Player (placed on the user's computer when they install the Flash plugin) can display SWF files without the help of an HTML file. As a result, if your movie is not destined to be viewed in a web browser, you don't have to worrying about publishing an HTML file along with your movie.

GIF

GIF stands for Graphic Interchange Format. Developed originally by CompuServe back in the late 1980s, GIFs are the workhorse image of the Web. The format itself can only display a maximum of 256 colors. As a result, GIFs are best used for relatively simple images with flat colors and are generally smaller in size (in terms of kilobytes) than other formats such as JPEG. One of the great things about GIFs is that they come in a few different forms:

- Transparent GIFs are partially transparent, causing the background upon which they are placed to be visible.

- Interlaced GIFs are structured in such a way that they come into focus slowly as the browser loads the image.

- Animated GIFs are simply a series of images saved in the same file. When an animated image is loaded by a browser, all the images in the file are displayed in sequence, creating an animation—sort of like a digital flipbook.

You can export a Flash movie as an animated GIF for distribution to users who don't have the Flash plug-in installed on their computer. A Flash movie published as an animated GIF is generally larger in size than if it had been published as a SWF file. In addition, any interactivity in a Flash movie exported to an animated GIF will be lost.

JPEG

JPEG stands for Joint Photographic Experts Group. JPEGs came along after GIFs and were designed specifically to display photographic or continuous color images. Their main strength is that they can display millions of colors. As a result, JPEGs tend to have larger file sizes than GIFs. A good way to think about it is that as the quality of the JPEG increases, so does its file size. Unfortunately, JPEGs only come in one flavor: no transparency, no interlacing, and definitely no animation.

By default, Flash exports the first frame of a movie as a static JPEG. There is, however, a trick for forcing Flash to export an alternate frame (opposed to the first one). This is covered in "Setting JPEG Publish Options."

PNG

PNG stands for Portable Network Group. Developed in part by Macromedia and established as a web standard by the World Wide Web Consortium, PNGs are a little less straightforward than GIFs or JPEGs. They were designed to combine the best of both GIFs and JPEGs. As a result, they can support indexed-color (256 colors), grayscale, true-color images (millions of colors), and transparency. The problem with PNGs is that they have spotty browser support. Microsoft Internet Explorer (4.0 and later) and Netscape Navigator (4.04 and later) partially support the display of PNG images. Because PNG is the native file type of Fireworks, Flash MX has some sophisticated tools geared specifically toward their manipulation and management.

Much like in the case of JPEGs, Flash exports a single static PNG image.

Windows Projector

A Windows Projector is probably one of the coolest formats available. Basically, it's a self-executing EXE file that doesn't need a browser or a plug-in to view it. This has some definite advantages over the other file types. First, you can distribute the Windows Projector without having to worry whether the intended audience has the necessary Flash plug-in, a compatible web browser, or even an Internet connection. They are self-contained little packages that are great for distribution of media such as CD-ROMs or DVDs.

Macintosh Projector

The Macintosh Projector is the Mac equivalent of the Windows Projector. A self-executing HQX file, the Macintosh Projector doesn't need the Flash plug-in or a browser to be viewed.

QuickTime

Publishing your Flash movie to QuickTime creates a MOV file that plays in the QuickTime Player. This format retains the vast majority of your movie's interactive features. However, users need to have the QuickTime plug-in installed to view Flash files published as MOV files.

> If you don't have QuickTime (version 4 or later) installed on your computer, you won't be able to publish your Flash movie in QuickTime format.

When rendered, your Flash creation occupies a single track in the QuickTime movie.

Manipulating Individual Publish Format Settings

Now that you've explored each of the various file formats to which your Flash movie can be published, let's look at the publishing settings of those various file formats. All of the work you'll do in this section is through the Publish Settings dialog box, which is accessed by going to File → Publish Settings.

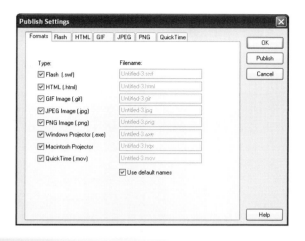

As you select individual file types in the Formats tab of the Publish Settings dialog box, you'll notice that additional tabs (labeled with the specific file type) are added. By clicking any of these tabs, you get access to that file type's settings. When you are finished manipulating the settings of all the file types to which you are publishing your Flash movie, click OK.

By selecting the Use Default Names option, your file is published with the same name you assigned to your FLA file. If this option is deselected, you can name the file uniquely.

> Because neither the Windows Projector nor the Macintosh Projector has any unique publishing settings, they aren't discussed in the following sections. However, when you export a movie to Windows Projector or Macintosh Projector, its properties are set by the choices you make under the Flash tab.

Working with Flash Settings

After you select Flash (SWF) in the Formats tab of the Publish Settings dialog box, you'll be able to click the Flash tab to access those settings.

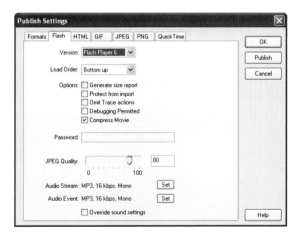

The options include the following:

Version Specifies the version of Flash Player (1, 2, 3, 4, 5, or 6) with which your published movie will be compatible. You'll have to be careful to which version you are publishing if you've used newer Flash features not supported in older Flash Player versions. For the most part, when it comes to backward compatibility with older plug-ins, you need to be most concerned with the ActionScript you are using.

Load Order Sets the order (either Bottom Up or Top Down) in which the layers in each individual frame load (and are displayed). Your choice is particularly important if the Flash file is being loaded over a slow modem. In that case, you might want to set the load order to reflect the position of the larger elements (large graphics, audio, and so on) so that they load first. If, for instance, you set the load order to Top Down, and the top layer in your movie is occupied by your ActionScript (which will load extremely quickly), you'll find that script layer will load and run before some of the more bandwidth-intensive elements (that occupy lower layers in the movie) even get a chance to load.

If, on the other hand, the movie is being accessed over a fast connection, your choice really won't matter that much because the layers will load so fast that there won't be any perceivable difference between the options.

Generate Size Report Tells Flash to output a SimpleText (Mac) or TXT (PC) file that reports upon the bandwidth intensity of the various portions of the movie.

Protect from Import Prevents your published SWF file from being imported back into Flash—a handy option for those conscious about their work being digitally plagiarized.

Omit Trace Actions Ignores any trace actions (which automatically open the Output window) that you've added to your movie. For more information on the trace function, refer to Chapter 18.

Debugging Permitted Allows the Debugger to work on the published file. In addition, when selected, this option also allows remote debugging via a browser using the Flash Debug Player plug-in or ActiveX control.

Compress Movie Compresses the movie so that its file size and download time are reduced. Beware, however, that movies that have been compressed using this option can only be played with the Flash 6 Player.

Password Allows you to enter the password needed either to open the Debugger (remotely or locally) or import the movie back into Flash. This option is only enabled if you selected either the Protect from Import or Debugging Permitted option.

JPEG Quality Lets you adjust the level of compression applied to all bitmaps in your Flash movie. Alternatively, you can also enter a value (from 0 to 100) into the field to the right of the slider. The lower the value you set, the more compression will result. The kicker is that although lower quality means smaller image size, it also means that the images will have a lower visual quality. The trick is finding the right balance between appearance and file size.

Audio Stream By clicking the Set button, you access the Sound Settings dialog box. From here, you can manipulate the settings of your movie's audio. The Compression drop-down menu lets you set the type of compression used on your audio. Each of the options (MP3, ADPCM, RAW, Disable, and Speech) has unique options you can manipulate.

If you are having trouble remembering the theory behind audio (compression, bit rate, sample rate, and so on), see Chapter 19. You can also refer to Chapter 20 for a more in-depth look at the various compression options.

Audio Event By clicking the Set button, you open the Sound Settings dialog box. From here, you'll be able to set the various compression properties of any event sounds in your movie.

For a refresher on event and stream audio, see Chapter 21.

Override Sound Settings Uses the settings you established in the Flash tab of the Publish Settings dialog box, automatically overriding any compression schemes set in the Library.

Manipulating HTML Settings

If your Flash movie is destined for distribution over the Web, it needs to be embedded in an HTML file. Before Flash 5 came along, you had to use another program, called Aftershock, to generate an HTML file into which your Flash movie was embedded. However, with Flash 5, Macromedia integrated the functionality of Aftershock into the Publish Settings dialog box, which is your one-stop tool for creating the HTML file that accompanies a published SWF file.

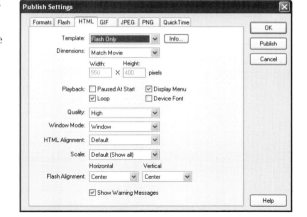

If you don't have the Flash option selected in the Formats tab of the Publish Settings dialog box, you don't have access to HTML as a file type. Likewise, if you select HTML from the Formats tab, Flash is automatically selected.

After you select HTML in the Formats tab of the Publish Settings dialog box, you'll be able to click the HTML tab to access the HTML-related settings.

The settings include the following:

Template Lets you choose from a set of predefined HTML templates that will be used to display the Flash movie.

Most of the time, you won't need to choose anything but the Flash Only (Default) template. However, some of the other templates are geared toward alternate file types, such as QuickTime, and will be useful in other situations. (For more information on each of the specific templates, see Flash MX's help feature.)

To get information about a specific template, select it from the drop-down menu and then click the Info button (to the right of the drop-down menu).

Dimensions Controls the HTML document's WIDTH and HEIGHT values in the OBJECT and EMBED tags. It's important to understand that the value you enter into the Width and Height fields (just below the Dimensions drop-down menu) doesn't actually affect that size of your Flash movie, just the area of the web page through which your movie is viewed. The way in which the movie fits in this area is determined by the Scale setting (discussed later). These are the options in the Dimensions drop-down menu:

- Match Movie retains the same width and height of the actual movie.

- To enter a width and height value in pixels, choose Pixels from the drop-down menu and then enter a value into the Width and Height fields.

- By choosing Percent and entering a value into the width and height fields, you set a percentage of the browser window that the movie fills.

Playback Controls how the Flash movie plays when it's downloaded:

- By choosing the Paused at Start option, your movie automatically stops at the first frame. A button with a `play()` action can restart the movie. In addition, selecting Play from the movie's Ctrl+click (Mac) or right-click (Win) menu can restart the movie.

- When selected, the Loop option forces the movie to loop *ad infinitum*.

- The Display Menu option lets you determine whether the movie's Ctrl+click (Mac) or right-click (Win) menu is active.

- When selected, the Device Font option, which only applies to movies when they're played on a Windows machine, replaces any font that the user doesn't have installed on their system with anti-aliased system fonts. This increases the legibility of small text as well as decreases the overall size of the movie.

Quality Determines the quality at which your movie is played. Basically, the options determine whether your movie sacrifices speed for quality or vice versa:

- By turning off any anti-aliasing, Low sacrifices speed over visual quality.

- Auto Low starts the movie playing without anti-aliasing but bumps the quality up to High if the user's computer can cope with the improved quality while still maintaining quick playback.

- Auto High begins playback at High quality but shifts into Low mode if the user's computer can't cope with the increased visual quality and playback speed.

- By choosing Medium, your movie is partially anti-aliased with no bitmap smoothing. The option results in a higher visual quality than Low, but a lower visual quality than High.

- When you select High, you force your movie to be anti-aliased. If the movie contains bitmaps that aren't animated, they are smoothed. On the other hand, if the bitmaps are animated in any way, they won't be smoothed.

- When you choose Best, you force your movie to be played at the highest visual quality possible with little regard for playback speed.

Window Mode Sets options for movies played in Internet Explorer 4.0 (and later) with the Flash ActiveX control:

- By choosing Window, your movie is played in its own rectangular window on a web page. It's important to note that this option results in the fastest animation speed.

- The Opaque Windowless option pushes any Dynamic HTML elements (specifically, layers) behind, so they don't appear over the Flash movie.

- The Transparent Windowless option displays the background of the HTML page on which the movie is embedded through all transparent areas of the movie.

The Transparent Windowless option often results in slower playback.

HTML Alignment Positions your Flash movie within the web page. The default option centers the Flash movie horizontally and vertically within the web page. The other options align the Flash movie along the left, right, top, and bottom edges of the browser window.

Scale Works in conjunction with the option you set with the Dimensions drop-down menu:

- The Default (Show All) option expands the size of your movie (without distortion) to fit the entire specified area while still maintaining the movie's aspect ratio. As a result, even if you choose this option, you might have borders appear on either of the movie's two sides.

- By choosing No Border, your movie is expanded (without distortion) to fill the entire area defined by the Dimensions setting. As with the Show All option, the movie maintains its aspect ration. However, the difference is that when you choose No Border, your movie may actually expand to be larger than the area defined by the Dimensions settings in order to maintain the movie's aspect ratio. As a result, the edges of your movie might appear as if they've been cut off.

- Exact Fit displays the entire movie in the specified area without reserving the original aspect ratio. As a result, your movie might be somewhat distorted.

Flash Alignment Determines the placement of the movie within the Dimensions area. You set it by choosing an option from the Horizontal drop-down menu and the Vertical drop-down menu.

Show Warning Messages Tells Flash to alert you to any conflicts created by your various publishing settings.

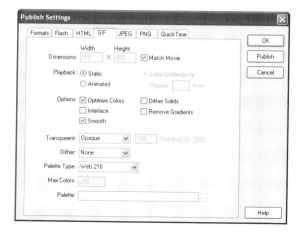

Working with GIF Settings

By selecting the GIF option from the Formats tab and then clicking the GIF tab, you can set GIF-specific options.

The settings include the following:

Dimensions Allows you to set the dimensions of the static image or animated GIF that is published by entering values (in pixels) into the Width and Height fields. If you want the dimensions of the GIF to match those of the Flash movie, select the Match Movie option.

Playback If you want to export a single frame of the Flash movie, select the Static option. By default, Flash exports the first frame of your movie as the static GIF image. If you want to force Flash to export an alternate frame, attach a `#Static` frame label to the desired frame by using the Property Inspector. (If you've forgotten how to attach frame labels, see Chapter 9.)

If you want to export the Flash movie as a GIF animation, select the Animated option. If you want to avoid publishing the entire movie as an animated GIF, attach a `#First` label to the initial frame in the range you want to publish and a `#Last` frame label to the final frame in the range.

From there, you can select Loop Continuously (to have the animation play over and over again without stopping) or enter the number of repetitions for the animation into the Repeat field.

Optimize Colors Tells Flash to remove any unused colors from the GIF's color table. This can reduce the final file size.

> If you have chosen Adaptive from the Palette drop-down menu, selecting the Optimize Color option has no effect.

Interlace Publishes the movie as an interlaced GIF. An interlaced GIF is structured in such a way that it comes into focus slowly as the browser loads the image.

Smooth Anti-aliases all of the artwork in the movie when it's published to GIF format. Be advised that this option results in a larger file size.

Dither Solids Applies dithering to both colors and gradients.

Remove Gradients Converts all of your gradients to solid colors. Because gradients don't translate well to GIF format, leaving this option unchecked could result in some odd (and visually unappealing) results.

Transparent   Determines the level at which the background of the movie is transparent, as well as how the Flash movie's Alpha settings are converted:

- By choosing Opaque, the movie is published as a GIF with a solid background.
- By choosing Transparent, the movie is published as a GIF with a transparent background.

> Choosing the Transparent option in conjunction with the Smooth option can result in semi-transparent halos around all objects.

- By choosing the Alpha option, you control the transparency of individual objects. By entering a Threshold value between 0 and 255, you make all colors below the value completely transparent and colors above the threshold partially transparent. A value of 128 corresponds to 50% Alpha.

Dither   Generates colors not in the current palette by combining pixels from a 256-color palette into patterns that approximate other colors. The options in the Dither drop-down menu let you set the method by which the pixels are combined when the movie is exported to GIF:

- By choosing None, dithering is turned off, and colors not in the basic color table are replaced with solid colors from the table that most closely approximate the specified color. Although not dithering can produce smaller files, it often results in strange colors.
- Choosing Ordered results in good quality images with a relatively small file size.
- Choosing Diffusion results in the best quality image. However, file size and load time are increased.

Palette Type   Lets you choose the type of palette is used when the GIF is published:

- The Web 216 palette is composed of 216 colors that are identical on both Windows and Macintosh machines.
- By choosing Adaptive, you set a custom palette of colors derived from the actual colors in the image. When you choose Adaptive, you can also limit the number of colors by entering a value (up to 256) in the Max Colors field.
- The Web Snap Adaptive palette is almost the same as the Adaptive palette. The only difference is that it converts similar colors to the Web 216 color palette.
- By selecting the Custom option, you can specify a custom-created palette by clicking the button (…) just to the right of the Palette field and browsing for an ACT file.

Setting JPEG Publish Options

If you want to publish a single frame of your Flash movie as a JPEG file, select JPEG Image from the Formats tab, and click the JPEG tab to manipulate its publishing settings. Much like in the case of a GIF, you can force Flash to export a frame other than the first one by attaching a #Static frame label to the desired frame with the Property Inspector (below left).

> Because the Dimensions in the JPEG tab are exactly the same as those in the GIF tab, we're going to skip them in this section. However, if you need to refresh your memory, see the previous section.

You can also set the following additional options:

Quality Adjusts the level of compression applied to the published JPEG. Alternatively, you can also enter a value (from 0 to 100) into the field to the right of the slider. The lower the value you set, the greater compression will result.

Progressive Creates a JPEG similar to an interlaced GIF.

Working with PNG Publishing Settings

If you want to publish a single frame of your Flash movie as a PNG file, select PNG Image from the Formats tab, and click the PNG tab to manipulate its publishing settings. Much like in the case of GIFs and JPEGs, you can force Flash to export a frame other than the first one by attaching a #Static frame label to the desired frame with the Property Inspector (below right).

> Because the majority of options for PNG are the same as those for publishing a GIF, we're not going to go over them again. If you want to refresh your memory, see the "Working with GIF Settings" section.

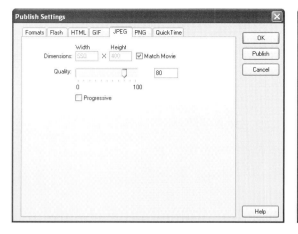
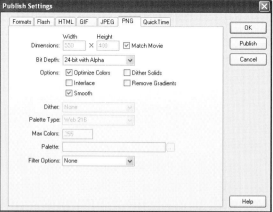

You have the following additional options:

Bit Depth Determines the amount of colors in the published PNG image:

- Choosing the 8-bit option results in an image with a maximum of 256 colors.

- The 24-bit option results in an image that can display a maximum of 16.7 million colors. As one would expect, this produces larger files sizes but renders your Flash movie far more accurately.

- The 24-bit with Alpha includes support for 16.7 million colors as well as an additional 8-bit channel for transparency support. When you choose this option, the unfilled areas in a PNG image turn transparent when the file is published.

Filter Options Determines the compression algorithm used on the PNG image:

- By choosing None, no compression algorithm is applied to the image. The None option results in a significantly larger image.

- The Sub option, which transmits the difference between each byte and the value of the corresponding byte of the prior pixel, works best on images that have repeating information (such as stripes or checks) along the horizontal axis.

- The Up option works in the opposite manner than the Sub option and is therefore most effective on images that feature vertically repeating information.

- The Average option, which uses a pixel's two adjacent neighbors to predict its value, works best on images that have a mix of both horizontally and vertically repeating information.

- The Path option generates a linear function of the pixels above, to the left, and to the upper left and then makes a prediction based on the neighboring pixel closest to the computed value.

Setting QuickTime Publish Options

If you'd like to publish your Flash creation as a QuickTime movie (MOV), select the QuickTime option from the Formats tab and click the QuickTime tab.

You can then manipulate the following options:

Dimensions Allows you to set the dimensions of the Quick-Time movie that is published by entering values (in pixels) into the Width and Height fields. If you want the dimensions of the QuickTime movie to match those of the actual Flash movie, select the Match Movie option.

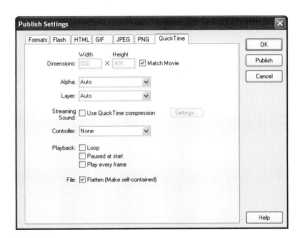

Alpha Lets you control the transparency of the Flash information in the QuickTime movie:

- By choosing Auto, the Flash movie becomes transparent if it is on top of any other tracks in the QuickTime movie (such as additional QuickTime video tracks), but it becomes opaque if it is the bottom or the only track in the movie.

- The Alpha-Transparent option makes the Flash track transparent, thereby displaying the contents of any additional lower tracks.

- When you choose the Copy option, the Flash track is rendered as completely opaque, thereby blocking all lower tracks.

Layer Controls the position of your Flash content relative to any QuickTime content in the exported movie. Choose Top if you want the Flash content to occupy the top layer and bottom if you want it to occupy the bottom layer. When you choose Auto, the Flash track is placed in front of other tracks in the QuickTime file if the Flash objects in the movie itself are in front of video objects. If they aren't, the Flash track is placed behind all other tracks in the QuickTime file.

Streaming Sound Forces Flash to export all of the streaming audio in the movie to a Quick-Time soundtrack. In the process, the audio recompresses using the standard QuickTime audio settings. To manipulate the default settings, click the Settings button to open the Sound Settings dialog box.

From here, you can set the compressor used, the bit rate, and the audio to mono or stereo.

If you are having trouble remembering the theory behind audio, see Chapter 19.

Controller If you've ever viewed a QuickTime file, you probably noticed that it had an interactive controller at the bottom of the player. With it you can do such things as pause, play, and adjust volume. The Controller drop-down menu lets you determine whether you want the standard controller to be displayed (by choosing Standard), no controller (None), or the QuickTime VR controller (QuickTime VR).

Loop Sets the QuickTime movie to loop indefinitely.

Paused at Start Sets the QuickTime movie to not automatically play. The user can begin playback by clicking the Play button in the controller.

Play Every Frame Overrides the frame rate and plays every frame without any of the skipping characteristics of QuickTime's attempt to maintain time. It's important to note that when this option is selected, the audio track is turned off.

Flatten (Make Self-Contained) If this option is unselected, the Flash content won't be combined with the QuickTime movie itself. Instead, the file content is published as a separate file and referenced thusly by QuickTime. If all of the files are not located in the same place, the QuickTime movie will be unable to display the Flash content. When you select the Flatten (Make Self-Contained) option, all of the content is combined into one file.

Previewing Your Flash Movie

If you've gone to the trouble of painstakingly manipulating the publishing settings of each of the file types to which your Flash movie will be published, it would be a shame if you couldn't preview your movie to see how it looks. To preview your movie in any of the various file types you selected in the Formats section of the Publish Settings dialog box, select File → Publish Preview and select from the available list of file types.

> You'll only be able to access those file types that were selected in the Formats section of the Publish Settings dialog box.

Flash automatically loads the selected file type.

PROFILING YOUR MOVIE

To get a graphical representation of how your movie performs, check out the Bandwidth Profiler—accessible by going to View → Bandwidth Profiler when you are testing your movie (Control → Test Movie).

With it, you can see the size (in kilobytes) of each frame in the movie. To simulate how your movie will play over different modems, go to View → Streaming when you are testing your movie. You can set the specific modem to test by choosing one of the options from the Debug menu.

Publishing Your Flash Movie

Now that you've manipulated the publishing settings of your various file types and previewed those files (and done any necessary tweaking), you can publish your Flash movie. Having gone to all the trouble to get here, the publishing process is rather anticlimactic. All you have to do is go to File → Publish and Flash does all the work—all of the various file types you set in the Publish Settings dialog box will be published simultaneously to the folder on your hard drive where you saved the FLA file on which they're based.

Besides the Publish command, there is also an Export command in the File menu. The Export command is almost the same as the Publish command; the difference is that, by using the Export command, you bypass the Publish Settings dialog box and are faced with an Export Movie dialog box where you set the file type and export location. The drawback of exporting is that you don't have access to the file type's publishing settings.

Publishing Accessible Content

Although there are a myriad of different file types to which you can publish your movie—all of which extend the scope of your audience—there is one aspect of publishing and distributing Flash movies that we haven't discussed yet.

In recent years, there has been a growing desire to make web content accessible—that is, usable for individuals with a variety of disabilities. One of the most pressing concerns is that, up until now, Flash movies couldn't be interpreted by screen reader—a type of software the "reads" the contents of a computer screen and then "speaks" it back to a visually impaired user. This problem derives from the fact that visual information (opposed to text) involves a subjective interpretation. In other words, one person's description of an image will probably differ from another individual's description of the same image. As a result, screen readers, which are simple pieces of software, are completely incapable of describing visual imagery. So, visually impaired individuals are not only cut off from visual content, but they are often also cut off from navigation schemes—many of which depend heavily on graphical interface elements (buttons, menus, and so on).

So, where does this leave visually impaired individuals who want to access Flash content? Well, in Flash MX, you can attach information to certain elements in your movie that can then be interpreted by screen readers—cool, huh? That way, *you* determine how your visual creation will be described.

There are, however, some pretty heavy caveats that need to be addressed. First, to make an object accessible to screen readers, it *must* have an instance name. As a result, there are a limited number of objects that can be made accessible to a screen reader: dynamic text, input text fields, Button symbols, Movie Clips, and entire movies.

> To make Static Text accessible, you must first convert it to Dynamic Text.

Second, and perhaps most importantly, users must be running a Windows operating system, complete with screen reader software and the Flash 6 plug-in, to access accessible content created in Flash MX.

This having been said, let's take a look at how you go about making your movie accessible so that you aren't excluding a portion of your potential audience:

1. First, select the object you want to make accessible to the screen reader.

2. Go to Window → Accessibility to open the Accessibility panel.

> If the object you've selected cannot be made accessible, you won't have access to any options in the Accessibility panel.

3. If you want to make the currently selected object accessible, click the Make Object Accessible option.

4. If the object you selected is a Movie Clip, you'll also see a Make Child Objects Accessible option. If you select this, all the various elements within the Movie Clip will also become accessible.

5. Enter a name into the Name field. The name, which will be "read" and vocalized by the screen reader, is the most basic aspect of making your object accessible.

   If you are making some Dynamic Text accessible, you won't have access to its Name—the actual text will be automatically used.

6. Enter a description for the selected element into the Description field.

7. If you want to add a keystroke to individual Button symbols, Movie Clip, or Input Text fields, enter a shortcut into the Shortcut field. There are, however, a few guidelines to which you need to stick:

   • Spell out the abbreviations of key names such as Shift, Ctrl, and Alt.

   • Use capital letters for alphabetic characters.

   • Use the plus (+) sign between key names—Alt+5, Ctrl+H, or Shift+9.

> To provide a keyboard shortcut, you must use the ActionScript Key object to detect user keypresses during movie playback. For more information on how to capture user keypresses, see Chapter 16.

8. When you've finished setting the accessibility options, simply close the Accessibility panel.

This process is good for making certain objects accessible to a screen reader (a process that is sometimes also referred to as *exposing*), but what if you want to make the *entire* movie accessible? All you need to do is follow these steps:

1. Deselect all the elements on the Stage.

2. Go to Window → Accessibility.

3. If it isn't already, select the Make Movie Accessible option.

4. If you want all the accessible objects within the movie to be exposed to screen readers, select the Make Child Objects Accessible option.

5. Enter a name for the movie into the Name field.

6. Enter a description for the movie into the Description field.

7. From here, if you want, select the Auto Label option. By doing this, Flash will use text that's integrated into Buttons or Input Text fields as the object's name.

8. When you're finished, close the Accessibility panel.

Creating Printable Movies

By this point you are probably convinced that Flash content, because it is based on vectors, looks pretty cool. You've heard it all: based on mathematically computations, scalable, incredibly crisp—yadda, yadda, yadda. What you probably haven't realized is that, because it's vector based, Flash movies look equally cool when they're printed. Wow, this is great—you can create all sorts of content that looks just as good on a screen as it does when printed.

> The processes described in this section set your movie so that it is printed as vectors—thereby maintaining the crisp, clean appearance. If you elect to skip this section, your movie can still be printed. However, it will print like any other 72dpi image—very low quality.

There are two methods you can use to configure your movie so that it prints out as vectors. First, you can designate specific frames in the Timeline that will print—all the frames that aren't designated as printable will not print. Second, you can designate certain areas within certain frames that will print—all the space outside of the printable area will not print.

> The kicker about creating a printable movie is that you are controlling how your content is being printed using the right-click context menu. Users can still print your movie using their browser's Print command—you've got no control over that.

Before you learn how to configure your movie to be printable, there are a couple of important details about which you should aware:

- All elements must be fully loaded to be printed.
- For a Movie Clip to be printed, it must be either on the Stage or in the work area, and it must have an instance name.
- Flash Players earlier than 4.025 (Win) or 4.020 (Mac) do not support frame printing.

This having been said, let's take a look at how you go about configuring your Flash movie so that it's printable.

Setting Printable Frames

To designate specific frames as printable, follow these steps:

1. In the Timeline, select the specific frame you want to make printable.
2. If it isn't already, open the Property Inspector by going to Window → Properties.
3. Enter **#p** into the Frame Label field to set that frame as printable.
4. Repeats steps 1 and 3 on any additional frames you want to make printable.

Setting Printable Areas

To designate a specific area in a frame as printable, follow these steps:

1. Select the frame you want to designate as a printable area—the frame itself must not have already been designated as printable with the **#p** label.

2. Select the frame that contains the object you want to use to designate the frame as printable.

3. If it isn't already, open the Property Inspector by going to Window → Properties.

4. Enter **#b** into the Label field.

Inspirational Design Model

As you've no doubt figured out, you can distribute your Flash creations in many different ways. One of the most unexpected methods of distribution—console games—wasn't discussed in this chapter because it's out of reach for average Flash users. Still, it's an incredibly interesting use of Flash.

Take, for instance, the use of Flash in the user interface for the popular LucasArts game Star Wars Starfighter, a flight action/adventure game for PlayStation 2 and Xbox. When LucasArts designed the in-game interface for Starfighter, the developers realized they lacked a functional out-of-game user interface. Enter Macromedia Flash.

So, LucasArts approached a small company in San Francisco called Secret Level (www.secretlevel.com) that was developing a Software Development Kit (called Strobe) that integrated Flash content into PlayStation 2 games. Pleased with the possibility of what Flash could bring to Starfighter, LucasArts contracted Orange Design (www.orangedesign.com) to design an out-of-game interface with Flash that was then integrated using Secret Level's Strobe. The result is a creative and unorthodox use of Flash that shows the possibilities of publishing and distributing your SWF creations.

> For more information on how Flash was used in Starfighter, see the Gamasutra article at www.gamasutra.com/features/20010801/corry_01.htm. You'll need to register to read the article, but it's free.

Summary

In this chapter you learned about the various file types to which you can output your dazzling Flash creations. You also learned about each of their publishing settings. From there, you looked at how to preview your movie and then publish it. You also learned about the difference between publishing and exporting a file. The chapter finished off by creating accessible movies and by creating printable movies.

CHAPTER 28

Working with Flash and Video

It is standard practice now to develop software applications that are *versatile*. Not only do you expect them to perform their particular job, but you also expect them to work cooperatively with other applications. This increases their effectiveness as well as your creative possibilities. It's this kind of versatility that puts the *multi* in multimedia.

Flash is no exception to this standard. In fact, due to its popularity as well as the SWF file format's wide applicability, Flash is one of the most portable ones available today. Not only can Flash incorporate many kinds of media into an animation or interactive movie, but it can also create and work with files that are usable in a variety of non-Flash applications.

This chapter explores the possibilities of Flash in a very different kind of setting: video. Flash movies can be exported as video. Also, with the release of Flash MX, videos can be imported into the Flash environment and controlled interactively like any other part of a Flash production. Video and Flash are fundamentally unlike. Video has no vectors, no tweening, no painting tools, and, above all else, no interactivity. However, video does have its own advantages. Whereas Flash is great at displaying stylized, cartoon-like images, video can show your audience images that are very lifelike and realistic. And unlike Flash, video can be broadcast on television and incorporated into movies.

As Flash continues to develop, it's very likely that the application will branch out beyond the Web and become a more important part of media production in general. This chapter introduces you to some of the beginning concepts of this role. It covers these topics:

- **Importing video into Flash**

- **The Sorenson Spark codec**

- **Using ActionScript to control video playback**

- **Preparing the components of a Flash animation for video**

- **Working with Flash video tracks**

- **Working with Flash audio tracks**

- **Getting Flash animations into a video application**

- **Reassembling an animation outside Flash**

- **Preparing your animation for videotape**

Understanding Video in the Flash Environment

One of the most sweeping changes in Flash MX is the addition of support for digital video. When using previous releases of Flash, developers had to simulate video. They usually did this by putting still-image sequences inside a Movie Clip to create a sort of digital flipbook. From a functional standpoint, this technique worked fairly well, but it tended to increase the size of the final movie appreciably because there was no way to compress (reduce the file size of) the "video."

Well, all that has changed. Flash MX's support of video is a significant step forward for both the application and its community of users. What was once the best means of delivering animated content on the Web is now also one of the best means of distributing video content. Anyone whose browser is equipped with the Flash 6 plug-in is now able to see both traditional Flash movies *and* Flash movies that contain real video footage. One plug-in covers it all! Now that we've got your attention, let's take a closer look at how all this works in Flash MX.

Sorenson Spark Codec

The "wizard behind the curtain" responsible for video in Flash MX is a video compression/decompression codec named Spark. Developed by Sorenson Media (www.sorenson.com), Spark enables you to put high-quality video into your Flash movies without entailing significant cost in terms of bandwidth or file size.

When you bring video into Flash, Spark automatically compresses it. The codec is actually part of Flash MX; any video files that are imported and embedded in a Flash document must have this compression applied to them.

Spark applies *temporal* compression to your video. This type of compression looks at areas of change in a video file and encodes each frame based on the amount of change from one frame to the next. If a frame doesn't exhibit a significant change, its information is simply copied from the preceding frame. This kind of encoding is also known as *interframe*. When the change between video frames *is* significant, however, Sorenson Spark automatically inserts a video *keyframe* into the video file. A keyframe is a complete picture of a frame, and, like the keyframes in your Flash Timeline, marks a significant change in content. So, to put it all in perspective, Spark uses a combination of keyframes and interframes (temporal compression) to deliver high-quality video while maintaining smaller video file sizes.

The version of Spark included in Flash MX is known as Sorenson Spark Standard Edition. If you enjoy working with Spark, you may be interested in upgrading to Sorenson Spark Pro. This expanded codec offers several advantages over the basic codec. Spark Pro is available to you within the application Sorenson Squeeze. Squeeze can compress your video files in Macromedia Flash Video format (FLV). Squeeze and the Spark Pro codec present a clear advantage over standard Spark because they allow you to compress your video using a Variable Bit Rate (VBR). Files compressed with VBR are generally much smaller because they are compressed "intelligently." Video frames that contain complex changes in color or motion are allowed more bandwidth than simple frames. This allows the file to use compression where it needs it most, yielding a video file that's much smaller overall. Visit `www.sorenson.com/sparkpro.html` for more details on Sorenson Squeeze.

> Sorenson Squeeze can also compress files for QuickTime video in MOV format, and for Flash Player 6 in SWF format.

Importing Video

To get video into the Flash authoring environment, you must first import it—just as you do sounds, bitmap images, and other media. Flash supports a wide variety of digital video formats. For both Macintosh and Windows platforms, you must have QuickTime 4 (or higher) installed on your computer in order to import most kinds of video into Flash MX. If you are a Windows user, you can benefit from the added support of DirectX 7 (or higher), which allows you to import additional Windows-specific video formats.

Table 28.1 gives you a summary of video import file formats supported by Flash MX.

FILE TYPE	PLATFORMS
Audio Video Interleaved (`.avi`)*	Macintosh, Windows
Digital Video (`.dv`)	Macintosh, Windows
Moving Picture Experts Group (`.mpg`, `.mpeg`)*	Macintosh, Windows
QuickTime Movie (`.mov`)	Macintosh, Windows
Windows Media File (`.wmv`, `.asf`)*	Windows
Macromedia Flash Video (`.flv`)**	Macintosh, Windows

Table 28.1

Video File Formats Supported for Import to Flash MX

* These formats are supported in Windows only if DirectX 7 (or higher) is installed.
** Macromedia Flash Video (`.flv`) files can be imported directly into Flash MX without the help of QuickTime or DirectX, but they must be compressed using Sorenson Squeeze.

If Flash is unable to import a particular video format, it will display a message alerting you to the fact. In some situations, you may be able to import the video but not the audio. In that case, you do have the option to import the video without sound.

> Even with Sorenson Spark and the other great advances in video compression technology, you should still take steps to ensure that you have made your video as "compression friendly" as possible. This means optimizing video and audio content and targeting the video to the bandwidth requirements of your audience. To read more about this, see "About the Sorenson Spark Codec" in the help files that ship with Flash MX.

To import a video into Flash:

1. Choose either File → Import (Cmd/Ctrl+R), which will import your video and place it directly onto your movie's Stage; or or File → Import to Library, which will drop the video into the Library of the current document and leave you with the task of placing it in your movie yourself.

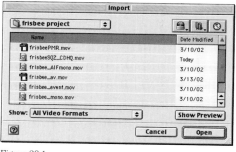

Figure 28.1

Only video files available to Flash are listed in the Import dialog box.

2. In the Import dialog box, choose All Video Formats from the Show drop-down menu (Figure 28.1). This acts as a filter, displaying only the video files that are available to Flash. Select the video you want to import and click Open.

3. Flash asks whether you want to embed the video in your movie or create a link and treat this video as an external video file. Make your selection and then click OK. (See the next sections of this chapter for the specifics of working with video in each context.)

Using Embedded Video Files

When you import a video clip into Flash, you have the option to make it an embedded video clip. This means the video becomes a permanent part of your Flash document and will appear in your movie's Library along with Movie Clips, graphic symbols, buttons, and the like.

To import a video file as an embedded video file:

1. Go through the initial steps of importing a video, as described in the preceding section. Flash will prompt you to import the video as either an embedded or a linked file. Choose the Embed Video in Macromedia Flash Document option and click OK.

The Import Video Settings dialog box appears (see Figure 28.2). Here you will make several choices that affect the amount and nature of compression applied to your video.

2. Use the Quality slider to control the amount of compression applied to the video. Higher settings afford better video quality but produce larger file sizes. Low settings do the opposite, yielding smaller files at the expense of quality. Settings at 60 or higher for Quality generally give good results.

3. Set the frequency of keyframes using the Keyframe Interval slider. Generally, you want to use as few keyframes as possible, since Spark will set keyframes for you as needed.

4. Use the Scale slider to adjust the size (pixel dimensions) of your video by percentage. Smaller dimensions yield smaller file sizes and tend to play more smoothly. If you know a video must be scaled down for your movie, be sure to do this in order to save on file size and improve performance once the video has been compressed.

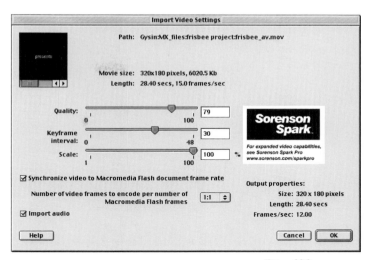

Figure 28.2

The Import Video Settings dialog box presents you with an array of compression settings for your embedded video.

5. Select Synchronize Video to Macromedia Flash Document to lock video playback speed with that of your movie's Timeline. To let the video and your movie play with their individual frame rates intact, deselect this option.

6. Select a ratio for Number of Video Frames to Encode per Number of Flash Frames. This specifies the ratio of imported video frames to main Flash Timeline frames. For example, to play one video frame per one Flash Timeline frame, select 1:1; to play one video frame for every four Timeline frames, choose 1:4; and so on.

7. Click the Import Audio check box to include a video file's audio track. If a video has no audio component, or the audio track isn't supported by Flash, this option will display a small warning message saying that the audio cannot be imported.

8. When finished, click OK. If you chose to import the video directly to the Stage, a warning appears, asking if you want to expand the frame count of the main Timeline to accommodate the length of the video. Do one of the following:

    • Click Yes so that the frame count extends to fit the length of your video.

    • Click No to leave the frame count as is. You can add frames later as needed.

   The imported video file appears in your movie's Library with a video icon 📹 beside its filename. Once the video is in the Library, you can incorporate it into your movie. To read about how this is done, see "Using ActionScript to Control Video Playback" later in this chapter.

Using Linked Video Files

When you import a video clip into Flash, you have the option to make it an external, or *linked,* video clip. This means that the video is linked to your Flash movie rather than being a direct part of it. A Flash movie that uses linked video clips cannot be published as an SWF file, because SWF doesn't support linked video clips. Flash movies using linked video must be published as QuickTime movies (QuickTime Flash). The resulting QuickTime file will be able to play both the Flash track and the linked video as a separate QuickTime track. (See Chapter 27 to read more about publishing in QuickTime movie format.)

To import a video file as a linked video file:

1. Go through the initial steps of importing a video, which are listed in the earlier "Importing Video" section. Flash will prompt you to import the video as either an embedded or a linked file. Choose the Link to External Video File option and then click OK.

2. If you chose to import the video directly to the Stage, a warning appears, asking if you want to expand the frame count of the main Timeline to accommodate the length of the video. Do one of the following:

   - Click Yes so that the frame count extends to fit the length of your video.

   - Click No to leave the frame count as is. You can add frames later as needed.

The imported video file appears in your movie's Library with a linked video icon beside its file name.

Using ActionScript to Control Video Playback

Now that you've brought a video into your Flash movie, you might be wondering how to manage its playback—how to make the video start, stop, rewind, skip ahead, and so on. The good news is that the imported video will behave like other elements within the Flash environment.

The best way to control your video is to create a video Movie Clip. Such a clip is a lot like an ordinary Movie Clip, except that it has the frames of the video stretched across its Timeline. Also, like ordinary Movie Clips, a video Movie Clip can be controlled via ActionScript. This means that you can use scripting commands within Flash to dictate the playback of the video Movie Clip's Timeline.

To create a video Movie Clip, you must have a video imported into your movie's Library. If you don't have a video of your own, we have provided a few that you can use. Open the Chapter 28 folder on this book's companion CD-ROM. If you want to use a QuickTime video, you can use mxVideo.mov. If you want to try using an FLV video, use mxVideo.flv. This video can be either an embedded or a linked video file. You will also want to have a few buttons on hand for use as controls to start and stop the video playback.

To create a video Movie Clip:

1. Choose Insert → New Symbol (Cmd/Ctrl+F8). Name the symbol **video_mc**, select Movie Clip as its behavior, and click OK.

2. Flash switches to Symbol Editing mode. In the Movie Clip Timeline, rename Layer 1 as **video**. Then insert a new layer and name it **actions**.

3. Highlight the Video layer and drag your video clip from the Library onto the Stage. Flash is likely to warn you that the current Timeline doesn't have enough frames to display your entire video and ask if you would like to add frames. Click Yes to add the necessary number of frames. Your video should now appear on the Stage, and your Timeline should have new frames stretching far enough to accommodate the length of the video. See Figure 28.3.

4. Use the Align panel (Cmd/Ctrl+K) to place your video in the horizontal and vertical center of the Movie Clip Stage. Now that your clip is in place, you can add some ActionScript to help monitor its playback.

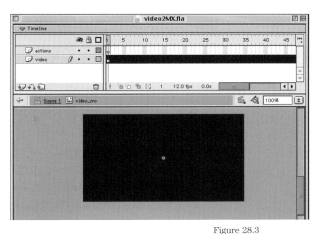

Figure 28.3

Frames are added to accommodate the video.

5. Select the keyframe in the Actions layer and open the Actions panel. Enter a `stop()` action and close the panel. At the very least, this is the only command your video Movie Clip requires. With `stop()` placed at frame 1 of its Timeline, the clip won't start playing until prompted to do so.

6. Save your movie and return to the main Timeline. Drag an instance of `video_mc` to the Stage and use the Property Inspector to assign it the instance name **trailer** (or something different if you prefer). This lesson uses `trailer` throughout.

7. Now that your clip has a unique name, you can add buttons that will allow you to interactively control the playback of the Movie Clip. Drag two buttons from your Library to the Stage: one for Play and one for Stop. Select the Play button, open the Actions panel, and enter the following statements:

```
on(press){
    frame = trailer._currentframe;
    trailer.gotoAndPlay(frame + 1);
}
```

The function of this script should be fairly self-explanatory. When the button is pressed, it stores the playback head location of the `trailer` clip and sends it to play at the *next* frame. When sitting in frame 1, the `trailer` Timeline is stopped. Since there are no other actions to stop the clip at the next frame, the video is allowed to play freely after this script jumps it ahead to frame 2. Also, if the clip is ever paused somewhere other than frame 1, the clip can always resume playback at the next frame.

8. Select the Stop button, open the Actions panel (if it's not open already), and enter the following statements:

```
on(press){
    trailer.gotoAndStop(1);
}
```

Again, a very straightforward script. When pressed, this button sends the clip instance back to frame 1 of its Timeline. Since there is a `stop()` action waiting there, the clip will halt when it arrives at frame 1.

9. Select Control → Test Movie or press Cmd+Return (Mac) or Ctrl+Enter (Win) to give these buttons a try. You will notice that the Play button sets the clip in motion, and the Stop button both halts it and sends it back to frame 1.

Additionally, you can add all sorts of controls to manipulate video playback. Here are just a few samples:

Pause Add the following to pause the video:

```
on(press){
    trailer.stop();
}
```

Fast Forward This example involves a few more elements. Attached to a Fast Forward button you have two handlers that toggle the variable `ffwd` on and off:

```
on(press){
    ffwd = 1;
}
on(release){
    ffwd = 0;
}
```

Then, to respond to the change in variable value, you assign a function for the video Movie Clip instance `trailer`. This script is attached to frame 1 of the main Timeline. When `ffwd` is "on," it sends the clip ahead by four frames. This number can be increased or decreased to change the speed of the fast-forward:

```
trailer.onLoad = function(){
    ffwd = 0;
}
trailer.onEnterFrame = function(){
    if(ffwd == 1){
        frame = trailer._currentframe
        trailer.gotoAndPlay(frame+4);
    }
}
```

There is a lot you can do to control the playback of a video within Flash. Using actions and methods of the MovieClip object, you should be able to invent all sorts of interesting techniques and video shuttle widgets. Check out the file(s) named `video2MX.fla` or `video2MX.swf` in the Chapter 28 folder on this book's companion CD-ROM. They'll show you these and other examples in the context of an actual movie.

Managing Video Files in Your Movie

There are a few techniques that can be helpful for managing your video media inside and outside a Flash document. After you edit or change an embedded video file outside Flash, you can update the file rather than re-import it.

To update an embedded video clip:

1. Select the video clip in the Library.

2. Ctrl+click (Mac) or right-click (Win) the video in the Library and choose Properties from the context menu.

3. Click Update in the Update Video Properties dialog box. The embedded clip is updated with the edited file.

Alternatively, you can replace the selected clip with an entirely different video clip. Click Import and choose a different clip in the Import dialog box. That clip will replace the embedded clip in your Library.

You might also want to replace the embedded video clip that is used for an embedded video instance. To change clips in a video instance:

1. Select the clip on the Stage that you would like to change.

2. Open the Property Inspector (Cmd/Ctrl+F3) to display the instance information for the selected clip.

3. Click the Swap button and choose the clip you would like to exchange for the clip on the Stage.

4. Click OK, and the clip instance is updated accordingly.

When publishing a Flash movie as an SWF file, the soundtrack of any embedded video clip(s) will be exported using the Stream sound settings. (These are the settings for Stream in the Flash tab of the Publish Settings dialog box.) Be sure that these options are set at the appropriate rate for your target audience. To read more about audio compression settings in Flash, see Chapter 21.

Publishing a Flash Movie on Videotape

Given the power and flexibility of the Flash authoring application, you may wonder why anyone would even consider putting their SWF masterpiece on videotape. After all, video is a noninteractive, linear medium. One of Flash's greatest assets is its ability to deliver animations and information in an audience-directed format: Your viewers can decide how the piece is presented. Plus, with the visibility of the Flash plug-in on the Web, your pieces are available to a worldwide audience of unprecedented size.

Video can be helpful in several situations, however. It may not provide the kind of interactivity found on the Web, but video does allow you to use Flash for applications in which the computer and interactivity are not part of the media equation. If you would like to use Flash to create animated shorts or cartoon for television, you have to go to video. Flash can be transferred to video for projected playback at concert venues and art galleries, and it can used as source material for video-mix artists and performers. Or, if you are involved in any kind of video postproduction work, you can use Flash to animate title sequences or special effects and to composite the Flash animation with your video footage to create interesting layered effects. As always, Flash gives you an endless variety of possibilities.

The steps for transferring a Flash animation to video are outlined in this chapter. Depending on the specific kind of video you want to produce, you may find that some modifications are needed in order to get the best results for your particular project. In general, the process includes the following steps:

- Prepare the Flash Timeline graphics, including Movie Clips

- Prepare the audio tracks if you plan to use the Flash audio

- Export the Flash animation as QuickTime video (Macintosh) or AVI (Windows)

- Import the animation to a video editing application and make any needed adjustments or edits depending on your specific goals

That's the process in a nutshell. Let's dive into the specifics and get things under way.

Preparing the Flash Timeline

The first part of the transfer-to-video process involves preparing your movie's Timeline. In this case, *preparing* means simplifying so that the Timeline is free of actions, Movie Clips, and any other items in your work that would not apply to a linear medium (such as navigational buttons).

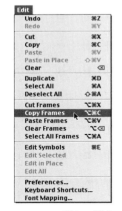

Figure 28.4

Use Edit → Copy Frames and Edit → Paste Frames to rebuild an animation so that it is completely linear and free of actions.

Actions must usually be cut simply because they can interrupt the flow of a linear animation. For example, if you have any kind of gotoAndPlay() loops that send the movie back to a previous frame, you'll need to delete these actions from your Timeline. If the actions are somehow integral to the overall animation, you can work around this situation by copying and pasting the frames in the loop. For instance, if you have an animation of a knock-knock joke, you may have a gotoAndPlay() action that sends the movie back to frame 1 to repeat the "Knock, knock! Who's there?" part of the joke. Because this action won't work when you transfer to video, your best strategy is to copy and paste the frames you need to repeat. Choose Edit → Copy Frames, then Edit → Paste Frames, to reconstruct the animation structure as needed (see Figure 28.4). To learn more about manipulating frames in the Timeline, see Chapter 9.

It's okay to use this technique with a Flash animation that uses scenes. The animation will be exported in the order the scenes are listed in the Scene panel (select Window → Scene or press Shift+F2).

Additionally, if your animation uses Movie Clips, you will need to do some tweaking. As self-contained animations, Movie Clips work fine in the Flash Player or in QuickTime Flash movies but are not supported in linear video applications. Consequently, you have to include them on their own layer(s) in the main Timeline. Using the same copy-and-paste technique described earlier, you can move animated components out of a Movie Clip Timeline and into your main Timeline.

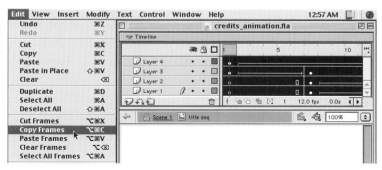

Figure 28.5

You can copy all frames of a Movie Clip to the Clipboard.

To transfer a Movie Clip animation to the main Timeline:

1. Open the Movie Clip's Timeline by using the Edit Symbols pop-up menu or by double-clicking the Movie Clip's icon in the Library. Flash jumps into Symbol Editing mode.

2. While pressing Shift, click each layer's name or label to select the frames that make up the Movie Clip animation. Take note of how many layers are used in the Movie Clip.

3. Choose Edit → Copy Frames to copy the frames to the Clipboard (see Figure 28.5). Return to Movie Editing mode.

4. Now you're ready to add the elements of the Movie Clip to your main Timeline. Insert new layers as needed to accommodate the components of the Movie Clip. If your Movie Clip used four layers, insert four new layers.

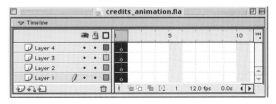

5. Click the frame in the topmost new layer where you would like to paste the Movie Clip. Then, Shift+click the lowest new layer to select the first frame for each, as shown above:

6. Choose Edit → Paste Frames to paste the Movie Clip frames into the new layers, starting at the frame you just highlighted. See Figure 28.6 for the results.

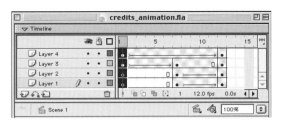

Figure 28.6

Movie Clip frames pasted into the main Timeline

This is a fairly simple process, but it may require some additional tweaking depending on how you used the Movie Clip in the original animation.

Some Advice about Monitors

Another point to consider if you are planning to display your video on a television monitor is the *aspect ratio*. The aspect ratio for television is 4:3, meaning that for every 4 units of width, there are 3 units of height. The standard size for television and video is 640×480 pixels. You can adjust your Flash movie to a 4:3 aspect ratio by choosing Modify → Document to set the width and height accordingly. Or, if your movie already conforms to this ratio but is smaller (for example, 160×120), you can make the adjustments when you export the video.

Concerning screen size and television monitors, be aware that not all monitors will play a video in exactly the same way. On some, information at the edge of the screen may be lost; for this reason, you want to be sure that your animation contains nothing significant at the edge of the Stage. There are two "safe zones" that will help you avoid problems with inconsistent monitors: the *action-safe zone* and the *title-safe zone*. The action-safe zone is exactly 90% of the total screen size; so for a 640×480 animation, you'll want to keep important images and animation within the area 576×432. The title-safe zone is reserved for text and is exactly 80% of the total screen size. This translates to an area of 512×384. Both these safe zones are centered within the total area of the Stage. See Figure 28.7.

Figure 28.7

To prepare a Flash animation for playback on a television monitor, be sure that important elements fall within the action-safe and title-safe zones.

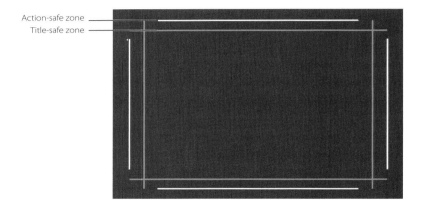

Action-safe zone
Title-safe zone

Preparing the Flash Audio

Flash can work as an animator alone, and dealing with audio at this point may not be a concern. If your plan is to bring an animation in and composite or edit it together with existing video footage, it's probably best not to incorporate sound in the Flash movie itself, but to wait and add your audio elements in the video application. However, if you plan to deliver your entire Flash animation (including the soundtrack) as a video, you'll need to follow some additional steps to prepare your movie.

When you export a Flash movie as video, there are several sound-related issues that you should be aware of:

Mixing When you created your Flash animation, chances are you used the Edit Envelope dialog box (shown just below) to adjust the relative volume level of each sound in your movie. This is a crucial step because it allows you to assign each sound its proper place in the audio spectrum. Some sounds, like narration and dialog, are important and need to be heard clearly whenever they are present. Other sounds, like music and sound effects, can be adjusted accordingly so that they don't impede on other audio elements.

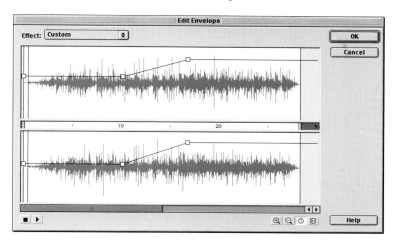

Your goal is to use the envelopes to create an ideal sound balance for your movie's audio components. Before you export to video, revisit these settings and be sure that your levels are correct. Once the Flash animation has been exported, the audio track is permanently mixed and cannot be changed. To tweak the audio, you would have to go back to your Flash file, readjust the audio, and re-export the movie. To learn more about options concerning the Edit Envelope window, see Chapter 20.

Synchronization Sync is a big topic when it comes to discussions of audio and video. It's very important because, if these elements lose sync, your animation will begin to look like a poorly dubbed monster movie. Regardless of the sync settings in your original animation, when you prepare to export to video, you should use the Property Inspector (choose Window → Properties or press Cmd/Ctrl+F3) to set all of the audio to Stream sync. This will lock your audio to the movie's frame rate and ensure tight synchronization. Also, be sure that each sound has enough frames to play in its entirety. Stream sounds will only be heard for the duration of the frames they occupy. To learn more about Flash synchronization options, see Chapter 21.

A WORD OF CAUTION ABOUT EMBEDDED AUDIO

Exporting sound from your Flash movie has its pros and cons. One of the benefits is that your synchronization will be preserved and you don't have to worry about reconstructing your audio track in a separate application later. Another plus is that your final video will be complete, with all its audio and visual elements neatly packed in a single digital video file.

However, if you plan to take your Flash video into another application such as Adobe Premiere for additional editing, you should take an additional step to prepare the audio. The streaming audio tracks that are embedded within a Flash video file won't work in Premiere. Any audio that is included with your Flash video will be distorted beyond recognition when it's brought into Premiere for editing. To avoid audio distortion in your video, you must bring the audio and video elements into Premiere *separately*. In the Mac OS, you can use Quick-Time Pro to extract the audio track from your video. In Windows, you can export two separate versions of your Flash movie: one that is silent and one that is sound-only. To read more about these techniques, see "QuickTime Video (Macintosh)" and "Video for Windows (AVI)" in the next section of this chapter.

Exporting Flash as Video

After completing all of the previously outlined steps, you are ready for the next phase of production: exporting your movie as video. If you are working on a Macintosh, you have the option to export your animation as QuickTime video. If you are a Windows user, Flash allows you to export under the AVI format. Both processes will convert your vector-based animation to a raster-based video file that can be opened and manipulated in a video editing application.

QuickTime Video (Macintosh)

If you work on a Macintosh, Flash allows you to export your animation as a QuickTime video file. You should note the fundamental difference between the different QuickTime file types, QuickTime Flash and QuickTime video. One of the enhancements in version 4 of QuickTime was its support for Flash files. Consequently, Flash can be exported as *QuickTime Flash*, which allows the movie to retain all of its interactive properties and act like a regular Flash file. To learn more about publishing interactive QuickTime Flash movies for both Macintosh and Windows, see Chapter 27.

Of all Flash's export options, the QuickTime video format is the least like Flash itself. It is raster-based (composed entirely of pixels) and has no interactive properties. However, it is the easiest format for transferring a Flash animation to video. Assuming that you have followed the steps outlined in the preceding section, your animation should be ready to export.

To export a Flash animation as QuickTime video:

1. Select File → Export Movie. A window appears, asking you to name the exported movie and browse to the location where you would like to save it (Figure 28.8). Select Quick-Time Video from the Format drop-down menu and give the file a name. Note that in the Name field, Flash appends a `.mov` extension to the untitled file to signify that it will be a digital video file.

2. Click Save, and the Export QuickTime Video dialog box appears (Figure 28.9). This interface is where you set all the options for your exported video, as follows:

Figure 28.8

When you export a movie, you will be prompted to choose an export format and location for the exported file.

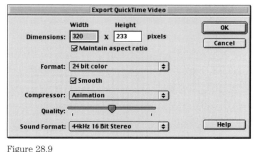

Figure 28.9

Export options

Dimensions Use these fields to specify width and height for the final video. Unless your Flash animation contains bitmap images, it can be scaled up or down without distortion to produce the final video. When the Maintain Aspect Ratio box is checked, your movie will be constrained to the proportions defined in the Document Properties dialog box.

Format Choose from the following color options for your movie:

*   Black and white: very low quality

*   4-bit color: low quality

*   8-bit color: 256 colors (marginal quality)

*   16-bit color: comparable to the Macintosh setting "Thousands of Colors"

*   24-bit color: comparable to the Macintosh setting "Millions of Colors"

*   32-bit color: same as 24-bit color, plus it supports Alpha Channel information for transparency effects

Smooth The Smooth option applies anti-aliasing to the exported QuickTime movie. Smooth can produce a higher-quality video image but may also lead to some distortion. Deselect this option if any unacceptable changes occur to your video.

Compressor These options allow you to take advantage of one of QuickTime's video-compression codecs. For vector-only Flash movies, you will experience good results with the Animation compression option. The Cinepak and Sorenson codecs are good for CD-ROM distribution. To learn more about individual QuickTime codecs, see the Quick-Time website: www.apple.com/quicktime/specifications.html.

Quality The slider will control how much compression is applied to the video. If you position the slider to the far right, the compression is minimal, affording better quality. As you move the slider to the left, more compression is added and quality suffers.

Sound Format Use this drop-down menu to set the parameters for the quality of sound exported from your movie. To learn more about sampling rates, bit depths, and other sound-related issues, see Chapter 19. This option can also be set to Disable if you wish to export your movie without its sound components.

If you plan to bring the exported video into another application outside of Flash, your best bet is to export the audio at the highest possible quality. It can always be down-sampled later if necessary.

3. Once you've set all your options, click OK, and Flash will begin the exporting process. This can sometimes take a while, especially if you are exporting a long animation or a complex soundtrack, or you are applying compression.

Your final QuickTime file will appear in the location you set; you'll see the capital-Q filmstrip icon ![icon] and a .mov extension after the filename. This file is suited for distribution as digital video on a CD-ROM or the Internet, or as source material for a video project, depending on what settings you applied.

IF YOUR VIDEO HAS A SOUNDTRACK

If you would like to go one step further and learn how this video file can be stored on videotape using Adobe Premiere, see the section "Preparing the Video for Tape" later in this chapter. If you plan to do this, *and your video has a soundtrack,* you'll have to take one additional step. The soundtrack of a QuickTime video that has been exported from Flash doesn't perform well in Premiere (see the sidebar "A Word of Caution about Embedded Audio" earlier in this chapter). Namely, the Flash audio track gets distorted to the point of being unrecognizable. In order to have a clear-sounding audio track, you must first strip the audio from the video file using QuickTime Pro and then bring the new audio-only track into Premiere and reconnect the two components. Sound like a pain? It is, sort of. But currently, it's the only way to make this work.

To distill the soundtrack from a QuickTime video:

1. Open the video file in QuickTime Pro. If you don't have QuickTime Pro, you can purchase a registration key that will unlock the "pro" features within your standard, free

version of QuickTime. To learn more about this, see the Apple website,
`www.apple.com/quicktime/buy`.

2. Choose File → Export (Cmd+E). A dialog box appears, where you set the
   following options:

   • Choose a name and destination for the exported soundtrack.

   • Select Sound to AIFF from the Export menu.

   • Choose the sample rate and bit-depth settings you require from the
     Use menu. We recommend that you keep this file at the highest possible
     quality.

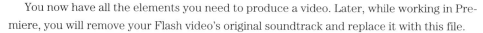

3. When finished, click Save, and QuickTime will export the track as an AIFF
   file to the location you specified in step 2.

   You now have all the elements you need to produce a video. Later, while working in Premiere, you will remove your Flash video's original soundtrack and replace it with this file.

Video for Windows (AVI)

If you're working with Flash on the Windows platform, you'll need to export your video in
AVI (Audio Video Interleaved) format. Like QuickTime video, AVI is a raster-based video format that will transfer nicely into a video editing application.

   To export a Flash animation as an AVI:

1. Select File → Export Movie. A window appears, asking you to name the exported movie
   and browse to the location where you would like to save it. Give the file a name and
   select Windows AVI from the Save as Type drop-down menu. When finished with these
   choices, click Save.

2. The Export Windows AVI dialog box appears
   (see Figure 28.10). This is where you set all
   the options for your exported video.

   Dimensions Use these Width and Height fields
   to specify dimensions for the final video. Unless
   your Flash animation contains bitmap images,
   a video file can be scaled up or down without distortion. When the Maintain Aspect Ratio
   box is checked, your movie will be constrained to the proportions defined in the Movie
   Properties dialog box.

Figure 28.10

**The Export
Windows AVI
dialog box**

   Video Format Choose from the following color options for your movie:

   • 8-bit color: low quality.

   • 16-bit color: Windows High Color setting.

- 24-bit color: Windows True Color setting.

- 32-bit color: like 24-bit color, plus it supports Alpha Channel information for transparency effects. This feature is not widely supported. Check the documentation for your video software before exporting a 32-bit video file.

Compress Video When checked, this will open an additional dialog box (after the current dialog box has been OK'd) that allows you to apply compression to your video. In this format, compression is recommended to help keep file sizes down.

Smooth Check the Smooth box to turn on anti-aliasing. Note that this may add unwanted pixels or noise to the final video image.

Sound Format Use this drop-down list to set the parameters for the quality of sound exported from your movie. To learn more about sampling rates, bit depths, and other sound-related issues, see Chapter 19. This option can also be set to Disable when you wish to export your movie without its sound components.

> If you plan to do additional editing of your video in another application such as Adobe Premiere, we recommend that you select Disable as the Sound Format option. The soundtrack of an AVI video that has been exported from Flash doesn't perform well in Premiere (see the earlier sidebar "A Word of Caution About Embedded Audio"). Namely, the Flash audio track gets distorted to the point of being unrecognizable. To have a clear-sounding audio track, you must export separate versions of your Flash movie: one as a silent AVI video, and one as a sound-only WAV file. To learn how to export a WAV version of your Flash movie, see the next section, "Exporting Your Movie as a WAV (Windows)."

3. Click OK to acknowledge all these video settings and to export your animation as an AVI video.

4. If you enabled compression in step 2, an additional dialog box appears (see Figure 28.11).

   Compressor Choose the compression codec that best suits the video equipment and software with which you are working. Consult the documentation that ships with your video editing system (or software) for specifics on working with compressed AVI footage. If you intend to view or distribute the animation as a stand-alone AVI, the Cinepak codec is a good choice.

   Compression Quality This slider sets the amount of compression applied to a file.

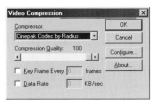

Figure 28.11

The Video Compression dialog box offers a list of possible compressors.

Key Frame Every To insert a keyframe at regular intervals, check this box and enter a number in the field. Keyframes help the compressor handle video information. Adding a keyframe at an interval equal to your movie's frame rate can be helpful. For example, a movie at 30 frames/second should have one keyframe every 30 frames.

Data Rate Checking this setting limits the amount of data a video generates when it plays back. A data rate of 150KB/second can help video stream smoothly from a CD-ROM drive.

5. Click OK when you are finished with the compression settings. Flash will export the AVI to the location you defined back in step 1.

When exporting is completed, you'll have a digital video file that is ready for use in a video editing application or in part of a CD-ROM. If you want to go one step further and transfer your video to tape, see the upcoming section on preparing your video.

Exporting Your Movie as a WAV File (Windows)

If you plan to bring your Flash video into Adobe Premiere, you must import it as two separate elements: a silent AVI video and a sound-only WAV file. This allows you to avoid the distortion that happens to Flash video soundtracks inside Premiere.

> To be certain that your movie is ready to be exported as a WAV, see the earlier section "Preparing the Flash Audio" before proceeding.

To export your Flash movie as a WAV file:

1. Select File → Export Movie. A window appears, asking you to name the exported movie and browse to the location where you want to save it. Name the file and select WAV Audio from the Save as Type drop-down menu. When finished with these choices, click Save.

2. The Export Windows WAV dialog box appears. This is where you set all the options for your exported soundtrack. Choose the highest possible sampling rate and bit depth from the Sound Format menu (you can always lower the quality later), and check the Ignore Event Sounds box.

3. Click OK, and Flash exports the sound as a WAV file to the location you specified in step 1. You now have all the elements you need to produce a video. Later, while working in Premiere, you will remove your Flash video's original soundtrack and replace it with this file.

Preparing the Video for Tape

And now, for your next trick... You may feel like a circus performer jumping between so many different windows, rearranging frames, and setting video compression options. The process can indeed be a bit crazy, but you are almost finished. This section outlines the steps involved in using Adobe Premiere to transfer a Flash QuickTime video or AVI to videotape. The nitty-gritty details of this process go far beyond the scope of this book—there are too many variables to account for in both the video setup of various computers and the intricacies of Premiere. What this section will do, however, is give you the basic, core information to get you started so that you can adapt the ideas to your video equipment and particular projects.

At the time of this writing, Adobe Premiere is in version 6.0. It is a video editing software package designed to assemble and create professional-quality video pieces using digital video footage. Premiere cannot record video from the original source, but it can *capture* recorded video from a digital video camera or camcorder. Premiere is equipped with an array of editing tools and effects for creating video shorts or feature-length movies. Once you have finished editing, Premiere also enables you to release your creation in a variety of formats, including videotape and various digital video codecs suitable for CD-ROM and Internet delivery.

This section assumes a familiarity with Premiere and its windows and features. If you are new to Premiere, select Help → Help Topics to access the HTML-based help files.

Importing Flash Components to a Video Editor

The first step is to launch Premiere and start a New Premiere Project. When you first launch the program, it will prompt you to define your settings in the Load Project Settings dialog box. You can select from one of the presets if there is an option that suits your needs. Or you can click Custom to display the New Project Settings dialog box (see Figure 28.12) and start from scratch.

Figure 28.12

Premier's New Project Settings dialog box allows you to define all the technical parameters for a video editing project.

1. In the New Project Settings dialog box, use the drop-down menu in the upper left-hand corner to set the following options for your Premiere project:

   General Select an editing mode that will work with your system—either QuickTime, or Video for Windows. Set a timebase that is either equal to or a multiple of the frame rate for your video. For Flash animations exported at 12 frames per second, set a timebase of 24.

Video Select a compressor, color depth, frame size, frame rate, and quality. For videotape, keep the quality at 100%.

Audio Set the sample rate, bit depth, and compression options for your project's audio track(s).

Keyframe and Rendering Use this to control the specifics of how Premiere renders and plays back your video.

Capture This is unnecessary since Flash has already generated your video footage.

2. Click OK to accept the settings you defined and to open the new project file.

3. Save the project.

Once your project has been created, you are ready to start working with the video you exported from Flash. To do this, you must import the files you need. Unlike Flash, Premiere doesn't store the files it imports in any kind of Library. When you import a video resource in Premiere, you are simply noting a path to that file on your computer's hard drive. Premiere will access the file when it is called upon in your video composition. Otherwise, the file sits on your hard disk and is never actually a permanent part of the Premiere project file. For this reason, be sure that you don't delete any source video files that are used in Premiere projects.

To import the video footage you exported from Flash:

1. Select File → Import File.

2. The Import dialog box appears. Use this window to browse to the video source file you wish to import. When you have found and selected the file, click Open to import the footage. If you plan to use your Flash footage with other video or audio clips, you can import multiple clips. Shift+click (Mac) or Ctrl+click (Win) the source video files to select the ones you need.

3. An icon representing the imported file(s) appears in the Project window.

Once you have imported the video you require, you can begin to build your project.

Assembling Your Animation as a Video Composition

You have defined your project and imported some source footage, and now you are ready to put the video together. Premiere makes this part of the process very easy. You can assemble an entire video piece by simply dragging and dropping the clips you need into the Premiere Timeline. Premiere's Timeline is similar to the Flash Timeline: Once a clip is in the Timeline, it is officially part of the video project and will appear in the final piece.

To place a video clip in the Premiere Timeline:

1. Select the video clip in the Project window. Your mouse cursor will change from the pointer to the hand cursor.

2. Drag the clip from the window to the Timeline. Drop it in the Video 1 channel. The clip should snap into position and align itself at the first possible opening. If the clip contains audio, you will see its audio track appear directly beneath the clip in the Audio 1 channel.

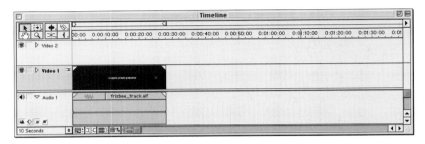

If this audio track was carried over from your Flash movie, be sure to delete it, for it will be drastically distorted in Premiere and will sound horrible in your final video production.

3. *(Optional if your clip includes sound)* Click the Toggle Sync Mode button. This will "unlock" the video and audio components of the files in your Timeline. Once they are unlocked, select the audio track and press Delete to clear the track from the Timeline.

4. Import the audio track that you created for your Flash video (if you haven't already). If you are working on a Mac, this is the track you created using QuickTime Pro. For Windows users, this is the sound-only WAV version of your movie that you exported from Flash.

5. Drag the audio track for your Flash movie from the Project window into the Audio 1 channel of Premiere's Timeline. Because this track was "distilled" from your original Flash movie, it will exactly match the length of the Flash track in the Video 1 channel.

6. Select Timeline → Preview or press Return/Enter to preview the video. Premiere will do the preview operation and then play the video for you in the Program side of the Monitor window. This is an essential step. Premiere won't be able to play your video until it has been previewed.

At this point, you have many options, depending on your specific goals. If you plan to use the Flash video as a solo piece, your work is finished; you are ready to go to videotape. If you intend to combine the video with additional footage, keep on going; you can continue to import clips, drop them in the Timeline, and use the Source window to set any in points or out points you need to perform video edits.

Exporting and Printing to Video

Premiere allows you to transfer the video you have edited to videotape. This process is called *printing to video.* Depending on the equipment you own, it can be done in a variety of ways. Premiere enables you to play back directly from the Timeline into a camcorder, VCR, or various DV (digital video) devices. Due to the variety of computer systems, video capture cards, and so on, discussing the specifics of each scenario is beyond the scope of this book. But here are some general tips:

Project settings When you play back directly to a VCR or other video device, Premiere uses the settings defined in the Project Settings dialog box. Make sure that these options afford the best possible playback on your system.

Lead time Be sure to include either a black matte or color bars at the start of the video. This allows the playback device to have a chance to establish sync with the tape before playing your animation. Adobe also recommends a minimum of 30 seconds of color bars and tone if your project will go out to a postproduction house for duplication.

To print a project to video:

1. Preview your project (Timeline → Preview) if you haven't already done so.

2. Set up your recording equipment and be sure that you have a tape on which to record.

3. Choose File → Export Timeline → Print to Video. The Print to Video dialog box appears (see Figure 28.13). Specify the following options:

Figure 28.13

The Print to Video dialog box allows you to set options for transferring your project from digital video to videotape.

   - In the Color Bars field, enter the number of seconds for which you would like to display colored bars.

   - In the Play Black field, enter the number of seconds for black matte.

   - Choose either Zoom Screen (Mac) or Full Screen (Win) to scale the video to full size. The Macintosh version allows you to do this using either hardware (via video capture card) or software.

   - Check Loop Playback for continuous video playback.

4. When you have finished, start your recording device and click OK. Premiere will take care of the rest.

When you are ready to stop playback, press the Escape key, and Premiere will cease video playback. You should be able to rewind your videotape and view the finished Flash animation on video. Cool!

Inspirational Design Model

As Flash continues to grow as a multimedia authoring tool, it will start popping up in some rather unusual and unorthodox places. Given its history, the only place you might expect to see Flash is the Web, or perhaps a CD-ROM. However, if you live in the U.K., you may have had the opportunity to see Flash on the telly (that's TV for those of us on the other side of the Atlantic).

Kerb (www.kerb.co.uk), a new media agency in the U.K. that specializes in all things Flash, created the first animated television series that was developed entirely in Flash. The series, *Hellz Kitchen* (see Figure 28.14), is currently being hosted on the Bravo Network website (www.bravo.co.uk/toonz/hellz/hellz_archive.html). *Hellz Kitchen* was commissioned by the Bravo Network and was scheduled to appear on television in the U.K. in 2001.

Figure 28.14

Hellz Kitchen by Kerb tells the tale of a bunch (pun intended) of criminally deranged and trigger-happy vegetables.

Summary

This chapter presented several options involving Flash and video. Now that Flash MX supports both embedded and linked video files, it's possible for you to bring video directly into a Flash movie. This adds new dimensions to movies and gives you the best of both worlds: Flash vector images and video raster images. You were also exposed to the process of taking a vector-based Flash animation, exporting it as a raster-based digital video file, and transferring the new file to videotape. This process eliminates the interactivity of the Flash movie but opens the door to an entirely new set of options for displaying or showing your Flash animations.

CHAPTER 29

Using Flash for CD-ROM Development

One of Flash's greatest strengths is its ability to deliver high-quality audio and animation in a single, compact file. This characteristic makes Flash ideally suited for the Internet and other applications in which bandwidth is a major concern. What is often forgotten, though, is that Flash can also be distributed in ways that are not limited by download-time or plug-in issues.

One of the best ways to distribute your Flash movies is to pass them to your audience on a CD-ROM as stand-alone or self-contained applications. In this format, Flash can either rely on the stand-alone Flash Player or be completely independent and run on both Macintosh and Windows platforms without additional software. Plus, with the capacity of a CD-ROM, you are able to deliver a greater amount of information without the concerns of bandwidth that you encounter on the Web.

While no single delivery method can do it all, you will find that each has its particular advantages and allows you to distribute your movies in new ways that open the door to many new possibilities. This chapter will cover the following topics:

- **Stand-alone Flash Player movies**

- **Self-contained Flash projectors**

- **Publishing movies for CD-ROM delivery**

- **Using ActionScript FSCommands**

- **Designing and scripting interface elements for a CD-ROM**

Stand-Alone Flash Files

Although Flash most commonly appears on the Internet in the context of a website, don't forget that there are other options that help you to reach your audience. Flash can produce two types of stand-alone movies that enable you to share your work without requiring that your audience go to the Web. The first is a standard SWF file. If your audience has the stand-alone Flash Player application, they will be able to see your movie without the aid of a web browser. The other type of stand-alone movie is a self-contained *Flash projector*. This is a self-running application that allows your movie to run on any computer, whether the Flash Player is installed or not.

One of the best advantages of both stand-alone options is that you can create all your movies so that they will run on all platforms. Regardless of the operating system that you use to run Flash, you'll be able to create final files that match the playback capabilities of your audience. This characteristic makes Flash one of the most portable multimedia applications currently available.

Distributing Movies with the Flash Player

The Flash Player application comes with Flash. It can be used to play any SWF file without the assistance of a web browser. The Flash Player (see Figure 29.1) offers several menu commands with which you control the playback and appearance of a movie. You can find the application in the Players folder, inside the folder where Flash resides on your computer's hard drive. For Macintosh users, the stand-alone player is named *SAFlashPlayer*; for Windows folks, it's named *SAFlashPlayer.exe*.

Figure 29.1

A movie running with the Flash Player application

Since the Flash Player will play any SWF file, it's very easy to distribute your movies in a compact manner, over a variety of platforms, and with minimal fuss. The average computer user won't have this application, however. Thus, it isn't the best delivery option if you're trying to target a large number of people—unless you're sure they all have the Flash Player application installed (meaning that they already own the Flash authoring application). To make your movie deliverable to the widest possible audience, use a self-contained Flash projector.

Delivering Movies as Self-Contained Flash Projectors

Self-contained Flash projectors are quite possibly the best way to distribute your movies outside the Web. A self-contained projector is an executable file—a self-contained application that will run your movie just as you created it on either Windows or a Macintosh operating system. Anyone using Windows or a Mac (which is just about everybody) will be able to see your Flash masterpiece without the help of any additional software or web-browser plug-in. Fantastic! Plus, by putting a self-contained projector on a CD-ROM, you're able to hand it out to fans, clients, customers, students, and so on, in a format that is easily accessible on any computer with a CD-ROM drive. Figure 29.2 shows a Flash projector in context.

Figure 29.2

A self-contained projector can run in its own window or on the full screen (as shown here).

Creating Flash Projectors

Creating, or, more appropriately, *publishing,* a Flash projector is very simple. And, because Flash allows you to create both Macintosh and Windows projectors, you can take care of creating both files in a single step. One minor disadvantage is that the self-contained projector will be a few hundred kilobytes larger than the SWF version of the same movie. This is because the projector file must contain information necessary for playing your movie using the resources of the operating system on which the projector is running.

To publish a self-contained Flash projector:

1. When you've finished finished creating the movie, choose File → Save to save it with any final changes in place.

2. Choose File → Publish Settings. The Publish Settings dialog box appears (see Figure 29.3).

Figure 29.3

The Publish Settings dialog box contains the options for creating self-contained projectors.

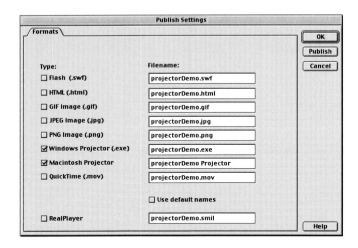

3. Check the box next to Windows Projector or Macintosh Projector depending on what kind of projector you need to create. Check both boxes if you would like to create both varieties. You can give each version a name in the adjacent Filename field. Be sure to leave the `.exe` suffix on the name of your Windows projector.

4. To finally publish the projector, do one of the following:

   • Click the Publish button. This will publish your projector immediately. This option is helpful if you need to publish several different kinds of movies in one sitting.

   • Click OK to accept the selections you've just made in the Publish Settings dialog box. Then select File → Publish (Shift+F12) to publish your projector(s).

   The Publishing window appears, showing the progress made toward publishing your movie. When it is finished, your projector file(s) should be sitting in the same folder as the Flash file you are currently using.

5. Quit Flash (File → Quit/Exit). After being published, Flash stand-alone projectors are given a circular icon showing the new Flash MX *f* 🅕 . Double-click the projector's circular icon to launch the self-contained projector application. The file is now ready to be burned onto a CD-ROM.

Using Flash to Create CD-ROM Interfaces

Although publishing your self-contained projector is the final step of the process, there are many additional things you can do with your movie to make it look and act more like a self-sufficient application. With the help of a few ActionScript commands, you can take your

Flash movie and turn it into an independent multimedia production that is controlled in precisely the ways you define. Not only does this give your piece a more professional look and feel, but it allows you to set the stage for the ways in which your audience chooses to view your work.

FSCommands

FSCommands are an element of ActionScript that allow Flash and the Flash Player to communicate with the application that is hosting your movie. In the context of this chapter, that application is either the Macintosh or Windows operating system. By issuing FSCommands in your movie, you can set many different parameters for the movie's presentation, and the options available to the audience who is viewing it. ActionScript's FSCommands are as follows:

`fullscreen` This command takes one of two arguments, `true` or `false`. When set to `true`, the projector will fill the entire monitor window and display no menu bar at the top of the screen. When set to `false`, the projector will appear in a window whose size is set by the dimensions specified in the Movie Properties dialog box.

`allowscale` This command, when set to `true`, allows the movie to stretch to fit the size of the window (or monitor) playing it. When set to `false`, the window that contains the movie can be stretched as needed, but the movie itself will not be scaled.

`showmenu` When set to `true`, this command enables the options in the context menu (Ctrl+click/right-click) for a projector file. These options allow your audience to play, stop, rewind, zoom, and change the display quality of the projector file. When set to `false`, all options are grayed out or removed, with the exception of "About Macromedia Flash Player."

A word of caution: `showmenu` has been known to behave unpredictably on some operating systems. Be sure to test your movie on a variety of platforms before distributing it to your audience.

`trapallkeys` This command, when set to `true`, will disable the keyboard. When set to `false` (the default), the movie can accept input from the keyboard.

Watch out—by setting `trapallkeys` to `true`, you are effectively cutting off the keyboard. If you do this to prevent nonscripted interaction with your movie, be sure to include a button or other element with the `fscommand("quit")` statement, for shutting down the projector.

`exec` Use the `exec` command to launch another application from the Flash projector. The new application will appear over the projector file. The argument for this command is specified as a string containing either the relative or absolute path to the application you would like to launch. For example:

```
on(release){
    fscommand("exec", "Burroughs:Applications (Mac OS 9):SimpleText");
}
```

This statement shows the absolute path to launch the SimpleText application on a Macintosh computer. The different components of the path are separated by the colon (:) character.

In Windows, the components are separated with the forward slash (/). For example:

```
fscommand("exec", "C:/Program Files/Accessories/Wordpad.exe");
```

quit This command takes no arguments. When it's issued, your computer will close the projector file.

Concerning syntax, all FSCommands (`quit`, `exec`, and so on) and their arguments are entered as strings. For example:

```
fscommand ("fullscreen", "true");
```

This statement sets a projector to play in full-screen mode. The command `fullscreen` and its argument `true` are listed in quotation marks, making each a text string. If you don't enter the arguments as strings, Flash won't be able to communicate properly with the operating system and perform the actions you specify.

The best place for FSCommands is in a frame on the main Timeline. Put them in the first frame of the movie so that they are executed before any other scripts are called. If you place your FSCommands in your movie's first frame, they will require no handler and will be one of the first movie parameters loaded into memory.

Letterbox Projectors and CD Interface Elements

Using FSCommands is the first step toward creating a truly unique CD-ROM for your Flash movie. This section introduces you to a few design-related techniques that you can employ to create a stylish and functional movie for cross-platform distribution.

The first technique involves creating a letterbox-style projector. *Letterbox* is a term used to describe the appearance of a video image. When you go to a movie theater, you see films on a screen that is quite different from the monitor on your television or computer. Rather than the standard 4:3 aspect ratio, movie screens have a 16:9 aspect ratio. These screens are much wider than they are tall and accommodate a broader field of view. Consequently, when studio films are re-released on video for consumers' televisions and VCRs, they are often modified to fit the 4:3 aspect ratio.

In some cases, though, this isn't done. To preserve the 16:9 cinematic aspect ratio, videos can be released in letterbox format. Roughly the top one-third and the bottom one-third of the screen are left black, and the image fills the entire width of the display. Ultimately, this format makes the image smaller than if it were in the 4:3 ratio but preserves the original proportions of the film. Although letterbox is used as a technical convention, it has a very stylish look and can lend an interesting visual quality to Flash projector files.

Creating the letterbox effect is very simple and involves only a few small modifications to your movie:

1. Select Modify → Document. The Document Properties dialog box appears. Set your movie dimensions so that they conform to the 16:9 aspect ratio (such as 320×180 or 640×360).

> Changing the movie dimensions of a finished animation often creates problems with the alignment and position of movie elements. So it's best to adjust the dimensions *before* you create the Flash movie.

2. Set the background color of the movie to black, even if you want your movie to have a different background color. When you create a self-contained projector, the background color of the movie is used to determine the color of the monitor when you play the movie in full-screen mode. Click OK to close the Document Properties dialog box.

3. Create a new layer in your movie and name it **letterbox**. Drag this layer so that it's at the bottom of all other layers in the Timeline. Select Insert → New Symbol and create a new graphic symbol that is a rectangle exactly the same size as your Stage. Make the rectangle whatever color you want for your movie background. Drag the rectangle onto the `letterbox` layer, positioning it in the center of the Stage. Lock the layer once it's in position.

4. Create another new layer and name it **actions**. Insert a new keyframe in frame 1 of this layer, highlight it, and select Window → Actions to display the Actions panel. Enter the following statements:

```
fscommand ("allowscale", "false");
fscommand ("fullscreen", "true");
```

The first statement in this script prohibits the movie from being scaled, and preserves the dimensions set in the movie's properties. To scale the movie so that it fills the width of the screen, you can set `"allowscale"` to `true`, but the letterbox effect is more dramatic when it is `false`.

The second statement in the script, sets your projector so that it plays back full-screen—meaning that it fills the entire monitor, covering the computer's desktop and any applications that are running. The `"fullscreen"` statement is crucial to the success of the letterbox technique, because it uses the background color of your movie (black) to create the matte that surrounds the 16:9 area of your Stage.

5. Publish your movie as a self-contained projector and see the letterbox effect in context.

By setting the movie dimensions to a 16:9 ratio, you established the initial effect. The black background color created the black mask. Then, by using a symbol as a colored backdrop for the movie, you created the impression that the Stage's color is something other than black. The size of the backdrop matches your Stage size, and the letterbox effect is complete. See Figure 29.4 for an illustration.

Figure 29.4

A letterbox projector playing in full-screen mode

This technique treats the rectangular symbol like background scenery in a theater production. In the same way that a stage crew might change props during a play, you can change the color or other attributes of the background symbol in your movie.

You can also create custom menus for your movie. Using the button techniques outlined in Chapter 13, you can create a series of buttons (menu bar) to serve as navigational controls for your projector. Then, with some basic ActionScript, you can attach commands to the buttons that will start, stop, rewind, skip, and perform all the necessary behaviors you require for navigation and other kinds of interactivity. To learn more about actions that allow your audience to interactively navigate through your movie, see Chapter 12 or the ActionScript Reference section.

Something interesting that you can do with a menu bar is allow your audience to toggle it off and on—it's there when they want it, and gone when they don't. This is especially useful for full-screen projectors, where you don't want a permanent menu or other navigational element cluttering your screen and distracting from your movie. There are many ways to toggle something off and on; consider the following example:

```
onClipEvent(keyDown){
    if(Key.getCode()==Key.SPACE){
        _visible=1;
    }
}
```

```
onClipEvent(keyUp){
    if(Key.getCode()==Key.SPACE){
        _visible=0;
    }
}
```

This script creates a simple toggle behavior for the menu bar Movie Clip to which the script is attached. Any time a key is pressed, keyDown and keyUp events are generated. The script tests to see whether the key in question happens to be the spacebar. If it is, then the clip is shown while the spacebar is down, and hidden when it is up. Of course, while the clip is visible, all the navigation buttons it contains are available. This allows your audience to toggle the menu "on" with the spacebar, and then click the buttons within the Movie Clip that make your movie do whatever it is that the users need to do: rewind, skip to another section, quit, and so on.

To make the foregoing script work properly, you must set the _visible property for the Movie Clip equal to 0 (or false) at the outset of the movie. Attach this script to a menu bar Movie Clip, and you'll be able to use the spacebar to toggle the menu on and off.

To see both the letterbox projector technique and a spacebar menu toggle in a self-contained projector, see the file projectorDemo (Macintosh) or projectorDemo.exe (Windows) in the Chapter 29 folder on the companion CD-ROM for this book. To examine the source file and to witness these scripts in context, see projectorDemo.fla in the same folder.

Inspirational Design Model

One of the best ways to find the inspiration needed to produce your own CD-ROM is to see just how easy it is to create the disc. A task that may have once seemed daunting and mysterious is actually very doable, provided that you have the necessary resources. The following list provides a good variety of information and advice for all your CD-ROM burning needs.

www.macdisk.com/cdromen.php3 This Macintosh-focused site provides a great deal of information about cross-platform CD burning. Windows users can read about MacImage, a utility used to help produce hybrid CD-ROMs on a PC.

www.roxio.com Roxio is the manufacturer of Toast 5 Titanium, the premiere tool for cross-platform (hybrid) CD burning in a Macintosh environment. To learn more about using Toast 5 Titanium, see Hands On 8.

www.nero.com Nero is the Windows-compatible CD-burning tool for creating hybrid CDs in a Windows environment. It's manufactured by Ahead Software. To read more about Nero, see "Beyond Burning Basics" in Hands On 8.

www.simplythebest.net/info/cdburninfo.html This informational website offers technical details on the CD-burning process and other related topics.

Summary

This chapter demonstrates Flash as a highly portable application, and shows how easy it is to distribute your movies in media other than the Internet. You learned how to create a self-contained Flash projector: an executable file or application that will run your movie on a Macintosh or Windows-based computer without any additional software. Related to the self-contained file, ActionScript FSCommands were also introduced in this chapter. These statements allow you to write scripts that directly communicate between your movie and the system hosting it.

After you have created your movie and included the commands you need for it to run as a self-contained file, you're ready to publish your projector(s) and burn a CD-ROM. Hands On 8 will take you through the steps.

Creating a Macintosh/Windows Hybrid CD Using Flash and Toast 5 Titanium

A hybrid CD-ROM is a CD that can be read by both Macintosh and Windows-based computers. Technically speaking, it contains HFS formatting for the Macintosh information *and* ISO 9660 for DOS/Windows. Most importantly, the hybrid CD specifies which files are viewable for each platform. The CD will appear on each OS exactly as you specify. Mac users will see only the Macintosh-based files you want them to see, and Windows users will see only the files readable by their system. By creating a hybrid CD, you can take both flavors of a Flash projector and store them in a medium that will deliver your movie to anyone with either a Macintosh or a Windows system.

This lesson discusses the steps involved in creating a hybrid CD using Roxio Toast 5 Titanium (formerly manufactured by Adaptec, among others). Toast 5 is an excellent application; we selected it for its ease of use and its ability to handle many of the issues surrounding multiplatform CDs. The topics in this tutorial are more about cross-platform CD burning in general than an in-depth discussion of the Toast application. So if you have another CD-burning application that you prefer, don't worry. The ideas presented here should translate to your application.

> Toast 5 Titanium runs only on Macintosh systems. Windows users can see their cross-platform CD-burning options in the section "Beyond Burning Basics" at the end of this tutorial.

To prepare for this tutorial, you should have two Flash self-contained projector files—one for the Macintosh and one for Windows. If you don't have these files, follow the steps in Chapter 29 for creating Flash projectors. With your completed projector files and a CD-R or CD-RW in place, you'll be ready to begin.

Phase 1: Preparing Your Files

Begin by launching the Toast 5 Titanium application. It's a good idea to put all your Macintosh files in a temporary partition on your computer before burning a CD. This allows the files to be drawn from a clean, unfragmented portion of your hard drive.

To create a temporary partition:

1. Select Utilities → Create Temporary Partition. The Create Temporary Partition dialog box appears.

2. Give the partition the same name you want the Macintosh CD to bear. Enter a number in the Size field to set the size of the partition. It should be large enough to hold all the files you wish to burn. Click OK when you are finished.

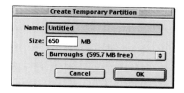

The partition appears on your desktop as a small rectangular icon that reads "toast."

With the partition in place, you can put your files in order. Copy all the Macintosh files onto the new partition. Then, open the partition and arrange the files in the configuration you want them to have on the CD. You can also set the shape, size, and position of the window this way. Any changes you make at this stage will set the appearance of the CD when it is opened from your audience's desktop.

To prepare the Windows files, create a new folder on your desktop, and name it with the title you want for the Windows version of your CD. Copy the Windows projector (and any other files you might need) to this location.

You're now ready to organize the disc.

Phase 2: Laying Out the Disc

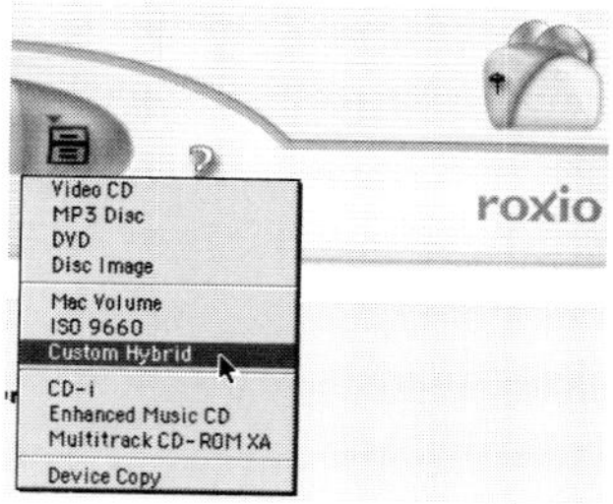

Figure H8.1

You can access this context menu by holding the mouse button down over Toast's Other button.

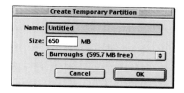

Your files are organized, and you can now set them up in Toast as a hybrid CD. Move your mouse cursor over the Other button in the main Toast window. You will see the context menu icon appear alongside the cursor as though you were performing a Ctrl+click. Click the button and hold the mouse button down. In the context menu that appears (see Figure H8.1), select Custom Hybrid.

The Custom Hybrid option changes the appearance of the window and shows you two options: one for Macintosh and one for ISO.

To set the Macintosh data:

1. Click the Select Mac button. The Select Volume dialog box appears. Select the volume that contains your Macintosh files.

2. If you want the projector (or any other file, for that matter) to launch automatically, check the AutoStart box (Figure H8.2). In the adjacent field, select the file that you want to start up automatically, and Toast will take care of the technical stuff.

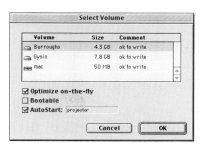

Figure H8.2

You can choose to have your projector launched automatically.

3. Click OK to finish and return to the main window. You will see the cumulative size of all Macintosh data in the Mac section of the Toast window. Now, let's move on to the Windows files.

To select files for the Windows portion of the CD:

1. Click the Select ISO button. The ISO 9660 window appears.

2. Drag the folder containing the Windows files into the main section of the window labeled with the Files tab. A disc icon appears and shows a hierarchical structure of the Windows files (see Figure H8.3). If you need to add additional files, simply click the Add button and browse to the extra files.

> One of the benefits of burning a hybrid CD in this fashion is the ability of the hybrid format to share common files between the Macintosh and ISO portions of the disc. Shared files should be copied to the Macintosh partition while you are preparing the files for your CD (at the outset of the burning process). To share files, simply drag them from the Macintosh partition to the Files tab of the ISO 9660 window. Toast will label the names of these files in blue so that you can see they are shared between the two sections of your CD.

3. Click on the Settings tab. Choose Joliet (MS-DOS+Windows) from the Naming menu. This option allows you to use long filenames (and names with spaces) on the Windows CD.

4. *(Optional)* To make a file on the CD launch automatically in Windows, you have to create a file called `autorun.inf`. This little file tells the computer to start an application immediately after reading the contents of the CD. You can create the file using BBEdit, Notepad, or a similar program that's capable of editing pure ASCII. The text for the `autorun.inf` file is as follows:

```
[autorun]
open=flashProjector.exe
icon=iconGraphic.ico
```

Figure H8.3

Windows files added to the hybrid CD

Replace `flashProjector.exe` with the name of the file you want to launch. If you would like the CD itself to have a graphic icon, specify the name of the graphic file in the second line. Be sure to include the graphic on the CD. After entering these statements, save the file as `autorun.inf` and put it with the other Windows files.

5. If you decided to use an `autorun.inf` file, there is one more step you should take. Click the Layout tab. Highlight the `autorun.inf` file and click Move to Top so that the file will be the first one on the list. This makes it easier for the computer to find the file when it first reads the contents of the disc.

6. Click the Done button to return to Toast's main window. The total file size of the Windows data is now listed in the ISO section.

That's it! Your CD has all of its contents, and you should be ready to burn the disc.

Phase 3: Burning and Testing the CD-ROM

At this point, all your files have been collected and assembled in Toast. Let the burning begin! To burn your hybrid CD:

1. Be sure that you have a recordable disc (either CD-R or CD-RW) in the burner. Click the red Record button.

2. After a little prep time, the Record dialog box appears. In the Speed menu, select the speed that works best for your burning device. If you would like to do a test burn, you can check the Simulation Mode box. Otherwise, click Write Disc, and away it goes.

3. When the disc is finished, Toast will ask if you want to verify the disc. This is recommended and takes only a little while. When Toast finishes verifying, it will ask you to eject the disc.

Testing a disc is a crucial part of CD-ROM development. The best way to do this is to run your CD on as many different machines as possible. As you do this, take note of how it performs. Do all of the features work? Is there anything that performs sluggishly? Look for recurring problems and troubleshoot accordingly.

Beyond Burning Basics

Now you know how to create a hybrid CD-ROM that will enable you to distribute your Flash masterpieces to the far ends of the earth. This tutorial outlined the basic concepts, and here are a few additional ideas that can help you get the most out of your CD-ROMs:

- *Using Windows?* Can't find a cross-platform CD-burning solution? You need look no farther than Nero by Ahead Software (`www.nero.com`). Nero will run on Windows 95, 98, Me, NT 4, 2000, and XP systems. Furthermore, it supports CD-ROM burning in a variety of formats, including ISO/HFS hybrid. To create a hybrid CD with Nero, your PC must be connected to a SCSI hard disk that contains the Macintosh-native, HFS partition that you wish to write to CD. Visit the Nero website for more information about system and hardware requirements and the CD/CD-RW burning devices that are supported.

- *Multisession CDs* can be used to create cross-platform CD-ROMs. Most burning applications like Toast can burn multisession discs. This means that only a portion of the CD is used, leaving room for more data in the future. You can burn two separate sessions, one for Mac data and one for Windows data. This will achieve similar cross-platform results.

- *Enhanced CDs* are CDs that contain both audio and data. You can create an enhanced CD that is also a hybrid; that's three for the price of one! Burn your audio first as a session rather than as an entire disc. Then, burn your hybrid data (Flash projectors, HTML files, and so on) to the same disc. CD audio players cannot detect multiple sessions, so all they see is the first chunk of information on the disc—your music. But when you put the disc in a computer, it will be able to see everything and play your music, animations, and whatever else your audience desires. This technique is especially helpful for musicians, bands, and multimedia artists who need to distribute a diverse body of work in a single, compact format.

- *AutoStart* (Mac) and *Autorun* (Windows) are features that must be enabled on the host computer in order for the CD-ROM to function properly. Due to the threat of computer viruses and worms, it's likely that many people have these options turned off on their systems. Because there is no way to get around this, it's a good idea to include some sort of instruction for launching your projector(s) if it isn't handled automatically.

Appendix and Reference

In this section, *you will find some supplemental information to help you enhance your Flash and ActionScript skills. The Appendix provides step-by-step instructions for creating navigational widgets and preloaders. The ActionScript Reference gives you the highlights and essentials of ActionScript.*

Adding Cool Bells and Whistles

On the whole, you can use two strategies when it comes to your Flash learning experience. First, you could master the hard-core theory and techniques and apply those to forging your own Flash creations. Alternatively, you could start off by learning how to make specific things. Through that process, you would learn the theory and techniques needed to go on and craft your own stuff. Some people prefer to learn in one way; others prefer to learn the other way. As a result, we've tried to cover both strategies. We've helped you master the theory and technique behind Flash as well as showing you how to make specific kinds of gadgets. Unfortunately, as you've probably figured out by now, there is *so* much you can do with Flash. As a result, there are some techniques that just didn't fit into any of the chapters.

Never fear, we aren't going to let these fall totally by the wayside. This appendix features step-by-step tutorials for creating some of the coolest Flash widgets and doohickeys that didn't quite fit into any one place in the book. Granted, if we were to write a tutorial on every cool thing you could create in Flash, we'd be sitting at our computers until the next Ice Age descended. As a result, the appendix itself is populated with selected tutorials.

The following topics will be covered:

- **Building navigational widgets**
- **Using preloaders to enhance your audience's experience**
- **Using an array to create a dynamic greeting**

Building Navigational Widgets

Interactive design of any kind (whether HTML-, Flash-, or CD-ROM-based) either succeeds or fails based on its navigation. Now, we're not just talking about buttons here—navigation has as much to do with how you audience moves about your site as it does with how you represent your content. As a result, efficient navigation can take any form.

So, what's the big deal with efficient navigation? Well, without efficient (and sometimes innovative) navigation systems, your audience could have trouble locating the information they're looking for and go elsewhere.

In the following section, you are going to look at how to create several useful navigational widgets that will ultimately enhance your audience's experience.

Producing a Drop-Down, Drag-Out Menu System

A drop-down, drag-out menu is a commonly used navigation technique that enables you to conveniently nest a number of different menu items under one button. This is usually how it works: When the user moves their mouse over a button, a series of additional buttons (usually stacked vertically) appear. From there, they can move their mouse over and click any of the newly appeared buttons (let's call them *secondary buttons*). If the user moves their mouse off of any of the secondary buttons, they disappear, leaving only the main menu button.

 An example of a drop-down, drag-out menu has been included in the Appendix A directory of the book's CD-ROM (in both SWF and FLA formats).

Creating the Visual Elements

The process by which you create a drop-down, drag-out menu is quite easy. It just takes a Movie Clip, a number of Button symbols, and some rudimentary ActionScript:

1. Because the menu is a self-contained Movie Clip, the first step is to create the Movie Clip itself. Go to Insert → New Symbol, click the Movie Clip radio button, enter **menu** into the Name field, and click OK.

2. Now, when the Symbol Editor opens, you need to start off by creating the main menu button—let's call it the *primary button*. Go to Insert → New Symbol, click the Button radio button, enter **primary menu button** into the Name field, and then click OK.

3. Now, when you're dumped into a second Symbol Editor, create a menu button of some kind. For this tutorial, it might be easiest to create a straightforward rectangular button like this one: **BUTTON**

4. Now, it's time to create the secondary buttons. Go to Insert → Symbol, click the Button radio button, enter **secondary menu button** into the Name field, and then click OK.

5. When the Symbol Editor opens, create the first button (in the vertical stack). Because of the nature of the menu (something that will be looked at momentarily), it's best to

create a button you can nestle up to the right side of the primary button without any gaps. This image illustrates what your secondary button should look like in relation to your primary menu button: **BUTTON** **BUTTON 1**

6. Now, repeat the process described in steps 4–5 until you have as many secondary buttons as you want to appear when the user moves their mouse over the primary menu button. Remember to give each button a unique name when you create it.

Putting the Visual Elements Together

Now that you've got the primary menu button and all of the secondary buttons created, it's time to put them together:

1. Switch back to the menu Movie Clip you created at the beginning of this tutorial (which until now has remained unused). In the first keyframe of the Movie Clip's single layer (which you should rename to **primary menu button**), place the primary menu button.

2. Select the second frame of the primary menu button layer, and insert a frame by going to Insert → Frame.

3. Add an additional layer (rename it to **secondary button 1**).

4. Add a keyframe to the second frame of the secondary button 1 layer by going to Insert → Keyframe.

5. Select the newly created keyframe, and insert the secondary button symbol. Make sure the left side of the secondary button symbol is flush with the right side of the primary menu button symbol that's sitting in the primary menu button layer—as was shown previously.

6. Now, add a new layer (rename it to **secondary button 2**), select the second frame, and add a keyframe.

7. Now, add the next secondary button you created to the second keyframe of the secondary button 2 layer. Make sure the top of this secondary button is flush (no overlap) with the bottom of the first secondary button you added.

8. Continue the process of adding additional layers and adding successive secondary buttons into the layer's second keyframe.

9. At this point, you should have something that looks a little like this:

    BUTTON **BUTTON 1**
    BUTTON 2
    BUTTON 3
    BUTTON 4

Creating the ActionScript

Now that you've got all the visual elements in place, it's time to add the ActionScript that will control the menu system:

1. First, select the primary menu button and open the Actions window (Window → Actions).

All the ActionScripting described in this tutorial is done in Normal mode. If you want to do it by hand, feel free to work instead in Expert mode.

2. Add a `goto()` action (which is located in the Movie Control category). Then, with the Parameters panel open, and the event section of the script selected in the ActionScript text box, select Roll Over as the event.

3. Then, select the action line of the script, make sure Frame Number is selected in the Type drop-down menu, enter **2** into the Frame field, and make sure that the Go to and Play radio button is selected. This will cause the playhead to jump to frame 2—giving the appearance that the secondary buttons appear when the user moves their mouse over the primary menu button.

4. At this point, if you were to test the Movie Clip, you'd see that it loops, making the secondary button rapidly appear and disappear as the playhead travels from frame 1 to frame 2 and then back to frame 1. What you need to do is force the Movie Clip to stop on frame 1 and wait until the user moves their mouse over the primary menu button (whose action will push the playhead to frame 2—giving the appearance that the secondary menu buttons appear). You can do this with a simple `stop()` action. So, create a new layer in the Movie Clip and call it **actions**.

5. Select the first (empty) keyframe and open the Actions panel (Window → Actions).

6. Expand the Movie Control category and add a `stop()` action.

7. Now you need to do the same thing to frame 2 so that the playhead doesn't automatically flip back to frame 1. Select the second frame in the actions layer, and go to Insert → Keyframe.

8. Open the Actions panel (Window → Actions) and add a `stop()` action from the Movie Control category.

9. At this stage, it's time to create the mechanism by which the secondary menu buttons disappear if the user moves their mouse away from them. To do this, you are going to create an invisible rectangular button that will be slightly larger than the entire menu (with all the secondary buttons visible) to which a simple `goto()` action will be attached that will send the playhead back to frame 1—giving the illusion that the secondary buttons disappear. The button will reside below the entire menu so that it will be activated when the user moves their mouse off the secondary buttons. To do this, the first thing you need to do is create the invisible button. Go to Insert → New Symbol, select the Button option, and enter **invisible button** into the Name field.

10. When the Symbol Editor opens, select the hit frame, insert a keyframe, and draw a rectangle that is about 25 pixels larger than the entire menu (with the secondary buttons visible).

> Because the button only has one state (hit)—thereby making it invisible—it doesn't matter at all what color is used when it's drawn in the Symbol Editor.

11. Return to the menu Movie Clip. Add a new layer, and call it **invisible button**. Click and drag the new layer so that it is at the bottom of the layer stack.

12. Select frame 2 of the invisible button layer, and add a keyframe.

13. When the newly created keyframe still selected, click and drag the invisible button symbol from the Library onto the Stage. Position it so it is directly behind the menu. When you've done this, the scene should look something like this:

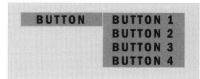

14. Now, you need to add the ActionScript that will push the playhead back to frame 1 (simulating the disappearance of the secondary menu buttons) when the user moves their mouse off the secondary menu buttons onto the invisible button you've just added. First, select the invisible button, and then open the Actions window (Window → Actions).

15. Add a goto() action. Then, in the Parameters panel with the event section of the script selected in the ActionScript text box, select Roll Over as the event.

16. Then, select Frame Number from the Type drop-down menu, enter **1** into the Frame field, and make sure that the Go to and Play radio button is selected.

Congratulations, you've made a simple drop-down, drag-out menu. Go back to the main Timeline, and drag the menu Movie Clip onto the Stage. To test your creation, go to Control → Test Movie.

Making a Draggable Pop-up Window

In HTML-based web design, you can use Dynamic HTML (DHTML) to create a pop-up browser window whose size you can set. This is handy for providing your users with information that is far better suited to a small, constrained space that is somewhat tangential.

In Flash, you can simulate the same sort of thing by creating a Movie Clip that appears when the user clicks a button (or some other element) and whose position can be changed by a simple click-and-drag movement. The cool thing about doing this sort of thing in Flash is that, unlike in HTML where the appearance of the pop-up browser window is fixed, you can create a draggable pop-up window that looks any way you want.

In the following sections, you're going to explore how to create one of these draggable pop-up windows.

> Because the Movie Clip is part of the larger Flash movie, your users won't be able to drag it outside the confines of the SWF file.

An example of a draggable pop-up window has been included in the Appendix A directory of the book's CD-ROM (in both SWF and FLA formats).

Creating the Window and Buttons

The first step in the process of creating a draggable pop-up menu is to create the button upon which the user will need to click to drag the pop-up window around the screen. The look of this button will be determined by the look of your pop-up window. For the purposes of this tutorial, you're going to create a simple rectangular button that will be attached to the upper-right corner of the pop-up window proper:

1. Go to Insert → New Symbol. When the Create New Symbol dialog box opens, make sure the Button option is selected, enter **drag button** into the Name field, and click OK.

2. When the Symbol Editor opens, create a simple rectangular button that looks something like this: **DRAG ME**

> Although you can incorporate any kind of rollover change to the button, it certainly isn't necessary for the functionality of the pop-up window.

3. Now that you've created the button upon which the user will click to drag the pop-up window, it's time to create the window. Go to Insert → New Symbol. When the Create New Symbol dialog box opens, select the Movie Clip option, enter **pop-up window** into the Name field, and click OK.

4. When the Symbol Editor opens, rename the single existing layer **window**. From here, select frame 1 (which is automatically a keyframe) of the window layer, and draw the rectangle that will serve as the window.

5. Now, add a second layer, and call it **actions**.

6. With the first keyframe of the actions layer selected, open the Actions panel (Window → Actions), expand the Movie Control category, and add a `stop()` action.

7. Now, add an additional layer, and call it **drag button**.

8. Now, with the first keyframe of the drag button layer selected, move the drag button symbol from the Library onto the Stage. Position it so that it is sitting just outside the top-right corner of the window. At this point, the Movie Clip (complete with the pop-up window and drag button symbols) should look something like this:

Where you position the drag button symbol relative to the pop-up window symbol is up to you. Remember, however, that it should probably be in close proximity to the window so that users associate the two.

9. Now it's time to add the ActionScript that will let the user drag the pop-up window around the screen when they click the drag button. First, select the drag button symbol. Then open the Actions window by going to Window → Actions.

10. In either Normal or Expert mode (it's up to you), attach the following script to the drag button:

```
on (press) {
 startDrag ("");
}
on (release) {
 stopDrag ();
}
```

If you are entering the script in Normal mode, the startDrag() and stopDrag() actions are located in the Movie Control category.

11. Now that you've created the button by which the user will drag the window around, as well as the window itself, it's time to create a button that will close down the pop-up window once it has been opened. First, go to Insert → New Symbol. When the Create New Symbol dialog box opens, select the Button option, enter **close button** into the Name field, and click OK.

12. When the Symbol Editor opens, create the button that the user will click to close the pop-up window.

13. When you're finished, return to the pop-up window Movie Clip, create a new layer called **close button**, select the new layer's first keyframe, and drag the close Button symbol from the Library onto the Stage. Position it where you'd like it to reside in the window. At this point, the pop-up window Movie Clip should look something like this:

As in the case of the drag Button symbol, where you position the close button symbol relative to the pop-up window symbol is pretty much up to you. Remember, however, that it should probably be near the window so that users associate the two.

14. From here, you can add the ActionScript to the button that will close the pop-up window. First, select the close Button symbol, and then go to Window → Actions.

15. When the Actions window opens, add the following script either in Normal or Expert mode:

```
on (release) {
    _root.window._visible = false;
}
```

Instead of putting `false` as the value for the `_visible` property, you can also put 0.

Essentially, this script will set the visibility of the pop-up window Movie Clip to `false` (making it invisible) when the user clicks the Close button.

Integrating the Window into Your Movie

Now, your pop-up Movie Clip is pretty much finished. From here, however, you have to integrate it with the main Timeline. This will include a button (to which some elementary Action-Script will be attached) on which the user will need to click to make the window "pop up." Also, you'll need to include some script in the first keyframe of the main Timeline that will make the pop-up Movie Clip initially invisible—it certainly wouldn't do any good if the window was already visible before the user clicked the button to make it pop up, now would it? Follow these steps:

1. First, switch back to the main Timeline. Create a new layer called **actions**, and add a `stop()` action to its first keyframe.

2. Then, go to Insert → New Symbol. When the Create New Symbol dialog box opens, select the Button option, enter **open button** in the Name field, and click OK.

3. When the Symbol Editor opens, create the button upon which the user will click to make the pop-up window "pop up."

4. When you've finished, switch back to the main Timeline. Create a new layer and call it **open button**. With the first keyframe of the newly created layer selected, drag the Open button onto the Stage.

5. When you've got the Open button positioned exactly where you want, you can add the ActionScript that will make the pop-up window appear. Select the Open button and go to Window → Actions.

6. When the Actions window opens, add the following script (either in Normal or Expert mode):

```
on (release) {
    window._visible = true;
}
```

> Instead of putting true as the value for the _visible property, you can also put 1.

This script will set the visibility of the pop-up window Movie Clip to true (making it visible) when the user clicks the Open button.

7. Now, you need to make sure the pop-up window Movie Clip is invisible when the movie starts playing. To do with, you'll add a simple script to the first keyframe of the main Timeline. First, select the first keyframe in the actions layer , and go to Window → Actions.

8. From here, add the following script *above* the stop() action you had previously added:
   ```
   window._visible = false;
   ```

9. This script will set the visibility of the pop-up window Movie Clip to false (making it invisible) when the playhead enters frame 1. From there, it will wait until the user clicks the Open button—thereby making it appear (pop up).

10. Now that all the necessary ActionScript is in place, it's time to add the last component to the main Timeline—the pop-up window. To do this, first create a new layer called **pop up window**.

11. From here, simply select the first keyframe in the pop-up window layer, and drag the pop-up window Movie Clip from the Library onto the Stage.

12. Now, for one of the most important parts: You need to give the pop-up window Movie Clip an instance name. To do this, select the symbol on the Stage, and open the Property Inspector by going to Window → Properties. Enter **window** into the Instance Name field.

Voila! You've now created a draggable pop-up window. To test your amazing creation, go to Control → Test Movie, and marvel at the power of Flash.

Opening a Local HTML File from a Flash CD-ROM

One of the greatest aspects of Flash development is that the software enables you to create stand-alone Flash projectors that will run on both Macintosh and Windows platforms. This feature makes it possible for you to distribute your Flash work via cross-platform or hybrid CD-ROMs, thereby greatly increasing the scope of Flash projects that you produce. CD-ROMs afford more storage space for large files and dodge many of the plug-in or connection speed issues that can be so problematic when trying to deliver Flash content over the Web.

> To learn more about Flash and CD-ROM development, see Chapter 29.

When working with Flash to produce a CD-ROM you will find that the process of authoring your movie is similar to what you do when targeting a production for an Internet audience. There are a few minor differences, though. You will encounter one difference when trying to access a local HTML file stored on your CD-ROM. If your Flash movie contains certain content that is best displayed in a web browser, all you need to do is ask Flash to target the URL and it will open the file in a browser window. The problem when it comes to CD-ROM

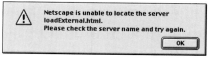

development is that Flash is geared to do this in a web environment, not from a local computer. The getURL() action that works so well on the Web is comparatively crippled when working with local files on a CD-ROM. If you have ever tried this, you are likely to be acquainted with an error message.

Another difference with CD-ROM development is that when Flash is on the Internet, your SWF movie will generally be stored in the same place, and by pointing to a particular URL, you can direct your audience to the movie you want to present. Unfortunately, this is not the case with CD-ROM delivery. Every computer and every CD-ROM drive is different. For Macintoshes, users can name their hard drives. The default *Macintosh HD* name that ships with a new G4 or iMac is not guaranteed to be the name of the computer. For Windows, this is equally complicated. CD-ROM drives are named with letters and vary greatly from one system to the next. One solution would be to hard-code the path, as in:

```
getURL("file:///Macintosh%20HD/Desktop%20Folder/FlashCD/index.html");
```

This works great—for one computer. Obviously if you are going to distribute your work to a large audience it is essential to make sure everyone can access the local HTML files you need to include with your project. To do this, you must be able to retrieve the absolute path to the file you want to display. That way, no matter which computer plays your disc, regardless of how it is set up, your movie will be able to find the correct files on the CD-ROM. Therefore, in the world of CD-ROM development, an absolute path is crucial to the creation of an error-free disc. The reason is that all files for the project are generally stored on the CD-ROM. If you can point the movie to the root directory of the CD-ROM, finding any supporting or related files is easy. This is because the hierarchy of the CD-ROM does not change; once the disc is burned, it is final. The different configurations of your audiences' computers are not, however, and that's why you need the absolute path.

Retrieving an Absolute Path

To retrieve the absolute path, you can write a function. This way, anytime you need to get the path, the function can do the work for you. Here's how:

1. Create a new movie (File→ New). Save the file and name it **HTML_Launcher**. Click the empty keyframe at frame 1, Layer 1 and choose Window → Actions. Enter the following statement:

```
trace(_url);
```

Select Control → Test Movie. The Output window spits out a long string of information. This is the absolute path to the file HTML_Launcher. The _url property returns the absolute path to the SWF file as a string. Notice that the phrase `HTML%5Flauncher.swf` is written at the end of the URL string. Where this is the name of file itself, everything that comes before it is the absolute path that gets you to the file.

> The character sequence %5F is the URL-encoded equivalent of the underscore character (_). When Flash deals with URLs, all information is encoded in this fashion. To learn more about working with encoded strings see the `escape()` and `unescape()` functions in Flash MX's Reference panel.

2. Now that you have retrieved a URL for the movie, you have something with which to work. The idea is that if you can get to the location of the movie, then you should be able to find all of its associated files.

   Return to the Actions panel where you entered the `trace()` action earlier, delete it, and enter the following statements:

   ```
   function moviePath(){
   var lastSlash=_url.lastIndexOf("/");
   var path=_url.substring(0,lastSlash+1);
   return path;
   }
   ```

   This function will return the absolute path of the folder where the movie `HTML_Launcher` resides. Now that you have seen the ActionScript that will do this, you can examine it in detail:

   - The first line declares the function under the name `moviePath()`. This particular function requires no arguments, so the parentheses that follow it are blank.

   - The second line initializes the variable `lastSlash`. The string method `lastIndexOf` stores the position of the last occurrence of the slash character (/) as it appears in the URL to this movie.

   - The third line initializes the variable `path`. The method `subString()` creates a new string based on the movie's URL. This new string starts from the beginning of the URL, at position 0, and ends at the last occurrence of the slash character plus 1. The +1 expression ensures that the slash will be included in the new string `path`. If the slash were not included, the path would not list the URL to the movie location properly.

   - The `return` statement in the fourth line allows your function to pass the string contained in the `path` variable to other parts of your movie.

   Now that the function is in place, you can call it from any location in your movie. It is important to note that the function is located in frame 1, Scene 1 of the movie. This makes the function one of the first things that Flash will read as it starts to play the movie, thus making it accessible at anytime throughout the movie's playback.

Launching the External HTML File

Before you can continue with this lesson you need to prepare a few things. First, go to the Appendix A folder in this book's CD-ROM and copy the file loadExternal.html to the same location where HTML_Launcher resides. Alternately, you can create your own HTML document if you prefer. In any case, this will simulate having a local HTML file on CD-ROM for the time being. Also, you will need to create a button. The look and feel of the button is up to you. Once those tasks are complete, you can continue:

1. Drag your button to the Stage. Select the button and choose Window → Actions to display the Actions panel. Enter the following statements in the panel:

```
on(release){
 var link=_root.moviePath():
 getURL(link+"loadExternal.html");
}
```

These statements are what call the function and execute the action to launch the HTML file. The variable link calls the custom function moviePath() and stores its value: the absolute path to your movie. Because the function was created on the main Timeline, the _root reference is included to properly target the function. Then the getURL() action opens the HTML file. It concatenates the path (stored in link) with the name of HTML file. getURL() accepts its arguments as string data. Because the link variable already contains string information from the moviePath() function, it is easily joined with the name of the HTML file to create a path that points directly to that file.

2. Save the movie and select Control → Test Movie. Click the button and watch the HTML file open in your computer's default browser!

3. To test and see how flexible this is, try the following experiment: Quit Flash and navigate to the folder where your movie and the HTML file are saved. Copy or move HTML_Launcher.swf and loadExternal.html together to a different location. Open the SWF movie, click the button, and see what happens. Because the ActionScript you wrote will dynamically generate an absolute path for the location of the movie, you can run it from anywhere! This should illustrate the effectiveness of the function. Because the _url property will always tell you the location of the movie, you can strip the filename from the end of the URL and use the absolute path to access supporting files, other movies, and so on.

The important thing to remember is that this function will get you to the folder where the main movie resides. From there, it is up to you to point to the correct file. For example, if your movie were in the root directory of a CD-ROM and your HTML files were in a subfolder named `webDocs`, you would have to change your script a bit. The new script would read:

```
getURL(link+"webDocs/loadExternal.html");
```

The actions attached to the button must reflect the correct path to the file. However, because the location of files on the CD-ROM cannot be changed once the disc is burned, you are safe with a hard-coded path like this. As long as you correctly enter the paths in your ActionScript, you will always be able to access the files you need.

Although this rendition of the lesson was geared toward loading an external HTML file, Flash MX now supports several different kinds of external media. It is now possible to load JPEG images and MP3 sounds directly into your Flash movies from an external location. Use the techniques described in this section to ensure your movie is always able to locate the directory where these external files are saved. For example:

```
var photo=root.moviePath();
loadMovie(photo+"loader_images/image1.jpg","frame");
```

Here, the `moviePath()` function is called and stored in the variable `photo`. The resulting path is plugged into the `loadMovie()` action, where files in the folder `loader_images` are imported and loaded into the clip instance named `frame`. To read more about loading JPEG images from an external location, see Chapter 17; to read about loading external MP3 files, see Chapter 22.

Using Preloaders to Enhance Your Audience's Experience

As Flash has grown in complexity, so have the files that it produces. In fact, Flash movies can now be far too bandwidth intensive to play immediately. As a result, a device called a *preloader* has come into widespread use. Essentially, a preloader is a small animation that plays while your movie is loaded. When the process is finished, the preloader stops and the main movie begins playing. So, a preloader gives your audience something to watch while the main movie loads. Otherwise, they would be stuck staring at a blank screen in their browser window (something that can easily be mistaken for a computer crash) while your movie loads.

Generally speaking, there are two kinds of preloaders: simple and complex. A simple preloader features a looping animation that plays repeatedly, giving no indication as to the portion of the movie left to load. A complex preloader, on the other hand, not only features a looping animation of some sort but also contains a dynamic indication of the amount of the movie that has loaded—like a loader bar or a percentage indication.

In this section, you are going to create both a simple and a complex preloader.

Creating a Simple Preloader

The simple preloader, which features a straightforward looping animation, is the easiest way to entertain your viewers while your main movie loads.

> Because the preloader animation plays while the main movie is loading, it must be small enough (in terms of file size) to download and play immediately. If not, your audience will have to wait for the preloader to load—which defeats its purpose.

An example of a simple preloader has been included in the Appendix A directory of the book's CD-ROM (in both SWF and FLA formats).

The process by which you create a simple preloader involves using a Movie Clip and some relatively straightforward ActionScript:

1. First, make sure the movie to which you want to add the preloader is open.

2. Open the Scene panel by going to Window → Scene. (For the purposes of this tutorial, we'll assume your entire movie resides in a single scene.)

3. Now, rename the existing scene to **main movie**.

4. Before you continue, select the final frame in your main movie, open the Property Inspector (Window → Properties), and enter **final** into the Label field. The reason for this will become apparent a number of steps down the line.

5. Now, add a second scene (by clicking the Add Scene button) called **preloader**. Make sure the preloader scene is *above* the main movie scene in the Scene panel.

6. Select the preloader scene.

7. Select the single layer (Layer 1), and rename it to **actions**.

8. Select frame 5 in the newly named actions layer, and enter a keyframe by going to Insert → Keyframe.

9. With the newly created blank keyframe selected, and the keyframe still selected, open the Property Inspector (Window → Properties).

10. Enter **check** into the Label field.

11. Now, select frame 10 in the actions layer and add another keyframe.

12. With the Property Inspector, add the label **loop** to the newly created keyframe.

13. Select frame 5 (check), and open the Actions panel (Window → Actions).

14. Make sure you're in Expert mode (which can be accessed by selecting Expert Mode from the Actions panel's View Options drop-down menu). Now, enter the following script into the ActionScript text box:

```
if (_framesloaded<_totalframes) {
  gotoAndPlay("loop");
```

```
  } else {
    gotoAndPlay("main movie", 1);
  }
```

Essentially, this script will check the number of frames loaded against the total frames in the movie. If the total number of frames loaded at the point that the script executes is less than the total number of frames in the movie, the playhead will go back to the loop frame. On the other hand, if the total number of frames loaded at the point that the script executes is equal to the total number of frames in the movie, the playhead will skip to frame 1 in the main movie scene.

15. Now it's time to insert the necessary ActionScript that will make sure the movie will continue to recheck whether the main movie has loaded (after the initial check). First, select frame 10 (loop).

16. Open the Actions panel, expand the Movie Control category, and add a `goto()` action to the ActionScript text box.

17. In the Parameters pane, select <current scene> from the Scene drop-down menu, select Frame Number from the Type drop-down menu, enter **1** into the Frame field, and make sure the Go to and Play radio button is selected. By doing this, the movie will automatically jump back to the first frame in the movie. From there, the playhead will progress to frame 5 and reexecute the script that checks to see if all the frames have been loaded.

18. Now that you've got the necessary scripts set up that will check whether the main movie has loaded, you need to add the actual looping animation that will entertain your audience while the ActionScript is doing its thing.

19. Create a Movie Clip of a simple animation. For example, you could create an animation of the word *Loading* that fades in and out. The only real limitations you have (beyond your own design constraints) is that the Movie Clip must be small enough (in terms of file size) that it will load and play immediately.

> You probably want to craft your preloader animation so that it will loop smoothly (without any jumps as it reaches the final frame and returns to the first frame).

20. Now, return to the main Timeline in the preloader scene.

21. Create a new layer and call it **preloader animation**.

22. Click and drag the preloader animation layer so that it is below the actions layer.

23. Now, with the first keyframe in the preloader animation layer selected, click and drag your animation Movie Clip from the Library onto the Stage. From here, you can position it exactly where you want.

24. The final thing that you need to do is add a `stop()` action to the final keyframe of the main movie scene so that, once it plays through, the playhead won't go back to frame 1 in the first scene (the preloader scene). To do this, switch to the main movie scene. Add a new layer and call it **actions**.

25. Select the first keyframe in the newly created actions layer, open the Actions panel (Window → Actions), expand the Movie Control category, and add a `stop()` action to the ActionScript text box.

Congratulations—you've just created a simple preloader. The Movie Clip will continue to loop while the movie checks (and, if necessary, rechecks) whether all the frames in the main movie scene have loaded.

> Because you are running the entire movie off your hard drive, you'll find that the main movie scene will load almost instantaneously, and therefore the preloader animation will barely play. If you want to actually see your preloader in action, test your movie (Control → Test Movie) and then go to View → Bandwidth Profiler. From here choose View → Show Streaming. This will simulate the movie as if it were streamed. Remember, you can choose the speed of the simulated modem from the View menu while you are testing the movie.

Creating a Complex Preloader

A simple preloader is fine if you want to provide minimum feedback to your audience while your main movie is loading. But let's face it, a simple looping animation can get pretty boring if the user has absolutely no clue as to the amount of the movie that has loaded (or what is left to load). This is where a complex preloader comes in. When you create a complex preloader, you create a dynamic animation that changes based on the amount of the movie that has loaded.

There are lots of different ways to create a complex preloader. In this tutorial, you are going to learn how to create a preloader in which a hollow horizontal bar gradually fills as the movie loads.

 An example of a complex preloader has been included in the Appendix A directory of the book's CD-ROM (in both SWF and FLA formats).

> The preloader created in this tutorial is not what you might expect. Instead of filling from left to right, it actually starts out in the center and fills outward both to the left and to the right. The reasons for the difference are purely aesthetic. There are so many preloader bars out there that fill from left to right that you'll attract attention with something a little out of the ordinary.

In this tutorial, you'll be employing the extremely useful `getBytesLoaded` and `getBytesTo-`
`tal` methods to determine the amount of your movie that's loaded and to drive the progress
of actual load bar animation:

1. With the movie open in which you want to add a preloader, create a new scene (before
   the actual movie proper), and call it **preloader**.

2. Now, create a Movie Clip called **preloader bar** by going to Insert → New Symbol, selecting the Movie Clip radio button, entering the name into the Name field, and clicking OK.

3. When the Symbol Editor opens, draw a filled horizontal rectangle. Ultimately, the rectangle will act as the actual preloader bar. As a result, you'll probably want to make sure
   it's long—say 5 centimeters (2 inches)—and thin.

> Don't group the preloader bar symbol's stroke and fill.

4. Now, open the Library (Window → Library), select the preloader bar Movie Clip, and
   duplicate it (by choosing Duplicate from the Library Options drop-down menu).

5. When the Duplicate Symbol dialog box opens, enter **preloader bar outline** into the
   Name field, and click OK.

6. Next, open the preloader bar outline Movie Clip by either double-clicking it in the
   Library or choosing it from the Edit Symbols drop-down menu located in the Scene and
   Symbol bar (located in the top-right corner of your screen).

7. Select the preloader bar outline symbol's fill and delete it. When you do this, you'll be
   left with an empty outline.

8. Now, switch back to the preloader bar Movie Clip. First, change the name of the layer
   with the horizontal rectangle to **bar**. Then, add a second keyframe in frame 2.

9. Add a new layer and change its name to **actions**.

10. In Expert mode, attach the following script to the first keyframe of the actions layer:
    ```
    setProperty (this, _xscale, (_root.getBytesLoaded() /
        _root.getBytesTotal()*100));
    ```

11. Essentially, this script checks the percentage of the movie that has loaded (by dividing
    the movie's total bytes by the bytes that have already loaded).

12. Now, switch back to the main Timeline. Rename the existing layer **loader**, and add an
    additional layer called **actions**.

13. With the first keyframe of the loader layer selected, drag the preloader bar outline Movie
    Clip onto the Stage. Use the Align panel (Window → Align) to align it horizontally/center
    and vertically/center to the Stage. By doing this, the preloader bar outline symbol will be
    placed in the middle of the Stage.

14. Select the second frame in the loader layer, and go to Insert → Keyframe.

15. Now, with the second keyframe of the loader layer still selected, drag the preloader bar Movie Clip onto the Stage. Use the Align panel to align it horizontally/center and vertically/center to the Stage. By doing this, you not only stick the symbol in the middle of the Stage, but you also place it in the same space as the preloader bar outline symbol—which is absolutely vital!

16. OK, now that you've placed the various preloader bar graphics, it's time to create the script that checks to see if all the frames in the main movie have loaded. Using Expert mode, attach the following script to the second keyframe in the actions layer:

```
if (_root.getBytesLoaded() != _root.getBytesTotal()) {
    gotoAndPlay (2);
}
else {
    gotoAndPlay ("intro", 1);
}
```

17. Basically, this script forces the movie to stay in frame 2 (and continually run and rerun the script) if the amount of bytes does not equal the total bytes of the main movie. Now, if the amount of bytes loaded does equal the main movie's total amount of bytes, the script makes the movie jump forward to the main movie.

> In this example, the gotoAndPlay() action references the first frame in a scene called intro. When it comes to making your own preloader, you'll need to enter the name of the second scene in your movie (which contains the main movie itself that needs to be preloaded) instead of intro.

18. Now, test your movie by going to Control → Test Movie. As was the case of the simple preloader you created earlier, because you are running the entire movie off your hard drive, you'll find that the main movie scene will load almost instantaneously, and therefore the preloader animation will barely play. If you want to actually see your preloader in action, go to View → Bandwidth Profiler. From here choose View → Show Streaming. This will simulate the movie as if it were being streamed.

Using an Array to Create a Dynamic Greeting

One of the most useful aspects of ActionScript is that you can use it to make your movie less predictable. Rather than have text and graphics appear in the same place, at the same time, and in the same color with each repeated visit to your website, you can pleasantly surprise your audience with a little variety. In this section you will learn how to use ActionScript to create a simple *array* that displays a different greeting each time someone navigates to the home page of a website or interactive interface.

An array is an informational structure organized into compartments, with each compartment holding a piece (or pieces) of information. An array is like a dresser (bureau, wardrobe, chest of drawers, or whatever you'd like to call it). It is one large structure that holds containers (the drawers). Each container can then hold information (the clothing). For example, a dresser has drawers for socks, underwear, T-shirts, and sweaters. Each drawer is a discreet location for each article of clothing. An array works in much the same way. Where a dresser has drawers, an array has *slots*; each slot can contain a piece of information: a string, a number, a variable, or even another array. And because an array is a single item, wherever it goes, it carries with it all of the information it contains. This makes it much easier to move information around as a group rather than as individual pieces. So, in a nutshell, arrays make it easier to store and work with collections of information because they keep their contents neat and organized.

The variety of applications for arrays is almost dizzying. In fact, the usefulness of arrays could fill not one but several books! This section shows you how to create an array in ActionScript and use it to affect some interesting and dynamic changes in a Flash movie.

To complete this exercise, you will need to retrieve some files from this book's CD-ROM. Go to the Appendix A directory and copy the entire ARRAY folder onto your computer's desktop. This project requires several SWF files. It simulates the interactive interface or website for an international club or cultural service organization. You will make changes to this project so that every time a visitor goes to the first section of the movie, a new translation of *hello* is displayed in the upper-left corner of the movie. Open the file `international_club.fla` and select Control → Test Movie. As you click the buttons that line the bottom of the movie, you will notice that different words appear at the top. However, when you click the yellow button to return to the first section, Greeting, you see no text at all. This is where you will create your array.

To create an array that displays a greeting:

1. Open `banner.fla` included the ARRAY folder. At this point the entire ARRAY folder should be saved on your computer. Click the middle of the Stage. If it is not open already, press Cmd/Ctrl+F3 to open the Property Inspector. You will notice that what you clicked is not the Stage, but a Movie Clip instance named `text_clip`. You will create your array in a script attached to this Movie Clip.

2. With the Movie Clip still selected, choose Window → Actions to open the Actions panel.

3. Enter the following statements:

```
onClipEvent(load){
    greeting=new Array();
}
```

This script creates a new array named `greeting` when the Movie Clip is loaded onto the Stage.

4. Click after the semicolon character to start a new line and type:

```
greeting[0]="Hello!";
```

The script should now read:

```
onClipEvent(load){
    greeting=new Array();
    greeting[0]="Hello!";
}
```

This line is very important. It creates the first slot in your array and stores in it the string `Hello!` Arrays identify their slots with numbers, and they start counting at 0.

5. You can now add a few more slots to your array and fill each with another new string:

```
onClipEvent(load){
    greeting=new Array();
    greeting[0]="Hello!";
    greeting[1]="Bonjour!";
    greeting[2]="Hola!";
}
```

6. The `greeting` array has a more international flavor now. By adding strings in slots 1 and 2, the array now contains a grand total of three slots: 0, 1, and 2.

7. Now that the array has a few items, you can put them to use. Click after the last semicolon, press Return/Enter, and add the following statements:

```
choice=Math.floor(Math.random()*greeting.length);
text=greeting[choice];
```

These lines should fall between the line that contains `Hola!` and the last curly brace.

So what do these statements do? Good question; actually they are some of the most important in the entire movie:

- `choice` is a variable that stores a random number generated by the expression on the other side of the assignment operator (=). The random number will always be between 0 and the last number in the array.

- The `length()` method (part of ActionScript's array object) retrieves the length of, or number of items in, an array. This number is multiplied by a random number in the range of 0 to .999... and then rounded down to the next-lower integer. Given the current length of the array, this will always be an integer between 0 and 2. That information is used in the next line.

- With the help of the array access operator, the array item stored in slot `choice` is retrieved from the `greeting` array and plugged into the variable `text`. For example, if `choice` is 2, the variable `text` will be set to the value of the `greeting` array's slot 2, or `Hola!` Of course the variable `text` is used for the text field inside the `banner` Movie Clip. Whatever value is stored in `text` will appear in the text field; in this case, it's `Hola!`

8. Take the opportunity to test this. Select Control → Test Movie. The movie will appear on your screen and display one of the three greetings in the array. Close the movie and test it again. You have a one-in-three chance of seeing the same thing; though, hopefully you'll see a different greeting this time. If you don't believe it, test your movie over and over. Each time you are likely to see a different greeting appear on your screen.

9. Add a few more lines to your script. The final script should look like Figure A.1.

10. Save your movie and test it again. If you repeat the testing process several times, you will see a greater variety of greetings. This script still works even though the size of the array has more than doubled. Why? Because you are using the item count or `length` property of the array to set the bounds for your selection. As the slots in the array increase, so does the range of numbers it has to choose from when this script makes its random selection.

11. To test this movie in context, close the `banner.fla` file and open `international_club.swf`. Select Control → Test Movie and navigate to the various sections of this movie. Be sure to click the yellow greeting button frequently. Notice that each time this button is clicked a new greeting appears. This works because `banner.swf` is being loaded at `_level1` of the Flash Player. Each time the movie is loaded, the Movie Clip with your array script is also loaded, thereby creating the array, making a greeting choice, and printing it to the text field.

To see some of the other little scripting tricks going on with this movie, look at the scripts attached to the brown, red, and green buttons on the Timeline of the `international_club.fla` file.

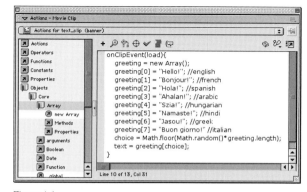

Figure A.1

The final script increases the number of international greetings to eight.

ActionScript Reference

Welcome to the ActionScript Reference section. This section is unlike any other throughout the rest of the book, but we hope you'll find it just as useful. Rather than present information in a step-by-step fashion, we've intended this reference to be used on an "as-needed" basis. If there is a term you want to use but are unsure of the syntax, or if you want to do something but are not certain which ActionScript elements will be most useful, this is the section for you.

This section is organized by category of the Action-Script language:

Actions The built-in commands of ActionScript. You use actions for navigation and Timeline control.

Functions Information processors that perform common tasks.

Properties Terms that set and retrieve the attributes of Timelines, Buttons, and Movie Clips.

Operators Used to evaluate and change the value of expressions.

Object and Timeline References Terms that allow you to target and define and the scope of elements in your movies.

Predefined Objects Used to manipulate the data associated with Flash's built-in objects (MovieClip, Sound, Color, and so on).

If you aren't sure how to find a particular term, this organization will prove to be most helpful. Think about what it is you want to do; do you want to change the way something looks? Then perhaps you will find it in the "Properties" section. Are you interested in controlling the playback of a Timeline? See the "Actions" section. Conversely, there may be times when you know the term but are unsure the category to which it belongs. You can overcome this easily. If you wanted to find the entry for `start-Drag()`, for instance, where would you begin to look? Well, `startDrag()` controls the drag-and-drop ability of Movie Clips. This is a type of Timeline control, so "Actions" would be the category to check. Once you have narrowed things down to a particular category, entries are listed alphabetically.

This is not a complete ActionScript reference. ActionScript was a big language before the release of Flash MX, and it is even larger now given all of the program's enhancements. A truly complete reference would probably use more pages than this entire book. What you will find here is a guide to terms we have deemed to be the *essential* elements of the ActionScript language. These are the terms that, if you had to pack your "ActionScript suitcase" to live abroad for a year, you would take with you. It's not everything, but it includes the things you can't do without.

Sample Entry

The key to getting the most out of this section is understanding how each entry is constructed. This section describes a sample entry.

Title and Version (1+, 2+, 3+, 4+, 5+, 6)

COMPONENTS:
`term(argument,"stringArgument")`
`argumentObject.term`

Each term is listed in this regular, sans-serif type, while any arguments you must specify are in sans-serif *italics*. Any arguments that must be specified as strings appear in quotes.

EXAMPLE:
This section is not listed for each entry. In some cases, it is not needed because the term is self-explanatory. For others, there are so many examples throughout the rest of the book, another example seems like overkill. For many entries, however, this section presents a contextual example of the term in action. Feel free to use this code in your own movies. Expand it, change it, tear it to pieces, do whatever you need to do to get things running properly. For some entries, there is not enough room to print parts of the script on a single line. In these cases, the character ➡ will be used to show you that the code should continue on the same line but can't because of the size limitations of this book's pages.

Actions

Actions are the built-in commands of ActionScript. Use actions to create conditional statements and loop routines and to direct the performance and playback of a Flash movie.

break (4+)

COMPONENTS:
`break`

This action works within a loop and causes a script to jump out of the loop to the first statement after the loop when the action is encountered. This action is helpful if you would like to exit a loop before it has finished.

EXAMPLE:
```
onClipEvent(load){
    taxRate=.0875;
    grandTotal=subTotal*taxRate;
    for(i=1;i<10;i++){
        if(eval("_root.selQty"+i)==0){
            this.attachMovie("alertClip",
            ➥"alert",1);
            break;
        }
        totalQty+=eval("_root.selQty"+i);
    }
}
```
The loop in this script uses break to jump out of the loop and creates a new instance of the clip alertClip if any of the variables named selQty1, selQty2...selQty9 are equal to zero. In practical application, the alertClip would be some sort of alert box informing the audience that there is a problem with how they entered data and telling them how to remedy the situation. break is placed carefully within the script. It causes the script to cease before the crucial statement updating the totalQty variable is executed. And it is called *after* the alert clip has been attached. See also the continue action.

continue (4+)

COMPONENTS:
continue

This statement disrupts the current flow of a loop. However, unlike break, the loop is not abandoned entirely; continue resumes with the next iteration of the loop. continue behaves differently depending on the kind of loop statement. In a while or do...while loop, the loop condition is checked before the loop resumes. In a for loop, the loop count is incremented and then the loop condition is checked. In a for...in loop, the loop resumes with the next property. To avoid errors, pay close attention to the flow of your loop statement when using continue.

EXAMPLE:
```
onClipEvent(load){
    taxRate=.0875;
    grandTotal=subTotal*taxRate;
    for(i=1;i<10;i++){
        if(eval("_root.selQty"+i)==0){
            continue;
        }
        totalQty+=eval("_root.selQty"+i);
    }
}
```
The loop in this script uses continue to jump out of the loop and resume iterations if any of the variables named selQty1, selQty2...selQty9 are equal to zero. See also the break action.

do...while (4+)

COMPONENTS:
```
do{
    statements;
} while(condition);
```
This loop syntax executes the statements and then checks the condition. The loop repeats in this fashion for as long as the condition is true. The syntax of the do...while loop ensures that the statements will be executed at least once before the condition is tested.

EXAMPLE:
```
x=0;
trace("the first 10 integers are:");
do{
    trace(x);
    x++
}while(x<10);
```
This script prints the phrase the first 10 integers are: followed by the numbers 0 1 2 3 4 5 6 7 8 9. The 11th time through the loop, x equals 10. Because 10 is not less than 10, the condition evaluates false and the loop ceases.

duplicateMovieClip (4+)

COMPONENTS:
duplicateMovieClip("target","instance",depth)

The `duplicateMovieClip()` action copies an instance of a Movie Clip. The action takes three arguments: *target*, the name of the instance to be duplicated entered as a string; *instance*, the name (also a string) assigned to the new duplicate; and *depth*, the clip layer where the duplicate is to be placed. The *depth* argument does not assign a movie `_level` for the new clip, but rather an internal depth (stacking level) in relation to the `target` clip. If, for example, the `target` clip is at a depth of 1, a duplicate can be placed below it at depth 0, or above it at depth 2. Internal depths are like virtual layers in the Timeline that host the clips. Clips with higher depth numbers will cover, or appear to be on top of, clips at a lower depth. Duplicated clips inherit the properties of the `target` clip but do not inherit any variables from the `target` Timeline. You can delete a duplicate clip with the `removeMovieclip()` action.

for (5+)

COMPONENTS:

```
for(initialize;condition;increment){
    statement(s);
}
```

The `for` action offers a compact alternative to the `while` loop syntax. Rather than use two additional lines to initialize a variable and increment the loop, a `for` loop places all elements of the loop syntax on a single line. The *initialize* argument sets an initial value for the loop counter variable; *condition* defines the condition that must evaluate as `true` for the loop to continue executing; and *increment* updates the counter variable. For as many times as *condition* is true, the loop will cause the *statement(s)* argument to execute.

After executing *statement(s)*, the `for` loop is updated before its condition is retested. If you require the loop to have multiple variables (that is, more than one counter or updater), separate them with commas.

EXAMPLE:

The following two loops are equivalent; each will execute until both `hi` and `lo` equal 5. Notice how the `for` syntax is much more economical:

```
for(hi=10,lo=0;hi!=lo;hi--,lo++){
    trace("hi: "+hi);
    trace("lo: "+lo);
}


hi=10;
lo=0;
while(hi!=lo){
    trace("hi: "+hi);
    trace("lo: "+lo);
    hi--;
    lo++;
}
```

for...in (5+)

COMPONENTS:

```
for(variable in object){
    statement(s);
}
```

The for...in loop structure performs actions or executes *statement(s)* over a series of properties belonging to an object or an array. The loop executes *statement(s)* for each property (stored in *variable*) that exists in the specified *object*. Use this action to cycle through the properties of an object and to either set, update, or retrieve information.

EXAMPLE:

```
for(item in _level0){
    clip=_root[item];
    if(typeof clip=="movieclip"){
        trace("path: "+targetPath(clip));
        // actions to prep clips, etc...
    }
}
```

This series of statements checks all elements of the _root Timeline. If an element is a Movie Clip, its target path is printed to the Output window. Additionally, you can use this as a "housekeeping" script to perform other actions with each Movie

Clip, such as set its X and Y coordinates, visibility, and so on.

fscommand (3+)

COMPONENTS:

fscommand("*command*","*arguments*")

Use fscommand to communicate with the application hosting a Flash movie. fscommand facilitates interaction between a movie and the stand-alone Flash Player. To read more about how fscommand can add to your stand-alone projectors, see Chapter 29. This term can also facilitate communication between a movie and a web browser via JavaScript or VBScript commands.

function (5+)

COMPONENTS:

```
function funName(arg1,arg2...argX){
    statement(s);
}
```

The function action constructs functions. A function is a data processing routine that can be performed many times. Use functions to create custom routines that do common or repetitive tasks in your movies. To create a function, you must specify a name for it (*funName*) and a job for it to perform (*statement(s)*). Optionally, you can specify arguments if they are necessary to pass parameters to the function.

EXAMPLE:

A simple function requires no arguments. The following function sends the main Timeline back to its beginning when invoked:

```
function rewind(){
    gotoAndStop(1);
}
```

More complicated functions such as the next one require arguments but have greater flexibility and power.

This function first checks to see if the correct number of arguments has been specified. If not, it prints a message to the Output window and exits

the function. If arguments have been correctly specified, it returns the product of the arguments:

```
function times (op1, op2){
    if(op1==undefined || op2==undefined){
        trace("needs arguments");
        return;
    }else{
        return op1*op2;
    }
}
```

return produces a value, but it is not immediately accessible. To have the function return a result you can use, assign it to a variable, such as in this statement:

```
prod=_root.times(2,2);
```

For the previous function, the variable prod would contain the value 4. The function would return 4, and that value would then be passed to the prod variable.

getURL (2+/4+)

COMPONENTS:

getURL("*target*","*window*","*varMethod*")

The getURL() action allows Flash to work outside the movie where the action is called. It can:

- Open a URL on the Internet
- Pass data to a server-side script
- Communicate with a host Director movie

getURL takes up to three arguments. *target* specifies the file to be opened or the command to be sent; *window* allows you to target a specific window in a browser or frameset. Each argument is specified as a string. ActionScript supports the following reserved names:

_self targets the current frame in the active window.

_blank targets a new default browser window.

_parent targets the current window and replaces only the frameset where the movie is currently sitting.

_top targets the current window and replaces all framesets with the new URL.

The third argument, *varMethod* (only supported in Flash Player versions 4 and above), allows you to pass information to a server-side application using either the GET or POST methods. To learn more about these methods, see Chapter 17.

gotoAndPlay (2+)

COMPONENTS:
gotoAndPlay(*frameNumber*)
gotoAndPlay("*frameLabel*")
gotoAndPlay("*scene*",*frameNumber*)
gotoAndPlay("*scene*","*frameLabel*")

This action sends the movie's playback to the specified frame, scene, or frame label and resumes playing from the new location. Specify *frameNumber* as an integer and both *frameLabel* and *scene* as strings (in quotes). If no scene is noted in the first argument slot, Flash applies the action to the present scene.

gotoAndStop (2+)

COMPONENTS:
gotoAndStop(*frameNumber*)
gotoAndStop("*frameLabel*")
gotoAndStop("*scene*","*frameNumber*")
gotoAndStop("*scene*","*frameLabel*")

This action sends the movie's playback head to the specified frame, scene, or frame label and halts playback at the new location. Specify *frameNumber* as an integer and both *frameLabel* and *scene* as strings (in quotes). If no scene is noted in the first argument slot, Flash applies the action to the present scene.

if (4+)

COMPONENTS:
if(*conditionalExpression*){
    statement(s);
}

Use the if action to compose a conditional statement. The *conditionalExpression* argument must be an expression that returns a Boolean value. When the condition evaluates as true, the *statement(s)* is

executed; when it returns false, it is ignored. Additionally, use the else action in conjunction with an if conditional statement. else provides alternative statements to be executed if the statements that come before it evaluate false.

loadMovie (3+)

COMPONENTS:
loadMovie("*URL*","*target*","*varMethod*")

Use the loadMovie() action to load additional SWF files. Parameters for this action are always entered as strings (in quotes). The *URL* argument allows you to enter either an absolute or relative path to the file you want to load. Use target to specify where the movie should be loaded. Movies can be loaded at new document levels (_level1, _level4, and so on), or they can replace levels if they already exist. For instance, the main Timeline can be replaced by loading at _level0 or _root. The target argument can also specify a Movie Clip to be filled by the new SWF file. It is also possible to pass variables when loading a new movie. Specify either GET or POST for the *varMethod* argument to pass information to the new movie. GET is recommended for small variable loads, and POST is best for larger quantities.

loadMovieNum (4+)

COMPONENTS:
loadMovieNum("*URL*",*level*,"*varMethod*")

The loadMovieNum() action is nearly identical to loadMovie(). The main difference is that with loadMovieNum(), the document level to be loaded is specified as a number rather than a string. This makes it easier to dynamically load levels, but it makes it impossible to load new movies into Movie Clip instances. If the specified level does not exist, it will be created for the new movie. If the level does exist, then the movie currently playing there will be replaced.

EXAMPLE:
The following statements are equivalent:
loadMovieNum("act1.swf",1,"GET");
loadMovie("act1.swf","_level1","GET");

The following loop cycles through document levels 0 to 8 and checks to see if each exists. The variable `top` stores the number of the last level present in the movie. When the loop is complete, `high.swf` is loaded into the next available document level:

```
l=0;
top=0;
do{
    if(eval("_level"+l)){
        trace("found@"+l);
        top++;
    } else {
        trace("not found@"+l);
    }
} while(l++<8);
trace("top=_level"+(top-1));
loadMovieNum("high.swf",top);
```

If there were movies present at levels 0 and 1 when this script was executed, `high.swf` would be loaded into `_level2`.

loadVariables (4+)

COMPONENTS:

`loadVariables("URL","target","varMethod")`

The `loadVariables()` action loads variables from the file specified in the *URL* argument into the movie level or Movie Clip specified by *target*. Flash can read variable data from text, CGI, ASP, PHP, and other server-side file types. All variables are passed as string data and should reside at the same domain as the movie that requests them when called in a web browser. Specify either GET or POST for the *varMethod* argument to pass information to the *target* Timeline. GET is recommended for small, variable loads, and POST is best for larger quantities.

loadVariablesNum (4+)

COMPONENTS:

`loadVariablesNum("URL",level,"varMethod")`
`loadVariablesNum()` and `loadVariables()` are almost identical. The difference is that with `load-VariablesNum()`, the target to receive the variables is specified as a number rather than a string. This

makes it easier to dynamically generate level numbers that will receive variables. Variables cannot be passed to Movie Clips using this action, however.

nextFrame (2+)

COMPONENTS:

`nextframe()`

This navigational action sends the playback head forward one frame and stops in the new location. For simple navigation, this is a quick alternative to a `gotoAndStop(_currentframe+1)` statement.

nextScene (2+)

COMPONENTS:

`nextScene()`

The `nextScene()` action is helpful for managing simple navigation between the scenes of a movie. When called, it will send the playback head to frame 1 of the next scene in the movie and halt playback at that point. Scene order is established by the order of items in the Scene panel. `nextScene()` will not work when attached to a Movie Clip and must be issued from the main Timeline of a movie scene.

play (2+)

COMPONENTS:

`play()`

The `play()` action represents one of the most fundamental tasks in Flash: playing an animation or Timeline. `play()` sets an animation in motion and allows it to continue playback until it is stopped by another action or until the Timeline runs out of frames. After using a `nextScene()` or `prevScene()` action to skip a movie ahead, you can use `play()` to cue the Timeline of the new scene.

prevFrame (2+)

COMPONENTS:

`prevFrame()`

This navigational action will send the playback head back one frame and stop in the new location. For simple navigation, this is a quick alternative to a `gotoAndStop(_currentframe-1)` statement.

prevScene (2+)

COMPONENTS:

prevScene()

The prevScene() action is helpful for managing simple navigation between the scenes of a movie. When called, it sends the playback head to frame 1 of the previous scene in the movie and halts playback at that point. Scene order is established by the order of items in the Scene panel. prevScene() will not work when attached to a Movie Clip and must be issued from the main Timeline of a movie scene.

print (5+)

COMPONENTS:

print("target","printArea")

Use this action to print either an entire movie or portions of a movie. Define the Timeline you want to print in the target argument. Unless specified, Flash will print all frames in the target Timeline. To specify frames for printing, mark each with a frame label titled #p in the Property Inspector. PostScript printers will print vectors and bitmaps alike; non-PostScript printers will convert vectors to bitmaps before printing. Alpha and color effects cannot be printed using the print() action; use printAsBitmap() instead.

The printArea argument allows you to define the area to be printed. This argument takes one of three different string values:

> "**bmovie**" tells Flash to use the content of a marked frame to define the print area. To designate a frame that defines the print area, attach a frame label that reads #b and insert a graphic to serve as the print boundaries or crop markers.

> "**bmax**" uses a size combination of all printable frames to define the print area. Use this option if the printed content is dynamically generated and varies from frame to frame.

> "**bframe**" treats every printable frame separately. Printed content will fill the entire page, and the elements of each frame will be scaled to fit accordingly.

EXAMPLE:

This script prints all frames in the directions clip instance and limits their print area to the frame with the #b frame label:

print("_root.directions", "bmovie");

If you want to designate specific frames that print, attach a #p frame label to each.

printAsBitmap (5+)

COMPONENTS:

printAsBitmap("target","printArea")

This action is identical to the print() action but with one exception: It prints raster (pixel-based) graphics instead of vectors. Despite the lower output quality, if you must print graphics containing alpha or color effects, this is the action to use. See the print() action for parameter specifics.

printAsBitmapNum (5+)

COMPONENTS:

printAsBitmapNum(level,"printArea")

This action is almost identical to the printAsBitmap() action. The main difference is that rather than specifying the target as a string, you specify a level as a number. Use this action if you need to target a printable movie level. As an alternative, rather than specify the movie level as an integer, you can use a variable that holds numeric data.

EXAMPLE:

In this example, a variable passes information from the custom output function to the printAsBitmapNum() action:

printNfo=output();
printAsBitmap(printNfo,"bFrame");

printNum (5+)

COMPONENTS:

printNum(level,"printArea")

This action is almost identical to the print() action. The main difference is that rather than specifying a target as a string, you specify a level as a number. Use this action if you need to target a printable movie level. As an alternative, rather than specify the movie level as an integer, you can use a variable that holds numeric data.

EXAMPLE:

The following statements are synonymous:

```
printNum(3,"bmax");
print("_level3","bmax");
```

removeMovieClip (4+)

COMPONENTS:

```
removeMovieClip("target")
```

Use the removeMovieClip() action to delete a Movie Clip from a Flash movie. Specify the name of the instance or path to the instance you want to remove using the *target* argument. This action works only on clips that were inserted in a movie using attachMovie() or duplicateMovieClip().

EXAMPLE:

When attached to a clip created via duplicate-MovieClip(), this script will delete the clip when it is clicked. Because this refers to the current clip, it is *not* entered as a string:

```
onClipEvent(mouseUp){
    if(this.hitTest(_root._xmouse,_root.
➥_ymouse,true)){
        removeMovieClip(this);
    }
}
```

setProperty (4+)

COMPONENTS:

```
setProperty("target",property,expression)
```

Use the setProperty() action to assign a value for one of Flash's predefined properties to a Movie Clip instance. Specify the instance you would like to affect for the *target* argument, specify a property (such as _alpha or _rotation) for *property*, and use *expression* to specify value for the property.

startDrag (4+)

COMPONENTS:

```
startDrag("target",lock,left,top,right,botm)
```

The startDrag() action makes the clip named by the *target* argument *draggable*. Draggable means that the Movie Clip instance can be moved around on the Stage by clicking and dragging it with the mouse cursor. The *lock* argument makes the cursor lock to the draggable clip's registration point when set to true, or it allows the cursor to drag from any point on the clip when set to false. This argument is optional; when not specified, it defaults to the false setting. The arguments *left*, *top*, *right*, and *botm* define the coordinate boundaries for the draggable clip. Boundaries are determined relative to the Timeline where the *target* clip resides. Coordinates are determined relative to the (0,0) origin of the Timeline where the clip resides. If the clip is sitting on the main Timeline, the origin is the upper-left corner of the Stage. If the *target* is nested within another Movie Clip instance, the origin is the host clip's registration point. Coordinate boundary arguments are optional as well. A clip can be made undraggable by using the stopDrag() action.

EXAMPLE:

See the stopDrag() action.

stop (2+)

COMPONENTS:

```
stop()
target.stop()
```

The stop() action will halt the playback of a Timeline when it is encountered. To stop a specific Timeline, enter its target reference for the *target* argument.

stopDrag (4+)

COMPONENTS:

```
stopDrag()
```

The stopDrag() action ceases a startDrag() action that is active in your movie. Because Flash allows for only one draggable clip at a time, this action takes no arguments and affects the current clip that has been targeted by a startDrag() action.

EXAMPLE:

The following statements create a simple drag-and-drop behavior for the clip instance `blob`. In this script, the clip is draggable until the mouse is released, or the clip is "dropped":

```
blob.onMouseDown=function(){
    startDrag("blob",false,0,0,550,400);
}

blob.onMouseUp=function(){
    stopDrag();
}
```

switch (6)

COMPONENTS:

```
switch(condition){
case(a):
    //statements if case a true
    break;
case(b):
    //statements if case b true
    break;
case(n):
    //statements if case n true
    break;
default:
    //default statements if no cases true
}
```

`switch` is a conditional statement structure that is an alternative to `if...else`. Use `switch` when you have several different conditions to test and each has its own set of statements to execute as a consequence. For *condition*, enter the conditional statement to be tested. For *case* (don't italicize "case"), enter each possible result of the condition. Following each `case`, enter the statement(s) you would like to execute if `case` returns `true`. Additionally, you must include a `break` statement to prevent your script from jumping to other cases after one returns `true`, and a `default` case if none of the specified conditions return `true`.

EXAMPLE:

In this example, a Movie Clip monitors the current playback position of the main Timeline. Depending on the main Timeline's current frame number, the Movie Clip is told to hold at frames 1, 2, or 3 of its Timeline:

```
onClipEvent(enterFrame){
    switch(_root._currentframe){
    case(1):
        gotoAndStop(1);
        break;
    case(10):
        gotoAndStop(2);
        break;
    case(20):
        gotoAndStop(3);
        break;
    default:
        stop();
    }
}
```

unloadMovie (3+)

COMPONENTS:

```
unloadMovie("target")
```

Use the `unloadMovie()` action to remove movies from stacking levels that were loaded using a `loadMovie()` or `loadMovieNum()` action. `unloadMovie()` can also remove the contents of clip instances from the Stage. Use the *target* argument to specify the movie or instance containing a movie that you would like to remove. Specify *target* as a string.

EXAMPLES:

This statement unloads the movie at movie level 2:

```
unloadMovie("_level2");
```

This statement unloads the contents of a clip instance:

```
unloadMovie("feature1");
```

When a clip is unloaded, the contents of the instance are removed but the instance itself remains on the Stage as an empty frame. The frame can be refilled with a new movie (SWF) using the `loadMovie()` action.

unloadMovieNum (3+)

COMPONENTS:

unloadMovieNum(*target*)

unloadMovieNum() is identical to unloadMovie(), with one exception: The *target* argument is entered as a number to specify the level you need to unload. As a result, unloadMovieNum() cannot unload Movie Clip instances. Use this action to dynamically unload movie levels.

EXAMPLE:

The following statements are equivalent:

```
unloadMovieNum(2);
unloadMovie("_level2");
```

updateAfterEvent (5+)

COMPONENTS:

updateAfterEvent()

This action is used in conjunction with the onClipEvent handlers mouseMove, mouseDown, mouseUp, keyDown, and keyUp and the MovieClip object events onMouseMove, onMouseDown, onMouseUp, onKeyDown, and onKeyUp. The updateAfterEvent() action forces Flash to redraw the screen independently of a movie's frame rate. Because it's not tied to a movie's fixed frame rate, updateAfterEvent() helps increase the responsiveness of keystroke and mouse actions that occur *between* frames. Use this for custom cursors, keyboard input, and other events that are cued via user input.

EXAMPLE:

This function, assigned to the instance cursor, makes the instance into a custom cursor. update-AfterEvent() ensures smooth cursor tracking:

```
cursor.onMouseMove=function(){
    cursor._x=_xmouse;
    cursor._y=_ymouse;
    updateAfterEvent();
}
```

while (4+)

COMPONENTS:

```
while(condition){
    statement(s);
}
```

The while() action creates looped statements. In a while() loop, you specify a *condition* to be tested. If the condition exists or is True, the loop will execute any *statement(s)* that it contains. If the condition does not exist or is False, the loop body is skipped. In a while loop, the condition is always tested before any statements are executed.

EXAMPLE:

It is standard to initialize loop variable(s) first, then present the condition and body of the loop. This loop duplicates the Movie Clip lite and scatters it across the Stage at various intervals:

```
var z;
z=0;
while(z<10){
    ry=Math.random()*400;
    duplicateMovieClip(lite,"lite"+z,z);
    _root["lite"+z]._x=50*z;
    _root["lite"+z]._y=ry;
    z++;
}
```

with (5+)

COMPONENTS:

```
with(object){
    statement(s);
}
```

The with action, introduced in Flash 5, replaced the tried-and-true tellTarget() action of Flash versions 3 and 4. Use the with action to access and manipulate the properties of the object or clip instance specified by *object*. For controlling clip instances, with prevents you from having to repeatedly enter long target path references.

EXAMPLE:

This script sets the transparency level and proportions of the menu instance to new values:

```
with(menu){
    _alpha=40;
    _xscale+=25;
    _yscale+=25;
}
```

This is an identical script using dot syntax:

```
_root.navigation.bar.menu._alpha=40;
_root.navigation.bar.menu._xscale+=25;
_root.navigation.bar.menu._yscale+=25;
```

Properties

ActionScript *properties* are the terms in the language that set and retrieve the status, attributes, position, and so on of different elements in your movie. You can assign properties to nearly every movie component. When assigned to elements individually, each is given its own unique set of characteristics.

 Buttons now fall under the control of Flash MX's new Button object. Any Button with an instance name can be manipulated via ActionScript to change its position, dimensions, and more. See the following entries for details.

_alpha (4+)

COMPONENTS:

Instance._alpha = value

The _alpha property gets and sets transparency values for Button objects and Movie Clip instances. Values range between 100 (opaque) and 0 (transparent). Transparent Movie Clips and Buttons are still active on the Stage and behave normally.

_currentFrame (4+)

COMPONENTS:

clipInstance._currentFrame

This property returns the frame number that a Timeline is currently playing when it is called. If no instance is specified, the property returns the current frame of the Timeline containing the script.

_dropTarget (4+)

COMPONENTS:

draggedClip._dropTarget

This read-only property returns the path of the Movie Clip over which *draggedClip* was dropped. Flash defines *over* if the draggable clip's registration point is anywhere over the bounds of the

target Movie Clip. _dropTarget returns the path in slash notation, but you can use the eval() function to convert the path to dot notation. For example:

```
onClipEvent(mouseUp){
    trace("slash: "+this._dropTarget);
    trace("dot: "+eval(this._dropTarget));
}
```

EXAMPLE:
When the current, draggable clip is "dropped," this script checks to see if it is over the instance hit. If it is not, then the draggable clip is sent back to the X Y position 100,100:

```
onClipEvent(mouseUp){
    stopDrag();
    if(eval(this.dropTarget)!=_root.hit){
        this._x=100;
        this._y=100;
    }
}
```

_framesloaded (4+)

COMPONENTS:

_framesloaded

loadedSWF._framesloaded

This property gets the number of frames that have been loaded from the main movie Timeline or an external SWF file. Use it to check that all movie assets have been loaded before beginning playback.

EXAMPLE:
```
if(_framesloaded==_totalframes){
    gotoAndPlay("start");
}else{
    gotoAndPlay(1);
}
```

This script monitors the progress of loading the main movie. If all frames have been loaded, it jumps to the marker start; otherwise, it loops back to frame 1.

_height (4+)

COMPONENTS:

instance._height=value

Use this property to test and set the height of *instance*. Specify *value* in pixels. This property applies to Movie Clip and Button instances alike.

_name (4+)

COMPONENTS:

instance._name="*name*";

This property gets and sets Movie Clip and Button instance names. You can test to see if an instance has a particular name and change the name of it as needed. To assign a new instance name, enter it as a string for the argument *name*.

NaN (5+)

COMPONENTS:

NaN

NaN stands for "not a number." This property represents a constant value for items that are not numbers or cannot be handled as numeric data.

_quality (5+)

COMPONENTS:

_quality="*value*"

This global property sets a display quality parameter for your movie. Display quality is determined by the amount of anti-aliasing applied to a movie. The *value* argument is entered as a string, and takes one of four possible arguments:

"LOW": No anti-aliasing is applied.

"MEDIUM": Anti-aliasing is applied sparingly to vectors only.

"HIGH": Vectors are anti-aliased; bitmaps are smoothed if there is no animation.

"BEST": Anti-aliasing is applied to both vectors and bitmaps.

_rotation (4+)

COMPONENTS:

instance._rotation=*value*

Use the _rotation property to control the amount (in degrees) you want to rotate *instance*. This property applies to both Buttons and Movie Clips.

When *value* is a positive number, the clip rotates clockwise. A negative value will rotate the clip counterclockwise. All rotations are applied relative to a Button or Movie Clip's orientation in its own Timeline.

_soundbuftime (4+)

COMPONENTS:

_soundbuftime=*seconds*

The _soundbuftime global property determines how many seconds of streaming audio should be loaded before it begins playback. Flash defaults to a setting of 5 seconds.

_target (4+)

COMPONENTS:

instance._target

This property returns the target path for either a Movie Clip or Button instance. The target path will be returned in the older Flash 4 slash syntax. To get a target path in dot syntax, use the targetPath() function.

_totalframes (4+)

COMPONENTS:

clipInstance._totalframes

This property returns the number of frames contained in a Movie Clip or the main Timeline. Use this property to create preloader movies that delay the main movie's playback until all frames in a movie (in other words, _totalframes) have been loaded. For an example, see the _framesloaded property.

_url (4+)

COMPONENTS:

instance._url

The _url property returns the URL (Uniform Resource Locator) of the SWF file that contains the Button or Movie Clip specified by *instance*. The URL is returned as a string that lists the absolute URL to the particular file.

EXAMPLE:

```
trace(this._url);
```

For a file loaded from your computer's hard drive, this statement will print the following:

```
file:///C/windows/Desktop/pathTest.swf
```

Or, for a file on the Web, it will print:

```
http://www.domain.com/folder/file.swf
```

_visible (4+)

COMPONENTS:

instance._visible=Boolean

This property determines whether a Button or Movie Clip *instance* is visible on the Stage. When set to true (default), the instance is fully visible; when set to false, the instance is hidden. Though hidden (invisible) Movie Clip instances are still able to respond to events and actions, Buttons that have been hidden via the _visible property are not.

_width (4+)

COMPONENTS:

instance._width=*value*

Use this property to test and set the width of the Button or Movie Clip specified by *instance*. *value* is specified in pixels.

_x (3+)

COMPONENTS:

instance._x

instance._x=*value*

The _x property allows you to return and set values for the horizontal coordinate position of the Button or Movie Clip specified by *instance*. The coordinate is determined by the instance's registration point and is relative to the movie or Timeline that's hosting *instance*:

- If *instance* is on the main Timeline, its coordinates are determined relative to the left side of the Stage. A Button or Movie Clip that's 225 pixels from the Stage's left side has an _x value of 225.

- If *instance* is nested inside a Movie Clip, its coordinates are determined relative to the registration point of the host clip. For example, a clip positioned 50 pixels to the right of the host's registration point has an _x value of 50; if it's 50 pixels to the left, _x is –50. Any changes made to the rotation or scaling of the host clip will affect the nested clip's _x value. For example, if a host clip were rotated 180°, _x values to the right of the host registration would be positive, and values to the left would be negative.

_xmouse (5+)

COMPONENTS:

instance._xmouse

This property gets the horizontal position of the mouse pointer relative to *instance*. _root._xmouse returns the position of the mouse relative to the left edge of the Stage; moverClip._xmouse returns the mouse position relative to the registration point of moverClip.

EXAMPLE:

This script keeps a Movie Clip in line with the horizontal position of the mouse, relative to the main Timeline:

```
onClipEvent(enterFrame){
    _x=_root._xmouse;


}
```

_xscale (4+)

COMPONENTS:

instance._xscale=*value*

Use this property to scale *instance* horizontally. All values are based on the original size of the Button or Movie Clip instance when it was created. Values are determined by a percentage of the original and adjusted symmetrically around the instance's registration point.

EXAMPLE:

This script continuously scales a clip by increments of 50%. Because scaling occurs symmetrically, the clip expands by 25% on both the left and right sides:

```
onClipEvent(enterFrame){
    _xscale=_xscale+50;
}
```

_y (3+)

COMPONENTS:

```
instance._y
instance._y=value
```

The _y property allows you to return and set values for the vertical coordinate position of the Button or Movie Clip specified by *instance*. The coordinate is determined by the instance's registration point and is relative to the movie that's hosting *instance*:

- If *instance* is on the main Timeline, its coordinates are determined relative to the top of the Stage. An instance that's 100 pixels below the top of the Stage has a _y value of 100.

- If *instance* is nested inside a Movie Clip, its coordinates are determined relative to the registration point of the host clip. For example, a clip positioned 50 pixels below the host's registration point has a _y value of 50; if it's 50 pixels above, _y is –50. Any changes made to the rotation or scaling of the host clip will affect the nested instance's _y value. For example, if a host clip were rotated 180°, _y values above the host registration would be positive, and values below would be negative.

_ymouse (5+)

COMPONENTS:

```
instance._ymouse
```

This property gets the vertical position of the mouse pointer relative to the Button or Movie Clip specified by *instance*. _root._ymouse returns the position of the mouse relative to the top of the Stage; launcher._ymouse returns the mouse position relative to the registration point of the button launcher.

_yscale (4+)

COMPONENTS:

```
instance._yscale=value
```

Use this property to scale *instance* vertically. All values are based on the original size of the Button or Movie Clip when it was created. Values are determined by a percentage of the original and adjusted symmetrically around the instance's registration point.

Functions

Functions are self-contained chunks of code that are part of the ActionScript language. They are unique routines that can evaluate the data they are given. Use ActionScript functions to perform common tasks that process and retrieve information in your Flash movies.

eval (5+)

COMPONENTS:

```
eval(expression)
```

Where *expression* is a string or produces a string, eval() converts *expression* to an identifier containing the variable value, property value, or Movie Clip reference held by the string. If *expression* contains no information, eval returns undefined.

EXAMPLE:

Use this function to help manage dynamically generated variables or instances:

```
j=1;
while(j<=5){
    this.duplicateMovieClip("cloud"+j,j);
    eval("_root.cloud"+j)._x=100*j;
    eval("_root.cloud"+j)._y=100*j;
    eval("_root.cloud"+j)._alpha=20*j;
    j++;
}
```

In this example, a Movie Clip is duplicated five times. Each new instance name (cloud1, cloud2, and so on) is evaluated as a string and turned into a Movie Clip reference that can be manipulated.

getProperty (4+)

COMPONENTS:

getProperty(*instance*,*property*)
Use this function to retrieve a property for the specified Movie Clip instance. The argument *instance* must be a valid reference to a Movie Clip instance.

getTimer (4+)

COMPONENTS:

getTimer()
The getTimer()function returns the number of milliseconds that have passed since a movie has started playing. It's useful for monitoring and setting timed actions or events.

EXAMPLE:

```
onClipEvent(load){
    start=getTimer();
}
onClipEvent(enterFrame){
    if(start+10000<getTimer()){
        orb.gotoAndStop(orb._currentframe+1);
        start=getTimer();
    }
}
```

This script is a good example of a simple timer. The variable start records the elapsed milliseconds when the Movie Clip is first loaded. At every frame, the current milliseconds are checked against the value of the start time plus 10,000. If the current milliseconds are greater than start+10000, meaning the movie has been running for 10 seconds, the orb Movie Clip is sent to the next frame and stopped, and the counter is reset. Ten seconds later, orb will be sent to its next frame, the counter will reset, and so on.

newline (4+)

COMPONENTS:

newline
This statement inserts a line break (carriage return) in a string of text. newline is useful for inserting line breaks in the contents of a text field.

String (5+)

COMPONENTS:

String(*expression*);
Use the string function to convert an expression to a string and return the string value.
Boolean values return as Boolean. String(true); returns "true".
Numbers return as number strings. String(365); returns "365".
Movie Clips return as strings naming their absolute path. String(this); returns "_root .main.sub1".
Objects return as the string value for the particular object. String() returns the same value as the toString() method, which will differ depending upon the contents of the object.

targetPath (5+)

COMPONENTS:

targetPath(*clipInstance*)
Use this function to return the absolute path to a Movie Clip instance. The path is returned as a string, written in dot notation.

EXAMPLE:

These statements assign a clip's absolute path to the variable me. You can use me in subsequent script statements whenever it is necessary to reference the path:

```
onClipEvent(load){
    me=targetPath(this);
}
```

Operators

Operators both evaluate and change the value of expressions.

-- (decrement) (4+)

COMPONENTS:

--*expression*
expression--

This operator will subtract 1 from *expression*. It can be used in two ways: as a pre-decrement and a post-decrement. Pre-decrement subtracts 1 from the expression and returns the new value. Post-decrement subtracts 1 from the expression but returns its original value.

EXAMPLE:
```
x=2;
y=--x;
```
Using pre-decrement, the final values are y = 1 and x = 1.
```
x=2;
y=x--;
```
Using post-decrement, the final values are y = 2 and x = 1.

++ (increment) (4+)

COMPONENTS:
```
++expression
expression++
```
This operator will add 1 to *expression*. It can be used in two ways: as a pre-increment and a post-increment. Pre-increment adds 1 to the expression and returns the new value. Post-increment adds 1 to the expression but returns its original value.

EXAMPLE:
```
x=1;
y=++x;
```
Using pre-decrement, the final values are y = 2 and x = 2.
```
x=1;
y=x++;
```
Using post-decrement, the final values are y = 1 and x = 2.

! (logical NOT) (4+)

COMPONENTS:
```
!expression
```
The NOT operator will always return the opposite Boolean value of the expression that follows it. You can use this to test when a condition does not exist or is not true.

EXAMPLES:
!1 evaluates as 0.
!0 evaluates as 1.

!= (inequality) (5+)

COMPONENTS:
```
expressionA!=expressionB
```
The inequality operator checks to see if two expressions are *not* equal and returns a Boolean value. If the expressions are not equal, it returns true; if they are equal, it returns false.

EXAMPLE:
Use the inequality operator as part of a preloader script. If a movie's frames are not loaded, the movie is sent back to frame 1:
```
if(_framesloaded!=_totalframes){
    gotoAndPlay(1);
}else{
    gotoAndPlay(5);
}
```

!== (strict inequality) (6)

COMPONENTS:
```
expressionA!==expressionB
```
The strict inequality operator, like the inequality operator, checks to see if two expressions are not equal and returns a Boolean value. The only difference is that with strict inequality, an expression's datatype is also considered in the evaluation.

EXAMPLE:
Given the following statements:
```
str="1";
num=new Number(1);
```
This comparison returns false because the string 1 and number 1 *are* equal:
```
str!=num;
```
This second comparison returns true because the string 1 and number 1 are not strictly equal:
```
str!==num;
```
Each expression has a different datatype.

% (modulo) (4+)

COMPONENTS:
```
expressionA%expressionB
```
This operator returns the remainder value of *expressionA* divided by *expressionB*.

EXAMPLE:

17%4 returns 1.

17 ÷ 4 = 4 with a remainder of 1. The modulo operator returns the remainder for the expression.

%= (modulo assignment) (4+)

COMPONENTS:

expressionA%=expressionB

This operator returns the remainder value of *expressionA* divided by *expressionB* and assigns the new value to *expressionA*.

EXAMPLE:

```
x=2;
y=13;
y%=x;
trace(y);
```

In this example, trace would print the number 1 to the Output window. y is divided by x, and the remainder (1) is assigned to y.

&& (logical AND) (4+)

COMPONENTS:

expressionA&&expressionB

The logical AND operator evaluates two expressions and returns a Boolean true or false based on the value of each.

true&&false evaluates as false.

true&&true evaluates as true.

false&&false evaluates as false.

For the AND operator to return true, both expressions must be true.

- (minus) (4+)

COMPONENTS:

expressionA-expressionB

This operator either subtract *expressionB* from *expressionA* or makes an expression have an opposite value.

EXAMPLES:

1.5-.4 returns 1.1.

4-3 returns 1.

-(4-3) returns −1.

-(1-2) returns 1.

* (multiply) (4+)

COMPONENTS:

*expressionA*expressionB*

This operator multiplies *expressionA* and *expressionB*.

*= (multiplication assignment) (4+)

COMPONENTS:

expressionA=expressionB*

This operator multiplies *expressionA* and *expressionB* and assigns the new value to *expressionA*.

EXAMPLE:

a*=b is equivalent to a=a*b.

The following statements reinitialize a as 200.

```
a=10
b=20
a*=b
```

?: (conditional) (4+)

COMPONENTS:

expression?trueResult:falseResult

The conditional operator is a single-line alternative to the if…else conditional syntax. A conditional expression is evaluated. If it is True, the first argument, *trueResult*, is returned; otherwise, the expression returns the second argument, *falseResult*.

EXAMPLE:

```
if(Key.getCode()==Key.RIGHT){
    nextFrame();
}else{
    stop();
}
```

This simple conditional advances the movie to the next frame if the right-arrow key is pressed. It can be rewritten as follows:

```
Key.RIGHT?nextFrame():stop();
```

// (single-line comment) (1+)

COMPONENTS:

//comments

The comment operator tells Flash to ignore the text that is between it and the end of the line on which it appears. Use comments to leave notes or explanations about your scripts. Flash will color all text behind the comment operator a light gray (default color).

/*...*/ (multiline comment) (5+)

COMPONENTS:

`/*comments begin...comments finish*/`

The multiline comment operator is useful if you have long blocks of text that must be ignored by Flash. Any text that appears between the opening asterisk and the closing asterisk will be ignored. Be sure to use both an opening and closing version of the operator around your comments.

/= (division assignment) (4+)

COMPONENTS:

`expressionA/=expressionB`

This operator returns the value of `expressionA` divided by `expressionB` and assigns the new value to `expressionA`.

EXAMPLE:

`x/=y` is equivalent to `x=x/y`.
`x` is reinitialized as the quotient of the expression `x/y`.

|| (logical OR) (4+)

COMPONENTS:

`expressionA||expressionB`

The OR operator evaluates `expressionA` and `expressionB` and returns a Boolean value. If either expression is true, the statement returns `true`. It returns `false` only if both expressions are false.
`1||0` evaluates `true` because one expression is true.
`0||1` evaluates `true` because one expression is true.
`1||1` evaluates `true` because both expressions are true.
`0||0` evaluates `false` because neither expression is true.

+ (addition) (4+)

COMPONENTS:

`expressionA+expressionB`
`"stringA"+"stringB"`

This operator returns the sum of `expressionA` and `expressionB`. It is also used to concatenate strings of information (only in Flash Player 5 or higher).

+= (addition assignment) (4+)

COMPONENTS:

`expressionA+=expressionB`
`expression+="string"`

This operator returns the sum of `expressionA` and `expressionB` and assigns the new value to `expressionA`. This operator works for numbers and strings.

EXAMPLES:

`x+=1` is equivalent to `x=x+1`.
`var x=10, y=20;`
`x+=y` returns 30.
The operator can also concatenate a string with a variable to produce a new value:
`x="Action";`
`trace(x+="Script");`
In this example, `trace` will print the word `Action-Script` in the Output window.

< (less than) (4+)

COMPONENTS:

`expressionA<expressionB`

If `expressionA` is less than `expressionB`, this comparison operator returns `true`. Otherwise, if A is either greater than or equal to B, it returns `false`. This operator also works with strings. Capital letters closest to A have the lowest value; lowercase letters closest to z have the highest value.

<= (less than or equal to) (4+)

COMPONENTS:

`expressionA<=expressionB`

If `expressionA` is less than or equal to `expressionB`, this comparison operator returns `true`. Otherwise, if A is greater than B, it returns `false`. This operator also works with strings. Capital letters closest to A have the lowest value; lowercase letters closest to z have the highest value.

= (assignment) (4+)

COMPONENTS:
identifier=expression

This operator assigns the value of *expression* to an identifier. An identifier is a name assigned to an object property, variable, or array element.

-= (subtraction assignment) (4+)

COMPONENTS:
expressionA-=expressionB

This operator returns the difference of *expressionA* and *expressionB* and assigns the new value to *expressionA*.

EXAMPLE:
y-=x is equivalent to y=y-x.
var x=10, y=20;
y-=x returns 10.

== (equality) (4+)

COMPONENTS
expressionA==expressionB

If *expressionA* is equal to *expressionB*, this comparison operator returns `true`; otherwise, it returns `false`.

=== (strict equality) (6)

COMPONENTS:
expressionA===expressionB

The strict equality operator, like the equality operator, checks to see if two expressions are equal and returns a Boolean value. The only difference is that with strict equality, an expression's datatype is also considered in the evaluation.

EXAMPLE:
Given the following statements:
str="1";
num=new Number(1);

The comparison str==num returns `true` because the string 1 and number 1 are equal. A second comparison, str===num returns `false` because the string 1 and number 1 are not strictly equal. Each expression has a different datatype.

> (greater than) (4+)

COMPONENTS:
expressionA>expressionB

If *expressionA* is greater than *expressionB*, this comparison operator returns `true`. Otherwise, if A is either less than or equal to B, it returns `false`. This operator also works with strings. Capital letters closest to A have the lowest value; lowercase letters closest to z have the highest value.

>= (greater than or equal to) (4+)

COMPONENTS:
expressionA>=expressionB

If *expressionA* is greater than or equal to *expressionB*, this comparison operator returns `true`. Otherwise, if A is less than B, it returns `false`. This operator also works with strings. Capital letters closest to A have the lowest value; lowercase letters closest to z have the highest value.

EXAMPLE:
The following comparisons return `true`:
2>=1
3>=3
"shockwave">="flash"

The following comparison returns `false`:
"Flash">="flash"

Flash is not greater than or equal to `flash` because uppercase letters come after lowercase letters.

typeof (5+)

COMPONENTS:
typeof *expression*

The `typeof` operator returns the datatype of *expression*. Datatypes (and the syntax in which they are returned) include `boolean`, `function`, `movieclip`, `number`, `object`, and `string`.

EXAMPLE:

```
obj = new Object;
trace("2: "+typeof 2);
trace("text: "+typeof "text");
trace("true: "+typeof true);
trace("obj: "+typeof obj);
```

These statements print the following to the Output window:

```
2: number
text: string
true: boolean
obj: object
```

2 is a number, `"text"` is a string, `true` is a Boolean value, and `obj` is a generic object. Items that contain no data will be returned as `undefined` or `null`.

Object and Timeline References

The object reference terms target Movie Clips, movie levels, variables, objects, and functions in your Flash movies. A thorough understanding of these terms is crucial to the success of writing accurate target paths. If a target path is ever in question, you can check it using the Movie Explorer, Debugger, or Insert Target Path button in the Actions panel.

_global (6)

COMPONENTS:

`_global.globalVariable`
`_global.globalFunction`

This reference allows you to create global variables, objects, and functions. *Global* means that a variable, object, or function is immediately available from any Timeline in your movie. Rather than specify a target path, such as `_root.myFunction`, the `_global` reference allows you to simply call `myFunction`. Use `_global` when you initialize a function or variable to make it available by name from any Timeline.

EXAMPLE:

In the following statement, the variable `startGame` is set to be available throughout a movie:

`_global.startGame=getTimer();`

This variable can be recalled throughout your movie by simply referencing `startGame`. If you did not use the `_global` reference, and the variable was created on the main Timeline, you would have to reference it using its target path: `_root.startGame`.

_level (4+)

COMPONENTS:

`_levelX`

This global property makes reference to the Timeline loaded at level *X*. The Flash Player can hold and play many Timelines at once. The main Timeline (the first movie loaded) is set at level 0. All subsequent Timelines are loaded at levels above it: level 1, level 2, and so on. Use the `_level` property to load and unload additional Timelines or to control their playback.

_parent (4+)

COMPONENTS:

`instance._parent`

A Timeline that contains another Timeline or Button is referred to as a `_parent`. This property references the Timeline or instance that *contains* the Button or Movie Clip instance where the call is made. For example, Movie Clips and Buttons sitting on the main Timeline refer to it as `_parent`. The main Timeline has no `_parent` because it is the lowest possible level (`_level0` or `_root`). This property is especially useful for creating relative target paths.

EXAMPLE:

If `arrow` were sitting on the main Timeline, this statement (called from the `arrow` Timeline) would halt the movie:

`_parent.stop();`

If `arrow` contained a nested instance named `fletcher`, this script (called from the `fletcher` Timeline) would also stop the main Timeline, make the `arrow` instance semi-transparent, and flip the head instance, which is also nested inside `arrow`:

```
_parent._parent.stop();
_parent._alpha=50;
_parent.head._rotation=180;
```

_root (4+)

COMPONENTS:

`_root.clipInstance`
`_root.action`
`_root.property`

The _root property refers to the main movie's Timeline. _root is synonymous with _level0. Use _root to create absolute target paths to `clipInstance` or to control the main Timeline from anywhere within the movie.

this (5+)

COMPONENTS:

`this.action`
`this.property`
`this.nestedClipA.nestedClipB`

`this` is a keyword used as a self-reference for the current Timeline. When called from inside a mouse event handler (attached to a Button), `this` refers to the Timeline where the Button resides. When attached to a Movie Clip and called from within an `onClipEvent` handler, `this` refers to the Timeline of the same clip. You can use `this` to control playback and set/retrieve properties of the current Timeline. It is also helpful for constructing target paths starting from the current Timeline.

Predefined Objects

The predefined objects control the properties and information associated with Flash's built-in objects: Array, Color, Date, Key, Math, Mouse, MovieClip, Object (Generic), Sound, String, and TextField. This list is *not* representative of all objects available to Flash and ActionScript. For a complete list of built-in objects, use Flash MX's Reference panel (Shift+F1).

Array Object (5+)

COMPONENTS:

`new Array()`
`new Array(length)`
`new Array(item0,item1,item2...itemx)`

Simply put, an array is an ordered list of data or information. Arrays are used for storing multiple pieces of data in a single location. You can use the properties and methods of the Array object to store, retrieve, and manipulate the items within an array.

To create an Array object, you can use the constructor function `new Array()`. For instance:

`list=new Array();`

This lone statement creates a new, empty array. The array constructor function can take optional arguments as well. Use a single integer in place of *length* to specify the length or number of slots in an array. For example:

`week=new Array(7);`

Here, the array `week` is empty but has seven vacant slots that can later be filled with items. Often, it is easiest to simply create an array and fill it with items from the start. For example:

`groceries=new Array("pasta","bread","milk");`

In this case, the array `groceries` is created and contains three items that happen to be string data. An array can also hold a mixture of data—for instance:

`home=new Array();`
`home[0]="Chicago";`
`home[1]=60657;`
`home[2]=["Lakeview","Wrigleyville"];`

In this example, the array `home` is created using the array access operator (`[]`). It contains the string `"Chicago"`, the number `60657`, and another array containing the strings `"Lakeview"` and `"Wrigleyville"`. Items in an array are referenced in the order they appear. The first item is referenced by 0, the second by 1, and so on. To access an array item by number, use the [] operator. For example, `trace(home[1])` returns 60657, the second item of the home array.

PROPERTIES:

`Array.length` returns the number of items (filled and empty) in an array.

METHODS:

`Array.concat()` creates a new array by adding additional items to an existing array.

`Array.pop()` clears and returns the last item of an array.

`Array.push()` appends additional item(s) to the end of an array.

`Array.shift()` clears and returns the first item of an array.

`Array.slice()` creates a new array using a portion of an existing array.

`Array.sort()` arranges the items of an array according to a user-created rule.

`Array.toString()` returns the items of an array as a string, using commas to separate the items.

`Array.unshift()` appends additional items to the beginning of an array.

Array.concat (5+)

COMPONENTS:

arrayObj`.concat(`*item1,item2,...itemx*`)`
Use this method to append items to the end of an existing array, creating an entirely new array.

EXAMPLE:

Create the array `letters1`:

`letters1=new Array("a","b","c");`

`letters2` is created by adding two items to `letters1`:

`letters2=letters1.concat("d","e");`

The `letters2` array consists of the following:

`["a","b","c","d","e"]`

Array.length (5+)

COMPONENTS:

arrayObj`.length`

This array property will both set and return the length, or number of items, contained in *arrayObj*. Because the first slot in an array is referenced by the number 0, an array's length is always one value greater than the position of the last array element. The `Array.length` property is updated as items are added or subtracted from an array and will always reflect the current state of the specified *arrayObj*, even if slots in the array are currently empty.

EXAMPLE:

Create a new array:

`alphabet=new Array("a","b","c");`

The following statement prints 3 in the Output window because the array `alphabet` contains three items:

`trace(alphabet.length);`

Array.pop (5+)

COMPONENTS:

arrayObj`.pop()`
Use this method to clear (delete) and return the last item of the specified *arrayObj*. When invoked, the final slot of the array is removed and the item that it contained is returned. This method is the opposite of `Array.shift()`, which clears and returns the first item in an array.

EXAMPLE:

In the following statements, the array `alphabet` has its last item removed:

`alphabet=new Array("a","b","c");`

`popped=alphabet.pop();`

The following statement prints c has been cleared to the Output window because c was the last item of the array:

`trace(popped+"has been cleared");`

Array.push (5+)

COMPONENTS:

arrayObj`.push(`*item1,item2...itemx*`)`

This method appends the specified items to the array *arrayObj*. Unlike the `Array.concat()` method, `push()` does not create a new array. And, unlike `Array.unshift()`, items are added to the end of the array rather than the beginning.

EXAMPLE:

Create a new array:

`alphabet=new Array("a","b","c");`

This statement adds d, e, and f to the array:

`alphabet.push("d","e","f")`

Array.shift (5+)

COMPONENTS:

arrayObj`.shift()`
Use this method to clear (delete) and return the first item of the specified *arrayObj*. When invoked,

the first slot of the array is removed and the item that it contained is returned. This method is the opposite of `Array.pop()`, which clears and returns the last item in an array.

EXAMPLES:

In the following statements, the array `alphabet` has its first item removed:

```
alphabet=new Array("a","b","c");
shifted=alphabet.shift();
```

The results are printed to the Output window. The next statement returns `a has been cleared` because `a` was the first item of the array:

```
trace(shifted+" has been cleared");
```

Array.slice (5+)

COMPONENTS:

arrayObj.slice(*startRef*,*endRef*)

Use the `Array.slice()` method to create a new array using a portion of the specified array *arrayObj*. To sample a portion of *arrayObj*, you must specify two arguments: *startRef* and *endRef*. Both numbers should be specified relative to 0, the start of the array. *startRef* represents the first item of *arrayObj* to be included in the new array. If *startRef* is negative, the first item will be counted starting from the last item in *arrayObj*. For example, –1 is the last array item, –2 is next to last, and so on. *endRef* is the item in *arrayObj* that comes *after* the last item of the new array. The *endRef* argument handles negative numbers in the same manner as *startRef*. If *endRef* is left blank, the default value is *arrayObj*.length, and all remaining items in *arrayObj* are included in the new array. Ultimately, the items in the new array are *startRef* through *endRef–1* for *arrayObj*.

EXAMPLE:

Create a new array:

```
nums=new Array("one","two","three",
➥"four","five");
```

These statements are equivalent. All create another new array with the last two elements of `nums`; they return `four,five`:

```
sub1=nums.slice(3,5);
sub2=nums.slice(3);
sub3=nums.slice(-2,5);
```

Array.sort (5+)

COMPONENTS:

arrayObj.sort()

arrayObj.sort(*sortFunction*)

The `Array.sort()` method sorts the items of *arrayObj* into a particular order. If no *sortFunction* argument is entered, the array items will be sorted in a loose alphabetic order where integers take highest precedence, followed by uppercase letters, then lowercase letters.

If *sortFunction* is specified, the array will be sorted according to the rules of the function. You must create *sortFunction* so that it will sort according to your needs. The function can be constructed as you see fit; however, there are a few simple rules you must follow. The function must be prepared to compare two values. If you want the first value to be sorted before the second, the function should return –1. If the first value should be sorted after the second, the function should return 1. For values that are equal and do not need to be sorted, the function should return 0. Items in the array are sorted so that the items with negative numbers have the highest precedence (are sorted first) and the positive ones have the lowest precedence (are sorted last). For example, consider sorting the values A and B in ascending order:

> A<B returns –1.
>
> A>B returns 1.
>
> A==B returns 0.

To sort in descending order, you only need to swap the return values. For low values (A<B), you return 1 (lowest precedence). High values (A>B) return –1 (highest precedence), and equal values return 0.

EXAMPLE:

The following example assumes there is a collection of objects (`plyr1`, `plyr2`, and so on), each having its own unique properties `points` and `id`. These objects are stored in the array `players`. The function `score` is used to sort, in descending order, the contents of `players` based on the value of `points` for each. `Array.sort()` calls the `score` function and then prints the name (`id` property) of each player in descending order according to the sorted version of the `players` array:

```
players=new Array(plyr1,plyr2,plyr3);

function score(a,b){
    if(a.points<b.points){
        return 1;
    }else if(a.points>b.points){
        return -1;
    }else return 0;
}

players.sort(score);

for(var i=0;i<players.length;i++){
    var prop=players[i];
    trace(prop.id+" scores "+prop.points);
```

Array.unshift (5+)

COMPONENTS:
arrayObj.unshift(*item1,item2...itemx*)

This method appends the specified items to the array *arrayObj*. Unlike the `Array.concat()` method, `unshift()` doesn't create a new array. And, unlike `Array.push()`, items are added to the beginning of the array rather than the end.

EXAMPLE:
Create a new array:

```
alphabet=new Array("d","e","f");
```

The following statement adds a, b, and c to the array:

```
alphabet.unshift("a","b","c");
```

Color Object (5+)

COMPONENTS:
new Color(*target*)

A Color object is a container for information that will manipulate and retrieve both the color content and the transparency value of the Movie Clip or the level specified by *target*. To invoke the methods of the Color object, you must first create a new object using the constructor `new Color()`.

METHODS:
`Color.getRGB()` retrieves the current RGB value of a Color object.
`Color.getTransform()` retrieves the current transform value for a Color object.
`Color.setRGB()` sets the RGB value of a Color object.
`Color.setTransform()` sets the current transform value for a Color object.

Color.getRGB (5+)

COMPONENTS:
colorObject.getRGB

Use this method to return the RGB value of the specified *colorObject*.

EXAMPLE:
These statements transfer the RGB values from one clip to another when the clip with the attached script is clicked by the mouse. The `getRGB()` method retrieves the color value from the `orb` Movie Clip's `orbColor` Color object and applies it to the current clip instance.

```
onClipEvent(mouseUp){
    if(this.hitTest(_root._xmouse,_root.
    ➥_ymouse,true)){
        colorTrans=new Color(this);
        colorTrans.setRGB(_root.orb.
        ➥orbColor.getRGB());
    }
}
```

Color.getTransform (5+)

COMPONENTS:
colorObject.getTransform()

This method of the Color object retrieves the current transform properties that are applied to the specified *colorObject*.

Color.setRGB (5+)

COMPONENTS:
colorObject.setRGB

Use this method to set the RGB value of the specified *colorObject*.

EXAMPLE:

This script sets the RGB value to red for the clip to which it is attached:

```
onClipEvent(load){
    clipColor=new Color(this);
    clipColor.setRGB(0xFF000000);
}
```

For another example, see the `Color.getRGB()` method.

Color.setTransform (5+)

COMPONENTS:

`colorObject.setTransform(transformObject)`
The `setTransform()` method allows you to manipulate the following color components of the specified `colorObject`: red, green, blue, and alpha. For each component, you can control both its percentage and its offset. To use this method, you must first create a generic object and assign the color properties specified in Table R.1. This object becomes the `transformObject`. Its properties are applied to `colorObject` when the `setTransform()` method is called.

Table R.1

Properties for a *transformObject*

PROPERTY NAME	PROPERTY RANGE	PROPERTY DESCRIPTION
ra	−100 to 100	Percentage of red
rb	−255 to 255	Red offset
ga	−100 to 100	Percentage of green
gb	−255 to 255	Green offset
ba	−100 to 100	Percentage of blue
bb	−255 to 255	Blue offset
aa	−100 to 100	Percentage of alpha
ab	−255 to 255	Alpha offset

Percentage is a value applied to a color component's initial value. For instance, setting ba=50 makes all blue in an object take on half its original value. Offset can either increase or decrease a color component's initial value. Setting gb=255 bumps an object's green values up to their maximum level. See "Scripting Color Changes" in Chapter 16 for an in-context example of these properties and methods.

Date Object (5+)

COMPONENTS:

```
new Date()
new Date(year,month,day,hours,minutes,
➥seconds,milliseconds);
```

ActionScript's Date object will retrieve the present date relative to either local time, or Universal Time, Coordinated. Local time measurements are based on the system clock settings of the computer playing a Flash movie. Universal Time, Coordinated (abbreviated UTC) is synonymous with Greenwich Mean Time (GMT)—time measured relative to the prime meridian. The UTC methods of the Date object will not be covered in this reference.

The Date object allows you to retrieve the current time, store it, and use date information as needed in your movies. There are two ways to create a Date object. You can use the constructor function `new Date()` to create an object for the current day and time, or you can create an object for a specific date using some of the Date object's arguments:

year, an integer value to specify the year. Use 0 to 99 to represent the years 1900 through 1999; for example, 73 means 1973. Use a four-digit number to represent the years 1000–1899 or the year 2000 and later, and use three-digit numbers for years prior to 1000 A.D.

month, an integer from 0 (January) to 11 (December) to specify the month.

day, an integer from 1 to 31 to specify the weekday. This argument is optional.

hours, an integer from 0 (midnight) to 23 (11 P.M.) to specify the hour. Note that the Date object doesn't support A.M. and P.M. time syntax. The *hours* argument is optional.

minutes, an integer from 0 to 59 to specify the minute. This argument is optional.

seconds, an integer from 0 to 59 to specify the second. This argument is optional.

milliseconds, an integer from 0 to 999 to specify the millisecond. This argument is optional. Milliseconds are important to Action-Script because *all* date information is stored in terms of milliseconds relative to midnight, January 1, 1970. Methods of the Date object allow you to manipulate these long, cumbersome numbers and translate them into more meaningful dates with the day of the week, month, time, and so on.

METHODS:

Once a Date object has been created, you can invoke the following methods with it to either set or retrieve date information:

Date.getDate() retrieves the day of the month.

Date.getDay() retrieves the day of the week.

Date.getFullYear() retrieves the year as a four-digit number.

Date.getHours() retrieves the hour of day.

Date.getMilliseconds() retrieves the milliseconds.

Date.getMinutes() retrieves the minute of the hour.

Date.getMonth() retrieves the month of the year.

Date.getSeconds() retrieves the seconds of the minute.

Date.getTime() retrieves the number of milliseconds since January 1, 1970.

Date.getYear() retrieves the year relative to 1900.

Date.setDate() sets the day of the month.

Date.setFullYear() sets the year as a four-digit number.

Date.setHours() sets the hour of day.

Date.setMilliseconds() sets the milliseconds.

Date.setMinutes() sets the minutes of the hour.

Date.setMonth() sets the month of the year.

Date.setSeconds() sets the seconds of the minute.

Date.setTime() sets the date in milliseconds relative to January 1, 1970.

Date.setYear() sets the year in either two-digit or four-digit format.

Date.toString() returns a string that lists the date in both local time and UTC.

EXAMPLE:

These statements create a new Date object for the current day and time; then they use various methods to format the date and display it in a "clock" created by text fields:

```
//create a new Date object
today=new Date();
//format each unit of time
//in an individual text field
hours=today.getHours();
minutes=today.getMinutes();
seconds=today.getSeconds();
```

The following statements are attached to a Button and will compute the number of days remaining until the birthday specified in the text fields **month** and **day**:

```
on(release){
    today=new Date();
    bDay=new Date(today.getFullYear(),
    ➡month-1,day)
    var wait=Math.ceil((bDay-today)/86400000);
    if(wait<0){
        printout="Happy belated birthday!";
    }else{
        printout=wait+" days until your
        ➡next birthday.";
    }
}
```

Here, there are two new Date objects: one for the current time, **today**, and another for the birthday specified in the text fields **month** and **day**. Note that because ActionScript numbers months starting with 0 (January equals 0), it's necessary to subtract 1 from the value that is entered into the **month** field. The difference between these dates is computed by Flash in terms of milliseconds. To return the result in a readable number, the final value is divided by 86,400,000 (the number of milliseconds in a day) and rounded to the next highest integer with the `Math.ceil()` method. The results are displayed in the field `printout` accordingly.

Date.getDate (5+)

COMPONENTS:

someDateObj`.getDate()`

Use the `getDate()` method to return the day of the month for *someDateObj*. The day will be returned as an integer from 1 to 31.

Date.getDay (5+)

COMPONENTS:

someDateObj`.getDay()`

Use the `getDay()` method to return the day of the week for *someDateObj*. Weekdays are returned as an integer from 0 (Sunday) to 6 (Saturday).

Date.getFullYear (5+)

COMPONENTS:

someDateObj`.getFullYear()`

The `getFullYear()` method returns the year for *someDateObj* as a four-digit integer.

Date.getHours (5+)

COMPONENTS:

someDateObj`.getHours()`

The `getHours()` method returns the hour of day for *someDateObj*. Hours are returned as integers from 0 (midnight) to 23 (11 P.M.). Note that the Date object does not support A.M. and P.M. time syntax.

Date.getMilliseconds (5+)

COMPONENTS:

someDateObj`.getMilliseconds()`

The `getMilliseconds()` method returns the milliseconds for *someDateObj*. Milliseconds are returned as an integer from 0 to 999.

Date.getMinutes (5+)

COMPONENTS:

someDateObj`.getMinutes()`

Use the `getMinutes()` method to return the minutes of the hour for *someDateObj*. Minutes are returned as an integer from 0 to 59.

Date.getMonth (5+)

COMPONENTS:

someDateObj`.getMonth()`

Use the `getMonth()` method to return the month of the year for *someDateObj*. The month is returned as an integer from 0 (January) to 11 (December).

Date.getSeconds (5+)

COMPONENTS:

someDateObj`.getSeconds()`

The `getSeconds()` method will return the seconds of the minute for *someDateObj*. Seconds are returned as an integer from 0 to 59.

Date.getTime (5+)

COMPONENTS:

someDateObj`.getTime()`

Flash stores all Date objects as a single number: elapsed milliseconds since midnight of January 1, 1970. The `getTime()` method will return the number of milliseconds for *someDateObj*. This measure allows you to access numbers for the easy comparison of two dates.

Date.getYear (5+)

COMPONENTS:

someDateObj`.getYear()`

Use this method to return the year of *someDateObj* relative to 1900. For example, the year 1973 is returned as 73, and the year 2002 is returned as 102.

Date.setDate (5+)

COMPONENTS:

someDateObj`.setDate(`*day*`)`

The `setDate` method allows you to set the day of the month for *someDateObj*. A date is specified in the argument *day* as an integer from 1 to 31.

Date.setFullYear (5+)

COMPONENTS:

someDateObj.setFullYear(*year,month,day*)

This method allows you to set the exact date of *someDateObj*. It takes the following arguments:

> *year*, a four-digit number to set the year
>
> *month*, an integer between 0 (January) and 11 (December) to set the month of the year
>
> *day*, an integer between 1 and 31 to set the day of the month

Date.setHours (5+)

COMPONENTS:

someDateObj.setHours(*hour*)

Use this method to set the hour of day for *someDateObj*. Hours are specified as an integer from 0 (midnight) to 23 (11 PM).

Date.setMilliseconds (5+)

COMPONENTS:

someDateObj.setMilliseconds(*mSeconds*)

Use this method to set the number of milliseconds for *someDateObj*. Milliseconds are specified as an integer between 0 and 999.

Date.setMinutes (5+)

COMPONENTS:

someDateObj.setMinutes(*minute*)

Use this method to set the minute of the hour for *someDateObj*. Minutes are specified as an integer between 0 and 59. Minute values outside the 0 to 59 range will update the previous or next hour of *someDateObj* accordingly. For example, a minute value of 60 is equivalent to the first minute of the next hour.

Date.setMonth (5+)

COMPONENTS:

someDateObj.setMonth(*month*)

Use this method to set the month of the year for *someDateObj*. Months are specified as an integer between 0 (January) and 11 (December). Month values outside the 0 to 11 range will update the previous or next year of *someDateObj* accordingly.

Date.setSeconds (5+)

COMPONENTS:

someDateObj.setSeconds(*second*)

Use this method to set the second of the minute for *someDateObj*. Seconds are specified as an integer between 0 and 59. Second values outside the 0 to 59 range will update the previous or next minute of *someDateObj* accordingly. For example, a second value of –1 is equivalent to the last (59th) second of the previous minute.

Date.setTime (5+)

COMPONENTS:

someDateObj.setTime(*mSeconds*)

Use this method to set the number of milliseconds for *someDateObj* relative to January 1, 1970. Milliseconds are specified as an integer and represent the elapsed seconds between the new Date object and the fixed marker in 1970.

Date.setYear (5+)

COMPONENTS:

someDateObj.setYear(*year,month,day*)

This method allows you to set the exact date of *someDateObj* and takes the following arguments:

> *year*, an integer value of 0 to 99 represents the years 1900 through 1999. Use a four-digit integer to represent the year 2000 and later and three-digit numbers for years prior to 1000 A.D.
>
> *month*, an integer between 0 (January) and 11 (December) to set the month of the year.
>
> *day*, an integer between 1 and 31 to set the day of the month.

Date.toString (5+)

COMPONENTS:

someDateObj.toString()

Use this method to convert the information in *someDateObj* to a readable format that includes the day of the week, month, calendar date, hours, minutes, seconds, GMT (or UTC) offset, and year.

Key Object (5+)

Key.*keyMethod*()

Key.*keyProperty*

The Key object monitors and controls keystrokes in your movies, and it provides an excellent means to create interactive controls using a computer keyboard. Key object methods are useful for recording the identity of pressed keys, and Key object properties provide shortcuts to identify many common keys for keyboard input. (For a complete listing of key codes, see Table R.4 at the end of the ActionScript Reference section.)

METHODS:

Key.getAscii() returns the ASCII value of the last key pressed.

Key.getCode() returns the key code value of the last key pressed.

Key.isDown() checks if the specified key is currently depressed.

PROPERTIES:

Table R.2 shows properties for the Key object.

Table R.2

Properties for a Key Object

SYNTAX	KEY	KEY CODE
Key.BACKSPACE	Backspace	8
Key.CAPSLOCK	Caps Lock	20
Key.CONTROL	Control	17
Key.DELETEKEY	Delete	46
Key.DOWN	Down arrow	40
Key.END	End	35
Key.ENTER	Enter (numeric keypad)	13
Key.ESCAPE	Esc	27
Key.HOME	Home	36
Key.INSERT	Insert	45
Key.LEFT	Left arrow	37
Key.PGDN	Page Down	34
Key.PGUP	Page Up	33
Key.RIGHT	Right arrow	39
Key.SHIFT	Shift	16
Key.SPACE	Spacebar	32
Key.TAB	Tab	9
Key.UP	Up arrow	38

Key.getAscii (5+)

COMPONENTS:

Key.getAscii()

Use this method to return the ASCII value of the last key pressed. Unlike getCode(), getAscii() can distinguish between uppercase and lowercase letters, but it cannot tell the difference between numbers on the regular keyboard and those on the numeric keypad. See Key.getCode() for an example of this method in context.

Key.getCode (5+)

COMPONENTS:

Key.getCode()

Use this method to return the key code value of the last key pressed. Key codes are built-in values that represent all keys on the keyboard with numeric codes. (For a complete listing of these, see Table R.4 at the end of the ActionScript Reference section.)

EXAMPLE:

Use the following function to retrieve key code and ASCII code values from Flash MX directly:

```
keyCheck=new Object();
keyCheck.onKeyDown=function(){
  trace("code: "+Key.getCode());
  trace("ascii: "+Key.getAscii());
}
Key.addListener(keyCheck);
```

The keyCheck object is registered as a listener that will respond to keystrokes, or more specifically, the onKeyDown event.

Key.isDown (5+)

COMPONENTS:

Key.isDown(*keyCode*)

Unlike the Key.getAscii() and Key.getCode() methods, this method tests whether the key specified in *keyCode* is being pressed or held down. It's useful for controls that rely on prolonged or constant key input. The argument for *keyCode* can be entered as a numeric key code value or as a property of the Key object (for example, Key.SPACE).

EXAMPLE:

This script demonstrates a simple Movie Clip navigation system using the arrow keys:

```
onClipEvent(enterFrame){
    if(Key.isDown(Key.UP)){
        this._y-=10;
    }else if(Key.isDown(Key.DOWN)){
        this._y+=10;
    }
    if(Key.isDown(Key.LEFT)){
        this._x-=10;
    }else if(Key.isDown(Key.RIGHT)){
        this._x+=10;
    }
}
```

Note in this example how up/down and left/right scripts are in separate if...else blocks. This enables the script to execute movement in two directions simultaneously—the clip can go either up or down *and* either left or right. Thus, the clip can move diagonally.

Math Object (5+)

COMPONENTS:

Math.*mathProperty*

Math.*mathMethod(expression)*

The Math object enables you to write scripts that perform numeric calculations. The object provides access to mathematical functions (via Math object methods) that can be used for ActionScript number-crunching in your movies.

METHODS:

Math.abs() calculates the absolute value.

Math.ceil() rounds a number to the next higher integer.

Math.floor() rounds a number to the next lower integer.

Math.max() calculates the larger of two numbers.

Math.min() calculates the smaller of two numbers.

Math.pow() raises a number to an exponential power.

Math.random() returns a random number between 0.0 and 1.0.

Math.round() rounds a number to the nearest integer.

Math.abs (5+)

COMPONENTS:

Math.abs(*expression*)

Use the Math.abs() method to return the *absolute value* of *expression*. The absolute value is the value of an expression relative to 0 without regard to whether it is positive or negative. Math.abs() converts negative values to positive values and leaves positive values untouched.

Math.ceil (5+)

COMPONENTS:

Math.ceil(*expression*)

The Math.ceil() method converts a floating-point number specified in *expression* to the nearest integer that is greater than or equal to *expression*. Math.ceil(0.00001) evaluates to 1. Math.ceil(1.9) evaluates to 2.

Math.floor (5+)

COMPONENTS:

Math.floor(*expression*)

The Math.floor() method converts a floating-point number specified in *expression* to the nearest integer that is less than or equal to *expression*. Math.floor(0.00001) evaluates to 0; Math.floor(1.9) evaluates to 1.

Math.max (5+)

COMPONENTS:

Math.max(*num1*,*num2*)

Use this method to return the larger of the two numbers specified in *num1* and *num2*.

Math.min (5+)

COMPONENTS:

Math.min(*num1*,*num2*)

Use this method to return the smaller of the two numbers specified in *num1* and *num2*.

Math.pow (5+)

COMPONENTS:

`Math.pow(num,exp)`

This method raises the number *num* to the power of *exp*.

Math.random (5+)

COMPONENTS:

`Math.random()`

`Math.random()` produces a random number that is greater than or equal to 0 and less than 1 (0.0 to 0.9999…). Use this method to randomly generate numbers that can be used for indeterminate functions, to make random selections, to arbitrarily position a Movie Clip on the Stage, and so on.

EXAMPLE:

This statement will generate a random integer between 0 and 10:

`Math.floor(Math.random()*11);`

Because `Math.random()` will never generate a number equal to 1, use an integer that's one number higher to set the upper range. `Math.floor()` will round the resulting value down to the nearest integer.

Similarly, you can establish both an upper and a lower range for the random number. These statements generate a random number between 50 and 100 and use it to set the `_alpha` value of a Movie Clip:

```
onClipEvent(load){
    vis=Math.floor(Math.random()*101)+50;
    this._alpha=vis;
}
```

Math.round (5+)

COMPONENTS:

`Math.round(expression)`

Use this method to round floating-point numbers to the nearest integer value. Numbers with decimal values equal to or greater than 0.5 will be rounded to the next higher integer value; decimal values less than 0.5 will be rounded to the next lower integer value.

EXAMPLE:

`Math.round(1.5)` returns 2.
`Math.round(1.4)` returns 1.
`Math.round(-1.5)` returns -1.
`Math.round(-1.6)` returns -2.

Mouse Object (5+)

COMPONENTS:

`Mouse.mouseMethod`

You can use the Mouse object to make the mouse cursor hidden or visible when it appears over the Flash Player. The methods of the Mouse object are usually used to replace the system default cursor (arrow) with a custom cursor Movie Clip.

METHODS:

`Mouse.hide()` hides the mouse cursor.
`Mouse.show()` shows the mouse cursor.

Mouse.hide (5+)

COMPONENTS:

`Mouse.hide()`

This method effectively hides the mouse cursor when it is positioned over the Flash Player (within a Flash movie's bounds). When the cursor is moved outside a movie, the default system cursor becomes visible again.

EXAMPLE:

These statements, when attached to a Movie Clip, will turn that clip into a custom mouse cursor. The `mouseMove` event is helpful in this situation to ensure that the Movie Clip moves smoothly with the cursor and doesn't skip between frames:

```
onClipEvent(load){
    Mouse.hide();
}
onClipEvent(mouseMove){
    this._x=_root._xmouse;
    this._y=_root._ymouse;

}
```

Mouse.show (5+)

COMPONENTS:

`Mouse.show()`

This method restores the appearance of the default mouse cursor after it has been hidden by the `Mouse.hide()` method.

MovieClip Object (5+/6)

COMPONENTS:

`clipInstance.methodName`

`targetPath.clipInstance.methodName`

The MovieClip object cannot create new Movie Clips. Movie Clips are created in Flash by selecting Insert → New Symbol and then selecting Movie Clip as the new symbol's behavior. Rather, the MovieClip object is ActionScript-based and provides a series of methods for controlling the playback of clip instances. Many of these are similar to the actions that you can use to control clip and movie Timeline playback. However, there are some methods that provide additional functionality beyond the scope of clip-related actions. Methods of the MovieClip object can be used on clip instances and movie Timelines alike. This includes both the main movie and SWF files that have been loaded into a new movie level. To use methods of the MovieClip object on a clip, simply attach the actions to the clip directly using the appropriate `onClipEvent` handler. If your movie requires that you control a clip from another location, such as a Button, the clip must have a unique instance name. It can be assigned in the Property Inspector or initialized when the clip is either duplicated or attached from the Library. Additionally, it is often necessary to specify the target path to the clip you want to control. A target path is required if your target clip resides at a different movie level (`_root`, `_level1`, `_level2`, and so on) or is nested within one or more Movie Clip instances. To read more about targeting clips and movie Timelines, see Chapter 16.

METHODS:

`MovieClip.attachMovie()` creates a new clip instance using a clip exported from the Library. `MovieClip.duplicateMovieClip()` creates a copy of the specified Movie Clip.

`MovieClip.getBytesLoaded()` returns the number of bytes loaded for the specified movie. `MovieClip.getBytesTotal()` returns the size, in bytes, of the specified movie. `MovieClip.getURL()` loads an external file found at the specified URL. `MovieClip.globalToLocal()` converts coordinates from Stage coordinates to clip instance coordinates. `MovieClip.gotoAndPlay()` sends the specified movie or instance to a frame in its Timeline and initiates playback from that point. `MovieClip.gotoAndStop()` sends the specified movie or instance to a frame in its Timeline and halts playback at that point. `MovieClip.hitTest()` returns Boolean True or False if the specified clip intersects with a movie coordinate or another clip. `MovieClip.loadMovie()` loads an external SWF movie into the specified clip instance. `MovieClip.loadVariables()` loads data found at a URL into the specified clip instance. `MovieClip.localToGlobal()` converts clip instance coordinates to Stage, or main movie, coordinates. `MovieClip.nextFrame()` sends the playback head of the specified clip or movie ahead one frame and stops it there. `MovieClip.play()` initiates playback of the specified clip or movie. `MovieClip.prevFrame()` sends the playback head of the specified clip or movie back one frame and stops it there. `MovieClip.removeMovieClip()` erases a dynamic clip instance created with either `duplicateMovieClip()` or `attachMovie()`. `MovieClip.startDrag()` makes a clip instance draggable. `MovieClip.stop()` halts playback of the specified clip or movie. `MovieClip.stopDrag()` disables a clip instance from being dragged by the mouse. `MovieClip.unloadMovie()` removes an external SWF file that was accessed via the `loadMovie()` action or method. `MovieClip.valueOf()` returns the absolute path to the specified clip instance in dot syntax.

MovieClip.attachMovie (5+)

COMPONENTS:

`clipInstance.attachMovie("id","name",depth)`

The `attachMovie()` method calls a new MovieClip instance to the Stage and positions it at the origin of `clipInstance`. The origin is the upper-left corner of the main movie or registration point of a MovieClip instance. To attach a clip, you must first export it from the Library by selecting Linkage from the Options menu. The exported name (specified in the Linkage Properties dialog box) is used for the argument *id*. Additionally, you must provide the clip with an instance name (*name*) and assign it a position in the internal clip stacking level (*depth*). *id* and *name* are entered as strings, and `depth` is specified as an integer.

EXAMPLE:

This script attaches the movie exported as `sun` and renames it as the instance `yellow`. Attaching a movie at the `_root` level will position it in the upper-left corner of the Stage. In this example, `yellow` is moved to the center of a 550×400–pixel Stage.

```
_root.attachMovie("sun","yellow",2);
_root.yellow._x=275;
_root.yellow._y=200;
```

MovieClip.duplicateMovieClip (5+)

COMPONENTS:

`instance.duplicateMovieClip("newName",depth)`

This method duplicates the specified *instance*, gives it a new instance name (*newName*), and assigns a position in the internal clip stacking level (*depth*). Enter the *newName* argument as a string, and enter *depth* as an integer. Although the syntax is slightly different, the functionality of this method is identical to the `duplicateMovieClip()` action. See the `duplicateMovieClip()` action for an in-context example.

MovieClip.getBytesLoaded (5+)

COMPONENTS:

`clipInstance.getBytesLoaded()`

Use this method to obtain the number of bytes that have been downloaded for the movie specified in `clipInstance`. If you want to retrieve the bytes for the main movie, no target is necessary, but it is good practice to specify `_root` or `this`. Because Movie Clips are considered part of their host movie, you cannot retrieve the number of bytes loaded for clip instances. This method is intended to monitor the load progress of main movies and external SWF files.

EXAMPLE:

This script fills the text field `loaded` with the number of kilobytes of the main movie that have been downloaded. The bytes value returned by `getBytesLoaded()` can be divided by 1,024 to obtain the number of kilobytes:

```
loaded=Math.round(_root.getBytesLoaded()/
➥1024)+"kB";
```

MovieClip.getBytesTotal (5+)

COMPONENTS:

`clipInstance.getBytesTotal()`

This method returns the size, in bytes, of the specified movie or MovieClip instance.

EXAMPLE:

This script fills the text field `total` with the total number of kilobytes of the main movie (the overall size of the movie in kilobytes). The bytes value returned by `getBytesTotal()` can be divided by 1,024 to obtain the number of kilobytes:

```
total=Math.round(_root.getBytesTotal()/
➥1024)+"kB";
```

MovieClip.getURL (5+)

COMPONENTS:

`clip.getURL("target","window","varMethod")`

This MovieClip object method has the same functionality as the `getURL()` action. It allows you to pass variables directly from the specified movie or clip instance to a URL. For a complete description and example, see the section about the `getURL()` action.

MovieClip.globalToLocal (5+)

COMPONENTS:

`clipInstance.globalToLocal(point)`

The `globalToLocal()`method performs a conversion from Stage coordinates to Movie Clip coordinates. It tells you where a certain coordinate point on the Stage appears, relative to the registration point of a Movie Clip. The *point* argument represents an object with the properties x and y. The object *point* is initialized to store coordinate values to be converted to local values. Conversions are based on the coordinate system of the specified instance *clipInstance*. The *point* object stores values for conversion and cannot set the position of a clip.

EXAMPLE:

Examine this script line by line to see how the conversion works.

Create a generic object named pnt:

`pnt=new Object();`

Assign its x and y properties the current x and y values for the current clip instance:

`pnt.x=this._x;`
`pnt.y=this._y;`

Print the current x and y values in a text field. This reflects their global, or Stage, position:

`_root.txt1="global: "+this._x+","+this._y;`

Perform the conversion from global to local coordinates on the pnt object:

`this.globalToLocal(pnt);`

Print the local coordinates for the current clip:

`_root.txt2="local: "+pnt.x+","+pnt.y;`

Because the properties were initialized as the location of the clip, a global-to-local conversion yields the coordinates (0, 0), or the registration point of this clip.

MovieClip.gotoAndPlay (5+)

COMPONENTS:

`clipInstance.gotoAndPlay(frameNum)`
`clipInstance.gotoAndPlay("frameLabel")`

This method sends the playback head of the specified movie or clip instance or movie level (noted in the argument *clipInstance*) to a location in its

Timeline and initiates playback from that point. You can set the location by supplying either a frame number as an integer or a frame label as a string.

MovieClip.gotoAndStop (5+)

COMPONENTS:

`clipInstance.gotoAndStop(frameNum)`
`clipInstance.gotoAndStop("frameLabel")`

This method sends the playback head of the specified movie or clip instance or movie level (noted in the argument *clipInstance*) to a location in its Timeline and halts its playback at that point. You can set the location by supplying either a frame number as an integer or a frame label as a string.

MovieClip.hitTest (5+)

COMPONENTS:

`clipInstance.hitTest(x,y,shapeFlag)`
`clipInstance.hitTest("target")`

This method returns a Boolean value and checks whether the specified clip *clipInstance* intersects with a coordinate point or another clip instance. To test intersection with a point, you must specify X and Y coordinates and enter a Boolean value for the *shapeFlag* argument. When false (the default setting if no value is entered), intersection will be based on the bounding box of *clipInstance*. When true, intersection occurs only with the actual pixels of *clipInstance*. Set *shapeFlag* to true to test intersection with irregularly shaped Movie Clips, or clips with large gaps. Alternately, to test for intersection with another clip, specify the target path to that clip as a string. No other arguments are required.

EXAMPLE:

The following syntax using the hitTest() method checks whether the current clip has collided with the border clip instance. If it has (true), the text field display shows HIT; otherwise, it shows nothing:

```
onClipEvent(enterFrame){
    if(this.hitTest("_root.border")){
        _root.display="HIT";
    }else _root.display="";
}
```

MovieClip.loadMovie (5+)

COMPONENTS:

`clipInstance.loadMovie("URL","varMethod")`

This method has the same functionality as the `loadMovie()` action. The only difference between the two is that as a MovieClip object method, it takes no *target* argument. Instead, it loads the SWF found at the specified URL into *clipInstance*. For an in-context example, and to learn about passing variables using the optional *varMethod* argument, see the section on the `loadMovie()` action.

MovieClip.loadVariables (5+)

COMPONENTS:

`clipInstance.loadVariables("URL","varMethd")`

This `MovieClip` method has the same functionality as the `loadVariables()` action. The main difference is that as a method, it takes no *target* argument and instead loads the variables found at the specified *URL* into *clipInstance*. For an in-context example, and to learn about passing variables using the optional *varMethd* argument, see the section on the `loadVariables()` action.

MovieClip.localToGlobal (5+)

COMPONENTS:

`clipInstance.localToGlobal(point)`

The `localToGlobal` method performs a conversion from Movie Clip coordinates to Stage coordinates. It tells you where a certain coordinate point in a Movie Clip appears, relative to the upper-left corner of the Stage. The *point* argument represents an object with the properties x and y. The object *point* is initialized to store coordinate values to be converted to Stage, or global, values. Conversions are based on the coordinate system of the specified instance *clipInstance*. The *point* object is used to store values for conversion and cannot set the position of a clip.

EXAMPLE:

Examine this script line by line to see how the conversion works. Create a generic object named `pnt`:

`pnt=new Object();`

Assign its x and y properties the current x and y values for the current clip instance:

`pnt.x=0;`

`pnt.y=0;`

Print the current x and y values in a text field. This reflects their global, or Stage, position:

`_root.txt1="global:"+this._x+","+this._y;`

Perform the conversion from local to global coordinates on the `pnt` object:

`this.localToGlobal(pnt);`

Print the local coordinates for the current clip:

`_root.txt2="local:"+pnt.x+","+pnt.y;`

Because the properties were initialized as the point (0, 0), a local-to-global conversion yields the coordinates (200, 130), or the position of this clip on the Stage.

MovieClip.nextFrame (5+)

COMPONENTS:

`clipInstance.nextFrame()`

This method sends the specified Movie Clip instance or movie level (*clipInstance*) ahead one frame in its Timeline and stops it there. It is particularly useful for creating frame-by-frame or slide-show sequences.

MovieClip.play (5+)

COMPONENTS:

`clipInstance.play()`

This method initiates playback of the specified Movie Clip instance or movie level. It is particularly useful for the interactive control of clips and movies from separate Timelines.

MovieClip.prevFrame (5+)

COMPONENTS:

`clipInstance.prevFrame()`

This method sends the specified Movie Clip instance or movie level (*clipInstance*) back one frame in its Timeline and stops it there. It is particularly useful for creating frame-by-frame or slide-show sequences.

MovieClip.removeMovieClip (5+)

COMPONENTS:

clipInstance.removeMovieClip()

This MovieClip object method has the same functionality as the removeMovieClip() action. It deletes from the Stage any clip instance that was created via attachMovie() or duplicateMovieClip(). This method takes no *target* argument; instead specify the target path to *clipInstance* to remove *clipInstance* from the Stage.

EXAMPLE:

When the current clip is clicked, this script will delete the instance alert from the current movie:

```
onClipEvent(mouseUp){
    if(this.hitTest(_root._xmouse,_root.
    ➡_ymouse,true)){
        _root.alert.removeMovieClip();
    }
}
```

MovieClip.startDrag (5+)

COMPONENTS:

clip.startDrag(*lock,left,top,right,bottom*)

Like the startDrag() action, the startDrag() method enables a clip to be dragged, or moved, about the Stage by the mouse cursor. When called, *clipInstance* becomes draggable. The *lock* argument is a Boolean value that specifies whether the clip's registration point should lock to the tip of the mouse cursor (true) or remain in its original position (false) when first clicked. The position arguments—*left*, *top*, *right*, and *bottom*—are entered as integers and determine the coordinate boundaries for the draggable *clipInstance*. For an example using the startDrag() action to create a slider, see "Creating a Slider to Scroll a Timeline" in Chapter 16.

MovieClip.stop (5+)

COMPONENTS:

clipInstance.stop()

This method ceases playback of the specified Movie Clip instance or movie level. It is particularly useful for the interactive control of clips and movies from separate Timelines.

MovieClip.stopDrag (5+)

COMPONENTS:

clipInstance.stopDrag()

Like the stopDrag() action, this method ceases the dragging of any clip instances in the current movie. For an example, see the startDrag() action.

MovieClip.unloadMovie (5+)

COMPONENTS:

clipInstance.unloadMovie()

This method unloads the SWF movie specified by *clipInstance*.

MovieClip.valueOf (5+)

COMPONENTS:

clipInstance.valueOf()

The valueOf method returns the absolute target path to the specified clip in dot syntax.

MovieClip Object Drawing Methods (6)

The drawing methods of the MovieClip object are new in Flash MX and can be used to dynamically draw Movie Clips with ActionScript. To read more about the MovieClip object drawing methods, see the Reference panel (Shift+F1) or the documentation that ships with Flash MX.

MovieClip.beginFill() sets the current fill style and fills the area within a Movie Clip.

MovieClip.createEmptyMovieClip() creates a new, empty Movie Clip.

MovieClip.curveTo() draws a curve in the current drawing style.

MovieClip.endFill() applies the fill established by the last beginFill() call.

MovieClip.lineStyle() defines the attributes of the line used when drawing a Movie Clip using ActionScript.

MovieClip.lineTo() draws a straight line in the current drawing style.

MovieClip.moveTo() resets the "pen" position when drawing a Movie Clip.

MovieClip.beginFill (6)

COMPONENTS:

`clipInstance.beginFill(rgb,alpha)`

Use this method to paint a fill color for the Movie Clip `clipInstance`. When painting, you must specify two things: an RGB color as a Hex color value in the format 0xrrggbb and a value between 0–100 for the opacity, or `alpha` of the fill.

MovieClip.createEmptyMovieClip (6)

COMPONENTS:

`target.createEmptyMovieClip("instance",depth)`

This method is the first step of drawing a Movie Clip with ActionScript. Use it to create a Movie Clip on the Timeline specified by `target`. For the new clip, assign an instance name (`instance`) as a string and give it a `depth` in the stacking level. There can only be one clip on a stacking level at a time, so be sure to create the clip at a depth that is available.

MovieClip.curveTo (6)

COMPONENTS:

`clipInstance.curveTo(hanX,hanY,ptX,ptY)`

The curveTo() method draws curves and arcs. The curved line is drawn from the current drawing position as set by the last lineTo(), curveTo(), or moveTo() call. If not otherwise specified, the curve begins at point (0,0) on the Timeline specified by `clipInstance`. To draw a curve, you must specify four things: X and Y coordinates (`hanX,hanY`) for the tangent handle that gives the curve its shape and X and Y coordinates (`ptX,ptY`) to set the destination of the curve. The resulting curve is drawn in the current line style as set by the last lineStyle() call.

MovieClip.endFill (6)

COMPONENTS:

`clipInstance.endFill()`

This method applies the fill established by the last beginFill() call to the specified `clipInstance`. If endFill() is called, and the drawing position has changed since the last moveTo() call, the path is closed and filled with the current fill style.

MovieClip.lineStyle (6)

COMPONENTS:

`clipInstance.lineStyle(stroke,rgb,alpha)`

Use this method to set the attributes for the outlines (strokes) of your vector images. Specify a line weight (`stroke`) as an integer. 0 represents hairline thickness; the maximum thickness is 255. Use a Hex color value (in the format 0xrrggbb) for `rgb` to set the color of the line, and specify an opacity (`alpha`) setting between 0–100. Once a lineStyle() call is made, all line attributes are fixed until a new call is made.

MovieClip.lineTo (6)

COMPONENTS:

`clipInstance.lineTo(x,y)`

The lineTo() method draws a straight line. The line is drawn from the current drawing position as set by the last lineTo(), curveTo(), or moveTo() call. If not otherwise specified, the line begins at point (0,0) on the Timeline specified by `clipInstance`. To draw a line you must specify the destination X and Y coordinates. The resulting line is drawn from the current position to point (x,y) in the current line style as set by the last lineStyle() call.

MovieClip.moveTo (6)

COMPONENTS:

`clipInstance.moveTo(x,y)`

The moveTo() method sets the initial drawing position of a line or curve. Specify the position as X and Y coordinates, relative to the registration point of `clipInstance`. After the drawing position has been set, the current drawing position is always determined by the coordinate destination of the last lineTo() or curveTo() call.

EXAMPLE:

This example uses ActionScript to dynamically draw a twilight scene. This first block draws a black square named sky. Note that when the shape is drawn using only beginFill(), it has no stroke:

```
_root.createEmptyMovieClip("sky",1);
_root.sky.beginFill(0x000000);
```

```
_root.sky.moveTo(0,0);
_root.sky.lineTo(0,200);
_root.sky.lineTo(200,200);
_root.sky.lineTo(200,0);
_root.sky.lineTo(0,0);
```

The second block draws a series of stars. They are randomly placed in a 190×190 box and randomly rotated in the range 0–45 degrees:

```
for(i=2; i<23; i++){
    var ptX=Math.floor(Math.random()*191);
    var ptY=Math.floor(Math.random()*191);
    var spin=Math.floor(Math.random()*46);
    _root.createEmptyMovieClip("star"+i,i);
    with(eval("_root.star"+i)){
        _rotation=spin;
        linestyle(2,0xcccc66,100);
        beginFill(0xcccc00)
        moveTo(ptX+7,ptY-7);
        lineTo(ptX,ptY-8);
        lineTo(ptX+5,ptY-13);
        lineTo(ptX+4,ptY-20);
        lineTo(ptX+10,ptY-16);
        lineTo(ptX+16,ptY-20);
        lineTo(ptX+15,ptY-13);
        lineTo(ptX+20,ptY-8);
        lineTo(ptX+13,ptY-7);
        lineTo(ptX+10,ptY);
        lineTo(ptX+7,ptY-7);
    }
}
```

This last block draws a crescent moon using the curveTo() drawing method. The moon has a dark purple stroke and a light-purple fill:

```
_root.createEmptyMovieClip("moon",i);
_root.moon.linestyle(8,0x663366,100);
_root.moon.beginFill(0x666699);
_root.moon.moveTo(40,50);
_root.moon.curveTo(116,12,150,40);
_root.moon.curveTo(190,73,160,160);
_root.moon.curveTo(162,109,126,74)
_root.moon.curveTo(85,35,40,50);
```

Object (Generic) Object Components (5+)

new Object()

Use this object to create a generic object that will hold information temporarily or to create custom objects. To create a generic or custom object, use the constructor function new Object(). For an example of this term in action, see the Color.setTransform(), MovieClip.localToGlobal(), or Sound.setTransform() methods.

Sound Object (5+/6)

COMPONENTS:

new Sound()
new Sound("*target*")

You can use the Sound object to control the playback of sounds in a Flash movie. To create a Sound object, you must use the constructor function new Sound(). Using this syntax, you create a global Sound object named globalSound that can control all sounds currently active in a movie:

globalSound=new Sound();

This syntax uses the *target* argument to create a Sound object named bkgdSound for the sounds at movie level 1:

bkgdSound=new Sound("_level1");

This final syntax creates a Sound object named clipSound for the sounds in the Movie Clip note:

clipSound=new Sound("_root.note");

Once a Sound object has been created, you can use the Sound object methods to control the volume and pan position of a sound. Additionally, individual sounds can be exported from the Library and attached to a specific Sound object using the attachSound() method. This technique offers complete control over all sound playback parameters, including *where* the sound starts and how many times it is looped (repeated).

EVENTS:

Sound.onSoundComplete takes place when a sound finishes its playback.

Sound.onLoad takes place when a sound is loaded into a Flash movie from an external source.

METHODS:

Sound.attachSound() pairs a sound exported from the Library with a Sound object.

Sound.getPan() retrieves the pan position for the given Sound object.

Sound.getTransform() retrieves the percentage of a sound's stereo channels currently being played in the left and right speakers.

Sound.getVolume() retrieves the volume level for the given Sound object.

Sound.setPan() assigns a pan position for the given Sound object.

Sound.setTransform() assigns the percentage of a sound's stereo channels to be played in the left and right speakers.

Sound.setVolume() assigns the volume level for the given Sound object.

Sound.start() cues the sound attached to the given Sound object.

Sound.stop() silences the sound attached to the given Sound object.

PROPERTIES:

Sound.duration returns the length of the specified sound in milliseconds.

Sound.position returns the number of milliseconds a sound has been playing.

Sound.attachSound (5+)

COMPONENTS:

soundObj.attachSound("identifier")

The attachSound() method pairs a sound exported from the Library with the specified Sound object. To export a sound, select the sound in the Library panel and choose Linkage from the Options menu. Check the Export for ActionScript box and assign it a name in the Identifier field. When invoking the attach-Sound() method, use this name as a string (in quotes) for the identifier argument, and the exported sound will be attached to the object you specify. Once the sound has been attached, it can be cued, stopped, and manipulated by controlling its Sound object. Only one sound can be attached to an object at a time. If you have multiple Sound objects at various movie levels, be sure to include a target argument to control the sounds attached to each.

EXAMPLE:

In this example, the sound brass is attached to the new Sound object fanfare and cued to play:

```
fanfare=new Sound();
fanfare.attachSound("brass");
fanfare.start();
```

Sound.duration (6)

COMPONENTS:

soundObj.duration

This property retrieves the total length, in milliseconds, for the sound attached to the specified soundObj.

EXAMPLE:

This script uses both the Sound.position and Sound.duration properties to create a progress bar that tracks the position of a sound. As the sound plays back, the progress bar (which is loaded at an _xscale value of 0) is scaled closer and closer to 100:

```
onClipEvent(load){
    bar_mc._xscale=0;
}
onClipEvent(enterFrame){
    played=_root.riff.position;
    total=_root.riff.duration;
    bar_mc._xscale=100*(played/total);
}
```

Sound.getPan (5+)

COMPONENTS:

soundObj.getPan()

Use this method to retrieve the current pan position for the specified Sound object. Pan position is measured between –100 (hard left) and 100 (hard right).

Sound.getTransform (5+)

COMPONENTS:

soundObj.getTransform(transformObj)

This method returns an object storing the properties ll, lr, rl, and rr of the object transformObj. These properties represent the channel percentages that are set by the setTransform() method for transformObj and applied to the sounds in or attached to *soundObj*. For more information about this method, see the entry for Sound .setTransform().

Sound.getVolume (5+)

COMPONENTS:

soundObj.getVolume()

This method retrieves the current volume level for the specified Sound object. Values are returned in the range of 0 (silence) to 100 (full volume).

EXAMPLE:

This function drops the volume of all sounds in a movie to 10% of their total possible volume if they are at full volume or restores them to full volume if they are turned down:

```
function volToggle(obj){
    if(obj.getVolume()==10){
        obj.setVolume(100);
    }else obj.setVolume(10);
}
```

Sound.onLoad (6)

COMPONENTS:

soundObj.onLoad=*function*

This event is triggered when the sound attached to *soundObj* has completely loaded into your movie via the loadSound() method. To make this event serve as a trigger to execute additional scripts, assign a function that executes the statements you require.

EXAMPLE:

You can use this event as a sort of preloader:

```
track1.onLoad=function(){
    track1.start(0,2);
    status.nextFrame();
}
```

When track1 finishes loading, it is cued, and the status Movie Clip jumps ahead to its next frame.

Sound.onSoundComplete (6)

COMPONENTS:

soundObj.onSoundComplete=*function*

This event is triggered when the sound attached to *soundObj* finishes playing. If the specified Sound

object is cued to loop, onSoundComplete will not occur until the sound has played through its loops. To make this event serve as the trigger to execute additional scripts, assign a function that executes the statements you require.

EXAMPLE:

You can use this event to do all sorts of things. One of the most logical "next steps" would be to cue the next song in a play list. For example:

```
track1.onSoundComplete=function(){
    track2.start();
}
```

When track1 finishes playing, track2 is cued.

Sound.position (6)

COMPONENTS:

soundObj.position

This property retrieves the current playback position, in milliseconds, for the sound attached to the specified *soundObj*. If *soundObj* is set to loop, the sound's position property resets to 0 with every loop iteration. For an example, see the Sound.duration property.

Sound.setPan (5+)

COMPONENTS:

soundObj.getPan(*panValue*)

This method sets the pan position for the sound or sounds associated with *soundObj*. The pan value can be set in the range of –100 (hard left) to 100 (hard right). When a sound is panned hard left, it is heard only in the left speaker. Conversely, panning a sound hard right isolates the sound in the right speaker.

EXAMPLE:

This script causes the Sound object movSnd to gradually pan its sound(s) to the left each time the button is clicked:

```
on(press){
    movSnd.setPan(movSnd.getPan()-10);
}
```

Rather than set a pan value explicitly, the getPan() method is used to retrieve the current pan value.

Then, `setPan()` adjusts the pan position to the current value minus 10. This script could just as easily pan sounds to the right by adding 10 to the current pan value.

Sound.setTransform (5+)

COMPONENTS:

`soundObj.setTransform(transformObj)`

`Sound.setTransform()` is one of the more interesting Sound object methods in ActionScript. It allows you to dynamically redistribute the left and right channel components of a stereo sound in the left and right speakers. This method enables you to completely rearrange the stereo makeup of a sound by telling Flash to play, for example, all of the left channel sound in the right speaker, none in the left, and all of the right channel sound in the left speaker, and 25% in the right.

To use this method, you must create a Transform object: a generic object with the properties `ll`, `lr`, `rl`, and `rr`. These properties are responsible for the distribution of the left and right channel components in the left and right speakers. See Table R.3 for a description of each.

Table R.3

Properties for a Sound Transform Object

PROPERTY NAME	PROPERTY RANGE	PROPERTY DESCRIPTION
ll	0–100	Percentage of the left channel sound to play in the left speaker
lr	0–100	Percentage of the right channel sound to play in the left speaker
rr	0–100	Percentage of the right channel sound to play in the right speaker
rl	0–100	Percentage of the left channel sound to play in the right speaker

After creating a Transform object, assign values for each of the four properties and pass them to the specified Sound object (`soundObj`) using the `setTransform()` method. For an in-context example, see "Scripting Special Effects" in Chapter 22.

Sound.setVolume (5+)

COMPONENTS:

`soundObj.getVolume(volumeValue)`

This method sets the volume level for the sound or sounds associated with `soundObj`. Volume can be set in the range of 0 (silence) to 100 (full volume). When a sound's volume is at 0, it will still play, but the sound will be inaudible and will sound as though it has been stopped. Although it is not documented by Macromedia, there is no real maximum volume level for sounds. However, if sounds are properly normalized before they are imported into a Flash movie, volume settings higher than 100 are likely to cause distortion.

EXAMPLE:

This script causes the Sound object `movSnd` to gradually decrease its volume each time the button is clicked:

```
on(press){
    movSnd.setVolume(movSnd.getVolume()-10);
}
```

Rather than set a volume value explicitly, the `getVolume()` method retrieves the current volume value. Then `setVolume()` adjusts the volume level to the current value minus 10. This script could just as easily increase the volume level by adding 10 to the current volume value.

Also see the example for `Sound.getVolume()`.

Sound.start (5+)

COMPONENTS:

`soundObj.start(secondsOffset,loops)`

Use this method to cue a sound that has been paired with the Sound object `soundObj` via `Sound.attachSound()`. This method takes up to two optional arguments: `secondsOffset` and `loops`. `secondsOffset` starts the sound at any time within the sound file. Specify a number, and the sound will start at that point—for example, 1.5 starts a sound one and a half seconds into the audio file. A value of 0 (default) plays a sound from the file's beginning. `loops` tells the sound how many times to repeat. A value of 1 (default) plays the sound once, 2 plays it twice, and so on. If you specify a value for `loopsOffset`, the sound will repeat from that point to its end for the number of loops that you specified.

EXAMPLE:

The following examples illustrate the `Sound.start()` method in several different forms. First, a Sound object must be created and have a sound attached from the Library:

```
groove=new Sound();
groove.attachSound("drums");
```

Then the sound is cued to play once from the beginning:

```
groove.start();
```

Or the sound is played once starting 1.8 seconds from the beginning:

```
groove.start(1.8);
```

Sound.stop (5+)

COMPONENTS:

soundObj.stop("*soundID*")

Use this method to silence sounds in a movie. Which sounds you stop depends on how you use the method. If *soundObj* is a global Sound object, this method silences all sounds in a movie. Specify a name (as a string) for *soundID* if you want to stop a sound that was attached with the `Sound .attachSound()` method.

EXAMPLE:

Because `bkgd` is a global Sound object, this statement stops all sounds in a movie:

```
bkgd.stop();
```

This statement stops the sound `drums` that is attached to the object `groove`:

```
groove.stop("drums");
```

String Object (5+)

COMPONENTS:

new String(*expression*)

The String object is a wrapper object that converts (if needed) the specified *expression* to a string and returns the result as a property within the String object. The String object can also be helpful for converting non-string datatypes to strings. However, these uses are often neither practical nor necessary. Assigning a value to a string using a literal (`stringName="text string"`) or performing conversions with the `String()` function is recommended by most ActionScript documentation. The power of the String object is in its methods. They can be invoked on any string and provide many options for manipulating string data.

METHODS:

`String.charAt()` returns the character in a string at a specified position.

`String.concat()` joins one or more strings to create a single string.

`String.indexOf()` locates the first occurrence of a specified item in a string.

`String.lastIndexOf()` locates the last occurrence of a specified item in a string.

`String.slice ()`extracts the specified portion of a string as a substring using positive and negative integers.

`String.substring()` extracts the specified portion of a string as a substring using only positive integers.

`String.toLowerCase()` returns a string containing only lowercase letters.

`String.toUpperCase()` returns a string containing only uppercase letters.

PROPERTIES:

`String.length` describes the number of characters in a string.

String.charAt (5+)

COMPONENTS:

string.charAt(*ref*)

Use this method to return the character in *string* at the reference position specified by *ref*. Reference positions are specified relative to 0. 0 represents the first character in the string, 1 represents the second, 2 represents the third, and so on.

EXAMPLE:

For the string `greeting`, this script returns G:

```
greeting="Good afternoon!";
trace(greeting.charAt(0));
```

The next statement returns ! because the string is 15 characters long and ! is at reference position 14.

```
trace(greeting.charAt(greeting.length-1));
```

String.concat (5+)

COMPONENTS:

string.concat(*item1*,*item2*...*itemx*)

Use the `String.concat()` method to join together, or concatenate, *string* with the elements specified for *item1*, *item2*, and so on.

EXAMPLE:

For the string one, this script creates `milestone`:

```
one="mile";
pair=one.concat("stone");
```

This statement creates `milestones`:

```
trio=one.concat("stone","s");
```

String.indexOf (5+)

COMPONENTS:

string.indexOf("*substring*",*ref*)

Use this method to search the elements of a string and return the position of the first occurrence of *substring* in *string*. As an optional argument, you can specify an integer for *ref*, the position where `indexOf()` will begin its search. `ref` must be a number between 0 (the string's first character) and `string.length-1` (the string's last character). `indexOf()` searches a string for *substring* from left to right, starting at either position 0 (the default) or `ref` (if specified). If *substring* isn't found, the method returns –1.

EXAMPLE:

This function strips a user's network ID—the name before the @ symbol—from a supplied e-mail address. The network ID is returned and is available for use in a movie to write greetings or keep a log of site visitors:

```
function netID(id){
    var at=id.indexOf("@");
    var user=id.substring(0,at);
    return user;
}
```

String.lastIndexOf (5+)

COMPONENTS:

string.lastIndexOf("*substring*",*ref*)

Use this method to search the elements of a string and return the position of the last occurrence of *substring* in *string*. As an optional argument, you can specify an integer for *ref*, the position where `lastIndexOf()`will begin its search. *ref* must be a number between 0 (the string's first character) and `string.length-1` (the string's last character). `lastIndexOf()`searches a string for *substring* from right to left (backwards) starting at either position `string.length-1` (the default) or *ref* (if specified). If *substring* is not found, the method returns –1. For an in-context example of this term, see "Opening a Local HTML File from a Flash CD-ROM" in the Appendix.

String.length (5+)

COMPONENTS:

string.length

Use the `length` property to return the number of characters in *string*. Because string characters are referenced starting at 0, a string's length will always be one value higher than the reference position of its last character. For example, in the string *"abc,"* the length is 3, but the reference position for *"c"* is 2 ("a" = 0, "b" = 1, "c" = 2). If a string contains a space, the space is counted as a character in the string's length.

EXAMPLE:

The following script, using the name of the author's dog, returns 6:

```
name="Darsie";
trace(name.length);
```

This script returns 10:

```
name="Darsie Dog";
trace(name.length);
```

String.slice (5+)

COMPONENTS:

string.slice(*startRef*,*endRef*)

Use the `slice()` method to extract a substring from *string*. To specify the contents of the substring, you must enter two arguments: *startRef* and *endRef*. *startRef* represents the reference position of the first character in the substring. *endRef* represents the reference position of the character in *string* immediately following the last character of the substring. If no `endRef` is specified, the length of the string (number of characters) is used as a default. Both numbers are entered as integers relative to 0, where 0 represents the first character of the string. Negative numbers are accepted as well, where –1 is the last character, –2 is the next-to-last character, and so on. Ultimately, the elements of the final substring are the characters in *string* between *startRef* and *endRef*-1.

EXAMPLE:

For the string `name`, a first name, last name, and middle initial are extracted as substrings:

```
name="Darsie D Dog"
firstName=name.slice(0,6);
initial=name.slice(7,8);
lastName=name.slice(9,12);
```

You can achieve the same results using the `substring()` method. The only difference is that `substring()` does not support negative numbers:

```
name="Darsie D Dog"
firstName=name.substring(0,6);
initial=name.substring(7,8);
lastName=name.substring(9);
```

Note that for the string `lastName`, no `endRef` is specified and the length of the string (`string.length`) is used as a default. Using negative numbers, the names could also be initialized using the following statements:

```
firstName=name.slice(-12,-6);
initial=name.slice(-5,-4);
lastName=name.slice(-3,12);
```

String.toLowerCase (5+)

COMPONENTS:

`string.toLowerCase()`

Use this method to convert all letter characters in *string* to lowercase. Note that this method

doesn't change *string*; rather, it yields a lowercase copy of *string*. For an example, see the `String.toUpperCase()`method.

String.toUpperCase (5+)

COMPONENTS:

`string.toUpperCase()`

Use this method to convert all letter characters in *string* to uppercase. Note that this method doesn't change *string*; rather, it yields an uppercase copy of *string*.

EXAMPLE:

In this script, `text` is reformatted to all uppercase characters. The ampersand (&) is unaffected:

```
text="UPPER & lower";
format1=text.toUpperCase();
format2=text.toLowerCase();
```

The script sets `format1` to UPPER & LOWER, and `format2` to upper & lower.

TextField Object (6)

Use the TextField object to manipulate the attributes of dynamic and input text fields with Action-Script. To do this, a text field must have a unique instance name. To assign an instance name, click the text field and open the Property Inspector (Window → Properties or Cmd/Ctrl+F3). Enter a name in the Instance Name field of the Property Inspector; this becomes the field's instance name.

PROPERTIES:

`TextField.hscroll` sets and returns the current horizontal scroll position.

`TextField.maxhscroll` defines the maximum horizontal scroll position.

`TextField.maxscroll` defines the maximum vertical scroll position.

`TextField.scroll` sets and returns the current vertical scroll position.

TextField.hscroll (6)

COMPONENTS:

`textField.hscroll=expression`

This `TextField` object property can both get and set the horizontal scrolling position for a text field object. You can use `hscroll` to create "ticker-style" side-scrolling text boxes for sports scores and stock quotes. An `hscroll` position of 0 will left-justify the text in a text field. See the `TextField.scroll` property for an example.

TextField.maxhscroll (6)

COMPONENTS:

textField.maxhscroll

This `TextField` object property returns the value for the rightmost position of text in a text field. If a text field does not contain enough text to go beyond the right edge of the text box, the `maxhscroll` property will return 0. This property cannot be set.

EXAMPLE:

This script makes the text in the `line` text field jump to the end, where the last word appears in the right corner of the text field:

```
on(press){
    edge=line.maxhscroll;
    line.hscroll=edge;
}
```

TextField.maxscroll (6)

COMPONENTS:

textField.maxscroll

This `TextField` object property returns the value for the topmost line in a text field when the bottommost line is visible. If a text field displays five lines, and there are 20 lines in a text block, the field's `maxscroll` property will be 16. Line 16 will be the top line when line 20 appears at the bottom of the field. This property cannot be set.

TextField.scroll (6)

COMPONENTS:

textField.scroll=*expression*

This `TextField` object property can both get and set the topmost line number displayed a text field. `scroll` creates interactive and animated scrolling text boxes.

EXAMPLE:

You can place any of these examples within an `on(mouseEvent)` or `onClipEvent(event)` handler, or you can use the events of the MovieClip and Button objects to scroll the contents of a text field object as you see fit.

To scroll a text field up:

`vertField.scroll+=1;`

To scroll a text field down:

`vertField.scroll-=1;`

To scroll a text field across (to the right):

`horizField.hscroll+=10;`

To reset the horizontal position of a text field:

`horizField.hscroll=0;`

Key Code Values for the Key Object

Table R.4 contains a complete listing of key code values for the Key object.

Table R.4

Key Code Values

ALPHABET KEYS	KEY CODE
A	65
B	66
C	67
D	68
E	69
F	70
G	71
H	72
I	73
J	74
K	75
L	76
M	77
N	78
O	79
P	80
Q	81

ALPHABET KEYS	KEY CODE
R	82
S	83
T	84
U	85
V	86
W	87
X	88
Y	89
Z	90

NUMBER KEYS	KEY CODE
0	48
1	49
2	50
3	51
4	52
5	53
6	54
7	55
8	56
9	57

NUMERIC KEYPAD KEYS	KEY CODE
keypad 0	96
keypad 1	97
keypad 2	98
keypad 3	99
keypad 4	100
keypad 5	101
keypad 6	102
keypad 7	103
keypad 8	104
keypad 9	105
Multiply (*)	106
Add (+)	107
Enter	13
Subtract (–)	109
Decimal (.)	110
Divide (/)	111

FUNCTION KEYS	KEY CODE
F1	112
F2	113
F3	114
F4	115
F5	116
F6	117
F7	118
F8	119
F9	120
F10	121
F11	122
F12	123

MISCELLANEOUS KEYS	KEY CODE
Backspace	8
Tab	9
Clear (Macintosh)	12
Enter	13
Shift	16
Control	17
Alt	18
Caps Lock	20
Esc	27
Spacebar	32
Page Up	33
Page Down	34
End	35
Home	36
Left arrow	37
Up arrow	38
Right arrow	39
Down arrow	40
Insert	45
Delete	46
Help	47
Num Lock	144
;:	186
=+	187
-_	189

Continued on next page

Continued from previous page

MISCELLANEOUS KEYS	KEY CODE
/?	191
`~	192
[{	219
|	220
]}	221
'"	222

Deprecated Terms

Since the release of Flash MX, the ActionScript elements listed in the left column of Table R.5 have been relegated to the scrap heap in favor of newer, more efficient syntax and terminology. Although these elements are still functional, it's best to avoid them whenever possible to ensure the future compatibility of your movies.

Table R.5

Deprecated Terms and Their Replacements

DEPRECATED TERM	NEW TERM
<> (inequality)	!= operator
add	+ operator
and	&&
call	function
chr	String.fromCharCode
eq	==
ge	>=
gt	>
_highquality	_quality property
ifFrameLoaded	_framesloaded property
int	Math.floor
le	<=
length	String.length
lt	<
maxscroll	textField.maxscroll
mbchr	String.fromCharCode
mblength	String.length
mbord	String.fromCharCode
mbsubstring	String.substr

DEPRECATED TERM	NEW TERM
ne	!= (inequality)
not	! (logical NOT)
or	|| (logical OR)
ord	String object
random	Math.random
scroll	textField.scroll
substring	String.substring
tellTarget	with
toggleHighQuality	_quality property

Index

Note to the Reader: Throughout this index **boldfaced** page numbers indicate primary discussions of a topic. *Italicized* page numbers indicate illustrations.

getVolume method, 438, **705**
getYear method, **692**
GIF (Graphic Interchange Format) format, **583**, **590–591**, *590*
_global, reference for, **685**
Global Intersection Style Color tool, 559
Global Intersection Style Thickness tool, 559
global variables, 300–301
globalToLocal method, **699**
Go to Line command, 286
Go to Location option, 130
Go to Symbol Definition option, 130
Goodnight Mr. Snoozleberg, 290, *290*
goto action, 646
gotoAndPlay action, 228, 285
    in MovieClip, **699**
    reference for, **670**
    for scenes, 198
gotoAndStop action, 228, 230
    in MovieClip, **699**
    reference for, **670**
    for scenes, 198
gotoFrame action, 488, 491, 493
gradient fills, 59
gradients, 59–60
    for GIF files, 590
    linear, **68–69**, *68*
    radial, **69**, *69*
Graphic Interchange Format (GIF) format, **583**, **590–591**, *590*
graphics
    ActionScripts for, **333–334**
        animation, **334–337**
        color, **339–342**, *340–341*
        scaling, **337–339**, *337*
    converting to symbols, **112–113**, *113*
    in Director, **478**
    symbols for, **109**
    vector and raster, 8
graphics tablets, 51
greater than signs (>) for comparisons, **684**
greetings, arrays for, **660–663**, *661, 663*

Grid option, 542
grids
    snapping objects to, 46
    in Swift 3D, 542
gripper region, 34
ground for garden scene, **149–150**, *150*
grouping objects, **92–93**, *93*
guide layers, **145–146**

H

Hand tool, 23
HandlerMan.swf file, 226
handlers, event, **221–222**
    in ActionScript, 278
    for mouse, **230–231**
    for Movie Clip, **235–236**
    problems in, 365
handsOn5.fla file, 378
height of bitmap fills, 59
_height property
    for Movie Clips, 333, 339
    reference for, **676–677**
Hellz Kitchen, 624, *624*
help, **36**, *36*
help documents, 29
Help menu, **20**
Hex colors, mixing, 64, **66–67**, *67*
Hidden option, 542
hide method, **696**
high cut filters for reverb, 523
High Quality Printing option, 505
hints, code, **283–286**, *283, 285*
history of Flash, **4–6**
Hit state for buttons, 109, 243, *244*, 246
hitTest method, **699**
Holm, Peter, 70
homer.txt file, 358
host processing in RTAS systems, 511
hot keys, 18
HSB colors, **67**, *67*
hscroll property, **709**
HTML buttons, **80**

T